Roget's II
The New
Thesaurus

Third Edition

BERKLEY BOOKS, NEW YORK

Based on the hardcover edition of *Roget's II: The New Thesaurus, Third Edition*. Copyright © 1995 by Houghton Mifflin Company. Reprinted by arrangement with Houghton Mifflin Company.

A Berkley Book / published by arrangement with
Houghton Mifflin Company

PRINTING HISTORY
Houghton Mifflin Company paperback edition published 1996
Berkley edition / February 1997

The Putnam Berkley World Wide Web site address is
http://www.berkley.com

ISBN: 0-425-15668-0

BERKLEY®
Berkley Books are published by
The Berkley Publishing Group, a member of Penguin Putnam Inc.,
200 Madison Avenue, New York, New York 10016.
BERKLEY and the "B" design are trademarks
belonging to Berkley Publishing Corporation.

PRINTED IN THE UNITED STATES OF AMERICA

10   9   8   7   6   5   4   3

HOW TO USE THIS BOOK

The Entries *Roget's II: The New Thesaurus, Third Edition,* contains two kinds of entries in a single alphabetical list. Main entries have definitions and synonym lists:

> **fabulous** *adjective* So remarkable as to elicit disbelief : amazing, astonishing, astounding, fantastic, fantastical, incredible, marvelous, miraculous, phenomenal, prodigious, stupendous, unbelievable, wonderful, wondrous. See GOOD in Index.

Other entries are cross-references to such main entries:

> **familiarity** *noun* See **acquaintance, friendship, impudence.**

Note that the entries being referred to are printed in boldface type. When an entry refers to two or more main entries, the main entries are listed in alphabetical order.

A main entry can contain both synonyms and cross-references:

> **fact** *noun* Something having real, demonstrable existence : actuality, event, phenomenon, reality. See REAL in Index. — See also **actuality, circumstance, information.**

At the entry **fact** a definition with a synonym list is given. Additional synonyms for different meanings of **fact** are listed at the main entries **actuality, circumstance,** and **information.**

Many words in English are used as more than one part of speech. For entries of this kind, the additional parts of speech are listed as boldface subentries. Like the main entry, the subentry can have synonym lists or cross-references, or both:

> **help** *verb* To give support or assistance. Also used with *out* : abet, aid, assist, boost, relieve, succor. *Idioms:* give (*or* lend) a hand, give a leg up. See HELP in Index. — See also **improve.**
>
> **help** *noun* The act or an instance of helping : abetment, aid, assist, assistance, hand, relief, succor, support. See HELP in Index. — See also **helper.**

Phrasal verbs, which consist of a verb followed by one or more prepositions, are also entered separately as subentries. Phrasal verbs can have both definitions and cross-references.

> **look** *verb* To direct the eyes on an object : consider, contemplate, eye, view. *Idiom:* clap (or lay or set) one's eyes on. See SEE in Index. — See also **appear, face, seek.**
>
> **look out** *verb* To be careful : beware, mind, watch out. *Idioms:* be on guard, be on the lookout, keep an eye peeled, take care (or heed). See AWARENESS, CAREFUL in Index.
>
> **look over** *verb* See **survey.**

Parts of an Entry   A main entry with a definition and a synonym list has several components.

> **fashionable** *adjective* Being or in accordance with the current fashion : à la mode, chic, dashing, mod, modish, posh, smart, stylish, swank, swanky, trig. *Informal:* classy, in, sharp, snappy, swish, tony, trendy. *Slang:* with-it. *Idioms:* all the rage, up to the minute. See STYLE, USUAL in Index.

The components of **fashionable** shown above are these:
- A part of speech, *adjective.*
- A definition, "Being or in accordance with the current fashion." If the entry had more than one definition, each would be numbered.
- Three groups of synonyms. The first group at **fashionable** is not labeled with any restriction of application. The second group is labeled *Informal* and the third group is labeled *Slang.*
- A group labeled *Idioms,* which contains phrases that are equivalent in meaning to the synonyms. Idioms are not entered separately.
- A reference to the Category Index that follows the Thesaurus. See page v for an explanation of the Category Index.

Cross-References   Each synonym group is listed and defined at only one entry. All the synonyms in that group are entered at their own alphabetical places as cross-references to the main entry, as described above. The cross-reference to a phrasal verb includes both the phrasal verb and the main entry:

> **fragmentize** *verb* See **break up** at **break.**

Variants   Variant spellings are given following the entry word. Variants that occur as frequently as the entry form are introduced by *or*. Variants that occur less frequently than the entry form are introduced by *also*. All variants given in this book are equally acceptable.

Variant wordings of idioms are given in parentheses:

> **fall** *verb* . . . **2.** To come to the
> ground suddenly and involuntarily :
> drop, go down, nose-dive, pitch,
> plunge, spill, topple, tumble. *Idiom:*
> take a fall (or header or plunge or
> spill or tumble). See RISE in Index.

Some verbs can be used with or without a preposition or an adverb. The optional word is shown in parentheses. For example, at **persuade** the synonym *sell (on)* indicates that both *sell* and *sell on* can be used to mean "To succeed in causing (a person) to act in a certain way."

Homographs   Words with the same spellings but different meanings and origins are called *homographs*. Homographs are given separate entry and distinguished by superscript numerals:

> **hide**[1] *verb* To put or keep out of
> sight . . .
> **hide**[2] *noun* The skin of an animal . . .

Labels   The following labels indicate the special status of a word:
Archaic   once common but now rarely used
Obsolete   once common but no longer used
Informal   not appropriate to formal discourse
Slang   characteristic of very casual speech, often exceptionally vivid, humorous, or irreverent
Regional   characteristic of a region of the United States
Other labels, such as *British* and *Architecture*, indicate words that are characteristic of a particular variety of English spoken outside the United States or of a specific subject area.

The Category Index   The Category Index is designed to take the user from a synonym list in the main body of the Thesaurus to words of related and opposite meaning elsewhere in the Thesaurus. A category reference, which appears in small capitals at the end of every synonym list, refers to an entry in the Category Index.

> **favorite** *adjective* **1.** Given special,
> usually doting treatment : darling,
> fair-haired, favored, pet[1]. See TREAT
> WELL in Index. **2.** Being a favorite :
> favored, popular, preferred, well-
> liked. See LIKE in Index.

The category reference LIKE is a direction to turn to the entry **LIKE** in the Category Index.

LIKE	**dislike**
noun	*noun*
admirer	disapproval
adoration	disgust
attraction	dislike
bent	drip
bias	
delight	*verb*
favorite	crawl
liking	disapprove
lure	disgust
public	dislike
taste	offend
adjective	*See also*
adorable	DESIRE
agreeable	EXCITE
attractive	HAPPY
biased	LOVE
delightful	PRAISE

The entries in the Category Index list entries in the Thesaurus that are related in meaning but not synonymous. These related words are divided into groups by part of speech.

Most category entries contain a subentry word that is opposite or contrastive in meaning to the main entry word, as **dislike** at **LIKE**. At some categories there is a third group consisting of words that are neutral in meaning. For example, the category **EXCESS** has subcategories of **insufficiency**, a contrastive term, and **enough**, a neutral term.

Some lists have only a main entry word and no subentries. An example is the category **WORDS**.

In some cases more than one meaning of a thesaurus entry appears at the same entry and part of speech in the Category Index. The number of different meanings is indicated by a number enclosed in parentheses. For example, at **SOUNDS** *noun* is found

hearing (3)

This means that the entry for the noun *hearing* in the thesaurus contains three meanings with three different synonym lists that fit in the category **SOUNDS**.

Most entries in the Category Index close with cross-references to other entries in the Category Index where other related words will be found. These cross-references are given in small capital letters. For example, **LIKE** has the cross-references DESIRE, EXCITE, HAPPY, LOVE, and PRAISE.

A

aback *adverb* See **unawares**.

abandon *verb* **1.** To give up or leave without intending to return or claim again : desert[3], forsake, leave[1], quit, throw over. *Idioms:* run out on, walk out on. See KEEP in Index. **2.** To cease trying to accomplish or continue : break off, desist, discontinue, give up, leave off, quit, relinquish, remit, stop. *Informal:* swear off. *Slang:* lay off. *Idioms:* call it a day, call it quits, hang up one's fiddle, have done with, throw in the towel. See CONTINUE in Index. — See also **abdicate, give over** at **give, relinquish**.

abandon *noun* **1.** A complete surrender of inhibitions : abandonment, incontinence, unrestraint, wantonness, wildness. See RESTRAINT in Index. **2.** A careless, often reckless disregard for consequences : carelessness, heedlessness, thoughtlessness. See CAREFUL in Index.

abandoned *adjective* **1.** Having been given up and left alone : bereft, derelict, deserted, desolate, forlorn, forsaken, lorn. See KEEP in Index. **2.** Lacking in moral restraint : dissipated, dissolute, fast, gay, incontinent, licentious, profligate, rakish, unbridled, unconstrained, uncontrolled, ungoverned, uninhibited, unrestrained, wanton, wild. See RESTRAINT in Index.

abandonment *noun* The act of forsaking : desertion. See KEEP in Index. — See also **abandon, abdication**.

abase *verb* See **humble**.

abasement *noun* See **degradation**.

abash *verb* See **embarrass**.

abashment *noun* See **embarrassment**.

abate *verb* See **decrease, deduct, subside**.

abatement *noun* See **decrease, deduction, wane**.

abbreviate *verb* See **shorten**.

abdicate *verb* To give up a possession, claim, or right : abandon, cede, demit, forswear, hand over, quitclaim, relinquish, render, renounce, resign, surrender, waive, yield. See KEEP in Index.

abdication *noun* A giving up of a possession, claim, or right : abandonment, demission, quitclaim, relinquishment, renunciation, resignation, surrender, waiver. See KEEP in Index.

abduct *verb* See **kidnap**.

abecedarian *noun* See **beginner**.

aberrance *noun* See **abnormality**.

aberrancy *noun* See **abnormality**.

aberrant *adjective* See **abnormal, errant**.

aberration *noun* See **abnormality, deviation, insanity**.

abet *verb* See **help**.

abetment *noun* See **help**.

abettor or **abetter** *noun* See **helper**.

abeyance *noun* The condition of being temporarily inactive : abeyancy, dormancy, intermission, latency, quiescence, suspension. See ACTION in Index.

abeyancy *noun* See **abeyance**.

abeyant *adjective* See **latent**.

abhor *verb* See **hate**.

abhorrence *noun* See **hate**.

abhorrent *adjective* See **filthy**.

abide *verb* See **endure, live[1], pause, remain**.

abide by *verb* See **follow**.

abiding *adjective* See **continuing**.

ability *noun* **1.** Physical, mental, financial, or legal power to perform : capability, capacity, competence, competency, faculty, might. See ABILITY in Index. **2.** Natural or acquired facility in a specific activity : adeptness, art, command, craft, expertise, expertness, knack, mastery, proficiency, skill, technique. *Informal:* know-how. See ABILITY, KNOWLEDGE in Index.

abjuration *noun* See **retraction.**

abjure *verb* See **retract.**

ablaze *adjective* See **burning.**

able *adjective* Having the ability to perform well : capable, competent, good, skilled, skillful. See ABILITY in Index.

able-bodied *adjective* See **lusty.**

abnormal *adjective* Departing from the normal : aberrant, anomalistic, anomalous, atypic, atypical, deviant, divergent, irregular, preternatural, unnatural. See GOOD, USUAL in Index.

abnormality *noun* The condition of being abnormal : aberrance, aberrancy, aberration, anomaly, deviance, deviancy, deviation, irregularity, preternaturalness, unnaturalness. See GOOD, USUAL in Index.

abode *noun* See **home.**

abolish *verb* To put an end to, especially formally and with authority : abrogate, annihilate, annul, cancel, invalidate, negate, nullify, set aside, vitiate, void. *Law:* extinguish. See CONTINUE in Index. — See also **annihilate.**

abolishment *noun* See **abolition.**

abolition *noun* An often formal act of putting an end to : abolishment, abrogation, annihilation, annulment, cancellation, defeasance, invalidation, negation, nullification, voidance. *Law:* avoidance, extinguishment. See CONTINUE in Index.

abominable *adjective* See **filthy.**

abominate *verb* See **hate.**

abomination *noun* See **hate.**

aboriginal *adjective* See **indigenous.**

abort *verb* See **miscarry.**

abound *verb* See **teem.**

about *adverb* See **approximately, back, backward.**

about-face *verb* See **double.**

abracadabra *noun* See **gibberish.**

abrade *verb* See **chafe.**

abridge *verb* See **shorten.**

abridgment *noun* See **synopsis.**

abrogate *verb* See **abolish.**

abrogation *noun* See **abolition.**

abrupt *adjective* **1.** Happening quickly and without warning : hurried, precipitant, precipitate, sudden. See FAST, SURPRISE in Index. **2.** Rudely unceremonious : blunt, brief, brusque, crusty, curt, gruff, short, short-spoken. See ATTITUDE in Index. — See also **steep¹.**

abruptly *adverb* See **short.**

abscond *verb* See **escape.**

absence *noun* **1.** Failure to be present : nonattendance. *Law:* nonappearance. See ABSENCE in Index. **2.** The condition of lacking a needed or usual amount : dearth, lack, want. See EXCESS in Index.

absent *adjective* **1.** Not present : away, gone, missing, wanting. See ABSENCE in Index. **2.** Deficient in a usual or needed amount : lacking, wanting. See EXCESS in Index. — See also **absent-minded.**

absent-minded *adjective* So lost in thought as to be unaware of one's surroundings : absent, abstracted, bemused, distrait, faraway, inattentive, preoccupied. *Idiom:* a million miles away. See ABILITY, AWARENESS in Index.

absent-mindedness *noun* See **trance.**

absolute *adjective* Having and exercising complete political power and control : absolutistic, arbitrary, autarchic, autarchical, autocratic, autocratical, despotic, dictatorial, monocratic, totalitarian, tyrannic, tyrannical, tyrannous. See OVER, POLITICS in Index. — See also **implicit, perfect, pure, unconditional, utter².**

absolutely *adverb* Without question : certainly, doubtless, doubtlessly, positively, undoubtedly. See CERTAIN, LIMITED in Index. — See also **completely, yes.**

absolution *noun* See **forgiveness.**

absolutism *noun* 1. A government in which a single leader or party exercises absolute control over all citizens and every aspect of their lives : autarchy, autocracy, despotism, dictatorship, monocracy, tyranny. See OVER, POLITICS in Index. 2. A political doctrine advocating the principle of absolute rule : authoritarianism, autocracy, despotism, dictatorship, totalitarianism. See OVER, POLITICS in Index.

absolutistic *adjective* See **absolute.**

absolve *verb* See **clear, excuse.**

absorb *verb* 1. To take in and incorporate, especially mentally : assimilate, digest, imbibe, take up. *Informal:* soak (up). See ACCEPT in Index. 2. To occupy the full attention of : consume, engross, immerse, monopolize, preoccupy. See AWARENESS, EXCITE in Index. — See also **drink.**

absorbed *adjective* Having one's thoughts fully occupied : deep, intent, preoccupied, rapt. *Idiom:* wrapped up in. See AWARENESS, EXCITE in Index.

absorbent *adjective* Having a capacity or tendency to absorb or

soak up : absorptive, assimilative, bibulous. See DRY in Index.

absorption *noun* 1. The process of absorbing and incorporating, especially mentally : assimilation, digestion. See ACCEPT in Index. 2. Total occupation of the attention or of the mind : engrossment, enthrallment, immersion, preoccupation, prepossession. See EXCITE in Index.

absorptive *adjective* See **absorbent.**

absquatulate *verb* See **escape.**

abstain *verb* See **refrain.**

abstemious *adjective* See **temperate.**

abstinence *noun* See **temperance.**

abstract *adjective* See **theoretical.**

  abstract *noun* See **synopsis.**

  abstract *verb* See **detach, review.**

abstracted *adjective* See **absent-minded.**

abstraction *noun* See **trance.**

abstruse *adjective* See **deep.**

absurd *adjective* See **foolish.**

absurdity *noun* See **foolishness, scream.**

abundance *noun* See **heap, plenty.**

abundant *adjective* See **generous.**

abuse *verb* 1. To hurt or injure by maltreatment : ill-treat, ill-use, maltreat, mishandle, mistreat, misuse. See HELP in Index. 2. To use wrongly and improperly : misapply, misappropriate, mishandle, misuse, pervert. See TREAT WELL in Index. 3. To take advantage of unfairly : exploit, impose, presume, use. See TREAT WELL in Index. — See also **revile.**

  abuse *noun* 1. Wrong, often corrupt use : misapplication, misappropriation, mishandling, misuse, perversion. See TREAT WELL in Index. 2. Physically harmful treatment : ill-treatment, maltreatment, mishandling, mistreatment, misusage. See HELP in Index. — See also **vituperation.**

abusive *adjective* Of, relating to, or characterized by verbal abuse : contumelious, invective, opprobrious, scurrilous, vituperative. See ATTACK, ATTITUDE in Index.

abut *verb* See **adjoin.**

abysm *noun* See **deep.**

abysmal *adjective* See **deep, yawning.**

abyss *noun* See **deep.**

abyssal *adjective* See **yawning.**

academic *adjective* See **pedantic, theoretical.**

accede *verb* See **assent.**

accelerate *verb* See **speed.**

accent *noun* See **emphasis, tone.**

accent *verb* See **emphasize.**

accentuate *verb* See **emphasize.**

accentuation *noun* See **emphasis.**

accept *verb* **1.** To receive (something given or offered) willingly and gladly : embrace, take (up), welcome. See ACCEPT in Index. **2.** To allow admittance, as to a group : admit, receive, take in. See ACCEPT in Index. — See also **assent, believe, endure, receive, understand.**

acceptable *adjective* **1.** Capable of being accepted : admissible, unobjectionable. See ACCEPT in Index. **2.** Of moderately good quality but less than excellent : adequate, all right, average, common, decent, fair, fairish, goodish, moderate, passable, respectable, satisfactory, sufficient, tolerable. *Informal:* OK, tidy. See GOOD in Index.

acceptance *noun* **1.** The act or process of accepting : acquiescence, agreement, assent, consent, nod, yes. *Informal:* OK. See ACCEPT in Index. **2.** Favorable regard : approbation, approval, favor. See ACCEPT, PRAISE in Index.

acceptant *adjective* See **receptive.**

acceptation *noun* See **meaning.**

accepted *adjective* Generally approved or agreed upon : conventional, orthodox, received, recognized, sanctioned. See ACCEPT, AGREE, STRAIGHT, USUAL in Index.

access *noun* See **admission, outburst, seizure.**

accessible *adjective* See **approachable, convenient, open.**

accession *noun* See **addition.**

accessory *noun* One who assists a lawbreaker in a wrongful or criminal act : accomplice, confederate, conspirator. See CRIMES, HELP in Index. — See also **attachment.**

accessory *adjective* See **auxiliary.**

accident *noun* An unexpected and usually undesirable event : casualty, contretemps, misadventure, mischance, misfortune, mishap. See HELP, SURPRISE in Index. — See also **chance.**

accidental *adjective* Occurring unexpectedly : casual, chance, contingent, fluky, fortuitous, inadvertent, odd. See SURPRISE in Index.

acclaim *verb* See **honor, praise.**

acclaim *noun* See **praise.**

acclamation *noun* See **praise.**

acclamatory *adjective* See **complimentary.**

acclimate *verb* See **adapt, harden.**

acclimation *noun* See **adaptation.**

acclimatization *noun* See **adaptation.**

acclimatize *verb* See **adapt, harden.**

acclivity *noun* See **ascent.**

accolade *noun* See **distinction, reward, trophy.**

accommodate *verb* To have the room or capacity for : contain, hold. See FULL in Index. — See also **adapt, harbor, harmonize, oblige.**

accommodating *adjective* See **obliging.**

accommodation *noun* See **adaptation, compromise.**

accompaniment *noun* 1. One that accompanies another : associate, attendant, companion, concomitant. See ACCOMPANIED in Index.
2. Something added to another for embellishment or completion : complement, enhancement, enrichment. See ACCOMPANIED in Index.

accompany *verb* To be with or go with (another) : attend, companion, company, escort. *Obsolete:* consort. *Idiom:* go hand in hand with. See ACCOMPANIED in Index.

accompanying *adjective* Occurring or existing with : attendant, attending, coincident, concomitant, concurrent. See ACCOMPANIED in Index.

accomplice *noun* See **accessory.**

accomplish *verb* To succeed in doing : achieve, attain, gain, reach, realize. *Slang:* score. See DO in Index.

accomplished *adjective* Proficient as a result of practice and study : finished, practiced. See ABILITY in Index.

accomplishment *noun* Something completed or attained successfully : achievement, acquirement, acquisition, attainment, effort, feat. See DO in Index.

accord *verb* See **agree, confer, grant.**

accord *noun* See **agreement, harmony, treaty.**

accordance *noun* See **agreement, conferment.**

accordant *adjective* See **agreeable.**

accost *verb* To approach for the purpose of speech : greet, hail[2], salute. See APPROACH, GREETING, SEEK in Index. — See also **confront.**

accouchement *noun* See **birth.**

account *noun* 1. A statement of causes or motives : explanation, justification, rationale, rationalization, reason. See EXPLAIN in Index.
2. A precise list of fees or charges : bill[1], check, invoice, reckoning, statement. *Informal:* tab. See PAY in Index. — See also **esteem, story, use, worth.**

account *verb* See **regard.**

account for *verb* To offer reasons for or a cause of : explain, justify, rationalize. See EXPLAIN in Index.

accountable *adjective* See **explainable, liable.**

accouter or **accoutre** *verb* See **furnish.**

accouterment or **accoutrement** *noun* See **outfit.**

accredit *verb* See **attribute, authorize.**

accretion *noun* See **buildup.**

accrue *verb* See **accumulate.**

acculturate *verb* See **socialize.**

accumulate *verb* To bring together so as to increase in mass or number : accrue, agglomerate, aggregate, amass, collect[1], cumulate, garner, gather, hive, pile up, roll up. See COLLECT in Index.

accumulation *noun* A quantity accumulated : aggregation, amassment, assemblage, collection, congeries, cumulation, gathering, mass. See COLLECT in Index.

accumulative *adjective* Increasing, as in force, by successive additions : additive, cumulative. See INCREASE in Index.

accuracy *noun* Freedom from error : accurateness, correctness, exactitude, exactness, preciseness, precision, rightness. See CORRECT in Index. — See also **veracity.**

accurate *adjective* 1. Having no errors : correct, errorless, exact,

precise, right, rigorous. See COR-
RECT, TRUE in Index. **2.** Conforming to fact : correct, exact, faithful,
precise, right, rigorous, true, veracious, veridical. See CORRECT,
HONEST, REAL, TRUE in Index.

accurateness *noun* See **accuracy.**

accursed *adjective* See **damned.**

accusation *noun* A charging of
someone with a misdeed : charge,
denouncement, denunciation, imputation, incrimination. *Law:* indictment. See ATTACK, LAW, PRAISE in
Index.

accusatorial *adjective* Containing, relating to, or involving an accusation : accusatory, denunciative,
denunciatory. See ATTACK, ATTI-
TUDE, PRAISE in Index.

accusatory *adjective* See
accusatorial.

accuse *verb* To make an accusation
against : arraign, charge, denounce,
incriminate, indict, tax. See
ATTACK, LAW, PRAISE in Index.

accused *noun* *Law.* A person
against whom an action is brought :
defendant, respondent. See LAW in
Index.

accuser *noun* One that accuses :
denouncer, indicter. See ATTACK,
LAW, PRAISE in Index. — See also
complainant.

accustom *verb* To make familiar
through constant practice or use :
condition, habituate, inure, wont.
See USUAL in Index.

accustomed *adjective* **1.** Familiar
through repetition : chronic, habitual, routine. See USUAL in Index.
2. In the habit : habituated, used,
wont. See USUAL in Index. — See
also **customary.**

ace *noun* See **expert.**
ace *verb* See **defeat.**
ace *adjective* See **excellent.**
acerb *adjective* See **sour.**

acerbic *adjective* See **biting, bitter,
sour.**

acerbity *noun* See **sarcasm.**

acetous *adjective* See **sour.**

ache *verb* See **desire, feel, hurt.**
ache *noun* See **pain.**

achieve *verb* See **accomplish.**

achievement *noun* See **accomplishment, feat.**

aching *adjective* See **painful.**

achy *adjective* See **painful.**

acicula *noun* See **point.**

acicular *adjective* See **pointed.**

aciculate *adjective* See **pointed.**

aciculated *adjective* See **pointed.**

acid *adjective* See **biting, sour.**

acidic *adjective* See **biting.**

acidity *noun* See **sarcasm.**

acidulous *adjective* See **sour.**

acknowledge *verb* **1.** To recognize,
often reluctantly, the reality or truth
of : admit, avow, concede, confess,
grant, own (up). *Slang:* fess up.
Chiefly Regional: allow. See
AFFIRM, KNOWLEDGE in Index.
2. To express recognition of :
admit, recognize. See AFFIRM,
KNOWLEDGE in Index.

acknowledgment or **acknowl-
edgement** *noun* The act of admitting to something : admission,
avowal, confession. See AFFIRM,
KNOWLEDGE, SHOW in Index. — See
also **recognition.**

acme *noun* See **climax.**

acquaint *verb* To make known
socially : introduce, present². See
KNOWLEDGE in Index. — See also
inform.

acquaintance *noun* **1.** Personal
knowledge derived from participation or observation : experience,
familiarity. See KNOWLEDGE in
Index. **2.** A person whom one knows
casually : friend. See KNOWLEDGE
in Index.

acquainted *adjective* See **familiar, informed.**

acquiesce *verb* See **assent.**

acquiescence *noun* See **acceptance, obedience.**

acquiescent *adjective* See **passive, willing.**

acquirable *adjective* See **available.**

acquire *verb* See **develop, get.**

acquirement *noun* See **accomplishment.**

acquisition *noun* See **accomplishment, addition.**

acquisitive *adjective* See **greedy.**

acquisitiveness *noun* See **greed.**

acquit *verb* See **act, clear.**

acquittal *noun* See **exculpation.**

acre *noun* See **land.**

acrid *adjective* See **biting, bitter.**

acridity *noun* See **sarcasm.**

acrimonious *adjective* See **resentful.**

acrimony *noun* See **resentment.**

act *noun* **1.** The process of doing : action. See ACTION in Index. **2.** Something done : action, deed, doing, thing, work. See DO in Index. **3.** A display of insincere behavior : acting, disguise, dissemblance, masquerade, pretense, sham, show, simulation. See HONEST, TRUE in Index. — See also **law, sketch.**

act *verb* **1.** To play the part of : do, enact, impersonate, perform, play, play-act, portray, represent. See ACTION, PERFORMING ARTS, SUBSTITUTE in Index. **2.** To conduct oneself in a specified way : acquit, bear, behave, carry, comport, demean[1], deport, do, quit. See BE in Index. **3.** To behave affectedly or insincerely or take on a false or misleading appearance of : counterfeit, dissemble, fake, feign, play-act, pose, pretend, put on, sham, simulate. See

HONEST, TRUE in Index. **4.** To perform the duties of another : function, officiate, serve. See DO, SUBSTITUTE in Index. — See also **function, stage.**

act up *verb* See **malfunction, misbehave.**

acting *adjective* See **temporary.**

acting *noun* The art and occupation of an actor : dramatics, stage. See ACTION, PERFORMING ARTS, SUBSTITUTE in Index. — See also **act.**

action *noun* See **act, behavior, combat, lawsuit.**

actionable *adjective* See **litigable.**

activate *verb* To arouse to action or put in motion : actuate, animate. See ACTION in Index.

active *adjective* In action or full operation : alive, functioning, going, operating, operative, running, working. See ACTION, AWARENESS in Index. — See also **energetic, vigorous.**

activity *noun* Energetic physical action : exercise, exertion. See ACTION in Index.

actor *noun* A theatrical performer : actress, player, thespian. See ACTION, PERFORMING ARTS, SUBSTITUTE in Index. — See also **participant.**

actress *noun* See **actor.**

actual *adjective* **1.** Occurring or existing in act or fact : existent, extant. See BE, REAL in Index. **2.** In agreement or correspondence with fact : real, true. See REAL in Index. — See also **authentic.**

actuality *noun* The quality of being actual or factual : fact, factuality, factualness, reality, truth. See REAL in Index. — See also **existence, fact.**

actualization *noun* See **effect.**

actualize *verb* See **realize.**

actually *adverb* In point of fact : indeed, really. See REAL, TRUE in Index. — See also **now, really.**

actuate *verb* See **activate, drive, use.**

acumen *noun* See **discernment.**

acuminate *verb* See **sharpen.**

acuminate *adjective* See **pointed.**

acumination *noun* See **point.**

acute *adjective* Possessing or displaying perceptions of great accuracy and sensitivity : incisive, keen[1], penetrating, perceptive, probing, sensitive, sharp, trenchant. See CAREFUL, SHARP in Index. — See also **critical, high, pointed, sharp.**

adage *noun* See **proverb.**

adamant *adjective* See **stubborn.**

adamantine *adjective* See **stubborn.**

adapt *verb* To make or become suitable to a particular situation or use : acclimate, acclimatize, accommodate, adjust, conform, fashion, fit[1], reconcile, square, suit, tailor. See CHANGE in Index.

adaptable *adjective* Capable of adapting or being adapted : adaptive, adjustable, elastic, flexible, malleable, pliable, pliant, supple. See CHANGE in Index.

adaptation *noun* **1.** The act of making suitable to an end or the condition of being made suitable to an end : accommodation, adaption, adjustment, conformation. See CHANGE in Index. **2.** *Biology.* Adjustment to a changing environment : acclimation, acclimatization. See CHANGE in Index.

adaption *noun* See **adaptation.**

adaptive *adjective* See **adaptable.**

add *verb* To combine (figures) to form a sum. Also used with *up* : cast, foot (up), sum (up), tot[2] (up), total, totalize. See INCREASE in Index.

added *adjective* See **additional.**

addition *noun* **1.** The act or process of adding : summation, totalization. See INCREASE in Index. **2.** Something tending to augment something else : accession, acquisition, augmentation. See INCREASE in Index.

additional *adjective* Being an addition : added, extra, fresh, further, more, new, other. See INCREASE in Index.

additionally *adverb* In addition : also, besides, further, furthermore, item, likewise, more, moreover, still, too, yet. *Idioms:* as well, to boot. See INCREASE in Index.

additive *adjective* See **accumulative.**

addle *verb* See **confuse.**

addled *adjective* See **confused.**

addlepated *adjective* See **confused.**

address *verb* **1.** To direct speech to : speak, talk. See WORDS in Index. **2.** To talk to an audience formally : lecture, prelect, speak. *Archaic:* bespeak. See WORDS in Index. **3.** To bring an appeal or request, for example, to the attention of : appeal, apply, approach, petition. *Obsolete:* sue. See REQUEST in Index. **4.** To mark (a written communication) with its destination : direct, superscribe. See START in Index. — See also **apply, send.**

address *noun* See **bearing, courtship, speech, tact.**

adduce *verb* See **present[2].**

adept *adjective* See **expert.**

adept *noun* See **expert.**

adeptness *noun* See **ability.**

adequacy *noun* See **enough.**

adequate *adjective* See **acceptable, sufficient.**

adhere *verb* See **bond, follow.**

adherence *noun* See **bond**.

adherent *noun* See **follower**.

adhesion *noun* See **bond**.

adhesive *adjective* See **sticky**.

adieu *noun* See **parting**.

ad interim *adjective* See **temporary**.

adipose *adjective* See **fatty**.

adjacent *adjective* See **adjoining, close**.

adjoin *verb* To be contiguous or next to : abut, border, bound[2], butt[2], join, meet[1], neighbor, touch, verge. See NEAR in Index.

adjoining *adjective* Sharing a common boundary : adjacent, conterminous, contiguous, next. See NEAR in Index.

adjourn *verb* See **defer**[1].

adjournment *noun* See **delay**.

adjudge *verb* See **judge**.

adjudicate *verb* See **judge**.

adjunct *noun* See **attachment**.

adjust *verb* To alter for proper functioning : fix, regulate, set[1], tune (up). *Music:* attune. See CHANGE, HELP in Index. — See also **adapt**.

adjustable *adjective* See **adaptable**.

adjustment *noun* See **adaptation**.

adjutant *noun* See **assistant**.

ad-lib *adjective* See **extemporaneous**.

ad-lib *verb* See **improvise**.

ad-lib *noun* See **improvisation**.

admeasure *verb* See **allot**.

admeasurement *noun* See **distribution**.

administer *verb* 1. To have charge of (the affairs of others) : administrate, direct, govern, head, manage, run, superintend, supervise. See OVER in Index. 2. To oversee the provision or execution of : administrate, carry out, dispense, execute. See OVER in Index. 3. To provide as a remedy : apply, dispense, give. See GIVE in Index. — See also **give**.

administrable *adjective* See **governable**.

administrant *noun* See **executive**.

administrate *verb* See **administer**.

administration *noun* 1. Authoritative control over the affairs of others : direction, government, management, superintendence, supervision. See OVER in Index. 2. The giving of a medication, especially by prescribed dosage : application, dispensation. See GIVE in Index. — See also **government**.

administrative *adjective* Of, for, or relating to administration or administrators : directorial, executive, managerial, ministerial, supervisory. See OVER in Index.

administrator *noun* See **executive**.

admirable *adjective* Deserving honor, respect, or admiration : commendable, creditable, deserving, estimable, exemplary, honorable, laudable, meritorious, praiseworthy, reputable, respectable, worthy. See GOOD, PRAISE, RESPECT, VALUE in Index.

admiration *noun* See **esteem, wonder**.

admire *verb* 1. To regard with great pleasure or approval : appreciate. See LIKE, PRAISE in Index. 2. To have a high opinion of : consider, esteem, honor, regard, respect, value. *Idioms:* look up to, think highly (or much or well) of. See PRAISE in Index.

admirer *noun* One who ardently admires : devotee, enthusiast, fancier, lover. *Informal:* fan[2]. See LIKE, LOVE, PRAISE in Index. — See also **beau**.

admissible *adjective* See **acceptable, permissible**.

admission *noun* 1. The state of being allowed entry : admittance, entrance[1], ingress, ingression, introduction, intromission. See ACCEPT in Index. **2.** The right to enter or make use of : access, admittance, entrance[1], entrée, entry, ingress. See ENTER in Index. — See also **acknowledgment.**

admit *verb* To serve as a means of entrance for : intromit, let in. See ENTER in Index. — See also **accept, acknowledge, permit.**

admittance *noun* See **admission.**

admix *verb* See **mix.**

admixture *noun* See **mixture.**

admonish *verb* See **call down** at **call, warn.**

admonishing *adjective* See **cautionary.**

admonishment *noun* See **rebuke, warning.**

admonition *noun* See **rebuke, warning.**

admonitory *adjective* See **cautionary.**

ado *noun* See **fuss.**

adolescence *noun* See **youth.**

adolescent *noun* See **teenager.**

adopt *verb* To take, as another's idea, and make one's own : embrace, espouse, take on, take up. See ACCEPT, GIVE in Index. — See also **confirm.**

adoption *noun* A ready taking up of something : embracement, espousal. See ACCEPT, GIVE in Index.

adorable *adjective* Easy to love : lovable, sweet. See GOOD, LIKE, LOVE in Index.

adoration *noun* **1.** The act of adoring, especially reverently : idolization, reverence, veneration, worship. See LIKE, LOVE, SACRED in Index. **2.** Deep and ardent affection : devotion, love, worship. See LIKE, LOVE in Index.

adore *verb* **1.** To regard with great awe and devotion : idolize, revere,

reverence, venerate, worship. See SACRED in Index. **2.** To feel deep, devoted love for : love, worship. See LOVE in Index. **3.** To like or enjoy enthusiastically, often excessively : delight (in), dote on (or upon), love. *Slang:* eat up, groove on. See LIKE, LOVE in Index.

adorn *verb* To furnish with decorations : bedeck, deck[2] (out), decorate, dress (up), embellish, garnish, ornament, trim. See BEAUTIFUL in Index. — See also **grace.**

adornment *noun* Something that adorns : decoration, embellishment, garnishment, garniture, ornament, ornamentation, trim, trimming. See BEAUTIFUL in Index.

adroit *adjective* See **artful, dexterous, neat.**

adroitness *noun* See **dexterity.**

adscititious *adjective* See **incidental.**

adulate *verb* See **flatter.**

adulation *noun* See **flattery.**

adulator *noun* See **sycophant.**

adult *adjective* See **mature.**

adulterant *noun* See **contaminant.**

adulterate *verb* To make impure or inferior by deceptively adding foreign substances : debase, doctor, load, sophisticate. See CLEAN in Index.

adulterated *adjective* See **impure.**

adulteration *noun* See **contamination.**

adulterator *noun* See **contaminant.**

adumbrate *verb* To give an indication of something in advance : augur, bode, forecast, forerun, foreshadow, foretell, foretoken, portend, prefigure, presage, prognosticate. See FORESIGHT, SHOW in Index. — See also **draft, shade.**

advance *verb* To cause to move forward or upward, as toward a goal : forward, further, promote. See FOR-

WARD, HELP in Index. — See also **come, lend, promote, propose, rise.**

advance *noun* **1.** Forward movement : advancement, furtherance, headway, march[1], progress, progression. See BETTER, FORWARD in Index. **2.** A preliminary action intended to elicit a favorable response. Used in plural : approach, overture. See APPROACH in Index. — See also **increase.**

advance *adjective* Going before : antecedent, anterior, earlier, precedent, preceding, previous, prior. See PRECEDE in Index.

advanced *adjective* Ahead of current trends or customs : forward, precocious, progressive. See PRECEDE in Index. — See also **old.**

advancement *noun* A progression upward in rank : elevation, jump, promotion, rise, upgrade. See RISE in Index. — See also **advance.**

advantage *noun* **1.** A factor conducive to superiority and success : handicap, head start, odds, start, vantage. See HELP in Index. **2.** A dominating position, as in a conflict : better, bulge, draw, drop, edge, superiority, upper hand, vantage. *Informal:* inside track, jump. See OVER in Index. **3.** Something beneficial : avail, benefit, blessing, boon[1], favor, gain, profit. See HELP in Index. — See also **interest, use.**

advantage *verb* See **profit.**

advantageous *adjective* See **beneficial, profitable.**

advent *noun* See **arrival.**

adventitious *adjective* See **incidental.**

adventure *noun* An exciting, often hazardous undertaking : emprise, enterprise, venture. See SAFETY in Index.

adventure *verb* See **hazard, risk.**

adventurer *noun* One who engages in exciting, risky pursuits : daredevil, venturer. See SAFETY in Index. — See also **mercenary, speculator.**

adventuresome *adjective* See **adventurous.**

adventuresomeness *noun* See **daring.**

adventurous *adjective* Taking or willing to take risks : adventuresome, audacious, bold, daredevil, daring, enterprising, venturesome, venturous. See SAFETY in Index. — See also **dangerous.**

adventurousness *noun* See **daring.**

adversarial *adjective* See **opposing.**

adversary *noun* See **opponent.**

adverse *adjective* See **opposing, unfavorable.**

adversity *noun* See **misfortune.**

advert *verb* See **refer.**

advertise *verb* **1.** To make known vigorously the positive features of (a product) : ballyhoo, build up, cry (up), popularize, promote, publicize, talk up. *Informal:* pitch, plug. *Slang:* push. See KNOWLEDGE in Index. **2.** To make (information) generally known : blaze[2], blazon, broadcast, bruit, circulate, disseminate, noise, promulgate, propagate, spread. *Idioms:* spread far and wide, spread the word. See KNOWLEDGE in Index. — See also **announce.**

advertisement *noun* See **promotion.**

advertising *noun* The act or profession of promoting something, as a product : promotion, publicity. See KNOWLEDGE in Index.

advice *noun* An opinion as to a decision or course of action : counsel, recommendation. See OPINION in Index. — See also **news.**

advisable *adjective* Worth doing, especially for practical reasons :

expedient, recommendable, well[2].
See WISE in Index.

advise *verb* To give recommendations to (someone) about a decision or course of action : counsel, recommend. *Informal:* mentor. See OPINION in Index. — See also **confer, inform.**

advised *adjective* Resulting from deliberation and careful thought : calculated, considered, studied, studious. See WISE in Index. — See also **informed.**

advisement *noun* A careful considering of a matter : calculation, consideration, deliberation, lucubration, study. See THOUGHTS in Index.

adviser or **advisor** *noun* One who advises another, especially officially or professionally : consultant, counselor, mentor. *Law:* counsel. See OPINION in Index.

advisory *adjective* Giving advice : consultative, consultatory, consulting, consultive. See OPINION in Index.

advocate *verb* See **support.**

aegis *noun* See **patronage.**

aerate *verb* See **air.**

aerial *adjective* See **airy, filmy, lofty.**

aery *adjective* See **filmy.**

aesthetic or **esthetic** *adjective* See **tasteful.**

afeard also **afeared** *adjective* See **afraid.**

affability *noun* See **amiability.**

affable *adjective* See **amiable, gracious.**

affair *noun* See **business, love, matter, party.**

affect[1] *verb* To evoke a usually strong mental or emotional response from : get (to), impress, move, strike, touch. See TOUCH in Index.

affect[2] *verb* See **assume.**

affectation *noun* Artificial behavior adopted to impress others :

affectedness, air (used in plural), mannerism, pose, pretense. See HONEST, TRUE in Index.

affected *adjective* Artificially genteel : artificial, mannered, precious. *Informal:* la-di-da. See GOOD, HONEST, PLAIN, TRUE in Index. — See also **artificial, concerned.**

affectedness *noun* See **affectation.**

affecting *adjective* Exciting a deep, usually somber response : impressive, moving, poignant, stirring, touching. See TOUCH in Index.

affection *noun* See **attachment, emotion.**

affectionate *adjective* Feeling and expressing affection : devoted, doting, fond, loving. See ATTITUDE, LOVE in Index.

affective *adjective* See **emotional.**

affectivity *noun* See **emotion.**

afferent *adjective* See **sensory.**

affianced *adjective* See **engaged.**

affiliate *verb* See **associate.**

affiliate *noun* See **associate, subsidiary.**

affiliation *noun* See **association.**

affinity *noun* See **likeness.**

affirm *verb* See **assert, confirm.**

affirmation *noun* See **assertion, confirmation.**

affirmative *adjective* See **favorable, positive.**

affix *verb* See **attach, fix.**

afflatus *noun* See **inspiration.**

afflict *verb* To bring great harm or suffering to : agonize, anguish, curse, excruciate, plague, rack, scourge, smite, strike, torment, torture. See ATTACK, HELP in Index.

afflicted *adjective* See **miserable.**

affliction *noun* See **burden**[1]**, curse, distress, sickness.**

afflictive *adjective* See **painful.**

affluence *noun* See **riches.**

affluent *adjective* See **rich.**

afford *verb* See **offer.**

affray *noun* See **brawl.**
affright *verb* See **frighten.**
  affright *noun* See **fear.**
affront *verb* See **insult.**
  affront *noun* See **indignity.**
afield *adverb* See **wrong.**
afire *adjective* See **burning.**
aflame *adjective* See **burning.**
aforetime *adverb* See **earlier.**
afraid *adjective* Filled with fear or terror : aghast, apprehensive, fearful, fearsome, funky, panicky. *Regional:* afeard, ascared. See FEAR in Index.
afresh *adverb* See **anew.**
after *adjective* See **back, later.**
  after *adverb* See **later.**
afterlife *noun* See **immortality.**
aftermath *noun* See **effect.**
afterward *adverb* See **later.**
afterwards *adverb* See **later.**
again *adverb* See **anew.**
age *noun* **1.** A particular time notable for its distinctive characteristics : day, epoch, era, period, time (often used in plural). See TIME in Index. **2.** *Informal.* A long time. Used in plural : eon, eternity, long[1], year (used in plural). *Informal:* blue moon. *Idioms:* forever and a day, forever and ever, month of Sundays. See TIME in Index. **3.** Old age : agedness, elderliness, senectitude, senescence, year (used in plural). See YOUTH in Index.
  age *verb* To grow old : get along, get on. See YOUTH in Index. — See also **mature.**
aged *adjective* Brought to full flavor and richness by aging : mellow, ripe. See YOUTH in Index. — See also **old.**
agedness *noun* See **age.**
ageless *adjective* Existing unchanged forever : dateless, eternal, timeless. *Archaic:* eterne. See CHANGE in Index.

agency *noun* See **branch, mean[3].**
agenda *noun* See **program.**
agent *noun* See **mean[3], spy.**
age-old *adjective* See **old.**
agglomerate *verb* See **accumulate.**
agglomeration *noun* See **heap.**
aggrandize *verb* See **exalt, increase.**
aggrandizement *noun* See **exaltation, increase.**
aggravate *verb* See **annoy, intensify.**
aggravation *noun* See **annoyance.**
aggregate *verb* See **accumulate, amount.**
  aggregate *noun* See **total, whole.**
aggregation *noun* See **accumulation.**
aggress *verb* See **attack.**
aggression *noun* Hostile behavior : aggressiveness, belligerence, belligerency, combativeness, contentiousness, hostility, militance, militancy. See ATTACK in Index. — See also **attack.**
aggressive *adjective* **1.** Inclined to act in a hostile way : belligerent, combative, contentious, hostile, militant. See ATTACK, ATTITUDE in Index. **2.** Marked by boldness and assertiveness : assertive. See ATTITUDE, TRY in Index.
aggressiveness *noun* See **aggression.**
aggressor *noun* One who starts a hostile action : assailant, assailer, assaulter, attacker. See ATTACK in Index.
aggrieve *verb* See **distress, wrong.**
aghast *adjective* See **afraid.**
agile *adjective* See **nimble.**
agileness *noun* See **agility.**
agility *noun* The quality or state of being mentally agile : agileness, dexterity, dexterousness, nimbleness, quickness. See ABILITY in Index.

agitate *verb* **1.** To cause to move to and fro violently : churn, convulse, rock, shake. See CALM, REPETITION in Index. **2.** To impair or destroy the composure of : bother, discompose, disquiet, distract, disturb, flurry, fluster, perturb, rock, ruffle, shake (up), toss, unsettle, upset. *Informal:* rattle. See CALM in Index.

agitated *adjective* See **anxious.**

agitation *noun* **1.** The condition of being physically agitated : commotion, convulsion, turbulence. See CALM in Index. **2.** A state of discomposure : dither, fluster, flutter, perturbation, tumult, turmoil, upset. *Informal:* lather, stew. See CALM in Index. — See also **disturbance.**

agitator *noun* One who agitates, especially politically : fomenter, inciter, instigator. See CALM, CHANGE, POLITICS in Index.

agnate *adjective* See **related.**

agog *adjective* See **eager.**

agonize *verb* See **afflict, writhe.**

agonizing *adjective* See **tormenting.**

agony *noun* See **distress.**

agree *verb* **1.** To come to an understanding or to terms : accord, coincide, concur, get together, harmonize. See AGREE in Index. **2.** To be compatible or in correspondence : accord, check, chime, comport with, conform, consist, correspond, fit[1], harmonize, match, square, tally. *Informal:* jibe. *Archaic:* quadrate. See AGREE in Index. — See also **assent.**

agreeability *noun* See **amiability.**

agreeable *adjective* **1.** To one's liking : congenial, favorable, good, grateful, gratifying, nice, pleasant, pleasing, pleasurable, satisfying, welcome. See LIKE in Index. **2.** In keeping with one's needs or expectations : accordant, compatible, conformable, congenial, congruous, consistent, consonant, correspondent, corresponding, harmonious. See AGREE in Index. — See also **amiable, obliging, willing.**

agreeableness *noun* See **amiability.**

agreed *adverb* See **yes.**

agreement *noun* **1.** The act or state of agreeing or conforming : accordance, chime, conformance, conformation, conformity, congruence, congruity, correspondence, harmonization, harmony, keeping. See AGREE in Index. **2.** Harmonious mutual understanding : accord, concord, concordance, concurrence, consonance, harmony, rapport, tune, unity. *Idiom:* meeting of the minds. See AGREE in Index. **3.** An act or state of agreeing between parties regarding a course of action : accord, arrangement, bargain, compact[2], deal, pact, understanding. See AGREE in Index. **4.** A legally binding arrangement between parties : bond, compact[2], contract, convention, covenant, pact. See AGREE in Index. — See also **acceptance, treaty.**

ahead *adverb* See **early.**

aid *verb* See **help.**

aid *noun* See **help, helper, relief.**

aide *noun* See **assistant.**

ail *verb* See **worry.**

ailing *adjective* See **sickly.**

ailment *noun* See **disease, indisposition.**

aim *verb* **1.** To move (a weapon or blow, for example) in the direction of someone or something : cast, direct, head, level, point, set[1], train, turn, zero in. *Military:* lay[1]. See SEEK in Index. **2.** To strive toward a goal : aspire, seek. *Idiom:* set one's sights on. See SEEK, START in Index. — See also **intend.**

aim *noun* See **intention, thrust.**

aimless *adjective* Without aim, purpose, or intent : desultory, pointless, purposeless. See PURPOSE in Index.

air *noun* **1.** The gaseous mixture enveloping the earth : atmosphere. See HIGH, PLACE in Index. **2.** The celestial regions as seen from the earth : firmament, heaven (often used in plural), sky. *Archaic:* welkin. See HIGH in Index. **3.** A general impression produced by a predominant quality or characteristic : ambiance, atmosphere, aura, feel, feeling, mood, smell, tone. See BE in Index. — See also **affectation, bearing, melody, wind[1].**

air *verb* **1.** To expose to circulating air : aerate, ventilate, wind[1]. See BREATH, OPEN in Index. **2.** To utter publicly : express, put, state, vent, ventilate. *Idiom:* come out with. See SHOW, WORDS in Index.

airless *adjective* **1.** Oppressive due to a lack of fresh air : close, stifling, stuffy. See BREATH, OPEN in Index. **2.** Marked by an absence of circulating air : breathless, breezeless, still, windless. See BREATH in Index.

airy *adjective* **1.** Of or relating to air : aerial, atmospheric, pneumatic. See BREATH, HIGH in Index. **2.** Exposed to or characterized by the presence of freely circulating air or wind : blowy, breezy, gusty, windy. See BREATH in Index. **3.** Displaying light-hearted nonchalance : breezy, buoyant, debonair, jaunty. *Informal:* corky. *Idiom:* free and easy. See ATTITUDE, CAREFUL, GOOD in Index. — See also **filmy, lofty.**

akin *adjective* See **related.**

alabaster *adjective* See **fair.**

à la mode *adjective* See **fashionable.**

alarm *noun* A signal that warns of imminent danger : alarum, alert,

tocsin, warning. See WARN in Index. — See also **fear.**

alarm *verb* See **frighten, warn.**

alarmist *noun* One who needlessly alarms others : scaremonger. See POLITICS, WARN in Index.

alarum *noun* See **alarm.**

alcoholic *adjective* See **hard.**

alert *adjective* Vigilantly attentive : observant, open-eyed, vigilant, wakeful, wary, watchful, wide-awake. *Idiom:* on the ball. See AWARENESS in Index. — See also **clever.**

alert *noun* See **alarm.**

alert *verb* See **warn.**

alertness *noun* The condition of being alert : vigilance, wakefulness, wariness, watchfulness. See AWARENESS in Index.

alien *adjective* See **foreign.**

alien *noun* See **foreigner.**

alien *verb* See **transfer.**

alienate *verb* See **estrange, transfer.**

alienation *noun* See **breach, estrangement, grant, insanity.**

alight[1] *verb* See **land.**

alight on or **upon** *verb* See **come across** at **come.**

alight[2] *adjective* See **burning.**

align also **aline** *verb* See **ally, line.**

alike *adjective* See **like[2].**

alikeness *noun* See **likeness.**

aliment *noun* See **food.**

alimentary *adjective* See **nutritious, nutritive.**

alimentation *noun* See **living.**

alimony *noun* See **living.**

alive *adjective* **1.** Marked by or exhibiting life : animate, animated, live[2], living, vital. See LIVE in Index. **2.** Having existence or life : around, existent, existing, extant, living. See LIVE in Index. **3.** Full of animation and activity : replete, rife. See BIG, RICH in Index. — See also **active, aware.**

all *adjective* See **whole.**

all *noun* See **whole.**

all *adverb* See **completely.**

all-around *adjective* See **general, versatile.**

allay *verb* See **calm, relieve.**

allegation *noun* See **assertion.**

allege *verb* See **assert, present².**

allegiance *noun* See **fidelity.**

allegiant *adjective* See **faithful.**

alleviate *verb* See **relieve.**

alleviation *noun* See **relief.**

alliance *noun* An association, especially of nations for a common cause : Anschluss, bloc, cartel, coalition, confederacy, confederation, federation, league, organization, union. See CONNECT, GROUP, POLITICS in Index. — See also **association.**

allied *adjective* See **related.**

all-inclusive *adjective* See **general.**

allocate *verb* See **allot, appropriate.**

allocation *noun* See **allotment, distribution.**

allocution *noun* See **speech.**

allot *verb* To set aside or distribute as a share : admeasure, allocate, allow, apportion, assign, give, lot, measure out, mete (out). See COLLECT in Index.

allotment *noun* That which is allotted : allocation, allowance, dole, lot, measure, part, portion, quantum, quota, ration, share, split. *Informal:* cut. *Slang:* divvy. See COLLECT in Index.

all-out *adjective* See **thorough, utter².**

all-overs *noun* See **jitter.**

allow *verb* See **acknowledge, allot, permit.**

allowable *adjective* See **permissible.**

allowance *noun* See **allotment, concession, permission.**

alloyed *adjective* See **impure.**

all right *adverb* See **yes.** *adjective* See **acceptable.**

all-round *adjective* See **general, versatile.**

all the same *adverb* See **still.**

allure *verb* See **attract, seduce.**

allure *noun* See **attraction.**

allurement *noun* See **attraction, lure.**

allurer *noun* See **seducer.**

alluring *adjective* See **seductive.**

allusive *adjective* See **suggestive.**

alluvion *noun* See **flood.**

ally *verb* To be formally associated, as by treaty : align, confederate, federate, league. See CONNECT, POLITICS in Index. — See also **associate.**

ally *noun* One nation associated with another in a common cause : coalitionist, confederate, leaguer. See CONNECT, POLITICS in Index. — See also **associate.**

almost *adverb* See **approximately.**

alms *noun* See **donation.**

almsman *noun* See **beggar.**

almswoman *noun* See **beggar.**

alone *adjective* Lacking the company of others : companionless, lone, lonely, lonesome, single, solitary, unaccompanied. See INCLUDE in Index. — See also **solitary, unique.**

alone *adverb* Without the presence or aid of another : single-handedly, singly, solely, solitarily, solo. *Idioms:* all by one's lonesome, by oneself. See INCLUDE in Index. — See also **solely.**

aloneness *noun* The quality or state of being alone : isolation, loneliness, singleness, solitariness, solitude. See INCLUDE in Index.

aloof *adjective* See **cool, detached.**

aloofness *noun* See **detachment.**

already *adverb* See **earlier.**

also *adverb* See **additionally**.

alter *verb* See **change, sterilize**.

alterable *adjective* See **changeable**.

alteration *noun* See **change**.

altercation *noun* See **argument**.

alternate *verb* See **rotate**.

alternate *noun* See **substitute**.

alternation *noun* See **rotation**.

alternative *noun* See **choice**.

altitude *noun* See **elevation**.

alto *adjective* See **low**.

altogether *adverb* See **completely**.

altruism *noun* See **benevolence**.

altruistic *adjective* See **benevolent**.

amalgam *noun* See **mixture**.

amalgamate *verb* See **mix**.

amalgamation *noun* See **mixture**.

amaranthine *adjective* See **endless**.

amass *verb* See **accumulate**.

amassment *noun* See **accumulation**.

amateur *noun* One lacking professional skill and ease in a particular pursuit : dabbler, dilettante, nonprofessional, smatterer, uninitiate. See ABILITY in Index.

amateurish *adjective* Lacking the required professional skill : dilettante, dilettantish, nonprofessional, unprofessional, unskilled, unskillful. See ABILITY in Index.

amative *adjective* See **erotic**.

amativeness *noun* See **desire**.

amatory *adjective* See **erotic**.

amaze *verb* See **surprise**.

amaze *noun* See **wonder**.

amazement *noun* See **wonder**.

amazing *adjective* See **fabulous**.

ambiance also **ambience** *noun* See **air, environment**.

ambidexterity *noun* See **insincerity**.

ambidextrous *adjective* See **insincere**.

ambiguity *noun* An expression or term liable to more than one interpretation : double-entendre, equiv-ocality, equivocation, equivoque, tergiversation. See CLEAR in Index.
— See also **equivocation, vagueness**.

ambiguous *adjective* **1.** Liable to more than one interpretation : cloudy, equivocal, inexplicit, nebulous, obscure, uncertain, unclear, vague. See CERTAIN, CLEAR in Index. **2.** Not affording certainty : borderline, chancy, clouded, doubtful, dubious, dubitable, equivocal, inconclusive, indecisive, indeterminate, problematic, problematical, questionable, uncertain, unclear, unsure. *Informal:* iffy. *Idioms:* at issue, in doubt, in question. See CERTAIN, CLEAR in Index.

ambiguousness *noun* See **vagueness**.

ambit *noun* See **circumference, range**.

ambition *noun* A strong desire to achieve something : ambitiousness, aspiration, emulation. See DESIRE in Index. — See also **intention**.

ambitious *adjective* Full of ambition : aspiring, emulous. See DESIRE in Index.

ambitiousness *noun* See **ambition**.

amble *verb* See **stroll**.

amble *noun* See **walk**.

ambrosial *adjective* See **delicious**.

ambulance chaser *noun* See **lawyer**.

ambulate *verb* See **walk**.

ambuscade *verb* See **ambush**.

ambuscade *noun* See **ambush**.

ambush *verb* To attack suddenly and without warning : ambuscade, bushwhack, surprise, waylay. See ATTACK in Index. **ambush** *noun* An attack or stratagem for capturing or tricking an unsuspecting person : ambuscade, trap. See ATTACK in Index.

ameliorate *verb* See **improve**.

amelioration noun See **improvement, progress.**

amenability noun See **obedience.**

amenable adjective See **liable, obedient, receptive.**

amenableness noun See **obedience.**

amend verb See **correct, improve, revise.**

amendatory adjective See **corrective.**

amendment noun See **improvement, revision.**

amends noun See **compensation.**

amenity noun 1. Anything that increases physical comfort : comfort, convenience, facility (often used in plural). See COMFORT in Index. 2. A courteous act or courteous acts that contribute to smoothness and ease in dealings and social relationships. Used in plural : civility, courtesy, pleasantry, politeness, propriety (used in plural). See COURTESY in Index. — See also **amiability.**

amerce verb See **fine².**

amercement noun See **fine².**

amiability noun The quality of being pleasant and friendly : affability, agreeability, agreeableness, amenity, amiableness, congeniality, congenialness, cordiality, cordialness, friendliness, geniality, genialness, pleasantness, sociability, sociableness, warmth. See ATTITUDE, GOOD in Index.

amiable adjective Pleasant and friendly in disposition : affable, agreeable, congenial, cordial, genial, good-natured, good-tempered, pleasant, sociable, warm. See ATTITUDE, GOOD in Index.

amiableness noun See **amiability.**

amicable adjective See **friendly.**

amigo noun See **friend.**

amiss adjective Not in accordance with what is usual or expected : astray, awry, sour, wrong. See SURPRISE, THRIVE in Index.

amiss adverb See **wrong.**

amnesiac adjective See **forgetful.**

amnesic adjective See **forgetful.**

amnesty noun See **forgiveness.**

amorist noun See **gallant.**

amorous adjective See **erotic.**

amorousness noun See **love.**

amorphous adjective See **shapeless.**

amount noun See **import, quantity, total.**

amount verb 1. To come to in number or quantity : aggregate, number, reach, run into, total. *Idiom:* add up to. See INCREASE in Index. 2. To be equivalent or tantamount : constitute, correspond, equal. *Idiom:* have all the earmarks. See BE in Index.

amour noun See **love.**

amour-propre noun See **egotism, pride.**

ample adjective See **broad, full, generous, roomy.**

amplification noun See **increase.**

amplify verb See **elaborate, elevate, increase.**

amplitude noun See **bulk, size.**

amuck also **amok** adjective See **runaway.**

amulet noun See **charm.**

amuse verb To occupy in an agreeable or pleasing way : divert, entertain, recreate, regale. See EXCITE in Index.

amusement noun 1. The condition of being amused : entertainment, recreation. See EXCITE in Index. 2. Something, especially a performance or show, designed to entertain : distraction, diversion, entertainment, recreation. See EXCITE in Index.

amusing adjective 1. Providing pleasure or entertainment : diverting, entertaining. See EXCITE in Index. **2.** Arousing laughter : comic, comical, droll, funny, humorous, laughable, risible, zany. See LAUGHTER in Index.

analogize *verb* See **liken.**

analogous *adjective* See **like².**

analogue *noun* See **parallel.**

analogy *noun* See **likeness.**

analysis *noun* **1.** The separation of a whole into its parts for study : anatomy, breakdown, dissection. See ASSEMBLE, INVESTIGATE in Index. **2.** A close or systematic study : examination, inspection, investigation, review, survey. See INVESTIGATE in Index.

analytic *adjective* See **logical.**

analytical *adjective* See **logical.**

analyze *verb* **1.** To separate into parts for study : anatomize, break down, dissect, resolve. See ASSEMBLE, INVESTIGATE in Index. **2.** To study closely or systematically : examine, inspect, investigate. See INVESTIGATE in Index.

anarchy *noun* See **disorder.**

anathema *noun* See **curse, hate.**

anathematize *verb* See **curse.**

anatomize *verb* See **analyze.**

anatomy *noun* See **analysis.**

ancestor *noun* **1.** A person from whom one is descended : antecedent, ascendant, father, forebear, forefather, foremother, mother, parent, progenitor. *Archaic:* predecessor. See KIN, PRECEDE in Index. **2.** One that precedes, as in time : antecedent, forerunner, precursor, predecessor, progenitor. See PRECEDE in Index.

ancestral *adjective* Of or from one's ancestors : hereditary, inherited, patrimonial. See KIN, PRECEDE in Index.

ancestry *noun* One's ancestors or their character or one's ancestral derivation : birth, blood, bloodline, descent, extraction, family, genealogy, line, lineage, origin, parentage, pedigree, seed, stock. See KIN, PRECEDE in Index.

anchor *verb* See **fasten.**

ancient *adjective* See **early, high, old.**

ancient *noun* See **senior.**

ancillary *adjective* See **auxiliary.**

anecdote *noun* See **yarn.**

anemic *adjective* See **pale, sickly.**

anesthetic also **anaesthetic** *adjective* See **insensitive.**

anew *adverb* Once more : afresh, again. See REPETITION in Index.

anfractuous *adjective* See **indirect, winding.**

angel *noun* See **innocent, patron, sponsor.**

angelic *adjective* See **innocent.**

angelical *adjective* See **innocent.**

anger *noun* A strong feeling of displeasure or hostility : choler, indignation, irateness, ire. See FEELINGS in Index.

anger *verb* **1.** To cause to feel or show anger : burn (up), enrage, incense¹, infuriate, madden, provoke. *Idioms:* make one hot under the collar, make one's blood boil, put one's back up. See FEELINGS in Index. **2.** To be or become angry : blow up, boil over, bristle, burn, explode, flare up, foam, fume, rage, seethe. *Informal:* steam. *Idioms:* blow a fuse, blow a gasket, blow one's stack (or top), breathe fire, fly off the handle, get hot under the collar, hit the ceiling (or roof), lose one's temper, see red. See FEELINGS in Index.

angle¹ *verb* See **hint.**

angle² *verb* See **bend, bias.**

angle *noun* See **phase, point of view, wrinkle.**

angry *adjective* Feeling or showing anger : choleric, indignant, mad. *Informal:* sore. *Idiom:* hot under the collar. See FEELINGS in Index.

angst *noun* See **anxiety.**

anguish *noun* See **distress.**

anguish *verb* See **afflict.**

anguishing *adjective* See **tormenting.**

angular *adjective* See **thin.**

anhydrous *adjective* See **dry.**

animal *adjective* See **physical.**

animalism *noun* See **physicality.**

animality *noun* See **physicality.**

animalize *verb* See **corrupt.**

animate *verb* See **activate, elate, encourage, fire, light¹, quicken.**

animate *adjective* See **alive.**

animated *adjective* See **alive, lively.**

animating *adjective* See **stimulating.**

animation *noun* See **elation, energy, spirit.**

animosity *noun* See **enmity.**

animus *noun* See **enmity.**

annals *noun* See **history.**

annex *verb* See **attach.**

annex *noun* See **extension.**

annihilate *verb* **1.** To destroy all traces of : abolish, blot out, clear, eradicate, erase, exterminate, extinguish, extirpate, kill¹, liquidate, obliterate, remove, root¹ (out *or* up), rub out, snuff out, stamp out, uproot, wipe out. *Idioms:* do away with, make an end of, put an end to. See HELP, MAKE in Index. **2.** To kill savagely and indiscriminately : butcher, decimate, massacre, slaughter. See CRIMES, HELP, MAKE in Index. — See also **abolish, overwhelm.**

annihilation *noun* Utter destruction : eradication, extermination, extinction, extinguishment, extirpation, liquidation, obliteration.

See CRIMES, HELP, MAKE in Index.
— See also **abolition.**

annotation *noun* See **commentary.**

announce *verb* To bring to public notice or make known publicly : advertise, annunciate, broadcast, declare, proclaim, promulgate, publish. See KNOWLEDGE, WORDS in Index. — See also **usher in** at **usher.**

announcement *noun* **1.** The act of announcing : annunciation, declaration, proclamation, promulgation, publication. See KNOWLEDGE in Index. **2.** A public statement : annunciation, declaration, edict, manifesto, notice, proclamation, pronouncement. See KNOWLEDGE in Index.

annoy *verb* **1.** To trouble the nerves or peace of mind of, especially by repeated vexations : aggravate, bother, bug, chafe, disturb, exasperate, fret, gall², get, irk, irritate, nettle, peeve, provoke, put out, rile, ruffle, vex. *Idioms:* get in one's hair, get on one's nerves, get under one's skin. See FEELINGS, PAIN in Index. **2.** To disturb by repeated attacks : bait, bedevil, beleaguer, beset, harass, harry, pester, plague, tease, torment, worry. See FEELINGS, PAIN in Index.

annoyance *noun* **1.** Something that annoys : aggravation, besetment, bother, irritant, irritation, nuisance, peeve, plague, torment, vexation. See FEELINGS, PAIN in Index. **2.** The act of annoying : botheration, bothering, exasperation, harassment, irritation, pestering, provocation, vexation. See FEELINGS, PAIN in Index. **3.** The feeling of being annoyed : aggravation, bother, botheration, exasperation, irritation, vexation. See FEELINGS, PAIN in Index.

annoying *adjective* See **vexatious.**

annul *verb* See **abolish, cancel.**

annular *adjective* See **round.**

annulment *noun* See **abolition.**

annunciate *verb* See **announce.**

annunciation *noun* See **announcement.**

anomalistic *adjective* See **abnormal.**

anomalous *adjective* See **abnormal.**

anomaly *noun* See **abnormality.**

anonymity *noun* See **obscurity.**

anonymous *adjective* Having an unknown name or author : nameless, unnamed, unsigned. See KNOWLEDGE in Index.

Anschluss *noun* See **alliance.**

answer *noun* **1.** Something spoken or written in return, as to a question or demand : rejoinder, reply, response. See ASK in Index.
2. Something worked out to explain, resolve, or provide a method for dealing with and settling a problem : determination, solution.
Mathematics: result. See ASK in Index.

answer *verb* To speak or act in response, as to a question : rejoin, reply, respond, retort, return, riposte. See ASK in Index. — See also **satisfy, serve.**

answerable *adjective* See **liable.**

antagonism *noun* See **enmity, opposition.**

antagonist *noun* See **opponent.**

antagonistic *adjective* See **opposing.**

ante *noun* See **bet.**

antecede *verb* See **precede.**

antecedence *noun* See **precedence.**

antecedent *noun* See **ancestor, cause.**

antecedent *adjective* See **advance, past.**

antedate *verb* See **precede.**

antediluvian *adjective* See **early, old.**

anterior *adjective* See **advance, past.**

anthropoid *adjective* See **manlike.**

anthropomorphic *adjective* See **manlike.**

anthropomorphous *adjective* See **manlike.**

antic *noun* See **prank¹.**

antic *adjective* See **fantastic.**

anticipant *adjective* See **expectant.**

anticipate *verb* See **expect, foresee.**

anticipated *adjective* See **due.**

anticipation *noun* The condition of looking forward to something, especially with eagerness : expectance, expectancy, expectation. See SURPRISE in Index. — See also **expectation.**

anticipative *adjective* See **expectant.**

anticipatory *adjective* See **expectant.**

antidote *noun* See **remedy.**

antipathetic *adjective* See **filthy, opposing.**

antipathy *noun* See **enmity, hate.**

antipodal *adjective* See **opposite.**

antipode *noun* See **opposite.**

antipodean *adjective* See **opposite.**

antipodes *noun* See **opposite.**

antiquated *adjective* See **old, old-fashioned.**

antique *adjective* See **old, old-fashioned.**

antiseptic *adjective* See **clean.**

antithesis *noun* See **opposite, opposition.**

antithetical *adjective* See **opposite.**

antonym *noun* See **opposite.**

antonymic *adjective* See **opposite.**

antonymous *adjective* See **opposite.**

anxiety *noun* A troubled or anxious state of mind : angst, anxiousness, care, concern, disquiet, disquietude, distress, nervousness, solicitude, unease, uneasiness, worry. See FEELINGS in Index.

anxious *adjective* In a state of anxiety or uneasiness : agitated, concerned, distressed, nervous, solicitous, uneasy, unsettled. See FEELINGS in Index.

anxiousness *noun* See **anxiety.**

A-one also **A-1** *adjective* See **excellent.**

apace *adverb* See **fast.**

apart *adjective* See **solitary.**

apart *adverb* See **separately.**

apartheid *noun* See **segregation.**

apathetic *adjective* Without emotion or interest : detached, impassive, incurious, indifferent, insensible, lethargic, listless, phlegmatic, stolid, unconcerned, uninterested, unresponsive. See FEELINGS in Index.

apathy *noun* Lack of emotion or interest : disinterest, impassivity, incuriosity, incuriousness, indifference, insensibility, insensibleness, lassitude, lethargy, listlessness, phlegm, stolidity, stolidness, unconcern, uninterest, unresponsiveness. See FEELINGS in Index.

ape *verb* See **imitate.**

aperture *noun* See **hole.**

apex *noun* See **climax, height, point.**

aphonic *adjective* See **dumb.**

aphorism *noun* See **proverb.**

aphoristic *adjective* See **pithy.**

aphrodisiac *adjective* See **erotic.**

aping *noun* See **mimicry.**

apish *adjective* See **imitative.**

aplomb *noun* See **balance, confidence.**

apocalypse *noun* See **revelation.**

apocalyptic *adjective* See **fateful.**

apocalyptical *adjective* See **fateful.**

apogee *noun* See **climax.**

apologetic *adjective* Expressing or inclined to express an apology : contrite, penitent, regretful, repentant, sorry. See REGRET in Index.

apologetic *noun* See **apology.**

apologia *noun* See **apology.**

apologize *verb* See **defend.**

apology *noun* **1.** A statement of acknowledgment expressing regret or asking pardon : excuse, mea culpa, regret (used in plural). See REGRET in Index. **2.** A statement that justifies or defends something, such as a past action or policy : apologetic, apologia, defense, justification, vindication. See ATTACK in Index.

apostasy *noun* See **defection.**

apostate *noun* See **defector.**

apostatize *verb* See **defect.**

apostle *noun* See **missionary.**

apostolic *adjective* See **missionary.**

apotheosis *noun* See **exaltation.**

apotheosize *verb* See **exalt.**

appall *verb* See **dismay.**

appalling *adjective* See **fearful, terrible.**

appanage also **apanage** *noun* See **birthright.**

apparatus *noun* See **device, outfit.**

apparel *noun* See **dress.**

apparel *verb* See **dress.**

apparent *adjective* **1.** Readily seen, perceived, or understood : clear, clear-cut, crystal clear, distinct, evident, manifest, noticeable, observable, obvious, patent, plain, pronounced, visible. See SEE in Index. **2.** Appearing as such but not necessarily so : external, ostensible, ostensive, outward, seeming, superficial. See SURFACE in Index.

apparently *adverb* On the surface : evidently, externally, ostensibly, ostensively, outwardly, seemingly, superficially. *Idioms:* on the

face of it, to all appearances. See SUR-
FACE in Index.

apparition *noun* See **ghost.**

appeal *noun* **1.** An earnest or
urgent request : entreaty, imploration, plea, prayer[1], supplication. See
ASK in Index. **2.** An application to a
higher authority, as for sanction or a
decision : petition. *Law:* prayer[1].
See ASK, LAW in Index. — See also
attraction.

appeal *verb* To make an earnest
or urgent request : beg, beseech,
crave, entreat, implore, plead, pray,
sue, supplicate. *Archaic:* conjure.
See ASK in Index. — See also **address,
attract, petition.**

appealer *noun* One that asks a
higher authority for something, as a
favor or redress : appellant, petitioner, suitor. See ASK, LAW in
Index.

appear *verb* **1.** To come into view :
emerge, issue, loom, materialize,
show. *Idioms:* make (or put in) an
appearance, meet the eye. See SEE in
Index. **2.** To have the appearance
of : look, seem, sound[1]. *Idiom:*
strike one as (being). See SURFACE in
Index. — See also **dawn.**

appearance *noun* **1.** The act of
coming into view : emergence. See
SEE in Index. **2.** The way something
or someone looks : aspect, look,
mien. See SURFACE in Index. — See
also **arrival, image.**

appease *verb* See **pacify, satisfy.**

appellant *noun* See **appealer.**

appellation *noun* See **name.**

appellative *noun* See **name.**

append *verb* See **attach.**

appendage *noun* See **attachment.**

appertain *verb* See **apply.**

appetence *noun* See **desire.**

appetency *noun* See **desire.**

appetite *noun* A desire for food or
drink : hunger, stomach, taste,

thirst. See DESIRE in Index. — See
also **desire, taste.**

appetizing *adjective* See **delicious.**

applaud *verb* To express approval,
especially by clapping : cheer, clap,
root2. *Idiom:* give someone a hand.
See PRAISE in Index. — See also
praise.

applause *noun* Approval expressed
by clapping : hand, ovation, plaudit. See PRAISE in Index. — See also
praise.

apple-polish *verb* See **fawn.**

apple-polisher *noun* See
sycophant.

applesauce *noun* See **nonsense.**

appliance *noun* See **device.**

applicability *noun* See **relevance.**

applicable *adjective* See **relevant.**

applicant *noun* A person who
applies for or seeks something, such
as a job or position : aspirant, candidate, hopeful, petitioner, seeker.
See SEEK in Index.

application *noun* A document used
in applying, as for a job : form. See
SEEK, WORDS in Index. — See also
**administration, diligence, duty, exer-
cise, relevance.**

apply *verb* **1.** To devote (oneself or
one's efforts) : address, bend,
buckle down, concentrate, dedicate,
devote, direct, focus, give, turn. See
COLLECT, WORK in Index. **2.** To be
pertinent : appertain, bear on (or
upon), concern, pertain, refer, relate.
Idioms: have a bearing on, have to do
with. See RELEVANT in Index. **3.** To
ask for employment, acceptance, or
admission : petition, put in. See
SEEK in Index. — See also **address,
administer, resort, use.**

appoint *verb* To select for an office
or position : designate, make,
name, nominate, tap[1]. See CHOICE
in Index. — See also **furnish.**

appointee *noun* A person who is appointed to an office or position : designee, nominee. See CHOICE in Index.

appointment *noun* The act of appointing to an office or position : designation, nomination. See CHOICE in Index. — See also **engagement, furnishing, position.**

apportion *verb* See **allot.**

apportionment *noun* See **distribution.**

apposite *adjective* See **relevant.**

appositeness *noun* See **relevance.**

appraisal *noun* See **estimate.**

appraise *verb* See **estimate.**

appraisement *noun* See **estimate.**

appreciable *adjective* See **perceptible.**

appreciate *verb* To recognize the worth, quality, importance, or magnitude of : cherish, esteem, prize[1], respect, treasure, value. *Idiom:* set store by. See PRAISE in Index. — See also **admire.**

appreciation *noun* A being grateful : gratefulness, gratitude, thankfulness, thanks. See GRATEFUL in Index. — See also **esteem.**

appreciative *adjective* See **grateful.**

apprehend *verb* See **arrest, know, perceive, understand.**

apprehension *noun* See **arrest, fear, grasp.**

apprehensive *adjective* See **afraid.**

apprise *verb* See **inform.**

approach *verb* To come near in space or time : near. *Idioms:* come close to, draw near to. See APPROACH in Index. — See also **address, rival, start.**

approach *noun* **1.** The act or fact of coming near : coming, convergence, imminence, nearness. See APPROACH in Index. **2.** A method used in dealing with something :

attack, course, line, modus operandi, plan, procedure, tack, technique. See MEANS in Index. — See also **advance.**

approachable *adjective* Easily approached : accessible, responsive, welcoming. See APPROACH, ATTITUDE in Index.

approaching *adjective* See **coming.**

approbate *verb* See **permit.**

approbation *noun* See **acceptance, permission.**

approbatory *adjective* See **complimentary.**

appropriate *adjective* Suitable for a particular person, condition, occasion, or place : apt, becoming, befitting, correct, felicitous, fit[1], fitting, happy, meet[2], proper, right, tailor-made. See RIGHT in Index. — See also **convenient, just.**

appropriate *verb* To set aside or apart for a specified purpose : allocate, assign, designate, earmark. See COLLECT, MONEY in Index. — See also **assume.**

appropriation *noun* See **grant, usurpation.**

approval *noun* See **acceptance, confirmation, permission.**

approve *verb* To be favorably disposed toward : countenance, favor, hold with. *Informal:* go for. *Idiom:* take kindly to. See PRAISE in Index. — See also **confirm, permit.**

approximate *verb* See **estimate, rival.**

approximately *adverb* Near to in quantity or amount : about, almost, nearly, roughly. *Idiom:* on the order of. See NEAR in Index.

approximation *noun* See **estimate.**

appurtenance *noun* See **attachment.**

apropos *adjective* See **relevant.**

apt *adjective* See **appropriate, inclined.**

aptitude *noun* See **talent.**

aptness *noun* See **talent.**

aquiver *adjective* See **tremulous.**

arbiter *noun* See **judge.**

arbitrary *adjective* **1.** Determined or marked by whim or caprice rather than reason : capricious, whimsical. See SURPRISE in Index.
2. Based on individual judgment or discretion : discretionary, judgmental, personal, subjective. See OPINION, SURPRISE in Index. — See also **absolute.**

arbitrate *verb* See **judge.**

arbitrator *noun* See **judge.**

arc *verb* See **bend.**

arcadian also **Arcadian** *adjective* See **country.**

arcane *adjective* See **mysterious.**

arced *adjective* See **bent.**

arch *verb* See **bend, stoop.**

archaic *adjective* See **old, old-fashioned.**

arched *adjective* See **bent.**

archenemy *noun* See **enemy.**

archetypal *adjective* See **typical.**

archetype *noun* See **original.**

archetypic *adjective* See **typical.**

archetypical *adjective* See **typical.**

archfiend *noun* See **fiend.**

architect *noun* See **originator.**

archive *noun* See **depository.**

arciform *adjective* See **bent.**

arctic *adjective* See **frigid.**

ardent *adjective* See **eager, enthusiastic, hot, passionate.**

ardor *noun* See **enthusiasm, passion.**

ardorless *adjective* See **frigid.**

arduous *adjective* See **burdensome, difficult.**

arduously *adverb* See **hard.**

area *noun* **1.** A part of the earth's surface : belt, district, locality, neighborhood, quarter, region, tract, zone. *Informal:* neck of the woods. See TERRITORY in Index. **2.** A sphere of activity, experience, study, or interest : arena, bailiwick, circle, department, domain, field, orbit, province, realm, scene, subject, terrain, territory, world. *Slang:* bag. See TERRITORY in Index. — See also **locality, neighborhood.**

arena *noun* See **area.**

argot *noun* See **dialect, language.**

arguable *adjective* See **debatable.**

argue *verb* **1.** To put forth reasons for or against something, often excitedly : contend, debate, dispute, moot. See AFFIRM, WORDS in Index. **2.** To engage in a quarrel : bicker, contend, dispute, fight, quarrel, quibble, spat, squabble, tiff, wrangle. *Informal:* hassle, tangle. *Idioms:* cross swords, have it out, have words, lock horns. See CONFLICT in Index. — See also **assert, indicate.**

argue into *verb* See **persuade.**

argument *noun* **1.** A discussion, often heated, in which a difference of opinion is expressed : altercation, bicker, clash, contention, controversy, debate, difficulty, disagreement, dispute, fight, polemic, quarrel, run-in, spat, squabble, tiff, word (used in plural), wrangle. *Informal:* hassle, rhubarb, tangle. See CONFLICT in Index. **2.** A course of reasoning : case, point. See REASON in Index. — See also **reason, subject.**

argumentation *noun* The presentation of an argument or arguments : debate, disputation, forensics. See AFFIRM, WORDS in Index.

argumentative *adjective* Given to arguing : combative, contentious, disputatious, eristic, litigious, polemic, polemical, quarrelsome, scrappy. See CONFLICT in Index.

argumentativeness *noun* The quality or state of being argumentative : combativeness, contentiousness, disputatiousness, litigiousness, scrappiness. See CONFLICT in Index.

aria *noun* See **melody.**

arid *adjective* See **dry, dull.**

arise *verb* See **begin, dawn, get up** at **get, rise, stem.**

aristocracy *noun* See **society.**

aristocratic *adjective* See **noble.**

arithmetic *noun* See **figure.**

arm *noun* See **branch, extension.**

armistice *noun* See **truce.**

armpit *noun* See **pit**[1].

army *noun* See **crowd.**

aroma *noun* See **flavor, fragrance, smell.**

aromatic *adjective* See **fragrant.**

aromatize *verb* See **scent.**

around *adverb* See **back, backward, through.**

around *adjective* See **alive.**

around-the-clock *adjective* See **continual.**

arouse *verb* To induce or elicit (a reaction or emotion) : awake, awaken, kindle, raise, rouse, stir[1] (up), waken. See EXCITE in Index. — See also **wake**[1].

arraign *verb* See **accuse.**

arrange *verb* **1.** To put into a deliberate order : array, deploy, dispose, marshal, order, organize, range, sort, systematize. See ORDER in Index. **2.** To plan the details or arrangements of : lay out, prepare, schedule, work out. See PLANNED in Index. **3.** To bring about or come to an agreement concerning : conclude, fix, negotiate, set[1], settle. See AGREE in Index. — See also **harmonize, settle.**

arrangement *noun* **1.** A way or condition of being arranged : categorization, classification, deployment, disposal, disposition, distribution, formation, grouping, layout, lineup, order, organization, placement, sequence. See ORDER in

Index. **2.** A plan made in preparation for an undertaking. Often used in plural : preparation (often used in plural), provision (often used in plural). See PLANNED in Index. — See also **agreement, compromise.**

arrant *adjective* See **flagrant, utter**[2].

array *verb* See **arrange, dress up** at **dress.**

array *noun* See **attire, display, group.**

arrearage *noun* See **debt.**

arrears *noun* See **debt.**

arrest *verb* To take into custody as a prisoner : apprehend, seize. *Informal:* nab, pick up. *Slang:* bust, collar, pinch, run in. See LAW in Index. — See also **grip, stop.**

arrest *noun* A seizing and holding by law : apprehension, seizure. *Slang:* bust, collar, pickup, pinch. See LAW in Index.

arresting *adjective* See **noticeable.**

arrival *noun* **1.** The act of arriving : advent, appearance, coming. See START in Index. **2.** One that arrives : comer, visitor. See ENTER in Index. — See also **success.**

arrive *verb* To come to a particular place : check in, get in, pull in, reach, show up, turn up. *Slang:* blow in. *Idiom:* make (or put in) an appearance. See START in Index. — See also **succeed.**

arrive at *verb* To reach (a goal or objective) : attain, come to, gain, get to. *Informal:* hit on (or upon). See START in Index.

arrogance *noun* The quality of being arrogant : haughtiness, hauteur, insolence, loftiness, lordliness, overbearingness, presumption, pride, pridefulness, proudness, superciliousness, superiority. See ATTITUDE in Index.

arrogant *adjective* Overly convinced of one's own superiority and importance : haughty, high-and-mighty, insolent, lofty, lordly, overbearing, overweening, prideful, proud, supercilious, superior. *Idiom:* on one's high horse. See ATTITUDE in Index.

arrogate *verb* See **assume.**

arrogation *noun* See **usurpation.**

art *noun* Deceitful cleverness : artfulness, artifice, craft, craftiness, cunning, foxiness, guile, slyness, wiliness. See HONEST, MEANS in Index. — See also **ability, business.**

artful *adjective* **1.** Showing art or skill in performing or doing : adroit, deft, dexterous, skillful. See ABILITY, KNOWLEDGE in Index. **2.** Deceitfully clever : crafty, cunning, foxy, guileful, scheming, sharp, sly, tricky, wily. See ABILITY, HONEST, MEANS in Index.

artfulness *noun* See **art.**

article *noun* See **element, object.**

articulacy *noun* See **eloquence.**

articulate *adjective* See **eloquent, vocal.**

articulate *verb* See **integrate, pronounce, say.**

articulateness *noun* See **eloquence.**

articulation *noun* See **expression, voicing.**

artifice *noun* See **art, trick.**

artificial *adjective* **1.** Made by human beings instead of nature : manmade, manufactured, synthetic. See CULTURE in Index. **2.** Made to imitate something else : imitation, manmade, mock, simulated, synthetic. *Informal:* pretend. See REAL in Index. **3.** Not genuine or sincere : affected, feigned, insincere, phony, pretended. See TRUE in Index. — See also **affected, plastic.**

artificiality *noun* See **insincerity.**

artistic *adjective* See **tasteful.**

artless *adjective* Free from guile, cunning, or deceit : guileless, ingenuous, innocent, naive, natural, simple, unaffected, unsophisticated, unstudied, unworldly. See HONEST in Index. — See also **rustic.**

artsy-craftsy *adjective* See **arty.**

arty *adjective* *Informal.* Pretentiously artistic : artsy-craftsy. See PLAIN in Index.

ascared *adjective* See **afraid.**

ascend *verb* To move upward on or along : climb, go up, mount, scale². See RISE in Index. — See also **rise.**

ascendance *noun* See **dominance.**

ascendancy *noun* See **dominance.**

ascendant *adjective* See **ruling.**

ascendant *noun* See **ancestor.**

ascension *noun* See **ascent, rise.**

ascent *noun* **1.** The act of moving upward on or along : ascension, climb. See RISE in Index. **2.** An upward slope : acclivity, rise. See RISE in Index. — See also **rise.**

ascertain *verb* See **discover.**

ascertainment *noun* See **discovery.**

ascribe *verb* See **attribute.**

ascription *noun* See **attribution.**

aseptic *adjective* See **dull.**

asepticism *noun* See **dullness.**

ashen *adjective* See **pale.**

ashy *adjective* See **pale.**

aside *noun* See **digression.**

ask *verb* **1.** To put a question to (someone) : examine, inquire, query, question, quiz. See ASK in Index. **2.** To seek an answer to (a question) : pose, put, raise. See ASK in Index. — See also **demand, invite, request.**

askance *adverb* See **skeptically.**

asleep *adjective* See **dead, sleeping.**

aspect *noun* See **appearance, expression, face, phase.**

asperity *noun* See **difficulty.**

asperse *verb* See **libel.**

aspersion *noun* See **libel.**

asphyxiate *verb* See **choke.**

aspirant *noun* One who aspires : aspirer, hopeful. See SEEK in Index. — See also **applicant.**

aspiration *noun* See **ambition, dream.**

aspire *verb* To have a fervent hope or aspiration : dream. *Idioms:* reach for the stars, set one's heart on. See SEEK in Index. — See also **aim.**

aspirer *noun* See **aspirant.**

aspiring *adjective* See **ambitious.**

ass *noun* See **fool.**

assail *verb* See **attack, beat, revile.**

assailable *adjective* See **vulnerable.**

assailant *noun* See **aggressor.**

assailer *noun* See **aggressor.**

assailment *noun* See **attack.**

assault *verb* See **attack, beat, rape.**

assault *noun* See **attack.**

assaulter *noun* See **aggressor.**

assay *verb* See **attempt, estimate, test.**

assay *noun* See **attempt, test.**

assemblage *noun* See **accumulation, assembly.**

assemble *verb* **1.** To bring together : call, cluster, collect[1], congregate, convene, convoke, gather, get together, group, muster, round up, summon. See COLLECT in Index. **2.** To come together : cluster, collect[1], congregate, convene, forgather, gather, get together, group, muster. See COLLECT in Index. — See also **make.**

assembler *noun* See **builder.**

assembly *noun* A number of persons who have come or been gathered together : assemblage, body, company, conclave, conference, congregation, congress, convention, convocation, crowd, gathering, group, meeting, muster, troop. *Informal:* get-together. See COLLECT in Index. — See also **convention.**

assent *verb* To respond affirmatively; receive with agreement or compliance : accede, accept, acquiesce, agree, consent, nod, subscribe, yes. See AGREE in Index.

assent *noun* See **acceptance.**

assert *verb* **1.** To put into words positively and with conviction : affirm, allege, argue, asseverate, aver, avouch, avow, claim, contend, declare, hold, maintain, say, state. *Idiom:* have it. See AFFIRM in Index. **2.** To defend, maintain, or insist on the recognition of (one's rights, for example) : claim, vindicate. See ATTACK in Index.

assertion *noun* The act of asserting positively : affirmation, allegation, asseveration, averment, claim, declaration, statement. See AFFIRM in Index.

assertive *adjective* See **aggressive, emphatic.**

assess *verb* See **estimate, impose.**

assessment *noun* See **estimate, tax.**

asset *noun* See **resource.**

asseverate *verb* See **assert.**

asseveration *noun* See **assertion.**

assiduity *noun* See **diligence.**

assiduous *adjective* See **diligent.**

assiduousness *noun* See **diligence.**

assign *verb* See **allot, appropriate, attribute, fix, station, transfer.**

assignation *noun* See **engagement.**

assignment *noun* See **attribution, distribution, grant, task.**

assimilate *verb* See **absorb, liken.**

assimilation *noun* See **absorption.**

assimilative *adjective* See **absorbent.**

assist *verb* See **help.**

assist *noun* See **help.**

assistance *noun* See **help.**

assistant *noun* A person who holds a position auxiliary to another and assumes some of the superior's responsibilities : adjutant, aide, auxiliary, coadjutant, coadjutor, deputy, helper, lieutenant, second[2]. See HELP in Index.

assistant *adjective* See **auxiliary.**

assize *noun* See **law.**

associate *verb* **1.** To unite or be united in a relationship : affiliate, ally, bind, combine, conjoin, connect, join, link, relate. See CONNECT in Index. **2.** To come or bring together in one's mind or imagination : bracket, connect, correlate, couple, identify, link. See SAME in Index. **3.** To be with as a companion : consort, fraternize, hang around, hobnob, run (around), troop. *Slang:* hang out. *Idiom:* rub elbows (or shoulders) . See NEAR in Index.

associate *noun* **1.** One who is united in a relationship with another : affiliate, ally, cohort, colleague, confederate, copartner, fellow, partner. See CONNECT in Index. **2.** One who shares interests or activities with another : chum, companion, comrade, crony, fellow, mate. *Informal:* buddy, pal. See NEAR in Index. — See also **accompaniment.**

association *noun* The state of being associated : affiliation, alliance, combination, conjunction, connection, cooperation, partnership. See NEAR in Index. — See also **conference, suggestion, union.**

assort *verb* To distribute into groups according to kinds : categorize, class, classify, group, pigeonhole, separate, sort (out). See COLLECT in Index.

assorted *adjective* See **various.**

assortment *noun* A collection of various things : conglomeration, gallimaufry, hodgepodge, jumble, medley, mélange, miscellany, mish-

mash, mixed bag, mixture, olio, patchwork, potpourri, salmagundi, variety. *Slang:* grab bag. See COLLECT in Index.

assuage *verb* See **pacify, relieve.**

assuagement *noun* See **relief.**

assume *verb* **1.** To take upon oneself : incur, shoulder, tackle, take on, take over, undertake. See ACCEPT in Index. **2.** To lay claim to for oneself or as one's right : appropriate, arrogate, commandeer, preempt, seize, take, usurp. See GIVE in Index. **3.** To take on or give a false appearance of : affect[2], counterfeit, fake, feign, pretend, put on, sham, simulate. *Idiom:* make believe. See TRUE in Index. — See also **don, suppose.**

assumed *adjective* Being fictitious and not real, as a name : made-up, pseudonymous. See TRUE in Index.

assuming *adjective* See **impudent.**

assumption *noun* Something taken to be true without proof : postulate, postulation, premise, presupposition, supposition, theory, thesis. See REASON in Index. — See also **impudence, usurpation.**

assumptive *adjective* See **impudent, presumptive.**

assurance *noun* See **confidence, promise, safety, sureness.**

assure *verb* See **convince, guarantee.**

assured *adjective* See **confident, sure.**

assuredly *adverb* See **yes.**

assuredness *noun* See **sureness.**

astonish *verb* See **surprise.**

astonishing *adjective* See **fabulous.**

astonishment *noun* See **marvel, wonder.**

astound *verb* See **surprise.**

astounding *adjective* See **fabulous.**

astray *adverb* See **wrong.**

astray *adjective* See **amiss, stray.**

astringent *adjective* See **biting.**

astute *adjective* See **shrewd.**

astuteness *noun* See **discernment.**

asylum *noun* See **cover, home, refuge.**

asymmetric *adjective* See **irregular.**

asymmetrical *adjective* See **irregular.**

asymmetry *noun* See **irregularity.**

athirst *adjective* See **eager, thirsty.**

athletic *adjective* See **muscular.**

atingle *adjective* See **thrilled.**

atmosphere *noun* See **air, environment, flavor.**

atmospheric *adjective* See **airy.**

atrium *noun* See **court.**

atrocious *adjective* See **offensive, outrageous.**

atrociousness *noun* See **enormity, flagrancy.**

atrocity *noun* See **enormity, flagrancy, outrage.**

atrophy *noun* See **deterioration.**

atrophy *verb* See **deteriorate.**

attach *verb* **1.** To join one thing to another : affix, clip², connect, couple, fasten, fix, moor, secure. See ASSEMBLE in Index. **2.** To add as a supplement or an appendix : affix, annex, append, subjoin. See INCREASE in Index.

attachment *noun* **1.** A subordinate element added to another entity : accessory, adjunct, appendage, appurtenance, supplement. See INCREASE in Index. **2.** The condition of being closely tied to another by affection or faith : affection, devotion, fondness, liking, love, loyalty (used in plural). See CONNECT in Index.

attack *verb* **1.** To set upon with violent force : aggress, assail, assault, beset, fall on (or upon), go at, have at, sail into, storm, strike. *Informal:* light into, pitch into. See ATTACK in Index. **2.** To start work on vigor-

ously : go at, sail in, tackle, wade in (or into). *Idiom:* hop to it. See WORK in Index.

attack *noun* The act of attacking : aggression, assailment, assault, attempt, offense, offensive, onrush, onset, onslaught, strike. See ATTACK in Index. — See also **approach, seizure.**

attackable *adjective* See **vulnerable.**

attacker *noun* See **aggressor.**

attain *verb* See **accomplish, arrive at** at **arrive.**

attainable *adjective* See **available.**

attainment *noun* See **accomplishment.**

attaint *noun* See **stain.**

attempt *verb* To make an attempt to do or make : assay, endeavor, essay, seek, strive, try. *Idioms:* have a go at, have (or make or take) a shot at, have (or take) a whack at, make a stab at, take a crack at. See TRY in Index.

attempt *noun* A trying to do or make something : crack, effort, endeavor, essay, go, offer, stab, trial, try. *Informal:* shot. *Slang:* take. *Archaic:* assay. See TRY in Index. — See also **attack.**

attend *verb* See **accompany, follow, hear, serve, tend².**

attendant *noun* See **accompaniment, helper.**

attendant *adjective* See **accompanying.**

attending *adjective* See **accompanying.**

attention *noun* Concentration of the mental powers on something : attentiveness, concentration, consideration, heedfulness, regardfulness. See EXCITE in Index. — See also **notice.**

attentive *adjective* **1.** Concentrating the mental powers on some-

thing : heedful, intent, regardful.
Idiom: all ears (*or* eyes). See EXCITE
in Index. **2.** Full of polite concern
for the well-being of others : considerate, courteous, gallant, polite,
solicitous, thoughtful. See CARE-
FUL, TREAT WELL in Index.

attentiveness *noun* See **attention,
consideration.**

attenuate *verb* See **dilute, enervate,
thin.**

attenuation *noun* See **debilitation.**

attest *verb* See **certify, confirm, indicate, testify.**

attestant *noun* See **witness.**

attestation *noun* See **confirmation.**

attester *or* **attestor** *noun* See
witness.

attire *noun* Showy and elaborate
clothing or apparel : array, finery,
frippery, regalia. See PUT ON in
Index. — See also **dress.**

attire *verb* See **dress, dress up** at
dress.

attitude *noun* See **position, posture,
sentiment.**

attitudinize *verb* See **pose, posture.**

attorney *noun* See **lawyer.**

attract *verb* To direct or impel to
oneself by some quality or action :
allure, appeal, draw, entice, lure,
magnetize, take. *Informal:* pull. See
LIKE in Index. — See also **interest.**

attraction *noun* The power or quality of attracting : allure, allurement, appeal, attractiveness, call,
charisma, charm, draw, enchantment, enticement, fascination, glamour, lure, magnetism, witchery.
Informal: pull. See LIKE in Index.

attractive *adjective* Pleasing to the
eye or mind : bewitching, enchanting, engaging, enticing, fascinating,
fetching, glamorous, lovely, prepossessing, pretty, sweet, taking, tempting, winning, winsome. See LIKE

in Index. — See also **beautiful,
becoming.**

attractiveness *noun* See **attraction.**

attribute *verb* To regard as belonging to or resulting from another :
accredit, ascribe, assign, charge,
credit, impute, lay[1], refer. See GIVE
in Index.

attribute *noun* See **quality,
symbol.**

attribution *noun* The act of attrib-
uting : ascription, assignment,
credit, imputation. See GIVE in
Index.

attrition *noun* See **penitence.**

attune *verb* See **adjust, harmonize.**

atypic *adjective* See **abnormal,
unusual.**

atypical *also* **atypic** *adjective* See
abnormal, unusual.

au courant *adjective* See **contemporary.**

audacious *adjective* See **adventurous, brave, impudent.**

audaciousness *noun* See **daring,
impudence.**

audacity *noun* See **daring, impudence.**

audience *noun* See **hearing, public.**

audition *noun* See **hearing.**

aught *noun* See **nothing.**

augment *verb* See **increase.**

augment *noun* See **increase.**

augmentation *noun* See **addition,
increase.**

augur *verb* See **adumbrate,
prophesy.**

augur *noun* See **prophet.**

augural *adjective* See **prophetic.**

augury *noun* See **omen.**

august *adjective* See **exalted,
grand.**

au naturel *adjective* See **nude.**

aura *noun* See **air.**

aureate *adjective* See **sonorous.**

auricular *adjective* See **confidential.**

aurora *noun* See **dawn**.

auspex *noun* See **prophet**.

auspice *noun* See **patronage**.

auspicious *adjective* See **favorable**, **opportune**.

austere *adjective* See **bleak**.

austerity *noun* See **severity**.

autarchic *adjective* See **absolute**.

autarchical *adjective* See **absolute**.

autarchy *noun* See **absolutism**.

authentic *adjective* **1.** Not counterfeit or copied : actual, bona fide, genuine, good, indubitable, original, real, true, undoubted, unquestionable. See TRUE in Index. **2.** Worthy of belief, as because of precision or faithfulness to an original : authoritative, convincing, credible, faithful, true, trustworthy, valid. See TRUE in Index.

authenticate *verb* See **confirm**, **prove**.

authentication *noun* See **confirmation**.

authenticity *noun* The quality of being authentic : genuineness, realness, truthfulness, validity. See TRUE in Index.

author *noun* See **originator**.

authoritarian *adjective* Characterized by or favoring absolute obedience to authority : autocratic, despotic, dictatorial, totalitarian, tyrannic, tyrannical. See OVER in Index. — See also **dictatorial**.

authoritarian *noun* One who imposes or favors absolute obedience to authority : autocrat, despot, dictator, martinet, totalitarian, tyrant. See OVER in Index.

authoritarianism *noun* See **absolutism**.

authoritative *adjective* **1.** Exercising authority : commanding, dominant, lordly, masterful. See OVER, STRONG in Index. **2.** Having or arising from authority : conclusive, official, sanctioned, standard. See TRUE in Index. — See also **authentic**, **definitive**.

authority *noun* **1.** The right and power to command, decide, rule, or judge : command, control, domination, dominion, jurisdiction, mastery, might, power, prerogative, sovereignty, sway. *Informal:* say-so. See OVER in Index. **2.** A person or group having the right and power to command, decide, rule, or judge : official. *Idioms:* powers that be, the Man. See OVER in Index. — See also **expert**, **faculty**.

authorization *noun* See **permission**.

authorize *verb* To give authority to : accredit, commission, empower, enable, entitle, license, qualify. See ALLOW in Index. — See also **permit**.

autochthonal *adjective* See **indigenous**.

autochthonic *adjective* See **indigenous**.

autochthonous *adjective* See **indigenous**.

autocracy *noun* See **absolutism**, **tyranny**.

autocrat *noun* See **authoritarian**.

autocratic *adjective* See **absolute**, **authoritarian**.

autocratical *adjective* See **absolute**.

autograph *verb* See **sign**.

automatic *adjective* See **perfunctory**, **spontaneous**.

autonomous *adjective* See **free**.

autonomy *noun* See **freedom**.

auxiliary *adjective* **1.** Giving or able to give help or support : accessory, ancillary, assistant, collateral, contributory, subsidiary, supportive. See HELP in Index. **2.** Used or held in reserve : backup, emergency, reserve, secondary, standby, sup-

plemental, supplementary. See
INCREASE in Index.

auxiliary *noun* See **assistant**.

avail *verb* See **profit**.

avail *noun* See **advantage, use**.

available *adjective* Capable of
being obtained or used : acquirable,
attainable, gettable, obtainable, procurable. *Idioms:* on hand, to be had.
See GET in Index.

avarice *noun* See **greed**.

avaricious *adjective* See **greedy**.

avariciousness *noun* See **greed**.

avenge *verb* To exact revenge for or
from : pay back, pay off, redress,
repay, requite, vindicate. *Informal:*
fix. *Archaic:* wreak. *Idioms:* even
the score, get back at, get even with,
pay back in kind (or in one's own
coin), settle (or square) accounts,
take an eye for an eye. See FORGIVE-
NESS in Index.

avenue *noun* See **way**.

aver *verb* See **assert**.

average *noun* Something, as a type,
number, quantity, or degree, that
represents a midpoint between
extremes on a scale of valuation :
mean[3], median, medium, norm, par.
See USUAL in Index.

average *adjective* See **acceptable, common, ordinary**.

averment *noun* See **assertion**.

averse *adjective* See **indisposed**.

averseness *noun* See **indisposition**.

aversion *noun* See **hate**.

avert *verb* See **prevent, turn**.

avid *adjective* See **eager, greedy,
voracious**.

avidity *noun* See **greed, voracity**.

avoid *verb* To keep away from :
burke, bypass, circumvent, dodge,
duck, elude, escape, eschew, evade,
get around, shun. *Idioms:* fight shy
of, give a wide berth to, have no
truck with, keep (or stay or steer)
clear of. See SEEK in Index.

avoidance *noun* See **abolition,
escape**.

avoirdupois *noun* See **heaviness**.

avouch *verb* See **assert**.

avow *verb* See **acknowledge, assert**.

avowal *noun* See **acknowledgment**.

await *verb* See **expect**.

awake *adjective* See **aware,
wakeful**.

awake *verb* See **arouse, wake**[1].

awaken *verb* See **arouse, wake**[1].

award *noun* See **reward, trophy**.

award *verb* See **confer, grant**.

aware *adjective* Marked by comprehension, cognizance, and perception : alive, awake, cognizant, sensible, sentient, wise[1]. *Slang:* hip.
Idiom: on to. See KNOWLEDGE in
Index.

awareness *noun* The condition of
being aware : cognizance, consciousness, perception, sense. See
KNOWLEDGE in Index.

awash *adjective* See **big**.

away *adjective* See **absent**.

awe *noun* See **wonder**.

awe *verb* See **surprise**.

awesome *adjective* See **rare**.

awful *adjective* See **terrible**.

awful *adverb* See **very**.

awfully *adverb* See **very**.

awkward *adjective* **1.** Lacking dexterity and grace in physical movement : clumsy, gawky, graceless,
inept, lumpish, maladroit, ungainly,
ungraceful. *Slang:* klutzy. *Idiom:* all
thumbs. See ABILITY in Index.
2. Difficult to handle or manage :
bulky, clumsy, ungainly, unhandy,
unmanageable, unwieldy. See EASY
in Index. **3.** Characterized by embarrassment and discomfort : constrained, uncomfortable, uneasy. See
FEELINGS in Index. — See also **unfortunate, unskillful**.

awry *adverb* See **wrong**.

awry *adjective* See **amiss**.

ax *noun* See **dismissal.**
  ax *verb* See **dismiss.**
axiom *noun* See **law.**
aye also **ay** *noun* See **yes.**
  aye also **ay** *adverb* See **yes.**

B

babble *verb* To talk rapidly, incoherently, or indistinctly : blather, chatter, gabble, gibber, jabber, prate, prattle. See WORDS in Index. — See also **chatter.**
  babble *noun* Unintelligible or foolish talk : blather, blatherskite, double talk, gabble, gibberish, jabber, jabberwocky, jargon, nonsense, prate, prattle, twaddle. See WORDS in Index. — See also **chatter.**
babbling *adjective* See **laughing.**
babe *noun* See **baby, beauty, innocent.**
babel *noun* See **noise.**
baby *noun* **1.** A very young child : babe, bambino, infant, neonate, newborn, nursling. *Idiom:* bundle of joy. See KIN, YOUTH in Index. **2.** A person who behaves in a childish, weak, or spoiled way : milksop, milquetoast, mollycoddle, weakling. *Idiom:* mama's boy (or girl). See YOUTH in Index.
  baby *verb* To treat with indulgence and often overtender care : cater, coddle, cosset, indulge, mollycoddle, overindulge, pamper, spoil. See TREAT WELL in Index.
babyish *adjective* Of or like a baby : cherubic, childlike, infantile, infantine. See YOUTH in Index. — See also **childish.**
back *noun* The part or area farthest from the front : rear[1], rearward. See PRECEDE in Index.

back *verb* **1.** To move in a reverse direction : backpedal, backtrack, fall back, retreat, retrocede, retrograde, retrogress. *Idiom:* retrace one's steps. See FORWARD in Index. **2.** To present evidence in support of. Also used with *up* : buttress, corroborate, substantiate. See SUPPORT in Index. — See also **confirm, finance, support.**
back down or **out** *verb* To abandon a former position or commitment : renege, retreat. *Slang:* cop out, fink out. See RESIST in Index.
back *adjective* Located in the rear : hind, hindmost, posterior, postern, rear[1]. *Nautical:* after. See PRECEDE in Index. — See also **remote.**
back *adverb* In or toward a former location or condition : about, around, backward, backwards, rearward, round. See APPROACH in Index. — See also **backward.**
backbite *verb* See **libel.**
backbreaking *adjective* See **burdensome.**
backer *noun* See **patron, sponsor.**
backfire *verb* To produce an unexpected and undesired result : boomerang. See SURPRISE in Index.
background *noun* See **history.**
backing *noun* See **capital, endorsement, patronage.**
backlog *noun* See **hoard.**
backpack *verb* See **hike.**
backpedal *verb* See **back.**
backset *noun* See **reverse.**
backside *noun* See **bottom.**
backslide *verb* See **relapse.**
  backslide *noun* See **lapse.**
backsliding *noun* See **lapse.**
backtrack *verb* See **back.**
backup *adjective* See **auxiliary.**
backward *adjective* **1.** Directed or facing toward the back or rear : retrograde, retrogressive. See PRECEDE

in Index. **2.** Not progressing and developing as fast as others, as in economic and social aspects : lagging, underdeveloped, undeveloped. See PRECEDE in Index. **3.** Having only a limited ability to learn and understand : dull, simple, simple-minded, slow, slow-witted. *Informal:* soft. *Offensive:* feeble-minded, half-witted, retarded, weak-minded. See ABILITY in Index. — See also **depressed, ignorant, modest, unprogressive.**

backward *adverb* Toward the back : about, around, back, backwards, rearward. See PRECEDE in Index. — See also **back.**

backwardness *noun* See **shyness.**

backwards *adverb* See **back, backward.**

bad *adjective* **1.** Below a standard of quality : bum[1], poor, unsatisfactory. *Idioms:* below par, not up to scratch (or snuff). See GOOD in Index. **2.** Bringing, predicting, or characterized by misfortune : evil, ill, inauspicious, unfavorable, unpropitious. See LUCK in Index. **3.** Impaired because of decay : putrid, rotten. See BETTER, TASTE, THRIVE in Index. — See also **evil, harmful, naughty, unpleasant.**

bad *noun* See **evil.**

badge *noun* See **decoration, sign.**

badger *verb* See **bait, besiege.**

badinage *noun* See **ribbing.**

badlands *noun* See **barren.**

bad name *noun* See **disgrace.**

badness *noun* See **evil.**

bad odor *noun* See **disgrace.**

bad-tempered *adjective* See **ill-tempered.**

baffle *verb* See **frustrate.**

bag *verb* See **bulge, take.**

bag *noun* See **area, forte.**

baggage *noun* See **slut.**

bail[1] *noun* See **bond, bondsman.**

bail[2] *verb* See **dip.**

bail out *verb* See **eject.**

bailiwick *noun* See **area.**

bailsman *noun* See **bondsman.**

bairn *noun* See **child.**

bait *verb* To torment with persistent insult or ridicule : badger, bullyrag, heckle, hector, hound, taunt. *Informal:* needle, ride. *Idiom:* wave the red flag in front of the bull. See TREAT WELL in Index. — See also **annoy, tantalize.**

bait *noun* See **lure.**

bake *verb* See **burn.**

baking *adjective* See **hot.**

balance *noun* **1.** A stable state characterized by the cancellation of all forces by equal opposing forces : counterpoise, equilibrium, equipoise, stasis. See ORDER in Index. **2.** A stable, calm state of the emotions : aplomb, collectedness, composure, coolness, equanimity, imperturbability, imperturbableness, nonchalance, poise, sang-froid, self-possession, unflappability. *Slang:* cool. See CALM, FEELINGS in Index. **3.** What remains after a part has been used or subtracted : leavings, leftover, remainder, remains, remnant, residue, rest[2]. See LEFTOVER in Index. — See also **proportion.**

balance *verb* **1.** To put in balance : counterbalance, equalize, stabilize, steady. See ORDER in Index. **2.** To act as an equalizing weight or force to : compensate, counteract, counterbalance, counterpoise, countervail, make up, offset, set off. See ORDER in Index. **3.** To place or be placed on a narrow or insecure surface : perch, poise. See POSTURE in Index. — See also **compare, compensate.**

balanced *adjective* See **even**[1], **sane, symmetrical.**

bald *adjective* See **bare.**

balderdash *noun* See **nonsense**.

bald-faced *adjective* See **shameless**.

baleful *adjective* See **malign**.

balk *verb* See **frustrate**.

balk *noun* See **beam**.

balky *adjective* See **contrary**.

balloon *verb* See **bulge**.

ballot *verb* See **elect**.

balloter *noun* See **elector**.

ball up *verb* See **botch, confuse**.

ballyhoo *verb* See **advertise, promote**.

ballyhoo *noun* See **promotion**.

balm *verb* See **calm**.

balmy[1] *adjective* See **gentle**.

balmy[2] *adjective* See **foolish**.

baloney *noun* See **nonsense**.

bambino *noun* See **baby**.

bamboozle *verb* See **deceive**.

ban *verb* See **censor, forbid**.

ban *noun* See **forbiddance**.

banal *adjective* See **trite**.

banality *noun* See **cliché**.

bananas *adjective* See **insane**.

band[1] *noun* A long narrow piece, as of material : bandeau, fillet, strip[2], stripe. See MATTER in Index. — See also **circle**.

band *verb* To encircle with or as if with a band : begird, belt, cincture, compass, encompass, engirdle, gird, girdle, girt, ring[1]. *Archaic:* engird. See EDGE in Index.

band[2] *noun* A group of people acting together in a shared activity : company, corps, party, troop, troupe. See PERFORMING ARTS in Index. — See also **gang, group**.

band *verb* To assemble or join in a group : combine, gang up, league, unite. See COLLECT in Index.

bandage *verb* See **dress**.

bandeau *noun* See **band**[1].

banderole or **banderol** also **bannerol** *noun* See **flag**[1].

bandit *noun* See **larcenist**.

bandy *verb* See **discuss, exchange**.

bane *noun* See **curse, destruction, poison, ruin**.

baneful *adjective* See **fateful, virulent**.

bang *noun* See **blast, blow**[2]**, report, slam, thrill**.

bang *verb* To strike, set down, or close in such a way as to make a loud noise : clap, crash, slam, whack. See SOUNDS in Index. — See also **blast, crack**.

bang *adverb* See **directly**.

banish *verb* To force to leave a country or place by official decree : deport, exile, expatriate, expel, ostracize, transport. See ACCEPT in Index. — See also **dismiss**.

banishment *noun* See **exile**.

bank[1] *noun* See **heap**.

bank *verb* See **heap**.

bank[2] *verb* To place (money) in a bank : deposit, lay away, salt away. *Informal:* sock away. See KEEP, MONEY in Index.

bank on or **upon** *verb* See **depend on** at **depend**.

bankroll *verb* See **finance**.

bankrupt *verb* See **destroy, ruin**.

bankruptcy *noun* See **failure**.

banner *noun* See **flag**[1].

banner *adjective* See **excellent**.

banneret *noun* See **flag**[1].

banquet *noun* See **feast**.

bantam *adjective* See **little**.

banter *noun* See **ribbing**.

banter *verb* See **joke**.

baptize *verb* See **name**.

bar *noun* Something that impedes or prevents entry or passage : barricade, barrier, block, blockage, clog, hamper, hindrance, hurdle, impediment, obstacle, obstruction, snag, stop, traverse, wall. See HELP, OPEN in Index. — See also **court, stick**.

bar *verb* To shut in with or as if with bars : confine, lock, wall. See FREE in Index. — See also **exclude, obstruct.**

barbarian *noun* See **boor.**

barbarian *adjective* See **coarse, uncivilized.**

barbaric *adjective* See **coarse, uncivilized.**

barbarism *noun* See **corruption.**

barbarity *noun* See **cruelty.**

barbarous *adjective* See **fierce, uncivilized.**

bard *noun* See **poet.**

bare *adjective* 1. Without the usual covering : bald, naked, nude. See PUT ON in Index. 2. Without addition, decoration, or qualification : bald, dry, plain, simple, unadorned, unvarnished. See PLAIN in Index. 3. Just sufficient : scant. See EXCESS in Index. — See also **empty, nude.**

bare *verb* To make bare : denude, disrobe, divest, expose, strip¹, uncover. See PUT ON in Index. — See also **reveal.**

barefaced *adjective* See **shameless.**

barely *adverb* By a very little; almost not : hardly, just, scarce, scarcely. See NEAR in Index.

bareness *noun* See **nudity.**

bargain *noun* 1. An agreement, especially one involving a sale or exchange : compact², contract, covenant, deal, transaction. See AGREE in Index. 2. Something offered or bought at a low price : *Informal:* buy, deal. *Slang:* steal. See MONEY, TRANSACTIONS in Index. — See also **agreement.**

bargain *verb* See **contract, haggle.**

bargain for or **on** *verb* See **expect.**

bark *verb* See **crack, snap.**

bark *noun* See **report.**

barnyard *adjective* See **obscene.**

baronial *adjective* See **grand.**

baroque *adjective* See **ornate.**

barrage *noun* A concentrated outpouring, as of missiles, words, or blows : bombardment, burst, cannonade, fusillade, hail¹, salvo, shower, storm, volley. See ATTACK in Index.

barrage *verb* To direct a barrage at : bombard, cannonade, fusillade, pepper, shower. See ATTACK in Index.

barrel *noun* See **heap.**

barrel *verb* See **rush.**

barren *adjective* 1. Unable to produce offspring : childless, impotent, infertile, sterile, unfruitful. See RICH in Index. 2. Lacking or unable to produce growing plants or crops : infertile, sterile, unfruitful, unproductive. See RICH in Index. — See also **empty, futile.**

barren *noun* A tract of unproductive land. Often used in plural : badlands, desert¹, waste, wasteland, wilderness. See RICH in Index.

barrenness *noun* See **emptiness, nothingness, sterility.**

barricade *noun* See **bar.**

barrier *noun* See **bar, wall.**

barrister *noun* See **lawyer.**

basal *adjective* See **elementary, radical.**

base¹ *noun* 1. The lowest or supporting part or structure : basis, bed, bottom, foot, footing, foundation, fundament, ground, groundwork, seat, substratum, underpinning (often used in plural). See OVER in Index. 2. A center of organization, supply, or activity : complex, headquarters, station. *Military:* installation. See PLACE in Index. — See also **basis, theme.**

base *verb* To provide a basis for : build, establish, found, ground, pred-

icate, rest¹, root¹, underpin. See
OVER in Index.

base² *adjective* See **lowly, shoddy,
sordid.**

baseborn *adjective* See **illegitimate, lowly.**

baseless *adjective* Having no basis
or foundation in fact : bottomless,
groundless, idle, unfounded, unwarranted. See TRUE in Index.

bash *noun* See **blast, blow², party.**
bash *verb* See **hit.**

bashful *adjective* See **modest.**

bashfulness *noun* See **shyness.**

basic *adjective* See **elemental, elementary, essential, radical.**
basic *noun* See **element.**

basically *adverb* See **essentially.**

basin *noun* The region drained by
a river system : watershed. See
TERRITORY in Index. — See also
depression.

basis *noun* **1.** That on which something immaterial, such as an argument or a charge, rests : base¹,
footing, foundation, fundament,
ground (often used in plural), groundwork, underpinning (often used in
plural). See OVER in Index. **2.** A fundamental principle or underlying
concept : base¹, cornerstone, foundation, fundament, fundamental,
root¹, rudiment (often used in plural). See OVER in Index. **3.** A justify-
ing fact or consideration : foundation, justification, reason, warrant.
See TRUE in Index. **4.** An established position from which to operate or deal with others : footing,
status, term (often used in plural).
See CONNECT in Index. — See also
base¹.

bask *verb* See **luxuriate.**

bass *adjective* See **low.**

bastard *adjective* See **illegitimate.**

bastardize *verb* See **corrupt.**

bastardy *noun* See **illegitimacy.**

baste *verb* See **beat.**

bat¹ *verb* See **blink.**

bat² *noun* See **bender.**

batch *noun* See **group.**

bate *verb* See **subside.**

bathe *verb* See **wash.**

bathetic *adjective* See **sentimental.**

bathos *noun* See **sentimentality.**

batten *verb* See **clean up at clean.**

batter *verb* To injure or damage, as
by abuse or heavy wear : knock
about (or around), mangle¹, maul,
rough up. See ATTACK, HELP,
STRIKE in Index. — See also **beat.**

battle *noun* See **combat, competition.**
battle *verb* See **contend.**

battle-ax or **battle-axe** *noun* See
scold.

battle cry *noun* See **cry.**

batty *adjective* See **insane.**

bauble *noun* See **novelty.**

bawd *noun* See **prostitute.**

bawdiness *noun* See **obscenity.**

bawdry *noun* See **obscenity.**

bawdy *adjective* See **obscene.**

bawl *verb* To cry loudly, as a
healthy child does from pain or
distress : howl, wail, yowl. See
SOUNDS in Index. — See also **cry,
roar.**
bawl out *verb* *Informal.* To reprimand loudly or harshly : berate,
rate². *Informal:* tell off. *Idioms:* give
hell to, give it to. See ATTACK in
Index. — See also **call down at call.**
bawl *noun* See **roar.**

bawling *noun* See **cry.**

bay¹ *noun* A body of water partly
enclosed by land but having a wide
outlet to the sea : bight, cove, inlet.
See TERRITORY in Index.

bay² *noun* See **howl.**
bay *verb* See **howl.**

be *verb* To have reality or life :
breathe, exist, live¹, subsist. See BE
in Index. — See also **exist.**

beak *noun* See **bill²**, **nose.**

beam *noun* **1.** A large, oblong piece of wood or other material, used especially for construction : balk, rafter, timber. See MATTER in Index. **2.** A series of particles or waves traveling close together in parallel paths : ray, shaft. See LIGHT in Index.

beam *verb* To emit a bright light : blaze¹, burn, gleam, glow, incandesce, radiate, shine. See LIGHT in Index. — See also **smile.**

beamy *adjective* See **bright.**

bean *noun* See **head.**

bear *verb* **1.** To hold up : carry, support, sustain. See OVER in Index. **2.** To hold and turn over in the mind : harbor, nourish, nurse. See THOUGHTS in Index. **3.** To be endowed with as a visible characteristic or form : carry, display, exhibit, have, possess. See SHOW in Index. **4.** To give birth to : bring forth, deliver, have. *Chiefly Regional:* birth. *Idiom:* be brought abed (or to bed) of. See RICH in Index. **5.** To bring forth (a product) : give, produce, yield. See RICH in Index. **6.** To exert pressure : press, push. See OVER in Index. **7.** To proceed in a specified direction : go, head, make, set out, strike out. See APPROACH in Index. — See also **act, bring, carry, endure, support.**

bear on or **upon** *verb* See **apply.**

bear out *verb* See **confirm, prove.**

bear up *verb* To withstand stress or difficulty : endure, hold up, stand up. See CONTINUE in Index.

bearable *adjective* Capable of being tolerated : endurable, sufferable, tolerable. See CONTINUE in Index.

beard *verb* See **defy.**

bearer *noun* A person who carries messages or is sent on errands : car-

rier, conveyer, courier, envoy, messenger, runner, transporter. See OVER in Index.

bearing *noun* **1.** Behavior through which one reveals one's personality : address, air, demeanor, manner, mien, presence, style. *Archaic:* port. See BE, STYLE in Index. **2.** One's place and direction relative to one's surroundings. Often used in plural : location, orientation, position, situation. See PLACE in Index. — See also **heading, relevance.**

beast *noun* See **fiend.**

beat *verb* **1.** To hit heavily and repeatedly with violent blows : assail, assault, baste, batter, belabor, buffet, drub, hammer, pound, pummel, smash, thrash, thresh. *Informal:* lambaste. *Slang:* clobber. *Idiom:* rain blows on. See ATTACK, STRIKE in Index. **2.** To punish with blows or lashes : flog, hide², lash, thrash, whip. *Informal:* trim. *Slang:* lay into, lick. See ATTACK, REWARD in Index. **3.** To shape, break, or flatten with repeated blows : forge¹, hammer, pound. See REPETITION, STRIKE in Index. **4.** To mix rapidly to a frothy consistency : whip, whisk. See ASSEMBLE, REPETITION in Index. **5.** To indicate (time or rhythm), as with repeated gestures or sounds : count. *Idioms:* keep time, mark time. See REPETITION in Index. **6.** To make rhythmic contractions, sounds, or movements : palpitate, pound, pulsate, pulse, throb. See REPETITION, SOUNDS in Index. — See also **defeat, flap, nonplus, surpass.**

beat down *verb* See **glare.**

beat off *verb* See **parry.**

beat *noun* **1.** A stroke or blow, especially one that produces a sound : clunk, pound, thud, thump. See ATTACK, SOUNDS,

STRIKE in Index. **2.** A periodic contraction or sound of something coursing : palpitation, pulsation, pulse, throb. See REPETITION, SOUNDS in Index. **3.** An area regularly covered, as by a policeman or reporter : circuit, round, route. See TERRITORY in Index. — See also **rhythm.**

beat *adjective* See **exhausted.**

beating *noun* A punishment dealt with blows or lashes : flogging, hiding, lashing, thrashing, whipping. *Informal:* trimming. *Slang:* licking. See ATTACK, REWARD in Index. — See also **defeat.**

beatitude *noun* See **happiness.**

beau *noun* A man who courts a woman : admirer, courter, suitor, swain, wooer. See SEX in Index. — See also **boyfriend.**

beau geste *noun* See **courtesy.**

beau ideal *noun* See **model.**

beauteous *adjective* See **beautiful.**

beautiful *adjective* Having qualities that delight the eye : attractive, beauteous, comely, fair, good-looking, gorgeous, handsome, lovely, pretty, pulchritudinous, ravishing, sightly, stunning. *Scots:* bonny. *Idiom:* easy on the eyes. See BEAUTIFUL in Index.

beautify *verb* See **grace.**

beauty *noun* A person regarded as physically attractive : belle (used of a woman), lovely, stunner. *Slang:* babe, doll, hunk (used of a man), knockout, looker, stud (used of a man). See BEAUTIFUL in Index. — See also **virtue.**

becalm *verb* See **calm.**

becloud *verb* See **obscure.**

become *verb* To come to be : come, get, grow, turn (out), wax. See CHANGE in Index. — See also **fit¹, flatter, suit.**

becoming *adjective* Pleasingly suited to the wearer : attractive, flattering. See BEAUTIFUL in Index. — See also **appropriate, correct.**

bed *noun* See **base¹.**

bed *verb* See **harbor, retire, take.**

bedaub *verb* See **smear.**

bedaze *verb* See **daze.**

bedazzle *verb* See **daze.**

bedeck *verb* See **adorn.**

bedevil *verb* See **annoy, besiege.**

bedim *verb* See **obscure.**

bedraggled *adjective* See **shabby.**

bee *noun* See **fancy.**

beef *noun* See **brawn, complaint.**

beef *verb* See **complain.**

beef up *verb* See **increase.**

beetle *verb* See **bulge.**

befall *verb* See **chance, come.**

befit *verb* See **fit¹, suit.**

befitting *adjective* See **appropriate, convenient, correct.**

befog *verb* See **obscure.**

before *adverb* See **earlier.**

beforehand *adverb* See **earlier, early.**

beforetime *adverb* See **earlier.**

befoul *verb* See **blacken, dirty.**

befuddle *verb* To muddle or stupefy with or as if with alcoholic drink : besot, fuddle. See DRUGS in Index. — See also **confuse.**

befuddlement *noun* See **daze.**

beg *verb* To ask or ask for as charity : bum¹, cadge. *Informal:* panhandle. *Slang:* mooch. See REQUEST in Index. — See also **appeal.**

beget *verb* See **father, produce.**

beggar *noun* One who begs habitually or for a living : almsman, almswoman, cadger, mendicant. *Informal:* panhandler. *Slang:* bummer, moocher. See REQUEST in Index. — See also **pauper, supplicant.**

beggarly *adjective* See **poor.**

beggary *noun* The condition of being a beggar : mendicancy, mendicity. See RICH in Index. — See also **poverty**.

begin *verb* To come into being : arise, commence, originate, start. See START in Index. — See also **start**.

beginner *noun* One who is just starting to learn or do something : abecedarian, fledgling, freshman, greenhorn, initiate, neophyte, novice, novitiate, tenderfoot, tyro. *Slang:* rookie. See START in Index.

beginning *noun* The act or process of bringing or being brought into existence : commencement, inauguration, inception, incipience, incipiency, initiation, launch, lead-off, opening, origination, start. *Informal:* kickoff. See START in Index. — See also **birth, origin**.

beginning *adjective* Of, relating to, or occurring at the start of something : inceptive, incipient, initial, initiatory, introductory, leadoff. See START in Index. — See also **early, elementary**.

begird *verb* See **band¹, surround**.

begrime *verb* See **dirty**.

begrudge *verb* See **envy**.

beguile *verb* See **charm, deceive**.

behave *verb* See **act, function**.

behavior *noun* **1.** The manner in which one behaves : action (often used in plural), comportment, conduct, deportment, way. See BE in Index. **2.** The way in which a machine or other thing performs or functions : functioning, operation, performance, reaction, working (often used in plural). See ACTION, MACHINE in Index.

behemoth *noun* See **giant**.

behemoth *adjective* See **giant**.

behest *noun* See **command**.

behind *noun* See **bottom**.

behind *adverb* See **late, slow**.

behindhand *adjective* See **late**.

behindhand *adverb* See **late, slow**.

behold *verb* See **see**.

beholden *adjective* See **obliged**.

beholder *noun* See **watcher**.

behoove *verb* See **suit**.

being *noun* See **effect, essence, existence, human being, thing**.

belabor *verb* See **beat**.

belated *adjective* See **late**.

belatedly *adverb* See **late**.

belatedness *noun* See **lateness**.

belay *verb* See **stop**.

belch *verb* See **erupt**.

beldam or **beldame** *noun* See **witch**.

beleaguer *verb* See **annoy, besiege**.

beleaguerment *noun* See **siege**.

belie *verb* See **distort, refute**.

belief *noun* **1.** Mental acceptance of the truth or actuality of something : credence, credit, faith. See OPINION in Index. **2.** Something believed or accepted as true by a person : conviction, feeling, idea, mind, notion, opinion, persuasion, position, sentiment, view. See OPINION in Index. — See also **confidence**.

believability *noun* See **verisimilitude**.

believable *adjective* Worthy of being believed : colorable, credible, creditable, plausible. See TRUE in Index.

believe *verb* **1.** To regard (something) as true or real : accept. *Slang:* buy, swallow. See OPINION in Index. **2.** To have confidence in the truthfulness of : credit, trust. *Idiom:* take at one's word. See OPINION in Index. **3.** To have an opinion : consider, deem, hold, opine, think. *Informal:* figure, judge. *Idiom:* be of the opinion. See OPINION in Index. — See also **feel, repute**.

believe in *verb* See **depend on** at **depend**.

belittle *verb* To think, represent, or speak of as small or unimportant : decry, denigrate, deprecate, depreciate, derogate, detract, discount, disparage, downgrade, minimize, run down, slight, talk down. *Idiom:* make light (*or* little) of. See ATTACK, SHOW in Index.

belittlement *noun* The act or an instance of belittling : denigration, deprecation, depreciation, derogation, detraction, disparagement, minimization. See ATTACK, SHOW in Index.

belle *noun* See **beauty**.

bellicose *adjective* See **belligerent, military**.

bellicoseness *noun* See **belligerence, fight**.

bellicosity *noun* See **belligerence, fight**.

belligerence *noun* Warlike or hostile attitude or nature : bellicoseness, bellicosity, belligerency, combativeness, contentiousness, hostility, militance, militancy, pugnaciousness, pugnacity, truculence, truculency. See ATTACK in Index. — See also **aggression, fight**.

belligerency *noun* See **aggression, belligerence, conflict, fight**.

belligerent *adjective* **1.** Having or showing an eagerness to fight : bellicose, combative, contentious, hostile, militant, pugnacious, quarrelsome, scrappy, truculent, warlike. See ATTACK in Index. **2.** Of or engaged in warfare : combatant, hostile, militant. *Idiom:* at war. See ATTACK in Index. — See also **aggressive**.

belligerent *noun* See **fighter**.

bellow *verb* See **roar**.

bellow *noun* See **roar**.

belly *verb* See **bulge**.

bellyache *verb* See **complain**.

bellyacher *noun* See **grouch**.

belong *verb* To have a proper or suitable place : fit[1], go. See ORDER in Index.

belonging *noun* See **effect**.

beloved *adjective* See **darling**.

beloved *noun* See **darling**.

belt *noun* See **area, blow**[2], **drink**.

belt *verb* See **band**[1], **drink, hit**.

bemire *verb* See **muddy**.

bemuse *verb* See **daze**.

bemused *adjective* See **absent-minded**.

bemusement *noun* See **trance**.

benchmark *noun* See **standard**.

bend *verb* **1.** To swerve from a straight line : angle[2], arc, arch, bow[2], crook, curve, round, turn. See STRAIGHT in Index. **2.** To cause to move, especially at an angle : angle[2], deflect, refract, turn. See STRAIGHT in Index. **3.** To be unable to hold up : give. See HELP in Index. — See also **apply, stoop**.

bend *noun* Something bent : bow[2], crook, curvature, curve, round, turn. See STRAIGHT in Index.

bender *noun* *Slang.* A drinking bout : binge, brannigan, carousal, carouse, drunk, spree. *Slang:* bat[2], booze, jag, tear[1]. See DRUGS, RESTRAINT in Index.

bending *adjective* See **crooked**.

benediction *noun* See **grace**.

benefaction *noun* See **benevolence, donation**.

benefactor *noun* See **donor, patron**.

benefactress *noun* See **donor**.

benefic *adjective* See **beneficial**.

beneficence *noun* See **benevolence, donation**.

beneficent *adjective* See **beneficial, benevolent**.

beneficial *adjective* Affording benefit : advantageous, benefic, beneficent, benignant, favorable, good, helpful, profitable, propitious, salutary, toward, useful. See HELP in Index.

benefit *verb* To derive advantage : capitalize, gain, profit. See HELP in Index. — See also **profit**.

benefit *noun* See **advantage, favor, interest, use**.

benevolence *noun* 1. Kindly, charitable interest in others : altruism, beneficence, benignancy, benignity, charitableness, charity, goodwill, grace, kindheartedness, kindliness, kindness, philanthropy. See ATTITUDE, KIND in Index. 2. A charitable deed : benefaction, beneficence, benignity, favor, kindliness, kindness, oblation, office (often used in plural), philanthropy. See GIVE, KIND in Index.

benevolent *adjective* 1. Characterized by kindness and concern for others : altruistic, beneficent, benign, benignant, good, goodhearted, kind[1], kindhearted, kindly. See ATTITUDE, KIND in Index. 2. Of or concerned with charity : altruistic, charitable, eleemosynary, philanthropic, philanthropical. See GIVE, KIND in Index.

benighted *adjective* See **ignorant**.

benightedness *noun* See **ignorance**.

benign *adjective* See **benevolent, favorable**.

benignancy *noun* See **benevolence**.

benignant *adjective* See **beneficial, benevolent**.

benignity *noun* See **benevolence**.

bent *adjective* Deviating from a straight line : arced, arched, arciform, bowed, curved, curvilinear, rounded. See STRAIGHT in Index. — See also **set[1]**.

bent *noun* An inclination to something : bias, cast, disposition, leaning, partiality, penchant, predilection, predisposition, proclivity,

proneness, propensity, squint, tendency, trend, turn. See APPROACH, LIKE in Index. — See also **talent**.

benumb *verb* See **daze, deaden, paralyze**.

benumbed *adjective* See **dull**.

bequeath *verb* See **hand down** at **hand, leave[1]**.

berate *verb* See **bawl out** at **bawl**.

bereft *adjective* See **abandoned**.

berth *noun* See **position**.

berth *verb* See **harbor**.

beseech *verb* See **appeal**.

beseem *verb* See **suit**.

beset *verb* See **annoy, attack, besiege, surround**.

besetment *noun* See **annoyance**.

besides *adverb* See **additionally**.

besiege *verb* 1. To surround with hostile troops : beleaguer, beset, blockade, invest, siege. *Idiom:* lay siege to. See ATTACK in Index. 2. To trouble persistently from or as if from all sides : badger, bedevil, beleaguer, beset, harass, harry, hound, importune, pester, plague, solicit. See ATTACK in Index. — See also **close in** at **close**.

besiegement *noun* See **siege**.

besmear *verb* See **blacken, smear**.

besmirch *verb* See **blacken, dirty**.

besoil *verb* See **dirty**.

besot *verb* See **befuddle**.

besotted *adjective* See **drunk**.

bespatter *verb* See **blacken, splash, spot**.

bespeak *verb* See **address, book, indicate**.

bespeckle *verb* See **speckle**.

besprinkle *verb* See **speckle, sprinkle**.

best *adjective* 1. Surpassing all others in quality : optimal, optimum, superlative, unsurpassed. See BETTER in Index. 2. Much more than half : better, greater, larger, largest, most. See BETTER, BIG in Index.

best *noun* The superlative or most preferable part of something : choice, cream, crème de la crème, elite, flower, pick, prize[1], top. *Idioms:* cream of the crop, flower of the flock, pick of the bunch (*or* crop). See BETTER in Index. — See also **regard.**

best *verb* See **defeat, surpass.**

bestain *verb* See **stain.**

bestial *adjective* See **fierce.**

bestiality *noun* See **corruption, cruelty.**

bestialize *verb* See **corrupt.**

bestow *verb* See **confer, donate, give, harbor.**

bestowal *noun* See **conferment.**

bestowment *noun* See **conferment.**

bestride *verb* See **stride.**

bet *verb* To make a bet : gamble, game, lay[1], play, wager. *Idiom:* put one's money on something. See GAMBLING in Index. — See also **gamble.**

bet *noun* Something risked on an uncertain outcome : ante, pot, stake (often used in plural), wager. See GAMBLING in Index. — See also **gamble.**

bête noire *noun* See **hate.**

bethink *verb* See **remember.**

betide *verb* See **come.**

betimes *adverb* See **early, intermittently.**

betoken *verb* See **indicate.**

betray *verb* **1.** To be treacherous to : double-cross. *Slang:* rat (on), sell out. *Idiom:* sell down the river. See TRUST in Index. **2.** To disclose in a breach of confidence : blab, divulge, expose, give away, let out, reveal, tell, uncover, unveil. *Informal:* spill. *Archaic:* discover. *Idioms:* let slip, let the cat out of the bag, spill the beans, tell all. See SHOW in Index. — See also **deceive.**

betrayal *noun* An act of betraying : double cross, treachery. *Slang:* sellout. See TRUST in Index.

betrayer *noun* One who betrays : double-crosser, Judas, traitor. *Informal:* rat. See TRUST in Index.

betrothal *noun* See **engagement.**

betrothed *adjective* See **engaged.**

betrothed *noun* See **intended.**

better *adjective* Of greater excellence than another : preferable, superior. See BETTER in Index. — See also **best.**

better *verb* See **improve, surpass.**

better *noun* See **advantage, superior.**

better *adverb* To a greater extent : more. See BIG in Index.

better half *noun* See **spouse.**

betterment *noun* See **improvement, progress.**

bettor *also* **better** *noun* One who bets : gambler, gamester, player. See GAMBLING in Index.

beveled *adjective* See **bias.**

beverage *noun* See **drink.**

bevy *noun* See **group.**

beware *verb* See **look out** at **look.**

bewilder *verb* See **confuse.**

bewilderedness *noun* See **daze.**

bewilderment *noun* See **daze.**

bewitch *verb* See **charm.**

bewitching *adjective* See **attractive, seductive.**

bias *noun* An inclination for or against that inhibits impartial judgment : one-sidedness, partiality, partisanship, prejudice, prepossession, tendentiousness. See AFFECT, LIKE, STRAIGHT in Index. — See also **bent.**

bias *verb* **1.** To cause to have a prejudiced view : jaundice, prejudice, prepossess, warp. See AFFECT, STRAIGHT in Index. **2.** To direct (material) to the interests of a particular group : skew, slant. *Informal:* angle[2]. See STRAIGHT in Index.

bias *adjective* Angled at a slant : beveled, biased, diagonal, oblique, slanted, slanting. See STRAIGHT in Index.

biased also **biassed** *adjective* Exhibiting bias : one-sided, partial, partisan, prejudiced, prejudicial, prepossessed, tendentious. See LIKE, STRAIGHT in Index. — See also **bias**.

bibelot *noun* See **novelty.**

bibulous *adjective* See **absorbent.**

bicker *verb* See **argue.**

bicker *noun* See **argument.**

bid *verb* See **command, go, invite.**

bid *noun* See **invitation, offer.**

biddable *adjective* See **obedient.**

bidding *noun* See **command.**

biddy also **biddie** *noun* See **witch.**

bide *verb* See **pause, remain.**

biff *verb* See **hit.**

biff *noun* See **blow[2].**

biform *adjective* See **double.**

bifurcate *verb* See **branch.**

big *adjective* **1.** Notably above average in amount, size, or scope : considerable, extensive, good, great, healthy, large, large-scale, sizable. *Informal:* tidy. See BIG in Index. **2.** Full to the point of flowing over : awash, brimful, brimming, overflowing. See BIG, RICH in Index. — See also **generous, important, mature, pregnant.**

Big Brother *noun* See **dictator.**

biggish *adjective* See **sizable.**

bighead *noun* See **egotism.**

bigheaded *adjective* See **egotistic.**

bigheadedness *noun* See **egotism.**

big-hearted *adjective* See **generous.**

big-heartedness *noun* See **generosity.**

big house *noun* See **jail.**

bight *noun* See **bay[1].**

big-league *adjective Informal.* Being among the leaders in one's field : blue-chip, major, major-league. *Informal:* bigtime, heavyweight. See IMPORTANT in Index.

big name *noun* See **celebrity.**

bigness *noun* See **size.**

bigoted *adjective* See **intolerant.**

bigotry *noun* See **prejudice.**

big shot *noun* See **dignitary.**

bigtime or **big-time** *adjective* See **big-league.**

big-timer *noun* See **dignitary.**

big wheel *noun* See **dignitary.**

bigwig *noun* See **dignitary.**

bilge *noun* See **nonsense.**

bilk *verb* See **cheat.**

bilk *noun* See **cheat.**

bill[1] *verb* To present a statement of fees or charges to : invoice. See MONEY, REQUEST in Index.

bill *noun* See **account, law, program, sign.**

bill[2] *noun* **1.** The horny projection forming a bird's jaws : beak. See MOUTH in Index. **2.** The projecting rim on the front of a cap : brim, peak, visor. See CONVEX, PROTECTION in Index.

billboard *noun* See **sign.**

billet *noun* See **position.**

billet *verb* See **harbor.**

billingsgate *noun* See **vituperation.**

binary *adjective* See **double.**

bind *verb* See **associate, commit, dress, tie.**

bind *noun* See **predicament.**

bine *noun* See **shoot.**

binge *noun* A period of uncontrolled self-indulgence : fling, orgy, rampage, spree. *Slang:* jag. See RESTRAINT in Index. — See also **bender.**

bird *noun* See **hiss.**

birdbrained *adjective* See **giddy.**

bird-dog also **birddog** *verb* See **follow.**

birth *noun* **1.** The act or process of bringing forth young : accouchement, birthing, childbearing, childbirth, delivery, labor, lying-in, parturition, travail. See START in Index. **2.** The initial stage of a developmental process : beginning, commencement, dawn, genesis, inception, nascence, nascency, onset, opening, origin, outset, spring, start. See START in Index. — See also **ancestry, nobility.**

birth *verb* See **bear.**

birthing *noun* See **birth.**

birthright *noun* **1.** A privilege granted a person, as by virtue of birth : appanage, perquisite, prerogative, right. *Law:* droit. See OWNED in Index. **2.** Any special privilege accorded a firstborn : heritage, inheritance, legacy, patrimony. See OWNED in Index.

bistered *adjective* See **dark.**

bit¹ *noun* **1.** A tiny amount : crumb, dab¹, dash, dot, dram, drop, fragment, grain, iota, jot, minim, mite, modicum, molecule, ort, ounce, particle, scrap¹, scruple, shred, smidgen, speck, tittle, trifle, whit. *Chiefly British:* spot. See BIG in Index. **2.** A small portion of food : crumb, morsel, mouthful, piece. *Informal:* bite. See BIG in Index. **3.** A rather short period : space, spell³, time, while. See BIG in Index. **4.** *Informal.* A particular kind of activity : *Slang:* routine. See ACTION in Index. — See also **item.**

bit² *noun* An instrument or means of restraining : brake, bridle, leash, restraint, snaffle. See RESTRAINT in Index.

bit *verb* See **restrain.**

bitch *verb* See **complain.**

bitchy *adjective* See **malevolent.**

bite *verb* **1.** To seize, as food, with the teeth : champ, chomp, gnash, gnaw. See ATTACK, INGESTION in Index. **2.** To consume gradually, as by chemical reaction or friction : corrode, eat, erode, gnaw, wear, wear away. See ATTACK in Index. — See also **sting.**

bite *noun* A light meal : morsel, snack. See INGESTION in Index. — See also **bit¹, edge.**

biting *adjective* So sharp as to cause mental pain : acerbic, acid, acidic, acrid, astringent, caustic, corrosive, cutting, mordacious, mordant, pungent, scathing, sharp, slashing, stinging, trenchant, truculent, vitriolic. See ATTACK, RESPECT in Index.

bitter *adjective* **1.** Having a noticeably sharp pungent taste or smell : acerbic, acrid, harsh, sour. See TASTE in Index. **2.** Causing sharp, often prolonged discomfort : brutal, hard, harsh, rough, severe. See COMFORT in Index. **3.** Difficult to accept : distasteful, indigestible, painful, unpalatable. See LIKE in Index. — See also **resentful.**

bitterness *noun* See **resentment.**

bizarre *adjective* See **eccentric, fantastic.**

blab *verb* See **betray, gossip.**

blab *noun* See **chatter, gossip.**

blabber *verb* See **chatter.**

blabber *noun* See **chatter.**

blabby *adjective* See **gossipy.**

black *adjective* **1.** Of the darkest achromatic visual value : ebon, ebony, inky, jet¹, jetty, onyx, pitch-black, pitchy, sable, sooty. See COLORS in Index. **2.** Having little or no light : dark, pitch-dark. See LIGHT in Index. — See also **dirty, evil, gloomy, malevolent.**

black *verb* See **dirty.**

black out *verb* To suffer temporary lack of consciousness : faint,

keel over, pass out, swoon. See
AWARENESS in Index. — See also
censor.

black-a-vised *adjective* See **dark**.

blackball *verb* To exclude from
normal social or professional activities : blacklist, boycott, ostracize,
shut out. See ACCEPT in Index.
— See also **veto**.

blacken *verb* To contaminate the
reputation of : befoul, besmear,
besmirch, bespatter, cloud, denigrate, dirty, smear, smudge, smut,
soil, spatter, stain, sully, taint, tarnish. *Idioms:* give a black eye
to, sling (*or* throw) mud on. See
ATTACK, CLEAN in Index. — See
also **dirty**.

black eye *noun* A bruise surround-
ing the eye : *Informal:* mouse.
Slang: shiner. See HEALTH, HELP in
Index. — See also **stain**.

blackish *adjective* Somewhat
black : dark, dusky. See COLORS in
Index.

blackjack *verb* See **coerce**.

blacklist *verb* See **blackball**.

blackout *noun* A temporary loss
of consciousness : faint, swoon.
Pathology: syncope. See AWARE-
NESS in Index.

black look *noun* See **frown**.

blade *noun* See **edge**.

blamable *also* **blameable** *adjective* See **blameworthy**.

blame *verb* To find fault with :
censure, criticize, fault, rap[1].
Informal: cut up, pan. *Slang:* knock.
See PRAISE in Index. — See also **fix**.

blame *noun* **1.** Responsibility for
an error or crime : culpability,
fault, guilt, onus. See START in
Index. **2.** A comment expressing
fault : censure, condemnation, criticism, denunciation, reprehension,
reprobation. *Informal:* pan. *Slang:*
knock. See PRAISE in Index.

blamed *adjective* See **damned**.

blameful *adjective* See **blameworthy**.

blameless *adjective* See **exemplary,
innocent**.

blameworthy *adjective* Deserving
blame : blamable, blameful, censurable, culpable, guilty, reprehensible. *Idiom:* at fault. See PRAISE in
Index.

blanch *also* **blench** *verb* See **pale**.

bland *adjective* See **flat, insipid,
neutral, suave**.

blandish *verb* See **coax, flatter**.

blandishment *noun* See **flattery**.

blandness *noun* See **dullness,
insipidity**.

blank *adjective* See **empty, expressionless, vacant**.

blanket *verb* See **cover**.

blankness *noun* See **emptiness**.

blare *verb* See **scream**.

blaring *adjective* See **loud**.

blarney *noun* See **flattery**.

blaspheme *verb* See **swear**.

blasphemous *adjective* See
sacrilegious.

blasphemy *noun* See **sacrilege,
swearword**.

blast *noun* **1.** A violent release of
confined energy, usually accompanied by a loud sound and shock
waves : blowout, blowup, burst,
detonation, explosion, fulmination.
See EXPLOSION in Index. **2.** An ear-
splitting, explosive noise : bang,
boom, roar, thunder. See SOUNDS in
Index. **3.** *Slang.* A big, exuberant
party : celebration, shindig,
shindy. *Slang:* bash, blowout. See
GROUP, RESTRAINT, WORK in Index.
— See also **wind[1]**.

blast *verb* **1.** To make an ear-
splitting explosive noise : bang,
boom, roar, thunder. See SOUNDS in
Index. **2.** To spoil or destroy :

blight, dash, nip[1]. See HELP in Index.
— See also **explode**.

blasted *adjective* See **damned**.

blatant *adjective* See **shameless**, **vociferous**.

blather *verb* See **babble**.
blather *noun* See **babble**, **nonsense**.

blatherskite *noun* See **babble**.

blaze[1] *verb* See **beam, burn, glare**.
blaze *noun* See **fire, glare**.

blaze[2] *verb* See **advertise**.

blazing *adjective* See **passionate**.

blazon *verb* See **advertise**.

bleach *verb* See **pale**.

bleak *adjective* Cold and forbidding : austere, dour, grim, hard, harsh, severe, stark. See ATTITUDE, HOT in Index. — See also **gloomy**.

blear *verb* See **obscure**.
blear *adjective* See **unclear**.

bleary *adjective* See **exhausted**, **unclear**.

bleed *verb* See **ooze**.

blemish *noun* See **defect, stain**.
blemish *verb* See **injure**.

blench *verb* See **flinch**.

blend *verb* See **harmonize, mix**.
blend *noun* See **mixture**.

bless *verb* See **sanctify**.

blessed *adjective* See **damned**, **holy**.

blessedness *noun* See **happiness**, **holiness**.

blessing *noun* See **advantage**, **grace**.

blight *verb* See **blast**.

blind *adjective* **1.** Without the sense of sight : eyeless, sightless, unseeing. See SEE in Index. **2.** Unwilling or unable to perceive : dull, purblind, uncomprehending, unperceptive. See SEE in Index. **3.** Screened from the view of oncoming drivers : concealed, hidden. See SHOW in Index. — See also **drunk**.
blind *verb* See **daze**.

blind alley *noun* A course leading nowhere : cul-de-sac, dead end. See OPEN in Index.

blindness *noun* The condition of not being able to see : sightlessness. See SEE in Index.

blink *verb* **1.** To open and close the eyes rapidly : bat[1], nictate, nictitate, twinkle, wink. See REPETITION, SEE in Index. **2.** To shine with intermittent gleams : flash, flicker, glimmer, twinkle, wink. See CONTINUE, LIGHT in Index. **3.** To pretend not to see. Also used with *at* : connive at, disregard, ignore, pass over, wink at. *Idioms:* be blind to, close (or shut) one's eyes to, look the other way, turn a blind eye to. See SEE in Index.
blink *noun* **1.** A brief closing of the eyes : nictation, nictitation, wink. See SEE in Index. **2.** A sudden quick light : coruscation, flash, flicker, glance, gleam, glimmer, glint, spark[1], twinkle, wink. See LIGHT in Index.

bliss *noun* See **happiness**.

blister *verb* See **slam**.

blistering *adjective* See **hot**.

blithe *adjective* See **gay, light**[2].

blitheness *noun* See **gaiety**.

blithesome *adjective* See **gay**.

blithesomeness *noun* See **gaiety**.

blitzkrieg *noun* See **charge**.

bloc *noun* See **alliance, combine**.

block *verb* To cut off from sight. Also used with *out* : conceal, hide[1], obscure, obstruct, screen, shroud, shut off (or out). See SHOW in Index. — See also **fill, obstruct**.
block in or **out** *verb* See **draft**.
block *noun* See **bar, head**.

blockade *noun* See **siege**.
blockade *verb* See **besiege**.

blockage *noun* See **bar**.

blockhead *noun* See **dullard**.

blockheaded *adjective* See **stupid**.

blocky *adjective* See **stocky.**

blond also **blonde** *adjective* See **fair.**

blood *noun* The fluid circulated by the heart through the vascular system : gore. See BLOOD in Index. — See also **ancestry, murder, nobility.**

bloodbath also **blood bath** *noun* See **massacre.**

bloodcurdling *adjective* See **horrible.**

bloodless *adjective* See **insensitive, pale.**

bloodletting *noun* See **massacre.**

bloodline *noun* See **ancestry.**

bloodshed *noun* See **massacre.**

bloodstain *verb* See **bloody.**

bloodsucker *noun* See **parasite.**

bloodsucking *adjective* See **parasitic.**

bloodthirsty *adjective* See **murderous.**

bloody *adjective* **1.** Of or covered with blood : gory. See BLOOD in Index. **2.** Attended by or causing bloodshed : gory, sanguinary, sanguineous. See BLOOD in Index. — See also **damned, murderous.**

bloody *verb* To cover with blood : bloodstain, ensanguine, imbrue. See BLOOD in Index.

bloody-minded *adjective* See **murderous.**

bloom¹ *noun* **1.** The showy reproductive structure of a plant : blossom, floret, flower. See BETTER in Index. **2.** A condition or time of vigor and freshness : blossom, efflorescence, florescence, flower, flush, prime. See BETTER in Index. **3.** A fresh rosy complexion : blush, color, flush, glow. See BETTER in Index.

bloom *verb* To bear flowers : blossom, blow³, burgeon, effloresce, flower. See BETTER, RICH in Index. — See also **flourish.**

bloom² *noun* See **stick.**

bloomer *noun* See **blunder.**

blooming *adjective* See **damned, fresh, ruddy, utter².**

blooper *noun* See **blunder.**

blossom *noun* See **bloom¹.**

blossom *verb* See **bloom¹, flourish.**

blot *noun* See **smear, stain.**

blot *verb* See **cancel.**

blot out *verb* See **annihilate.**

blotch *noun* See **smear.**

blotch *verb* See **spot.**

blow¹ *verb* To be in a state of motion, as air : puff, winnow. See BREATH in Index. — See also **boast, botch, burst, explode, go, pant, treat, waste.**

blow in *verb* See **arrive.**

blow up *verb* See **anger.**

blow *noun* See **boast, wind¹.**

blow² *noun* A sudden sharp, powerful stroke : bang, clout, crack, hit, lick, pound, slug³, sock, swat, thwack, welt, whack, wham, whop. *Informal:* bash, biff, bop, clip¹, wallop. *Slang:* belt, conk, paste. See ATTACK, STRIKE in Index. — See also **shock¹.**

blow³ *verb* See **bloom¹.**

blow-by-blow *adjective* See **detailed.**

blower *noun* See **braggart.**

blowhard *noun* See **braggart.**

blowout *noun* See **blast.**

blowup *noun* See **blast, outburst.**

blowy *adjective* See **airy.**

blubber *verb* See **cry.**

blubbering *noun* See **cry.**

bludgeon *verb* See **intimidate.**

blue *adjective* See **depressed, gloomy, racy, sad.**

blue blood *noun* See **nobility, society.**

blue-blooded *adjective* See **noble.**

blue-chip *adjective* See **big-league.**

bluecoat *noun* See **policeman.**

blue moon *noun* See **age.**

bluenose *noun* See **prude.**

bluenosed *adjective* See **genteel.**

blueprint *noun* See **design.**

  blueprint *verb* See **design.**

blue-ribbon *adjective* See **excellent.**

blues *noun* See **gloom.**

bluff *verb* See **deceive.**

blunder *noun* A stupid, clumsy mistake : bull², bungle, foozle, fumble, muff, stumble. *Informal:* blooper, boner. *Slang:* bloomer, goof. See CORRECT in Index.

  blunder *verb* To move awkwardly or clumsily : bumble¹, stumble. See ABILITY, MOVE in Index. — See also **botch, muddle.**

blunderer *noun* A clumsy person : botcher, bungler, dub, foozler. *Slang:* screwup. *Idiom:* bull in a china shop. See ABILITY in Index.

blunt *verb* See **deaden, dull.**

  blunt *adjective* See **abrupt, dull.**

blur *verb* See **obscure.**

blurry *adjective* See **filmy.**

blurt *verb* See **exclaim.**

blush *verb* To become red in the face : color, crimson, flush, glow, mantle, redden. See EXPRESS in Index.

  blush *noun* See **bloom¹, glance.**

bluster *verb* See **roar.**

board *verb* See **harbor, take.**

  board *noun* See **stage.**

boast *verb* To talk with excessive pride : brag, crow, gasconade, rodomontade, vaunt. *Informal:* blow¹. See PRAISE in Index. — See also **command.**

  boast *noun* An act of boasting : brag, braggadocio, fanfaronade, gasconade, rodomontade, vaunt. *Informal:* blow¹. See PRAISE in Index.

boaster *noun* See **braggart.**

boastful *adjective* Characterized by or given to boasting : braggart, rodomontade. See ATTITUDE, PRAISE in Index.

bobby *noun* See **policeman.**

bode *verb* See **adumbrate.**

bodiless *adjective* See **immaterial.**

bodily *adjective* Of or relating to the human body : corporal, corporeal, fleshly, personal, physical, somatic. See BODY in Index.

body *noun* **1.** The physical frame of a dead person or animal : cadaver, carcass, corpse, remains. *Slang:* stiff. See BODY in Index. **2.** The main part : bulk. *Anatomy:* corpus. See BIG in Index. **3.** A separate and distinct portion of matter : bulk, mass, object. See MATTER in Index. — See also **assembly, force, group, human being, quantity.**

body forth *verb* See **embody.**

body politic *noun* See **state.**

boff *noun* See **hit.**

boffo *noun* See **hit.**

boffola *noun* See **hit.**

bog *noun* See **swamp.**

  bog *verb* See **hinder.**

bogey also **bogy** or **bogie** *noun* See **ghost.**

bogeyman *noun* See **ghost.**

boggle *verb* See **botch, stagger.**

bogle *noun* See **ghost.**

bogus *adjective* See **counterfeit.**

boil *verb* **1.** To cook (food) in liquid heated to the point of steaming : parboil, simmer, stew. See INGESTION in Index. **2.** To be in a state of emotional or mental turmoil : bubble, burn, churn, ferment, seethe, simmer, smolder. See CALM in Index.

boil away *verb* See **evaporate.**

boil down *verb* To reduce in complexity or scope : simplify. See INCREASE, SIMPLE in Index.

boil over *verb* See **anger.**

boiling *adjective* See **hot.**

boisterous *adjective* See **vociferous.**

bold *adjective* See **adventurous, brave, impudent, noticeable, steep¹.**

boldfaced *adjective* See **impudent.**

boldness *noun* See **daring, impudence.**

bollix up *verb* See **botch.**

bolster *verb* See **sustain.**

bolt *noun* See **jump.**

bolt *verb* See **gulp, jump, run, rush.**

bomb *noun* See **failure.**

bomb *verb* See **fail.**

bombard *verb* See **barrage.**

bombardment *noun* See **barrage.**

bombast *noun* Pretentious, pompous speech or writing : claptrap, fustian, grandiloquence, magniloquence, orotundity, rant, turgidity. See PLAIN, STYLE, WORDS in Index.

bombastic *adjective* See **sonorous.**

bombed *adjective* See **drunk.**

bona fide *adjective* See **authentic.**

bond *noun* **1.** Something that physically confines the legs or arms : chain (used in plural), fetter, handcuff (often used in plural), hobble, iron (used in plural), manacle, restraint, shackle. *Archaic:* gyve. See FREE in Index. **2.** That which unites or binds : knot, ligament, ligature, link, nexus, tie, vinculum, yoke. See CONNECT in Index. **3.** The close physical union of two objects : adherence, adhesion, cohesion. See CONNECT in Index. **4.** Money supplied for the temporary release of an arrested person that guarantees appearance of that person for trial : bail¹. See LAW in Index. — See also **agreement.**

bond *verb* To hold fast : adhere, cleave², cling, cohere, stick. See CONNECT in Index.

bondage *noun* See **slavery.**

bondsman *noun* One who posts bond : bail¹, bailsman. See LAW in Index.

bone *verb* *Informal.* To study or work hard, especially when pressed for time. Also used with *up* : cram, grind. *Idiom:* burn the midnight oil. See WORK in Index.

bone-dry *adjective* See **dry.**

boner *noun* See **blunder.**

bong *verb* See **ring².**

bonkers *adjective* See **insane.**

bonny *adjective* See **beautiful, good.**

bonus *noun* See **reward.**

bony *adjective* See **thin.**

boo *noun* See **hiss.**

booby trap *noun* See **pitfall.**

boodle *noun* See **bribe, plunder.**

book *noun* A printed and bound work : tome, volume. See WORDS in Index.

book *verb* To cause to be set aside, as for one's use, in advance : bespeak, engage, reserve. See GET in Index. — See also **list¹.**

booking *noun* A commitment, as for a performance by an entertainer : engagement. *Slang:* gig. See PERFORMING ARTS in Index.

bookish *adjective* See **pedantic, studious.**

boom *verb* See **blast, prosper, rumble.**

boom *noun* See **blast.**

boomerang *verb* See **backfire.**

booming *adjective* See **flourishing.**

boomy *adjective* See **flourishing.**

boon¹ *noun* See **advantage.**

boon² *adjective* See **gay.**

boor *noun* An unrefined, rude person : barbarian, chuff, churl, Philistine, vulgarian, yahoo. See GOOD in Index.

boorish *adjective* See **coarse.**

boost *verb* See **elevate, help, increase, promote, raise.**

boost *noun* See **increase, lift.**
boot¹ *verb* See **dismiss, eject.**
 boot *noun* See **dismissal, ejection, thrill.**
boot² *verb* See **profit.**
bootleg *verb* See **smuggle.**
bootlegger *noun* See **smuggler.**
bootless *adjective* See **futile.**
bootlessness *noun* See **futility.**
bootlick *verb* See **fawn.**
booty *noun* See **plunder.**
booze *noun* See **bender.**
 booze *verb* See **drink.**
boozed *adjective* See **drunk.**
boozehound *noun* See **drunkard.**
boozer *noun* See **drunkard.**
boozy *adjective* See **drunk.**
bop *verb* See **hit.**
 bop *noun* See **blow².**
border *noun* **1.** A fairly narrow line or space forming a boundary : borderline, brim, brink, edge, edging, fringe, margin, periphery, rim, verge. *Chiefly Military:* perimeter. See EDGE in Index. **2.** The line or area separating geopolitical units : borderland, boundary, frontier, march², marchland. See EDGE, TERRITORY in Index.
 border *verb* To put or form a border on : bound², edge, fringe, margin, rim, skirt, verge. See EDGE in Index. — See also **adjoin.**
 border on or **upon** *verb* See **rival.**
borderland *noun* See **border.**
borderline *noun* See **border, verge.**
 borderline *adjective* See **ambiguous.**
bore *verb* To fatigue with dullness or tedium : tire, weary. See EXCITE in Index.
 bore *noun* See **drip.**
boreal *adjective* See **frigid.**
boredom *noun* The condition of being bored : ennui. See EXCITE in Index.
boring *adjective* Arousing no inter-

est or curiosity : drear, dreary, dry, dull, humdrum, irksome, monotonous, stuffy, tedious, tiresome, uninteresting, weariful, wearisome, weary. See EXCITE in Index.
bosom *noun* See **heart.**
 bosom *verb* See **embrace.**
boss *noun* **1.** Someone who directs and supervises workers : director, foreman, foreperson, forewoman, head, manager, overseer, superintendent, supervisor, taskmaster, taskmistress. *Informal:* straw boss. *Slang:* chief. See OVER in Index. **2.** A professional politician who controls a party or political machine : chief, leader. See OVER in Index. — See also **chief.**
 boss *verb* To command or issue commands in an arrogant manner : dictate, dominate, domineer, order, rule, tyrannize. See OVER in Index. — See also **supervise.**
 boss *adjective* See **excellent.**
bossy *adjective* See **dictatorial.**
botch *verb* To harm irreparably through inept handling; make a mess : ball up, blunder, boggle, bungle, foul up, fumble, gum up, mess up, mishandle, mismanage, muddle, muff, spoil. *Informal:* bollix up, muck up. *Slang:* blow¹, goof up, louse up, screw up, snafu. *Idiom:* make a muck of. See CORRECT, HELP in Index.
 botch *noun* A ruinous state of disorder : foul-up, mess, muddle, shambles. *Informal:* hash. *Slang:* screwup, snafu. See CORRECT, ORDER in Index.
botcher *noun* See **blunderer.**
bother *verb* See **agitate, annoy.**
 bother *noun* Needless trouble : botheration, fuss, pother. See EASY in Index. — See also **annoyance.**
botheration *noun* See **annoyance, bother.**

bothering *noun* See **annoyance.**

bothersome *adjective* See **vexatious.**

bottom *noun* **1.** A side or surface that is below or under : underneath, underside, undersurface. See OVER in Index. **2.** *Informal.* The part of one's back on which one rests in sitting : buttock (used in plural), derrière, posterior, rump, seat. *Informal:* backside, behind, rear[1]. *Slang:* bun (used in plural), fanny, tush. *Chiefly British:* bum[2]. See OVER in Index. — See also **base[1], center, low.**

bottom *adjective* Opposite to or farthest from the top : lowermost, lowest, nethermost, undermost. See OVER in Index.

bottomless *adjective* See **baseless.**

boulevard *noun* See **way.**

bounce *verb* **1.** To spring back after colliding with something : rebound. See APPROACH, MOVE in Index. **2.** To move in a lively way : bound[1], jump, leap, spring. See MOVE in Index. — See also **dismiss, eject.**

bounce back

bounce *noun* **1.** An act of bouncing or a bouncing movement : bound[1], rebound. See APPROACH, MOVE in Index. **2.** A sudden lively movement : bound[1], jump, leap, spring. See MOVE in Index. — See also **dismissal, ejection, flexibility, resilience, spirit.**

bouncy *adjective* See **lively.**

bound[1] *verb* See **bounce.**

bound *noun* See **bounce.**

bound[2] *verb* See **adjoin, border, determine.**

bound *noun* See **end, limit.**

bound[3] *adjective* See **obliged.**

boundary *noun* See **border.**

bounden *adjective* See **obliged.**

boundless *adjective* See **endless.**

boundlessness *noun* See **infinity.**

bounteous *adjective* See **generous.**

bounteousness *noun* See **generosity, plenty.**

bountiful *adjective* See **generous.**

bountifulness *noun* See **generosity, plenty.**

bounty *noun* See **reward.**

bouquet *noun* Cut flowers that have been arranged in a usually small bunch : nosegay, posy. See THING in Index. — See also **fragrance.**

bout *noun* See **siege, turn.**

boutade *noun* See **fancy.**

boutique *noun* See **store.**

bow[1] *verb* See **defer[2], stoop, succumb.**

bow *noun* An inclination of the head or body, as in greeting, consent, courtesy, submission, or worship : curtsy, genuflection, kowtow, nod, obeisance. See COURTESY in Index.

bow[2] *verb* See **bend.**

bow *noun* See **bend.**

bowdlerize *verb* See **censor.**

bowed *adjective* See **bent.**

bowl over *verb* See **stagger.**

box[1] *noun* See **predicament.**

box[2] *noun* See **slap.**

box *verb* See **slap.**

box office *noun* See **take.**

boy *noun* *Informal.* A grown man referred to familiarly, jokingly, or as a member of one's set or group : fellow. *Informal:* chap. See BEINGS, CONNECT in Index.

boycott *verb* See **blackball.**

boyfriend also **boy friend** *noun* A man who is the favored companion of a woman : beau. *Informal:* fellow. See CONNECT, SEX in Index.

brace *verb* See **gird.**

brace *noun* See **couple, support.**

bracer *noun* See **tonic.**

bracing *adjective* See **tonic.**

bracket *noun* See **class**.
  bracket *verb* See **associate**.
brag *verb* See **boast**.
  brag *noun* See **boast, braggart**.
  brag *adjective* See **excellent**.
braggadocio *noun* See **boast, braggart**.
braggart *noun* One given to boasting : boaster, brag, braggadocio, bragger, vaunter. *Informal:* blowhard. *Slang:* blower. See PRAISE in Index.
  braggart *adjective* See **boastful**.
bragger *noun* See **braggart**.
brain *noun* See **head, intelligence, mind**.
brainchild *noun* See **invention**.
brainless *adjective* See **mindless**.
brainpower *noun* See **intelligence**.
brainsick *adjective* See **insane**.
brainsickness *noun* See **insanity**.
brainstorm *noun* See **inspiration**.
brainwash *verb* See **indoctrinate**.
brain wave *noun* See **inspiration**.
brainwork *noun* See **thought**.
brainy *adjective* See **intelligent**.
brake *noun* See **bit²**.
  brake *verb* See **restrain**.
branch *noun* **1.** Something resembling or analogous to a tree branch : arm, fork, offshoot. See PART in Index. **2.** An area of study that is part of a larger body of learning : discipline, specialty. See PART in Index. **3.** A part of a family, tribe, or other group, or of such a group's language, that is believed to stem from a common ancestor : division, offshoot, subdivision. See PART in Index. **4.** A component of government that performs a given function : agency, arm, department, division, organ, wing. See PART in Index. **5.** *Chiefly Regional.* A small stream : brook¹, creek. *Chiefly Regional:* kill², run. See DRY in Index. — See also **subsidiary**.

branch *verb* To separate into branches or branchlike parts. Also used with *out* : bifurcate, diverge, divide, fork, ramify, subdivide. See PART in Index.
brand *noun* See **mark**.
  brand *verb* See **mark, stigmatize**.
brandish *verb* See **display, flourish**.
brand-new *adjective* See **fresh**.
brannigan *noun* See **bender**.
brash *adjective* See **impudent, rash¹, tactless**.
brashness *noun* See **impudence, temerity**.
brass *noun* See **impudence, money**.
brassbound *adjective* See **stubborn**.
brass ring *noun* See **catch**.
brass-tacks *adjective* See **pithy**.
brassy *adjective* See **impudent, shameless**.
brattle *verb* See **rattle**.
brave *adjective* Having or showing courage : audacious, bold, courageous, dauntless, doughty, fearless, fortitudinous, gallant, game, hardy, heroic, intrepid, mettlesome, plucky, stout, stouthearted, unafraid, undaunted, valiant, valorous. *Informal:* spunky. *Slang:* gutsy, gutty. See FEAR in Index.
  brave *noun* See **bully**.
  brave *verb* See **defy**.
braveness *noun* See **courage**.
bravery *noun* See **courage**.
braw *adjective* See **good**.
brawl *noun* A quarrel, fight, or disturbance marked by very noisy, disorderly, and often violent behavior : affray, broil², donnybrook, fray, free-for-all, melee, riot, row², ruction, tumult. *Informal:* fracas. *Slang:* rumble. See ATTACK in Index.
brawl *verb* To quarrel noisily : broil², caterwaul, row², wrangle. See ATTACK in Index.

brawn *noun* Solid and well-developed muscles : bulk, muscularity. *Informal:* beef. See BODY in Index. — See also **strength**.

brawny *adjective* See **muscular**.

bray *verb* See **crush**.

brazen *adjective* See **impudent, shameless**.

brazenfaced *adjective* See **shameless**.

brazenness *noun* See **impudence**.

breach *noun* 1. An act or instance of breaking a law or regulation or of nonfulfillment of an obligation or promise, for example : contravention, infraction, infringement, transgression, trespass, violation. See RIGHT in Index. 2. An opening, especially in a solid structure : break, gap, hole, perforation, rupture. See OPEN in Index. 3. An interruption in friendly relations : alienation, break, disaffection, estrangement, fissure, rent², rift, rupture, schism, split. See ASSEMBLE, HELP in Index.

breach *verb* To make a hole or other opening in : break (through), gap, hole, perforate, pierce, puncture. See OPEN in Index. — See also **violate**.

bread *noun* See **food, living, money**.

bread and butter *noun* See **living**.

breadth *noun* See **width**.

break *verb* 1. To crack or split into two or more fragments by means of or as a result of force, a blow, or strain : fracture, rift, rive, shatter, shiver², smash, splinter, sunder. See HELP in Index. 2. To make or become unusable or inoperative : fail, ruin. *Slang:* bust. See HELP in Index. 3. To impair severely something such as the spirit, health, or effectiveness of : crush, destroy, overwhelm, ruin. See HELP in Index. 4. To desist from, cease, or

discontinue (a habit, for example) : cut out, give up, leave off, stop. *Slang:* kick. See CONTINUE in Index. 5. To find the key to (a code, for example) : crack, decipher, decrypt, puzzle out. See KNOWLEDGE in Index. 6. To interrupt regular activity for a short period : recess. *Idioms:* take a break, take a breather, take five (or ten). See CONTINUE in Index. 7. To give way mentally and emotionally. Also used with *down* : collapse, crack, snap. *Informal:* crack up, fold. See EXPLOSION in Index. — See also **breach, collapse, come out** at **come, communicate, demote, disobey, divide, gentle, penetrate, ruin, violate**.

break down *verb* See **analyze, break up** at **break, decay, destroy, fail, take down** at **take**.

break in *verb* To enter forcibly or illegally : burglarize. *Law:* trespass. See CRIMES, ENTER in Index. — See also **interrupt**.

break off *verb* See **abandon, separate, suspend**.

break out *verb* To become manifest suddenly and in full force : burst (forth or out), erupt, explode, flare (up). See EXPLOSION, START in Index. — See also **escape**.

break up *verb* 1. To reduce or become reduced to pieces or components : break down, crumble, decompose, disintegrate, dissolve, fragment, fragmentize. See CONTINUE, HELP in Index. 2. *Informal.* To express great amusement or mirth : guffaw, roar. *Slang:* howl. See LAUGHTER in Index. — See also **divide, separate**.

break *noun* 1. A cessation of continuity or regularity : discontinuance, discontinuation, discontinuity, disruption, interruption, pause, suspension. See CONTINUE in Index.

2. A pause or interval, as from work or duty : intermission, recess, respite, rest[1], time-out. *Informal:* breather. See CONTINUE in Index. — See also **breach, crack, escape, gap, opportunity.**

breakable *adjective* See **fragile.**

breakage *noun* An act, instance, or consequence of breaking : damage, destruction, impairment, wreckage. See HELP in Index.

breakdown *noun* A sudden sharp decline in mental, emotional, or physical health : collapse. *Informal:* crackup. See EXPLOSION in Index. — See also **analysis, collapse, decay, failure.**

break-in *noun* See **trespass.**

breakneck *adjective* See **fast.**

breakout *noun* See **escape.**

breast *noun* See **heart.**

breath *noun* **1.** The act or process of breathing : respiration. See BREATH in Index. **2.** Air breathed out, evidenced by vapor, odor, or heat : exhalation. See BREATH in Index. — See also **shade, spirit.**

breathe *verb* **1.** To draw air into the lungs in the process of respiration. Also used with *in* : inhale, inspire. See BREATH in Index. **2.** To expel air in the process of respiration. Also used with *out* : exhale, expire. See BREATH in Index. **3.** To breathe in and out : respire. See BREATH in Index. — See also **be, confide.**

breather *noun* See **break.**

breathless *adjective* See **airless.**

breed *verb* See **father, grow, produce, reproduce.**

breed *noun* See **kind[2].**

breeding *noun* See **reproduction.**

breeze *noun* **1.** A gentle wind : zephyr. See BREATH in Index. **2.** *Informal.* An easily accomplished task : child's play, cinch, pushover, snap, walkaway, walkover. *Slang:*

duck soup. See EASY in Index. — See also **wind[1].**

breeze *verb Informal.* To move swiftly and effortlessly : zip. *Slang:* waltz. See EASY in Index.

breezeless *adjective* See **airless.**

breezy *adjective* See **airy.**

brew *verb* See **threaten.**

bribe *noun* Money, property, or a favor given, offered, or promised to a person or accepted by a person in a position of trust as an inducement to dishonest behavior : fix, graft, payola. *Informal:* payoff. *Slang:* boodle. See CRIMES, MONEY, PERSUASION in Index.

bribe *verb* To give, offer, or promise a bribe to : buy (off). *Informal:* pay off. *Idiom:* grease someone's palm (or hand). See CRIMES, MONEY, PERSUASION in Index.

bridal *noun* See **wedding.**

bridle *noun* See **bit[2].**

bridle *verb* See **restrain.**

brief *adjective* **1.** Not long in time or duration : short. See BIG, FAST in Index. **2.** Marked by or consisting of few words that are carefully chosen : compendious, concise, laconic, lean[2], short, succinct, summary, terse. See BIG, STYLE, WORDS in Index. — See also **abrupt, quick.**

brief *noun* See **synopsis.**

briery also **briary** *adjective* See **thorny.**

brig *noun* See **jail.**

bright *adjective* Giving off or reflecting light readily or in large amounts : beamy, brilliant, effulgent, incandescent, irradiant, lambent, lucent, luminous, lustrous, radiant, refulgent, shiny. See LIGHT in Index. — See also **cheerful, clever, colorful, favorable.**

brighten *verb* See **clear, light[1].**

brilliance *noun* See **fire, glitter.**

brilliancy *noun* See **fire, glitter.**

brilliant *adjective* Extemely bright : glaring, glary. See LIGHT in Index. — See also **bright, favorable, glorious, intelligent.**

brim *noun* See bill², border.

brimful *adjective* See **big, full.**

brimming *adjective* See **big, full.**

bring *verb* 1. To cause to come along with oneself : bear, carry, convey, fetch, take, transport. See ACCOMPANIED in Index. 2. To achieve (a certain price). Also used with *in* : fetch, realize, sell for. See GET in Index. — See also **cause, persuade.**

bring about *verb* See **cause.**

bring around or **round** *verb* See **persuade, revive.**

bring down *verb* See **drop, overthrow.**

bring forth *verb* See **bear.**

bring in *verb* See **return.**

bring off *verb* See **effect.**

bring on *verb* See **cause.**

bring out *verb* See **publish.**

bring up *verb* To take care of and educate (a child) : raise, rear². See CARE FOR in Index. — See also **broach, refer.**

brink *noun* See **border, verge.**

brio *noun* See **spirit.**

brisk *adjective* See **energetic, nimble, vigorous.**

bristle *verb* See **anger, teem.**

brittle *adjective* See **fragile.**

broach *verb* To put forward (a topic) for discussion : bring up, introduce, moot, put forth, raise. See START in Index.

broad *adjective* 1. Extending over a large area from side to side : wide. See WIDE in Index. 2. Large in expanse : ample, expansive, extensive, spacious. See WIDE in Index. 3. Not narrow or conservative in thought, expression, or conduct : broad-minded, liberal, open-minded, progressive, tolerant. See ATTITUDE, WIDE in Index. — See also **general, obscene, unsubtle.**

broadcast *verb* See **advertise, announce.**

broaden *verb* To make or become broad or broader : widen. See WIDE in Index. — See also **extend.**

broad-minded *adjective* See **broad.**

broadness *noun* See **width.**

broad-spectrum *adjective* See **general.**

Brobdingnagian *adjective* See **giant.**

broil¹ *verb* See **burn.**

broil² *noun* See **brawl.**

broil *verb* See **brawl.**

broiling *adjective* See **hot.**

broke *adjective* See **poor.**

broken-down *adjective* See **shabby.**

broker *noun* See **go-between.**

bromide *noun* See **cliché.**

bromidic *adjective* See **trite.**

Bronx cheer *noun* See **hiss.**

brood *noun* See **progeny, young.**

brood *verb* To focus the attention on something moodily and at length : cark, dwell, fret, mope, worry. *Informal:* stew. See CONCERN, THOUGHTS in Index.

brook¹ *noun* See **branch.**

brook² *verb* See **endure.**

brother *noun* See **friend.**

brouhaha *noun* See **sensation.**

browbeat *verb* See **intimidate.**

browbeater *noun* See **bully.**

brownnose or **brown-nose** *verb* See **fawn.**

brown study *noun* See **trance.**

browse *verb* To look through reading matter casually : dip into, flip through, glance at (or over or through), leaf (through), riffle (through), run through, scan, skim, thumb (through). See INVESTIGATE, WORDS in Index.

bruise *verb* To make a bruise or bruises on : contuse. See HELP in Index.

bruit *verb* See **advertise.**

brume *noun* See **haze.**

brummagem *adjective* See **gaudy.**

brunet *adjective* See **dark.**

brush¹ *noun* Light and momentary contact with another person or thing : flick, graze, skim. See TOUCH in Index.

brush *verb* To make light and momentary contact with, as in passing : flick, graze, kiss, shave, skim. See TOUCH in Index.

brush² *noun* A brief, hostile exposure to or contact with something such as danger or opposition : clash, encounter, run-in, skirmish. See TOUCH in Index.

brusque also **brusk** *adjective* See **abrupt.**

brutal *adjective* See **bitter.**

brutality *noun* See **cruelty.**

brutalize *verb* See **corrupt.**

bubble *noun* See **illusion.**

bubble *verb* See **boil, foam, wash.**

bubbling *adjective* See **laughing.**

buck *verb* See **contest.**

buck up *verb* See **encourage.**

bucket *verb* See **rush.**

buckle *verb* See **cave in** at **cave, succumb.**

buckle down *verb* See **apply.**

buckram *adjective* See **stiff.**

bucolic *adjective* See **country.**

bud¹ *noun* See **child, germ.**

bud² *noun* See **friend.**

buddy *noun* See **associate, friend.**

budge *verb* See **stir¹.**

budget *noun* See **quantity.**

buff¹ *verb* See **gloss.**

buff² *noun* See **enthusiast.**

buffet *noun* See **slap.**

buffet *verb* See **beat, slap.**

bug *noun* See **defect, enthusiast, germ, indisposition.**

bug *verb* See **annoy, tap².**

bugbear *noun* See **hate.**

buggy *adjective* See **insane.**

build *verb* To make or form (a structure) : construct, erect, put up, raise, rear². See MAKE in Index.
— See also **base¹, form, increase, make.**

build in *verb* To construct or include as an integral or permanent part : incorporate, integrate. See INCLUDE in Index.

build up *verb* See **advertise, gain, increase, promote.**

build *noun* See **constitution.**

builder *noun* **1.** A person or business that makes or builds something : assembler, constructor, erector, maker, manufacturer, producer. See MAKE in Index. **2.** A person instrumental in the growth of something, especially in its early stages : contributor, creator, developer, pioneer. See MAKE in Index.

building *noun* A usually permanent construction, such as a house or store : edifice, pile, structure. See MAKE in Index.

building block *noun* See **element.**

buildup also **build-up** *noun* The result or product of building up : accretion, development, enlargement, multiplication, proliferation. See INCREASE in Index. — See also **increase, promotion.**

built *adjective* See **shapely.**

built-in *adjective* Serving as part of a whole, as a nondetachable part of a larger unit : component, constituent, incorporated. See INCLUDE in Index. — See also **constitutional.**

bulge *noun* A part that protrudes or extends outward : jut, knob, knot, overhang, projection, protrusion,

protuberance. See CONVEX in Index.
— See also **advantage.**

bulge verb To curve outward past
the normal or usual limit : bag, balloon, beetle, belly, jut, overhang,
pouch, project, protrude, protuberate, stand out, stick out. See CON-
VEX in Index.

bulk noun Great extent, amount, or
dimension : amplitude, magnitude,
mass, size, volume (often used in
plural). See BIG in Index. — See also
body, brawn, quantity, weight.

bulky adjective **1.** Extremely large;
having great mass : massive, oversize, oversized. See BIG in Index.
2. Having a large body, especially in
girth : heavy, hefty, hulking,
hulky, husky², stout. See BIG in
Index. — See also **awkward.**

bull¹ noun See **nonsense, policeman.**

bull² noun See **blunder.**

bulldoze verb See **intimidate.**

bulldozer noun See **bully.**

bullheaded adjective See
obstinate.

bullheadedness noun See
obstinacy.

bully noun One who is habitually
cruel to smaller or weaker people :
browbeater, bulldozer, hector, intimidator. Archaic: brave. See OVER in
Index.

bully verb See **intimidate.**

bully adjective See **excellent.**

bullyrag verb See **bait, intimidate.**

bum¹ noun See **wastrel.**

bum verb See **beg, idle.**

bum adjective See **bad.**

bum² noun See **bottom.**

bumble¹ verb See **blunder, muddle.**

bumble² verb See **hum.**

bumble noun See **hum.**

bumbling adjective See **unskillful.**

bummer noun See **beggar, shame.**

bump verb To proceed with sudden,
abrupt movements : jerk, jolt. See
REPETITION in Index. — See also
collide, demote, eject.

bump into verb See **come across**
at **come.**

bump off verb See **murder.**

bump noun **1.** A small raised area
of skin resulting from a light blow or
an insect sting, for example :
bunch, knot, lump¹, swelling. See
CONVEX in Index. **2.** An unevenness
or elevation on a surface : hump,
knob, knot, lump¹, nub, protuberance. See CONVEX in Index. — See
also **collision.**

bumpkin noun See **clodhopper.**

bun noun See **bottom.**

bunch noun See **bump, crowd,
group.**

bundle noun See **fortune, group.**

bundle up verb See **wrap.**

bungle verb See **botch, muddle.**

bungle noun See **blunder.**

bungler noun See **blunderer.**

bunk¹ verb See **harbor.**

bunk² noun See **nonsense.**

bunkum also **buncombe** noun See
nonsense.

Bunyanesque adjective See **giant.**

buoy verb See **elate, sustain.**

buoyancy noun See **resilience.**

buoyant adjective See **airy.**

burble verb See **wash.**

burbling adjective See **laughing.**

burden¹ noun **1.** Something carried
physically : cargo, freight, haul,
load. Sports: impost. See HEAVY,
OVER in Index. **2.** Something hard
to bear physically or emotionally :
affliction, cross, trial, tribulation.
See HEAVY, OVER in Index. **3.** A
duty or responsibility that is a source
of anxiety, worry, or hardship :
millstone, onus, tax, weight.
Informal: headache. See HEAVY,
OVER in Index. — See also **duty.**

burden *verb* See **charge.**
burden² *noun* See **import, thrust.**
burdensome *adjective* Requiring great or extreme bodily, mental, or spiritual strength : arduous, back-breaking, demanding, difficult, effortful, exacting, exigent, formidable, hard, heavy, laborious, onerous, oppressive, rigorous, rough, severe, taxing, tough, trying, weighty. See HEAVY in Index.
burg *noun* See **city.**
burgeon *verb* See **bloom¹, increase.**
burglar *noun* See **larcenist.**
burglarize *verb* See **break in** at **break.**
burglary *noun* See **trespass.**
burial *noun* An act of placing a body in a grave or tomb : entombment, inhumation, interment. See SHOW in Index.
buried *adjective* See **ulterior.**
burke *verb* See **avoid, repress.**
burlesque *noun* See **mockery.**
burlesque *verb* See **imitate.**
burly *adjective* See **muscular.**
burn *verb* **1.** To undergo combustion : blaze¹, combust, flame, flare. See HOT in Index. **2.** To undergo or cause to undergo damage by or as if by fire : char, scorch, sear, singe. See HOT in Index. **3.** To feel or look hot : bake, broil¹, roast, swelter. See HOT in Index. — See also **anger, beam, boil, irritate, sting.**
burn out *verb* See **run down** at **run.**
burn *noun* Damage or a damaged substance that results from burning : char, scorch, sear, singe. See HOT in Index.
burning *adjective* **1.** Compelling immediate attention : crying, dire, emergent, exigent, imperative, instant, pressing, urgent. See BIG in Index. **2.** On fire : ablaze, afire, aflame, alight², conflagrant, fiery,

flaming. *Idioms:* in a blaze, in flames. See HOT in Index. — See also **fervid, hot, passionate.**
burnish *verb* See **gloss.**
burnish *noun* See **gloss.**
burr also **bur** *noun* See **hum.**
burr also **bur** *verb* See **hum.**
burrow *noun* See **hole.**
burst *verb* To come open or fly apart suddenly and violently, as from internal pressure : blow¹ (out), explode, pop¹. *Slang:* bust. See EXPLOSION in Index. — See also **break out** at **break, explode.**
burst out *verb* See **exclaim.**
burst *noun* See **barrage, blast, outburst.**
bursting *adjective* See **eager, full.**
bury *verb* To place (a corpse) in or as if in a grave : entomb, inhume, inter, lay¹. *Idiom:* lay (or put) to rest. See SHOW in Index. — See also **hide¹.**
bush *noun* See **wild.**
bushed *adjective* See **exhausted.**
bushel *noun* See **heap.**
bushwhack *verb* See **ambush.**
business *noun* **1.** Activity pursued as a livelihood : art, calling, career, craft, employment, job, line, métier, occupation, profession, pursuit, trade, vocation, work. *Slang:* racket. *Archaic:* employ. See ACTION in Index. **2.** Commercial, industrial, or professional activity in general : commerce, industry, trade, trading, traffic. See ACTION in Index. **3.** Something that concerns or involves one personally : affair, concern, lookout. See RELEVANT in Index. — See also **company, matter, patronage.**
businesslike *adjective* See **serious.**
businessperson *noun* See **dealer.**
buss *verb* See **kiss.**
buss *noun* See **kiss.**
bust *verb* See **arrest, break, burst, collapse, demote, gentle, ruin, slap.**

bust *noun* See **arrest, failure, slap.**
bustle *noun* See **stir**[1].
  bustle *verb* See **fuss, rush.**
busy *adjective* **1.** Involved in activity or work : employed, engaged, occupied. See ACTION in Index.
2. Excessively filled with detail : cluttered, crowded, fussy. See SIMPLE in Index.
  busy *verb* To make busy : employ, engage, occupy. See ACTION in Index.
busybody *noun* See **meddler.**
but *adverb* See **solely.**
butcher *noun* See **murderer.**
  butcher *verb* See **annihilate.**
butchery *noun* See **massacre.**
butt[1] *noun* See **push.**
butt[2] *verb* See **adjoin.**
butt[3] *noun* See **dupe, joke, target.**
butt[4] *noun* See **end.**
butter up *verb* See **flatter.**
butt in *verb* See **meddle.**
buttinsky *noun* See **meddler.**
buttock *noun* See **bottom.**
button-down also **buttoned-down** *adjective* See **conventional.**
buttress *noun* See **support.**
  buttress *verb* See **back.**
buxom *adjective* See **shapely.**
buy *verb* To acquire in exchange for money or something of equal value : purchase. See GET, MONEY in Index. — See also **believe, bribe.**
  buy *noun* Something bought or capable of being bought : purchase. See GET, MONEY in Index. — See also **bargain.**
buyable *adjective* See **corruptible.**
buyer *noun* See **patron.**
buzz *verb* See **hum, telephone.**
  buzz *noun* See **call, hum.**
by-and-by *noun* See **future.**
bygone *adjective* See **old-fashioned.**
bypass *verb* See **avoid, skirt.**
  bypass *noun* See **escape.**

byproduct or **by-product** *noun* See **derivative.**
bystander *noun* See **watcher.**
byword *noun* See **proverb.**
byzantine also **Byzantine** *adjective* See **complex.**

C

cabal *noun* See **plot.**
cabalistic *adjective* See **mysterious.**
cabbage *noun* See **money.**
cache *noun* See **hoard.**
  cache *verb* See **hide**[1].
cachinnate *verb* See **laugh.**
cachinnation *noun* See **laugh.**
cackle *verb* See **laugh.**
  cackle *noun* See **laugh.**
cacophonous or **cacophonic** or **cacophonical** *adjective* See **inharmonious.**
cadaver *noun* See **body.**
cadaverous *adjective* See **ghastly, pale, wasted.**
cadence *noun* See **rhythm.**
cadenced *adjective* See **rhythmical.**
cadency *noun* See **rhythm.**
cadge *verb* See **beg.**
cadger *noun* See **beggar.**
caducity *noun* See **senility.**
cage *verb* See **enclose.**
cagey also **cagy** *adjective* See **shrewd.**
cajole *verb* See **coax.**
cake *verb* See **harden.**
calaboose *noun* See **jail.**
calamitous *adjective* See **fatal.**
calamity *noun* See **disaster.**
calculate *verb* To ascertain by mathematics : cast, cipher, compute, figure, reckon. See REASON in Index. — See also **estimate.**
calculated *adjective* Planned, weighed, or estimated in advance : considered, deliberate, intentional,

premeditated. See PURPOSE in
Index. — See also **advised.**

calculating *adjective* Coldly planning to achieve selfish aims :
designing, scheming. See ATTITUDE
in Index.

calculation *noun* The act, process,
or result of calculating : computation, figuring, reckoning. See REA-
SON in Index. — See also **advisement,
caution.**

calendar *noun* See **program.**

caliber *noun* See **merit, quality.**

caliginous *adjective* See **dark.**

call *verb* **1.** To demand to appear,
come, or assemble : convene, convoke, muster, send for, summon. See
REQUEST in Index. **2.** To describe
with a word or term : characterize,
designate, label, name, style, tag,
term. See SPECIFIC, WORDS in
Index. — See also **assemble, name,
predict, roar, telephone, visit.**

call down *verb* To criticize for a
fault or an offense : admonish, castigate, chastise, chide, dress down,
rap[1], rebuke, reprimand, reproach,
reprove, scold, tax, upbraid.
Informal: bawl out, lambaste. *Slang:*
chew out. *Idioms:* bring (or call or
take) to task, call on the carpet, haul
(or rake) over the coals, let someone
have it. See ATTACK, PRAISE in
Index.

call for *verb* To be a proper or sufficient occasion for : justify, occasion, warrant. See RIGHT in Index.
— See also **demand.**

call off *verb* See **cancel.**

call *noun* A telephone communication : buzz, ring[2]. See WORDS in
Index. — See also **attraction, cause,
demand, shout, visit.**

call girl *noun* See **prostitute.**

calligraphic *adjective* See **graphic.**

calling *noun* See **business, vocation.**

callous *adjective* See **cold-blooded.**

call to arms *noun* See **cry.**

call to battle *noun* See **cry.**

calm *adjective* Not excited or emotionally agitated : peaceful, placid,
serene, tranquil. See CALM in Index.
— See also **cool, still.**

calm *noun* Lack of emotional agitation : calmness, peace, peacefulness, placidity, placidness, quietude,
serenity, tranquillity. See CALM in
Index. — See also **stillness.**

calm *verb* To make or become
calm. Also used with *down* : allay,
balm, becalm, lull, quiet, settle, still,
tranquilize. See CALM in Index.
— See also **pacify.**

calmness *noun* See **calm, stillness.**

calumniate *verb* See **libel.**

calumniation *noun* See **libel.**

calumnious *adjective* See **libelous.**

calumny *noun* See **libel.**

camouflage *verb* See **disguise.**

campaign *noun* See **drive.**

campestral *adjective* See **country.**

camp follower *noun* See **prostitute.**

can *verb* See **conserve, dismiss.**

can *noun* See **jail.**

canard *noun* See **lie[2].**

cancel *verb* **1.** To remove or invalidate by or as if by running a line
through or wiping clean : annul,
blot (out), cross (off or out), delete,
efface, erase, expunge, obliterate, rub
(out), scratch (out), strike (out), undo,
wipe (out), x (out). *Law:* vacate. See
CONTINUE in Index. **2.** To decide
not to go ahead with (something previously arranged) : call off. *Slang:*
scratch, scrub. See CONTINUE in
Index. **3.** To make ineffective
by applying an opposite force or
amount : counteract, negate, neutralize, nullify. See ACTION in
Index. — See also **abolish.**

cancellation also **cancelation**
noun See **abolition, erasure.**

candid *adjective* See **frank.**

candidate *noun* See **applicant**.

candy *verb* See **sweeten**.

cane *noun* See **stick**.

canker *verb* See **corrupt, poison**.
  canker *noun* See **poison**.

cannonade *verb* See **barrage**.
  cannonade *noun* See **barrage**.

canny *adjective* See **economical, shrewd**.

can of worms *noun* See **problem**.

canon *noun* See **law**.

canonical *adjective* See **orthodox**.

cant[1] *noun* See **inclination**.
  cant *verb* See **incline**.

cant[2] *noun* See **dialect, language**.

cantankerous *adjective* See **ill-tempered**.

cap *verb* See **climax, cover, top**.
  cap *noun* See **height**.

capability *noun* See **ability**.

capable *adjective* See **able**.

capacious *adjective* See **full, roomy**.

capacity *noun* See **ability, grasp**.

caper *noun* See **prank**[1].
  caper *verb* See **gambol**.

capital *adjective* See **excellent, flagrant, primary**.
  capital *noun* Money or property used to produce more wealth : backing, capitalization, financing, funding, grubstake, stake, subsidization. See HELP, MONEY in Index.
  — See also **fund, resource**.

capitalist *noun* See **financier**.

capitalization *noun* See **capital**.

capitalize *verb* See **benefit, finance**.

capitulate *verb* See **succumb**.

capitulation *noun* See **surrender**.

caprice *noun* See **fancy**.

capricious *adjective* Following no predictable pattern : changeable, erratic, fantastic, fantastical, fickle, freakish, inconsistent, inconstant, mercurial, temperamental, ticklish, uncertain, unpredictable, unstable, unsteady, variable, volatile, whimsical. See CHANGE, CONTINUE in Index. — See also **arbitrary**.

capsize *verb* See **overturn**.

capsized *adjective* See **upside-down**.

captain *verb* See **lead**.

captious *adjective* See **critical**.

captivate *verb* See **charm**.

capture *verb* To obtain possession or control of : gain, get, take, win. *Slang:* cop. See GET in Index. — See also **take**.

carbon copy *noun* See **copy**.

carcass *noun* See **body**.

card *noun* See **character, joker**.

cardinal *adjective* See **primary**.

care *noun* 1. A cause of distress or anxiety : concern, trouble, worry. See CONCERN in Index. 2. Cautious attentiveness : carefulness, caution, gingerliness, heed, heedfulness, mindfulness, regard. See CAREFUL in Index. 3. The function of watching, guarding, or overseeing : charge, custody, guardianship, keeping, superintendence, supervision, trust. See CARE FOR in Index. — See also **anxiety, caution, thoroughness, treatment**.
  care *verb* To have an objection : mind, object. See CONCERN in Index.
  care for *verb* See **tend**[2].

career *noun* See **business**.

carefree *adjective* See **light**[2].

careful *adjective* 1. Cautiously attentive : heedful, mindful, observant, watchful. See CAREFUL in Index. 2. Showing or marked by attentiveness to all aspects or details : fastidious, meticulous, painstaking, punctilious, scrupulous. See CAREFUL in Index. — See also **wary**.

carefulness *noun* See **care, caution, thoroughness**.

careless *adjective* **1.** Lacking or marked by a lack of care : feckless, heedless, inattentive, irresponsible, reckless, thoughtless, unconcerned, unmindful, unthinking. See CARE-FUL in Index. **2.** Indifferent to correctness, accuracy, or neatness : messy, slapdash, slipshod, sloppy, slovenly, untidy. See CAREFUL in Index. — See also **mindless**.

carelessness *noun* See **abandon**.

caress *verb* To touch or stroke affectionately : cuddle, fondle, pat, pet[1]. See TOUCH in Index.

caretaker *noun* See **guardian**.

careworn *adjective* See **haggard**.

cargo *noun* See **burden[1]**.

caricature *noun* See **mockery**.

   caricature *verb* See **imitate**.

cark *verb* See **brood, worry**.

carnage *noun* See **massacre**.

carnal *adjective* See **physical**.

carnality *noun* See **physicality**.

carol *verb* See **sing**.

carom *verb* See **glance**.

carousal *noun* See **bender**.

carouse *noun* See **bender**.

   carouse *verb* See **revel**.

carp *verb* See **quibble**.

   carp at *verb* See **nag**.

carper *noun* See **critic**.

carping *adjective* See **critical**.

carriage *noun* See **posture, transportation**.

carrier *noun* See **bearer**.

carry *verb* **1.** To move while supporting : bear, convey, lug[2], transport. *Informal:* tote. *Slang:* schlep. See OVER in Index. **2.** To hold on one's person : bear, have, possess. *Informal:* pack. See OWNED in Index. **3.** To have as an accompaniment, a condition, or a consequence : entail, involve. See START in Index. **4.** To have for sale : keep, stock. See KEEP in Index. — See also

act, bear, bring, communicate, conduct, extend, pass, support.

carry away *verb* To move or excite greatly : electrify, enrapture, thrill, transport. *Slang:* send. See EXCITE in Index.

carry off *verb* See **kill[1]**.

carry on *verb* To continue without halting despite difficulties or setbacks : go on, hang on, keep on, persevere, persist. *Idioms:* hang in there, keep going, keep it up. See CONTINUE in Index. — See also **conduct, misbehave, participate, rave, wage**.

carry out *verb* See **administer, effect, enforce, follow, wage**.

carry through *verb* See **effect**.

cartel *noun* See **alliance, combine**.

carve *verb* See **cut, engrave**.

Casanova *noun* See **gallant, philanderer**.

case *noun* See **argument, example, lawsuit**.

   case *verb* See **examine**.

caseharden *verb* See **harden**.

cash *noun* See **money**.

cashier *verb* See **dismiss**.

Cassandra *noun* See **pessimist**.

cast *verb* See **add, aim, calculate, design, shed, throw**.

   cast about *verb* See **seek**.

   cast out *verb* See **dismiss**.

   cast *noun* See **bent, expression, form, kind[2], throw, tint**.

castigate *verb* See **call down** at call, punish.

castigation *noun* See **punishment**.

castle in the air *noun* See **illusion**.

castrate *verb* See **sterilize**.

castration *noun* See **sterilization**.

casual *adjective* See **accidental, easygoing**.

casualness *noun* See **ease**.

casualty *noun* See **accident, fatality, victim**.

casuistry *noun* See **fallacy**.

cataclysm *noun* See **disaster, flood, revolution.**

cataclysmal *adjective* See **fatal.**

cataclysmic *adjective* See **fatal.**

catacomb *noun* See **grave**[1].

catalog or **catalogue** *noun* See **list**[1].

catalog or **catalogue** *verb* See **list**[1].

catalyst *noun* An agent that stimulates or precipitates a reaction, development, or change : ferment, leaven, leavening, yeast. See CHANGE in Index.

cataract *noun* See **flood.**

catastrophe *noun* See **disaster.**

catastrophic *adjective* See **fatal.**

catcall *noun* See **hiss.**

catch *verb* **1.** To get hold of (something moving) : clutch[1], grab, seize, snatch. *Informal:* nab. *Idiom:* lay hands on. See GET in Index. **2.** To gain control of or an advantage over by or as if by trapping : enmesh, ensnare, ensnarl, entrap, snare, tangle, trammel, trap, web. See FREE in Index. **3.** To become or cause to become stuck or lodged : fix, lodge, stick. See MOVE in Index. **4.** To perceive, especially barely or fleetingly : descry, detect, discern, espy, glimpse, spot, spy. See SEE in Index. — See also contract, fasten, hit, seize, snap, take, understand.

catch up *verb* To come up even with another : overtake. See SEEK, WIN in Index. — See also **grip, involve.**

catch *noun* **1.** The act of catching, especially a sudden taking and holding : clutch[1], grab, seizure, snatch. See GET in Index. **2.** A device for fastening or for checking motion : clasp, fastener, hook. See MOVE in Index. **3.** *Informal.* A tricky or unsuspected condition : rub, snag.

See LIMITED in Index. **4.** *Informal.* A person or thing worth catching : plum, prize[1]. *Slang:* brass ring. See DESIRE in Index.

catching *adjective* See **communicable.**

catechism *noun* See **test**[1].

catechization *noun* See **test**[1].

categorical *adjective* See **definite.**

categorization *noun* See **arrangement.**

categorize *verb* See **assort, class.**

category *noun* See **class.**

cater *verb* See **baby, humor.**

caterwaul *verb* See **brawl.**

catharsis *noun* See **elimination.**

cathartic *adjective* See **eliminative.**

catholic *adjective* See **universal.**

catholicon *noun* See **panacea.**

catlike *adjective* See **stealthy.**

catnap *noun* See **nap.**

catnap *verb* See **nap.**

cat's cradle *noun* See **tangle.**

cat's-paw also **catspaw** *noun* See **cat's-paw, pawn**[2].

cause *noun* **1.** That which produces an effect : antecedent, occasion. See START in Index. **2.** A basis for an action or a decision : ground (often used in plural), motivation, motive, reason, spring. See START in Index. **3.** That which provides a reason or justification : call, ground (often used in plural), justification, necessity, occasion, reason, wherefore, why. *Idiom:* why and wherefore. See START in Index. **4.** A goal or set of interests served with dedication : crusade. See START in Index. — See also **lawsuit.**

cause *verb* To be the cause of : bring, bring about, bring on, effect, effectuate, generate, induce, ingenerate, lead to, make, occasion, result in, secure, set off, stir[1] (up), touch off, trigger. *Idioms:* bring to pass (or effect), give rise to. See START in Index.

caustic *adjective* See **biting**.

causticity *noun* See **sarcasm**.

caution *noun* Careful forethought to avoid harm or risk : calculation, care, carefulness, chariness, gingerliness, precaution, wariness. See FEAR in Index. — See also **care, prudence, warning**.

caution *verb* See **warn**.

cautionary *adjective* Giving warning : admonishing, admonitory, monitory, warning. See WARN in Index.

cautious *adjective* See **wary**.

cave *noun* A hollow beneath the earth's surface : cavern, grotto. See CONVEX in Index.

cave in *verb* To fall in : buckle, collapse, crumple, give, go. *Idiom:* give way. See EXPLOSION in Index. — See also **collapse**.

caveat *noun* See **warning**.

cavern *noun* See **cave**.

cavernous *adjective* See **hollow, yawning**.

cavil *verb* See **quibble**.

caviler *noun* See **critic**.

cavity *noun* See **hole**.

cavort *verb* See **gambol**.

cease *verb* See **stop, suspend**.

cease *noun* See **end**.

cease-fire or **ceasefire** *noun* See **truce**.

ceaseless *adjective* See **continual, endless**.

ceaselessness *noun* See **endlessness**.

cede *verb* See **abdicate, relinquish, transfer**.

ceiling *noun* See **limit**.

celebrate *verb* **1.** To mark (a day or an event) with ceremonies of respect, festivity, or rejoicing : commemorate, keep, observe, solemnize. See REMEMBER in Index.

2. To show joyful satisfaction in an event, especially by merrymaking : rejoice, revel. *Idioms:* kill the fatted calf, make merry. See LAUGHTER in Index. — See also **honor**.

celebrated *adjective* See **eminent**.

celebration *noun* **1.** The act of observing a day or an event with ceremonies : commemoration, observance. See REMEMBER in Index.

2. The act of showing joyful satisfaction in an event : festivity, merrymaking, rejoicing, revel (often used in plural), revelry. See LAUGHTER in Index. — See also **blast, party, praise**.

celebrity *noun* A famous person : hero, lion, luminary, name, notable, personage, personality. *Informal:* big name. See KNOWLEDGE in Index. — See also **fame**.

celerity *noun* See **haste**.

celestial *adjective* See **heavenly**.

censor *verb* **1.** To examine (material) and remove parts considered harmful or improper for publication or transmission : bowdlerize, expurgate, screen. See INCLUDE, SHOW in Index. **2.** To keep from being published or transmitted : ban, black out, hush (up), stifle, suppress. *Idiom:* keep (or put) a lid on. See SHOW in Index.

censorious *adjective* See **critical**.

censurable *adjective* See **blameworthy**.

censure *verb* See **blame, deplore**.

censure *noun* See **blame**.

center *noun* **1.** A point or an area equidistant from all sides of something : median, middle, midpoint, midst. See EDGE in Index. **2.** A point of origin from which ideas or influences, for example, originate : bottom, core, focus, heart, hub, quick, root^1. See START in Index.

3. A place of concentrated activity, influence, or importance : focus,

headquarters, heart, hub, seat. See
EDGE in Index.

center *verb* See **concentrate**.

center *adjective* See **central**.

central *adjective* At, in, near, or
being the center : center, medial,
median, mid, middle. See EDGE in
Index. — See also **middle, pivotal**.

cerebral *adjective* See **intellectual,
mental**.

cerebrate *verb* See **think**.

cerebration *noun* See **thought**.

ceremonial *adjective* See **ritual**.

ceremonial *noun* See **ceremony**.

ceremonious *adjective* Fond of or
given to ceremony : conventional,
courtly, formal, punctilious. See
COURTESY in Index. — See also
ritual.

ceremoniousness *noun* See
ceremony.

ceremony *noun* 1. A formal act or
set of acts prescribed by ritual : ceremonial, liturgy, observance, office,
rite, ritual, service. See RITUAL in
Index. 2. Strict observance of social
conventions : ceremoniousness,
formality, protocol, punctiliousness.
See COURTESY in Index. — See also
ritual.

certain *adjective* 1. Bound to happen : inescapable, inevitable, sure,
unavoidable. See CERTAIN in
Index. 2. Established beyond a
doubt : hard, inarguable, incontestable, incontrovertible, indisputable,
indubitable, irrefutable, positive,
sure, unassailable, undeniable,
undisputable, unquestionable. See
CERTAIN, TRUE in Index. — See also
definite, firm¹, sure.

certainly *adverb* See **absolutely**.

certainty *noun* A clearly established
fact : cinch, sure thing. See CER-
TAIN, TRUE in Index. — See also
sureness.

certify *verb* To confirm formally as
true, accurate, or genuine : attest,
testify, vouch (for), witness. *Idiom:*
bear witness to. See AFFIRM in
Index. — See also **guarantee**.

certitude *noun* See **sureness**.

cessation *noun* See **end, stop**.

cesspit *noun* See **pit¹**.

cesspool *noun* See **pit¹**.

chafe *verb* To make (the skin) raw
by or as if by friction : abrade, excoriate, fret, gall², irritate. See HELP in
Index. — See also **annoy, fuss**.

chaff *verb* See **joke**.

chaff *noun* See **ribbing**.

chagrin *noun* See **embarrassment**.

chagrin *verb* See **embarrass**.

chain *noun* See **bond, series**.

chain *verb* See **hamper**.

challenge *verb* See **contest, dare,
defy, object, rival**.

challenge *noun* See **dare, defiance, objection**.

champ *verb* See **bite, chew**.

champion *adjective* See **excellent**.

champion *verb* See **support**.

chance *noun* 1. The quality shared
by random, unintended, or unpredictable events or this quality
regarded as the cause of such
events : fortuitousness, fortuity,
fortune, hap, hazard, luck. See CER-
TAIN in Index. 2. The likeliness of a
given event occurring : likelihood,
odds, possibility, probability, prospect (used in plural). See LIKELY in
Index. 3. An unexpected random
event : accident, fluke, fortuity,
hap, happenchance, happenstance,
hazard. See CERTAIN, SURPRISE in
Index. — See also **opportunity, risk**.

chance *verb* To take place by
chance : befall, hap, happen. See
HAPPEN in Index. — See also **hazard**.

chance on or **upon** *verb* See
come across at **come**.

chance *adjective* See **accidental, random.**

chancy *adjective* See **ambiguous, dangerous.**

change *verb* **1.** To make or become different : alter, modify, mutate, turn, vary. See CHANGE in Index. **2.** To give up in return for something else : commute, exchange, interchange, shift, substitute, switch, trade. *Informal:* swap. See CHANGE, SUBSTITUTE in Index. **3.** To leave or discard for another : shift, switch. See CHANGE, SUBSTITUTE in Index.

change *noun* **1.** The process or result of making or becoming different : alteration, modification, mutation, permutation, variation. See CHANGE in Index. **2.** The process or result of changing from one appearance, state, or phase to another : changeover, conversion, metamorphosis, mutation, shift, transfiguration, transformation, translation, transmogrification, transmutation, transubstantiation. See CHANGE in Index. **3.** The act of exchanging or substituting : commutation, exchange, interchange, shift, substitution, switch, trade, transposition. *Informal:* swap. See CHANGE, SUBSTITUTE in Index.
— See also **transition.**

changeable *adjective* Capable of or liable to change : alterable, fluid, inconstant, mutable, uncertain, unsettled, unstable, unsteady, variable, variant. *Archaic:* various. See CHANGE in Index. — See also **capricious, mobile.**

changeless *adjective* See **consistent, even[1].**

changeover *noun* See **change.**

channel *verb* See **concentrate, conduct.**

chant *verb* See **sing.**

chaos *noun* See **disorder.**

chaotic *adjective* See **confused.**

chap *noun* See **boy.**

char *verb* See **burn.**

char *noun* See **burn.**

character *noun* **1.** The combination of emotional, intellectual, and moral qualities that distinguishes an individual : complexion, disposition, makeup, nature, personality. See BE in Index. **2.** Moral or ethical strength : fiber, honesty, integrity, principle. See STRONG in Index. **3.** A person portrayed in fiction or drama : persona, personage. See REAL in Index. **4.** A person who is appealingly odd or curious : oddity, original. *Informal:* card, oddball. See USUAL in Index. **5.** A conventional mark used in a writing system : sign, symbol. See MARKS in Index.
— See also **dignitary, quality, reference, reputation.**

character assassination *noun* See **libel.**

characteristic *adjective* See **distinctive.**

characteristic *noun* See **quality.**

characterize *verb* See **call, distinguish.**

charade *noun* See **pretense.**

charge *verb* **1.** To place a burden or heavy load on : burden[1], cumber, encumber, freight, lade, load, saddle, tax, weight. See OVER in Index. **2.** To cause to be filled, as with a particular mood or tone : freight, imbue, impregnate, permeate, pervade, saturate, suffuse, transfuse. See FULL in Index. — See also **accuse, attribute, command, commit, entrust, fill, load.**

charge *noun* A swift advance or attack : blitzkrieg, rush. See APPROACH in Index. — See also **accusation, care, command, cost,**

dependent, detention, duty, load, toll[1].

chariness *noun* See **caution**.

charisma *noun* See **attraction**.

charitable *adjective* See **benevolent, humanitarian, tolerant**.

charitableness *noun* See **benevolence, tolerance**.

charity *noun* See **benevolence, donation, grace, tolerance**.

charlatan *noun* See **fake**.

charm *verb* **1.** To act upon with or as if with magic : bewitch, enchant, enthrall, entrance[2], spell[2], spellbind, voodoo, witch. See PERSUASION in Index. **2.** To please greatly or irresistibly : beguile, bewitch, captivate, enchant, entrance[2], fascinate. See LIKE in Index.

charm *noun* A small object worn or kept for its supposed magical power : amulet, fetish, juju, periapt, phylactery, talisman. See SUPERNATURAL in Index. — See also **attraction, spell[2]**.

charmer *noun* See **seducer**.

charming *adjective* See **delightful**.

chart *noun* See **table**.

chart *verb* See **design, plot**.

charter *verb* See **hire**.

chary *adjective* See **economical, wary**.

chase *verb* See **hunt, pursue**.

chase *noun* See **pursuit**.

chasm *noun* See **deep**.

chaste *adjective* Morally beyond reproach, especially in sexual conduct : decent, modest, nice, pure, virgin, virginal, virtuous. See GOOD, RESTRAINT, SEX in Index.

chasten *verb* See **correct**.

chastise *verb* See **call down** at **call, punish**.

chastisement *noun* See **punishment**.

chastity *noun* The condition of being chaste : decency, innocence, modesty, purity, virginity, virtue, virtuousness. See GOOD, RESTRAINT, SEX in Index.

chat *noun* See **chatter, conversation**.

chat *verb* See **converse[1]**.

chattel *noun* See **effect**.

chatter *verb* To talk volubly, persistently, and usually inconsequentially : babble, blabber, chitchat, clack, jabber, palaver, prate, prattle, rattle (on), run on. *Informal:* go on, spiel. *Slang:* gab, gas, jaw, yak. *Idioms:* run off at the mouth, shoot the breeze (or bull). See WORDS in Index. — See also **babble, rattle**.

chatter *noun* Incessant and usually inconsequential talk : babble, blab, blabber, chat, chitchat, jabber, palaver, prate, prattle, small talk. *Slang:* gab, gas, yak. See WORDS in Index.

chatty *adjective* See **conversational, talkative**.

chaw *verb* See **chew**.

cheap *adjective* Low in price : inexpensive, low, low-cost, low-priced. See MONEY, VALUE in Index. — See also **shoddy, stingy**.

cheapen *verb* See **debase, depreciate**.

cheapskate *noun* See **miser**.

cheat *verb* To get money or something else from by deceitful trickery : bilk, cozen, defraud, gull, mulct, rook, swindle, victimize. *Informal:* chisel, flimflam, take, trim. *Slang:* diddle[1], do, gyp, stick, sting. See HONEST in Index. — See also **philander**.

cheat *noun* **1.** An act of cheating : fraud, swindle, victimization. *Informal:* flimflam. *Slang:* gyp. See HONEST in Index. **2.** A person who cheats : bilk, cheater, cozener, defrauder, rook, sharper, swindler, trickster, victimizer. *Informal:* chiseler, crook, flimflammer. *Slang:* diddler, gyp, gypper. See HONEST in Index.

cheater *noun* See **cheat.**

check *noun* See **account, examination, restriction, stop.**

check *verb* See **agree, examine, frustrate, restrain, stop, test.**

check in *verb* See **arrive.**

check out *verb* See **die.**

checkmate *verb* See **frustrate.**

checkup *noun* See **examination.**

cheek *noun* See **impudence.**

cheekiness *noun* See **impudence.**

cheeky *adjective* See **impudent.**

cheer *noun* See **happiness.**

cheer *verb* See **applaud, delight, encourage.**

cheerful *adjective* Being in or showing good spirits : bright, cheery, chipper, happy, lighthearted, sunny. See HAPPY in Index. — See also **glad.**

cheerfulness *noun* See **happiness.**

cheering *adjective* See **encouraging.**

cheerless *adjective* See **gloomy, sad.**

cheery *adjective* See **cheerful, glad.**

cheesy *adjective* See **shoddy.**

chef *noun* See **cook.**

chef-d'oeuvre *noun* See **masterpiece.**

cherish *verb* To have the highest regard for : prize[1], treasure. *Idiom:* hold dear. See VALUE in Index. — See also **appreciate.**

cherubic *adjective* See **babyish.**

chew *verb* To bite and grind with the teeth : champ, chomp, chump[2], crump, crunch, masticate, munch. *Regional:* chaw. See MOUTH in Index.

chew on or **over** *verb* See **ponder.**

chew out *verb* See **call down** at **call.**

chic *adjective* See **fashionable.**

chicanery *noun* See **indirection.**

chicken *noun* See **coward.**

chicken *adjective* See **cowardly.**

chicken feed *noun* See **peanut.**

chickenhearted *adjective* See **cowardly.**

chickenheartedness *noun* See **cowardice.**

chide *verb* See **call down** at **call.**

chief *adjective* See **primary, principal.**

chief *noun* One who is highest in rank or authority : boss, chieftain, director, head, headman, hierarch, leader, master. *Slang:* honcho. *Idiom:* cock of the walk. See OVER in Index. — See also **boss.**

chieftain *noun* See **chief.**

child *noun* A young person between birth and puberty : bud[1], innocent, juvenile, moppet, tot[1], youngster. *Informal:* kid. *Scots:* bairn. See KIN, YOUTH in Index. — See also **descendant, innocent, minor.**

childbearing *noun* See **birth.**

childbirth *noun* See **birth.**

childish *adjective* Of or characteristic of a child, especially in immaturity : babyish, immature, infantile, juvenile, puerile. See YOUTH in Index.

childless *adjective* See **barren.**

childlike *adjective* See **babyish.**

child's play *noun* See **breeze.**

chill *adjective* See **cold, cool.**

chill *noun* See **cold.**

chilliness *noun* See **cold.**

chilly *adjective* See **cold, cool.**

chime *noun* See **agreement.**

chime *verb* See **agree, ring[2].**

chime in *verb* See **interrupt.**

chimera *noun* See **illusion.**

chimeric *adjective* See **illusive, imaginary.**

chimerical *adjective* See **illusive, imaginary.**

chink *noun* See **crack.**

chintzy *adjective* See **gaudy.**

chip in *verb* See **contribute, interrupt.**

chipper *adjective* See **cheerful, lively.**

chisel *verb* See **cheat.**

chiseler *noun* See **cheat.**

chitchat *noun* See **chatter.**

  chitchat *verb* See **chatter.**

chivalric *adjective* See **gallant.**

chivalrous *adjective* See **gallant, gracious.**

chivalrousness *noun* See **gallantry.**

chivalry *noun* See **gallantry.**

chockablock *adjective* See **full.**

choice *noun* 1. The act of choosing : election, option, preference, selection. See CHOICE in Index. 2. The power or right of choosing : alternative, option. See CHOICE in Index. — See also **best, elect.**

  choice *adjective* Of fine quality : fine[1], first-class, prime, select, superior. See BETTER in Index. — See also **delicate, select.**

choke *verb* 1. To interfere with or stop the normal breathing of, especially by constricting the windpipe : strangle, throttle. See BREATH in Index. 2. To stop the breathing of : asphyxiate, smother, stifle, suffocate. See BREATH in Index. — See also **fail, fill, repress.**

  choke off *verb* See **suppress.**

  choke *noun* See **plug.**

choler *noun* See **anger.**

choleric *adjective* See **angry, testy.**

chomp *verb* See **bite, chew.**

choose *verb* 1. To make a choice from a number of alternatives : cull, elect, opt (for), pick (out), select, single (out). See CHOICE in Index. 2. To have the desire or inclination to : desire, like[1], please, want, will, wish. *Idioms:* have a mind, see fit. See DESIRE in Index.

choosy *adjective* See **nice.**

chop[1] *verb* See **cut back** at **cut.**

  chop down *verb* See **cut.**

  chop *noun* See **slap.**

chop[2] *verb* See **swerve.**

chore *noun* See **task.**

chortle *verb* See **chuckle.**

chosen *adjective* See **select.**

  chosen *noun* See **elect.**

chow *noun* See **food.**

  chow *verb* See **eat.**

christen *verb* See **name.**

chronic *adjective* 1. Of long duration : continuing, lingering, persistent, prolonged, protracted. See CONTINUE in Index. 2. Subject to a disease or habit for a long time : confirmed, habitual, habituated, inveterate. See CONTINUE in Index. — See also **accustomed.**

chronicle *noun* See **history, story.**

chubby *adjective* See **plump**[1].

chuck *verb* See **discard, eject.**

chuckle *verb* To laugh quietly : chortle. See LAUGHTER, SOUNDS in Index.

chuff *noun* See **boor.**

chum *noun* See **associate, friend.**

chumminess *noun* See **friendship.**

chummy *adjective* See **familiar.**

chump[1] *noun* See **dullard.**

chump[2] *verb* See **chew.**

chunk *noun* See **lump**[1].

chunky *adjective* See **stocky.**

church *noun* See **faith.**

  church *adjective* See **spiritual.**

churchly *adjective* See **spiritual.**

churchman *noun* See **preacher.**

churchwoman *noun* See **preacher.**

churl *noun* See **boor.**

churlish *adjective* See **coarse.**

churn *verb* See **agitate, boil.**

chutzpah also **hutzpah** *noun* See **impudence.**

cinch *noun* See **breeze, certainty.**

  cinch *verb* See **guarantee.**

cincture *verb* See **band**[1].

cinerarium *noun* See **grave¹**.
cipher *noun* See **nonentity**.
cipher *verb* See **calculate**.
circle *noun* **1.** A closed plane curve everywhere equidistant from a fixed point or something shaped like this : band¹, circuit, disk, gyre, ring¹, wheel. *Archaic:* orb. See GEOMETRY in Index. **2.** A course, process, or journey that ends where it began or repeats itself : circuit, cycle, orbit, round, tour, turn. See REPETITION in Index. **3.** A group of people sharing an interest, activity, or achievement : crowd, group, set². See GROUP in Index. — See also **area, crowd**.
circle *verb* See **surround, turn**.
circuit *noun* See **beat, circle, circumference, conference, revolution**.
circuitous *adjective* See **indirect**.
circular *adjective* See **indirect, round**.
circulate *verb* See **advertise, distribute, flow, get around** at **get, spread**.
circulation *noun* See **distribution, revolution**.
circumference *noun* A line around a closed figure or area : ambit, circuit, compass, perimeter, periphery. See EDGE in Index.
circumlocutionary *adjective* See **tautological**.
circumnavigate *verb* See **skirt**.
circumscribe *verb* See **limit**.
circumscription *noun* See **restriction**.
circumspect *adjective* See **wary**.
circumspection *noun* See **prudence**.
circumstance *noun* **1.** One of the conditions or facts attending an event and having some bearing on it : detail, fact, factor, particular. See REAL in Index. **2.** Something that happens : event, happening, incident, occasion, occurrence,

thing. See HAPPEN in Index. — See also **condition, event**.
circumstantial *adjective* See **detailed**.
circumvent *verb* See **avoid, skirt**.
circumvention *noun* See **escape**.
circumvolution *noun* See **revolution**.
circumvolve *verb* See **turn**.
cite *verb* See **name, present²**.
citify *verb* To imbue with city ways, manners, and customs : metropolitanize, urbanize. See URBAN in Index.
citizen *noun* A person owing loyalty to and entitled to the protection of a given state : national, subject. See GROUP, POLITICS in Index.
city *noun* A large and important town : metropolis, municipality. *Informal:* burg, town. See URBAN in Index.
city *adjective* Of, in, or belonging to a city : metropolitan, municipal, urban. See URBAN in Index.
civic *adjective* See **public**.
civil *adjective* See **courteous, public**.
civility *noun* See **amenity, courtesy**.
civilization *noun* See **culture**.
civilize *verb* See **socialize**.
civilized *adjective* See **cultured**.
civilizing *adjective* See **cultural**.
clack *noun* See **snap**.
clack *verb* See **chatter, rattle, snap**.
clad *verb* See **face**.
claim *verb* To assert one's right to : demand. *Idiom:* lay claim to. See GIVE, OWNED, REQUEST in Index. — See also **assert, demand**.
claim *noun* A legitimate or supposed right to demand something as one's rightful due : pretense, pretension, title. *Slang:* dibs. See OWNED, REQUEST in Index. — See also **assertion, demand, interest**.

claimant *noun* One who sets forth a claim to a royal title : claimer, pretender. See OWNED in Index. — See also **complainant**.

claimer *noun* See **claimant**.

clamber *verb* See **scramble**.

clamor *verb* See **roar**.

clamor *noun* See **noise, roar, vociferation**.

clamorous *adjective* See **vociferous**.

clampdown *noun* See **suppression**.

clan *noun* See **family**.

clandestine *adjective* See **secret**.

clandestinely *adverb* See **secretly**.

clandestineness *noun* See **secrecy**.

clandestinity *noun* See **secrecy**.

clap *verb* See **applaud, bang, crack**.

clap *noun* See **report**.

claptrap *noun* See **bombast, nonsense**.

clarification *noun* See **explanation, purification**.

clarifier *noun* See **purifier**.

clarify *verb* To make clear or clearer : clear (up), elucidate, illuminate, illustrate. *Idiom:* shed (or throw) light on (or upon). See CLEAR in Index. — See also **refine**.

clarity *noun* The quality of being clear and easy to perceive or understand : clearness, distinctness, limpidity, limpidness, lucidity, lucidness, pellucidity, pellucidness, perspicuity, perspicuousness, plainness. See CLEAR in Index. — See also **purity**.

clash *verb* To strike together with a loud, harsh noise : crash, smash. See SOUNDS in Index. — See also **conflict**.

clash *noun* A loud striking together : crash, smash. See SOUNDS in Index. — See also **argument, brush², conflict**.

clasp *noun* See **catch, embrace, hold**.

clasp *verb* See **embrace, grasp**.

class *noun* **1.** A subdivision of a larger group : category, classification, order, set². See GROUP in Index. **2.** A division of persons or things by quality, rank, or grade : bracket, grade, league, order, rank¹, tier. See GROUP, VALUE in Index. **3.** *Informal.* High style in quality, manner, or dress : quality, refinement. See STYLE in Index. — See also **quality**.

class *verb* To assign to a class or classes : categorize, classify, distribute, grade, group, pigeonhole, place, range, rank¹, rate¹. See GROUP, VALUE in Index. — See also **assort**.

classic *adjective* See **typical, vintage**.

classical *adjective* See **typical, vintage**.

classification *noun* See **arrangement, class**.

classified *adjective* See **confidential**.

classify *verb* See **assort, class**.

classy *adjective* See **fashionable**.

clatter *verb* See **rattle**.

clean *adjective* **1.** Free from dirt, stain, or impurities : antiseptic, cleanly, immaculate, spotless, stainless, unsoiled, unsullied. See CLEAN in Index. **2.** Without imperfections or blemishes, as a line or contour : perfect, regular. See BEAUTIFUL in Index. **3.** Not lewd or obscene : decent, modest, wholesome. See DECENT in Index. — See also **innocent, neat, sportsmanlike**.

clean *verb* See **refine, tidy**.

clean out *verb* See **empty, ruin**.

clean up *verb* *Slang.* To make a large profit : batten, profit. *Idiom:* make a killing. See MONEY in Index.

clean *adverb* See **completely**.

cleaner *noun* See **purifier**.

cleanliness *noun* See **purity**.

cleanly *adjective* See **clean**.

cleanly *adverb* See **fair**.

cleanness *noun* See **purity**.

cleanse *verb* See **purify, refine**.

cleanser *noun* See **purifier**.

clear *adjective* 1. Free from what obscures or dims : crystal clear, crystalline, limpid, lucid, pellucid, see-through, transparent. See CLEAR, TOUCH in Index. 2. Free from clouds or mist, for example : cloudless, fair, fine[1], sunny, unclouded. See CLEAR in Index. 3. Free from flaws or blemishes : flawless, unblemished, unmarked. See BEAUTIFUL in Index. 4. Free from obstructions : free, open, unblocked, unimpeded, unobstructed. See OPEN in Index. 5. Freed from contact or connection : free. See FREE, STRIKE in Index. — See also **apparent, decided, definite, empty, sharp, transparent, unsubtle**.

clear *verb* 1. To become brighter or fairer. Also used with *up* : brighten, lighten[1]. See CLEAR in Index. 2. To free from an entanglement : disengage, disentangle, disinvolve, extricate, untangle. See FREE in Index. 3. To rid of obstructions : free, open, unblock. See OPEN in Index. 4. To free from a charge or imputation of guilt : absolve, exculpate, exonerate, vindicate. *Law:* acquit, purge. See LAW in Index. 5. To pass by or over safely or successfully : hurdle, negotiate, surmount. See THRIVE in Index. — See also **annihilate, clarify, empty, pass, return, rid, settle, tidy**.

clear out *verb* See **run**.

clear up *verb* See **resolve**.

clear *adverb* See **completely**.

clearance *noun* See **elimination**.

clear-cut *adjective* See **apparent, decided, definite**.

clearness *noun* See **clarity**.

clear-sightedness *noun* See **discernment**.

cleavage *noun* See **crack**.

cleave[1] *verb* See **cut**.

cleave[2] *verb* See **bond**.

cleft *noun* See **crack**.

clemency *noun* See **grace**.

clement *adjective* See **tolerant**.

clench *verb* See **grasp**.

clench *noun* See **hold**.

clergyman *noun* See **preacher**.

clergywoman *noun* See **preacher**.

cleric *noun* See **preacher**.

clerical *noun* See **preacher**.

clerk *noun* See **preacher, seller**.

clever *adjective* 1. Mentally quick and original : alert, bright, intelligent, keen[1], quick, quick-witted, sharp, sharp-witted, smart. *Idiom:* smart as a whip. See ABILITY in Index. 2. Amusing or pleasing because of wit or originality : scintillating, smart, sparkling, witty. See LAUGHTER in Index. — See also **dexterous**.

cliché *noun* A trite expression or idea : banality, bromide, commonplace, platitude, stereotype, truism. See SURPRISE in Index.

clichéd *adjective* See **trite**.

click *noun* See **snap**.

click *verb* See **relate, snap, succeed**.

client *noun* See **patron**.

clientele *noun* See **patronage**.

climacteric *noun* See **crisis**.

climacteric *adjective* See **critical**.

climactic *adjective* Of or constituting a climax : crowning, culminating, peak. See HIGH, OVER in Index.

climate *noun* See **environment, temper**.

climax *noun* The highest point or state : acme, apex, apogee, crest, crown, culmination, height, meridian, peak, pinnacle, summit, top, zenith. *Informal:* payoff. *Medicine:* fastigium. See HIGH in Index.

climax *verb* To reach or bring to a climax : cap, crest, crown, culminate, peak, top (off or out). See EXCITE in Index.

climb *verb* See **ascend, rise.**
climb *noun* See **ascent.**

clinch *verb* See **embrace.**
clinch *noun* See **embrace.**

clincher *noun* See **trump.**

cling *verb* See **bond.**

clinging *adjective* See **tight.**

clink *noun* See **jail.**

clip¹ *verb* See **cut back** at **cut, hit, skin, slap.**
clip *noun* See **blow², slap, speed.**

clip² *verb* See **attach, embrace.**

clique *noun* See **crowd.**

cloak *verb* See **clothe, cover, wrap.**
cloak *noun* See **façade, wrap.**

cloak-and-dagger *adjective* See **secret.**

clobber *verb* See **beat, overwhelm.**

clock *verb* See **time.**

clod *noun* See **dullard, lump¹.**

clodhopper *noun* A clumsy, unsophisticated person : bumpkin, rustic, yokel. See ABILITY in Index.

clog *verb* See **fill.**
clog *noun* See **bar.**

cloister *verb* See **seclude.**

clomp *verb* See **thud.**

close *adjective* 1. Not far from another in space, time, or relation : adjacent, contiguous, immediate, near, nearby, nigh, proximate. *Idioms:* at hand, under one's nose, within a stone's throw, within hailing distance. See NEAR in Index. 2. Nearly equivalent or even : neck and neck, nip and tuck, tight. See NEAR in Index. 3. Not deviating from correctness, accuracy, or completeness : exact, faithful, full, rig-

orous, strict. See CAREFUL in Index.
— See also **airless, familiar, stingy, taciturn, thick, tight.**

close *verb* 1. To move (a door, for example) in order to cover an opening : shut. See OPEN in Index. 2. To bring or come to a natural or proper end : complete, conclude, consummate, end, finish, terminate, wind up, wrap up. See START in Index. 3. To come together : converge, meet¹. See OPEN in Index.
— See also **fill.**

close in *verb* To surround and advance upon : besiege, enclose, envelop, hedge, hem. See OPEN in Index.

close off *verb* See **isolate.**
close out *verb* See **sell off** at **sell.**
close *noun* See **court, end.**
close *adverb* To a point near in time, space, or relation : closely, hard, near, nearby, nigh. See NEAR in Index.

close-fisted *adjective* See **stingy.**

closely *adverb* See **close.**

close-minded *adjective* See **intolerant.**

close-mouthed *adjective* See **taciturn.**

closeness *noun* See **friendship.**

closet *verb* See **imprison.**

closing *adjective* See **last¹.**
closing *noun* See **end.**

closure *noun* See **end.**

clot *verb* See **coagulate.**

clothe *verb* To cover as if with clothes : cloak, drape, mantle, robe. See PUT ON in Index. — See also **dress, wrap.**

clothes *noun* See **dress.**

clothing *noun* See **dress.**

cloud *verb* See **blacken, obscure.**
cloud *noun* See **crowd.**

clouded *adjective* See **ambiguous.**

cloudiness *noun* See **vagueness.**

cloudless *adjective* See **clear.**

cloud nine *noun* See **heaven.**

cloudy *adjective* See **ambiguous, filmy, turbid, unclear.**

clout *noun* See **blow², influence, muscle.**

clout *verb* See **hit.**

clown *noun* See **joker.**

clown *verb* See **joke.**

cloy *verb* See **satiate.**

club *noun* See **union.**

clue also **clew** *noun* See **hint, lead.**

clump *noun* See **group, lump¹.**

clump *verb* See **lump¹, thud.**

clumsy *adjective* See **awkward, tactless, unskillful.**

clunk *noun* See **beat.**

clunk *verb* See **thud.**

cluster *noun* See **group.**

cluster *verb* See **assemble.**

clutch¹ *noun* See **catch, hold.**

clutch *verb* See **catch, grasp.**

clutch² *noun* See **group.**

clutching *adjective* See **jealous.**

clutter *noun* See **disorder.**

cluttered *adjective* See **busy.**

coach *verb* See **educate.**

coaction *noun* See **cooperation.**

coadjutant *noun* See **assistant.**

coadjutor *noun* See **assistant.**

coagulate *verb* To change or be changed from a liquid into a soft, semisolid, or solid mass : clot, congeal, curdle, gelatinize, jell, jelly, set¹. See SOLID in Index.

coalesce *verb* See **combine.**

coalition *noun* See **alliance, combine, unification.**

coalitionist *noun* See **ally.**

coarse *adjective* **1.** Lacking in delicacy or refinement : barbarian, barbaric, boorish, churlish, crass, crude, gross, ill-bred, indelicate, philistine, rough, rude, tasteless, uncivilized, uncouth, uncultivated, uncultured, unpolished, unrefined, vulgar. See COURTESY, SMOOTH in Index. **2.** Consisting of or covered with

large particles : grainy, granular, gritty, rough. See SMOOTH in Index. — See also **obscene, rough.**

coarseness *noun* See **obscenity.**

coast *verb* See **slide.**

coax *verb* To persuade or try to persuade by gentle persistent urging or flattery : blandish, cajole, honey, wheedle. *Informal:* soft-soap, sweet-talk. See PERSUASION in Index.

cock-and-bull story *noun* See **lie².**

cockcrow *noun* See **dawn.**

cockeyed *adjective* See **drunk, foolish.**

coddle *verb* See **baby.**

coequal *noun* See **peer².**

coerce *verb* To compel by pressure or threats : blackjack, dragoon, force. *Informal:* hijack, strong-arm. See PERSUASION in Index. — See also **force.**

coercion *noun* See **force.**

coercive *adjective* See **forcible.**

coetaneous *adjective* See **contemporary.**

coeval *adjective* See **contemporary.**

coeval *noun* See **contemporary.**

coexistent *adjective* See **contemporary.**

cogent *adjective* See **convincing, sound².**

cogitate *verb* See **ponder, think.**

cogitation *noun* See **thought.**

cogitative *adjective* See **thoughtful.**

cognate *adjective* See **related.**

cognizance *noun* See **awareness, notice.**

cognizant *adjective* See **aware.**

cognomen *noun* See **name.**

cohere *verb* See **bond.**

coherence *noun* See **consistency.**

cohesion *noun* See **bond.**

cohort *noun* See **associate, follower.**

coil *verb* See **wind².**

coincide *verb* To occur at the same time : concur, synchronize. See

NEAR in Index. — See also **agree.**

coincident *adjective* See **accompanying, simultaneous.**

cold *adjective* **1.** Marked by a low temperature : chill, chilly, cool, nippy, shivery. See HOT in Index. **2.** Not affected by or showing emotion : cold-blooded, emotionless, unaffected, unemotional, unmoved. See ATTITUDE, HOT in Index. **3.** Lacking all friendliness and warmth : frigid, frosty, glacial, icy. See ATTITUDE, HOT in Index. — See also **frigid, unconscious.**

cold *noun* Relative lack of physical warmth : chill, chilliness, coldness, coolness. See HOT in Index.

cold-blooded *adjective* Completely lacking in compassion : callous, cold-hearted, compassionless, hard, hard-boiled, hardened, hardhearted, heartless, obdurate, stonyhearted, unfeeling. See ATTITUDE in Index. — See also **cold.**

cold feet *noun* See **fear.**

cold-hearted *adjective* See **coldblooded.**

coldness *noun* See **cold.**

coldshoulder *verb* See **snub.**

cold shoulder *noun* See **snub.**

collaborate *verb* See **cooperate.**

collaboration *noun* See **cooperation.**

collaborative *adjective* See **cooperative.**

collapse *verb* **1.** To suddenly lose all health or strength : break (down), cave in, crack, drop, give out, succumb. *Informal:* crack up. *Slang:* conk out. *Idiom:* give way. See HEALTH in Index. **2.** To undergo sudden financial failure : break, bust, crash, fail, go under. *Informal:* fold. *Idioms:* go belly up, go bust, go on the rocks, go to the wall. See MONEY in Index. — See also **break, cave in** at **cave, surrender.**

collapse *noun* An abrupt disastrous failure : breakdown, crash, debacle, smash, smashup, wreck. See MONEY in Index. — See also **breakdown, fall.**

collar *noun* See **arrest.**

collar *verb* See **arrest.**

collate *verb* See **compare.**

collateral *adjective* See **auxiliary, parallel, subordinate.**

colleague *noun* See **associate, peer².**

collect¹ *verb* See **accumulate, assemble, compose.**

collect² *noun* See **prayer¹.**

collected *adjective* See **cool.**

collectedness *noun* See **balance.**

collection *noun* See **accumulation, group.**

collide *verb* To come together or come up against with force : bump, crash. See CONFLICT in Index.

collision *noun* Violent forcible contact between two or more things : bump, concussion, crash, impact, jar, jolt, percussion, shock¹, smash. See CONFLICT in Index.

colloquial *adjective* See **conversational.**

colloquium *noun* See **conference.**

colloquy *noun* See **conversation.**

collude *verb* See **plot.**

collusion *noun* See **plot.**

colony *noun* See **possession.**

colophon *noun* See **mark.**

color *noun* **1.** The property by which the sense of vision can distinguish between objects, as a red apple and a green apple, that are very similar or identical in form and size : hue, shade, tint, tone. See COLORS in Index. **2.** Something that imparts color : colorant, coloring, dye, dyestuff, pigment, stain, tincture. See COLORS in Index. — See also **bloom¹, complexion, façade, flag¹, verisimilitude.**

color *verb* **1.** To impart color to : dye, stain, tincture, tint. See COLORS in Index. **2.** To give a deceptively attractive appearance to : gild, gloss (over), gloze (over), sugarcoat, varnish, veneer, whitewash. *Idioms:* paper over, put a good face on. See TRUE in Index. — See also **blush, dip, distort.**

colorable *adjective* See **believable.**

colorant *noun* See **color.**

colorfast *adjective* See **fast.**

colorful *adjective* **1.** Full of color : bright, gay, rich, vivid. See COLORS in Index. **2.** Evoking strong mental images through distinctiveness : picturesque, vivid. See STRONG in Index.

coloring *noun* See **color, complexion, façade.**

colorless *adjective* See **dull, neutral, pale.**

colorlessness *noun* See **dullness.**

colossal *adjective* See **giant.**

column *noun* See **line.**

comb *verb* See **scour¹.**

combat *verb* See **contend.**

combat *noun* A hostile encounter between opposing military forces : action, battle, engagement. See CONFLICT in Index.

combatant *noun* See **fighter.**

combatant *adjective* See **belligerent.**

combative *adjective* See **aggressive, argumentative, belligerent.**

combativeness *noun* See **aggression, argumentativeness, belligerence, fight.**

combination *noun* The result of combining : composite, compound, conjugation, unification, union, unity. See ASSEMBLE in Index. — See also **association, combine.**

combinational *adjective* Of, relating to, or tending to produce combination : combinative, combinato-

rial, conjugational, conjugative, conjunctional, connectional, connective. See ASSEMBLE in Index.

combinative *adjective* See **combinational.**

combinatorial *adjective* See **combinational.**

combine *verb* To bring or come together into a united whole : coalesce, compound, concrete, conjoin, conjugate, connect, consolidate, couple, join, link, marry, meld, unify, unite, wed, yoke. See ASSEMBLE in Index. — See also **associate, band², embody.**

combine *noun* **1.** A group of individuals united in a common cause : bloc, cartel, coalition, combination, faction, party, ring¹. See GROUP in Index. **2.** A combination of businesses closely interconnected for common profit : cartel, pool, syndicate, trust. See GROUP, MONEY in Index.

combust *verb* See **burn.**

come *verb* **1.** To take place : befall, betide, come about, come off, develop, hap, happen, occur, pass, transpire. *Idiom:* come to pass. See HAPPEN in Index. **2.** To take place at a set time : fall, occur. See HAPPEN in Index. **3.** To happen to one : befall, betide. See HAPPEN in Index. **4.** To go forward, especially toward a conclusion. Also used with *along* : advance, get along, march¹, move, proceed, progress. See APPROACH in Index. **5.** To have as one's home or place of origin : hail², originate. See START in Index. — See also **become, stem.**

come about *verb* See **come.**

come across *verb* To find or meet by chance : bump into, chance on (*or* upon), come on (*or* upon), find, happen on (*or* upon), light on (*or* upon), run across, run into, stumble

on (or upon), tumble on. *Archaic:*
alight on (or upon). *Idiom:* meet up
with. See MEET in Index. — See also
contribute.

come around or **round** *verb* See
recover.

come back *verb* See **return**.

come by *verb* See **get, visit**.

come in *verb* See **enter, run**.

come into *verb* See **inherit**.

come off *verb* See **come, succeed**.

come on or **upon** *verb* See **come
across** at **come**.

come out *verb* **1.** To be made pub-
lic : break, get out, out, transpire.
Informal: leak (out). *Idiom:* come to
light. See KNOWLEDGE, SHOW in
Index. **2.** To make one's formal
entry, as into society : debut.
Idiom: make one's bow. See KNOWL-
EDGE in Index.

come over *verb* See **visit**.

come through *verb* See **survive**.

come to *verb* See **arrive at** at
arrive.

comeback *noun* A return to former
prosperity or status : recovery. See
APPROACH, WIN in Index. — See
also **retort**.

comedian *noun* See **joker**.

comedic *adjective* See **humorous**.

comedown *noun* See **descent**.

comedy *noun* See **humor**.

come-hither *adjective* See
seductive.

comeliness *noun* See **decency**.

comely *adjective* See **beautiful,
correct**.

come-on *noun* See **lure**.

comer *noun* One showing much
promise : rising star, up-and-
comer. See ABILITY in Index. — See
also **arrival**.

comestible *adjective* See **edible**.

comestible *noun* See **food**.

comeuppance *noun* See **due**.

comfort *verb* To give hope to in
time of grief or pain : console, solace, soothe. See HELP in Index. — See
also **relieve**.

comfort *noun* A consoling in time
of grief or pain : consolation, solace. See HELP in Index. — See also
amenity, prosperity.

comfortable *adjective* Affording
pleasurable ease : cozy, easeful,
easy, snug. *Informal:* comfy, soft.
See GOOD in Index. — See also **prosperous, sufficient**.

comfortless *adjective* See **uncomfortable**.

comfy *adjective* See **comfortable**.

comic *noun* See **joker**.

comic *adjective* See **amusing,
laughable**.

comical *adjective* See **amusing,
laughable**.

comicality *noun* See **humor**.

comicalness *noun* See **humor**.

coming *adjective* **1.** In the relatively
near future : approaching, forthcoming, upcoming. See NEAR in
Index. **2.** Showing great promise :
promising, up-and-coming. *Idiom:*
on the way up. See INCREASE in
Index. — See also **following, future**.

coming *noun* See **approach,
arrival**.

coming-out *noun* See **presentation**.

command *verb* **1.** To give orders
to : bid, charge, direct, enjoin,
instruct, order, tell. See OVER,
WORDS in Index. **2.** To have at one's
disposal : boast, enjoy, have, hold,
possess. See OWNED in Index. — See
also **dominate, lead**.

command *noun* An authoritative
indication to be obeyed : behest,
bidding, charge, commandment, dictate, direction, directive, injunction,
instruction (often used in plural),
mandate, order, word. See OVER,

WORDS in Index. — See also **ability, authority, domination, lead.**

commandeer *verb* See **assume, seize.**

commanding *adjective* See **authoritative, dominant.**

commandment *noun* See **command.**

comme il faut *adjective* See **correct.**

commemorate *verb* See **celebrate, memorialize.**

commemoration *noun* See **celebration, memorial.**

commemorative *adjective* See **memorial.**

commence *verb* See **begin, dawn, start.**

commencement *noun* See **beginning, birth.**

commend *verb* See **compliment, entrust, praise.**

commendable *adjective* See **admirable.**

commendation *noun* See **compliment, praise.**

commendatory *adjective* See **complimentary.**

commensurable *adjective* See **proportional.**

commensurate *adjective* See **proportional.**

comment *noun* An expression of fact or opinion : note, obiter dictum, observation, remark. See WORDS in Index. — See also **commentary.**

comment *verb* To state facts, opinions, or explanations : note, observe, remark. See WORDS in Index.

commentary *noun* **1.** Critical explanation or analysis : annotation, comment, exegesis, interpretation, note. See WORDS in Index. **2.** A narrative of experiences undergone by the writer. Often used in plural : memoir, reminiscence (often used in plural). See WORDS in Index.

commentator *noun* See **critic.**

commerce *noun* See **business.**

commingle *verb* See **mix.**

commiserate *verb* See **feel.**

commiseration *noun* See **pity.**

commiserative *adjective* See **pitying.**

commission *noun* See **mission.**

commission *verb* See **authorize.**

commit *verb* **1.** To be responsible for or guilty of (an error or crime) : perpetrate. *Informal:* pull off. See DO, LAW in Index. **2.** To place officially in confinement : consign, institutionalize. *Informal:* send up. See FREE in Index. **3.** To be morally bound to do : bind, charge, obligate, pledge. See OBLIGATION in Index. — See also **entrust.**

commitment *noun* See **duty.**

commix *verb* See **mix.**

commixture *noun* See **mixture.**

commodious *adjective* See **roomy.**

commodity *noun* See **good.**

common *adjective* **1.** Belonging to, shared by, or applicable to all alike : communal, conjoint, general, joint, mutual, public. See GROUP in Index. **2.** Occurring quite often : everyday, familiar, frequent, regular, routine, widespread. See USUAL in Index. **3.** Commonly encountered : average, commonplace, general, normal, ordinary, typical, usual. See SURPRISE in Index. — See also **acceptable, general, inferior, lowly, notorious, ordinary.**

common *noun* A tract of cultivated land belonging to and used by a community : green. See GROUP in Index. — See also **commonalty.**

commonality *noun* See **commonalty.**

commonalty *noun* The common people : common (used in plural), commonality, commoner (used in plural), crowd, hoi polloi, mass (used in plural), mob, pleb (used in plural), plebeian (used in plural), populace, public, ruck[1], third estate. See OVER in Index.

commoner *noun* See **commonalty**.

commonly *adverb* See **usually**.

commonplace *adjective* See **common, ordinary, trite**.

commonplace *noun* See **cliché, usual**.

common sense *noun* The ability to make sensible decisions : judgment, sense, wisdom. *Informal:* gumption, horse sense. See ABILITY in Index.

commonsensible *adjective* See **sane**.

commonsensical *adjective* See **sane**.

commotion *noun* See **agitation, disturbance**.

communal *adjective* See **common**.

communalize *verb* See **socialize**.

communicable *adjective* Capable of transmission by infection : catching, contagious, infectious, taking. See MOVE in Index. — See also **outgoing**.

communicate *verb* **1.** To make known : break, carry, convey, disclose, get across, impart, pass, report, tell, transmit. See KNOWLEDGE in Index. **2.** To cause (a disease) to pass to another or others : carry, convey, give, pass, spread, transmit. See MOVE in Index. — See also **express, relate, say**.

communication *noun* **1.** The exchange of ideas by writing, speech, or signals : communion, intercommunication, intercourse. *Obsolete:* converse[1]. See KNOWLEDGE in Index. **2.** Something communicated,

as information : message, word. See WORDS in Index. — See also **touch**.

communicative *adjective* See **outgoing**.

communion *noun* See **communication, faith**.

community *noun* See **public**.

commutation *noun* See **change**.

commute *verb* See **change**.

comp *noun* See **pass**.

compact[1] *adjective* See **pithy, stocky, thick**.

compact *verb* See **contract, squeeze**.

compact[2] *noun* See **agreement, bargain**.

compactness *noun* See **thickness**.

companion *noun* See **accompaniment, associate, mate**.

companion *verb* See **accompany**.

companionable *adjective* Liking company : convivial, sociable, social. *Chiefly British:* matey. See ATTITUDE in Index. — See also **social**.

companionless *adjective* See **alone**.

companionship *noun* See **company, friendship**.

company *noun* **1.** A commercial organization : business, concern, corporation, enterprise, establishment, firm[2], house. *Informal:* outfit. See GROUP in Index. **2.** A person or persons visiting one : guest, visitant, visitor. See ACCOMPANIED in Index. **3.** A pleasant association among people : companionship, fellowship, society. See CONNECT, GROUP in Index. — See also **assembly, band**[2].

company *verb* See **accompany**.

comparable *adjective* See **like**[2].

comparative *adjective* Estimated by comparison : relative. See SAME in Index.

compare *verb* **1.** To examine in order to note the similarities and differences of : balance, collate. See SAME in Index. **2.** To be equal or alike : correspond, equal, match, measure up, parallel, touch. *Informal:* stack up. See SAME in Index. — See also **liken.**

comparison *noun* See **likeness.**

compass *noun* See **circumference, grasp, range.**

compass *verb* See **band**[1]**, know, surround, understand.**

compassion *noun* See **pity.**

compassionate *adjective* See **humanitarian, pitying.**

compassionate *verb* See **feel.**

compassionless *adjective* See **cold-blooded.**

compatible *adjective* See **agreeable.**

compatriot *noun* See **countryman.**

compeer *noun* See **peer**[2]**.**

compel *verb* See **force.**

compendious *adjective* See **brief.**

compensate *verb* **1.** To make up for : balance, counterbalance, counterpoise, countervail, neutralize, offset, outweigh, redeem, set off. See SUBSTITUTE in Index. **2.** To give compensation to : indemnify, pay, recompense, redress, reimburse, remunerate, repay, requite. See PAY in Index. — See also **balance, pay, reward.**

compensation *noun* Something to make up for loss or damage : amends, indemnification, indemnity, offset, quittance, recompense, redress, reimbursement, remuneration, reparation, repayment, requital, restitution, satisfaction, setoff. See SUBSTITUTE in Index. — See also **payment, wage.**

compensative *adjective* See **compensatory.**

compensatory *adjective* Affording compensation : compensative, remunerative. See SUBSTITUTE in Index.

compete *verb* To strive against (others) for victory : contend, contest, emulate, rival, vie. See CONFLICT in Index.

competence *noun* See **ability, faculty.**

competency *noun* See **ability, faculty.**

competent *adjective* See **able, sufficient.**

competition *noun* **1.** A vying with others for victory or supremacy : battle, contest, corrivalry, race, rivalry, strife, striving, struggle, tug of war, war, warfare. See CONFLICT in Index. **2.** A trial of skill or ability : contest, meet[1]. See CONFLICT in Index. — See also **competitor.**

competitive *adjective* Given to competition : emulous. See CONFLICT in Index.

competitor *noun* One that competes : competition, contender, contestant, corrival, opponent, rival. See CONFLICT in Index.

complain *verb* To express negative feelings, especially of dissatisfaction or resentment : grouch, grump, whine. *Informal:* crab, gripe, grouse, kick. *Slang:* beef, bellyache, bitch. See FEELINGS, HAPPY in Index.

complainant *noun* One that makes a formal complaint, especially in court : accuser, claimant, plaintiff. See LAW in Index.

complainer *noun* See **grouch.**

complaint *noun* An expression of dissatisfaction or a circumstance regarded as a cause for such expression : grievance. *Informal:* gripe, grouse. *Slang:* beef, kick. **Idiom:** bone to pick. See HAPPY in Index. — See also **disease, indisposition.**

complaisant *adjective* See **obliging**.

complement *noun* Something that completes another : supplement. See AGREE, PART in Index. — See also **accompaniment**.

complement *verb* To supply what is lacking : complete, fill in (or out), round (off or out), supplement. See AGREE, PART in Index.

complemental *adjective* See **complementary**.

complementary *adjective* Forming or serving as a complement : complemental, supplemental. See AGREE, PART in Index.

complete *adjective* **1.** Lacking nothing essential or normal : entire, full, intact, integral, perfect, whole. See PART in Index. **2.** Not shortened by omissions : unabbreviated, unabridged, uncensored, uncut, unexpurgated. See PART in Index. **3.** Having reached completion : done, through. See PART in Index. — See also **round, thorough, utter²**, **whole**.

complete *verb* See **close, complement**.

completely *adverb* **1.** To the fullest extent : absolutely, all, altogether, dead, entirely, flat, fully, just, perfectly, quite, thoroughly, totally, utterly, well², wholly. *Informal:* clean, clear. *Idioms:* in toto, through and through. See BIG, LIMITED in Index. **2.** In a complete manner : exhaustively, intensively, thoroughly. *Idioms:* in and out, inside out, up and down. See LIMITED, PART in Index.

completeness *noun* The state of being entirely whole : entirety, integrity, oneness, totality, wholeness. See PART in Index.

completion *noun* See **end**.

complex *adjective* **1.** Consisting of two or more interconnected parts : composite, compound. See SIMPLE in Index. **2.** Difficult to understand because of intricacy : byzantine, complicated, convoluted, daedal, Daedalian, elaborate, intricate, involute, involved, knotty, labyrinthine, tangled. See SIMPLE in Index.

complex *noun* **1.** A usually large entity composed of interconnected parts : system. See PART in Index. **2.** An exaggerated concern : *Informal:* hang-up. See FEAR in Index. — See also **base¹**.

complexion *noun* Skin tone, especially of the face : color, coloring. See COLORS in Index. — See also **character, disposition**.

complexity *noun* Something complex : complication, intricacy. See SIMPLE in Index.

compliance *noun* See **obedience**.

compliancy *noun* See **obedience**.

compliant *adjective* See **obedient**.

complicate *verb* To make complex, intricate, or perplexing : embarrass, entangle, involve, perplex, ravel, snarl², tangle. See SIMPLE in Index.

complicated *adjective* See **complex, elaborate**.

complication *noun* See **complexity**.

compliment *verb* To pay a compliment to : commend, congratulate, praise. *Idiom:* take off one's hat to. See PRAISE in Index. — See also **praise**.

compliment *noun* An expression of admiration or congratulation : commendation, congratulation (often used in plural), praise, tribute. See PRAISE in Index. — See also **courtesy, praise**.

complimentary *adjective* Serving to compliment : acclamatory, approbatory, commendatory, congratulatory, laudatory. See PRAISE in Index. — See also **free.**

comply verb See **follow.**

component noun See **element.**

component adjective See **built-in.**

comport verb See **act.**

comport with verb See **agree.**

comportment noun See **behavior.**

compose verb **1.** To form by artistic effort : create, indite, produce, write. See MAKE in Index. **2.** To bring one's emotions under control : collect[1], contain, control, cool, simmer down. *Idiom:* cool it. See RESTRAINT in Index. — See also **constitute, form.**

composed adjective See **cool.**

composite adjective See **complex.**

composite noun See **combination.**

composition noun **1.** Something that is the result of creative effort : opus, piece, production, work. See MAKE in Index. **2.** A relatively brief discourse written especially as an exercise : essay, paper, theme. See WORDS in Index. — See also **compromise.**

compos mentis adjective See **sane.**

composure noun See **balance.**

compound verb See **combine.**

compound adjective See **complex.**

compound noun See **combination.**

comprehend verb See **contain, know, understand.**

comprehensible adjective See **understandable.**

comprehension noun See **grasp.**

comprehensive adjective See **general.**

compress verb See **contract, squeeze.**

compression noun See **constriction.**

comprise verb See **contain.**

compromise noun A settlement of differences through mutual conces-

sion : accommodation, arrangement, give-and-take, medium, settlement. *Law:* composition. See AGREE in Index.

compromise verb To make a concession : concede. *Idioms:* give and take, go fifty-fifty, meet someone halfway. See AGREE in Index. — See also **risk.**

compulsion noun See **force.**

compulsory adjective See **forced, required.**

compunction noun See **penitence, qualm.**

compunctious adjective See **remorseful.**

computation noun See **calculation, figure.**

compute verb See **calculate.**

comrade noun See **associate.**

comradeship noun See **friendship.**

con verb See **examine, memorize, study.**

concatenate verb See **integrate.**

concave adjective See **hollow.**

concavity noun See **depression.**

conceal verb See **block, cover, hide[1].**

concealed adjective See **blind, ulterior.**

concealment noun See **secrecy.**

concede verb See **acknowledge, compromise, give in** at **give, grant.**

conceit noun See **egotism, fancy.**

conceit verb See **like[1].**

conceited adjective See **egotistic, vain.**

conceivable adjective See **earthly.**

conceive verb See **design, imagine, understand.**

concentrate verb To direct toward a common center : center, channel, converge, focalize, focus. See EDGE in Index. — See also **apply.**

concentrated adjective Not diffused or dispersed : exclusive, intensive, undivided, unswerving, whole. See COLLECT, EDGE, PART in Index. — See also **heavy, strong.**

concentration *noun* A converging at a common center : confluence, conflux, convergence. See EDGE in Index. — See also **attention.**

concept *noun* See **idea.**

conception *noun* See **idea.**

conceptual *adjective* See **imaginary.**

concern *noun* Curiosity about or attention to someone or something : concernment, interest, interestedness, regard. See CONCERN in Index. — See also **anxiety, business, care, company, consideration, gadget, importance.**

concern *verb* See **apply, worry.**

concerned *adjective* Having concern : affected, interested, involved. See CONCERN in Index. — See also **anxious.**

concernment *noun* See **concern, importance, relevance.**

concert *noun* See **harmony.**

concession *noun* An accommodation made in the light of special or extenuating circumstances : allowance. See AGREE in Index.

conciliate *verb* See **pacify, reconcile.**

conciliation *noun* See **reconciliation.**

concise *adjective* See **brief.**

conclave *noun* See **assembly.**

conclude *verb* See **arrange, close, decide, infer, settle.**

concluding *adjective* See **last**[1].

conclusion *noun* See **decision, deduction, end.**

conclusive *adjective* See **authoritative, decisive, definitive.**

conclusively *adverb* See **last**[1].

concoct *verb* See **invent.**

concomitant *adjective* See **accompanying.**

concomitant *noun* See **accompaniment.**

concord *noun* See **agreement, harmony, treaty.**

concordance *noun* See **agreement.**

concourse *noun* See **junction.**

concrete *adjective* See **physical, real.**

concrete *verb* See **combine, harden.**

concupiscence *noun* See **desire.**

concupiscent *adjective* See **erotic.**

concur *verb* See **agree, coincide.**

concurrence *noun* See **agreement.**

concurrent *adjective* See **accompanying, contemporary.**

concurrently *adverb* See **together.**

concussion *noun* See **collision.**

condemn *verb* To pronounce judgment against : damn, doom, sentence. See LAW in Index. — See also **deplore.**

condemnable *adjective* See **deplorable.**

condemnation *noun* See **blame.**

condemned *adjective* Sentenced to terrible, irrevocable punishment : doomed, fated, foredoomed, lost. See LAW, RELIGION in Index.

condensation *noun* See **synopsis.**

condense *verb* See **shorten, thicken.**

condescend *verb* **1.** To descend to a level considered inappropriate to one's dignity : deign, stoop, vouchsafe. See OVER, RISE in Index. **2.** To treat in a superciliously indulgent manner : patronize. *Informal:* high-hat. *Idiom:* speak (or talk) down to. See ATTITUDE, OVER, RESPECT, RISE in Index.

condescendence *noun* See **condescension.**

condescension *noun* Superciliously indulgent treatment, especially of those considered inferior : condescendence, patronization. See ATTITUDE, RESPECT, RISE in Index.

condiment *noun* See **flavoring**.

condition *noun* **1.** Manner of being or form of existence : mode, situation, state, status. See BE in Index. **2.** Something indispensable : essential, must, necessity, need, precondition, prerequisite, requirement, requisite, sine qua non. See NECESSARY in Index. **3.** Existing surroundings that affect an activity. Used in plural : circumstance (often used in plural), environment. *Slang:* scene. See BE in Index. — See also **provision, trim**.

condition *verb* See **accustom**.

conditional *adjective* Depending on or containing a condition or conditions : provisional, provisory, tentative. See LIMITED in Index. — See also **dependent**.

conditioned *adjective* See **dependent**.

condolatory *adjective* See **pitying**.

condolence *noun* See **pity**.

condonation *noun* See **forgiveness**.

condone *verb* See **forgive**.

conduce *verb* See **contribute**.

conducive *adjective* See **contributive**.

conduct *verb* **1.** To control the course of (an activity) : carry on, direct, manage, operate, run, steer. See OVER in Index. **2.** To serve as a conduit : carry, channel, convey, transmit. See ALLOW in Index. — See also **guide, wage**.

conduct *noun* See **behavior**.

conductor *noun* See **guide**.

confab *noun* See **conversation**.

confab *verb* See **converse¹**.

confabulate *verb* See **converse¹**.

confabulation *noun* See **conversation**.

confabulator *noun* See **conversationalist**.

confabulatory *adjective* See **conversational**.

confederacy *noun* See **alliance**.

confederate *verb* See **ally**.

confederate *noun* See **accessory, ally, associate**.

confederation *noun* See **alliance, union**.

confer *verb* **1.** To meet and exchange views to reach a decision : advise, consult, deliberate, parley, talk. *Informal:* powwow. See COLLECT, MEET, WORDS in Index. **2.** To give formally or officially : accord, award, bestow, grant, present². See GIVE in Index.

conferee also **conferree** *noun* One who participates in a conference : discussant, discusser. See MEET, WORDS in Index.

conference *noun* **1.** A meeting for the exchange of views : colloquium, discussion, parley, seminar. *Informal:* powwow. *Slang:* rap session. See MEET, WORDS in Index. **2.** An exchanging of views : discussion, ventilation. *Slang:* rap³. See WORDS in Index. **3.** A group of athletic teams that play each other : association, circuit, league, loop. See GROUP in Index. — See also **assembly, conferment, convention, deliberation**.

conferment *noun* The act of conferring, as of an honor : accordance, bestowal, bestowment, conference, conferral, grant, presentation. See GIVE in Index.

conferral *noun* See **conferment**.

confess *verb* See **acknowledge**.

confession *noun* See **acknowledgment, religion**.

confessor *noun* See **confidant**.

confidant *noun* One in whom secrets are confided : confessor, confidante, repository. See SHOW, WORDS in Index. — See also **friend**.

confidante *noun* See **confidant, friend**.

confide *verb* To tell in confidence :
breathe, whisper. See SHOW, WORDS
in Index. — See also **entrust.**

confidence *noun* **1.** Absolute certainty in the trustworthiness of
another : belief, dependence, faith,
reliance, trust. See BELIEF in Index.
2. A firm belief in one's own powers : aplomb, assurance, self-
assurance, self-confidence, self-
possession. See ATTITUDE, BELIEF
in Index. — See also **sureness.**

confident *adjective* Having a firm
belief in one's own powers :
assured, secure, self-assured, self-
confident, self-possessed. See ATTI-
TUDE, BELIEF in Index. — See also
sure.

confidential *adjective* **1.** Known
about by very few : auricular,
inside, private, secret. *Informal:*
hush-hush. See SHOW in Index.
2. Indicating intimacy and mutual
trust : familiar, intimate[1]. See
ATTITUDE, NEAR in Index. **3.** Of or
being information available only to
authorized persons : classified,
privileged, restricted. See SHOW in
Index.

configuration *noun* See **form.**

configure *verb* See **form.**

confine *verb* See **bar, imprison, jail,
limit.**

confine *noun* See **end, limit.**

confinement *noun* See **detention,
restriction.**

confining *adjective* See **tight.**

confirm *verb* **1.** To assure the certainty or validity of : attest,
authenticate, back (up), bear out,
corroborate, evidence, justify, substantiate, testify (to), validate, verify,
warrant. See SUPPORT, TRUE in
Index. **2.** To accept officially :
adopt, affirm, approve, pass, ratify,
sanction. See ACCEPT, LAW in
Index. **3.** To make firmer in a partic-

ular conviction or habit : fortify,
harden, strengthen. See STRONG in
Index. — See also **prove.**

confirmation *noun* **1.** An act of
confirming officially : affirmation,
approval, ratification, sanction. See
LAW in Index. **2.** That which con-
firms : attestation, authentication,
corroboration, demonstration, evidence, proof, substantiation, testament, testimonial, testimony, validation, verification, warrant. See
TRUE in Index.

confirmed *adjective* Firmly established by long standing : deep-
rooted, deep-seated, entrenched,
hard-shell, ineradicable, ingrained,
inveterate, irradicable, set[1], settled.
See CONTINUE in Index. — See also
chronic.

confiscate *verb* See **seize.**

confiscation *noun* See **seizure.**

conflagrant *adjective* See **burning.**

conflagration *noun* See **fire.**

conflict *noun* **1.** A state of open, prolonged fighting : belligerency, confrontation, hostility (used in plural),
strife, struggle, war, warfare. See
CONFLICT in Index. **2.** A state of
disagreement and disharmony :
clash, confrontation, contention,
difference, difficulty, disaccord,
discord, discordance, dissension,
dissent, dissentience, dissidence,
dissonance, faction, friction, inharmony, schism, strife, variance, war,
warfare. See CONFLICT in Index.

conflict *verb* To fail to be in
accord : clash, contradict, disaccord, discord, jar. *Idiom:* go (*or* run)
counter to. See AGREE in Index.

confluence *noun* See **concentration, junction.**

conflux *noun* See **concentration.**

conform *verb* See **adapt, agree,
conventionalize, fit[1], follow,
harmonize.**

conformable *adjective* See **agreeable, obedient.**

conformance *noun* See **agreement.**

conformation *noun* See **adaptation, agreement.**

conformist *adjective* See **conventional.**

conformity *noun* See **agreement.**

confound *verb* See **confuse, embarrass, nonplus.**

confounded *adjective* See **confused, damned.**

confront *verb* To meet face-to-face, especially defiantly : accost, encounter, face, front. See MEET in Index. — See also **encounter.**

confrontation *noun* A face-to-face, usually hostile meeting : encounter, face-off. See MEET in Index. — See also **conflict.**

confuse *verb* **1.** To cause to be unclear in mind or intent : addle, befuddle, bewilder, confound, discombobulate, dizzy, fuddle, jumble, mix up, muddle, mystify, perplex, puzzle. *Informal:* throw. **Idiom:** make one's head reel (or swim or whirl). See CLEAR, FEELINGS in Index. **2.** To put into total disorder : ball up, disorder, jumble, mess up, muddle, scramble, snarl². *Slang:* snafu. **Idiom:** play havoc with. See ORDER in Index. **3.** To take (one thing) mistakenly for another : confound, mistake, mix up. See CORRECT in Index. — See also **embarrass.**

confused *adjective* **1.** Characterized by physical confusion : chaotic, disordered, helter-skelter, higgledy-piggledy, topsy-turvy, upside-down. *Informal:* mixed-up. See ORDER in Index. **2.** Mentally uncertain : addled, addlepated, confounded, confusional, muddleheaded, perplexed, turbid. *Informal:* mixed-up. See CLEAR in Index.

confusedness *noun* See **disorder.**

confusion *noun* See **disorder, embarrassment.**

confusional *adjective* See **confused.**

confute *verb* See **refute.**

congeal *verb* See **coagulate, harden.**

congener *noun* See **parallel.**

congenial *adjective* See **agreeable, amiable.**

congeniality *noun* See **amiability.**

congenialness *noun* See **amiability.**

congenital *adjective* See **constitutional, innate.**

congeries *noun* See **accumulation.**

congest *verb* See **fill.**

conglomeration *noun* See **assortment.**

congratulate *verb* See **compliment, pride.**

congratulation *noun* See **compliment.**

congratulatory *adjective* See **complimentary.**

congregate *verb* See **assemble.**

congregation *noun* See **assembly.**

congress *noun* See **assembly, convention, union.**

congruence *noun* See **agreement.**

congruity *noun* See **agreement, consistency.**

congruous *adjective* See **agreeable, symmetrical.**

conjectural *adjective* See **supposed.**

conjecture *verb* See **guess.**

conjecture *noun* See **guess, theory.**

conjoin *verb* See **associate, combine.**

conjoint *adjective* See **common.**

conjugal *adjective* See **marital.**

conjugality *noun* See **marriage.**

conjugate *verb* See **combine.**

conjugation *noun* See **combination.**

conjugational *adjective* See combinational.

conjugative *adjective* See combinational.

conjunction *noun* See association.

conjunctional *adjective* See combinational.

conjuration *noun* See magic.

conjure *verb* See appeal.

conk *noun* See blow², head.
  conk *verb* See hit.
  conk out *verb* See collapse, fail.

connate *adjective* See related.

connatural *adjective* See constitutional, related.

connect *verb* See associate, attach, combine, relate.

connection *noun* See association, contact, joint, relation, suggestion.

connectional *adjective* See combinational.

connective *adjective* See combinational.

conniption *noun* See temper.

conniption fit *noun* See temper.

connivance also **connivence** *noun* See plot.

connive *verb* See plot.
  connive at *verb* See blink.

connotation *noun* See meaning, suggestion.

connotative *adjective* See suggestive.

connote *verb* See mean¹.

connubial *adjective* See marital.

connubiality *noun* See marriage.

conquer *verb* See defeat.

conquering *adjective* See victorious.

conqueror also **conquerer** *noun* One that conquers : conquistador, master, victor, winner. See WIN in Index.

conquest *noun* The act of conquering : triumph, victory, win. See WIN in Index.

conquistador *noun* See conqueror.

consanguine *adjective* See related.

consanguineous *adjective* See related.

conscience *noun* See decency.

conscienceless *adjective* See unscrupulous.

conscious *adjective* See mindful.

consciousness *noun* See awareness.

conscript *verb* See draft.

conscription *noun* See draft.

consecrate *verb* See devote, sanctify.

consecrated *adjective* See sacred.

consecution *noun* See order, series.

consecutive *adjective* Following one after another in an orderly pattern : sequent, sequential, serial, subsequent, successional, successive. See PRECEDE, TIME in Index.

consensus *noun* See unanimity.

consent *noun* See acceptance, permission.
  consent *verb* See assent, permit.

consequence *noun* See effect, importance.

consequent *adjective* See logical.

consequential *adjective* See important, influential.

conservancy *noun* See conservation.

conservation *noun* The careful guarding of an asset : conservancy, husbandry, management, preservation. See KEEP in Index.

conservative *adjective* **1.** Strongly favoring retention of the existing order : orthodox, right, rightist, right-wing, Tory, traditionalist, traditionalistic. See KEEP in Index. **2.** Kept within sensible limits : discreet, moderate, reasonable, restrained, temperate. See PLAIN, RESTRAINT in Index. — See also preservative, unprogressive.

conservative *noun* One who strongly favors retention of the existing order : orthodox, rightist, rightwinger, Tory, traditionalist. See KEEP in Index.

conservator *noun* See **guardian.**

conserve *verb* **1.** To protect (an asset) from loss or destruction : husband, preserve, save. See KEEP in Index. **2.** To prepare (food) for storage and future use : can, preserve, put up. See KEEP in Index. — See also **economize.**

consider *verb* See **admire, believe, deal with** at **deal, hear of** at **hear, look, ponder, regard.**

considerable *adjective* See **big, important.**

considerably *adverb* To a considerable extent : far, much, quite, well[2]. *Idioms:* by a long shot (or way), by a wide margin, by far. See BIG in Index.

considerate *adjective* See **attentive.**

consideration *noun* Thoughtful attention : attentiveness, concern, regard, solicitude, thoughtfulness. See ATTITUDE, CONCERN, KIND, TREAT WELL in Index. — See also **advisement, attention, esteem, payment.**

considered *adjective* See **advised, calculated.**

consign *verb* See **commit, entrust, send.**

consist *verb* To have an inherent basis : dwell, exist, inhere, lie[1], repose, reside, rest[1]. See START in Index. — See also **agree.**

consistence *noun* See **consistency.**

consistency *noun* Logical agreement among parts : coherence, congruity, consistence. See AGREE in Index.

consistent *adjective* Remaining continually unchanged : changeless, constant, invariable, same,

unchanging, unfailing. See CHANGE in Index. — See also **agreeable.**

consistently *adverb* See **usually.**

consolation *noun* See **comfort.**

console *verb* See **comfort.**

consolidate *verb* See **combine.**

consolidation *noun* See **unification.**

consonance *noun* See **agreement, harmony.**

consonant *adjective* See **agreeable, harmonious.**

consort *verb* See **accompany, associate.**

consort *noun* See **spouse.**

conspicuous *adjective* See **noticeable.**

conspiracy *noun* See **plot.**

conspirator *noun* See **accessory.**

conspire *verb* See **plot.**

constable *noun* See **policeman.**

constancy *noun* See **fidelity.**

constant *adjective* See **consistent, continual, even[1], faithful, firm[1].**

consternate *verb* See **dismay.**

consternation *noun* See **dismay.**

constituent *adjective* See **built-in.**

constituent *noun* See **element.**

constitute *verb* To be the constituent parts of : compose, form, make (up). See BE in Index. — See also **amount, establish, found.**

constitution *noun* The physical or constitutional characteristics of a person : build, habit, habitus, physique. See BODY in Index. — See also **foundation.**

constitutional *adjective* Forming an essential element, as arising from the basic structure of an individual : built-in, congenital, connatural, elemental, inborn, inbred, indigenous, indwelling, ingrained, inherent, innate, intrinsic, native, natural. See BE, NATIVE, START in Index. — See also **essential.**

constitutional *noun* A usually brief and regular journey on foot,

especially for exercise : turn, walk.
See MOVE in Index.

constitutive *adjective* See **essential**.

constrain *verb* To check the freedom and spontaneity of : constrict, cramp², inhibit. See FREE, TIGHTEN in Index. — See also **force, restrain**.

constrained *adjective* See **awkward**.

constraint *noun* See **force, restriction**.

constrict *verb* To make smaller or narrower : constringe, narrow. See TIGHTEN, WIDE in Index. — See also **constrain, contract, squeeze**.

constriction *noun* 1. A becoming narrow or narrower : *Pathology:* stricture. See WIDE in Index. 2. A compressing of something : compression, squeeze. See TIGHTEN in Index.

constringe *verb* See **constrict, contract, squeeze**.

construct *verb* See **build, make**.

construction *noun* See **explanation**.

constructor or **constructer** *noun* See **builder**.

construe *verb* See **explain, interpret, translate**.

consuetude *noun* See **custom**.

consult *verb* See **confer**.

consultant *noun* See **adviser**.

consultation *noun* See **deliberation**.

consultative *adjective* See **advisory**.

consultatory *adjective* See **advisory**.

consulting *adjective* See **advisory**.

consultive *adjective* See **advisory**.

consume *verb* 1. To eat completely or entirely : devour, dispatch, eat up. *Informal:* polish off, put away. See INGESTION in Index. 2. To do away with completely and destructively : devour, eat (up), swallow (up), waste. See HELP in Index. — See

also **absorb, eat, exhaust, go, waste**.

consumer *noun* One who consumes goods and services : customer, user. See GIVE, USED in Index.

consummate *verb* See **close**.

consummate *adjective* See **perfect, utter²**.

consummation *noun* See **end, fulfillment**.

consumption *noun* A quantity consumed : usage, use. See GIVE, USED in Index. — See also **tuberculosis**.

consumptive *adjective* See **tubercular**.

contact *noun* 1. A coming together so as to be touching : contingence, touch. See TOUCH in Index. 2. An acquaintance who is in a position to help : connection, source. See CONNECT in Index. — See also **touch**.

contact *verb* To bring into or make contact with : touch. See TOUCH in Index. — See also **reach**.

contagion *noun* See **poison**.

contagious *adjective* See **communicable**.

contain *verb* 1. To be filled by : have, hold. See INCLUDE in Index. 2. To have as a part : comprehend, comprise, embody, embrace, encompass, have, include, involve, subsume, take in. See INCLUDE in Index. — See also **accommodate, compose**.

contaminant *noun* One that contaminates : adulterant, adulterator, contamination, contaminator, impurity, poison, pollutant. See CLEAN in Index.

contaminate *verb* To make physically impure : defile, foul, poison, pollute. See CLEAN in Index. — See also **taint**.

contamination *noun* The state of being contaminated : adulteration, pollution, sophistication. See CLEAN in Index. — See also **contaminant.**

contaminative *adjective* See **unwholesome.**

contaminator *noun* See **contaminant.**

contemn *verb* See **despise.**

contemplate *verb* See **intend, look, ponder.**

contemplation *noun* See **look, thought.**

contemplative *adjective* See **thoughtful.**

contemporaneous *adjective* See **contemporary.**

contemporary *adjective* **1.** Belonging to the same period of time as another : coetaneous, coeval, coexistent, concurrent, contemporaneous, synchronic, synchronous. See TIME in Index. **2.** Characteristic of recent times or informed of what is current : au courant, current, mod, modern, up-to-date, up-to-the-minute. See KNOWLEDGE, NEW in Index. — See also **present¹, simultaneous.**

contemporary *noun* **1.** One of the same time or age as another : coeval. See TIME in Index. **2.** A person of the present age : modern. See NEW, TIME in Index.

contempt *noun* See **defiance, despisal.**

contemptible *adjective* See **filthy.**

contemptuous *adjective* See **disdainful.**

contend *verb* To strive in opposition : battle, combat, duel, fight, struggle, tilt, war, wrestle. See CONFLICT in Index. — See also **argue, assert, compete.**

contender *noun* See **competitor.**

content *adjective* See **fulfilled.**

content *verb* See **satisfy.**

contention *noun* See **argument, conflict, thesis.**

contentious *adjective* See **aggressive, argumentative, belligerent.**

contentiousness *noun* See **aggression, argumentativeness, belligerence, fight.**

conterminous *adjective* See **adjoining.**

contest *verb* To take a stand against : buck, challenge, dispute, oppose, resist, traverse. See SUPPORT in Index. — See also **compete.**

contest *noun* See **competition.**

contestant *noun* See **competitor.**

contestation *noun* See **thesis.**

contested *adjective* See **debatable.**

contexture *noun* See **texture.**

contiguous *adjective* See **adjoining, close.**

continent *adjective* See **temperate.**

contingence *noun* See **contact.**

contingency *noun* See **possibility.**

contingent *adjective* See **accidental, dependent, probable.**

continual *adjective* Existing or occurring without interruption or end : around-the-clock, ceaseless, constant, continuous, endless, eternal, everlasting, incessant, interminable, nonstop, ongoing, perpetual, persistent, relentless, round-the-clock, timeless, unceasing, unending, unfailing, uninterrupted, unremitting. See CONTINUE in Index.

continuance *noun* See **continuation.**

continuation *noun* Uninterrupted existence or succession : continuance, continuity, continuum, duration, endurance, persistence, persistency. See CONTINUE in Index. — See also **renewal.**

continue *verb* To begin or go on after an interruption : pick up, renew, reopen, restart, resume, take up. See CONTINUE in Index. — See also **endure.**

continuing *adjective* Existing or remaining in the same state for an indefinitely long time : abiding, durable, enduring, lasting, long-lasting, long-lived, long-standing, old, perdurable, perennial, permanent, persistent. See CONTINUE in Index. — See also **chronic.**

continuity *noun* See **continuation.**

continuous *adjective* See **continual.**

continuum *noun* See **continuation.**

contort *verb* See **deform.**

contour *noun* See **outline.**

contrabandist *noun* See **smuggler.**

contract *verb* **1.** To enter into a formal agreement : bargain, covenant. See AGREE in Index. **2.** To become affected with a disease : catch, develop, get, sicken, take. *Idiom:* come down with. See GET in Index. **3.** To reduce in size, as by drawing together : compact¹, compress, constrict, constringe, shrink. See INCREASE in Index. — See also **pledge.**

contract *noun* See **agreement, bargain.**

contradict *verb* See **conflict, deny.**

contradiction *noun* See **denial, opposition.**

contradictory *adjective* See **opposite.**

contradictory *noun* See **opposite.**

contradistinction *noun* See **opposition.**

contralto *adjective* See **low.**

contraposition *noun* See **opposition.**

contrapositive *noun* See **opposite.**

contraption *noun* See **device, gadget.**

contrariety *noun* See **opposition.**

contrariness *noun* See **opposition.**

contrarious *adjective* See **contrary.**

contrary *adjective* Given to acting in opposition to others : balky, contrarious, difficult, froward, impossible, ornery, perverse, wayward. See ATTITUDE, SUPPORT in Index. — See also **opposite.**

contrary *noun* See **opposite.**

contrast

contrast *noun* Striking difference between compared individuals : counterpoint. See SAME in Index.

contravene *verb* See **deny, violate.**

contravention *noun* See **breach.**

contretemps *noun* See **accident.**

contribute *verb* **1.** To give in common with others : chip in, donate, subscribe. *Informal:* kick in. *Slang:* come across. See GIVE in Index. **2.** To have a share, as in an act or result; have a hand in : conduce, partake, participate, share. *Idiom:* take part. See PARTICIPATE, START in Index. — See also **donate.**

contribution *noun* See **donation.**

contributive *adjective* Tending to contribute to a result : conducive, contributory. See PARTICIPATE in Index.

contributor *noun* See **builder, donor, patron.**

contributory *adjective* See **auxiliary, contributive.**

contrite *adjective* See **apologetic, remorseful.**

contriteness *noun* See **penitence.**

contrition *noun* See **penitence.**

contrivance *noun* See **device, gadget, invention.**

contrive *verb* See **design, invent.**

contrived *adjective* See **forced.**

control *verb* To exercise authority or influence over : direct, dominate, govern, rule. *Idioms:* be at the helm, be in the driver's seat, hold sway over, hold the reins. See OVER in Index. — See also **compose, govern.**

control *noun* See **authority, domination, government, reserve.**

controllable *adjective* See **governable.**

controlled *adjective* See **reserved.**

controlling *adjective* See **dominant.**

controversy *noun* See **argument.**

controvert *verb* See **deny.**

contumacious *adjective* See **defiant.**

contumacy *noun* See **defiance.**

contumelious *adjective* See **abusive, impudent.**

contumely *noun* See **indignity, vituperation.**

contuse *verb* See **bruise.**

conundrum *noun* See **mystery.**

convalesce *verb* See **recover.**

convene *verb* See **assemble, call.**

convenience *noun* See **amenity.**

convenient *adjective* **1.** Suited to one's end or purpose : appropriate, befitting, expedient, fit[1], good, meet[2], proper, suitable, tailor-made, useful. See AGREE, GOOD in Index. **2.** Being within easy reach : accessible, handy, nearby. *Idioms:* close (or near) at hand, close by. See NEAR in Index.

convention *noun* **1.** A formal assemblage of the members of a group : assembly, conference, congress, convocation, meeting. See ASSEMBLE in Index. **2.** An accepted way of doing something : form. See USUAL in Index. — See also **agreement, assembly, treaty.**

conventional *adjective* Conforming to established practice or standards : button-down, conformist, establishmentarian, orthodox, straight, traditional. *Slang:* square. See USUAL in Index. — See also **accepted, ceremonious.**

conventionalize *verb* To make conventional : conform, stylize. See USUAL in Index.

converge *verb* See **close, concentrate.**

convergence *noun* See **approach, concentration, junction.**

conversant *adjective* See **familiar.**

conversation *noun* Spoken exchange : chat, colloquy, confabulation, converse[1], dialogue, discourse, speech, talk. *Informal:* confab. *Slang:* jaw. See WORDS in Index.

conversational *adjective* In the style of conversation : chatty, colloquial, confabulatory, informal. See WORDS in Index. — See also **talkative.**

conversationalist *noun* One given to conversation : confabulator, conversationist, discourser, talker. See WORDS in Index.

conversationist *noun* See **conversationalist.**

converse[1] *verb* To engage in spoken exchange : chat, confabulate, discourse, speak, talk. *Informal:* confab, visit. See WORDS in Index.

converse *noun* See **communication, conversation.**

converse[2] *adjective* See **opposite.**

converse *noun* See **opposite.**

conversion *noun* A fundamental change in one's beliefs : metanoia, rebirth, regeneration. See CHANGE in Index. — See also **change.**

convert *verb* To change into a different form, substance, or state : metamorphose, mutate, transfigure, transform, translate, transmogrify, transmute, transpose, transubstantiate. See CHANGE in Index.

convey *verb* See **bring, carry, communicate, conduct, express, pass, say, transfer.**

conveyance *noun* See **grant, transportation.**

conveyer *noun* See **bearer.**

conviction *noun* See **belief, sureness.**

convince *verb* To cause (another) to

believe or feel sure about something : assure, persuade, satisfy, win over. See PERSUASION in Index. — See also **persuade**.

convincing *adjective* Serving to convince : cogent, persuasive, satisfactory, telling. See PERSUASION in Index. — See also **authentic**.

convivial *adjective* See **companionable, gay, social**.

conviviality *noun* See **gaiety**.

convocation *noun* See **assembly, convention**.

convoke *verb* See **assemble, call**.

convoluted *adjective* See **complex**.

convulse *verb* See **agitate**.

convulsion *noun* See **agitation, revolution, throe**.

cook *verb* To prepare (food) for eating by the use of heat : do. See INGESTION in Index.

cook up See **invent**.

cook *noun* A person who prepares food for eating : chef. See INGESTION in Index.

cool *adjective* **1.** Not easily excited, even under pressure : calm, collected, composed, cool-headed, detached, even[1], even-tempered, imperturbable, nonchalant, possessed, unflappable, unruffled. See CALM in Index. **2.** Not friendly, sociable, or warm in manner : aloof, chill, chilly, distant, offish, remote, reserved, reticent, solitary, standoffish, unapproachable, uncommunicative, undemonstrative, withdrawn. See ATTITUDE, HOT in Index. — See also **cold, marvelous**.

cool *verb* See **compose**.

cool *noun* See **balance**.

cooler *noun* See **jail**.

cool-headed *adjective* See **cool**.

coolness *noun* See **balance, cold**.

coop *noun* See **jail**.

coop *verb* See **enclose**.

cooperate *verb* To work together toward a common end : collaborate. See CONFLICT in Index.

cooperation *noun* Joint work toward a common end : coaction, collaboration, synergy, teamwork. See CONFLICT in Index. — See also **association**.

cooperative *adjective* Working together toward a common end : collaborative, synergetic, synergic, synergistic. See CONFLICT in Index.

coordinate *verb* See **harmonize**.

cop *noun* See **policeman**.

cop *verb* See **capture, steal**.

cop out *verb* See **back down** at back.

copartner *noun* See **associate**.

copious *adjective* See **generous**.

copper *noun* See **policeman**.

copulate *verb* See **take**.

copy *noun* **1.** An inferior substitute imitating an original : ersatz, imitation, pinchbeck, simulation. See SUBSTITUTE in Index. **2.** Something closely resembling another : carbon copy, duplicate, facsimile, image, likeness, reduplication, replica, replication, reproduction, simulacrum. *Archaic:* simulacre. *Law:* counterpart. See SAME in Index.

copy *verb* To make a copy of : duplicate, imitate, replicate, reproduce, simulate. See SAME in Index. — See also **follow**.

coquet *verb* See **flirt**.

coquetry *noun* See **flirtation**.

coquette *noun* See **flirt**.

coquettish *adjective* See **flirtatious**.

cordial *adjective* See **amiable**.

cordiality *noun* See **amiability**.

cordialness *noun* See **amiability**.

core *noun* See **center, heart**.

cork *noun* See **plug**.

cork *verb* See **fill**.

corkscrew *verb* See **wind[2]**.

corky *adjective* See **airy**.

corner *noun* See **monopoly,
predicament.**

cornerstone *noun* See **basis.**

corny *adjective* See **trite.**

corollary *noun* See **effect.**

corporal *adjective* See **bodily.**

corporation *noun* See **company.**

corporeal *adjective* See **bodily,
physical.**

corps *noun* See **band², force.**

corpse *noun* See **body.**

corpulent *adjective* See **fat.**

corpus *noun* See **body, quantity.**

correct *verb* 1. To make right what
is wrong : amend, emend, mend,
rectify, redress, reform, remedy,
right. See CORRECT in Index. 2. To
castigate for the purpose of improving : chasten. See PRAISE in Index.
— See also **punish.**

correct *adjective* Conforming to
accepted standards : becoming,
befitting, comely, comme il faut,
decent, decorous, de rigueur, nice,
proper, respectable, right, seemly.
See COURTESY in Index. — See also
accurate, appropriate.

correction *noun* See **punishment.**

corrective *adjective* Tending to
correct : amendatory, emendatory,
reformative, reformatory, remedial.
See CORRECT in Index.

corrective *noun* See **remedy.**

correctly *adverb* See **fair.**

correctness *noun* See **accuracy,
decency, veracity.**

correlate *verb* See **associate.**

correlate *noun* See **parallel.**

correlation *noun* See **relation.**

correlative *noun* See **parallel.**

correspond *verb* See **agree,
amount, compare, fit¹.**

correspondence *noun* See **agreement, likeness.**

correspondent *noun* See **parallel.**

correspondent *adjective* See
agreeable.

corresponding *adjective* See
agreeable, like².

corrival *noun* See **competitor.**

corrivalry *noun* See **competition.**

corroborate *verb* See **back, confirm, prove.**

corroboration *noun* See
confirmation.

corrode *verb* See **bite.**

corrosive *adjective* See **biting.**

corrosiveness *noun* See **sarcasm.**

corrupt *adjective* 1. Utterly reprehensible in nature or behavior :
degenerate, depraved, flagitious, miscreant, perverse, rotten, unhealthy,
villainous. See CLEAN, GOOD in
Index. 2. Marked by dishonesty,
especially in matters of public
trust : dishonest, venal. *Informal:*
crooked. See HONEST in Index.
3. Ruthlessly seeking personal
advantage : mercenary, praetorian,
venal. *Informal:* crooked. See SELF
in Index.

corrupt *verb* To ruin utterly in
character or quality : animalize,
bastardize, bestialize, brutalize, canker, debase, debauch, demoralize,
deprave, pervert, stain, vitiate, warp.
See CLEAN, HELP in Index. — See
also **taint.**

corruptible *adjective* Capable of
being bribed : buyable, purchasable, venal. See CRIMES, PERSUA-
SION in Index.

corruption *noun* 1. Degrading,
immoral acts or habits : bestiality,
depravity, flagitiousness, immorality, perversion, turpitude, vice, villainousness, villainy, wickedness.
See CLEAN in Index. 2. Departure
from what is legally, ethically, and
morally correct : corruptness, dishonesty, improbity. *Informal:* crookedness. See HONEST in Index. 3. A
term that offends against established
usage standards : barbarism, sole-

cism, vulgarism. See STYLE in Index.

corruptive *adjective* See **unwholesome.**

corruptness *noun* See **corruption.**

coruscate *verb* See **flash.**

coruscation *noun* See **blink.**

cosmic *adjective* See **universal.**

cosmopolitan *adjective* See **sophisticated, universal.**

cosmos *noun* See **universe.**

cosset *verb* See **baby.**

cost *noun* **1.** An amount paid or to be paid for a purchase : charge, price. *Informal:* tab. See TRANSACTIONS in Index. **2.** Something expended to obtain a benefit or desired result : disbursement, expenditure, expense, outlay. See TRANSACTIONS in Index. **3.** A loss sustained in the accomplishment of or as the result of something : expense, price, sacrifice, toll[1]. See TRANSACTIONS in Index.

cost *verb* To require a specified price : go for, sell for. See TRANSACTIONS in Index.

costive *adjective* See **stingy.**

costly *adjective* Bringing a high price : dear, expensive, high, high-priced. See TRANSACTIONS, VALUE in Index. — See also **valuable.**

costume *noun* See **disguise, dress.**

coterie *noun* See **crowd.**

cotton *verb* See **fawn, get along at get.**

couch *verb* See **phrase.**

counsel *verb* See **advise.**

counsel *noun* See **advice, adviser, deliberation, lawyer.**

counselor also **counsellor** *noun* See **adviser, lawyer.**

count *verb* **1.** To note (items) one by one so as to get a total : enumerate, number, numerate, reckon, tally, tell. See COUNT in Index. **2.** To be of significance or importance : import, matter, signify, weigh. See IMPORTANT in Index. — See also **beat.**

count on *verb* See **depend on at depend, expect.**

count out *verb* See **exclude.**

count *noun* A noting of items one by one : enumeration, numeration, reckoning, tally. *Archaic:* tale. See COUNT in Index.

countenance *noun* See **expression, face.**

countenance *verb* See **approve, encourage.**

counter *noun* See **opposite.**

counter *verb* See **oppose, retaliate.**

counter *adjective* See **opposite.**

counteract *verb* See **balance, cancel.**

counteraction *noun* See **retaliation.**

counterattack *noun* See **retaliation.**

counterbalance *verb* See **balance, compensate.**

counterblow *noun* See **retaliation.**

counterfactual *adjective* See **false.**

counterfeit *adjective* Fraudulently or deceptively imitative : bogus, fake, false, fraudulent, phony, sham, spurious, suppositious, supposititious. See TRUE in Index.

counterfeit *verb* To make a fraudulent copy of : fake, falsify, forge[1]. See TRUE in Index. — See also **act, assume, fake.**

counterfeit *noun* A fraudulent imitation : fake, forgery, phony, sham. See TRUE in Index.

counterfeiter *noun* See **forger.**

countermeasure *noun* See **remedy.**

counterpart *noun* One that has the same functions and characteristics as another : opposite number, vis-à-vis. See SAME in Index. — See also **copy, mate, parallel.**

counterpoint *noun* See **contrast.**

counterpoise *noun* See **balance**.
  counterpoise *verb* See **balance**,
  compensate.

countervail *verb* See **balance**,
  compensate.

countless *adjective* See
  incalculable.

country *noun* A rural area : countryside, God's country. See URBAN
  in Index. — See also **state, territory**.
  country *adjective* Of or relating to
  the countryside : arcadian, bucolic,
  campestral, pastoral, provincial,
  rural, rustic. *Informal:* hick. See
  URBAN in Index.

countryman *noun* A person who is
  from one's own country : compatriot, countrywoman, fellow citizen.
  See GROUP in Index.

countryside *noun* See **country**.

countrywoman *noun* See
  countryman.

couple *noun* Two items of the same
  kind together : brace, couplet, doublet, duet, duo, match, pair, two,
  twosome, yoke. See GROUP, SAME
  in Index. — See also **pair**.
  couple *verb* See **associate, attach,
  combine, take**.

couplet *noun* See **couple**.

coupling *noun* See **joint**.

courage *noun* The quality of mind
  enabling one to face danger or hardship resolutely : braveness, bravery, courageousness, dauntlessness,
  doughtiness, fearlessness, fortitude,
  gallantry, gameness, heart, intrepidity, intrepidness, mettle, nerve,
  pluck, pluckiness, spirit, stoutheartedness, undauntedness, valiance,
  valiancy, valiantness, valor.
  Informal: spunk, spunkiness. *Slang:*
  gut (used in plural), gutsiness,
  moxie. See FEAR in Index.

courageous *adjective* See **brave**.

courageousness *noun* See
  courage.

courier *noun* See **bearer**.

course *verb* See **flow**.
  course *noun* See **approach, heading, series**.

court *verb* **1.** To attempt to gain the
  affection of : pursue, spark[2], woo.
  Informal: romance. See SEEK, SEX in
  Index. **2.** To behave so as to bring on
  (danger, for example) : invite, provoke, tempt. See SEEK in Index.

court *noun* **1.** An area partially or
  entirely enclosed by walls or build-
  ings : atrium, close, courtyard,
  enclosure, quad, quadrangle, yard.
  See PLACE in Index. **2.** A judicial
  assembly : bar, tribunal. See LAW
  in Index.

courteous *adjective* Characterized
  by good manners : civil, genteel,
  mannerly, polite, well-bred, well-
  mannered. See COURTESY in Index.
  — See also **attentive**.

courteousness *noun* See **courtesy**.

courter *noun* See **beau**.

courtesan *noun* See **prostitute**.

courtesy *noun* **1.** Well-mannered
  behavior toward others : civility,
  courteousness, genteelness, gentility, mannerliness, politeness, politesse. See COURTESY in Index.
  2. An act requiring special generosity : beau geste, compliment, favor.
  See GIVE in Index. — See also
  amenity.

courtier *noun* See **sycophant**.

courtly *adjective* See **ceremonious,
  gracious**.

courtship *noun* Romantic atten-
  tions : address (often used in plural), suit. See SEEK, SEX in Index.

courtyard *noun* See **court**.

cove *noun* See **bay**[1].

covenant *noun* See **agreement, bargain, promise**.
  covenant *verb* See **contract,
  pledge**.

cover *verb* **1.** To extend over the surface of : blanket, cap, overlay, spread. See PUT ON in Index. **2.** To journey over (a specified distance) : make. *Informal:* do. See MOVE in Index. **3.** To observe, analyze, and relate the details of (an event) : report. See WORDS in Index. **4.** To prevent (something) from being known. Also used with *up* : cloak, conceal, enshroud, hide[1], hush (up), mask, shroud, veil. *Idioms:* keep under cover, keep under wraps. See SHOW in Index. — See also **face.**

cover *noun* Something that physically protects, especially from danger : asylum, covert, harbor, haven, protection, refuge, retreat, sanctuary, shelter. See ATTACK, SAFETY in Index. — See also **façade.**

coverage *noun* The reporting of news : reportage. See WORDS in Index.

covert *adjective* See **secret, ulterior.**

covert *noun* See **cover, hide-out.**

covertly *adverb* See **secretly.**

covertness *noun* See **secrecy.**

covet *verb* See **desire, envy.**

covetous *adjective* See **envious, greedy.**

covetousness *noun* See **envy, greed.**

cow *verb* See **intimidate.**

coward *noun* An ignoble, uncourageous person : craven, dastard, funk, poltroon. *Slang:* chicken, yellow-belly. See FEAR in Index.

cowardice *noun* Ignoble lack of courage : chickenheartedness, cowardliness, cravenness, dastardliness, faint-heartedness, funk, pusillanimity, unmanliness. *Slang:* gutlessness, yellowness, yellow streak. See FEAR in Index.

cowardliness *noun* See **cowardice.**

cowardly *adjective* Ignobly lacking in courage : chickenhearted, craven, dastardly, faint-hearted, lily-livered, pusillanimous, unmanly. *Slang:* chicken, gutless, yellow, yellow-bellied. See FEAR in Index.

coy *adjective* See **flirtatious, modest.**

coyness *noun* See **shyness.**

cozen *verb* See **cheat, deceive.**

cozener *noun* See **cheat.**

cozy also **cosy** *adjective* See **comfortable.**

crab *noun* See **grouch.**

crab *verb* See **complain.**

crabbed *adjective* See **ill-tempered.**

crabby *adjective* See **ill-tempered.**

crack *noun* **1.** A usually narrow partial opening caused by splitting and rupture : break, chink, cleavage, cleft, crevice, fissure, rift, split. See OPEN in Index. **2.** A flippant or sarcastic remark : dig, quip. *Slang:* wisecrack. See RESPECT, WORDS in Index. — See also **attempt, blow[2], flash, report, try.**

crack *verb* **1.** To make a sudden sharp, explosive noise : bang, bark, clap, pop[1], snap. See SOUNDS in Index. **2.** To undergo partial breaking : fissure, fracture, rupture, split. See HELP in Index. — See also **break, collapse.**

crack up *verb* See **break, collapse, crash.**

crack *adjective* See **expert.**

crackdown *noun* See **suppression.**

cracked *adjective* See **insane.**

crackerjack also **crackajack** *adjective* See **expert.**

crackerjack also **crackajack** *noun* See **expert.**

crackers *adjective* See **insane.**

crackle *verb* To make a series of short, sharp noises : crepitate, splutter, sputter. See SOUNDS in Index.

crackpot *noun* A person regarded as strange, eccentric, or crazy : crazy, eccentric, lunatic. *Informal:* crank,

loon, loony. *Slang:* cuckoo, ding-a-
ling, dingbat, kook, nut, screwball,
weirdie, weirdo. See WISE in Index.

crackup or **crack-up** *noun* See
breakdown, crash.

craft *noun* See **ability, art, business,
indirection.**

craftiness *noun* See **art, indirection.**

craftsmanship *noun* See **work.**

crafty *adjective* See **artful.**

cragged *adjective* See **rough.**

craggy *adjective* See **rough.**

cram *verb* See **bone, crowd.**

cramp[1] *noun* See **throe.**

cramp[2] *noun* See **restriction.**
  cramp *verb* See **constrain.**

cramped *adjective* See **tight.**

crank *noun* See **crackpot, grouch.**

cranky *adjective* See **eccentric, ill-
tempered.**

crap *noun* See **nonsense.**

crapulence *noun* See **drunkenness.**

crapulent *adjective* See **drunk.**

crapulous *adjective* See **drunk.**

crash *noun* A wrecking of a vehicle : smash, smashup, wreck.
Informal: crackup, pileup. See HELP
in Index. — See also **clash, collapse,
collision, slam.**
  crash *verb* To undergo wrecking :
smash. *Informal:* crack up, pile up.
See HELP in Index. — See also **bang,
clash, collapse, collide, retire.**
  crash *adjective Informal.*
Designed to meet emergency needs
as quickly as possible : hurry-up,
rush. See FAST in Index.

crashing *adjective* See **utter**[2].

crass *adjective* See **coarse.**

crave *verb* See **appeal, lust.**

craven *adjective* See **cowardly.**
  craven *noun* See **coward.**

cravenness *noun* See **cowardice.**

craving *noun* See **desire.**

crawl *verb* **1.** To move along in a
crouching or prone position : creep,
slide, snake, worm. See MOVE in

Index. **2.** To advance slowly :
creep, drag, inch. See FAST in
Index. **3.** To experience a repugnant tingling sensation : creep.
See FEAR, LIKE in Index. — See
also **teem.**

crawl *noun* A very slow rate of
speed : creep, snail's pace. See FAST
in Index.

crawly *adjective Informal.* Experiencing a repugnant tingling sensation : creepy. See FEAR, LIKE in
Index.

craze *verb* See **derange.**
  craze *noun* See **enthusiasm,
fashion.**

craziness *noun* See **foolishness,
insanity.**

crazy *adjective* See **enthusiastic,
foolish, insane.**
  crazy *noun* See **crackpot.**

cream *noun* See **best.**
  cream *verb* See **foam, overwhelm.**

creamy *adjective* See **fresh.**

crease *noun* See **fold, line.**
  crease *verb* See **fold, wrinkle.**

create *verb* See **compose, found,
produce.**

creation *noun* See **foundation,
myth, universe.**

creative *adjective* See **inventive.**

creativeness *noun* See **invention.**

creativity *noun* See **invention.**

creator *noun* See **builder,
originator.**

creature *noun* See **human being.**

credence *noun* See **belief.**

credibility *noun* See **verisimilitude.**

credible *adjective* See **authentic,
believable.**

credibleness *noun* See **verisimilitude.**

credit *verb* See **attribute, believe.**
  credit *noun* See **attribution, belief,
recognition.**

creditability *noun* See **verisimilitude.**

creditable *adjective* See **admirable, believable.**

creditableness *noun* See **verisimilitude.**

credulous *adjective* See **easy.**

creed *noun* See **religion.**

creek *noun* See **branch.**

creep *verb* See **crawl, sneak.**

creep *noun* See **crawl.**

creepy *adjective* See **crawly.**

crème de la crème *noun* See **best, society.**

crepitate *verb* See **crackle.**

crest *noun* See **climax, height.**

crest *verb* See **climax.**

cretin *noun* See **fool.**

crevice *noun* See **crack.**

crew *noun* See **force.**

crib *verb* See **pirate.**

cribber *noun* See **pirate.**

crime *noun* **1.** A serious breaking of the public law : illegality, misdeed, offense. *Law:* felony. See CRIMES in Index. **2.** A wicked act or wicked behavior : deviltry, diablerie, evil, evildoing, immorality, iniquity, misdeed, offense, peccancy, sin, wickedness, wrong, wrongdoing. See RIGHT in Index. **3.** Something that offends one's sense of propriety, fairness, or justice : offense, outrage, sin. See RIGHT in Index. — See also **shame.**

criminal *adjective* Of, involving, or being a crime : illegal, illegitimate, illicit, lawless, unlawful, wrongful. See CRIMES in Index.

criminal *noun* One who commits a crime : lawbreaker, malefactor, offender. *Law:* felon. See CRIMES in Index.

criminate *verb* See **implicate.**

crimp *verb* See **wrinkle.**

crimp *noun* See **fold.**

crimson *verb* See **blush.**

cringe *verb* See **fawn, flinch.**

cringe *noun* See **recoil.**

crinkle *noun* See **fold, line.**

crinkle *verb* See **wrinkle.**

cripple *verb* To deprive of a limb or bodily member or its use : dismember, maim, mutilate. See HELP in Index. — See also **disable.**

crisis *noun* **1.** A highly volatile dangerous situation requiring immediate remedial action : emergency, extremity, flash point. See POLITICS, SAFETY in Index. **2.** A decisive point : climacteric, crossroad (used in plural), exigence, exigency, head, juncture, pass, turning point, zero hour. See DECIDE in Index.

crisscross *verb* See **cross.**

criterion *noun* See **standard.**

critic *noun* **1.** A person who evaluates and reports on the worth of something : commentator, judge, reviewer. See VALUE in Index.
2. A person who finds fault, often severely and willfully : carper, caviler, criticizer, faultfinder, hypercritic, niggler, nitpicker, quibbler. See PRAISE in Index.

critical *adjective* **1.** Inclined to judge too severely : captious, carping, censorious, faultfinding, hypercritical, overcritical. See PRAISE in Index. **2.** Characterized by careful and exact evaluation : discerning, discriminating. See CAREFUL, VALUE in Index. **3.** So serious as to be at the point of crisis or necessary to resolve a crisis : acute, climacteric, crucial, desperate, dire. See SAFETY in Index.

criticism *noun* See **blame, review.**

criticize *verb* See **blame, review.**

criticizer *noun* See **critic.**

critique *noun* See **review.**

croak *verb* See **die.**

croaking *adjective* See **hoarse.**

croaky *adjective* See **hoarse.**

crocked *adjective* See **drunk.**

crone *noun* See **witch.**

crony *noun* See **associate.**

crook *verb* See **bend.**

crook *noun* See **bend, cheat.**

crooked *adjective* Having bends, curves, or angles : bending, curved, curving. See STRAIGHT in Index. — See also **corrupt.**

crookedness *noun* See **corruption, irregularity.**

crop *verb* See **cut back** at **cut, gather.**

crop *noun* See **harvest.**

cross *verb* **1.** To go across : pass, track, transit, traverse. See MOVE in Index. **2.** To pass through or over : crisscross, crosscut, cut across, decussate, intersect. See MEET in Index. — See also **cancel, frustrate.**

cross up *verb* See **destroy.**

cross *noun* See **burden**[1].

cross *adjective* See **ill-tempered.**

crosscut *verb* See **cross.**

cross-examine *verb* See **interrogate.**

cross-eye *noun* See **squint.**

cross-eyed *adjective* See **squinty.**

crossing *adjective* See **transverse.**

crossroad *noun* See **crisis.**

crosswise *adjective* See **transverse.**

crouch *verb* To stoop low with the limbs pulled in close to the body : huddle, hunch, hunker (down), squat. See HIGH in Index.

crow *verb* See **boast, exult.**

crowd *noun* **1.** An enormous number of persons gathered together : crush, drove, flock, horde, mass, mob, multitude, press, ruck[1], swarm, throng. See BIG, GROUP in Index. **2.** A very large number of things grouped together : army, cloud, drove, flock, horde, host, legion, mass, mob, multitude, ruck[1], score (used in plural), swarm, throng. See BIG, GROUP in Index. **3.** A particular social group : circle, clique, coterie, set[2]. *Informal:* bunch, gang.

See GROUP in Index. — See also **assembly, circle, commonalty.**

crowd *verb* **1.** To congregate, as around a person : flock, mob, press, throng. See COLLECT, TIGHTEN in Index. **2.** To fill to excess by compressing or squeezing tightly : cram, jam, load, mob, pack, stuff. *Informal:* jam-pack. See FULL, TIGHTEN in Index. **3.** To act on with a steady pushing force : crush, press. See PUSH in Index.

crowded *adjective* See **busy, thick, tight.**

crown *verb* See **climax, top.**

crown *noun* See **climax, height.**

crowning *adjective* See **climactic.**

crucial *adjective* See **critical, decisive.**

crucible *noun* See **trial.**

crucify *verb* See **torture.**

crud *noun* See **filth.**

crude *adjective* In a natural state and still not prepared for use : native, raw, unprocessed, unrefined. See CLEAN in Index. — See also **coarse, rude.**

cruel *adjective* So intense as to cause extreme suffering : ferocious, fierce, savage, vicious. See HELP, KIND in Index. — See also **fierce.**

cruelty *noun* A cruel act or an instance of cruel behavior : barbarity, bestiality, brutality, inhumanity, savagery, truculence, truculency. See ATTITUDE, KIND in Index.

crumb *noun* See **bit**[1].

crumble *verb* See **break up** at **break.**

crummy *also* **crumby** *adjective* See **shoddy.**

crump *verb* See **chew.**

crumple *verb* See **cave in** at **cave, wrinkle.**

crumple *noun* See **fold.**

crunch *verb* See **chew, grind.**

crusade *noun* See **cause, drive.**

crush verb 1. To press forcefully so as to break up into a pulpy mass : mash, mush, pulp, squash. See HELP in Index. 2. To break up into tiny particles : bray, granulate, grind, mill, powder, pulverize, triturate. See HELP in Index. — See also **break, crowd, overwhelm, squeeze, suppress.**

crush noun See **crowd, infatuation.**

crust noun See **impudence.**

crusty adjective See **abrupt.**

crutch noun See **support.**

cry verb To make inarticulate sounds of grief or pain, usually accompanied by tears : bawl, blubber, howl, keen[2], sob, wail, weep, yowl. See HAPPY, SOUNDS in Index. — See also **advertise, exclaim, roar.**

cry noun 1. A fit of crying : bawling, blubbering, sobbing, tear[2] (used in plural), wailing, weeping. See SOUNDS in Index. 2. A rallying term used by proponents of a cause : battle cry, call to arms, call to battle, motto, rallying cry, war cry. See WORDS in Index. — See also **demand, exclamation.**

crying adjective See **burning.**

crypt noun See **grave**[1].

cryptic adjective See **mysterious.**

crystal clear or **crystal-clear** adjective See **apparent, clear, transparent.**

crystalline adjective See **clear, transparent.**

cuckoo noun See **crackpot.**

cuckoo adjective See **insane.**

cuddle verb See **caress, snuggle.**

cue noun See **hint.**

cuff noun See **slap.**

cuff verb See **slap.**

cul-de-sac noun See **blind alley.**

cull verb See **choose, glean.**

culminate verb See **climax.**

culminating adjective See **climactic.**

culmination noun See **climax, fulfillment.**

culpability noun See **blame.**

culpable adjective See **blameworthy.**

cultivate verb See **grow, nurse, till.**

cultivated adjective See **cultured.**

cultivation noun See **culture.**

cultural adjective Promoting culture : civilizing, edifying, enlightening, humanizing, refining. See CULTURE in Index.

culture noun 1. Enlightenment and excellent taste resulting from intellectual development : civilization, cultivation, refinement. See CULTURE in Index. 2. The total product of human creativity and intellect : civilization, Kultur. See CULTURE in Index.

culture verb See **till.**

cultured adjective Characterized by discriminating taste and broad knowledge as a result of development or education : civilized, cultivated, educated, polished, refined, urbane, well-bred. See CULTURE in Index.

cumber verb See **charge.**

cumbersome adjective See **heavy.**

cumbrous adjective See **heavy.**

cumshaw noun See **gratuity.**

cumulate verb See **accumulate.**

cumulation noun See **accumulation.**

cumulative adjective See **accumulative.**

cumulus noun See **heap.**

cunning adjective See **artful.**

cunning noun See **art, deceit.**

cupidity noun See **greed.**

curative adjective Serving to cure : remedial, restorative, therapeutic. See HEALTH in Index.

curative noun See **remedy.**

curb noun See **restriction.**

curb verb See **restrain.**

curdle verb See **coagulate.**

cure *noun* An agent used to restore health : elixir, medicament, medication, medicine, nostrum, physic, remedy. See HEALTH in Index. — See also **remedy.**

cure *verb* To rectify (an undesirable or unhealthy condition) : heal, remedy. See HEALTH in Index.

cure-all *noun* See **panacea.**

cureless *adjective* See **hopeless.**

curiosity *noun* **1.** Mental acquisitiveness : curiousness, inquisitiveness, interest. *Idiom:* thirst for knowledge. See INVESTIGATE in Index. **2.** Undue interest in the affairs of others : curiousness, inquisitiveness. *Informal:* nosiness, snoopiness. See INVESTIGATE in Index.

curious *adjective* **1.** Eager to acquire knowledge : inquiring, inquisitive, investigative, questioning. See INVESTIGATE in Index. **2.** Unduly interested in the affairs of others : inquisitive, inquisitorial. *Informal:* nosy, snoopy. See INVESTIGATE in Index. — See also **eccentric, funny.**

curiousness *noun* See **curiosity.**

curl *verb* See **wave, wind².**

currency *noun* See **money.**

current *adjective* See **contemporary, present¹, prevailing.**

current *noun* See **flow.**

currently *adverb* See **now.**

curse *noun* **1.** A denunciation invoking a wish or threat of evil or injury : anathema, damnation, execration, imprecation, malediction. *Archaic:* malison. See WORDS in Index. **2.** A cause of suffering or harm : affliction, bane, evil, ill, plague, scourge, woe. See HELP in Index. — See also **jinx, swearword.**

curse *verb* To invoke evil or injury upon : anathematize, damn, imprecate. *Informal:* cuss. *Archaic:* exe-

crate, maledict. See WORDS in Index. — See also **afflict, jinx, swear.**

cursed also **curst** *adjective* See **damned.**

cursory *adjective* See **superficial.**

curt *adjective* See **abrupt.**

curtail *verb* See **shorten.**

curtailment *noun* See **decrease.**

curtain *noun* See **death.**

curtsy *noun* See **bow¹.**

curvaceous *adjective* See **shapely.**

curvature *noun* See **bend.**

curve *verb* See **bend, wave.**

curve *noun* See **bend.**

curved *adjective* See **bent, crooked.**

curvilinear *adjective* See **bent.**

curving *adjective* See **crooked.**

curvy *adjective* See **shapely.**

cusp *noun* See **point.**

cuspate *adjective* See **pointed.**

cuspated *adjective* See **pointed.**

cuspidate *adjective* See **pointed.**

cuspidated *adjective* See **pointed.**

cuss *verb* See **curse, swear.**

cuss *noun* See **swearword.**

custodian *noun* See **guardian.**

custody *noun* See **care, detention.**

custom *noun* A habitual way of behaving : consuetude, habit, habitude, manner, practice, praxis, usage, usance, use, way, wont. See USUAL in Index. — See also **patronage.**

custom *adjective* Made according to the specifications of the buyer : custom-built, customized, custom-made, made-to-order, tailor-made. See AGREE in Index.

customarily *adverb* See **usually.**

customariness *noun* See **usualness.**

customary *adjective* Commonly practiced or used : accustomed, habitual, regular, usual, wonted. See USUAL in Index.

custom-built *adjective* See **custom.**

customer *noun* See **consumer, patron.**

customized *adjective* See **custom.**

custom-made *adjective* See **custom.**

cut *verb* **1.** To penetrate with a sharp edge : gash, incise, pierce, slash, slit. See ENTER, HELP in Index. **2.** To separate into parts with or as if with a sharp-edged instrument : carve, cleave[1], dissever, sever, slice, slit, split. See ASSEMBLE in Index. **3.** To bring down, as with a saw or ax. Also used with *down* : chop down, fell[1], hew. See RISE in Index. **4.** To fail to attend on purpose : truant. *Informal:* skip. **Idioms:** go AWOL, play hooky (or truant). See SEEK in Index. — See also **cut back** at **cut, dilute, snub, swerve.**

cut across *verb* See **cross.**

cut back *verb* To decrease, as in length or amount, by or as if by severing or excising : chop[1], clip[1], crop, cut, cut down, lop[1], lower[2], pare, prune, shear, slash, trim, truncate. See INCREASE in Index.

cut down *verb* See **cut back** at **cut, drop, kill[1].**

cut in *verb* See **interrupt, intrude.**

cut off *verb* See **head off** at **head, isolate, kill[1].**

cut out *verb* See **break, go, supplant.**

cut up *verb* See **blame, misbehave.**

cut *noun* **1.** The result of cutting : gash, incision, slash, slice, slit, split. See ENTER, HELP in Index. **2.** A part severed from a whole : piece, portion, section, segment, slice. See PART in Index. **3.** An unexcused absence : truancy, truantry. *Informal:* hooky. See SEEK in Index. — See also **allotment, decrease, snub.**

cut-and-dried *adjective* See **ordinary.**

cutback *noun* See **decrease.**

cut-off *noun* See **stop.**

cutthroat *noun* See **murderer.**

cutthroat *adjective* See **murderous.**

cutting *adjective* See **biting.**

cutup *noun* See **mischief.**

cycle *noun* See **circle.**

cyclic *adjective* See **recurrent.**

cyclical *adjective* See **recurrent.**

cyclopean *adjective* See **giant.**

cynic *noun* A person who expects only the worst from people : misanthrope, misanthropist. See ATTITUDE in Index.

cynic *adjective* See **cynical.**

cynical *adjective* Marked by or displaying contemptuous mockery of the motives or virtues of others : cynic, ironic, ironical, sardonic, wry. See ATTITUDE, RESPECT in Index.

D

dab[1] *verb* See **smear.**

dab *noun* See **bit[1].**

dab[2] *noun* See **expert.**

dabbler *noun* See **amateur.**

dab hand *noun* See **expert.**

dad *noun* See **father.**

daddy *noun* See **father.**

daedal *adjective* See **complex.**

Daedalian or **Daedalean** *adjective* See **complex.**

daffy *adjective* See **insane.**

daft *adjective* See **insane.**

dainty *adjective* See **delicate, nice.**

dainty *noun* See **delicacy.**

dalliance *noun* See **flirtation.**

dally *verb* See **delay, flirt.**

dam *verb* See **obstruct.**

damage *noun* See **breakage, harm.**

damage *verb* See **injure.**

damn *verb* See **condemn, curse, swear.**

damn *noun* *Informal.* The least bit : hoot, iota, jot, ounce, shred,

whit. *Informal:* rap². *Slang:* diddly.
See BIG in Index.

damn *adjective* See **damned.**

damnation *noun* See **curse.**

damned *adjective* **1.** Condemned,
especially to hell : doomed, lost.
Idiom: gone to blazes. See REWARD
in Index. **2.** *Informal.* So annoying
or detestable as to deserve condemnation : accursed, blasted, blessed,
bloody, confounded, cursed, damn,
darn, execrable, infernal. *Informal:*
blamed. *Chiefly British:* blooming,
ruddy. See LIKE in Index. — See also
utter².

damp *adjective* Slightly wet :
dank, moist. See DRY in Index.

dampen *verb* See **muffle, wash.**

dance *verb* To move rhythmically
to music, using patterns of steps or
gestures : foot, step. *Slang:* hoof.
Idioms: cut a rug, foot it, trip the
light fantastic. See REPETITION,
WORK in Index. — See also **gambol.**

dance *noun* A party or gathering
for dancing : ball. *Informal:* hop.
See WORK in Index.

dancer *noun* A person who dances,
especially professionally : terpsichorean. *Slang:* hoofer. See REPETI-
TION in Index.

dander *noun* See **temper.**

dandy *adjective* See **excellent,
marvelous.**

danger *noun* Exposure to possible
harm, loss, or injury : endangerment, hazard, imperilment, jeopardy, peril, risk. See SAFETY in
Index.

dangerous *adjective* Involving possible risk, loss, or injury : adventurous, chancy, hazardous, jeopardous,
parlous, perilous, risky, treacherous,
unsafe, venturesome, venturous.
Slang: hairy. See SAFETY in Index.
— See also **grievous.**

dangle *verb* See **hang.**

dangly *adjective* See **hanging.**

dank *adjective* See **damp.**

dap *verb* See **glance.**

dapple *verb* See **speckle.**

dare *verb* To call on another to do
something requiring boldness :
challenge, defy. *Idiom:* throw down
the gauntlet. See REQUEST in Index.
— See also **defy, presume.**

dare *noun* An act of taunting
another to do something bold or
rash : challenge. See REQUEST in
Index.

daredevil *noun* See **adventurer.**

daredevil *adjective* See
adventurous.

daredevilry *noun* See **daring.**

daredeviltry *noun* See **daring.**

daring *adjective* See **adventurous.**

daring *noun* Willingness to take
risks : adventuresomeness, adventurousness, audaciousness, audacity,
boldness, daredevilry, daredeviltry,
daringness, venturesomeness, venturousness. See SAFETY in Index.

daringness *noun* See **daring.**

dark *adjective* **1.** Deficient in
brightness : caliginous, dim, dusky,
murky, obscure. See LIGHT in
Index. **2.** Of a complexion tending
toward brown or black : bistered,
black-a-vised, brunet, dusky,
swarthy. See COLORS in Index.
3. Characterized by or expressive of a
foreboding somberness : lowery,
sullen. See WARN in Index. — See
also **black, blackish, gloomy.**

dark *noun* Absence or deficiency
of light : darkness, dimness, duskiness, murkiness, obscureness, obscurity. See LIGHT in Index.

darken *verb* See **shade.**

darkness *noun* See **dark.**

darling *noun* A person who is much
loved : beloved, dear, honey, love,
minion, precious, sweet, sweetheart,
truelove. *Informal:* sweetie. *Idiom:*

light of one's life. See LOVE in Index.
— See also **favorite**.

darling *adjective* Regarded with
much love and tenderness :
beloved, dear, loved, precious. See
LOVE in Index. — See also **delightful,
favorite.**

darn *adjective* See **damned**.

dart *verb* See **fly, rush, throw**.

dash *verb* See **blast, rush, splash,
throw.**

  dash *noun* See **bit¹, point, shade,
  spirit, vigor.**

dashing *adjective* See **fashionable,
lively.**

dastard *noun* See **coward**.

dastardliness *noun* See **cowardice**.

dastardly *adjective* See **cowardly**.

data *noun* See **information**.

date *noun* See **engagement**.

  date *verb* See **see**.

dated *adjective* See **old-fashioned**.

dateless *adjective* See **ageless**.

daub *verb* See **smear**.

  daub *noun* See **smear**.

daunt *verb* See **dismay**.

dauntless *adjective* See **brave**.

dauntlessness *noun* See **courage**.

dawdle *verb* See **delay, idle**.

dawdler *noun* See **laggard**.

dawn *noun* The first appearance of
daylight in the morning : aurora,
cockcrow, dawning, daybreak, morn,
morning, sunrise, sunup. See START
in Index. — See also **birth**.

  dawn *verb* To begin to appear or
  develop : appear, arise, commence,
  emerge, originate. See START in
  Index.

  dawn on or **upon** *verb* See
  register.

dawning *noun* See **dawn**.

day *noun* See **age, life**.

daybreak *noun* See **dawn**.

daydream *noun* See **dream**.

  daydream *verb* See **dream**.

daydreaming *noun* See **trance**.

daze *verb* **1.** To confuse with bright
light : bedazzle, blind, dazzle. See
SEE in Index. **2.** To dull the senses,
as with a heavy blow, a shock, or
fatigue : bedaze, bemuse, benumb,
stun, stupefy. *Chiefly Regional:*
maze. See AWARENESS in Index.

  daze *noun* A stunned or bewil-
  dered condition : befuddlement,
  bewilderedness, bewilderment, discombobulation, fog, muddle, mystification, perplexity, puzzlement,
  stupefaction, stupor, trance. See
  AWARENESS in Index.

dazzle *verb* See **daze**.

  dazzle *noun* See **glare**.

dead *adjective* **1.** No longer alive :
asleep, deceased, defunct, departed,
extinct, gone, late, lifeless. *Idioms:*
at rest, pushing up daisies. See LIVE
in Index. **2.** Lacking physical feeling
or sensitivity : asleep, insensible,
insensitive, numb, unfeeling. See
AWARENESS in Index. — See also
exhausted, inanimate, utter², vanished.

  dead *adverb* See **completely,
  directly.**

deaden *verb* To render less sensitive : benumb, blunt, desensitize,
dull, numb. *Idiom:* take the edge off.
See AWARENESS in Index. — See also
muffle.

dead end *noun* See **blind alley**.

dead heat *noun* See **tie**.

deadliness *noun* See **fatality**.

deadlock *noun* See **tie**.

deadly *adjective* Causing or tending to cause death : deathly, fatal,
lethal, mortal, vital. See LIVE in
Index. — See also **ghastly, virulent**.

deadpan *adjective* See **expressionless.**

deafening *adjective* See **loud**.

deal *verb* See **distribute, give, push,
sell.**

deal with verb **1.** To behave in a specified way toward : handle, treat. See TREAT WELL in Index.
2. To be occupied or concerned with : consider, take up, treat. *Idiom:* have to do with. See RELEVANT in Index.

deal noun An indefinite amount or extent : quantity. *Informal:* lot. See BIG in Index. — See also **agreement, bargain.**

dealer noun A person engaged in buying and selling : businessperson, merchandiser, merchant, speculator, trader, tradesman, trafficker. See TRANSACTIONS in Index. — See also **pusher.**

dear noun See **darling.**

dear adjective See **costly, darling.**

dearth noun See **absence.**

death noun The act or fact of dying : decease, demise, dissolution, extinction, passing, quietus, rest[1]. *Slang:* curtain (used in plural). See LIVE in Index. — See also **fatality.**

deathless adjective See **immortal.**

deathlessness noun See **immortality.**

deathlike adjective See **ghastly.**

deathly adjective See **deadly, ghastly.**

debacle noun See **collapse.**

debar verb See **exclude, forbid.**

debark verb See **land.**

debase verb To lower in character or quality : cheapen, degrade, demean[2], downgrade. See BETTER in Index. — See also **adulterate, corrupt.**

debasement noun See **degradation.**

debatable adjective In doubt or dispute : arguable, contested, disputable, doubtful, exceptionable, moot, mootable, problematic, problematical, questionable, uncertain. See CERTAIN in Index.

debate verb See **argue.**

debate noun See **argument, argumentation.**

debauch verb See **corrupt, seduce.**

debaucher noun See **seducer.**

debilitate verb See **enervate.**

debilitation noun The depletion or sapping of strength or energy : attenuation, depletion, devitalization, enervation, enfeeblement, impoverishment. See STRONG in Index.

debility noun See **infirmity.**

debonair also **debonaire** adjective See **airy, light[2].**

debris noun See **ruin.**

debt noun **1.** Something, such as money, owed by one person to another : arrearage, arrears, due, indebtedness, liability, obligation. See OBLIGATION, PAY in Index.
2. A condition of owing something to another : arrearage, arrears, indebtedness, liability, obligation. See PAY in Index.

debunk verb See **discredit.**

debut also **début** also **début** noun See **presentation.**

debut verb See **come out at come.**

decadence noun See **deterioration.**

decamp verb See **escape.**

decampment noun See **escape.**

decant verb See **pour.**

decay verb To become or cause to become rotten or unsound : break down, decompose, deteriorate, disintegrate, molder, putrefy, rot, spoil, taint, turn. *Idioms:* go bad, go to pot, go to seed. See BETTER, THRIVE in Index.

decay noun The condition of being decayed : breakdown, decomposition, deterioration, disintegration, putrefaction, putrescence, putridness, rot, rottenness, spoilage. See BETTER, THRIVE in Index.

decaying adjective See **shabby.**

decease verb See **die.**

decease *noun* See **death.**

deceased *adjective* See **dead.**

deceit *noun* The act or practice of deceiving : cunning, deceitfulness, deception, double-dealing, duplicity, guile, shiftiness. See HONEST in Index.

deceitful *adjective* See **dishonest.**

deceitfulness *noun* See **deceit.**

deceive *verb* To cause to accept what is false, especially by trickery or misrepresentation : beguile, betray, bluff, cozen, delude, double-cross, dupe, fool, hoodwink, humbug, mislead, take in, trick. *Informal:* bamboozle, have. *Slang:* four-flush. *Idioms:* lead astray, play false, pull the wool over someone's eyes, put something over on, take for a ride. See HONEST in Index.

decency *noun* 1. Conformity to recognized standards, as of conduct or appearance : comeliness, correctness, decentness, decorousness, decorum, properness, propriety, respectability, respectableness, seemliness. See USUAL in Index. 2. A sense of propriety or rightness : conscience, grace. See RIGHT in Index. — See also **chastity.**

decent *adjective Informal.* Proper in appearance : presentable, respectable. See GOOD, USUAL in Index. — See also **acceptable, chaste, clean, correct, sufficient.**

decentness *noun* See **decency.**

deception *noun* See **deceit, trick.**

deceptive *adjective* See **fallacious.**

decide *verb* To make up or cause to make up one's mind : conclude, determine, resolve, settle. See DECIDE in Index. — See also **judge.**

decided *adjective* Without any doubt : clear, clear-cut, definite, distinct, pronounced, unquestionable. See CERTAIN in Index. — See also **decisive, definite, set¹.**

decidedness *noun* See **decision.**

deciding *adjective* See **decisive.**

decimate *verb* See **annihilate.**

decipher *verb* See **break, explain, resolve.**

decipherable *adjective* See **explainable.**

decipherment *noun* See **explanation.**

decision *noun* 1. A position reached after consideration : conclusion, determination, resolution. See DECIDE in Index. 2. Unwavering firmness of character, action, or will : decidedness, decisiveness, determination, firmness, purpose, purposefulness, resoluteness, resolution, resolve, toughness, will, willpower. See CERTAIN, STRONG in Index.

decisive *adjective* 1. Determining or having the power to determine an outcome : conclusive, crucial, deciding, determinative. See DECIDE, IMPORTANT in Index. 2. Not hesitating or wavering : decided, determined, firm¹, resolute. See DECIDE in Index. — See also **definitive.**

decisiveness *noun* See **decision.**

deck¹ *verb* See **drop.**

deck² *verb* See **adorn, dress up** at **dress.**

declaim *verb* See **rant.**

declaimer *noun* See **speaker.**

declamation *noun* See **oratory, speech.**

declamatory *adjective* See **oratorical, sonorous.**

declaration *noun* See **announcement, assertion.**

declare *verb* See **announce, assert, say.**

déclassé *adjective* See **lowly.**

declassed *adjective* See **lowly.**

declension *noun* See **deterioration.**

declination *noun* See **deterioration, failure.**

decline *verb* To be unwilling to accept, consider, or receive : dismiss, refuse, reject, spurn, turn down. *Slang:* nix. **Idiom:** turn thumbs down on. See ACCEPT in Index. — See also **deteriorate, drop, fade.**

decline *noun* See **deterioration, drop, failure, fall.**

declivity *noun* See **drop.**

décolleté *adjective* See **low.**

decompose *verb* See **break up** at **break, decay.**

decomposition *noun* See **decay.**

decontaminate *verb* See **sterilize.**

decorate *verb* See **adorn.**

decoration *noun* An emblem of honor worn on one's clothing : badge, medal. See REWARD in Index. — See also **adornment.**

decorous *adjective* See **correct.**

decorousness *noun* See **decency.**

decorticate *verb* See **skin.**

decorum *noun* See **decency, manner.**

decrease *verb* To grow or cause to grow gradually less : abate, diminish, drain, dwindle, ebb, lessen, let up, peter (out), rebate, reduce, tail away (or off), taper (off). See INCREASE in Index.

decrease *noun* The act or process of decreasing : abatement, curtailment, cut, cutback, decrement, diminishment, diminution, drain, reduction, slash, slowdown, taper. See INCREASE in Index.

decree *noun* See **law, ruling.**

decree *verb* See **dictate, judge.**

decrement *noun* See **decrease.**

decrepit *adjective* See **infirm, shabby.**

decrepitude *noun* See **infirmity.**

decry *verb* See **belittle.**

decrypt *verb* See **break.**

decumbent *adjective* See **flat.**

decussate *verb* See **cross.**

dedicate *verb* See **apply, devote.**

dedicated *adjective* See **sacred.**

deduce *verb* See **infer.**

deduct *verb* To take away (a quantity) from another quantity : abate, discount, rebate, subtract, take (off). *Informal:* knock off. See INCREASE in Index. — See also **infer.**

deduction *noun* **1.** An amount deducted : abatement, discount, rebate, reduction. See INCREASE in Index. **2.** A position arrived at by reasoning from premises or general principles : conclusion, illation, illative, inference, judgment. See REASON in Index.

deed *noun* See **act.**

deed *verb* See **transfer.**

deem *verb* See **believe, regard.**

de-emphasize *verb* See **soft-pedal.**

deep *adjective* **1.** Extending far downward or inward from a surface : abysmal, profound. See SURFACE in Index. **2.** Beyond the understanding of an average mind : abstruse, esoteric, profound, recondite. *Slang:* heavy. See EASY, SURFACE in Index. **3.** Resulting from or affecting one's innermost feelings : intense, profound, strong. See STRONG, SURFACE in Index. — See also **absorbed, low.**

deep *noun* Something of immeasurable and vast extent : abysm, abyss, chasm, depth (often used in plural), gulf. See HIGH in Index.

deepen *verb* See **intensify.**

deepness *noun* See **depth.**

deep-rooted *adjective* See **confirmed.**

deep-seated *adjective* See **confirmed.**

deep water *noun* See **predicament.**

defamation *noun* See **libel.**

defamatory *adjective* See **libelous.**

defame verb See **libel**.
default noun See **failure**.
default verb See **fail**.
defeasance noun See **abolition**.
defeat verb To win a victory over, as in battle or a competition : beat, best, conquer, master, overcome, prevail against (or over), rout, subdue, subjugate, surmount, triumph over, vanquish, worst. *Informal:* trim, whip. *Slang:* ace, lick. *Idioms:* carry (or win) the day, get (or have) the best of, get (or have) the better of, go someone one better. See WIN in Index. — See also **frustrate**.

defeat noun The act of defeating or the condition of being defeated : beating, drubbing, overthrow, rout, thrashing, vanquishment. *Informal:* massacre, trimming, whipping. *Slang:* dusting, licking. See WIN in Index.

defect noun Something that mars the appearance or causes inadequacy or failure : blemish, bug, fault, flaw, imperfection, shortcoming. See BEAUTIFUL, BETTER, HELP in Index. — See also **shortage**.

defect verb To abandon one's cause, usually to join another : apostatize, desert[3], renegade, tergiversate, turn. *Slang:* rat. *Idioms:* change sides, turn one's coat. See APPROACH, TRUST in Index.

defection noun An instance of defecting from or abandoning a cause : apostasy, recreance, recreancy, tergiversation. See APPROACH, TRUST in Index.

defective adjective Having a defect : faulty, imperfect. See BETTER in Index. — See also **deficient**.

defector noun A person who has defected : apostate, deserter, recreant, renegade, runagate, tergiversator, turncoat. *Informal:* rat. See APPROACH in Index.

defend verb 1. To keep safe from danger, attack, or harm : guard, preserve, protect, safeguard, secure, shield, ward. *Archaic:* fend. See ATTACK in Index. 2. To support against arguments, attack, or criticism : apologize, justify, maintain, vindicate. *Idioms:* speak up for, stand up for, stick up for. See SUPPORT in Index.

defendable adjective See **tenable**.
defendant noun See **accused**.
defense noun The act or a means of defending : guard, preservation, protection, protector, safeguard, security, shield, ward. See ATTACK in Index. — See also **apology**.

defenseless adjective See **helpless**.
defensible adjective See **justifiable**, **tenable**.

defer[1] verb To put off until a later time : adjourn, delay, hold off, hold up, postpone, remit, shelve, stay[1], suspend, table, waive. *Informal:* wait. *Idiom:* put on ice. See DO in Index.

defer[2] verb To conform to the will or judgment of another, especially out of respect or courtesy : bow[1], submit, yield. *Idioms:* give ground, give way. See PRECEDE, RESIST in Index.

deference noun See **honor**, **obedience**.

deferential adjective Marked by courteous submission or respect : duteous, dutiful, obeisant, respectful. See RESIST in Index.

deferment noun See **delay**.
deferral noun See **delay**.
defiance noun 1. The disposition boldly to defy or resist authority or an opposing force : contempt, contumacy, despite, recalcitrance, recalcitrancy. See RESIST in Index.
2. Behavior or an act that is inten-

tionally provocative : challenge, provocation. See ATTACK in Index.

defiant *adjective* Marked by defiance : contumacious, recalcitrant. See RESIST in Index.

deficiency *noun* See **shortage**.

deficient *adjective* Lacking an essential element : defective, incomplete, lacking, wanting. See BETTER, EXCESS in Index. — See also **insufficient**.

deficit *noun* See **shortage**.

defile *verb* See **contaminate, dirty, taint, violate**.

defilement *noun* See **impurity**.

definite *adjective* **1.** Clearly, fully, and sometimes emphatically expressed : categorical, clear, clear-cut, decided, explicit, express, positive, precise, specific, unambiguous, unequivocal. See CLEAR in Index. **2.** Known positively : certain, positive, sure. *Idiom:* for certain. See CERTAIN in Index. **3.** Having distinct limits : determinate, fixed, limited. See LIMITED in Index. — See also **decided**.

definitive *adjective* Serving the function of deciding or settling with finality : authoritative, conclusive, decisive, determinative, final. See DECIDE in Index.

deflate *verb* See **discredit**.

deflect *verb* See **bend, turn**.

deflower *verb* See **violate**.

deform *verb* To alter and spoil the natural form or appearance of : contort, disfigure, distort, misshape, twist. See BEAUTIFUL in Index.

deformity *noun* A disfiguring abnormality of shape or form : disfigurement, malformation. See BEAUTIFUL in Index.

defraud *verb* See **cheat**.

defrauder *noun* See **cheat**.

deft *adjective* See **artful, dexterous, neat**.

deftness *noun* See **dexterity**.

defunct *adjective* See **dead, vanished**.

defy *verb* To confront boldly and courageously : beard, brave, challenge, dare, face, front. *Idioms:* fly in the face of, snap one's fingers at, stand up to, thumb one's nose at. See RESIST in Index. — See also **dare, disobey**.

degeneracy *noun* See **deterioration**.

degenerate *adjective* See **corrupt**.

degenerate *verb* See **deteriorate, fade**.

degeneration *noun* See **deterioration**.

degradation *noun* A lowering in or deprivation of character or self-esteem : abasement, debasement, humiliation, mortification. See RESPECT, WIN in Index. — See also **demotion**.

degrade *verb* See **debase, demote, humble**.

degree *noun* **1.** One of the units in a course, as on an ascending or descending scale : grade, level, peg, point, rung, stage, step. *Informal:* notch. See BIG in Index. **2.** Relative intensity or amount, as of a quality or attribute : extent, magnitude, measure, proportion. See BIG in Index.

dehydrate *verb* See **dry**.

deific *adjective* See **divine**.

deign *verb* See **condescend**.

deject *verb* See **depress**.

dejected *adjective* See **depressed**.

dejection *noun* See **gloom**.

delay *verb* **1.** To cause to be later or slower than expected or desired : detain, hang up, hold up, lag, retard, set back, slow (down or up), stall[2]. See HELP, TIME in Index. **2.** To go or move slowly so that progress is hindered : dally, dawdle, dilly-

dally, drag, lag, linger, loiter, poke,
procrastinate, tarry, trail. *Idioms:*
drag one's feet (*or* heels), mark time,
take one's time. See FAST in Index.
— See also **defer[1]**.

delay *noun* **1.** The condition or
fact of being made late or slow :
detainment, holdup, lag, retardation.
See HELP, TIME in Index. **2.** The act
of putting off or the condition of
being put off : adjournment, deferment, deferral, postponement, stay[1],
suspension, waiver. See TIME in
Index.

delectable *adjective* See **delicious,
delightful.**

delectation *noun* See **delight,
enjoyment.**

delegate *noun* See **representative.**

delete *verb* See **cancel.**

deleterious *adjective* See **harmful.**

deletion *noun* See **erasure.**

deliberate *verb* See **confer, ponder,
think.**

deliberate *adjective* **1.** Done or
said on purpose : intended, intentional, purposeful, voluntary, willful, witting. See PURPOSE in Index.
2. Careful and slow in acting, moving, or deciding : leisurely, measured, unhurried. See FAST in Index.
— See also **calculated.**

deliberation *noun* An exchange of
views in an attempt to reach a decision : conference, consultation,
counsel, parley. See WORDS in
Index. — See also **advisement,
thought.**

deliberative *adjective* See
thoughtful.

delicacy *noun* Something fine and
delicious, especially a food :
dainty, morsel, tidbit, treat.
Informal: goody. See GOOD, INGES-
TION in Index. — See also **infirmity.**

delicate *adjective* **1.** Appealing to
refined taste : choice, dainty, ele-

gant, exquisite, fine[1]. See GOOD,
INGESTION in Index. **2.** So slight as
to be difficult to notice or appreciate : fine[1], finespun, nice, refined,
subtle. See BIG in Index. **3.** Showing sensitivity and skill in dealing
with others : diplomatic, discreet,
politic, sensitive, tactful. See ABIL-
ITY in Index. **4.** Requiring great tact
or skill : sensitive, ticklish, touch-
and-go, touchy, tricky. See EASY in
Index. — See also **fine[1], fragile, gentle, infirm.**

delicateness *noun* See **infirmity.**

delicious *adjective* Highly pleasing,
especially to the sense of taste :
ambrosial, appetizing, delectable,
heavenly, luscious, savory, scrumptious, tasteful, tasty, toothsome.
Slang: yummy. See GOOD, INGES-
TION in Index. — See also **delightful.**

delight *noun* A feeling of extreme
gratification aroused by something
good or desired : delectation, enjoyment, joy, pleasure. See HAPPY, LIKE
in Index.

delight *verb* To give great or keen
pleasure to : cheer, enchant, gladden, gratify, overjoy, please, pleasure, tickle. *Archaic:* joy. See
HAPPY, LIKE in Index. — See also
adore, rejoice.

delighted *adjective* See **glad.**

delightful *adjective* Giving great
pleasure or delight : charming,
delectable, delicious, enchanting,
heavenly, luscious. *Informal:* darling. See GOOD, HAPPY, LIKE in
Index.

delimit *verb* See **determine.**

delimitate *verb* See **determine.**

delineate *verb* See **represent.**

delineation *noun* See **outline,
representation.**

delineative *adjective* See
descriptive.

delinquency *noun* See **failure.**

deliquesce *verb* See **melt.**

delirious *adjective* See **frantic.**

deliver *verb* See **bear, give, rescue.**

deliverance *noun* See **rescue.**

delivery *noun* The act of delivering or the condition of being delivered : surrender, transfer. See GIVE in Index. — See also **birth, rescue.**

delude *verb* See **deceive.**

deluge *verb* See **flood.**

deluge *noun* See **flood.**

delusion *noun* See **illusion.**

delusive *adjective* See **fallacious, illusive, illusory.**

delusory *adjective* See **fallacious, illusive, illusory.**

delve *verb* See **dig, explore.**

demand *verb* **1.** To ask for urgently or insistently : call for, claim, exact, insist on (or upon), require, requisition. *Idiom:* cry out for. See REQUEST in Index. **2.** To have as a need or prerequisite : ask, call for, entail, involve, necessitate, require, take. See NECESSARY, OVER in Index. — See also **claim.**

demand *noun* **1.** The act of demanding : call, claim, cry, exaction, requisition. See REQUEST in Index. **2.** Something asked for or needed : exigence, exigency (often used in plural), need, want. See NECESSARY, OVER in Index.

demanding *adjective* See **burdensome, severe.**

demarcate *verb* See **determine.**

demean[1] *verb* See **act.**

demean[2] *verb* See **debase, humble.**

demeanor *noun* See **bearing.**

demented *adjective* See **insane.**

dementia *noun* See **insanity.**

demise *noun* See **death.**

demise *verb* See **die.**

demission *noun* See **abdication.**

demit *verb* See **abdicate, quit.**

demobilize *verb* See **discharge.**

democratic *adjective* See **popular.**

demolish *verb* See **destroy.**

demonstrate *verb* See **prove, show.**

demonstration *noun* See **confirmation, display.**

demoralize *verb* See **corrupt.**

demoralizing *adjective* See **unwholesome.**

demote *verb* To lower in rank or grade : break, bump, degrade, downgrade, reduce. *Slang:* bust. See RISE in Index.

demotion *noun* The act or an instance of demoting : degradation, reduction. See RISE in Index.

demur *verb* See **object.**

demur *noun* See **objection.**

demure *adjective* See **modest.**

demureness *noun* See **modesty.**

den *noun* See **hide-out, hole.**

denial *noun* A refusal to grant the truth of a statement or charge : contradiction, disaffirmance, disaffirmation, disclaimer, negation, rejection. *Law:* traversal. See AFFIRM in Index. — See also **refusal.**

denigrate *verb* See **belittle, blacken.**

denigration *noun* See **belittlement, libel.**

denominate *verb* See **name.**

denomination *noun* See **faith, name, religion.**

denotation *noun* See **meaning.**

denotative *adjective* See **designative.**

denote *verb* See **designate, mean**[1].

denotive *adjective* See **designative.**

denounce *verb* See **accuse, deplore.**

denouncement *noun* See **accusation.**

denouncer *noun* See **accuser.**

dense *adjective* See **stupid, thick.**

density *noun* See **thickness.**

denude *verb* See **bare.**

denunciation *noun* See **accusation, blame.**

denunciative *adjective* See **accusatorial.**

denunciatory *adjective* See **accusatorial.**

deny *verb* To refuse to admit the truth, reality, value, or worth of : contradict, contravene, controvert, disaffirm, gainsay, negate, negative, oppugn. *Law:* traverse. See AFFIRM in Index. — See also **refuse, repudiate.**

depart *verb* See **deviate, die, go.**

departed *adjective* See **dead.**

departing *adjective* See **parting.**

department *noun* See **area, branch.**

departure *noun* The act of leaving : egress, exit, exodus, going, withdrawal. See APPROACH in Index. — See also **deviation.**

depend *verb* See **hang.**

depend on or **upon** *verb* **1.** To place trust or confidence in : bank on (or upon), believe in, count on (or upon), reckon on (or upon), rely on (or upon), trust (in). See TRUST in Index. **2.** To be determined by or contingent on something unknown, uncertain, or changeable : hang on, hang upon, hinge on (or upon), rest on (or upon), turn on, turn upon. See START in Index. — See also **expect.**

dependable *adjective* Capable of being depended upon : reliable, responsible, solid, sound[2], trustworthy, trusty. See TRUST in Index.

dependence also **dependance** *noun* See **confidence.**

dependency also **dependancy** *noun* See **possession.**

dependent *adjective* Determined or to be determined by someone or something else : conditional, conditioned, contingent, relative, reliant, subject. See START in Index. — See also **subordinate.**

dependent also **dependant** *noun* A person who relies on another for support : charge, ward. See GIVE in Index.

depict *verb* See **represent.**

depiction *noun* See **representation.**

deplete *verb* To lessen or weaken severely, as by removing something essential : drain, exhaust, impoverish, sap[2], use up. See GIVE, INCREASE, RICH in Index. — See also **dry up** at **dry.**

depletion *noun* See **debilitation.**

deplorable *adjective* Worthy of severe disapproval : condemnable, disgraceful, shameful, unfortunate. See GOOD in Index. — See also **sorrowful.**

deplore *verb* To feel or express strong disapproval of : censure, condemn, denounce, reprehend, reprobate. See PRAISE in Index. — See also **regret.**

deploy *verb* See **arrange.**

deployment *noun* See **arrangement.**

depone *verb* See **testify.**

deponent *noun* See **witness.**

deport *verb* See **act, banish.**

deportation *noun* See **exile.**

deportee *noun* See **émigré.**

deportment *noun* See **behavior.**

depose *verb* See **testify.**

deposit *verb* To put down, especially in layers, by a natural process : precipitate. See INCREASE in Index. — See also **bank[2].**

deposit *noun* **1.** Matter that settles on a bottom or collects on a surface by a natural process : dreg (often used in plural), lees, precipitate, precipitation, sediment. See LEFTOVER in Index. **2.** A partial or initial payment : down payment. See MONEY, PAY in Index.

deposition *noun* See **testimony.**

depository *noun* A place where something is deposited for safekeeping : archive, magazine, repository,

store, storehouse, warehouse. See
KEEP in Index.

deprave *verb* See **corrupt.**

depraved *adjective* See **corrupt.**

depravity *noun* See **corruption.**

deprecate *verb* See **belittle,
disapprove.**

deprecation *noun* See **belittlement.**

deprecative *adjective* See
disparaging.

deprecatory *adjective* See
disparaging.

depreciate *verb* To become or
make less in price or value :
cheapen, depress, devaluate, devalue,
downgrade, lower^2, mark down,
reduce, write down. See INCREASE,
MONEY in Index. — See also **belittle.**

depreciation *noun* A lowering in
price or value : devaluation, markdown, reduction, write-down. See
INCREASE, MONEY in Index. — See
also **belittlement.**

depreciative *adjective* See
disparaging.

depreciatory *adjective* See
disparaging.

depredate *verb* See **sack^2.**

depress *verb* To make sad or
gloomy : deject, dispirit, oppress,
sadden, weigh down. See HAPPY in
Index. — See also **depreciate, lower^2.**

depressed *adjective* **1.** In low spirits : blue, dejected, desolate, dispirited, down, downcast, downhearted,
dull, dysphoric, gloomy, heavy-
hearted, low, melancholic, melancholy, sad, spiritless, tristful,
unhappy, wistful. *Idiom:* down at (or
in) the mouth. See HAPPY in Index.
2. Economically and socially below
standard : backward, deprived, disadvantaged, impoverished, underprivileged. See RICH in Index.

depressing *adjective* See **sad.**

depression *noun* **1.** An area sunk
below its surroundings : basin,

concavity, dip, hollow, pit^1, sag,
sink, sinkhole. See CONVEX in
Index. **2.** A period of decreased business activity and high unemploy-
ment : recession, slump. See RICH
in Index. — See also **gloom.**

deprival *noun* See **deprivation.**

deprivation *noun* The condition of
being deprived of what one once had
or ought to have : deprival, dispossession, divestiture, loss, privation.
See GIVE, RICH in Index.

deprive *verb* To take or keep something away from : dispossess,
divest, rob, strip^1. See GIVE in Index.

deprived *adjective* See **depressed.**

depth *noun* **1.** The extent or measurement downward from a surface :
deepness, drop. See SURFACE in
Index. **2.** Intellectual penetration or
range : deepness, profoundness,
profundity. See THOUGHTS in Index.
— See also **deep, intensity.**

deputy *noun* See **assistant, representative.**

derange *verb* To make insane :
craze, madden, unbalance, unhinge.
See SANE in Index. — See also **disorder, upset.**

derangement *noun* See **disorder,
insanity.**

derelict *adjective* See **abandoned,
negligent.**

dereliction *noun* See **failure.**

deride *verb* See **ridicule.**

de rigueur *adjective* See **correct.**

derision *noun* See **ridicule.**

derisive *adjective* See **sarcastic.**

derivation *noun* See **derivative,
origin.**

derivational *adjective* See
derivative.

derivative *adjective* Stemming
from an original source : derivational, derived, secondary. See KIN
in Index.

derivative *noun* Something derived from another : byproduct, derivation, descendant, offshoot, outgrowth, spinoff. See KIN in Index.

derive *verb* **1.** To arrive at through reasoning : educe, evolve, excogitate. See REASON in Index. **2.** To obtain from another source : draw, get, take. See KIN in Index. — See also **descend, stem.**

derived *adjective* See **derivative.**

derogate *verb* See **belittle.**

derogation *noun* See **belittlement.**

derogative *adjective* See **disparaging.**

derogatory *adjective* See **disparaging.**

derrière *noun* See **bottom.**

descend *verb* **1.** To bring oneself down to a lower level of behavior : lower[2], sink, stoop. See RISE in Index. **2.** To have hereditary derivation : derive, issue, spring. *Idiom:* trace one's descent. See KIN in Index. — See also **deteriorate, drop, fall.**

descendant *noun* One descended directly from the same parents or ancestors : child, offspring, progeny, scion. See KIN in Index.

descendent also **descendant** *adjective* See **descending.**

descending *adjective* Moving or sloping down : descendent, downward. See RISE in Index.

descent *noun* A sudden drop to a lower condition or status : comedown, down, downfall, downgrade. See RISE in Index. — See also **ancestry, drop, fall.**

describe *verb* To give a verbal account of : narrate, recite, recount, rehearse, relate, report, tell. See WORDS in Index. — See also **represent.**

description *noun* See **kind[2], representation, story.**

descriptive *adjective* Serving to describe : delineative, graphic, representative. See WORDS in Index.

descry *verb* See **catch, discern, notice.**

desecrate *verb* See **violate.**

desecration *noun* See **sacrilege.**

desegregate *verb* See **integrate.**

desegregation *noun* See **integration.**

desensitize *verb* See **deaden.**

desert[1] *noun* See **barren.**

desert[2] *noun* See **due.**

desert[3] *verb* See **abandon, defect.**

deserted *adjective* See **abandoned, lonely.**

deserter *noun* See **defector.**

desertion *noun* See **abandonment.**

deserve *verb* See **earn.**

deserved *adjective* See **just.**

deserving *adjective* See **admirable.**

desiccate *verb* See **dry, dry up** at **dry.**

design *verb* **1.** To form a strategy for : blueprint, cast, chart, conceive, contrive, devise, formulate, frame, lay[1], plan, project, scheme, strategize, work out. *Informal:* dope out. *Idiom:* lay plans. See PLANNED in Index. **2.** To work out and arrange the parts or details of : blueprint, lay out, map (out), plan, set out. See PLANNED in Index. — See also **intend.**

design *noun* A method for making, doing, or accomplishing something : blueprint, game plan, idea, layout, plan, project, schema, scheme, strategy. See PLANNED in Index. — See also **figure, intention.**

designate *verb* To make known or identify, as by signs : denote, indicate, mark, point out, show, specify. See SHOW in Index. — See also **appoint, appropriate, call, name.**

designation *noun* See **appointment, name.**

designative *adjective* Serving to designate or indicate : denotative, denotive, designatory, exhibitive, exhibitory, indicative, indicatory. See SHOW in Index.

designatory *adjective* See **designative.**

designee *noun* See **appointee.**

designing *adjective* See **calculating.**

desirable *adjective* Arousing erotic desire : sexy. See DESIRE, SEX in Index.

desire *verb* To have a strong longing for : ache, covet, hanker, long², pant, pine, want, wish, yearn. *Informal:* hone². See DESIRE in Index. — See also **choose.**

desire *noun* **1.** A strong wanting of what promises enjoyment or pleasure : appetence, appetency, appetite, craving, hunger, itch, longing, lust, thirst, wish, yearning, yen. See DESIRE in Index. **2.** Sexual hunger : amativeness, concupiscence, eroticism, erotism, itch, libidinousness, lust, lustfulness, passion, prurience, pruriency. See DESIRE, SEX in Index.

desist *verb* See **abandon.**

desolate *verb* See **devastate.**

desolate *adjective* See **abandoned, depressed, gloomy, lonely.**

desolation *noun* See **emptiness.**

despair *verb* To lose all hope : despond, give up. See HOPE in Index.

despair *noun* Utter lack of hope : desperateness, desperation, despond, despondence, despondency, hopelessness. See HOPE in Index.

despairing *adjective* See **despondent.**

desperate *adjective* See **critical, despondent, intense.**

desperateness *noun* See **despair.**

desperation *noun* See **despair.**

despicable *adjective* See **filthy.**

despisable *adjective* See **filthy.**

despisal *noun* The feeling of despising : contempt, despite, disdain, scorn. See RESPECT in Index.

despise *verb* To regard with utter contempt and disdain : contemn, disdain, scorn, scout². *Idioms:* have no use for, look down on (or upon). See RESPECT in Index. — See also **hate.**

despite *noun* See **defiance, despisal, indignity.**

despiteful *adjective* See **malevolent.**

despitefulness *noun* See **malevolence.**

despoil *verb* See **sack².**

despond *verb* See **despair.**

despond *noun* See **despair.**

despondence *noun* See **despair, gloom.**

despondency *noun* See **despair, gloom.**

despondent *adjective* Having lost all hope : despairing, desperate, forlorn, hopeless. See HOPE in Index.

despot *noun* See **authoritarian, dictator.**

despotic *adjective* See **absolute, authoritarian.**

despotism *noun* See **absolutism, tyranny.**

destine *verb* See **fate.**

destiny *noun* See **fate.**

destitute *adjective* See **empty, poor.**

destitution *noun* See **poverty.**

destroy *verb* **1.** To cause the complete ruin or wreckage of : bankrupt, break down, cross up, demolish, finish, ruin, shatter, sink, smash, spoil, torpedo, undo, wash up, wrack², wreck. *Slang:* total. *Idiom:* put the kibosh on. See HELP in Index. **2.** To pull down or break up so that reconstruction is impossible : demolish, dismantle, dynamite, knock down, level, pull down, pulverize, raze, tear down, wreck.

Aerospace: destruct. See HELP in Index. — See also **break, kill**[1], **murder.**

destroyer *noun* See **ruin.**

destruct *verb* See **destroy.**

destruction *noun* The act of destroying or state of being destroyed : bane, devastation, havoc, ruin, ruination, undoing, wrack[1], wreck, wreckage. See HELP, LEFTOVER in Index. — See also **breakage, ruin.**

destructive *adjective* Having the capability or effect of damaging irreparably : pernicious, ruinous. See HELP in Index. — See also **fatal.**

desuetude *noun* See **obsoleteness.**

desultory *adjective* See **aimless, random.**

detach *verb* **1.** To separate one thing from another thing : disconnect, disengage, uncouple. See ASSEMBLE in Index. **2.** To remove from association with : abstract, disassociate, disengage, dissociate, withdraw. See ASSEMBLE in Index. — See also **divide.**

detached *adjective* Lacking interest in one's surroundings or worldly affairs : aloof, disinterested, incurious, indifferent, unconcerned, uninterested, uninvolved. See ATTITUDE, CONCERN in Index. — See also **apathetic, cool, neutral, solitary.**

detachment *noun* **1.** The act or process of detaching : disconnection, disengagement, separation, uncoupling. See ASSEMBLE in Index. **2.** Dissociation from one's surroundings or worldly affairs : aloofness, distance, remoteness. See ATTITUDE, CONCERN, INCLUDE, NEAR in Index. **3.** A unit of troops on special assignment : detail. See GROUP in Index. — See also **division, fairness, force.**

detail *noun* A small, often specialized element of a whole : fine print, item, particular, technicality. See GROUP in Index. — See also **circumstance, detachment, element.**

detail *verb* See **stipulate.**

detailed *adjective* Characterized by attention to detail : blow-by-blow, circumstantial, full, minute[2], particular, thorough. See SPECIFIC in Index.

detain *verb* See **delay, hold, jail.**

detainment *noun* See **delay.**

detect *verb* See **catch, notice.**

detectable *adjective* See **perceptible.**

detective *noun* A person whose work is investigating crimes or obtaining hidden evidence or information : investigator, sleuth. *Informal:* eye. *Slang:* dick, gumshoe. See INVESTIGATE in Index.

detention *noun* The state of being detained by legal authority : charge, confinement, custody, ward. See FREE in Index.

deter *verb* See **dissuade.**

deteriorate *verb* To become lower in quality, character, or condition : atrophy, decline, degenerate, descend, retrograde, sink, worsen. *Idioms:* go bad, go to pot, go to seed, go to the dogs. See BETTER in Index. — See also **decay, fade.**

deterioration *noun* Descent to a lower level or condition : atrophy, decadence, declension, declination, decline, degeneracy, degeneration. See BETTER in Index. — See also **decay, failure.**

determent *noun* See **prevention.**

determinate *adjective* See **definite.**

determination *noun* See **answer, decision, ruling.**

determinative *adjective* See **decisive, definitive.**

determine *verb* To fix the limits of : bound[2], delimit, delimitate, demarcate, limit, mark (off *or* out), measure. See LIMITED in Index.
— See also **decide, discover, judge.**

determined *adjective* See **decisive, firm[1], set[1].**

deterrence *noun* See **prevention.**

deterrent *adjective* See **preventive.**

detest *verb* See **hate.**

detestable *adjective* See **filthy.**

detestation *noun* See **hate.**

detonate *verb* See **explode.**

detonation *noun* See **blast.**

detour *verb* See **skirt.**

detract *verb* See **belittle.**

detract from *verb* See **injure.**

detraction *noun* See **belittlement, libel.**

detractive *adjective* See **disparaging, libelous.**

detriment *noun* See **disadvantage, harm.**

detrimental *adjective* See **harmful.**

de trop *adjective* See **superfluous.**

devaluate *verb* See **depreciate.**

devaluation *noun* See **depreciation.**

devalue *verb* See **depreciate.**

devastate *verb* To destroy completely as or as if by conquering : desolate, ravage, waste. *Idiom:* lay waste. See HELP in Index.

devastation *noun* See **destruction.**

develop *verb* **1.** To bring (a product or idea, for example) into being : generate, produce. See KIN in Index. **2.** To be disclosed gradually : evolve, unfold. See SHOW in Index. **3.** To come gradually to have : acquire, form. See GET in Index. — See also **come, contract, elaborate, gain, mature.**

developed *adjective* See **mature.**

developer *noun* See **builder.**

development *noun* A progression from a simple form to a more complex one : evolution, evolvement, growth, progress, unfolding. See CHANGE in Index. — See also **buildup, event, progress.**

deviance *noun* See **abnormality.**

deviancy *noun* See **abnormality.**

deviant *adjective* See **abnormal.**

deviant *noun* One whose sexual behavior differs from the accepted norm : deviate, pervert. See SEX, USUAL in Index.

deviate *verb* To turn away from a prescribed course of action or conduct : depart, digress, diverge, stray, swerve, veer. *Archaic:* err. See APPROACH, CORRECT in Index.
— See also **digress, turn.**

deviate *noun* See **deviant.**

deviation *noun* A departing from what is prescribed : aberration, departure, divergence, divergency, diversion. See APPROACH, CORRECT in Index. — See also **abnormality, digression.**

device *noun* Something, as a machine, devised for a particular function : apparatus, appliance, contraption, contrivance. See MACHINE in Index. — See also **figure, invention, trick.**

devil *noun* See **fiend, mischief.**

devilish *adjective* See **fiendish.**

devilry *noun* See **mischief.**

deviltry *noun* See **crime, mischief.**

devious *adjective* See **erratic, indirect, underhand.**

deviousness *noun* See **indirection.**

devise *verb* See **design, invent, leave[1].**

devitalization *noun* See **debilitation.**

devitalize *verb* See **enervate.**

devoid *adjective* See **empty.**

devolve *verb* See **fall.**

devote *verb* To give over by or as if by vow to a higher purpose : consecrate, dedicate, hallow. See GIVE in Index. — See also **apply**.

devoted *adjective* See **affectionate, sacred**.

devotee *noun* One zealously devoted to a religion : enthusiast, fanatic, sectary, votary, zealot. See BELIEF, LOVE, RELIGION in Index. — See also **admirer, enthusiast**.

devotion *noun* A state of often extreme religious ardour : devoutness, pietism, piety, piousness, religionism, religiosity, religiousness. See RELIGION in Index. — See also **adoration, attachment**.

devotional *adjective* See **holy**.

devour *verb* See **consume, eat, eat up** at eat, **waste**.

devout *adjective* See **holy**.

devoutness *noun* See **devotion**.

dexterity *noun* Skillfulness in the use of the hands or body : adroitness, deftness, dexterousness, prowess, skill, sleight. See ABILITY in Index. — See also **agility**.

dexterous *adjective* Exhibiting or possessing skill and ease in performance : adroit, clever, deft, facile, handy, nimble, slick. See ABILITY in Index. — See also **artful**.

dexterousness *noun* See **agility, dexterity**.

diablerie *noun* See **crime, mischief**.

diabolic *adjective* See **fiendish**.

diabolical *adjective* See **fiendish**.

diagonal *adjective* See **bias**.

dial *noun* See **face**.

dial *verb* See **telephone**.

dialect *noun* A variety of a language that differs from the standard form : argot, cant[2], jargon, lingo, patois, vernacular. See WORDS in Index. — See also **language**.

dialogue or **dialog** *noun* See **conversation**.

diametric *adjective* See **opposite**.

diametrical *adjective* See **opposite**.

diaphanous *adjective* See **filmy**.

diatribe *noun* See **tirade**.

dibs *noun* See **claim**.

dick *noun* See **detective**.

dicker *verb* See **haggle**.

dictate *verb* To set forth expressly and authoritatively : decree, fix, impose, lay down, ordain, prescribe. *Idioms:* call the shots (or tune), lay it on the line. See OVER in Index. — See also **boss**.

dictate *noun* See **command, rule**.

dictator *noun* An absolute ruler, especially one who is harsh and oppressive : Big Brother, despot, führer, man on horseback, oppressor, strongman, totalitarian, tyrant. See OVER in Index. — See also **authoritarian**.

dictatorial *adjective* Tending to dictate : authoritarian, bossy, dogmatic, domineering, imperious, magisterial, masterful, overbearing, peremptory. See OVER in Index. — See also **absolute, authoritarian**.

dictatorship *noun* See **absolutism, tyranny**.

diction *noun* See **wording**.

dictionary *noun* See **vocabulary**.

didactic *adjective* Inclined to teach or moralize excessively : didactical, preachy. See TEACH in Index. — See also **moral**.

didactical *adjective* See **didactic, moral**.

diddle[1] *verb* See **cheat**.

diddle[2] *verb* See **idle**.

diddler *noun* See **cheat**.

diddly *noun* See **damn**.

die *verb* To cease living : decease, demise, depart, drop, expire, go, pass away, pass (on), perish, succumb. *Informal:* pop off. *Slang:* check out, croak, kick in, kick off. *Idioms:* bite the dust, breathe one's last, cash in, give up the ghost, go to one's grave, kick the bucket, meet one's end (or

Maker), pass on to the Great Beyond, turn up one's toes. See LIVE in Index.
— See also **disappear, fade, subside.**

die-hard also **diehard** *noun* See **reactionary.**

die-hard also **diehard** *adjective* See **reactionary, stubborn.**

die-hardism *noun* See **stubbornness.**

diet *noun* See **food.**

differ *verb* **1.** To be unlike or dissimilar : disagree, diverge, vary. *Idiom:* be at variance. See SAME in Index. **2.** To be of different opinion : disaccord, disagree, discord, dissent, vary. *Idiom:* join (or take) issue. See AGREE in Index.

difference *noun* The condition of being unlike or dissimilar : discrepance, discrepancy, disparity, dissimilarity, dissimilitude, distinction, divarication, divergence, divergency, unlikeness. See SAME in Index.
— See also **conflict, gap, variation.**

different *adjective* Not like another in nature, quality, amount, or form : disparate, dissimilar, divergent, diverse, unlike, variant, various. See SAME in Index. — See also **new.**

differentiate *verb* See **distinguish.**

differentiation *noun* See **distinction.**

difficult *adjective* Not easy to do, achieve, or master : arduous, hard, laborious, serious, tall, tough, uphill. See EASY in Index. — See also **burdensome, contrary, inconvenient.**

difficultly *adverb* See **hard.**

difficulty *noun* Something that obstructs progress and requires great effort to overcome : asperity, hardship, rigor, vicissitude (often used in plural). *Idioms:* a hard (or tough) nut to crack, a hard (or tough) row to hoe, heavy sledding. See EASY in Index. — See also **argument, conflict, predicament.**

diffidence *noun* See **modesty.**

diffident *adjective* See **modest.**

diffuse *verb* See **spread.**

diffuse *adjective* See **wordy.**

diffuseness *noun* See **wordiness.**

diffusion *noun* See **wordiness.**

dig *verb* **1.** To break, turn over, or remove (earth or sand, for example) with or as if with a tool : delve, excavate, grub, scoop, shovel, spade. See ENTER in Index. **2.** To make by digging : excavate, scoop, shovel. See MAKE in Index. **3.** To thrust against or into : jab, jog, nudge, poke, prod. See TOUCH in Index.
— See also **enjoy, explore, ram, uncover, understand.**

dig *noun* An act of thrusting into or against, as to attract attention : jab, jog, nudge, poke. See TOUCH in Index. — See also **crack, home.**

digest *verb* See **absorb.**

digestion *noun* See **absorption.**

dignify *verb* See **exalt, grace.**

dignitary *noun* An important, influential person : character, eminence, leader, lion, nabob, notability, notable, personage. *Informal:* big-timer, heavyweight, somebody, someone, VIP. *Slang:* big shot, big wheel, bigwig, muckamuck. See IMPORTANT in Index.

dignity *noun* See **honor.**

digress *verb* To turn aside, especially from the main subject in writing or speaking : deviate, divagate, diverge, ramble, stray, wander. *Idiom:* go off at (or on) a tangent. See APPROACH in Index. — See also **deviate.**

digression *noun* An instance of digressing : aside, deviation, divagation, divergence, divergency, excursion, excursus, irrelevancy, parenthesis, tangent. See APPROACH in Index.

digressive *adjective* Marked by or given to digression : discursive, excursive, parenthetic, parenthetical, rambling, tangential. See APPROACH in Index.

dilapidated *adjective* See **ruinous, shabby.**

dilate *verb* See **elaborate.**

dilatory *adjective* See **slow.**

dilemma *noun* See **predicament.**

dilettante *noun* See **amateur.**

dilettante *adjective* See **amateurish.**

dilettantish *adjective* See **amateurish.**

diligence *noun* Steady attention and effort, as to one's occupation : application, assiduity, assiduousness, industriousness, industry, sedulousness. See INDUSTRIOUS in Index.

diligent *adjective* Characterized by steady attention and effort : assiduous, industrious, sedulous, studious. See INDUSTRIOUS in Index.

dilly-dallier *noun* See **laggard.**

dilly-dally *verb* See **delay.**

dilute *verb* To lessen the strength of by or as if by admixture : attenuate, cut, thin, water (down), weaken. See STRONG in Index.

dilute *adjective* Lower than normal in strength or concentration due to admixture : thin, washy, watered-down, waterish, watery, weak. See STRONG in Index.

dim *verb* See **dull, obscure.**

dim *adjective* See **dark, dull, filmy, unclear.**

dimension *noun* See **size.**

diminish *verb* See **decrease.**

diminishment *noun* See **decrease.**

diminution *noun* See **decrease.**

diminutive *adjective* See **tiny.**

dimness *noun* See **dark.**

dimwit *noun* See **dullard.**

dimwitted *adjective* See **stupid.**

din *noun* See **noise.**

ding-a-ling *noun* See **crackpot.**

dingbat *noun* See **crackpot.**

ding-dong *noun* See **fool.**

dingy *adjective* See **shabby.**

dip *verb* **1.** To plunge briefly in or into a liquid : douse, duck, dunk, immerge, immerse, souse, submerge, submerse. See ENTER in Index. **2.** To immerse in a coloring solution : color, dye. See COLORS, ENTER in Index. **3.** To take a substance, as liquid, from a container by plunging the hand or a utensil into it : bail², lade, ladle, scoop (up). See GIVE in Index. — See also **drop.**

dip into *verb* See **browse.**

dip *noun* See **depression, fall, fool, plunge.**

diplomacy *noun* See **tact.**

diplomatic *adjective* See **delicate.**

dippy *adjective* See **foolish.**

dire *adjective* See **burning, critical, fateful, fearful.**

direct *adjective* **1.** Proceeding or lying in an uninterrupted line or course : straight, straightforward, through. See STRAIGHT in Index. **2.** Of unbroken descent or lineage : lineal. See CONTINUE in Index. — See also **frank, immediate.**

direct *verb* See **address, administer, aim, apply, command, conduct, control, guide.**

direct *adverb* See **directly.**

direction *noun* See **administration, command, government, guidance.**

directive *noun* See **command.**

directly *adverb* **1.** In a direct line : dead, direct, due, right, straight, straightaway. See STRAIGHT in Index. **2.** With precision or absolute conformity : bang, dead, direct, exactly, fair, flush, just, precisely, right, smack¹, square, squarely, straight. *Slang:* smack-dab. See PRECISE in Index. **3.** Without delay :

forthwith, immediately, instant, instantly, now, right away, right off, straightaway, straight off. *Idioms:* at once, first off. See TIME in Index. — See also **immediately.**

director *noun* See **boss, chief, executive, guide.**

directorial *adjective* See **administrative.**

direful *adjective* See **fateful, fearful.**

dirt *noun* See **filth, obscenity.**

dirtiness *noun* The condition or state of being dirty : filth, filthiness, foulness, griminess, grubbiness, smuttiness, squalor, uncleanliness, uncleanness. See CLEAN in Index. — See also **impurity, obscenity.**

dirty *adjective* Covered or stained with or as if with dirt or other impurities : black, filthy, grimy, grubby, smutty, soiled, unclean, uncleanly. See CLEAN in Index. — See also **obscene, rough.**

dirty *verb* To make dirty : befoul, begrime, besmirch, besoil, black, blacken, defile, smudge, smutch, soil, sully. See CLEAN in Index. — See also **blacken.**

dirty old man *noun* See **lecher.**

disable *verb* To render powerless or motionless, as by inflicting severe injury : cripple, immobilize, incapacitate, knock out, paralyze. *Idiom:* put out of action (*or* commission). See HELP in Index. — See also **unfit.**

disaccord *noun* See **conflict.**

disaccord *verb* See **conflict, differ.**

disacknowledge *verb* See **repudiate.**

disadvantage *noun* An unfavorable condition, circumstance, or characteristic : detriment, drawback, handicap, minus. See HELP in Index.

disadvantaged *adjective* See **depressed.**

disadvantageous *adjective* See **unfavorable.**

disaffect *verb* See **estrange.**

disaffection *noun* See **breach, estrangement.**

disaffirm *verb* See **deny.**

disaffirmance *noun* See **denial.**

disaffirmation *noun* See **denial.**

disagree *verb* See **differ.**

disagreeable *adjective* See **illtempered, unpleasant.**

disagreement *noun* See **argument, gap.**

disallow *verb* See **forbid, refuse.**

disallowance *noun* See **forbiddance, refusal.**

disappear *verb* **1.** To pass out of sight either gradually or suddenly : evanesce, evaporate, fade, fade out, vanish. See SHOW in Index. **2.** To cease to exist : die (away *or* out), expire. See LIVE in Index.

disappearance *noun* The act or an example of passing out of sight : evanescence, evaporation, fade-out, vanishment. See SHOW in Index.

disappoint *verb* To cause unhappiness by failing to satisfy the hopes, desires, or expectations of : discontent, disgruntle, dissatisfy, let down. See HAPPY in Index.

disappointing *adjective* Disturbing because of failure to measure up to a standard or produce the desired results : sorry, unlucky. See HAPPY in Index.

disappointment *noun* Unhappiness caused by the failure of one's hopes, desires, or expectations : discontent, discontentment, disgruntlement, dissatisfaction, letdown, regret. See HAPPY in Index.

disapprobation *noun* See **disapproval.**

disapproval *noun* Unfavorable opinion or judgment : disapprobation, disesteem, disfavor, displeasure. See LIKE in Index.

disapprove *verb* To have or express an unfavorable opinion of : deprecate, discountenance, disesteem, disfavor, frown on (or upon), object. *Idioms:* hold no brief for, not go for, take a dim view of, take exception to. See LIKE in Index.

disarrange *verb* See **disorder, tousle.**

disarrangement *noun* See **disorder.**

disarray *noun* See **disorder.**

disarray *verb* See **disorder.**

disassemble *verb* See **take down** at **take.**

disassociate *verb* See **detach.**

disaster *noun* An occurrence inflicting widespread destruction and distress : calamity, cataclysm, catastrophe, tragedy. See HELP in Index.

disastrous *adjective* See **fatal.**

disavow *verb* See **repudiate.**

disbelief *noun* The refusal or reluctance to believe : discredit, incredulity, incredulousness, unbelief. See BELIEF in Index.

disbelieve *verb* To give no credence to : discredit. *Idiom:* take no stock in. See BELIEF in Index.

disbelieving *adjective* See **incredulous.**

disburden *verb* See **rid, unload.**

disburse *verb* See **spend.**

disbursement *noun* See **cost.**

discard *verb* To let go or get rid of as being useless or defective, for example : dispose of, dump, junk, scrap[1], throw away, throw out. *Informal:* chuck, jettison, shuck (off). *Slang:* ditch. See KEEP in Index.

discarnate *adjective* See **immaterial.**

discern *verb* To perceive and fix the identity of, especially with difficulty : descry, distinguish, make

out, pick out, spot. See SEE in Index. — See also **catch, distinguish, notice.**

discernible *adjective* See **perceptible, visible.**

discerning *adjective* See **critical.**

discernment *noun* Skill in perceiving, discriminating, or judging : acumen, astuteness, clearsightedness, discrimination, eye, keenness, nose, penetration, perceptiveness, percipience, percipiency, perspicacity, sagacity, sageness, shrewdness, wit. See ABILITY, CAREFUL in Index.

discharge *verb* **1.** To release from military duty : demobilize, muster out, separate. See FREE, KEEP in Index. **2.** To pass or pour out : empty, flow, issue. See ENTER in Index. — See also **dismiss, excuse, free, fulfill, settle, unload.**

discharge *noun* See **dismissal, performance.**

disciple *noun* See **follower.**

disciplinary *adjective* See **punishing.**

discipline *noun* See **branch, punishment.**

discipline *verb* See **educate, punish.**

disclaim *verb* See **repudiate.**

disclaimer *noun* See **denial.**

disclose *verb* See **communicate, reveal.**

disclosure *noun* See **revelation.**

discolor *verb* See **stain.**

discombobulate *verb* See **confuse.**

discombobulation *noun* See **daze.**

discomfit *verb* See **embarrass.**

discomfiture *noun* See **embarrassment.**

discomfort *noun* See **inconvenience.**

discomfort *verb* See **embarrass, inconvenience.**

discommode *verb* See **inconvenience.**

discompose *verb* See **agitate.**

discomposure *noun* See **embarrassment.**

disconcert *verb* See **embarrass.**

disconnect *verb* See **detach.**

disconnection *noun* See **detachment.**

discontent *noun* See **disappointment.**

discontent *verb* See **disappoint.**

discontentment *noun* See **disappointment.**

discontinuance *noun* See **break, stop.**

discontinuation *noun* See **break, stop.**

discontinue *verb* See **abandon, stop, suspend.**

discontinuity *noun* See **break.**

discord *noun* See **conflict.**

discord *verb* See **conflict, differ.**

discordance *noun* See **conflict.**

discordant *adjective* See **incongruous, inharmonious.**

discount *verb* See **belittle, deduct.**

discount *noun* See **deduction.**

discountenance *verb* See **disapprove, embarrass.**

discourage *verb* To make less hopeful or enthusiastic : dishearten, dispirit. See HELP in Index. — See also **dissuade.**

discourse *noun* A formal, lengthy exposition of a topic : disquisition, dissertation, treatise. See WORDS in Index. — See also **conversation, speech.**

discourse *verb* See **converse¹.**

discourser *noun* See **conversationalist.**

discourteous *adjective* See **rude.**

discourtesy *noun* See **impudence.**

discover *verb* To obtain knowledge or awareness of something not known before, as through observation or study : ascertain, determine, find (out), hear, learn. See TEACH in Index. — See also **betray, reveal.**

discovery *noun* Something that has been discovered : ascertainment, find, finding, strike. See TEACH in Index.

discredit *verb* To cause to be no longer believed or valued : debunk, deflate, explode, puncture. *Informal:* shoot down. *Idioms:* knock the bottom out of, shoot full of holes. See VALUE in Index. — See also **disbelieve, disgrace, refute.**

discredit *noun* See **disbelief, disgrace.**

discreditable *adjective* See **disgraceful.**

discreet *adjective* See **conservative, delicate.**

discrepance *noun* See **difference, gap.**

discrepancy *noun* See **difference, gap.**

discrepant *adjective* In sharp opposition : incompatible, incongruent, incongruous, inconsistent. *Logic:* repugnant. See AGREE in Index. — See also **incongruous.**

discrete *adjective* See **distinct, individual.**

discretely *adverb* See **separately.**

discreteness *noun* See **individuality.**

discretion *noun* See **prudence, will.**

discretionary *adjective* See **arbitrary, optional.**

discriminate *adjective* See **discriminating.**

discriminate *verb* See **distinguish.**

discriminating *adjective* Able to recognize small differences or draw fine distinctions : discriminate, discriminative, discriminatory, select, selective. See PRECISE in Index. — See also **critical.**

discrimination *noun* The ability to distinguish, especially to recognize small differences or draw fine distinctions : refinement, selectiveness, selectivity. See PRECISE in Index. — See also **discernment, distinction.**

discriminative *adjective* See **discriminating.**

discriminatory *adjective* See **discriminating.**

discursive *adjective* See **digressive.**

discuss *verb* To speak together and exchange ideas and opinions about : bandy (about), moot, talk over, thrash out (or over), thresh out (or over), toss around. *Informal:* hash (over), kick around, knock about (or around). *Slang:* rap³. *Idiom:* go into a huddle. See WORDS in Index.

discussant *noun* See **conferee.**

discusser *noun* See **conferee.**

discussion *noun* See **conference.**

disdain *noun* See **despisal.**

disdain *verb* See **despise.**

disdainful *adjective* Showing scorn and disrespect toward (someone or something) : contemptuous, scornful. *Idiom:* on one's high horse. See RESPECT in Index.

disease *noun* A pathological condition of mind or body : ailment, complaint, disorder, ill, illness, infirmity, malady, sickness. See HEALTH in Index.

disembark *verb* See **land.**

disembarrass *verb* See **rid.**

disembodied *adjective* See **immaterial.**

disencumber *verb* See **rid.**

disengage *verb* See **clear, detach, undo.**

disengagement *noun* See **detachment.**

disentangle *verb* See **clear.**

disesteem *noun* See **disapproval.**

disesteem *verb* See **disapprove.**

disfavor *noun* See **disapproval.**

disfavor *verb* See **disapprove.**

disfigure *verb* See **deform.**

disfigurement *noun* See **deformity.**

disgorge *verb* See **erupt.**

disgrace *noun* Loss of or damage to one's reputation : bad name, bad odor, discredit, dishonor, disrepute, humiliation, ignominy, ill repute, obloquy, odium, opprobrium, shame. See RESPECT in Index.

disgrace *verb* To damage in reputation : discredit, dishonor, shame. *Idiom:* be a reproach to. See RESPECT in Index.

disgraceful *adjective* Meriting or causing shame or dishonor : discreditable, dishonorable, disreputable, ignominious, opprobrious, shameful. See RESPECT in Index. — See also **deplorable.**

disgracefulness *noun* See **infamy.**

disgruntle *verb* See **disappoint.**

disgruntlement *noun* See **disappointment.**

disguise *verb* To change or modify so as to prevent recognition of the true identity or character of : camouflage, dissemble, dissimulate, mask, masquerade. See SHOW in Index.

disguise *noun* Clothes or other personal effects, such as makeup, worn to conceal one's identity : costume. See SHOW in Index. — See also **act, façade.**

disguisement *noun* See **façade.**

disgust *verb* To offend the senses or feelings of : nauseate, repel, revolt, sicken. *Idiom:* turn one's stomach. See LIKE in Index.

disgust *noun* Extreme repugnance excited by something offensive : nausea. See LIKE in Index.

disgusted *adjective* See **sick.**

disgusting *adjective* See **filthy, offensive.**

disharmonious *adjective* See **inharmonious.**

dishearten *verb* See **discourage.**

dishevel *verb* See **tousle.**

disheveled *adjective* See **messy.**

dishonest *adjective* Given to or marked by deliberate concealment or misrepresentation of the truth : deceitful, lying, mendacious, untruthful. See HONEST in Index. — See also **corrupt.**

dishonesty *noun* Lack of integrity : improbity. See HONEST in Index. — See also **corruption, indirection.**

dishonor *noun* See **disgrace.**

dishonor *verb* See **disgrace.**

dishonorable *adjective* See **disgraceful.**

dishonorableness *noun* See **infamy.**

disinclination *noun* See **dislike, indisposition.**

disinclined *adjective* See **indisposed.**

disinfect *verb* See **sterilize.**

disingenuous *adjective* See **insincere, underhand.**

disingenuousness *noun* See **insincerity.**

disintegrate *verb* See **break up** at **break, decay.**

disintegration *noun* See **decay.**

disinterest *noun* See **apathy, fairness.**

disinterested *adjective* See **detached, fair, neutral.**

disinterestedness *noun* See **fairness.**

disinvolve *verb* See **clear.**

disjoin *verb* See **divide.**

disjoint *verb* See **divide.**

disjunction *noun* See **division.**

disjuncture *noun* See **division.**

disk also **disc** *noun* See **circle.**

dislike *verb* To have a feeling of aversion for : disrelish, mislike.

Archaic: distaste. **Idiom:** have no use for. See LIKE in Index.

dislike *noun* An attitude or feeling of aversion : disinclination, disrelish, distaste, mislike. See LIKE in Index.

dislocate *verb* See **disturb, slip.**

dislocation *noun* See **displacement.**

disloyal *adjective* See **faithless.**

disloyalty *noun* See **faithlessness.**

dismal *adjective* See **gloomy, sad.**

dismantle *verb* See **destroy, take down** at **take.**

dismay *verb* To deprive of courage or the power to act as a result of fear, anxiety, or disgust : appall, consternate, daunt, horrify, shake, shock[1]. See FEAR in Index.

dismay *noun* A sudden or complete loss of courage in the face of trouble or danger : consternation. See FEAR in Index.

dismember *verb* See **cripple.**

dismiss *verb* **1.** To end the employment or service of : cashier, discharge, drop, release, terminate. *Informal:* ax, fire, pink-slip. *Slang:* boot[1], bounce, can, sack[1]. **Idioms:** give someone his or her walking papers, give someone the ax, give someone the gate, give someone the pink slip, let go, show someone the door. See KEEP in Index. **2.** To direct or allow to leave : send (away). *Idioms:* send about one's business, send packing, show someone the door. See KEEP in Index. **3.** To rid one's mind of : banish, cast out, dispel, shut out. See KEEP in Index. — See also **decline, drop, eject.**

dismissal *noun* The act of dismissing or the condition of being dismissed from employment : discharge, termination. *Informal:* ax. *Slang:* boot[1], bounce, sack[1]. See KEEP in Index. — See also **ejection.**

dismount *verb* See **take down** at **take**.

disobedience *noun* The condition or practice of not obeying : insubordination, noncompliance. See RESIST in Index.

disobedient *adjective* Refusing or failing to obey : insubordinate, noncompliant. See RESIST in Index.

disobey *verb* To refuse or fail to obey : break, defy, flout, transgress, violate. *Idiom:* pay no attention to. See RESIST in Index.

disorder *noun* **1.** A lack of order or regular arrangement : chaos, clutter, confusedness, confusion, derangement, disarrangement, disarray, disorderedness, disorderliness, disorganization, jumble, mess, mix-up, muddle, muss, scramble, topsy-turviness, tumble. *Slang:* snafu. See ORDER in Index. **2.** A lack of civil order or peace : anarchy, lawlessness, misrule. See ORDER, PEACE in Index. — See also **disease, disturbance, sickness.**

disorder *verb* To put out of proper order : derange, disarrange, disarray, disorganize, disrupt, disturb, jumble, mess up, mix up, muddle, tumble, unsettle, upset. See ORDER in Index. — See also **confuse, tousle, upset.**

disordered *adjective* See **confused, insane.**

disorderedness *noun* See **disorder.**

disordering *noun* See **upset.**

disorderliness *noun* The state of being messy or unkempt : messiness, sloppiness, slovenliness, untidiness. See ORDER in Index. — See also **disorder, unruliness.**

disorderly *adjective* **1.** Lacking regular or logical order : messy, unsystematic. See ORDER in Index. **2.** *Law.* Upsetting civil order or peace : riotous, rowdy. See PEACE in Index. — See also **unruly.**

disorganization *noun* See **disorder, upset.**

disorganize *verb* See **disorder.**

disoriented *adjective* See **stray.**

disown *verb* See **repudiate.**

disparage *verb* See **belittle.**

disparagement *noun* See **belittlement.**

disparaging *adjective* Tending or intending to belittle : deprecative, deprecatory, depreciative, depreciatory, derogative, derogatory, detractive, low, pejorative, slighting, uncomplimentary. See PRAISE in Index.

disparate *adjective* See **different.**

disparity *noun* See **difference, gap, inequality.**

dispassion *noun* See **fairness.**

dispassionate *adjective* See **fair, neutral.**

dispassionateness *noun* See **fairness.**

dispatch *verb* See **consume, kill**[1], **send.**

dispatch *noun* See **haste.**

dispel *verb* See **dismiss, scatter.**

dispensable *adjective* See **unnecessary.**

dispensation *noun* See **administration, distribution.**

dispense *verb* See **administer, distribute, excuse.**

dispersal *noun* See **distribution.**

disperse *verb* See **distribute, lift, scatter, spread.**

dispersion *noun* See **distribution.**

dispirit *verb* See **depress, discourage.**

dispirited *adjective* See **depressed.**

dispiriting *adjective* See **sad.**

displace *verb* See **disturb, supplant.**

displacement *noun* A change in normal place or position : dislocation, disturbance, move, movement, rearrangement, shift. See MOVE in Index.

display *verb* To make a public and usually ostentatious show of : brandish, disport, exhibit, expose, flash, flaunt, parade, show (off), sport. See SHOW in Index. — See also **bear, express, reveal, show.**

display *noun* **1.** An act of showing or displaying : demonstration, exhibit, exhibition, manifestation, show. See SHOW in Index. **2.** An impressive or ostentatious exhibition : array, panoply, parade, pomp, show, spectacle. See SHOW in Index.

displease *verb* See **offend.**

displeasing *adjective* See **unpleasant.**

displeasure *noun* See **disapproval.**

disport *verb* See **display, play.**

disport *noun* See **play.**

disposal *noun* The act of getting rid of something useless or used up : dumping, elimination, jettison, riddance. See KEEP in Index. — See also **arrangement.**

dispose *verb* To have an impact on in a certain way : incline, influence, predispose, sway. See AFFECT, LIKE in Index. — See also **arrange.**

dispose of *verb* See **discard, settle.**

disposed *adjective* See **inclined.**

disposition *noun* A person's customary manner of emotional response : complexion, humor, nature, temper, temperament. See BE in Index. — See also **arrangement, bent, character.**

dispossess *verb* See **deprive.**

dispossession *noun* See **deprivation.**

disproportion *noun* See **inequality.**

disproportionateness *noun* See **inequality.**

disprove *verb* See **refute.**

disputable *adjective* See **debatable.**

disputation *noun* See **argumentation.**

disputatious *adjective* See **argumentative.**

disputatiousness *noun* See **argumentativeness.**

dispute *verb* See **argue, contest.**

dispute *noun* See **argument.**

disqualify *verb* See **unfit.**

disquiet *verb* See **agitate.**

disquiet *noun* See **anxiety, restlessness.**

disquieting *adjective* See **disturbing.**

disquietude *noun* See **anxiety, restlessness.**

disquisition *noun* See **discourse.**

disregard *verb* See **blink, ignore, neglect.**

disregard *noun* See **neglect, thoughtlessness.**

disregardful *adjective* See **thoughtless.**

disrelish *verb* See **dislike.**

disrelish *noun* See **dislike.**

disremember *verb* See **forget.**

disreputability *noun* See **infamy.**

disreputable *adjective* See **disgraceful.**

disreputableness *noun* See **infamy.**

disrepute *noun* See **disgrace.**

disrespect *noun* Lack of proper respect : irreverence, lese majesty. See RESPECT in Index. — See also **impudence.**

disrespectful *adjective* Having or showing a lack of respect : irreverent. See RESPECT in Index. — See also **rude.**

disrobe *verb* See **bare, strip**[1].

disrupt *verb* To break up the order or progress of : disturb, upset. See ORDER in Index. — See also **disorder.**

disruption *noun* See **break, upset.**

disruptive *adjective* See **disturbing.**

dissatisfaction *noun* See **disappointment.**

dissatisfy *verb* See **disappoint.**

dissect *verb* See **analyze.**

dissection *noun* See **analysis.**

dissemblance *noun* See **act.**

dissemble *verb* See **act, disguise.**

disseminate *verb* See **advertise, distribute, spread.**

dissemination *noun* See **distribution.**

dissension *noun* See **conflict.**

dissent *verb* See **differ.**

dissent *noun* See **conflict.**

dissenter *noun* See **separatist.**

dissentience *noun* See **conflict.**

dissertation *noun* See **discourse, thesis.**

disserve *verb* See **injure.**

disservice *noun* See **injustice.**

dissever *verb* See **cut, divide.**

disseverance *noun* See **division.**

disseverment *noun* See **division.**

dissidence *noun* See **conflict.**

dissident *noun* See **separatist.**

dissimilar *adjective* See **different.**

dissimilarity *noun* See **difference.**

dissimilitude *noun* See **difference.**

dissimulate *verb* See **disguise.**

dissipate *verb* See **lift, scatter, waste.**

dissipated *adjective* See **abandoned.**

dissociate *verb* See **detach.**

dissolute *adjective* See **abandoned.**

dissoluteness *noun* See **license.**

dissolution *noun* See **death, license.**

dissolve *verb* See **break up** at **break, fade, fade out** at **fade, melt.**

dissolve *noun* See **fade-out.**

dissonance *noun* See **conflict.**

dissonant *adjective* See **incongruous, inharmonious.**

dissuade *verb* To persuade (a person) not to do something : deter, discourage, divert. *Idiom:* talk out of. See PERSUASION in Index.

distaff *noun* See **femininity.**

distaff *adjective* See **feminine.**

distance *noun* 1. The fact or condition of being far removed or apart : farness, remoteness. See BIG, NEAR in Index. 2. An extent, measured or unmeasured, of linear space : length, space, stretch. *Informal:* piece, way. See BIG in Index. — See also **detachment, expanse, remove.**

distant *adjective* Far from others in space, time, or relationship : far, faraway, far-flung, far-off, remote, removed. *Idiom:* at a distance. See NEAR, TIME in Index. — See also **cool.**

distaste *noun* See **dislike.**

distaste *verb* See **dislike.**

distasteful *adjective* See **bitter, unpalatable.**

distill *verb* See **drip.**

distinct *adjective* Distinguished from others by nature or qualities : discrete, separate, several, various. See SAME in Index. — See also **apparent, decided, sharp.**

distinction *noun* 1. The act or an instance of distinguishing : differentiation, discrimination, separation. See SAME in Index. 2. Recognition of achievement or superiority or a sign of this : accolade, honor, kudos, laurel (often used in plural). See RESPECT in Index. — See also **difference, eminence, virtue.**

distinctive *adjective* Serving to identify or set apart an individual or group : characteristic, individual, peculiar, typical, vintage. See SAME in Index.

distinctiveness *noun* See **individuality.**

distinctness *noun* See **clarity.**

distinguish *verb* 1. To recognize as being different : differentiate, discern, discriminate, know, separate, tell. See SAME in Index. 2. To make

noticeable or different : characterize, differentiate, discriminate, individualize, mark, set apart, signalize,
singularize. See SAME in Index.
3. To cause to be eminent or recognized : elevate, ennoble, exalt,
honor, signalize. See RESPECT in
Index. — See also **discern, notice.**

distinguishable *adjective* See
perceptible.

distinguished *adjective* See
eminent.

distort *verb* To give an inaccurate
view of by representing falsely or
misleadingly : belie, color, falsify,
load, misrepresent, misstate, pervert,
twist, warp, wrench, wrest. *Idiom:*
give a false coloring to. See TRUE in
Index. — See also **deform.**

distract *verb* See **agitate.**

distraction *noun* See **amusement.**

distrait *adjective* See **absent-
minded.**

distraught *adjective* See **insane.**

distress *verb* To cause suffering or
painful sorrow to : aggrieve, grieve,
hurt, injure, pain, wound. See HAPPY
in Index. — See also **worry.**

distress *noun* **1.** A state of physical or mental suffering : affliction,
agony, anguish, hurt, misery, pain,
torment, torture, woe, wound,
wretchedness. See HAPPY in Index.
2. The condition of being in need of
immediate assistance : exigence,
exigency, hot water, trouble. See
HELP in Index. — See also **anxiety.**

distressed *adjective* See **anxious.**

distressful *adjective* See **disturbing.**

distressing *adjective* See
disturbing.

distribute *verb* **1.** To give out in
portions or shares : deal (out), dispense, divide, dole out, parcel out,
portion (out), ration (out), share.
Slang: divvy. See COLLECT in
Index. **2.** To pass (something) out :

circulate, disperse, disseminate,
hand out. See COLLECT in Index.
— See also **class, spread.**

distribution *noun* **1.** The act of dis-
tributing or the condition of being
distributed : admeasurement, allocation, assignment, apportionment,
dispensation, division. See COLLECT
in Index. **2.** The passing out or
spreading about of something : circulation, dispersal, dispersion, dissemination. See COLLECT in Index.
— See also **arrangement.**

district *noun* See **area, neighborhood, territory.**

distrust *noun* Lack of trust :
doubt, leeriness, mistrust, suspicion.
See TRUST in Index.

distrust *verb* To lack trust or confidence in : doubt, misdoubt, mistrust, suspect. See TRUST in Index.
— See also **doubt.**

distrustful *adjective* Lacking trust
or confidence : doubting, leery,
mistrustful, suspicious, untrusting.
See TRUST in Index.

disturb *verb* To alter the settled
state or position of : dislocate, displace, move, shake, shift. See MOVE
in Index. — See also **agitate, annoy,
disorder, disrupt.**

disturbance *noun* An interruption
of regular procedure or of public
peace : agitation, commotion, disorder, helter-skelter, stir[1], tumult,
turbulence, turmoil, uproar.
Informal: flap, to-do. See CALM,
ORDER in Index. — See also **displacement, insanity.**

disturbing *adjective* Troubling to
the mind or emotions : disquieting,
disruptive, distressful, distressing,
intrusive, perturbing, troublesome,
troublous, unsettling, upsetting,
worrisome. See HAPPY, PAIN in
Index.

disunion *noun* See **division.**

disunite *verb* See **divide, estrange.**
disunity *noun* See **division.**
disuse *noun* See **obsoleteness.**
ditch *verb* See **discard.**
dither *noun* See **agitation.**
 dither *verb* See **hesitate.**
dithyrambic *adjective* See **passionate.**
divagate *verb* See **digress.**
divagation *noun* See **digression.**
divarication *noun* See **difference.**
dive *verb* See **fall, plunge.**
 dive *noun* See **fall, joint, plunge.**
diverge *verb* See **branch, deviate, differ, digress.**
divergence *noun* See **deviation, difference, digression, division.**
divergency *noun* See **deviation, difference, digression, division.**
divergent *adjective* See **abnormal, different.**
divers *adjective* See **several, various.**
diverse *adjective* See **different, various.**
diverseness *noun* See **variety.**
diversification *noun* See **variety.**
diversified *adjective* See **general, various.**
diversion *noun* See **amusement, deviation, play.**
diversity *noun* See **variety.**
divert *verb* See **amuse, dissuade, turn.**
diverting *adjective* See **amusing.**
divest *verb* See **bare, deprive.**
divestiture *noun* See **deprivation.**
divide *verb* **1.** To make a division into parts, sections, or branches : break up, dissever, part, partition, section, segment, separate. See ASSEMBLE, PART in Index. **2.** To become or cause to become apart one from another : break, detach, disjoin, disjoint, disunite, divorce, part, separate, split (up). *Idioms:* part

company, set at odds. See ASSEMBLE in Index. — See also **branch, distribute.**
divination *noun* See **prophecy.**
divine *adjective* **1.** Of, from, like, or being a god or God : deific, godlike, godly, heavenly, holy. See RELIGION in Index. **2.** In the service or worship of God or a god : holy, religious, sacred. See RELIGION in Index. — See also **heavenly, marvelous.**
 divine *noun* See **preacher.**
 divine *verb* See **foresee, prophesy.**
diviner *noun* See **prophet.**
divine spark *noun* See **spirit.**
divinitory *adjective* See **prophetic.**
division *noun* **1.** The act or an instance of separating one thing from another : detachment, disjunction, disjuncture, disseverance, disseverment, disunion, divorce, divorcement, parting, partition, separation, severance, split. See ASSEMBLE, PART in Index. **2.** One of the parts into which something is divided : member, part, piece, portion, section, segment, subdivision. See PART in Index. **3.** The condition of being divided, as in opinion : disunion, disunity, divergence, divergency, schism. See ASSEMBLE in Index. — See also **branch, distribution, subsidiary.**
divorce *noun* See **division.**
 divorce *verb* See **divide.**
divorcement *noun* See **division.**
divulge *verb* See **betray.**
divvy *verb* See **distribute.**
 divvy *noun* See **allotment.**
dizziness *noun* A sensation of whirling or falling : giddiness, lightheadedness, vertiginousness, vertigo, wooziness. See AWARENESS in Index.
dizzy *adjective* Having a sensation of whirling or falling : giddy, lightheaded, reeling, vertiginous, woozy.

See AWARENESS in Index. — See also
giddy.

dizzy verb See confuse.

dizzying adjective See giddy.

do verb See act, cheat, cook, cover,
fulfill, manage, perform, serve,
stage.

do for verb See serve.

do in verb See exhaust, murder.

do up verb See wrap.

do noun See party.

docile adjective See gentle,
obedient.

docket noun See program.

doctor verb See adulterate, fake,
fix, treat.

doctored adjective See impure.

doctrinaire adjective Devoted to
certain doctrines without regard to
practicability : dogmatic. See
ABILITY in Index.

doctrine noun A principle taught or
advanced for belief, as by a religious
or philosophical group : dogma,
teaching, tenet. See BELIEF in Index.

doddering adjective See senile.

dodge noun See trick.

dodge verb See avoid, evade.

doff verb See remove.

dog verb To follow closely or persistently : heel[1], tag, trail. See PRE-
CEDE in Index. — See also follow.

dogged adjective See obstinate.

doggedness noun See obstinacy.

dogma noun See doctrine.

dogmatic adjective See dictatorial,
doctrinaire.

doing noun See act.

doldrums noun See gloom.

dole noun See allotment, relief.

dole out verb See distribute.

doleful adjective See sorrowful.

dolefulness noun See gloom.

do-little noun See wastrel.

doll noun See beauty.

doll up verb See dress up at dress.

dolorous adjective See sorrowful.

dolt noun See dullard.

doltish adjective See stupid.

domain noun See area.

dome noun See head.

domestic adjective **1.** Of or relating
to the family or household : familial, family, home, homely, household. See GROUP, KIN in Index.
2. Trained or bred to live with and be
of use to people : tame. See WILD
in Index. **3.** Of, from, or within a
country's own territory : home,
internal, national, native. See
NATIVE in Index.

domesticate verb To train to live
with and be of use to people :
domesticize, gentle, master, tame.
See WILD in Index.

domesticize verb See domesticate.

domicile noun See home.

domicile verb See harbor, live[1].

dominance noun The condition or
fact of being dominant : ascendance, ascendancy, domination,
paramountcy, predominance,
preeminence, preponderance,
preponderancy, prepotency, supremacy. See OVER in Index. — See also
domination.

dominant adjective Exercising controlling power or influence : commanding, controlling, dominating,
dominative, governing, paramount,
preponderant, regnant, reigning, ruling. See OVER in Index. — See also
authoritative, ruling.

dominate verb **1.** To occupy the
preeminent position in : predominate, preponderate, prevail, reign,
rule. *Idioms:* have the ascendancy,
reign supreme. See OVER in Index.
2. To rise above, especially so as to
afford a view of : command, overlook, tower above (or over). See
OVER in Index. — See also boss,
control.

dominating *adjective* See **dominant.**

domination *noun* The act of exercising controlling power or the condition of being so controlled : command, control, dominance, dominion, mastery, reign, rule, sway. See OVER in Index. — See also **authority, dominance.**

dominative *adjective* See **dominant.**

domineer *verb* See **boss.**

domineering *adjective* See **dictatorial.**

dominion *noun* See **authority, domination, ownership.**

don *verb* To put (an article of clothing) on one's person : assume, get on, pull on, put on, slip into, slip on. See PUT ON in Index.

donate *verb* To present as a gift to a charity or cause : bestow, contribute, give, hand out. See GIVE in Index. — See also **contribute.**

donation *noun* Something given to a charity or cause : alms, benefaction, beneficence, charity, contribution, gift, handout, offering, subscription. See GIVE in Index.

donator *noun* See **donor.**

done *adjective* See **complete, through.**

done for *adjective* See **through.**

done in *adjective* See **exhausted.**

Don Juan *noun* See **gallant, philanderer, seducer.**

donnish *adjective* See **pedantic.**

donnybrook *noun* See **brawl.**

donor *noun* A person who gives to a charity or cause : benefactor, benefactress, contributor, donator, giver. See GIVE in Index.

do-nothing *adjective* See **lazy.**

do-nothing *noun* See **wastrel.**

do-nothingism *noun* See **laziness.**

doodad *noun* See **gadget.**

doodle *verb* See **mess around** at **mess.**

doohickey *noun* See **gadget.**

doom *noun* See **fate.**

doom *verb* See **condemn, fate.**

doomed *adjective* See **condemned, damned.**

doomsayer *noun* See **pessimist.**

dope *noun* See **drug, fool.**

dope *verb* See **drug.**

dope out *verb* See **design, resolve.**

doped *adjective* See **drugged.**

dopey also **dopy** *adjective* See **foolish, lethargic, stupid.**

dormancy *noun* See **abeyance.**

dormant *adjective* See **latent.**

dose *verb* See **drug.**

dot *noun* See **bit¹, point.**

dot *verb* See **speckle.**

dotage *noun* See **senility.**

dote on *verb* See **adore.**

doting *adjective* See **affectionate, senile.**

dotty *adjective* See **insane.**

double *adjective* 1. Composed of two parts or things : biform, binary, dual, duple, duplex, duplicate, geminate, twofold. See PART in Index. 2. Twice as much or as large : twofold. See BIG in Index. 3. Being or acting so as to conceal one's real intentions : double-dealing, double-faced, two-faced. See HONEST in Index. — See also **twin.**

double *noun* One exactly resembling another : duplicate, image, picture, portrait, spitting image. *Slang:* ringer. See SAME in Index. — See also **mate.**

double *verb* 1. To make or become twice as great : duplicate, geminate, redouble, twin. See BIG, INCREASE in Index. 2. To turn sharply around. Also used with *back* : about-face, reverse. See APPROACH in Index. — See also **fold.**

double-cross *verb* See **betray, deceive.**

double cross also **double-cross** *noun* See **betrayal.**

double-crosser *noun* See **betrayer.**

double-dealing *adjective* See **double.**

double-dealing *noun* See **deceit.**

double-entendre *noun* See **ambiguity.**

double-faced *adjective* See **double.**

doublet *noun* See **couple.**

double talk *noun* See **babble, gibberish.**

doubt *verb* To be uncertain, disbelieving, or skeptical about : distrust, misdoubt, mistrust, question, wonder. *Idiom:* have one's doubts. See CERTAIN in Index. — See also **distrust.**

doubt *noun* A lack of conviction or certainty : doubtfulness, dubiety, dubiousness, incertitude, mistrust, question, skepticism, suspicion, uncertainty, wonder. See CERTAIN in Index. — See also **distrust.**

doubter *noun* See **skeptic.**

doubtful *adjective* 1. Experiencing doubt : dubious, skeptical, uncertain, undecided, unsure. *Idiom:* in doubt. See CERTAIN in Index. 2. Not likely : improbable, questionable, unapt, unlikely. See LIKELY in Index. — See also **ambiguous, debatable, shady.**

doubtfully *adverb* See **skeptically.**

doubtfulness *noun* See **doubt.**

doubting *adjective* See **distrustful.**

doubting Thomas *noun* See **skeptic.**

doubtless *adverb* See **absolutely.**

doubtlessly *adverb* See **absolutely.**

dough *noun* See **money.**

doughtiness *noun* See **courage.**

doughty *adjective* See **brave.**

dour *adjective* See **bleak, glum.**

douse *verb* See **dip, extinguish, wet.**

dovetail *verb* See **fit¹.**

dowdy *adjective* See **old-fashioned, tacky².**

dower *verb* See **gift.**

down *adjective* See **depressed, sick, slow.**

down *verb* See **drop, gulp.**

down *noun* See **descent.**

down-and-out or **down and out** *noun* See **pauper.**

down-and-out or **down and out** *adjective* See **poor.**

down-and-outer *noun* See **pauper.**

down-at-heel or **down-at-the-heel** *adjective* See **shabby.**

downcast *adjective* See **depressed.**

downfall *noun* See **descent, fall, ruin.**

downgrade *verb* See **belittle, debase, demote, depreciate.**

downgrade *noun* See **descent.**

downhearted *adjective* See **depressed.**

downheartedness *noun* See **gloom.**

down payment *noun* See **deposit.**

downpour *noun* See **flood.**

downright *adjective* See **frank, utter².**

downslide *noun* See **fall.**

downswing *noun* See **fall.**

down-to-earth *adjective* See **realistic.**

downtrend *noun* See **fall.**

downturn *noun* See **fall.**

downward *adjective* See **descending.**

doze *verb* See **nap.**

doze *noun* See **nap.**

dozy *adjective* See **sleepy.**

drab *adjective* See **dull.**

drabness *noun* See **dullness.**

draft *noun* 1. Compulsory enrollment in military service : conscription, induction, levy. See GIVE in

Index. **2.** A preliminary plan or version, as of a written work : outline, rough, skeleton, sketch. See PLANNED, WORDS in Index. — See also **drink, pull.**

draft *verb* **1.** To enroll compulsorily in military service : conscript, induct, levy. See GIVE in Index. **2.** To devise and set down : draw up, formulate, frame. See WORDS in Index. **3.** To draw up a preliminary plan or version of : adumbrate, block in (or out), outline, rough in (or out), sketch. See PLANNED in Index.

drag *noun* See **pull.**

drag *verb* See **crawl, delay, pull, trail.**

dragging *adjective* See **long[1].**

draggle *verb* See **trail.**

dragoon *verb* See **coerce.**

drain *verb* To remove (a liquid) by a steady, gradual process : draw (off), let out, pump, tap[2]. See INCREASE in Index. — See also **decrease, deplete, exhaust, fatigue.**

drain *noun* See **decrease.**

drained *adjective* See **exhausted.**

draining *adjective* See **tiring.**

dram *noun* See **bit[1], drop.**

dramatic *adjective* **1.** Of or relating to drama or the theater : dramaturgic, dramaturgical, histrionic, histrionical, theatric, theatrical, thespian. See PERFORMING ARTS in Index. **2.** Suggesting drama or a stage performance, as in emotionality or suspense : histrionic, histrionical, melodramatic, sensational, spectacular, theatric, theatrical. See EXCITE, STYLE, SURPRISE in Index.

dramatics *noun* See **acting, theatrics.**

dramatize *verb* See **stage.**

dramaturgic *adjective* See **dramatic.**

dramaturgical *adjective* See **dramatic.**

drape *verb* See **clothe, sprawl.**

draw *verb* See **attract, derive, drain, evoke, infer, pour, pull, return.**

draw back *verb* See **retreat.**

draw down *verb* See **exhaust.**

draw in *verb* See **engage, withdraw.**

draw out *verb* See **lengthen.**

draw up *verb* See **draft.**

draw *noun* See **advantage, attraction, pull, tie.**

drawback *noun* See **disadvantage.**

drawn *adjective* See **haggard, wasted.**

drawn-out *adjective* See **long[1].**

dread *noun* See **fear, wonder.**

dread *verb* See **fear.**

dreadful *adjective* See **fearful, terrible.**

dreadfully *adverb* See **very.**

dream *noun* **1.** An illusory mental image : daydream, fancy, fantasy, fiction, figment, illusion, phantasm, phantasma, reverie, vision. See REAL in Index. **2.** A fervent hope, wish, or goal : aspiration, ideal. See HOPE in Index. — See also **illusion.**

dream *verb* To experience dreams or daydreams : daydream, fantasize, muse[1], woolgather. See REAL in Index. — See also **aspire.**

dream up *verb* See **invent.**

dreamer *noun* A person inclined to be imaginative or idealistic but impractical : idealist, utopian, visionary. See ABILITY, HOPE in Index.

dreamlike *adjective* See **illusive.**

dreamy *adjective* Given to daydreams or reverie : moony, visionary, woolgathering. See REAL in Index. — See also **marvelous.**

drear *adjective* See **boring.**

dreariness *noun* See **dullness.**

dreary *adjective* See **boring, gloomy.**

dreg *noun* See **deposit, trash.**

drench *verb* See **wet.**

dress *verb* **1.** To put clothes on : apparel, attire, clothe, garb, garment, invest. *Informal:* tog. See PUT ON in Index. **2.** To apply therapeutic materials to (a wound) : bandage, bind. See CARE FOR in Index. — See also **adorn, till.**

dress down *verb* See **call down** at **call.**

dress up *verb* To dress in formal or special clothing : array, attire, deck² (out), prank². *Informal:* trick out (or up). *Slang:* doll up. See ORDER, PLAIN, PUT ON in Index.

dress *noun* **1.** Articles worn to cover the body : apparel, attire, clothes, clothing, garment (used in plural), habiliment (often used in plural), raiment. *Informal:* dud (used in plural), tog (used in plural). *Slang:* thread (used in plural). See PUT ON in Index. **2.** A set or style of clothing : costume, garb, guise, habiliment (often used in plural), outfit, turnout. *Informal:* getup, rig. See PUT ON in Index. **3.** A one-piece skirted outer garment for women and children : frock, gown. See PUT ON in Index.

dressy *adjective* See **formal.**

dribble *verb* See **drip, drool.**

dribble *noun* See **drip.**

driblet *noun* See **drop.**

drift *verb* See **heap, rove, slide, wash.**

drift *noun* See **flow, heap, import, thrust.**

drill *noun* See **practice.**

drill *verb* See **exercise, impress, indoctrinate.**

drink *verb* **1.** To take into the mouth and swallow (a liquid) : imbibe, pull on, quaff, sip, sup. *Informal:* swig, toss down (or off). *Slang:* belt. *Idiom:* wet one's whistle. See MOUTH in Index. **2.** To take

alcoholic liquor, especially excessively or habitually : guzzle, imbibe, tipple. *Informal:* nip², soak. *Slang:* booze, lush², tank up. *Idioms:* bend the elbow, hit the bottle. See DRUGS in Index. **3.** To salute by raising and drinking from a glass : pledge, toast. See DESIRE, REMEMBER in Index. **4.** To take in (moisture or liquid) : absorb, imbibe, soak (up), sop up, take up. See GIVE in Index.

drink *noun* **1.** Any liquid that is fit for drinking : beverage, drinkable, liquor, potable. See DRY in Index. **2.** An act of drinking or the amount swallowed : draft, potation, pull, quaff, sip, sup, swill. *Informal:* swig. *Slang:* belt. See MOUTH in Index.

drinkable *noun* See **drink.**

drip *verb* To fall or let fall in drops of liquid : distill, dribble, drop, trickle, weep. See RISE in Index.

drip *noun* **1.** The process or sound of dripping : dribble, trickle. See RISE, SOUNDS in Index. **2.** *Slang.* An unpleasant, tiresome person : bore. *Slang:* dweeb, jerk, nerd, pill, poop². See LIKE in Index.

drippy *adjective* See **sentimental.**

drive *verb* **1.** To force to move or advance with or as if with blows or pressure : propel, push, ram, shove, thrust. See MOVE in Index. **2.** To urge to move along : herd, run. See MOVE in Index. **3.** To set or keep going : actuate, impel, mobilize, move, propel, run. See MOVE in Index. **4.** To run and control (a motor vehicle) : motor, pilot, wheel. *Slang:* tool. See MOVE in Index. — See also **hunt, impress, labor, plunge, ram, work.**

drive *noun* **1.** A trip in a motor vehicle : ride, run. *Informal:* spin, whirl. See MOVE in Index. **2.** An organized effort to accomplish a pur-

pose : campaign, crusade, movement, push. See ACTION, SEEK in
Index. **3.** An aggressive readiness
along with energy to undertake taxing efforts : enterprise, hustle, initiative, punch. *Informal:* get-up-and-
go, gumption, push. See ACTION,
TIRED, TRY in Index. — See also **way.**

drivel *noun* See **drool, nonsense.**
  drivel *verb* See **drool.**

driver *noun* A person who operates
a motor vehicle : motorist, operator. See MOVE in Index.

driving *adjective* See **vigorous.**

droit *noun* See **birthright.**

droll *adjective* See **amusing.**

drollery *noun* See **humor.**

drollness *noun* See **humor.**

drone[1] *noun* See **wastrel.**

drone[2] *verb* See **hum.**
  drone *noun* See **hum.**

drool *verb* To let saliva run from
the mouth : dribble, drivel, salivate, slaver, slobber. See DRY,
MOUTH in Index.
  drool *noun* Saliva running from
the mouth : drivel, salivation,
slaver, slobber. See DRY, MOUTH in
Index.

droop *verb* See **slouch, wilt.**

drop *noun* **1.** A quantity of liquid
falling or resting in a spherical
mass : driblet, droplet, globule. See
DRY in Index. **2.** A small amount of
liquor : dram, jigger, shot, sip, tot[1].
Informal: nip[2], slug[1]. *Slang:* snort.
See BIG, INGESTION in Index. **3.** A
downward slope or distance :
decline, declivity, descent, fall,
pitch. See RISE in Index. — See also
advantage, bit[1]**, depth, fall.**
  drop *verb* **1.** To go from a more
erect posture to a less erect posture : fall, sink, slump. See RISE in
Index. **2.** To slope downward :
decline, descend, dip, fall, pitch,
sink. See RISE in Index. **3.** To cause

to fall, as from a shot or blow :
bring down, cut down, down, fell[1],
flatten, floor, ground, knock down,
level, prostrate, strike down, throw.
Slang: deck[1]. *Idiom:* lay low. See
RISE in Index. **4.** To cease consideration or treatment of : dismiss,
give over, give up, skip. *Idioms:* have
done with, wash one's hands of. See
KEEP in Index. **5.** To take or leave
out : eliminate, omit, remove. See
INCLUDE in Index. **6.** To suffer the
loss of : forfeit, lose. *Idiom:* kiss
good-by to. See GET in Index. — See
also **collapse, die, dismiss, drip, fall,
lower**[2]**.**
  drop by *verb* See **visit.**
  drop in *verb* See **visit.**
  drop off *verb* See **slip.**

droplet *noun* See **drop.**

drop-off *noun* See **fall.**

drossy *adjective* See **worthless.**

droughty *adjective* See **dry.**

drove *noun* See **crowd.**

drown *verb* See **flood.**

drowsy *adjective* See **sleepy.**

drub *verb* See **beat, overwhelm,
slam.**

drubbing *noun* See **defeat.**

drudge *verb* See **grind.**
  drudge *noun* One who works or
toils tirelessly : fag, grub, plodder,
slave. *Informal:* grind, workhorse.
See WORK in Index.

drudgery *noun* See **labor.**

drug *noun* **1.** A substance used in
the treatment of disease : medicament, medication, medicine, pharmaceutical. See DRUGS in Index.
2. A substance that affects the central nervous system and is often
addictive : hallucinogen, narcotic,
opiate. *Informal:* dope. See DRUGS
in Index.
  drug *verb* To administer or add a
drug to : dose, medicate, narcotize,

opiate, physic. *Informal:* dope (up).
See DRUGS in Index.

drugged *adjective* Stupefied, intoxicated, or otherwise influenced by
the taking of drugs : *Informal:*
doped. *Slang:* high, hopped-up, lit
(up), potted, spaced-out, stoned,
turned-on, wiped-out, zonked. See
DRUGS in Index.

drunk *adjective* Stupefied, excited,
or muddled with alcoholic liquor :
besotted, crapulent, crapulous,
drunken, inebriate, inebriated, intoxicated, sodden, tipsy. *Informal:*
cockeyed, stewed. *Slang:* blind,
bombed, boozed, boozy, crocked,
high, lit (up), loaded, looped, pickled,
pixilated, plastered, potted, sloshed,
smashed, soused, stinking, stinko,
stoned, tight, zonked. *Idioms:* drunk
as a skunk, half-seas over, high as a
kite, in one's cups, three sheets in (or
to) the wind. See DRUGS in Index.

drunk *noun* See **bender, drunkard.**

drunkard *noun* A person who is
habitually drunk : drunk, inebriate,
sot, tippler. *Slang:* boozehound,
boozer, lush[2], rummy[1], soak, souse,
sponge, stiff. See DRUGS in Index.

drunken *adjective* See **drunk.**

drunkenness *noun* The condition
of being intoxicated with alcoholic
liquor : crapulence, inebriation,
inebriety, insobriety, intoxication,
tipsiness. See DRUGS in Index.

dry *adjective* 1. Having little or no
liquid or moisture : anhydrous,
arid, bone-dry, moistureless, sere,
waterless. See DRY in Index.
2. Having little or no precipitation :
arid, droughty, rainless, thirsty. See
DRY in Index. 3. With little or no
emotion or expression : impassive,
matter-of-fact, unemotional. See
ATTITUDE, EXCITE in Index. — See
also **bare, boring, dull, harsh, sour,
thirsty.**

dry *verb* To make or become free
of moisture. Also used with *out* :
dehydrate, desiccate, exsiccate,
parch. See DRY in Index. — See also
harden.

dry up *verb* 1. To make or become
no longer fresh or shapely because of
loss of moisture : mummify, sear,
shrivel, wither, wizen. See DRY in
Index. 2. To make or become no
longer active or productive :
deplete, desiccate, give out, play out,
run out. See CONTINUE in Index.

dryness *noun* See **dullness,
temperance.**

dual *adjective* See **double, twin.**

dub *verb* See **name.**

dub *noun* See **blunderer.**

dubiety *noun* See **doubt.**

dubious *adjective* See **ambiguous,
doubtful.**

dubiously *adverb* See **skeptically.**

dubiousness *noun* See **doubt.**

dubitable *adjective* See **ambiguous.**

duck *verb* See **avoid, dip, evade.**

duck *noun* See **plunge.**

duck soup *noun* See **breeze.**

ductile *adjective* See **flexible,
malleable.**

ductility *noun* See **flexibility.**

dud *noun* See **dress, failure.**

dudgeon *noun* See **offense.**

due *adjective* 1. Owed as a debt :
outstanding, owed, owing, payable,
receivable, unpaid, unsettled. See
PAY in Index. 2. Known to be about
to arrive : anticipated, expected,
scheduled. See SURPRISE in Index.
— See also **just.**

due *noun* Something justly
deserved : comeuppance, desert[2]
(often used in plural), guerdon, recompense, reward, wage (often used
in plural). *Informal:* lump[1] (used in
plural). *Idioms:* what is coming to
one, what one has coming. See
REWARD in Index. — See also **debt.**

due *adverb* See **directly.**

duel *verb* See **contend.**

due process *noun* See **justice.**

duet *noun* See **couple.**

dulcet *adjective* See **melodious.**

dulcify *verb* See **pacify.**

dull *adjective* **1.** Lacking responsiveness or alertness : benumbed, insensible, insensitive, numb, stuporous, torpid, unresponsive, wooden. See AWARENESS in Index. **2.** Not physically sharp or keen : blunt. See SHARP in Index. **3.** Lacking liveliness, charm, or surprise : arid, aseptic, colorless, drab, dry, earthbound, flat, flavorless, lackluster, lifeless, lusterless, matter-of-fact, pedestrian, prosaic, spiritless, sterile, stodgy, unimaginative, uninspired. See EXCITE in Index. **4.** Lacking vividness in color : dim, drab, flat, muddy, murky. See COLORS in Index. **5.** Lacking gloss and luster : dim, flat, lackluster, lusterless, mat. See LIGHT in Index. — See also **backward, blind, boring, depressed, insensitive, slow.**

dull *verb* **1.** To make or become less sharp-edged : blunt, turn. *Idiom:* take the edge off. See SHARP in Index. **2.** To make or become less keen or responsive : dim, hebetate, stupefy. See AWARENESS in Index. — See also **deaden, obscure.**

dullard *noun* A mentally dull person : blockhead, chump[1], clod, dolt, dummkopf, dummy, dunce, numskull, thickhead. *Slang:* dimwit, dumbbell, dumbo. See ABILITY in Index.

dullness also **dulness** *noun* A lack of excitement, liveliness, or interest : asepticism, blandness, colorlessness, drabness, dreariness, dryness, flatness, flavorlessness, insipidity, insipidness, jejuneness, lifelessness, sterileness, sterility, stodginess, vapidity, vapidness, weariness. See EXCITE in Index. — See also **lethargy.**

dumb *adjective* Lacking the power or faculty of speech : aphonic, inarticulate, mute, speechless, voiceless. See WORDS in Index. — See also **speechless, stupid.**

dumbbell *noun* See **dullard.**

dumbfound also **dumfound** *verb* See **stagger.**

dumbness *noun* See **silence.**

dumbo *noun* See **dullard.**

dummkopf *noun* See **dullard.**

dummy *noun* See **dullard.**

dump *verb* See **discard, sell off** at **sell, unload.**

dumping *noun* See **disposal.**

dumps *noun* See **gloom.**

dumpy *adjective* See **stocky.**

dunce *noun* See **dullard.**

dunk *verb* See **dip.**

dunk *noun* See **plunge.**

duo *noun* See **couple, pair.**

dupable *adjective* See **easy.**

dupe *noun* A person who is easily deceived or victimized : butt[3], fool, gull, lamb, pushover, victim. *Informal:* sucker. *Slang:* fall guy, gudgeon, mark, monkey, patsy, pigeon, sap[1]. *Chiefly British:* mug. See WISE in Index. — See also **pawn[2].**

dupe *verb* See **deceive.**

duple *adjective* See **double.**

duplex *adjective* See **double.**

duplicate *noun* See **copy, double, mate.**

duplicate *verb* See **copy, double, repeat.**

duplicate *adjective* See **double.**

duplicitous *adjective* See **underhand.**

duplicity *noun* See **deceit.**

durability *noun* See **soundness.**

durable *adjective* See **continuing.**

duration *noun* See **continuation, life, term.**

duress *noun* See **force.**

dusk *noun* See **evening.**

duskiness *noun* See **dark.**

dusky *adjective* See **blackish, dark.**

dust *verb* See **sprinkle.**

dusting *noun* See **defeat.**

dusty *adjective* See **fine¹.**

Dutch *noun* See **predicament.**

duteous *adjective* See **deferential.**

dutiful *adjective* See **deferential.**

duty *noun* **1.** An act or course of action that is demanded of one, as by position, custom, law, or religion : burden¹, charge, commitment, imperative, must, need, obligation, responsibility. See OBLIGATION in Index. **2.** The condition of being put to use : application, employment, service, use, utilization. See USED in Index. — See also **task, tax.**

dwarf *adjective* See **tiny.**

dweeb *noun* See **drip.**

dwell *verb* See **brood, consist, live¹.**

dwelling *noun* See **home.**

dwindle *verb* See **decrease.**

dye *noun* See **color.**

dye *verb* See **color, dip.**

dyestuff *noun* See **color.**

dynamic *adjective* See **energetic, forceful, vigorous.**

dynamical *adjective* See **energetic, forceful, vigorous.**

dynamite *verb* See **destroy.**

dynamo *noun* See **eager beaver.**

dysphoria *noun* See **gloom.**

dysphoric *adjective* See **depressed.**

E

eager *adjective* Intensely desirous or interested : agog, ardent, athirst, avid, bursting, impatient, keen¹, solicitous, thirsting, thirsty. *Informal:* raring. *Idioms:* champing at the bit, ready and willing. See CONCERN in Index.

eager beaver *noun* *Informal.* An intensely energetic, enthusiastic person : dynamo, hustler. *Informal:* go-getter, live wire. See CONCERN in Index.

ear *noun* See **hearing.**

earlier *adverb* **1.** At a time in the past : already, before, erstwhile, formerly, once, previously. *Archaic:* aforetime, beforetime. See PRECEDE in Index. **2.** Up to this time : before, heretofore, previously, yet. See PRECEDE in Index. **3.** Until then : before, beforehand. See PRECEDE in Index.

earlier *adjective* See **advance, past.**

earliest *adjective* See **first.**

early *adjective* **1.** At or near the start of a period, development, or series : beginning, first, initial. See START in Index. **2.** Of, existing, or occurring in a distant period : ancient, antediluvian, primitive. See START in Index. **3.** Developing, occurring, or appearing before the expected time : precocious, premature, untimely. See TIME in Index.

early *adverb* Before the expected time : ahead, beforehand, betimes. *Idioms:* ahead of time, in advance, with time to spare. See TIME in Index.

earmark *verb* See **appropriate.**

earn *verb* **1.** To receive, as wages, for one's labor : gain, get, make, win. *Informal:* pull down. *Idioms:* earn (or make) a living, earn one's keep. See GIVE, MONEY in Index. **2.** To acquire as a result of one's behavior or effort : deserve, gain, get, merit, win. *Informal:* rate¹. See GET in Index. — See also **return.**

earnest¹ *adjective* See **grave², serious.**

earnest² *noun* See **pawn¹.**

earnestness *noun* See **seriousness.**

earnings *noun* See **gain, wage.**

earshot *noun* See **hearing.**

earsplitting *adjective* See **loud.**

earth *noun* The celestial body where humans live. Often uppercase : world. See PLACE in Index. — See also **mankind.**

earthbound also **earth-bound** *adjective* See **dull, earthly.**

earthen *adjective* See **earthly, earthy.**

earthlike *adjective* See **earthy.**

earthly *adjective* **1.** Relating to or characteristic of the earth or of human life on earth : earthbound, earthen, earthy, mundane, secular, tellurian, telluric, temporal, terrene, terrestrial, worldly. See BODY, CULTURE, PLACE in Index. **2.** Capable of being anticipated, considered, or imagined : conceivable, imaginable, likely, mortal, possible, thinkable. *Idioms:* humanly possible, within the bounds (or range or realm) of possibility. See POSSIBLE in Index.

earthquake *noun* See **tremor.**

earthy *adjective* Consisting of or resembling soil : earthen, earthlike, terrestrial. See MATTER in Index. — See also **earthly, racy.**

ease *noun* **1.** Freedom from constraint, formality, embarrassment, or awkwardness : casualness, easiness, informality, naturalness, poise, spontaneity, unceremoniousness, unrestraint. See RESTRAINT, TIGHTEN in Index. **2.** The ability to perform without apparent effort : easiness, effortlessness, facileness, facility, readiness. See EASY in Index. — See also **prosperity, relief, rest¹.**

ease *verb* **1.** To reduce in tension, pressure, or rigidity : let up, loose, loosen, relax, slack, slacken, untighten. See TIGHTEN in Index. **2.** To make less difficult : expedite, facilitate. *Idioms:* clear (or prepare) the way for, grease the wheels, open the door for (or to). See EASY in Index **3.** To maneuver gently and slowly into place : glide, slide, slip. See CAREFUL, EASY in Index. — See also **edge, relieve, subside.**

ease off *verb* See **weaken.**

easeful *adjective* See **comfortable.**

easiness *noun* See **ease.**

easy *adjective* **1.** Posing no difficulty : effortless, facile, simple, smooth. *Informal:* snap. *Idioms:* easy as ABC, easy as falling off a log, easy as one-two-three, easy as pie, like taking candy from a baby, nothing to it. See EASY in Index. **2.** Easily imposed on or tricked : credulous, dupable, exploitable, gullible, naive, susceptible. See WISE in Index. — See also **comfortable, easygoing, gradual, light², prosperous, smooth, tolerant, wanton.**

easygoing also **easy-going** *adjective* Unconstrained by rigid standards or ceremony : casual, easy, informal, natural, relaxed, spontaneous, unceremonious, unrestrained. *Informal:* laid-back. See PLAIN, TIGHTEN in Index.

easy street *noun* See **prosperity.**

eat *verb* To take (food) into the body as nourishment : consume, devour, fare, ingest, partake. *Slang:* chow. *Idioms:* break bread, have (or take) a bite. See INGESTION in Index. — See also **bite, consume.**

eat up *verb* *Slang.* To be avidly interested in : devour, feast on, relish. See CONCERN in Index. — See also **adore, consume, exhaust.**

eatable *adjective* See **edible.**

eats *noun* See **food.**

eavesdrop *verb* See **spy.**

ebb *verb* See **decrease, recede, subside.**

ebb *noun* See **wane.**

ebon *adjective* See **black.**

ebony *adjective* See **black.**

ebullient *adjective* See **exuberant.**

eccentric *adjective* Deviating from the customary : bizarre, cranky, curious, erratic, freakish, idiosyncratic, odd, outlandish, peculiar, quaint, queer, quirky, singular, strange, unnatural, unusual, weird. *Slang:* kooky, screwball. *British Slang:* rum, rummy2. See USUAL in Index.

eccentric *noun* See **crackpot.**

eccentricity *noun* Peculiar behavior : idiosyncrasy, peculiarity, quirk, quirkiness, singularity. See USUAL in Index.

ecclesiastic *noun* See **preacher.**

ecclesiastical *adjective* See **spiritual.**

echinate *adjective* See **thorny.**

echo *noun* **1.** Repetition of sound via reflection from a surface : repercussion, reverberation. See SOUNDS in Index. **2.** Imitative reproduction, as of the style of another : imitation, reflection, reflex, repetition. See SAME in Index. **3.** One who mindlessly imitates another : imitator, mimic, parrot. See SAME in Index.

echo *verb* **1.** To send back the sound of : rebound, reecho, reflect, repeat, resound, reverberate. See SOUNDS in Index. **2.** To copy (another) slavishly : image, imitate, mimic, mirror, parrot, reflect, repeat. See SAME in Index.

echoic *adjective* Imitating sounds : imitative, onomatopoeic, onomatopoetic. See SAME, SOUNDS in Index.

echoism *noun* The formation of words in imitation of sounds : ono-

matopoeia. See SAME, SOUNDS in Index.

eclipse *verb* See **obscure.**

economical *adjective* Careful in the use of material resources : canny, chary, frugal, provident, prudent, saving, Scotch, sparing, thrifty. See CAREFUL, SAVE in Index.

economize *verb* To use without wasting : conserve, save, spare. See SAVE in Index.

economy *noun* Careful use of material resources : frugality, providence, prudence, thrift, thriftiness. See SAVE in Index.

ecstasy *noun* See **heaven.**

ecumenical *adjective* See **universal.**

edacious *adjective* See **greedy, voracious.**

edacity *noun* See **voracity.**

eddy *verb* See **swirl.**

edge *noun* **1.** The cutting part of a sharp instrument : blade. See SHARP in Index. **2.** A cutting quality : bite, incisiveness, keenness, sharpness, sting. See SHARP in Index. — See also **advantage, border, skirt, verge.**

edge *verb* To advance carefully and gradually : ease, sidle. See CAREFUL, MOVE in Index. — See also **border, insinuate, sharpen.**

edging *noun* See **border.**

edgy *adjective* Feeling or exhibiting nervous tension : fidgety, jittery, jumpy, nervous, restive, restless, skittish, tense, twitchy. *Slang:* uptight. *Idioms:* a bundle of nerves, all wound up, on edge. See TIGHTEN in Index.

edible *adjective* Fit to be eaten : comestible, eatable, esculent. See INGESTION in Index.

edible *noun* See **food.**

edict *noun* See **announcement, law, ruling.**

edification *noun* See **illumination.**

edifice *noun* See **building.**

edify *verb* See **illuminate.**

edifying *adjective* See **cultural, educational.**

educable *adjective* Capable of being educated : teachable, trainable. See TEACH in Index.

educate *verb* To impart knowledge and skill to : coach, discipline, instruct, school, teach, train, tutor. See TEACH in Index. — See also **inform.**

educated *adjective* Having an education : enlightened, informed, lettered, literate. See KNOWLEDGE in Index. — See also **cultured, informed.**

education *noun* **1.** The act, process, or art of imparting knowledge and skill : instruction, pedagogics, pedagogy, schooling, teaching, training, tuition, tutelage, tutoring. See TEACH in Index. **2.** Known facts, ideas, and skill that have been imparted : erudition, instruction, knowledge, learning, scholarship, science. See KNOWLEDGE in Index.

educational *adjective* Serving to educate or inform : edifying, educative, enlightening, illuminative, informative, instructional, instructive. See TEACH in Index.

educative *adjective* See **educational.**

educator *noun* One who educates : instructor, pedagogue, teacher, trainer, tutor. See TEACH in Index.

educe *verb* See **derive, evoke.**

eerie or **eery** *adjective* See **weird.**

efface *verb* See **cancel.**

effect *noun* **1.** Something brought about by a cause : aftermath, consequence, corollary, end product, event, fruit, harvest, issue, outcome, precipitate, ramification, result, resultant, sequel, sequence, sequent, upshot. See CAUSE in Index. **2.** The power or capacity to produce a desired result : effectiveness, effectuality, effectualness, efficaciousness, efficacy, efficiency, influence, potency. See AFFECT in Index. **3.** The condition of being in full force or operation : actualization, being, materialization, realization. See BE in Index. **4.** One's portable property. Used in plural : belonging (often used in plural), good (used in plural), lares and penates, personal effects, personal property, possession (used in plural), property, thing (often used in plural). *Informal:* stuff. *Law:* chattel, movable (often used in plural). See OWNED in Index.

effect *verb* To bring about and carry to a successful conclusion : bring off, carry out, carry through, effectuate, execute, put through. *Informal:* swing. See DO in Index. — See also **cause, enforce.**

effective *adjective* **1.** Producing or able to produce a desired effect : effectual, efficacious, efficient, productive. See THRIVE in Index. **2.** In effect : operational, operative. See BE in Index. — See also **forceful.**

effectiveness *noun* See **effect.**

effectual *adjective* See **effective.**

effectuality *noun* See **effect.**

effectualness *noun* See **effect.**

effectuate *verb* See **cause, effect.**

effectuation *noun* See **performance.**

effeminacy *noun* The quality of being effeminate : effeminateness, femininity, sissiness, unmanliness, womanishness. See GENDER in Index.

effeminate *adjective* Having qualities more appropriate to women than to men : epicene, feminine, sissified, sissyish, unmanly, womanish. See GENDER in Index.

effeminateness *noun* See **effeminacy.**

effervesce verb See **foam**.

effervescent adjective See **exuberant**.

efficacious adjective See **effective**.

efficaciousness noun See **effect**.

efficacy noun See **effect**.

efficiency noun The quality of being efficient : productivity. See INDUSTRIOUS, THRIVE in Index. — See also **effect**.

efficient adjective Acting effectively with minimal waste : productive. See INDUSTRIOUS, THRIVE in Index. — See also **effective**.

effloresce verb See **bloom**[1].

efflorescence noun See **bloom**[1].

efflux noun See **spate**.

effort noun The use of energy to do something : endeavor, exertion, pain (used in plural), strain[1], striving, struggle, trouble, while. Informal: elbow grease. See WORK in Index. — See also **accomplishment, attempt, task**.

effortful adjective See **burdensome, forced**.

effortless adjective See **easy, smooth**.

effortlessness noun See **ease**.

effrontery noun See **impudence**.

effulgent adjective See **bright**.

effuse verb See **pour**.

egg on verb See **provoke**.

ego noun See **egotism, pride, self**.

egocentric adjective Concerned with the person rather than with society : egoistic, egoistical, individualistic. See SELF in Index. — See also **egotistic**.

egocentric noun See **egotist**.

egocentricity noun See **egoism**.

egocentrism noun See **egoism**.

egoism noun Concern only for oneself : egocentricity, egocentrism, egomania, self-absorption, self-centeredness, self-involvement, selfishness. See SELF in Index. — See also **egotism**.

egoist noun See **egotist**.

egoistic adjective See **egocentric, egotistic**.

egoistical adjective See **egocentric, egotistic**.

egomania noun See **egoism**.

egomaniac noun See **egotist**.

egomaniacal adjective See **egotistic**.

egotism noun 1. An exaggerated belief in one's own importance : egoism, self-importance. Informal: bighead, bigheadedness, swelled head. See SELF-LOVE in Index. 2. A regarding of oneself with undue favor : amour-propre, conceit, ego, egoism, narcissism, pride, vainglory, vainness, vanity. Slang: ego trip. See SELF-LOVE in Index.

egotist noun A conceited, self-centered person : egocentric, egoist, egomaniac, narcissist. Informal: swellhead. See SELF, SELF-LOVE in Index.

egotistic adjective 1. Thinking too highly of oneself : conceited, egoistic, egoistical, egotistical, narcissistic, vain, vainglorious. Informal: bigheaded, stuck-up, swellheaded. See SELF-LOVE in Index. 2. Concerned only with oneself : egocentric, egoistic, egoistical, egomaniacal, egotistical, self-absorbed, self-centered, self-involved, selfish, self-seeking, self-serving. Idiom: wrapped up in oneself. See SELF in Index.

egotistical adjective See **egotistic**.

ego trip noun See **egotism**.

egregious adjective See **flagrant**.

egregiousness noun See **flagrancy**.

egress noun See **departure**.

eidolon noun See **ghost**.

ejaculate verb See **exclaim**.

ejaculation noun See **exclamation**.

eject *verb* **1.** To put out by force : bump, dismiss, evict, expel, oust, throw out. *Informal:* chuck. *Slang:* boot[1] (out), bounce, kick out. *Idioms:* give someone the boot, give someone the heave-ho (or old heave-ho), send packing, show someone the door, throw out on one's ear. See KEEP in Index. **2.** To catapult oneself from a disabled aircraft : bail out, jump. See APPROACH in Index. — See also **erupt**.

ejection *noun* The act of ejecting or the state of being ejected : dismissal, ejectment, eviction, expulsion, ouster. *Slang:* boot[1], bounce. See KEEP in Index.

ejectment *noun* See **ejection**.

elaborate *adjective* Complexly detailed : complicated, fancy, intricate. See PLAIN in Index. — See also **complex**.

elaborate *verb* **1.** To express at greater length or in greater detail : amplify, develop, dilate, enlarge, expand, expatiate, labor. See EXPLAIN in Index. **2.** To disclose bit by bit : develop, evolve. *Idioms:* fill in the details, go into detail. See SHOW in Index.

élan *noun* See **spirit**.

élan vital *noun* See **spirit**.

elapse *verb* See **go**.

elastic *adjective* See **adaptable**, **flexible**.

elasticity *noun* See **flexibility**, **resilience**.

elate *verb* To raise the spirits of : animate, buoy (up), elevate, exhilarate, flush, inspire, inspirit, lift, uplift. *Obsolete:* exalt. See HAPPY in Index.

elate *adjective* See **elated**.

elated *adjective* Feeling great delight and joy : elate, elevated, overjoyed. *Slang:* up. See HAPPY in Index.

elatedness *noun* See **elation**.

elation *noun* High spirits : animation, elatedness, euphoria, exaltation, exhilaration, inspiration, lift, uplift. See HAPPY in Index.

elbow grease *noun* See **effort**.

elbowroom *noun* See **freedom**, **room**.

elder *noun* See **senior**, **superior**.

elder *adjective* See **senior**.

elderliness *noun* See **age**.

elderly *adjective* See **old**.

elect *verb* To select by vote for an office : ballot, vote (in). See CHOICE, POLITICS in Index. — See also **choose**.

elect *noun* One that is selected : choice, chosen, pick, select. See CHOICE in Index.

elect *adjective* See **select**.

election *noun* See **choice**.

elective *adjective* See **optional**.

elector *noun* One who votes : balloter, voter. See CHOICE, POLITICS in Index.

electrify *verb* See **carry away** at **carry**, **startle**.

eleemosynary *adjective* See **benevolent**.

elegance *noun* Refined, effortless beauty of manner, form, and style : elegancy, grace, polish, urbanity. See BEAUTIFUL, STYLE in Index.

elegancy *noun* See **elegance**.

elegant *adjective* Of such tasteful beauty as to elicit admiration : exquisite, graceful. See BEAUTIFUL, STYLE in Index. — See also **delicate**.

element *noun* **1.** A fundamental irreducible constituent of a whole : basic, essential, fundamental, rudiment (often used in plural). *Idiom:* part and parcel. See PART in Index. **2.** One of the individual entities contributing to a whole : building block, component, constituent, factor, ingredient, integrant, part. See

PART in Index. **3.** An individually considered portion of a whole : article, detail, item, particular, point. See PART in Index.

elemental *adjective* Of or being an irreducible element : basic, elementary, essential, fundamental, primitive, ultimate, underlying. See SURFACE in Index. — See also **constitutional.**

elementary *adjective* Of or treating the most basic aspects : basal, basic, beginning, rudimental, rudimentary. See SIMPLE, START in Index. — See also **elemental.**

elephantine *adjective* See **giant, ponderous.**

elevate *verb* **1.** To move (something) to a higher position : boost, heave, hoist, lift, pick up, raise, rear[2], take up, uphold, uplift, upraise, uprear. See RISE in Index. **2.** To increase markedly in level or intensity, especially of sound : amplify, heighten, raise. See INCREASE in Index. — See also **distinguish, elate, exalt, promote.**

elevated *adjective* **1.** Being positioned above a given level : raised. See RISE in Index. **2.** Being on a high intellectual or moral level : high-minded, moral, noble. See HIGH in Index. **3.** Abnormally increased, especially in intensity : heightened, high, raised. See INCREASE in Index. **4.** Exceedingly dignified in form, tone, or style : eloquent, exalted, grand, high, high-flown, lofty. See HIGH, STYLE in Index. — See also **elated, exalted.**

elevation *noun* The distance of something from a given level : altitude, height. See HIGH in Index. — See also **advancement, exaltation.**

elicit *verb* See **evoke.**

eligibility *noun* See **qualification.**

eligible *adjective* **1.** Satisfying certain requirements, as for selection : fit[1], fitted, qualified, suitable, worthy. See ABILITY in Index. **2.** Deemed suitable for marriage : marriageable. *Archaic:* marriable. See MARRIAGE in Index.

eliminate *verb* **1.** To get rid of, especially by banishment or execution : eradicate, liquidate, purge, remove, wipe out. *Idioms:* do away with, put an end to. See HELP, KEEP in Index. **2.** To discharge (wastes or foreign substances) from the body : evacuate, excrete. *Medicine:* purge. See KEEP in Index. — See also **drop, exclude.**

elimination *noun* **1.** The act or process of eliminating : clearance, eradication, liquidation, purge, removal, riddance. See KEEP in Index. **2.** The act or process of discharging bodily wastes or foreign substances : evacuation, excretion, purgation. *Medicine:* catharsis. See KEEP in Index. — See also **disposal.**

eliminative *adjective* Of, relating to, or tending to eliminate : cathartic, eliminatory, evacuant, evacuative, excretory, purgative. See KEEP in Index.

eliminatory *adjective* See **eliminative.**

elite or **élite** *noun* See **best, society.**

elite or **élite** *adjective* See **noble.**

elitist or **élitist** *adjective* See **snobbish.**

elitist or **élitist** *noun* See **snob.**

elixir *noun* See **cure.**

elocution *noun* See **oratory.**

elocutionary *adjective* See **oratorical.**

elongate *verb* See **lengthen.**

elongate *adjective* See **long[1].**

elongated *adjective* See **long[1].**

elongation *noun* See **extension.**

eloquence *noun* Vivid, effective, or persuasive communication in speech or artistic performance : articulacy, articulateness, eloquentness, expression, expressiveness, expressivity, facundity. See WORDS in Index.

eloquent *adjective* Fluently persuasive and forceful : articulate, facund, silver-tongued, smooth-spoken. See WORDS in Index. — See also **elevated, expressive.**

eloquentness *noun* See **eloquence.**

elucidate *verb* See **clarify.**

elucidation *noun* See **explanation.**

elucidative *adjective* See **explanatory.**

elude *verb* See **avoid, escape, lose.**

elusive *adjective* See **evasive.**

emaciated *adjective* See **wasted.**

emanate *verb* See **stem.**

emancipate *verb* See **free.**

emancipation *noun* See **liberty.**

embark *verb* See **start.**

embarrass *verb* To cause (a person) to be self-consciously distressed : abash, chagrin, confound, confuse, discomfit, discomfort, disconcert, discountenance, faze, mortify. *Idioms:* put on the spot, throw for a loop. See PAIN in Index. — See also **complicate.**

embarrassment *noun* Self-conscious distress : abashment, chagrin, confusion, discomfiture, discomposure. See PAIN in Index. — See also **excess.**

embed also **imbed** *verb* See **fix.**

embellish *verb* See **adorn, grace.**

embellishment *noun* See **adornment.**

embitter *verb* To make or become bitter : sour. See HAPPY in Index.

embittered *adjective* See **resentful.**

embitterment *noun* See **resentment.**

emblem *noun* See **symbol.**

emblematic *adjective* See **symbolic.**

emblematical *adjective* See **symbolic.**

embodiment *noun* A physical entity typifying an abstraction : exteriorization, externalization, incarnation, manifestation, materialization, objectification, personalization, personification, substantiation, type. *Rhetoric:* prosopopeia. See SUBSTITUTE in Index.

embody *verb* **1.** To represent (an abstraction, for example) in or as if in bodily form : body forth, exteriorize, externalize, incarnate, manifest, materialize, objectify, personalize, personify, substantiate. See SUBSTITUTE in Index. **2.** To make a part of a united whole : combine, incorporate, integrate. See INCLUDE in Index. — See also **contain.**

embolden *verb* See **encourage.**

embosom *verb* See **embrace.**

embrace *verb* To put one's arms around affectionately : clasp, enfold, hold, hug, press, squeeze. *Slang:* clinch. *Archaic:* bosom, clip[2], embosom. See TOUCH in Index. — See also **accept, adopt, contain.**

embrace *noun* The act of embracing : clasp, hug, squeeze. *Slang:* clinch. See TOUCH in Index.

embracement *noun* See **adoption.**

embrangle *verb* See **involve.**

embranglement *noun* See **entanglement.**

embroil *verb* See **involve.**

embroilment *noun* See **entanglement.**

embryo *noun* See **germ.**

emend *verb* See **correct, revise.**

emendate *verb* See **revise.**

emendation *noun* See **revision.**

emendatory *adjective* See **corrective.**

emerge *verb* See **appear, dawn.**

emergence *noun* See **appearance**.

emergency *noun* See **crisis**.
emergency *adjective* See **auxiliary**.

emergent *adjective* See **burning**.

emigrant *noun* One who emigrates : immigrant, migrant, transmigrant. See APPROACH in Index.

emigrate *verb* To leave one's native land and settle in another : immigrate, migrate, transmigrate. See APPROACH in Index.

emigration *noun* Departure from one's native land to settle in another : exodus, immigration, migration, transmigration. See APPROACH in Index.

émigré *noun* One forced to emigrate, usually for political reasons : deportee, exile, expatriate, expellee. See APPROACH in Index. — See also **foreigner**.

eminence *noun* A position of exalted widely recognized importance : distinction, eminency, fame, glory, illustriousness, luster, mark, notability, note, preeminence, prestige, prominence, prominency, renown. See IMPORTANT, KNOWLEDGE, RESPECT in Index. — See also **dignitary, hill**.

eminency *noun* See **eminence**.

eminent *adjective* Widely known and esteemed : celebrated, distinguished, famed, famous, great, illustrious, notable, noted, preeminent, prestigious, prominent, redoubtable, renowned. See KNOWLEDGE, RESPECT in Index.

eminently *adverb* See **very**.

emit *verb* To discharge material, as vapor or fumes, usually suddenly and violently : give, give forth, give off, give out, issue, let off, let out, release, send forth, throw off, vent. See FREE, MOVE in Index. — See also **shed**.

emolument *noun* See **wage**.

emote *verb* See **emotionalize**.

emotion *noun* A complex and usually strong subjective response, such as love or hate : affection, affectivity, feeling, sentiment. See FEELINGS in Index.

emotional *adjective* **1.** Readily stirred by emotion : feeling, sensitive. See FEELINGS in Index. **2.** Relating to, arising from, or appealing to the emotions : affective, emotive. See FEELINGS in Index.

emotionalize *verb* To make an emotional display : emote, gush. See FEELINGS in Index.

emotionless *adjective* See **cold**.

emotive *adjective* See **emotional**.

empathetic *adjective* See **understanding**.

empathic *adjective* See **understanding**.

empathize *verb* See **identify, sympathize**.

empathy *noun* See **pity, sympathy**.

emphasis *noun* Special weight placed upon something considered important : accent, accentuation, stress. See IMPORTANT in Index.

emphasize *verb* To accord emphasis to : accent, accentuate, feature, highlight, italicize, play up, point up, stress, underline, underscore. See IMPORTANT in Index.

emphatic *adjective* **1.** Expressed or performed with emphasis : forceful, resounding. See STRONG in Index. **2.** Bold and definite in character : assertive, forceful, insistent. See STRONG in Index.

emphatically *adverb* See **flatly**.

emplace *verb* See **position**.

emplacement *noun* See **position**.

employ *verb* To obtain the use or services of : engage, hire, retain, take on. *Idiom:* put on the payroll.

See GET, WORK in Index. — See also **busy, use.**

employ *noun* See **business, employment.**

employable *adjective* See **open, usable.**

employed *adjective* Having a job : hired, jobholding, retained, working. See WORK in Index. — See also **busy.**

employee also **employe** *noun* One who is employed by another : hireling, jobholder, worker. *Informal:* hire, hired hand. See OVER, WORK in Index.

employer *noun* One that employs persons for wages : hirer. See OVER, WORK in Index.

employment *noun* **1.** The act of employing for wages : engagement, hire. See GET, WORK in Index. **2.** The state of being employed : employ, hire. See WORK in Index. — See also **business, duty, exercise.**

empoison *verb* See **poison.**

emporium *noun* See **store.**

empower *verb* See **authorize, enable.**

emprise *noun* See **adventure.**

emptiness *noun* **1.** Total absence of matter : vacancy, vacuity, vacuum, void. See FULL in Index. **2.** Total lack of ideas, meaning, or substance : barrenness, blankness, hollowness, inanity, vacancy, vacuity, vacuousness. See FULL in Index. **3.** A desolate sense of loss : blankness, desolation, hollowness, vacuum, void. See FULL in Index. — See also **nothingness.**

empty *adjective* **1.** Containing nothing : bare, blank, clear, vacant, vacuous, void. See FULL in Index. **2.** Lacking value, use, or substance : hollow, idle, otiose, vacant, vain. See FULL in Index. **3.** Not having a desirable element : barren, destitute, devoid, innocent, lacking, void,

wanting. *Idiom:* in want of. See FULL in Index. — See also **vacant.**

empty *verb* To remove the contents of. Also used with *out* : clean out, clear, evacuate, vacate, void. See FULL in Index. — See also **discharge.**

empty-headed *adjective* See **giddy, vacant.**

empyreal *adjective* See **heavenly.**

emulate *verb* See **compete, follow.**

emulation *noun* See **ambition.**

emulative *adjective* See **imitative.**

emulous *adjective* See **ambitious, competitive.**

enable *verb* To give the means, ability, or opportunity to do : empower, permit. See ALLOW in Index. — See also **authorize.**

enact *verb* See **act, establish, stage.**

enactment *noun* See **law.**

enamored *adjective* See **infatuated.**

enceinte *adjective* See **pregnant.**

enchant *verb* See **charm, delight.**

enchanting *adjective* See **attractive, delightful.**

enchantment *noun* See **attraction.**

enchantress *noun* See **seductress, witch.**

encircle *verb* See **surround.**

enclose *verb* To confine within a limited area : cage, coop (in *or* up), fence (in), immure, mew (up), pen², shut in, shut up, wall (in *or* up). See FREE in Index. — See also **close in** at **close.**

enclosure *noun* See **court.**

encomium *noun* See **praise.**

encompass *verb* See **band¹, contain, surround.**

encounter *verb* To come up against : confront, face, meet¹, run into. See MEET in Index. — See also **confront, engage.**

encounter *noun* See **brush², confrontation.**

encourage *verb* **1.** To impart strength and confidence to : buck up, cheer (up), hearten, nerve, perk up. See HELP in Index. **2.** To impart courage, inspiration, and resolution to : animate, cheer (on), embolden, inspire, inspirit, motivate. See HELP in Index. **3.** To lend supportive approval to : countenance, favor, smile on (or upon). See SUPPORT in Index. — See also **promote.**

encouragement *noun* Something that encourages : inspiration, motivation, stimulation. See HELP in Index. — See also **stimulus.**

encouraging *adjective* Inspiring confidence or hope : cheering, heartening, hopeful, likely, promising. See HELP in Index.

encroachment *noun* See **trespass.**

encumber *verb* See **charge, hinder.**

end *noun* **1.** A demarcation point or boundary beyond which something does not extend or occur : bound^2 (often used in plural), confine (used in plural), limit. See EDGE in Index. **2.** A concluding or terminating : cease, cessation, close, closing, closure, completion, conclusion, consummation, ending, end of the line, finish, period, stop, stopping point, termination, terminus, wind-up, wrap-up. See CONTINUE in Index. **3.** The last part : close, conclusion, ending, finale, finish, last^1, termination, wind-up, wrap-up. See START in Index. **4.** Residual matter : butt^4, fragment, ort (often used in plural), scrap^1, shard, stub. See LEFT-OVER in Index. — See also **intention, length, tail.**

end *verb* See **close.**

endanger *verb* To subject to danger or destruction : imperil, jeopardize, menace, peril, risk, threaten. See SAFETY in Index.

endangerment *noun* See **danger.**

endeavor *verb* See **attempt.**

endeavor *noun* See **attempt, effort.**

endemic *adjective* See **indigenous.**

ending *noun* See **end.**

endless *adjective* **1.** Having no ends or limits : boundless, illimitable, immeasurable, infinite, limitless, measureless, unbounded, unlimited. See LIMITED in Index. **2.** Enduring for all time : amaranthine, ceaseless, eternal, everlasting, immortal, never-ending, perpetual, unending, world without end. *Archaic:* eterne. See CONTINUE in Index. — See also **continual.**

endlessness *noun* The quality or state of having no end : ceaselessness, eternality, eternalness, eternity, everlastingness, perpetuity, world without end. See CONTINUE in Index.

endmost *adjective* See **last^1.**

end of the line *noun* See **end.**

endorse *verb* See **permit, prove, sign, support.**

endorsement *noun* An indication of commendation or approval : backing, recommendation, support. See SUPPORT in Index. — See also **permission.**

endow *verb* See **gift.**

endowed *adjective* See **gifted.**

end product *noun* See **effect.**

endue *verb* See **gift.**

endurable *adjective* See **bearable.**

endurance *noun* The quality or power of withstanding hardship or stress : stamina, staying power. See CONTINUE in Index. — See also **continuation.**

endure *verb* **1.** To carry on through despite hardships : *Slang:* sweat out, tough out. See CONTINUE in Index. **2.** To put up with : abide, accept, bear, brook^2, go, stand (for), stomach, suffer, support, sustain, swallow, take, tolerate, withstand.

Informal: lump[2]. *Idioms:* take it, take it lying down. See ACCEPT in Index. **3.** To be in existence or in a certain state for an indefinitely long time : abide, continue, go on, hold out, last[2], persist, remain, stay[1]. See CONTINUE in Index. — See also **bear up** at **bear**.

enduring *adjective* See **continuing**.

enemy *noun* One who is hostile to or opposes the purposes or interests of another : archenemy, foe, nemesis. See LOVE in Index.

energetic *adjective* Possessing, exerting, or displaying energy : active, brisk, dynamic, dynamical, forceful, kinetic, lively, sprightly, strenuous, vigorous. *Informal:* peppy. See ACTION in Index. — See also **vigorous.**

energetically *adverb* See **hard.**

energize *verb* To give or impart vitality and energy to (someone or something) : exhilarate, invigorate, stimulate, vitalize. See HELP in Index.

energizing *adjective* See **tonic.**

energy *noun* Capacity or power for work or vigorous activity : animation, force, might, potency, power, puissance, sprightliness, steam, strength. *Informal:* get-up-and-go, go, pep, peppiness, zip. See ACTION in Index.

enervate *verb* To lessen or deplete the nerve, energy, or strength of : attenuate, debilitate, devitalize, enfeeble, sap[2], undermine, undo, unnerve, weaken. See STRONG in Index.

enervation *noun* See **debilitation.**

enfeeble *verb* See **enervate.**

enfeeblement *noun* See **debilitation.**

enfold *verb* See **embrace, wrap.**

enforce *verb* To compel observance of : carry out, effect, execute, implement, invoke. *Idioms:* put in force, put into action. See OBLIGATION, OVER in Index.

engage *verb* **1.** To get and hold the attention of : involve, occupy. See EXCITE in Index. **2.** To come or bring together and interlock : mesh. See CONNECT in Index. **3.** To involve (someone) in an activity : draw in. See PARTICIPATE in Index. **4.** To enter into conflict with : encounter, meet[1], take on. *Idiom:* do (or join) battle with. See CONFLICT, MEET in Index. — See also **book, busy, employ, participate, pledge, tie up** at **tie.**

engaged *adjective* Pledged to marry : affianced, betrothed, intended, plighted. See MARRIAGE in Index. — See also **busy.**

engagement *noun* **1.** The act or condition of being pledged to marry : betrothal, espousal, troth. See MARRIAGE in Index. **2.** A commitment to appear at a certain time and place : appointment, assignation, date, rendezvous, tryst. See AGREE in Index. — See also **booking, combat, employment, promise.**

engaging *adjective* See **attractive.**

engender *verb* See **produce.**

engineer *verb* See **wangle.**

engird *verb* See **band[1].**

engirdle *verb* See **band[1].**

englut *verb* See **gulp.**

engorge *verb* See **gulp, satiate.**

engorgement *noun* See **satiation.**

engrave *verb* **1.** To cut (a design or inscription) into a hard surface, especially for printing : carve, etch, grave[3], incise. See MARKS in Index. **2.** To produce a deep impression of : etch, fix, grave[3], impress, imprint, inscribe, stamp. See MARKS in Index.

engross *verb* See **absorb, write.**

engrossment *noun* See **absorption.**

engulf *verb* See **flood, overwhelm.**

enhance *verb* See **flatter, grace, intensify, promote.**

enhancement *noun* See **accompaniment.**

enigma *noun* See **mystery.**

enigmatic *adjective* See **mysterious.**

enjoin *verb* See **command, forbid.**

enjoy *verb* **1.** To receive pleasure from : like[1], relish, savor. *Informal:* go for. *Slang:* dig. See LIKE in Index. **2.** To have the use or benefit of : have, hold, possess. See OWNED in Index. — See also **command.**

enjoyable *adjective* Affording enjoyment : gratifying, pleasant, pleasing, pleasurable. See PAIN in Index.

enjoyment *noun* The condition of responding pleasurably to something : delectation, pleasure. See PAIN in Index. — See also **delight.**

enkindle *verb* See **fire, light[1].**

enlarge *verb* See **elaborate, increase.**

enlargement *noun* See **buildup, expansion, increase.**

enlighten *verb* See **illuminate, inform.**

enlightened *adjective* See **educated, informed.**

enlightening *adjective* See **cultural, educational.**

enlightenment *noun* See **illumination.**

enlist *verb* See **join.**

enliven *verb* See **light[1].**

enlivening *adjective* See **stimulating.**

enmesh *verb* See **catch.**

enmeshment *noun* See **entanglement.**

enmity *noun* Deep-seated hatred, as between longtime opponents or rivals : animosity, animus, antagonism, antipathy, hostility, ill will. See LOVE in Index.

ennoble *verb* See **distinguish, exalt.**

ennoblement *noun* See **exaltation.**

ennui *noun* See **boredom.**

enormity *noun* The quality of passing all moral bounds : atrociousness, atrocity, heinousness, monstrousness. See GOOD in Index. — See also **flagrancy, outrage.**

enormous *adjective* See **giant, outrageous.**

enormousness *noun* The quality of being enormous : hugeness, immenseness, immensity, prodigiousness, stupendousness, tremendousness, vastness. See BIG in Index.

enough *adjective* See **sufficient.**

enough *noun* An adequate quantity : adequacy, sufficiency. See EXCESS in Index.

enounce *verb* See **state.**

enrage *verb* See **anger.**

enrapture *verb* See **carry away** at **carry.**

enrich *verb* See **fertilize.**

enrichment *noun* See **accompaniment.**

enroll *verb* See **join, list[1].**

ensanguine *verb* See **bloody.**

ensconce *verb* See **establish, hide[1].**

enshroud *verb* See **cover, wrap.**

ensign *noun* See **flag[1].**

enslave *verb* To make subservient or subordinate : enthrall, subject, subjugate. See FREE in Index.

enslavement *noun* See **slavery.**

ensnare *verb* See **catch.**

ensnarement *noun* See **entanglement.**

ensnarl *verb* See **catch, entangle.**

ensue *verb* See **follow.**

ensure *verb* See **guarantee.**

entail *verb* See **carry, demand.**

entangle *verb* To twist together so that separation is difficult : ensnarl, foul, snarl[2], tangle. See ORDER in Index. — See also **complicate.**

entanglement *noun* The condition of being entangled or implicated : embranglement, embroilment, enmeshment, ensnarement, involvement. See FREE, PARTICIPATE in Index. — See also **tangle.**

enter *verb* To come or go into (a place) : come in, go in, penetrate. *Nautical:* put in. *Idioms:* gain entrance (or entry), set foot in. See ENTER in Index. — See also **join, penetrate, post³, start.**

enterprise *noun* See **adventure, company, drive, project.**

enterprising *adjective* See **adventurous, vigorous.**

entertain *verb* See **amuse, hear of** at **hear, ponder.**

entertaining *adjective* See **amusing.**

entertainment *noun* See **amusement.**

enthrall *verb* See **charm, enslave, grip.**

enthrallment *noun* See **absorption.**

enthusiasm *noun* **1.** Passionate devotion to or interest in a cause or subject, for example : ardor, fervor, fire, passion, zeal, zealousness. See CONCERN, FEELINGS in Index. **2.** A subject or activity that inspires lively interest : craze, mania, passion, rage. See CONCERN in Index.

enthusiast *noun* A person who is ardently devoted to a particular subject or activity : bug, devotee, fanatic, maniac, zealot. *Informal:* buff², fan², fiend. *Slang:* freak, nut. See CONCERN in Index. — See also **admirer, devotee.**

enthusiastic *adjective* Showing or having enthusiasm : ardent, fervent, keen¹, mad, rabid, warm, zealous. *Informal:* crazy. *Slang:* gung ho, nuts. See CONCERN in Index.

entice *verb* See **attract, seduce.**

enticement *noun* See **attraction, lure.**

enticer *noun* See **seducer.**

enticing *adjective* See **attractive, seductive.**

entire *adjective* See **complete, good, round, whole.**

entirely *adverb* See **completely, solely.**

entirety *noun* See **completeness, whole.**

entitle *verb* See **authorize, name.**

entity *noun* See **existence, system, thing.**

entomb *verb* See **bury.**

entombment *noun* See **burial.**

entourage *noun* See **retinue.**

entrance¹ *noun* The act of entering : entry, ingress. See ENTER in Index. — See also **admission.**

entrance² *verb* See **charm.**

entrap *verb* See **catch.**

entreat *verb* See **appeal.**

entreaty *noun* See **appeal.**

entrée *noun* See **admission.**

entrench *verb* See **fix.**

entrenched *adjective* See **confirmed.**

entrenchment *noun* See **trespass.**

entrepreneur *noun* See **originator.**

entrust also **intrust** *verb* **1.** To put in the charge of another for care, use, or performance : commend, commit, confide, consign, give (over), hand over, relegate, trust, turn over. *Idiom:* give in trust (or charge). See GIVE in Index. **2.** To place a trust upon : charge, trust. See TRUST in Index.

entry *noun* An item inserted, as in a diary, register, or reference book : insertion, posting. See WORDS in Index. — See also **admission, entrance¹.**

entwine *verb* See **wind².**

enucleate *verb* See **explain.**

enucleation *noun* See **explanation.**

enumerate *verb* To name or specify one by one : itemize, list[1], numerate, tick off. See COUNT, SPECIFIC in Index. — See also **count**.

enumeration *noun* See **count**.

enunciate *verb* See **pronounce, state**.

enunciation *noun* See **voicing**.

envelop *verb* See **close in** at **close, wrap**.

envenom *verb* See **poison**.

envious *adjective* Resentfully or painfully desirous of another's advantages : covetous, green-eyed, invidious, jealous. See DESIRE in Index.

enviousness *noun* See **envy**.

environ *verb* See **surround**.

environment *noun* **1.** A surrounding area : environs, locale, locality, neighborhood, precinct (used in plural), surroundings, vicinity. See NEAR, PLACE in Index. **2.** The totality of surrounding conditions and circumstances affecting growth or development : ambiance, atmosphere, climate, medium, milieu, mise en scène, surroundings, world. See BE, LIMITED, PLACE in Index. — See also **condition**.

environs *noun* See **environment, skirt**.

envisage *verb* See **imagine**.

envision *verb* See **foresee, imagine**.

envoy *noun* See **bearer**.

envy *noun* Resentful or painful desire for another's advantages : covetousness, enviousness, jealousy. See DESIRE in Index.

envy *verb* To feel envy towards or for : begrudge, covet, grudge. See DESIRE in Index.

enwrap *verb* See **wrap**.

eon *also* **aeon** *noun* See **age**.

ephemeral *adjective* See **transitory**.

epicene *adjective* See **effeminate**.

epicure *noun* See **sybarite**.

epicurean *adjective* See **sensuous, sybaritic**.

epicurean *noun* See **sybarite**.

epidemic *noun* See **outbreak**.

epidermis *noun* See **skin**.

epigrammatic *adjective* See **pithy**.

epigrammatical *adjective* See **pithy**.

episode *noun* See **event**.

epistle *noun* See **letter**.

epithet *noun* See **name, swearword**.

epitome *noun* See **synopsis**.

epitomize *verb* See **represent, review**.

epoch *noun* See **age**.

equable *adjective* See **even**[1].

equal *adjective* **1.** Agreeing exactly in value, quantity, or effect : equivalent, even[1], identical, same, tantamount. *Idioms:* on a par, one and the same. See SAME in Index. **2.** Having the necessary strength or ability : up to. See ABILITY in Index. **3.** Just to all parties : equitable, even[1], evenhanded, fair. See SAME in Index.

equal *noun* See **peer**[2].

equal *verb* To do or make something equal to : match, meet[1], tie. See SAME in Index. — See also **amount, compare**.

equality *noun* See **equivalence**.

equalize *verb* To make equal : equate, even[1], level, square. See SAME in Index. — See also **balance**.

equanimity *noun* See **balance**.

equate *verb* See **equalize, liken**.

equation *noun* See **equivalence**.

equilibrium *noun* See **balance**.

equip *verb* See **furnish**.

equipment *noun* See **outfit**.

equipoise *noun* See **balance**.

equitable *adjective* See **equal, fair**.

equitableness *noun* See **fairness**.

equity *noun* See **justice**.

equivalence *noun* The state of being equivalent : equality, equation, equivalency, par, parity, sameness. See SAME in Index.

equivalency *noun* See **equivalence**.

equivalent *adjective* See **equal, like²**.

equivalent *noun* See **peer²**.

equivocal *adjective* See **ambiguous, evasive, shady**.

equivocality *noun* See **ambiguity**.

equivocalness *noun* See **vagueness**.

equivocate *verb* **1.** To use evasive or deliberately vague language : euphemize, hedge, shuffle, tergiversate, weasel. *Informal:* pussyfoot, waffle. *Idioms:* beat about (or around) the bush, mince words. See CLEAR in Index. **2.** To stray from truthfulness or sincerity : palter, prevaricate, shuffle. See TRUE in Index.

equivocation *noun* The use or an instance of equivocal language : ambiguity, equivoque, euphemism, hedge, prevarication, shuffle, tergiversation, weasel word. *Informal:* waffle. See CLEAR in Index. — See also **ambiguity**.

equivoque *also* **equivoke** *noun* See **ambiguity, equivocation**.

era *noun* See **age**.

eradicate *verb* See **annihilate, eliminate**.

eradication *noun* See **annihilation, elimination**.

erase *verb* See **annihilate, cancel**.

erasure *noun* The act of erasing or the condition of being erased : cancellation, deletion, expunction, obliteration. See INCLUDE in Index.

erect *adjective* Directed or pointed upward : raised, upright, upstanding. See HORIZONTAL in Index.

erect *verb* To raise upright : pitch, put up, raise, rear², set up, upraise, uprear. See HORIZONTAL, RISE in Index. — See also **build**.

erector *noun* See **builder**.

eristic *adjective* See **argumentative**.

erode *verb* See **bite**.

erotic *adjective* **1.** Of, concerning, or promoting sexual love or desire : amatory, amorous, aphrodisiac, lascivious, salacious, sexual, sexy. See SEX in Index. **2.** Feeling or devoted to sexual love or desire : amative, amorous, concupiscent, lascivious, lecherous, lewd, libidinous, lustful, lusty, passionate, prurient, sexy. See SEX in Index.

eroticism *noun* See **desire**.

erotism *noun* See **desire**.

err *verb* To make an error or mistake : miscue, mistake, slip, slip up, stumble, trip up. See CORRECT in Index. — See also **deviate, offend**.

errand *noun* See **mission**.

errant *adjective* **1.** Traveling about, especially in search of adventure : roaming, roving, wandering. See MOVE in Index. **2.** Straying from a proper course or standard : aberrant. See CORRECT in Index.

erratic *adjective* Without a fixed or regular course : devious, stray, wandering. See PURPOSE in Index. — See also **capricious, eccentric, uneven**.

erratum *noun* See **error**.

erroneous *adjective* Containing an error or errors : fallacious, false, inaccurate, incorrect, mistaken, off, unsound, untrue, wrong. *Idioms:* all wet, in error, off base, off (or wide of) the mark. See CORRECT in Index.

erroneousness *noun* See **fallacy**.

error *noun* An act or thought that unintentionally deviates from what is correct, right, or true : erratum, inaccuracy, incorrectness, lapse, miscue, misstep, mistake, slip, slipup, trip. See CORRECT in Index. — See also **fallacy**.

errorless *adjective* See **accurate**.

ersatz *noun* See **copy**.

erstwhile *adjective* See **late**.

erstwhile *adverb* See **earlier**.

eruct *verb* See **erupt**.

erudite *adjective* See **learned**.

erudition *noun* See **education**.

erupt *verb* To send forth (confined matter) violently : belch, disgorge, eject, eruct, expel, spew. *Geology:* extravasate. See EXPLOSION in Index. — See also **break out** at **break**.

eruption *noun* The act of emerging violently from limits or restraints : explosion, outbreak, outburst. See EXPLOSION in Index. — See also **outburst**.

escalate *verb* See **increase**.

escalation *noun* See **increase**.

escape *verb* **1.** To break loose and leave suddenly, as from confinement or from a difficult or threatening situation : abscond, break out, decamp, flee, fly, get away, run away. *Informal:* skip (out). *Slang:* lam. *Regional:* absquatulate. *Idioms:* blow (or fly) the coop, cut and run, give someone the slip, make a getaway, take flight, take it on the lam. See FREE in Index. **2.** To fail to be fixed by the mind, memory, or senses of : elude. *Idiom:* slip away from. See OWNED in Index. — See also **avoid**.

escape *noun* **1.** The act or an instance of escaping, as from confinement or difficulty : break, breakout, decampment, escapement, flight, getaway. *Slang:* lam. See FREE in Index. **2.** The act, an instance, or a means of avoiding : avoidance, bypass, circumvention, evasion. See SEEK in Index. **3.** Freedom from worry, care, or unpleasantness : forgetfulness, oblivion, obliviousness. See SEEK in Index.

escaped *adjective* See **fugitive**.

escapee *noun* See **fugitive**.

escapement *noun* See **escape**.

eschew *verb* See **avoid**.

escort *verb* See **accompany, guide**.

escort *noun* See **guide**.

esculent *adjective* See **edible**.

esculent *noun* See **food**.

esoteric *adjective* See **deep**.

especial *adjective* See **special**.

espial *noun* See **notice**.

espousal *noun* See **adoption, engagement, wedding**.

espouse *verb* See **adopt, marry**.

esprit *noun* See **morale, spirit**.

esprit de corps *noun* See **morale**.

espy *verb* See **catch**.

essay *noun* See **attempt, composition, test**.

essay *verb* See **attempt, test**.

essence *noun* A basic trait or set of traits that define and establish the character of something : being, essentiality, nature, quintessence, substance, texture. See SURFACE in Index. — See also **heart**.

essential *adjective* **1.** Constituting or forming part of the essence of something : basic, constitutional, constitutive, fundamental, integral, vital. See BE, SURFACE in Index. **2.** Incapable of being dispensed with : indispensable, necessary, needful, required, requisite. See IMPORTANT, NECESSARY in Index. — See also **elemental**.

essential *noun* See **condition, element**.

essentiality *noun* See **essence**.

essentially *adverb* In regard to the essence of a matter : basically, fundamentally. *Idioms:* at bottom, at heart, in essence. See SURFACE in Index.

establish *verb* **1.** To place securely in a position or condition : ensconce, fix, install, seat, settle. See PUT IN in Index. **2.** To put in force or cause to be by legal authority : constitute, enact, legislate, make, promulgate. See ACTION, MAKE, POLITICS in Index. — See also base[1], found, prove.

establishment *noun* See **company, foundation.**

establishmentarian *adjective* See **conventional.**

estate *noun* See **holding, land.**

esteem *noun* A feeling of deference, approval, and liking : account, admiration, appreciation, consideration, estimation, favor, honor, regard, respect. See RESPECT in Index.

esteem *verb* See **admire, appreciate, regard.**

estimable *adjective* See **admirable.**

estimate *verb* **1.** To make a judgment as to the worth or value of : appraise, assay, assess, calculate, evaluate, gauge, judge, rate[1], size up, valuate, value. *Idiom:* take the measure of. See VALUE in Index. **2.** To calculate approximately : approximate, place, put, reckon, set[1]. See PRECISE in Index.

estimate *noun* **1.** The act or result of judging the worth or value of something or someone : appraisal, appraisement, assessment, estimation, evaluation, judgment, valuation. See VALUE in Index. **2.** A rough or tentative calculation : approximation, estimation. See PRECISE in Index.

estimation *noun* See **esteem, estimate.**

estrange *verb* To make distant, hostile, or unsympathetic : alienate, disaffect, disunite. *Idiom:* set at odds. See LOVE in Index.

estrangement *noun* The act of estranging or the condition of being estranged : alienation, disaffection.

See LOVE in Index. — See also **breach.**

estrus also **oestrus** *noun* See **heat.**

etcetera *noun* See **odds and ends.**

etch *verb* See **engrave.**

eternal *adjective* Without beginning or end : infinite, sempiternal. See LIMITED in Index. — See also **ageless, continual, endless.**

eternality *noun* See **endlessness, eternity.**

eternalize *verb* See **immortalize.**

eternalness *noun* See **endlessness, eternity.**

eterne *adjective* See **ageless, endless.**

eternity *noun* The totality of time without beginning or end : eternality, eternalness, infinity, perpetuity, sempiternity. See LIMITED in Index. — See also **age, endlessness, immortality.**

eternize *verb* See **immortalize.**

ethereal *adjective* See **filmy.**

ethic *noun* **1.** A rule or habit of conduct with regard to right and wrong or a body of such rules and habits : ethicality, moral (used in plural), morality. See RIGHT in Index. **2.** The moral quality of a course of action. Used in plural : ethicality, ethicalness, morality, propriety, righteousness, rightfulness, rightness. See RIGHT in Index.

ethical *adjective* In accordance with principles of right or good conduct : moral, principled, proper, right, righteous, rightful, right-minded, virtuous. See RIGHT in Index.

ethicality *noun* See **ethic.**

ethicalness *noun* See **ethic.**

ethos *noun* See **psychology.**

etiolate *verb* See **pale.**

etiquette *noun* See **manner.**

eulogize *verb* See **honor.**

euphemism *noun* See **equivocation.**

euphemize *verb* See **equivocate.**

eulogy *noun* See **praise.**

euphonic *adjective* See **melodious.**

euphonious *adjective* See **melodious.**

euphoria *noun* See **elation.**

evacuant *adjective* See **eliminative.**

evacuate *verb* See **eliminate, empty.**

evacuation *noun* See **elimination.**

evacuative *adjective* See **eliminative.**

evade *verb* To avoid fulfilling or answering completely : dodge, duck, hedge, sidestep, skirt. See SEEK in Index. — See also **avoid, lose.**

evaluate *verb* See **estimate.**

evaluation *noun* See **estimate.**

evanesce *verb* See **disappear.**

evanescence *noun* See **disappearance.**

evanescent *adjective* See **transitory.**

evangelist *noun* See **missionary.**

evangelize *verb* See **preach.**

evaporate *verb* To pass off as vapor, especially when heated : boil away, vaporize, volatilize. See SOLID in Index. — See also **disappear.**

evaporation *noun* See **disappearance.**

evasion *noun* See **escape.**

evasive *adjective* **1.** Characterized by or exhibiting evasion : elusive, slippery. See SEEK in Index. **2.** Deliberately ambiguous or vague : equivocal. See CLEAR in Index.

eve *noun* See **evening.**

even[1] *adjective* **1.** Having no irregularities, roughness, or indentations : flat, flush, level, planar, plane[1], smooth, straight. See SMOOTH in Index. **2.** On the same plane or line : flush, level. See SAME in Index. **3.** Having no change or variation : changeless, constant, equa-

ble, invariable, invariant, regular, same, steady, unchanging, uniform, unvarying. See SAME in Index. **4.** Owing or being owed nothing : quit, quits, square. See PAY in Index. **5.** Being an exact amount or number : exact. *Idiom:* on the nose. See PRECISE in Index. **6.** Neither favorable or unfavorable : balanced, fifty-fifty. See FAIR in Index. — See also **cool, equal.**

even *verb* To make even, smooth, or level : flat, flatten, level, plane[2], smooth, straighten. See SMOOTH in Index. — See also **equalize.**

even *adverb* **1.** To a more extreme degree : still, yet. See BIG in Index. **2.** Not just this but also : indeed. *Idiom:* not to mention. See TRUE in Index. **3.** In an exact manner : exactly, just, precisely. See PRECISE, SAME in Index.

even[2] *noun* See **evening.**

evenhanded *adjective* See **equal.**

evening *noun* The period between afternoon and nighttime : dusk, eve, eventide, gloaming, nightfall, twilight. *Archaic:* even[2], vesper. See START in Index.

event *noun* Something significant that happens : circumstance, development, episode, happening, incident, news, occasion, occurrence, thing. See HAPPEN in Index. — See also **circumstance, effect, fact.**

even-tempered *adjective* See **cool.**

eventide *noun* See **evening.**

eventual *adjective* See **potential.**

eventuality *noun* See **possibility.**

everlasting *adjective* See **continual, endless.**

everlasting life *noun* See **immortality.**

everlastingness *noun* See **endlessness, immortality.**

everyday *adjective* Of or suitable for ordinary days or routine occa-

sions : quotidian, workaday, workday. See GOOD, USUAL in Index.
— See also **common.**

everything *noun* See **whole.**

evict *verb* See **eject.**

eviction *noun* See **ejection.**

evidence *noun* See **confirmation, sign.**

evidence *verb* See **confirm, prove, show.**

evident *adjective* See **apparent.**

evidently *adverb* See **apparently.**

evil *adjective* Morally objectionable : bad, black, immoral, iniquitous, peccant, reprobate, sinful, vicious, wicked, wrong. See RIGHT in Index. — See also **bad, harmful, malevolent.**

evil *noun* **1.** That which is morally bad or objectionable : iniquity, peccancy, sin, wickedness, wrong. See RIGHT in Index. **2.** Whatever is destructive or harmful : bad, badness, ill. See HELP in Index. — See also **crime, curse.**

evildoing *noun* See **crime.**

evil eye *noun* See **spell².**

evince *verb* See **show.**

evocative *adjective* See **suggestive.**

evoke *verb* To call forth or bring out (something latent, hidden, or unexpressed) : draw (out), educe, elicit, summon. See SHOW in Index.

evolution *noun* See **development, movement.**

evolve *verb* See **derive, develop, elaborate.**

evolvement *noun* See **development.**

exact *adjective* See **accurate, close, even¹, precise, strict.**

exact *verb* See **demand, extort, impose.**

exacting *adjective* See **burdensome, nice, severe.**

exaction *noun* See **demand, toll¹.**

exactitude *noun* See **accuracy, veracity.**

exactly *adverb* See **directly, even¹.**

exactness *noun* See **accuracy, veracity.**

exaggerate *verb* To make (something) seem greater than is actually the case : hyperbolize, inflate, magnify, overcharge, overstate. *Idioms:* blow up out of proportion, lay it on thick, stretch the truth. See INCREASE in Index.

exaggeration *noun* The act or an instance of exaggerating : hyperbole, hyperbolism, overstatement, tall talk. See INCREASE in Index.

exalt *verb* To raise to a high position or status : aggrandize, apotheosize, dignify, elevate, ennoble, glorify, magnify, uplift. *Idiom:* put on a pedestal. See RISE in Index. — See also **distinguish, elate, honor, praise.**

exaltation *noun* The act of raising to a high position or status or the condition of being so raised : aggrandizement, apotheosis, elevation, ennoblement, glorification. See RISE in Index. — See also **elation, praise.**

exalted *adjective* Raised to or occupying a high position or rank : august, elevated, grand, high-ranking, lofty. See RISE in Index. — See also **elevated.**

exam *noun* See **examination, test.**

examination *noun* **1.** The act of examining carefully : check, checkup, inspection, perusal, scrutiny, study, view. *Informal:* going-over. See INVESTIGATE in Index. **2.** A medical inquiry into a patient's state of health : checkup, exam. See INVESTIGATE in Index. — See also **analysis, test.**

examine *verb* To look at carefully or critically : check (out), con, go over, inspect, peruse, scrutinize, study, survey, traverse, view. *Informal:* case. *Idiom:* give a going-

over. See INVESTIGATE in Index.
— See also **analyze, ask, test.**

example *noun* **1.** One that is representative of a group or class : case, illustration, instance, representative, sample, specimen. See SUBSTITUTE in Index. **2.** An instance that warns or discourages prospective imitators : lesson, warning. See WARN in Index. — See also **model, precedent.**

exasperate *verb* See **annoy.**

exasperation *noun* See **annoyance.**

excavate *verb* See **dig.**

exceed *verb* To go beyond the limits of : overreach, overrun, overstep, surpass, transcend. See EXCESS in Index. — See also **surpass.**

exceedingly *adverb* See **very.**

excel *verb* See **surpass.**

excellence *noun* The quality of being exceptionally good of its kind : fineness, superbness, superiority. See GOOD in Index. — See also **virtue.**

excellent *adjective* Exceptionally good of its kind : ace, banner, blue-ribbon, brag, capital, champion, fine[1], first-class, first-rate, prime, quality, splendid, superb, superior, terrific, tiptop, top. *Informal:* A-one, bully, dandy, great, swell, topflight, topnotch. *Slang:* boss. *Chiefly British:* tophole. See GOOD in Index.

except *verb* See **exclude, object.**

exception *noun* See **objection.**

exceptionable *adjective* See **debatable, objectionable.**

exceptional *adjective* See **rare.**

exceptionally *adverb* See **unusually, very.**

excess *noun* **1.** A condition of going or being beyond what is needed, desired, or appropriate : embarrassment, excessiveness, exorbitance, extravagance, extravagancy, extravagantness, overabundance, plethora, superabundance, superfluity, super-

fluousness, surfeit. See EXCESS in Index. **2.** Immoderate indulgence, as in food or drink : intemperance, overindulgence, surfeit. See EXCESS in Index. — See also **surplus.**

excess *adjective* See **superfluous.**

excessive *adjective* Exceeding a normal or reasonable limit : exorbitant, extravagant, extreme, immoderate, inordinate, overabundant, overmuch, undue. See EXCESS in Index.

excessiveness *noun* See **excess.**

exchange *verb* To give and receive : bandy, interchange. See GIVE in Index. — See also **change.**

exchange *noun* See **change.**

excitation *noun* See **heat.**

excite *verb* See **provoke.**

excited *adjective* See **thrilled.**

excitement *noun* See **heat.**

exclaim *verb* To speak suddenly or sharply, as from surprise or emotion : blurt (out), burst out, cry (out), ejaculate, rap out. See WORDS in Index.

exclamation *noun* A sudden, sharp utterance : cry, ejaculation, outcry. See WORDS in Index.

exclude *verb* To keep from being admitted, included, or considered : bar, count out, debar, eliminate, except, keep out, rule out, shut out. See INCLUDE in Index.

exclusive *adjective* **1.** Not divided among or shared with others : single, sole. See INCLUDE in Index. **2.** Catering to, used by, or admitting only the wealthy or socially superior : fancy, posh, swank, swanky. *Informal:* ritzy. See PLAIN in Index. — See also **concentrated, select.**

exclusively *adverb* See **solely.**

excogitate *verb* See **derive, ponder.**

excogitation *noun* See **thought.**

excogitative *adjective* See **thoughtful.**

excoriate *verb* See **chafe, slam.**

excrete *verb* See **eliminate.**

excretion *noun* See **elimination.**

excretory *adjective* See **eliminative.**

excruciate *verb* See **afflict.**

excruciating *adjective* See **tormenting.**

exculpate *verb* See **clear.**

exculpation *noun* A freeing or clearing from accusation or guilt : exoneration, vindication. *Law:* acquittal. See LAW in Index.

excursion *noun* See **digression, trip.**

excursionist *noun* See **tourist.**

excursive *adjective* See **digressive.**

excursus *noun* See **digression.**

excusable *adjective* See **justifiable, pardonable.**

excuse *verb* To free from an obligation or duty : absolve, discharge, dispense, exempt, let off, relieve, spare. See FREE in Index. — See also **forgive, justify.**

excuse *noun* An explanation offered to justify an action or make it better understood : plea, pretext. See EXPLAIN in Index. — See also **apology, forgiveness.**

exec *noun* See **executive.**

execrable *adjective* See **damned.**

execrate *verb* See **curse, hate.**

execration *noun* See **curse, hate.**

execute *verb* See **administer, effect, enforce, fulfill, interpret, perform.**

execution *noun* See **interpretation, performance.**

executive *noun* A person having administrative or managerial authority in an organization : administrant, administrator, director, manager, officer, official. *Informal:* exec. See OVER in Index.

executive *adjective* See **administrative.**

exegesis *noun* See **commentary, explanation.**

exegetic *adjective* See **explanatory.**

exemplar *noun* See **model.**

exemplary *adjective* Beyond reproach : blameless, good, irreprehensible, irreproachable, lily-white, unblamable. See RIGHT in Index. — See also **admirable, ideal.**

exemplify *verb* See **instance, represent.**

exempt *verb* See **excuse.**

exercise *noun* The act of putting into play : application, employment, exertion, implementation, operation, play, usage, use, utilization. See USED in Index. — See also **activity, practice.**

exercise *verb* **1.** To bring to bear steadily or forcefully : exert, ply^2, put out, throw, wield. See CAUSE in Index. **2.** To subject to or engage in forms of exertion in order to train, strengthen, or condition : drill, practice, train, work out. See WORK in Index. — See also **fulfill, use.**

exert *verb* See **exercise.**

exertion *noun* See **activity, effort, exercise.**

exhalation *noun* See **breath.**

exhale *verb* See **breathe.**

exhaust *verb* **1.** To use all of : consume, drain, draw down, eat up, expend, finish, play out, run through, spend, use up. *Informal:* polish off. See INCREASE in Index. **2.** To make extremely tired : fag (out), tire out, wear out. *Informal:* knock out, tucker (out). *Slang:* do in, poop^1 (out). *Idioms:* run ragged, take it out of. See TIRED in Index. — See also **deplete.**

exhausted *adjective* Extremely tired : bleary, dead, drained, fatigued, rundown, spent, tired out, wearied, weariful, weary, worn-down, worn-out. *Informal:* beat, bushed, tuckered (out). *Slang:* done in, fagged (out), pooped (out). *Idioms:*

all in, ready to drop. See HEALTH, TIRED in Index.

exhausting *adjective* See **tiring**.

exhaustion *noun* The condition of being extremely tired : fatigue, tiredness, weariness. See TIRED in Index.

exhaustive *adjective* See **thorough**.

exhaustively *adverb* See **completely**.

exhibit *verb* See **bear, display, show**.

exhibit *noun* See **display, exhibition**.

exhibition *noun* A large public display, as of goods or works of art : exhibit, exposition, show. See SHOW in Index. — See also **display**.

exhibitionism *noun* See **theatricalism**.

exhibitive *adjective* See **designative**.

exhibitory *adjective* See **designative**.

exhilarant *adjective* See **tonic**.

exhilarate *verb* See **elate, energize**.

exhilarating *adjective* See **tonic**.

exhilaration *noun* See **elation**.

exhort *verb* See **urge**.

exigence *noun* See **crisis, demand, distress, need**.

exigency *noun* See **crisis, demand, distress, need**.

exigent *adjective* See **burdensome, burning**.

exiguous *adjective* See **meager**.

exile *noun* Enforced removal from one's native country by official decree : banishment, deportation, expatriation, extradition, ostracism, transportation. See ACCEPT, REWARD in Index. — See also **émigré**.

exile *verb* See **banish**.

exist *verb* To have being or actuality : be, subsist. See BE in Index. — See also **be, consist**.

existence *noun* The fact or state of existing or of being actual : actuality, being, entity, reality. See BE, REAL in Index. — See also **life, thing**.

existent *adjective* See **actual, alive, present¹**.

existent *noun* See **thing**.

existing *adjective* See **alive, present¹**.

exit *noun* See **departure**.

exit *verb* See **go**.

exodus *noun* See **departure, emigration**.

exonerate *verb* See **clear**.

exoneration *noun* See **exculpation**.

exorbitance *noun* See **excess**.

exorbitant *adjective* See **excessive**.

exotic *adjective* See **foreign**.

expand *verb* See **elaborate, extend, increase, spread**.

expanse *noun* A wide and open area, as of land, sky, or water : distance, expansion, extent, reach, space, spread, stretch, sweep. See PLACE in Index.

expansible *adjective* See **extensible**.

expansile *adjective* See **extensible**.

expansion *noun* The act of increasing in dimensions, scope, or inclusiveness : enlargement, extension, spread. See INCREASE in Index. — See also **expanse**.

expansive *adjective* See **broad, general, outgoing**.

expatiate *verb* See **elaborate**.

expatriate *verb* See **banish**.

expatriate *noun* See **émigré**.

expatriation *noun* See **exile**.

expect *verb* To look forward to confidently : anticipate, await, bargain for (or on), count on, depend on (or upon), look for, wait (for). *Informal:* figure on. See SURPRISE in Index. — See also **require**.

expectance *noun* See **anticipation**.

expectancy noun See **anticipation, expectation.**

expectant adjective Having or marked by expectation : antici- pant, anticipative, anticipatory. See SURPRISE in Index. — See also **pregnant.**

expectation noun Something expected : anticipation, expec- tancy, prospect. See SURPRISE in Index. — See also **anticipation.**

expected adjective See **due.**

expecting adjective See **pregnant.**

expediency noun See **makeshift.**

expedient noun See **makeshift.**

expedient adjective See **advisa- ble, convenient.**

expedite verb See **ease, speed.**

expedition noun A journey under- taken with a specific objective : pilgrimage, safari, tour, trek, voyage. See MOVE in Index. — See also **haste.**

expeditious adjective See **fast, quick.**

expeditiousness noun See **haste.**

expel verb See **banish, eject, erupt.**

expellee noun See **émigré.**

expend verb See **exhaust, spend.**

expenditure noun See **cost.**

expense noun See **cost.**

expensive adjective See **costly.**

experience verb To participate in or partake of personally : feel, go through, have, know, meet[1] (with), see, suffer, taste (of), undergo. Archaic: prove. **Idiom:** run up against. See PARTICIPATE in Index. — See also **feel.**

experience noun See **acquain- tance.**

experienced adjective Skilled or knowledgeable through long prac- tice : old, practiced, seasoned, versed, veteran. **Idiom:** knowing the ropes. See ABILITY in Index.

experiment noun See **test.**

experiment verb See **test.**

experimental adjective See **pilot.**

experimentation noun See **test.**

expert noun A person with a high degree of knowledge or skill in a par- ticular field : ace, adept, authority, dab hand, master, past master, pro- fessional, proficient, wizard. Informal: whiz. Slang: crackerjack. Chiefly British: dab[2]. See ABILITY in Index.

expert adjective Having or dem- onstrating a high degree of knowl- edge or skill : adept, crack, master, masterful, masterly, professional, proficient, skilled, skillful. Slang: crackerjack. See ABILITY in Index.

expertise noun See **ability.**

expertness noun See **ability.**

expiatory adjective See **purgative.**

expire verb See **breathe, die, disap- pear, lapse.**

explain verb To make understanda- ble : construe, decipher, explicate, expound, interpret, spell out. Archaic: enucleate. **Idiom:** put into plain English. See EXPLAIN in Index. — See also **account for** at **account, resolve.**

explain away verb See **extenuate.**

explainable adjective Capable of being explained or accounted for : accountable, decipherable, explica- ble, illustratable, interpretable. See EXPLAIN in Index.

explanation noun Something that serves to explain or clarify : clarifi- cation, construction, decipherment, elucidation, exegesis, explication, exposition, illumination, illustra- tion, interpretation. Archaic: enucle- ation. See EXPLAIN in Index. — See also **account.**

explanative adjective See **explanatory.**

explanatory adjective Serving to explain : elucidative, exegetic, explanative, explicative, expositive, expository, hermeneutic, hermeneutical, illustrative, interpretative, interpretive. See EXPLAIN in Index.

expletive noun See **swearword.**

explicable adjective See **explainable.**

explicate verb See **explain.**

explication noun See **explanation.**

explicative adjective See **explanatory.**

explicit adjective See **definite.**

explode verb **1.** To release or cause to release energy suddenly and violently, especially with a loud noise : blast, blow[1] (up), burst, detonate, fire, fulminate, go off, touch off. See EXPLOSION in Index. **2.** To increase or expand suddenly, rapidly, or without control : mushroom, snowball. See INCREASE in Index. — See also **anger, break out** at **break, burst, discredit.**

exploit verb See **abuse, manipulate, use.**

exploit noun See **feat.**

exploitable adjective See **easy.**

exploration noun The act or an instance of exploring or investigating : investigation, probe, reconnaissance. See INVESTIGATE in Index.

explore verb To go into or through for the purpose of making discoveries or acquiring information : delve, dig, inquire, investigate, look into, probe, reconnoiter, scout[1]. See INVESTIGATE in Index.

explosion noun See **blast, eruption, outburst, report.**

expose verb To lay open, as to something undesirable or injurious : subject. *Idiom:* open the door to. See PROTECTION in Index. — See also **bare, betray, display, reveal.**

exposé noun See **revelation.**

exposed adjective See **open.**

exposition noun See **exhibition, explanation.**

expositive adjective See **explanatory.**

expository adjective See **explanatory.**

expostulate verb See **object.**

expostulation noun See **objection.**

exposure noun The condition of being laid open to something undesirable or injurious : liability, openness, susceptibility, susceptibleness, vulnerability, vulnerableness. See PROTECTION in Index. — See also **revelation.**

expound verb See **explain.**

express verb To give expression to, as by gestures, facial aspects, or bodily posture : communicate, convey, display, manifest. See SHOW in Index. — See also **air, phrase, represent, say, squeeze.**

express adjective See **definite, specific.**

expression noun **1.** The act or an instance of expressing in words : articulation, statement, utterance, verbalization, vocalization, voice. See WORDS in Index. **2.** Something that takes the place of words in communicating a thought or feeling : gesture, indication, sign, token. See SHOW in Index. **3.** A word or group of words forming a unit and conveying meaning : locution, phrase. See WORDS in Index. **4.** A disposition of the facial features that conveys meaning, feeling, or mood : aspect, cast, countenance, face, look, visage. See EXPRESS in Index. — See also **eloquence, representation, term.**

expressionless adjective Lacking expression : blank, deadpan, inexpressive, pokerfaced. See SHOW in Index.

expressive adjective Effectively conveying meaning, feeling, or mood : eloquent, meaning, meaningful, significant. See EXPRESS, SHOW in Index.

expressiveness *noun* See **eloquence.**

expressivity *noun* See **eloquence.**

expressway *noun* See **way.**

expropriate *verb* See **seize.**

expropriation *noun* See **seizure.**

expulsion *noun* See **ejection.**

expunction *noun* See **erasure.**

expunge *verb* See **cancel.**

expurgate *verb* See **censor.**

exquisite *adjective* See **delicate, elegant.**

exsiccate *verb* See **dry.**

extant *adjective* See **actual, alive.**

extemporaneous *adjective* Spoken, performed, or composed with little or no preparation or forethought : ad-lib, extemporary, extempore, impromptu, improvised, offhand, snap, spur-of-the-moment, unrehearsed. *Informal:* off-the-cuff. See PREPARED in Index.

extemporary *adjective* See **extemporaneous.**

extempore *adjective* See **extemporaneous.**

extemporization *noun* See **improvisation.**

extemporize *verb* See **improvise.**

extend *verb* **1.** To make or become more comprehensive or inclusive : broaden, expand, widen. See INCREASE in Index. **2.** To proceed on a certain course or for a certain distance : carry, go, lead, reach, run, stretch. See REACH in Index. — See also **go, increase, lengthen, offer, renew, spread.**

extended *adjective* See **general, long**[1].

extendible *adjective* See **extensible.**

extensible *adjective* Capable of being extended or expanded : expansible, expansile, extendible,

extensile, protractile, stretch, stretchable. See INCREASE in Index.

extensile *adjective* See **extensible.**

extension *noun* **1.** The act of making something longer or the condition of being made longer : elongation, prolongation, protraction. See LONG in Index. **2.** A part added to a main structure : annex, arm, wing. See PART in Index. — See also **expansion, range.**

extensive *adjective* See **big, broad, general.**

extent *noun* The measure of how far or long something goes in space, time, or degree : length, reach, span, stretch. See BIG in Index. — See also **degree, expanse, range, size.**

extenuate *verb* To conceal or make light of a fault or offense : explain away, gloss over, gloze (over), palliate, sleek over, whitewash. See SHOW in Index. — See also **thin.**

exteriorization *noun* See **embodiment.**

exteriorize *verb* See **embody.**

exterminate *verb* See **annihilate.**

extermination *noun* See **annihilation.**

external *adjective* See **apparent.**

externalization *noun* See **embodiment.**

externally *adverb* See **apparently.**

externalize *verb* See **embody.**

extinct *adjective* See **dead, vanished.**

extinction *noun* See **annihilation, death.**

extinguish *verb* To cause to stop burning or giving light : douse, put out, quench, snuff out. See CONTINUE in Index. — See also **abolish, annihilate, suppress.**

extinguishment *noun* See **abolition, annihilation.**

extirpate *verb* See **annihilate.**

extirpation *noun* See **annihilation.**

extol *verb* See **honor, praise.**

extolment *noun* See **praise.**

extort *verb* To obtain by coercion or intimidation : exact, squeeze, wrench, wrest, wring. *Slang:* shake down. See GET in Index.

extra *adjective* See **additional, superfluous.**

extra *adverb* See **very.**

extract *verb* See **glean, pull.**

extraction *noun* See **ancestry.**

extradition *noun* See **exile.**

extramundane *adjective* See **supernatural.**

extraneous *adjective* See **foreign, irrelevant.**

extraordinarily *adverb* See **unusually.**

extraordinary *adjective* See **rare.**

extrasensory *adjective* See **supernatural.**

extravagance *noun* Excessive or imprudent expenditure : extravagancy, lavishness, prodigality, profligacy, profuseness, profusion, squander, waste, wastefulness. See CAREFUL, SAVE in Index. — See also **excess, luxury.**

extravagancy *noun* See **excess, extravagance, luxury.**

extravagant *adjective* Characterized by excessive or imprudent spending : lavish, prodigal, profligate, profuse, spendthrift, wasteful. See CAREFUL, EXCESS, SAVE in Index. — See also **excessive, profuse.**

extravagantness *noun* See **excess.**

extravasate *verb* See **erupt.**

extraverted *adjective* See **outgoing.**

extreme *adjective* **1.** Most distant or remote, as from a center : farthermost, farthest, furthermost, furthest, outermost, outmost, ultimate, utmost, uttermost. See BIG, EDGE in Index. **2.** Holding especially political views that deviate drastically and fundamentally from conventional or traditional beliefs : extremist, fanatic, fanatical, rabid, radical, revolutionary, ultra. *Slang:* far-out. See CONCERN, EDGE, POLITICS in Index. — See also **excessive, ultimate.**

extreme *noun* Either of the two points at the ends of a spectrum or range : limit. See EDGE in Index. — See also **length.**

extremely *adverb* See **very.**

extremist *noun* One who holds extreme views or advocates extreme measures : fanatic, radical, revolutionary, revolutionist, ultra, zealot. See CONCERN, EDGE, POLITICS in Index.

extremist *adjective* See **extreme.**

extremity *noun* See **crisis.**

extricate *verb* See **clear.**

extrinsic *adjective* See **foreign.**

extroverted *adjective* See **outgoing.**

exuberant *adjective* Full of joyful, unrestrained high spirits : ebullient, effervescent, sparkling. See HAPPY in Index. — See also **profuse.**

exude *verb* See **ooze.**

exult *verb* To feel or express an uplifting joy over a success or victory : crow, glory, jubilate, triumph. See HAPPY in Index. — See also **rejoice.**

exultance *noun* See **exultation.**

exultancy *noun* See **exultation.**

exultant *adjective* Feeling or expressing an uplifting joy over a success or victory : jubilant, triumphant. See HAPPY in Index.

exultation *noun* The act or condition of feeling an uplifting joy over a success or victory : exultance, exultancy, jubilance, jubilation, triumph. See HAPPY in Index.

exuviate *verb* See **shed.**

eye *noun* An organ of vision : orb. See SEE in Index. — See also **detec-**

tive, discernment, loop, point of view, thick, vision.

eye *verb* See **gaze, look, watch.**

eye-catching *adjective* See **noticeable.**

eyeless *adjective* See **blind.**

eye opener *noun* See **revelation.**

eyesight *noun* See **vision.**

eyewitness *noun* See **witness.**

F

fable *noun* See **fiction, myth, yarn.**

fabric *noun* See **texture.**

fabricate *verb* See **fake, invent, make.**

fabricator *noun* See **forger, liar.**

fabulist *noun* See **liar.**

fabulous *adjective* So remarkable as to elicit disbelief : amazing, astonishing, astounding, fantastic, fantastical, incredible, marvelous, miraculous, phenomenal, prodigious, stupendous, unbelievable, wonderful, wondrous. See GOOD in Index. — See also **marvelous, mythical.**

façade also **facade** *noun* **1.** The forward outer surface of a building : face, front, frontage, frontal. *Architecture:* frontispiece. See PRECEDE in Index. **2.** A deceptive outward appearance : cloak, color, coloring, cover, disguise, disguisement, face, false colors, front, gloss, guise, mask, masquerade, pretense, pretext, semblance, show, veil, veneer, window-dressing. *Slang:* put-on. See SHOW in Index.

face *noun* **1.** The front surface of the head : countenance, feature (often used in plural), muzzle, visage. *Informal:* mug. *Slang:* kisser, map, pan, puss. See PRECEDE in Index. **2.** A facial contortion indicating dis-

pleasure, disgust, or pain : grimace, moue, mouth, pout. *Informal:* mug. See EXPRESS in Index. **3.** An outward appearance : aspect, countenance, look, physiognomy, surface, visage. See SURFACE in Index. **4.** The outer layer of an object : surface, top. See SURFACE in Index. **5.** The marked outer surface of an instrument : dial. See PRECEDE in Index. **6.** The level of credit or respect at which one is regarded by others : prestige, standing, status. See RESPECT in Index. — See also **expression, façade, impudence.**

face *verb* **1.** To have the face or front turned in a specific direction : front, look (on *or* upon). See PRECEDE in Index. **2.** To furnish with a covering of a different material : clad, cover, sheathe, side, skin. See SURFACE in Index. — See also **confront, defy, encounter.**

face-lift *noun* See **renewal.**

facelifting *noun* See **renewal.**

face-off *noun* See **confrontation.**

facet *noun* See **phase.**

facetious *adjective* See **humorous.**

facile *adjective* See **dexterous, easy, glib, nimble.**

facileness *noun* See **ease.**

facilitate *verb* See **ease.**

facility *noun* See **amenity, ease, fluency.**

facsimile *noun* See **copy.**

fact *noun* Something having real, demonstrable existence : actuality, event, phenomenon, reality. See REAL in Index. — See also **actuality, circumstance, information.**

faction *noun* See **combine, conflict.**

factitious *adjective* See **plastic.**

factor *noun* See **circumstance, element.**

factory *noun* See **work.**

factual *adjective* Based on fact : hard. See REAL in Index.

factuality *noun* See **actuality**.

factualness *noun* See **actuality**.

facultative *adjective* See **optional**.

faculty *noun* Conferred power : authority, mandate, right. *Law:* competence, competency. See ABILITY in Index. — See also **ability, talent**.

facund *adjective* See **eloquent**.

facundity *noun* See **eloquence**.

fad *noun* See **fashion**.

fade *verb* **1.** To lose strength or power : decline, degenerate, deteriorate, fail, flag², languish, sink, wane, waste (away), weaken. *Informal:* fizzle (out). *Idioms:* go downhill, hit the skids. See INCREASE, STRONG in Index. **2.** To become inaudible : die (away, out, or down), fade out. See INCREASE in Index. **3.** To disappear gradually by or as if by dispersal of particles : dissolve, melt (away). See INCREASE, SEE in Index. — See also **disappear**.

fade out *verb* To make (a film image) disappear gradually : dissolve. See INCREASE, SEE in Index. — See also **disappear, fade**.

fade *noun* See **fade-out**.

fadeaway *noun* See **fade-out**.

faded *adjective* See **shabby**.

fade-out or **fadeout** *noun* A gradual disappearance, especially of a film image : dissolve, fade, fadeaway. See INCREASE, SEE in Index. — See also **disappearance**.

fag *noun* See **drudge, labor**.

fag *verb* See **exhaust, labor**.

fagged *adjective* See **exhausted**.

fail *verb* **1.** To prove deficient or insufficient : give out, run out. *Idioms:* fall short, run dry, run short. See EXCESS in Index. **2.** To be unsuccessful : choke, fall through. *Informal:* fall down, flop. *Slang:* bomb. *Idioms:* fail of success, fall short. See THRIVE in Index. **3.** To cease functioning properly : break down, give out. *Slang:* conk out. See THRIVE in Index. **4.** To receive less than a passing grade : *Informal:* flunk. See THRIVE in Index. **5.** To not do (something necessary) : default, neglect, omit. See DO in Index. — See also **break, collapse, fade**.

failing *noun* See **weakness**.

fail-safe *adjective* See **foolproof**.

failure *noun* **1.** The condition of not achieving the desired end : unsuccess, unsuccessfulness. See THRIVE in Index. **2.** One that fails completely : bust, fiasco, loser, washout. *Informal:* dud, flop, lemon. *Slang:* bomb. See THRIVE in Index. **3.** A cessation of proper mechanical functions : breakdown, outage. See THRIVE in Index. **4.** Nonperformance of what ought to be done : default, delinquency, dereliction, neglect, omission. *Law:* nonfeasance. See DO in Index. **5.** A marked loss of strength or effectiveness : declination, decline, deterioration. See INCREASE in Index. **6.** The condition of being financially insolvent : bankruptcy, bust, insolvency. See MONEY in Index.

fain *adjective* See **willing**.

fainéant *adjective* See **lazy**.

fainéant *noun* See **wastrel**.

faint *adjective* So lacking in strength as to be barely audible : feeble, weak. See STRONG in Index. — See also **gentle, remote, unclear**.

faint *verb* See **black out** at **black**.

faint *noun* See **blackout**.

faint-hearted *adjective* See **cowardly**.

faint-heartedness *noun* See **cowardice**.

fair *adjective* **1.** Having light hair : blond, fair-haired, towheaded. See

COLORS in Index. **2.** Of a light color or complexion : alabaster, ivory, light[1], pale. See COLORS in Index. **3.** Free from bias in judgment : disinterested, dispassionate, equitable, fair-minded, impartial, indifferent, just, nonpartisan, objective, square, unbiased, unprejudiced. *Idiom:* fair and square. See FAIR in Index. — See also **acceptable, beautiful, clear, equal, favorable, sportsmanlike.**

fair *adverb* In a fair, sporting manner : cleanly, correctly, fairly, properly. See FAIR in Index. — See also **directly.**

fair-haired *adjective* See **fair, favorite.**

fairish *adjective* See **acceptable.**

fairly *adverb* To some extent : pretty, rather. *Idiom:* more or less. See BIG in Index. — See also **fair, really.**

fair-minded *adjective* See **fair.**

fair-mindedness *noun* See **fairness.**

fairness *noun* The quality or state of being just and unbiased : detachment, disinterest, disinterestedness, dispassion, dispassionateness, equitableness, fair-mindedness, impartiality, impartialness, justice, justness, nonpartisanship, objectiveness, objectivity. See FAIR in Index.

faith *noun* Those who accept and practice a particular religious belief : church, communion, denomination, persuasion, sect. See RELIGION in Index. — See also **belief, confidence, religion.**

faithful *adjective* Adhering firmly and devotedly, as to a person, a cause, or a duty : allegiant, constant, fast, firm[1], liege, loyal, staunch, steadfast, true. See CONTINUE, TRUST in Index. — See also **accurate, authentic, close.**

faithfulness *noun* See **fidelity.**

faithless *adjective* Not true to duty or obligation : disloyal, false, false-hearted, perfidious, recreant, traitorous, treacherous, unfaithful, untrue. See CONTINUE, TRUST in Index.

faithlessness *noun* Betrayal, especially of a moral obligation : disloyalty, false-heartedness, falseness, falsity, infidelity, perfidiousness, perfidy, traitorousness, treacherousness, treachery, unfaithfulness. See CONTINUE, TRUST in Index.

fake *verb* **1.** To impart a false character to (something) by alteration : doctor, fabricate, falsify, fictionalize, fictionize. See TRUE in Index. **2.** To contrive and present as genuine : counterfeit, feign, pretend, simulate. *Idioms:* make believe, put on an act. See TRUE in Index. — See also **act, assume, counterfeit, improvise.**

fake *noun* One who fakes : charlatan, faker, fraud, humbug, impostor, mountebank, phony, pretender, quack. See TRUE in Index. — See also **counterfeit.**

fake *adjective* See **counterfeit.**

faker *noun* See **fake, forger.**

fall *verb* **1.** To move downward in response to gravity : descend, drop. See RISE in Index. **2.** To come to the ground suddenly and involuntarily : drop, go down, nose-dive, pitch, plunge, spill, topple, tumble. *Idiom:* take a fall (*or* header *or* plunge *or* spill *or* tumble). See RISE in Index. **3.** To undergo a sharp, rapid descent in value or price : dive, drop, nose-dive, plummet, plunge, sink, skid, slump, tumble. *Idiom:* take a sudden downtrend (*or* downturn). See INCREASE in Index. **4.** To undergo moral deterioration : sink, slip. *Idiom:* go bad (*or* wrong). See RIGHT in Index. **5.** To come as by lot or inheritance : devolve, pass. See

REACH in Index. — See also **come, drop, subside, surrender.**

fall back *verb* See **back, retreat.**

fall down *verb* See **fail.**

fall off *verb* See **slip, subside.**

fall on or **upon** *verb* See **attack.**

fall through *verb* See **fail.**

fall *noun* **1.** The act of dropping from a height : descent, drop. See RISE in Index. **2.** A sudden involuntary drop to the ground : dive, nose-dive, pitch, plunge, spill, tumble. *Informal:* header. See RISE in Index. **3.** A disastrous overwhelming defeat or ruin : collapse, downfall, waterloo. See THRIVE in Index. **4.** A usually swift downward trend, as in prices : decline, descent, dip, dive, downslide, downswing, downtrend, downturn, drop, drop-off, nosedive, plunge, skid, slide, slump, tumble. See INCREASE in Index. — See also **drop.**

fallacious *adjective* **1.** Containing fundamental errors in reasoning : false, illogical, invalid, sophistic, specious, spurious, unsound. See CORRECT, TRUE in Index. **2.** Tending to lead one into error : deceptive, delusive, delusory, illusive, illusory, misleading. See HONEST, REAL in Index. — See also **erroneous.**

fallacy *noun* **1.** An erroneous or false idea : erroneousness, error, falsehood, falseness, falsity, untruth. See CORRECT, TRUE in Index. **2.** Plausible but invalid reasoning : casuistry, sophism, sophistry, speciousness, spuriousness. See CORRECT, TRUE in Index.

fallback *noun* See **retreat.**

fall guy *noun* See **dupe, scapegoat.**

false *adjective* Devoid of truth : counterfactual, specious, spurious, truthless, untrue, untruthful, wrong. See TRUE in Index. — See also **counterfeit, erroneous, faithless, fallacious.**

false colors *noun* See **façade.**

false-hearted *adjective* See **faithless.**

false-heartedness *noun* See **faithlessness.**

falsehood *noun* See **fallacy, lie², mendacity.**

false impression *noun* See **misunderstanding.**

falseness *noun* See **faithlessness, fallacy.**

falsifier *noun* See **liar.**

falsify *verb* See **counterfeit, distort, fake, lie².**

falsity *noun* See **faithlessness, fallacy, lie².**

falter *verb* See **hesitate, lurch.**

fame *noun* Wide recognition for one's deeds : celebrity, famousness, notoriety, popularity, renown, reputation, repute. See KNOWLEDGE in Index. — See also **eminence.**

famed *adjective* See **eminent, famous.**

familial *adjective* See **domestic.**

familiar *adjective* **1.** Having good knowledge of : acquainted, conversant, versant, versed. *Idiom:* up on. See KNOWLEDGE in Index. **2.** Very closely associated : chummy, close, friendly, intimate¹. *Informal:* thick. *Slang:* tight. *Idiom:* hand in glove with. See LOVE in Index. — See also **common, confidential, impudent.**

familiar *noun* See **friend.**

familiarity *noun* See **acquaintance, friendship, impudence.**

family *noun* **1.** A group of people sharing common ancestry : clan, house, kindred, lineage, stock, tribe. *Idioms:* flesh and blood, kith and kin. See KIN in Index. **2.** A group of usually related people living

together as a unit : house, household, ménage. See GROUP in Index.
— See also **ancestry, kin.**
family *adjective* See **domestic.**
family tree *noun* See **genealogy.**
famished *adjective* See **ravenous.**
famous *adjective* Widely known
and discussed : famed, leading,
notorious, popular, well-known. See
KNOWLEDGE in Index. — See also
eminent.
famousness *noun* See **fame.**
fan[1] *verb* See **spread.**
fan[2] *noun* See **admirer, enthusiast.**
fanatic *noun* See **devotee, enthusiast, extremist.**
fanatic *adjective* See **extreme.**
fanatical *adjective* See **extreme.**
fancier *noun* See **admirer.**
fanciful *adjective* Appealing to
fancy : fancy, fantastic, fantastical,
imaginative, whimsical. See PLAIN
in Index. — See also **fictitious,
imaginary.**
fancy *noun* An impulsive, often
illogical turn of mind : bee, boutade, caprice, conceit, freak, humor,
impulse, megrim, notion, vagary,
whim, whimsy. *Idiom:* bee in one's
bonnet. See THOUGHTS in Index.
— See also **dream, imagination,
liking, love.**
fancy *verb* See **imagine, like**[1]**.**
fancy *adjective* See **elaborate,
exclusive, fanciful.**
fancy-free *adjective* See **single.**
fanfaronade *noun* See **boast.**
fanny *noun* See **bottom.**
fantasize *verb* See **dream, imagine.**
fantastic *adjective* Conceived or
done with no reference to reality or
common sense : antic, bizarre, fantastical, far-fetched, grotesque. See
TRUE, USUAL in Index. — See also
**capricious, fabulous, fanciful, ficti-
tious, imaginary, marvelous.**

fantastical *adjective* See **capricious, fabulous, fanciful, fantastic,
fictitious, imaginary, marvelous.**
fantasy also **phantasy** *noun* See
dream, illusion, imagination, myth.
far *adjective* See **distant.**
far *adverb* See **considerably.**
faraway *adjective* See **absent-
minded, distant.**
farce *noun* See **mockery.**
farceur *noun* See **joker.**
farcical *adjective* See **laughable.**
farcicality *noun* See **humor.**
fare *verb* See **eat, go, manage.**
fare *noun* See **food.**
farewell *adjective* See **parting.**
farewell *noun* See **parting.**
far-fetched *adjective* See **fantastic.**
far-flung *adjective* See **distant,
widespread.**
farness *noun* See **distance.**
far-off *adjective* See **distant.**
far-out *adjective* See **extreme.**
far-ranging *adjective* See **general.**
far-reaching *adjective* See **general.**
farsighted or **far-sighted** *adjective* See **visionary.**
farsightedness or **far-sighted-
ness** *noun* See **vision.**
farthermost *adjective* See **extreme.**
farthest *adjective* See **extreme.**
fascinate *verb* See **charm, grip.**
fascinating *adjective* See
attractive.
fascination *noun* See **attraction.**
fashion *noun* The current custom :
craze, fad, furor, mode, rage, style,
trend, vogue. *Informal:* thing.
Idioms: the in thing, the last word,
the latest thing. See STYLE, USUAL
in Index. — See also **style, way.**
fashion *verb* See **adapt, make.**
fashionable *adjective* Being or in
accordance with the current fashion : à la mode, chic, dashing, mod,
modish, posh, smart, stylish, swank,
swanky, trig. *Informal:* classy, in,

sharp, snappy, swish, tony, trendy. *Slang:* with-it. *Idioms:* all the rage, up to the minute. See STYLE, USUAL in Index.

fast *adjective* **1.** Characterized by great celerity : breakneck, expeditious, fleet, quick, rapid, speedy, swift. *Informal:* hell-for-leather. *Idiom:* quick as a bunny (or wink). See FAST in Index. **2.** Permanently resistive to fading : colorfast, indelible. See CONTINUE in Index. — See also **abandoned, faithful, quick, sure, tight, wanton.**

fast *adverb* In a rapid way : apace, posthaste, quick, quickly. *Informal:* flat out, hell-for-leather, lickety-split, pronto. *Idioms:* full tilt, in a flash, in nothing flat, like a bat out of hell, like a blue streak, like a flash, like a house on fire, like a shot, like a streak, like greased lightning, like the wind, like wildfire. See FAST in Index.

fasten *verb* To make secure : anchor, catch, fix, moor, secure. *Idiom:* make fast. See MOVE in Index. — See also **attach, fix, tie.**

fastener *noun* See **catch.**

fastidious *adjective* See **careful, nice.**

fastidiousness *noun* See **thoroughness.**

fastigium *noun* See **climax.**

fastness *noun* See **stability.**

fat *adjective* Having too much flesh : corpulent, fatty, fleshy, gross, obese, overblown, overweight, porcine, portly, stout, weighty. See FAT in Index. — See also **fatty, profitable, thick.**

fat *noun* Adipose tissue : suet. See FAT in Index. — See also **surplus.**

fatal *adjective* Causing ruin or destruction : calamitous, cataclysmal, cataclysmic, catastrophic, destructive, disastrous, fateful, ruinous. See HELP in Index. — See also **deadly, fateful.**

fatality *noun* **1.** The quality or condition of causing death : deadliness, lethality. See LIVE in Index. **2.** A termination of life, usually as the result of an accident or a disaster : casualty, death. See LIVE in Index.

fate *noun* **1.** That which is inevitably destined : destiny, fortune, kismet, lot, portion, predestination. See CERTAIN in Index. **2.** A predestined tragic end : doom. See CERTAIN, LIVE, LUCK, START in Index.

fate *verb* **1.** To determine the future of in advance : destine, foreordain, predestinate, predestine, predetermine, preordain. See CERTAIN in Index. **2.** To predestine to a tragic end : doom, foredoom. See CERTAIN, LIVE, LUCK, START in Index.

fated *adjective* Governed and decided by or as if by fate : fateful. See CERTAIN in Index. — See also **condemned.**

fateful *adjective* **1.** So critically decisive as to affect the future : fatal, momentous. See DECIDE in Index. **2.** Portending future disaster : apocalyptic, apocalyptical, baneful, dire, direful, fire-and-brimstone, grave[2], hellfire, ominous, portentous, unlucky. See LUCK, WARN in Index. — See also **fatal, fated.**

father *noun* A male parent : sire. *Informal:* dad, daddy, pa, papa, pappy[2], pop[2]. *Slang:* old man. See KIN in Index. — See also **ancestor, original, originator.**

father *verb* To be the biological father of : beget, breed, get, procreate, sire. See KIN in Index. — See also **produce.**

fatherlike *adjective* See **fatherly.**

fatherly *adjective* Like a father : fatherlike, paternal. See KIN in Index.

fathom *verb* See **know, understand**.

fathomable *adjective* See **understandable**.

fatidic *adjective* See **prophetic**.

fatidical *adjective* See **prophetic**.

fatigue *noun* See **exhaustion**.

fatigue *verb* To diminish the strength and energy of : drain, jade, tire, wear, wear down, wear out, weary. See TIRED in Index.

fatigued *adjective* See **exhausted**.

fatiguing *adjective* See **tiring**.

fatty *adjective* Having the qualities of fat : adipose, fat, greasy, oily, oleaginous, unctuous. See FAT in Index. — See also **fat**.

fatuous *adjective* See **mindless**.

fault *noun* See **blame, defect, weakness**.

fault *verb* See **blame**.

faultfinder *noun* See **critic, grouch**.

faultfinding *adjective* See **critical**.

faultless *adjective* See **innocent, perfect**.

faulty *adjective* See **defective**.

favor *noun* 1. A kindly act : good turn, grace, indulgence, kindness, service. *Archaic:* benefit. See HELP in Index. 2. Favorable or preferential bias : favoritism, partiality, partialness, preference. See FAIR in Index. — See also **acceptance, advantage, benevolence, courtesy, esteem**.

favor *verb* 1. *Chiefly Regional.* To be similar to, as in appearance : resemble, take after. See SAME in Index. 2. To treat with inordinate gentleness and care : spare. *Idiom:* handle (or treat) with kid gloves. See TREAT WELL in Index. 3. To show partiality toward (someone) : prefer. *Idiom:* play favorites. See FAIR in Index. — See also **approve, encourage, oblige**.

favorable *adjective* 1. Indicative of future success or full of promise : auspicious, benign, bright, brilliant, fair, fortunate, good, propitious. See LUCK in Index. 2. Disposed to favor one over another : partial, preferential. See FAIR in Index. 3. Giving assent : affirmative, positive. See AFFIRM in Index. — See also **agreeable, beneficial, opportune**.

favored *adjective* See **favorite**.

favorite *adjective* 1. Given special, usually doting treatment : darling, fair-haired, favored, pet[1]. See TREAT WELL in Index. 2. Being a favorite : favored, popular, preferred, well-liked. See LIKE in Index.

favorite *noun* 1. One liked or preferred above all others : darling, pet[1]. *Idiom:* apple of one's eye. See LIKE in Index. 2. A competitor regarded as the most likely winner : *Informal:* shoo-in. See WIN in Index.

favoritism *noun* See **favor**.

fawn *verb* To support slavishly every opinion or suggestion of a superior : bootlick, cringe, grovel, kowtow, slaver, toady, truckle. *Informal:* apple-polish, brownnose, cotton. *Slang:* suck up. *Idioms:* curry favor, dance attendance, kiss someone's feet, lick someone's boots. See OVER in Index.

faze *verb* See **embarrass**.

fealty *noun* See **fidelity**.

fear *noun* Great agitation and anxiety caused by the expectation or the realization of danger : affright, alarm, apprehension, dread, fearfulness, fright, funk, horror, panic, terror, trepidation. *Slang:* cold feet. *Idiom:* fear and trembling. See FEAR in Index.

fear *verb* To be afraid of : dread. *Idiom:* have one's heart in one's mouth. See FEAR in Index.

fearful *adjective* Causing or able to cause fear : appalling, dire, direful, dreadful, fearsome, formidable, frightful, ghastly, redoubtable, scary, terrible, tremendous. See FEAR in Index. — See also **afraid, terrible.**

fearfulness *noun* See **fear.**

fearless *adjective* See **brave.**

fearlessness *noun* See **courage.**

fearsome *adjective* See **afraid, fearful.**

feasible *adjective* See **possible.**

feast *noun* A large meal elaborately prepared or served : banquet, junket. *Informal:* feed, spread. See INGESTION in Index.

feast on *verb* See **eat up** at **eat.**

feat *noun* A great or heroic deed : achievement, exploit, gest, masterstroke, stunt, tour de force. See ACTION in Index. — See also **accomplishment, trick.**

feather *noun* See **kind².**

featherbrained *adjective* See **giddy.**

feature *noun* A prominent article in a periodical : lead. *Chiefly British:* leader. See WORDS in Index. — See also **face, quality.**

feature *verb* See **emphasize, imagine.**

febrific *adjective* See **hot.**

febrile *adjective* See **hot.**

feckless *adjective* See **careless.**

fecund *adjective* See **fertile.**

fecundate *verb* See **fertilize.**

fecundity *noun* See **fertility.**

federate *verb* See **ally.**

federation *noun* See **alliance, union.**

fed up *adjective* See **sick.**

fee *noun* See **toll¹, wage.**

feeble *adjective* See **faint, infirm, tenuous.**

feeble-minded *adjective* See **backward.**

feebleness *noun* See **infirmity.**

feed *verb* See **live¹, nourish, promote.**

feed *noun* See **feast.**

feel *verb* **1.** To be physically aware of through the senses : experience, have. See KNOWLEDGE in Index. **2.** To undergo an emotional reaction : experience, have, know, savor, taste. See FEELINGS in Index. **3.** To view in a certain way : believe, hold, sense, think. See OPINION in Index. **4.** To experience or express compassion : ache, commiserate, compassionate, pity, sympathize, yearn. *Idioms:* be sorry, have (or take) pity. See PITY in Index. — See also **experience, grope, perceive, touch.**

feel out *verb* To test the attitude of : probe, sound³ (out). *Idioms:* put out feelers, send up a trial balloon. See INVESTIGATE in Index.

feel *noun* See **air, hang, touch.**

feeler *noun* Something, as a remark, used to determine the attitude of another : probe. *Idiom:* trial balloon. See INVESTIGATE in Index.

feeling *noun* Intuitive cognition : hunch, idea, impression, intuition, suspicion. See THOUGHTS in Index. — See also **air, belief, emotion, sensation, sensitiveness, sentiment, touch.**

feeling *adjective* See **emotional, understanding.**

feign *verb* See **act, assume, fake, pretend.**

feigned *adjective* See **artificial.**

feint *noun* See **trick.**

felicitous *adjective* See **appropriate.**

felicity *noun* See **happiness.**

feline *adjective* See **stealthy.**

fell¹ *verb* See **cut, drop.**

fell² *adjective* See **fierce.**

fell³ *noun* See **hide².**

fellow *noun* See **associate, boy, boyfriend, mate, peer**[2].

fellow citizen *noun* See **countryman**.

fellowship *noun* See **company, friendship, union**.

felon *noun* See **criminal**.

felony *noun* See **crime**.

female *adjective* See **feminine**.

femaleness *noun* See **femininity**.

feminine *adjective* Of, relating to, or characteristic of women : distaff, female, womanish, womanly. See GENDER in Index. — See also **effeminate**.

feminineness *noun* See **femininity**.

femininity *noun* **1.** The quality or condition of being feminine : femaleness, feminineness, womanliness. See GENDER in Index. **2.** Women in general : distaff, muliebrity, womanhood, womankind, womenfolk. See GENDER in Index. — See also **effeminacy**.

femme fatale *noun* See **seductress**.

fen *noun* See **swamp**.

fence *verb* See **enclose, wall**.

fend *verb* See **defend, manage, parry**.

feral *adjective* See **fierce, savage**.

ferment *verb* See **boil**.

ferment *noun* See **catalyst, unrest**.

ferocious *adjective* See **cruel, fierce**.

ferociousness *noun* See **intensity**.

ferocity *noun* See **intensity**.

fertile *adjective* **1.** Capable of reproducing : fecund, fruitful, productive, prolific. *Biology:* proliferous. See RICH in Index. **2.** Characterized by great productivity : fecund, fruitful, productive, prolific, rich. See RICH in Index.

fertility *noun* The quality or state of being fertile : fecundity, fruitfulness, productiveness, productivity, prolificacy, prolificness, richness. See RICH in Index.

fertilize *verb* To make fertile : enrich, fecundate. See RICH in Index.

fervency *noun* See **passion**.

fervent *adjective* See **enthusiastic, passionate**.

fervid *adjective* Characterized by intense emotion and activity : burning, fevered, feverish, heated, hectic. See EXCITE, FEELINGS, HOT in Index. — See also **passionate**.

fervor *noun* See **enthusiasm, heat, passion**.

Fescennine *adjective* See **obscene**.

fess up *verb* See **acknowledge**.

festinate *verb* See **rush**.

festival *noun* See **gaiety**.

festive *adjective* See **glad, merry**.

festiveness *noun* See **gaiety**.

festivity *noun* See **celebration, gaiety, party**.

fetch *verb* See **bring**.

fetching *adjective* See **attractive**.

fete also **fête** *noun* See **party**.

fetid *adjective* See **smelly**.

fetish *noun* See **charm, thing**.

fetter *noun* See **bond**.

fetter *verb* See **hamper**.

fettle *noun* See **trim**.

fevered *adjective* See **fervid**.

feverish *adjective* See **fervid, hot**.

fey *adjective* See **magic**.

fiancé *noun* See **intended**.

fiancée *noun* See **intended**.

fiasco *noun* See **failure**.

fib *verb* See **lie**[2].

fib *noun* See **lie**[2].

fibber *noun* See **liar**.

fiber *noun* See **character, texture, thread**.

fibril *noun* See **thread**.

fickle *adjective* See **capricious**.

fiction *noun* A narrative not based on fact : fable, story. See REAL in Index. — See also **dream, lie**[2]**, myth**.

fictional *adjective* See **fictitious**.

fictionalize *verb* See **fake.**

fictionize *verb* See **fake.**

fictitious *adjective* Consisting or suggestive of fiction : fanciful, fantastic, fantastical, fictional, fictive, invented, made-up. See REAL in Index.

fictive *adjective* See **fictitious.**

fiddle *verb* To move one's fingers or hands in a nervous or aimless fashion : fidget, fool, monkey, play, putter, tinker, toy, trifle, twiddle. See TOUCH in Index. — See also **tamper.**

fiddle away *verb* See **idle.**

fiddle-faddle *noun* See **trivia.**

fidelity *noun* Faithfulness or devotion to a person, a cause, obligations, or duties : allegiance, constancy, faithfulness, fealty, loyalty, steadfastness. See CONTINUE, OBLIGATION in Index. — See also **veracity.**

fidget *verb* See **fiddle.**

fidget *noun* See **jitter.**

fidgety *adjective* See **edgy.**

field *noun* See **area.**

fiend *noun* A perversely bad, cruel, or wicked person : archfiend, beast, devil, ghoul, monster, ogre, tiger, vampire. See KIND in Index. — See also **enthusiast.**

fiendish *adjective* Perversely bad, cruel, or wicked : devilish, diabolic, diabolical, ghoulish, hellish, infernal, ogreish, satanic, satanical. See KIND in Index.

fierce *adjective* Showing or suggesting a disposition to be violently destructive without scruple or restraint : barbarous, bestial, cruel, fell[2], feral, ferocious, inhuman, savage, truculent, vicious, wolfish. See KIND in Index. — See also **cruel, heavy, high, intense.**

fiercely *adverb* See **hard.**

fierceness *noun* See **intensity.**

fiery *adjective* See **burning, hot, passionate, spirited.**

fifty-fifty *adjective* See **even**[1].

fight *verb* See **argue, contend.**

fight *noun* **1.** A physical conflict involving two or more : fistfight, fisticuffs, scrap[2], scuffle, tussle. *Slang:* rumble. See CONFLICT in Index. **2.** The power or will to fight : bellicoseness, bellicosity, belligerence, belligerency, combativeness, contentiousness, pugnaciousness, pugnacity, truculence, truculency. See CONFLICT in Index. — See also **argument.**

fighter *noun* One who engages in a combat or struggle : belligerent, combatant, soldier, warrior. See CONFLICT in Index.

figment *noun* See **dream, myth.**

figure *noun* **1.** An element or a component in a decorative composition : design, device, motif, motive, pattern. See PART in Index. **2.** Arithmetic calculations. Used in plural : arithmetic, computation, number (used in plural). See COUNT in Index. — See also **form.**

figure *verb* See **believe, calculate.**

figure on *verb* See **expect.**

figure out *verb* See **resolve, work.**

figuring *noun* See **calculation.**

filament *noun* See **thread.**

filch *verb* See **steal.**

file *noun* See **line.**

fill *verb* **1.** To make or become full; put as much into as can be held : charge, freight, heap, load, pack, pile. See FULL in Index. **2.** To plug up something, as a hole, space, or container : block, choke, clog, close, congest, cork, plug, stop. See FULL in Index. — See also **satisfy.**

fill in or **out** *verb* See **complement, substitute.**

fill *noun* See **plug.**

fillet *noun* See **band**[1].

fill-in *noun* See **substitute.**

fillip *noun* See **stimulus.**

filmy *adjective* **1.** So light and insubstantial as to resemble air or a thin film : aerial, aery, airy, diaphanous, ethereal, gauzy, gossamer, gossamery, sheer², transparent, vaporous, vapory. See THICK in Index. **2.** Covered by or as if by a thin coating or film : blurry, cloudy, dim, hazy, misty. See CLEAR in Index.

filth *noun* Foul or dirty matter : dirt, grime, muck. *Slang:* crud. See CLEAN in Index. — See also **dirtiness, obscenity.**

filthiness *noun* See **dirtiness, obscenity.**

filthy *adjective* **1.** Heavily soiled; very dirty or unclean : foul, nasty, squalid, vile. See CLEAN in Index. **2.** So objectionable as to elicit despisal or deserve condemnation : abhorrent, abominable, antipathetic, contemptible, despicable, despisable, detestable, disgusting, foul, infamous, loathsome, lousy, low, mean², nasty, nefarious, obnoxious, odious, repugnant, rotten, shabby, vile, wretched. See GOOD in Index. — See also **dirty, obscene.**

finagle *verb* See **maneuver, wangle.**

final *adjective* See **definitive, last¹.**

finale *noun* See **end.**

finally *adverb* See **last¹, ultimately.**

finance *verb* To supply capital to or for : back, capitalize, fund, grubstake, stake, subsidize. *Informal:* bankroll. *Idiom:* put up money for. See HELP, MONEY in Index.

finance *noun* See **fund.**

financial *adjective* Of or relating to finances or those who deal in finances : fiscal, monetary, pecuniary. See MONEY in Index.

financier *noun* One who is occupied with or expert in large-scale financial affairs : capitalist.

Informal: moneyman. See MONEY in Index.

financing *noun* See **capital.**

find *verb* To look for and discover : locate, pinpoint, spot. See GET in Index. — See also **come across** at **come, discover.**

find *noun* See **discovery.**

finding *noun* See **discovery.**

fine¹ *adjective* **1.** Able to make or detect effects of great subtlety or precision : delicate, nice, subtle. See PRECISE in Index. **2.** Consisting of small particles : dusty, powdery, pulverous, pulverulent. See BIG in Index. — See also **choice, clear, delicate, excellent.**

fine² *noun* A sum of money levied as punishment for an offense : amercement, mulct, penalty. See REWARD in Index.

fine *verb* To impose a fine on : amerce, mulct, penalize. See REWARD in Index.

fineness *noun* See **excellence.**

fine print *noun* See **detail.**

finery *noun* See **attire.**

finespun *adjective* See **delicate.**

finesse *verb* See **trump, wangle.**

finest *noun* See **policeman.**

finger *verb* See **place, touch.**

finical *adjective* See **nice.**

finicky *adjective* See **nice.**

finish *verb* See **close, destroy, exhaust, kill¹, murder, run.**

finish *noun* See **end.**

finished *adjective* See **accomplished, through.**

fink *noun* See **informer.**

fink *verb* See **inform.**

fink out *verb* See **back down** at **back.**

fire *noun* **1.** The visible signs of combustion : blaze¹, conflagration, flame, flare-up. See HOT in Index. **2.** Liveliness and vivacity of imagination : brilliance, brilliancy, genius, inspiration. See GOOD in Index. **3.** Exceptional brightness and clarity, as of a cut and polished stone : brilliance, brilliancy, luminosity, radiance. See LIGHT in Index. — See also **enthusiasm, passion.**

fire *verb* To arouse the emotions of; make ardent : animate, enkindle, impassion, inspire, kindle, stir[1]. See EXCITE in Index. — See also **dismiss, explode, light[1], shoot, throw.**

fire-and-brimstone *adjective* See **fateful.**

fired up *adjective* See **thrilled.**

firm[1] *adjective* **1.** Unyielding to pressure or force : hard, incompressible, solid. See RESIST, STRONG in Index. **2.** Indicating or possessing determination, resolution, or persistence : constant, determined, resolute, steadfast, steady, stiff, tough, unbending, uncompromising, unflinching, unwavering, unyielding. See PURPOSE in Index. **3.** In a definite and final form; not likely to change : certain, fixed, flat, set[1]. See CHANGE in Index. — See also **decisive, faithful, sound[2], sure, tight.**

firm[2] *noun* See **company.**

firmament *noun* See **air.**

firmness *noun* See **decision, soundness, stability.**

first *adjective* Preceding all others in time : earliest, initial, maiden, original, pioneer, primary, prime, primordial. See START in Index. — See also **early, primary.**

first-class *adjective* See **choice, excellent.**

firsthand *adjective* See **immediate.**

first-rate *adjective* See **excellent.**

fiscal *adjective* See **financial.**

fish *verb* See **hint.**

fish story *noun* See **lie[2].**

fishwife *noun* See **scold.**

fishy *adjective* See **shady.**

fissure *noun* See **breach, crack.**

fissure *verb* See **crack.**

fistfight *noun* See **fight.**

fisticuffs *noun* See **fight.**

fit[1] *verb* **1.** To conform to another, especially in size and shape : dovetail. See AGREE in Index. **2.** To be in keeping with : become, befit, conform, correspond, go with, match, suit. See AGREE in Index. — See also **adapt, agree, belong, furnish, prepare.**

fit out or **up** *verb* See **furnish.**

fit *adjective* See **appropriate, convenient, eligible, healthy, just.**

fit[2] *noun* See **outburst, seizure, temper.**

fitful *adjective* See **intermittent.**

fitness *noun* See **qualification, trim.**

fitted *adjective* See **eligible.**

fitting *adjective* See **appropriate, just.**

fitting *noun* See **furnishing.**

fix *verb* **1.** To ascribe (a misdeed or an error, for example) to : affix, assign, blame, fasten, impute, pin on, place. See GIVE in Index. **2.** To implant so deeply as to make change nearly impossible : embed, entrench, fasten, infix, ingrain, lodge, root[1]. See MOVE in Index. **3.** To restore to proper condition or functioning : doctor, fix up, mend, overhaul, patch, repair[1], revamp, right. *Idiom:* set right. See HELP in Index. **4.** To prearrange the outcome of (a contest) unlawfully : tamper. *Idiom:* stack the deck. See CRIMES in Index. — See also **adjust, arrange, attach, avenge, catch, dictate, engrave, establish, fasten, prepare, settle, sterilize.**

fix up *verb* To improve in appearance, especially by refurbishing : smarten (up), spruce (up). See BETTER in Index. — See also **fix.**

fix *noun* See **bribe, predicament.**

fixation *noun* See **thing.**

fixed *adjective* Firmly in position : immobile, immovable, stationary, steadfast, steady, unmovable, unmoving. See MOVE in Index.
— See also **definite, firm¹, set¹.**

fizz *verb* See **foam, hiss.**

fizzle *verb* See **fade, hiss.**

flabbergast *verb* See **stagger.**

flabby *adjective* See **limp.**

flaccid *adjective* See **limp.**

flag¹ *noun* Fabric used especially as a symbol : banderole, banner, banneret, color (used in plural), ensign, jack, oriflamme, pennant, pennon, standard, streamer. See SUBSTITUTE in Index.

flag *verb* See **signal.**

flag² *verb* See **fade, wilt.**

flagitious *adjective* See **corrupt.**

flagitiousness *noun* See **corruption.**

flagrance *noun* See **flagrancy.**

flagrancy *noun* The quality or state of being flagrant : atrociousness, atrocity, egregiousness, enormity, flagrance, flagrantness, glaringness, grossness, outrageousness, rankness. See GOOD in Index.

flagrant *adjective* Conspicuously bad or offensive : arrant, capital, egregious, glaring, gross, rank². See GOOD in Index.

flagrantness *noun* See **flagrancy.**

flail *verb* See **thrash.**

flair *noun* See **talent.**

flamboyant *adjective* See **ornate, showy.**

flame *verb* See **burn.**

flame *noun* See **fire.**

flaming *adjective* See **burning, passionate.**

flank *noun* See **side.**

flap *verb* **1.** To move (one's arms or wings, for example) up and down : beat, flitter, flop, flutter, waggle, wave. See REPETITION in Index. **2.** To move or cause to move about while being fixed at one edge : flutter, fly, wave. See REPETITION in Index. — See also **fly.**

flap *noun* See **disturbance.**

flare *verb* See **break out** at **break, burn, fly.**

flare up *verb* See **anger.**

flare-up *noun* See **fire, outburst.**

flash *verb* To emit light suddenly in rays or sparks : coruscate, glance, gleam, glimmer, glint, glisten, glister, glitter, scintillate, shimmer, spangle, sparkle, twinkle, wink. See LIGHT in Index. — See also **blink, display, rush.**

flash *noun* A very brief time : crack, instant, minute¹, moment, second¹, trice, twinkle, twinkling, wink. *Informal:* jiff, jiffy. *Chiefly British:* tick. See BIG, TIME in Index. — See also **blink, glitter.**

flash point also **flashpoint** *noun* See **crisis.**

flashy *adjective* See **gaudy.**

flat *adjective* **1.** Lying down : decumbent, horizontal, procumbent, prone, prostrate, recumbent. See HORIZONTAL in Index. **2.** Having lost tang or effervescence : stale. See SOLID, TASTE in Index. **3.** Lacking an appetizing flavor : bland, flavorless, insipid, tasteless, unsavory. See TASTE in Index. — See also **dull, even¹, firm¹, utter².**

flat *adverb* See **completely, flatly.**

flat *verb* See **even¹.**

flatfoot *noun* See **policeman.**

flatly *adverb* In a direct, positive manner : emphatically, flat, positively. *Informal:* flat out. See STRONG in Index.

flatness *noun* See **dullness.**

flat out *adverb* See **fast, flatly.**

flat-out *adjective* See **utter².**

flatten *verb* See **drop, even¹.**

flatter *verb* **1.** To compliment excessively and ingratiatingly :

adulate, blandish, butter up, honey, slaver. *Informal:* soft-soap, sweet-talk. See PRAISE in Index. **2.** To look good on or with : become, enhance, suit. *Idiom:* put in the best light. See AGREE, BEAUTIFUL in Index.

flatterer *noun* See sycophant.

flattering *adjective* See becoming.

flattery *noun* Excessive, ingratiating praise : adulation, blandishment, blarney, incense², oil, slaver. *Informal:* soft soap. *Idiom:* honeyed words. See PRAISE in Index.

flatulent *adjective* See inflated.

flaunt *verb* See display.

flavor *noun* **1.** A distinctive property of a substance affecting the gustatory sense : relish, sapor, savor, smack², tang, taste, zest. See TASTE in Index. **2.** A distinctive yet intangible quality deemed typical of a given thing : aroma, atmosphere, savor, smack². See TASTE in Index. — See also **flavoring.**

flavor *verb* To impart flavor to : season. See TASTE in Index.

flavoring *noun* A substance that imparts taste : condiment, flavor, seasoner, seasoning, spice. See TASTE in Index.

flavorless *adjective* See dull, flat.

flavorlessness *noun* See dullness.

flaw *noun* See defect.

flaw *verb* See injure.

flawless *adjective* See clear, good, perfect.

flay *verb* See slam.

fleck *verb* See speckle.

fleck *noun* See point.

fledgling also **fledgeling** *noun* See beginner.

flee *verb* See escape.

fleece *verb* See skin.

fleecy *adjective* See hairy.

fleer *verb* See sneer.

fleer *noun* See sneer.

fleet *verb* See rush.

fleet *adjective* See fast, transitory.

fleeting *adjective* See transitory.

fleetness *noun* See haste.

Fleet Street *noun* See press.

flesh *noun* See mankind.

fleshless *adjective* See thin.

fleshliness *noun* See physicality.

fleshly *adjective* See bodily, physical.

fleshy *adjective* See fat.

flexibility *noun* The quality or state of being flexible : bounce, ductility, elasticity, flexibleness, give, malleability, malleableness, plasticity, pliability, pliableness, pliancy, pliantness, resilience, resiliency, spring, springiness, suppleness. *Obsolete:* flexure. See FLEXIBLE in Index.

flexible *adjective* **1.** Easily altered or influenced : ductile, elastic, flexile, impressionable, malleable, plastic, pliable, pliant, suggestible, supple. See FLEXIBLE in Index. **2.** Capable of withstanding stress without injury : elastic, flexile, resilient, springy, supple. *Physics:* plastic. See FLEXIBLE in Index. — See also **adaptable, malleable.**

flexibleness *noun* See flexibility.

flexile *adjective* See flexible, malleable.

flexuous *adjective* See malleable, winding.

flexure *noun* See flexibility.

flick *noun* See brush¹.

flick *verb* See brush¹.

flicker *verb* See blink, flutter.

flicker *noun* See blink.

flight *noun* See escape.

flighty *adjective* See giddy.

flimflam *verb* See cheat.

flimflam *noun* See cheat.

flimflammer *noun* See cheat.

flimsiness *noun* See infirmity.

flimsy *adjective* See **implausible, infirm, tenuous.**

flinch *verb* To draw away involuntarily, usually out of fear or disgust : blench, cringe, quail, recoil, shrink, shy[1], start, wince. See APPROACH, SEEK in Index.

flinch *noun* See **recoil.**

fling *noun* See **binge, throw, try.**

fling *verb* See **throw.**

flip *verb* See **toss.**

flip *adjective* See **impudent.**

flip through *verb* See **browse.**

flirt *verb* **1.** To make amorous advances without serious intentions : coquet, dally, toy, trifle. See SEX in Index. **2.** To treat lightly or flippantly : dally, play, toy, trifle. See WORK in Index.

flirt *noun* A woman who is given to flirting : coquette. *Informal:* vamp. See SEX in Index.

flirtation *noun* **1.** The practice of flirting : coquetry, dalliance. See SEX in Index. **2.** A usually brief romance entered into lightly or frivolously : dalliance. See SEX in Index.

flirtatious *adjective* Given to flirting : coquettish, coy, flirty. See SEX in Index.

flirty *adjective* See **flirtatious.**

flit *verb* See **flutter, fly, rush.**

flitter *verb* See **flap, flutter, fly.**

float *verb* See **fly, wash.**

flock *noun* See **crowd.**

flock *verb* See **crowd.**

flog *verb* See **beat.**

flogging *noun* See **beating.**

flood *noun* An abundant, usually overwhelming flow or fall, as of a river or rain : alluvion, cataclysm, cataract, deluge, downpour, freshet, inundation, Niagara, overflow, torrent. *Chiefly British:* spate. See BIG in Index. — See also **flow.**

flood *verb* **1.** To flow over completely : deluge, drown, engulf, flush, inundate, overflow, overwhelm, submerge, whelm. See FULL in Index. **2.** To affect as if by an outpouring of water : deluge, inundate, overwhelm, swamp, whelm. See FULL in Index. — See also **pour.**

floor *verb* See **drop, stagger.**

floozy also **floozie** *noun* See **slut.**

flop *verb* To drop or sink heavily and noisily : plop, plump[2], plunk. See RISE in Index. — See also **fail, flap, retire, slouch.**

flop *noun* See **failure.**

floppy *adjective* See **limp.**

florescence *noun* See **bloom**[1].

floret *noun* See **bloom**[1].

florid *adjective* See **ornate, ruddy.**

flounce *verb* See **strut.**

flounder *verb* See **muddle, wallow.**

flourish *verb* **1.** To grow rapidly and luxuriantly : bloom[1], blossom, thrive. See THRIVE in Index. **2.** To be in one's prime : flower, shine. *Idioms:* cut a figure, make a splash. See THRIVE in Index. **3.** To wield boldly and dramatically : brandish, sweep, wave. See EXPRESS in Index. — See also **prosper.**

flourishing *adjective* Improving, growing, or succeeding steadily : booming, boomy, prospering, prosperous, roaring, thrifty, thriving. See THRIVE in Index.

flout *verb* See **disobey.**

flow *verb* **1.** To move freely as a liquid : circulate, course, run, stream. See MOVE in Index. **2.** To come forth or emit in abundance : gush, pour, run, rush, stream, surge, well[1]. See MOVE in Index. **3.** To proceed with ease, especially of expression : glide, roll, sail. See MOVE in Index. — See also **discharge, stem, teem.**

flow *noun* Something suggestive of running water : current, drift, flood, flux, rush, spate, stream, surge, tide. See MOVE in Index.

flower *noun* See **best, bloom¹, society.**

flower *verb* See **bloom¹, flourish.**

flowery *adjective* See **sonorous.**

flowing *adjective* See **smooth.**

fluency *noun* Ready skill in expression : facility, fluidity. See ABILITY in Index.

fluent *adjective* See **smooth.**

fluff *noun* See **lapse.**

fluid *adjective* See **changeable, mobile, smooth.**

fluidity *noun* See **fluency.**

fluke *noun* See **chance.**

fluky *adjective* See **accidental.**

flummox *verb* See **nonplus.**

flunk *verb* See **fail.**

flurry *verb* See **agitate.**

flurry *noun* See **stir¹.**

flush *verb* See **blush, elate, flood.**

flush *noun* See **bloom¹, glow.**

flush *adjective* See **even¹, rich, ruddy.**

flush *adverb* See **directly.**

flushed *adjective* See **ruddy.**

fluster *verb* See **agitate.**

fluster *noun* See **agitation.**

flutter *verb* To move quickly, lightly, and irregularly like a bird in flight : flicker, flit, flitter, hover. See REPETITION in Index. — See also **flap, fly.**

flutter *noun* See **agitation.**

flux *noun* See **flow.**

flux *verb* See **melt.**

fly *verb* **1.** To move through the air with or as if with wings : flap, flit, flitter, flutter, sail, wing. See MOVE in Index. **2.** To pass quickly and lightly through the air : dart, float, sail, shoot, skim. See MOVE in Index. **3.** To react explosively or suddenly : flare (up). See EXPLOSION in Index. — See also **escape, flap, rush.**

flying *adjective* See **quick.**

foam *noun* A mass of bubbles in or on the surface of a liquid : froth, head, lather, spume, suds, yeast. See SOLID in Index.

foam *verb* To form or cause to form foam : bubble, cream, effervesce, fizz, froth, lather, spume, suds, yeast. See SOLID in Index. — See also **anger.**

foamy *adjective* Consisting of or resembling foam : frothy, lathery, spumous, spumy, sudsy, yeasty. See SOLID in Index.

fob off *verb* See **foist.**

focalize *verb* See **concentrate.**

focus *noun* See **center.**

focus *verb* See **apply, concentrate.**

foe *noun* See **enemy.**

fog *noun* See **daze, haze.**

fog *verb* See **obscure.**

foggy *adjective* See **unclear.**

fogy *noun* See **square.**

foible *noun* See **weakness.**

foil *verb* See **frustrate.**

foist *verb* To offer or put into circulation (an inferior or spurious item) : fob off, palm off, pass off, put off. See HONEST in Index. — See also **impose, insinuate.**

fold *noun* A line or an arrangement made by the doubling of one part over another : crease, crimp, crinkle, crumple, pleat, plica, plication, pucker, rimple, ruck², rumple, wrinkle. See SMOOTH in Index.

fold *verb* To bend together or make a crease in so that one part lies over another : crease, double, pleat, ply¹, ruck². See ORDER, SMOOTH in Index. — See also **break, collapse, succumb.**

folklore *noun* See **lore.**

follow *verb* **1.** To keep (another) under surveillance by moving along behind : dog, shadow, track, trail. *Informal:* bird-dog, tail. See PRE-

CEDE in Index. **2.** To take as a
model or make conform to a
model : copy, emulate, imitate,
model (on, upon, *or* after), pattern
(on, upon, *or* after). *Idioms:* follow in
the footsteps of, follow suit, follow
the example of. See SAME in Index.
3. To act in conformity with : abide
by, adhere, carry out, comply, conform, keep, mind, obey, observe.
Idiom: toe the line (*or* mark). See
ACCEPT, SAME in Index. **4.** To
occur after in time : ensue, succeed, supervene. *Idiom:* follow on (*or*
upon) the heels of. See PRECEDE,
TIME in Index. **5.** To occur as a consequence : attend, ensue, result.
See CAUSE, PRECEDE in Index. — See
also **understand.**

follow through *verb* See **follow
up** at **follow.**

follow up *verb* To strengthen the
effect of (an action) by further
action : follow through, pursue.
See CONTINUE in Index.

follower *noun* One who supports
and adheres to another : adherent,
cohort, disciple, henchman, minion,
partisan, satellite, supporter. See
OVER, PRECEDE in Index.

following *adjective* Occurring right
after another : coming, next. See
PRECEDE, TIME in Index.

following *noun* See **public,
retinue.**

folly *noun* See **foolishness.**

foment *verb* See **provoke.**

fomenter *noun* See **agitator.**

fond *adjective* See **affectionate.**

fondle *verb* See **caress.**

fondness *noun* See **attachment,
taste.**

food *noun* **1.** Something fit to be
eaten : aliment, bread, comestible,
diet, edible, esculent, fare, foodstuff,
meat, nourishment, nurture, nutriment, nutrition, pabulum, pap, prov-

ender, provision (used in plural), sustenance, victual. *Slang:* chow, eats,
grub. See INGESTION in Index.
2. That which sustains the mind or
spirit : aliment, bread, nourishment, nutriment, pabulum, pap, sustenance. See CARE FOR, INGESTION
in Index.

foodstuff *noun* See **food.**

fool *noun* One deficient in judgment
and good sense : ass, idiot, imbecile, jackass, mooncalf, moron, nincompoop, ninny, nitwit, simple,
simpleton, softhead, tomfool.
Informal: dope, gander, goose. *Slang:*
cretin, ding-dong, dip, goof, jerk,
nerd, schmo, schmuck, turkey. See
ABILITY in Index. — See also **dupe.**

fool *verb* See **deceive, fiddle, mess
around** at **mess, tamper.**

fool around *verb* See **joke, mess
around** at **mess, neck, philander.**

fool away *verb* See **waste.**

foolery *noun* See **foolishness.**

foolhardiness *noun* See **temerity.**

foolhardy *adjective* See **rash**[1].

foolish *adjective* So senseless as to
be laughable : absurd, harebrained,
idiotic, imbecilic, insane, lunatic,
mad, moronic, nonsensical, preposterous, silly, softheaded, tomfool,
unearthly, zany. *Informal:* cockeyed,
crazy, loony, loopy. *Slang:* balmy[2],
dippy, dopey, jerky, sappy, wacky.
See ABILITY, KNOWLEDGE in Index.
— See also **mindless.**

foolishness *noun* Foolish behavior : absurdity, folly, foolery, idiocy, imbecility, insanity, lunacy,
madness, nonsense, preposterousness, senselessness, silliness, tomfoolery, zaniness. *Informal:* craziness. See ABILITY in Index.

foolproof *adjective* Designed so as
to be impervious to human error or
misuse : fail-safe. See THRIVE in
Index.

foot *verb* See **add, dance, walk.**
 foot *noun* See **base¹.**
footfall *noun* See **tread.**
footing *noun* See **base¹, basis, place.**
footloose *adjective* See **single.**
footstep *noun* See **tread.**
foozle *noun* See **blunder.**
foozler *noun* See **blunderer.**
forage *verb* See **scour¹.**
foray *noun* See **invasion.**
 foray *verb* See **invade.**
forbear *verb* See **refrain.**
forbearance *noun* See **patience, tolerance.**
forbearing *adjective* See **patient, tolerant.**
forbid *verb* To refuse to allow : ban, debar, disallow, enjoin, inhibit, interdict, outlaw, prohibit, proscribe, taboo. See ALLOW in Index.
forbiddance *noun* A refusal to allow : ban, disallowance, inhibition, interdiction, prohibition, proscription, taboo. See ALLOW in Index.
forbidden *adjective* Not allowed : impermissible, taboo, verboten. See ALLOW in Index.
forbidding *adjective* So disagreeable as to discourage approach : inhospitable, unhospitable, uninviting. See WARN in Index.
force *noun* **1.** Power used to overcome resistance : coercion, compulsion, constraint, duress, pressure, strength, violence. See ATTACK in Index. **2.** The capacity to exert an influence : forcefulness, magnetism, power. See STRONG in Index. **3.** A group of people organized for a particular purpose : body, corps, crew, detachment, gang, team, unit. See GROUP in Index. — See also **energy, impact, muscle.**
 force *verb* To cause (a person or thing) to act or move in spite of resis-

tance : coerce, compel, constrain, make, obligate, oblige, pressure. See ATTACK in Index. — See also **coerce, rape.**
forced *adjective* **1.** Done under force : compulsory. See WILLING in Index. **2.** Not natural or spontaneous : contrived, effortful, labored, strained. See TRUE in Index.
forceful *adjective* Full of or displaying force : dynamic, dynamical, effective, forcible, hard-hitting, powerful, strong, vigorous. See STRONG in Index. — See also **emphatic, energetic.**
forcefully *adverb* See **hard.**
forcefulness *noun* See **force.**
forcible *adjective* Accomplished by force : coercive, violent. *Informal:* strong-arm. See ATTACK in Index. — See also **forceful.**
forcibly *adverb* See **hard.**
fore *noun* See **front.**
forearm *verb* See **gird.**
forebear *noun* See **ancestor.**
forebode *verb* See **threaten.**
foreboding *noun* See **threat.**
forecast *verb* See **adumbrate, predict.**
 forecast *noun* See **prediction.**
foredoom *verb* See **fate.**
foredoomed *adjective* See **condemned.**
forefather *noun* See **ancestor.**
foregoing *adjective* See **last¹, past.**
forehanded *adjective* See **wary.**
forehandedness *noun* See **prudence.**
foreign *adjective* **1.** Of, from, or characteristic of another place or part of the world : alien, exotic, strange. *Archaic:* outlandish. See NATIVE in Index. **2.** Not part of the essential nature of a thing : alien, extraneous, extrinsic. See NATIVE in Index.

foreigner *noun* A person coming
from another country or into a new
community : alien, émigré, newcomer, outlander, outsider, stranger.
See NATIVE in Index.

foreknow *verb* See **foresee.**

foreman *noun* See **boss.**

foremost *adjective* See **primary.**

foremother *noun* See **ancestor.**

forenoon *noun* See **morning.**

forensics *noun* See **argumentation.**

foreordain *verb* See **fate.**

forepart *noun* See **front.**

foreperson *noun* See **boss.**

forerun *verb* See **adumbrate.**

forerunner *noun* See **ancestor,
omen, precursor.**

foresee *verb* To know in advance :
anticipate, divine, envision, foreknow, see. See FORESIGHT, SEE in
Index.

foreshadow *verb* See **adumbrate.**

foreshadower *noun* See **precursor.**

foresight *noun* See **prudence,
vision.**

foresighted *adjective* See **visionary.**

foresightedness *noun* See **prudence.**

forestall *verb* See **prevent.**

forestallment *noun* See **prevention.**

foretaste *noun* See **taste.**

foretell *verb* See **adumbrate, predict, prophesy.**

foreteller *noun* See **prophet.**

forethought *noun* See **prudence.**

forethoughtfulness *noun* See
prudence.

foretoken *noun* See **omen.**

foretoken *verb* See **adumbrate.**

forewarn *verb* See **threaten, warn.**

forewarning *noun* See **threat.**

forewoman *noun* See **boss.**

foreword *noun* See **introduction.**

forfeit *verb* See **drop.**

forfend also **forefend** *verb* See
prevent.

forgather also **foregather** *verb*
See **assemble.**

forge[1] *verb* See **beat, counterfeit,
make.**

forge[2] *verb* See **plunge.**

forger *noun* One who makes a
fraudulent copy of something :
counterfeiter, fabricator, faker. See
TRUE in Index.

forgery *noun* See **counterfeit.**

forget *verb* To fail to remember :
Informal: disremember. *Idiom:* draw
a blank. See REMEMBER in Index.

forgetful *adjective* Unable to
remember : amnesiac, amnesic,
oblivious. See REMEMBER in Index.
— See also **mindless.**

forgetfulness *noun* See **escape.**

forgivable *adjective* See
pardonable.

forgive *verb* To grant forgiveness to
or for : condone, excuse, pardon,
remit. *Idiom:* forgive and forget. See
FORGIVENESS in Index.

forgiveness *noun* The act or an
instance of forgiving : absolution,
amnesty, condonation, excuse, pardon, remission. See FORGIVENESS in
Index.

forgo also **forego** *verb* See
relinquish.

fork *noun* See **branch.**
fork *verb* See **branch.**
fork out or **over** or **up** *verb* See
spend.

forlorn *adjective* See **abandoned,
despondent, lonely.**

form *noun* **1.** The external outline of
a thing : cast, configuration, figure,
pattern, shape. See SURFACE in
Index. **2.** A hollow device for shaping a fluid or plastic substance :
cast, matrix, mold. See SURFACE in
Index. — See also **application, convention, ritual, trim.**
form *verb* **1.** To give form to by or
as if by pressing and kneading :

model, mold, shape. See SURFACE in
Index. **2.** To create by combining
parts or elements : build, compose,
configure, pattern, shape, structure.
See MAKE in Index. — See also **constitute, develop.**

formal *adjective* Requiring elegant
clothes and fine manners : dressy,
full-dress. See PLAIN in Index. — See
also **ceremonious, ritual.**

formalistic *adjective* See **pedantic.**

formality *noun* See **ceremony,
ritual.**

formation *noun* See **arrangement.**

former *adjective* See **late, past.**

formerly *adverb* See **earlier.**

formidable *adjective* See **burdensome, fearful.**

formless *adjective* See **shapeless.**

formula *noun* See **ticket.**

formulaic *adjective* See **ordinary.**

formulate *verb* See **design, draft,
invent, phrase.**

forsake *verb* See **abandon.**

forsaken *adjective* See **abandoned.**

forswear also **foreswear** *verb* See
abdicate, lie².

forsworn or **foresworn** *adjective*
See **perjurious.**

forte *noun* Something at which a
person excels : long suit, métier,
specialty, strong point, strong suit.
Slang: bag, thing. See ABILITY in
Index.

forthcoming *adjective* See **coming.**

forthright *adjective* See **frank.**

forthwith *adverb* See **directly.**

fortify *verb* See **confirm, gird.**

fortitude *noun* See **courage.**

fortitudinous *adjective* See **brave.**

fortuitous *adjective* See **accidental.**

fortuitousness *noun* See **chance.**

fortuity *noun* See **chance.**

fortunate *adjective* See **favorable,
happy.**

fortunateness *noun* See **luck.**

fortune *noun* A large sum of
money : mint. *Informal:* bundle,
pretty penny, tidy sum, wad. *Slang:*
pile. See RICH in Index. — See also
chance, fate, luck, resource, riches.

forward *verb* See **advance, send.**

forward *adjective* See **advanced,
impudent.**

forwardness *noun* See **impudence.**

fossil *noun* See **square.**

foster *verb* See **nurse, promote.**

foul *adjective* See **filthy, obscene,
offensive, smelly.**

foul *verb* See **contaminate,
entangle.**

foul up *verb* See **botch.**

foulness *noun* See **dirtiness, impurity, obscenity.**

foul-smelling *adjective* See **smelly.**

foul-up *noun* See **botch.**

found *verb* To bring into existence
formally : constitute, create, establish, institute, organize, originate,
set up, start. See START in Index.
— See also **base¹.**

foundation *noun* The act of found-
ing or establishing : constitution,
creation, establishment, institution,
organization, origination, start-up.
See START in Index. — See also
base¹, basis.

foundational *adjective* See **radical.**

founder¹ *verb* See **sink.**

founder² *noun* See **originator.**

fount *noun* See **origin.**

fountain *noun* See **origin.**

fountainhead *noun* See **origin.**

four-flush *verb* See **deceive.**

fourth estate *noun* See **press.**

foxiness *noun* See **art.**

foxy *adjective* See **artful.**

fracas *noun* See **brawl.**

fractional *adjective* See **partial.**

fractious *adjective* See **unruly.**

fractiousness *noun* See **unruliness.**

fracture *verb* See **break, crack.**

fragile *adjective* Easily broken or damaged : breakable, brittle, delicate, frangible. See STRONG in Index. — See also **infirm.**

fragileness *noun* See **infirmity.**

fragility *noun* See **infirmity.**

fragment *noun* See **bit¹, end.**

fragment *verb* See **break up** at **break.**

fragmentary *adjective* See **partial.**

fragmentize *verb* See **break up** at **break.**

fragrance *noun* A sweet or pleasant odor : aroma, bouquet, perfume, redolence, scent. See SMELLS in Index.

fragrant *adjective* Having a pleasant odor : aromatic, redolent. See SMELLS in Index.

frail *adjective* See **infirm.**

frailness *noun* See **infirmity.**

frailty *noun* See **infirmity, weakness.**

frame *verb* See **design, draft, make.**

frame of mind *noun* See **mood.**

frame of reference *noun* See **phase.**

frangible *adjective* See **fragile.**

frank *adjective* Manifesting honesty and directness, especially in speech : candid, direct, downright, forthright, honest, ingenuous, man-to-man, open, plainspoken, straight, straightforward, straight-out, unreserved. *Informal:* straight-from-the-shoulder, straight-shooting. See CLEAR, SHOW in Index.

frantic *adjective* Marked by extreme excitement, confusion, or agitation : delirious, frenetic, frenzied, mad, wild. *Archaic:* madding. See CALM in Index.

frantically *adverb* See **hard.**

fraternity *noun* See **union.**

fraternize *verb* See **associate.**

fraud *noun* See **cheat, fake.**

fraudulent *adjective* See **counterfeit.**

fray *noun* See **brawl.**

freak *noun* A person or animal that is abnormally formed : monster, monstrosity. See USUAL in Index. — See also **enthusiast, fancy.**

freakish *adjective* Resembling a freak : freaky, grotesque, monstrous. See USUAL in Index. — See also **capricious, eccentric.**

freaky *adjective* See **freakish.**

freckle *verb* See **speckle.**

free *adjective* 1. Costing nothing : complimentary, gratis, gratuitous. *Idiom:* on the house. See MONEY in Index. 2. Having political independence : autonomous, independent, self-governing, sovereign. See DEPENDENCE, FREE in Index. — See also **clear, generous, loose, outspoken, unreserved, voluntary.**

free *verb* To set at liberty : discharge, emancipate, liberate, loose, manumit, release. *Slang:* spring. *Idiom:* let loose. See FREE in Index. — See also **clear.**

freebie also **freebee** *noun* See **pass.**

freedom *noun* 1. The condition of being politically free : autonomy, independence, independency, liberty, self-government, sovereignty. See DEPENDENCE, FREE in Index. 2. Ease of or space for movement : elbowroom, play. See TIGHTEN in Index. — See also **liberty.**

free-for-all *noun* See **brawl.**

freehanded *adjective* See **generous.**

freehandedness *noun* See **generosity.**

freeload *verb* *Slang.* To take advantage of the generosity of others : leech. *Informal:* sponge. See DEPENDENCE in Index.

freeloader *noun* See **parasite.**

freeloading *adjective* See **parasitic.**

freely *adverb* See **voluntarily**.

free-spoken *adjective* See **outspoken**.

freeway *noun* See **way**.

freezing *adjective* See **frigid**.

freight *noun* See **burden**[1].

freight *verb* See **charge, fill**.

frenetic *adjective* See **frantic**.

frenzied *adjective* See **frantic**.

frenziedly *adverb* See **hard**.

frequent *verb* To visit regularly : hang around, haunt, repair[2], resort. *Slang:* hang out. See PLACE in Index.

frequent *adjective* See **common**.

frequently *adverb* See **usually**.

fresh *adjective* **1.** Not previously used : brand-new, new. See NEW in Index. **2.** Bright and clear in complexion; not dull or faded : blooming, creamy, glowing, peaches-and-cream. See BEAUTIFUL in Index. — See also **additional, impudent, new**.

freshen *verb* See **refresh, tidy**.

freshet *noun* See **flood**.

freshman *noun* See **beginner**.

freshness *noun* See **novelty**.

fret *verb* See **annoy, brood, chafe**.

fretful *adjective* See **ill-tempered, impatient**.

friction *noun* See **conflict**.

friend *noun* A person whom one knows well, likes, and trusts : amigo, brother, chum, confidant, confidante, familiar, intimate[1], mate, pal. *Informal:* bud[2], buddy. *Slang:* sidekick. See LOVE in Index. — See also **acquaintance, patron**.

friendliness *noun* See **amiability**.

friendly *adjective* Of or befitting a friend or friends : amicable, neighborly, warmhearted. See ATTITUDE, LOVE in Index. — See also **familiar**.

friendship *noun* The condition of being friends : chumminess, closeness, companionship, comradeship, familiarity, fellowship, intimacy. See LOVE in Index.

fright *noun* See **fear, mess**.

fright *verb* See **frighten**.

frighten *verb* To fill with fear : affright, alarm, panic, scare, scarify[2], startle, terrify, terrorize. *Archaic:* fright. *Idioms:* make one's blood run cold, make one's hair stand on end, scare silly (or stiff), scare the daylights out of. See FEAR in Index.

frightful *adjective* See **fearful, terrible**.

frigid *adjective* **1.** Very cold : arctic, boreal, freezing, frosty, gelid, glacial, icy, polar, wintry. *Archaic:* frore. *Idiom:* bitter (or bitterly) cold. See HOT in Index. **2.** Deficient in or lacking sexual desire : ardorless, cold, inhibited, passionless, unresponsive. See SEX in Index. — See also **cold**.

frigidity *noun* See **frigidness**.

frigidness *noun* Extreme lack of warmth : frigidity, frostiness, gelidity, gelidness, iciness, wintriness. See HOT in Index.

frill *noun* See **luxury**.

fringe *noun* See **border, skirt**.

fringe *verb* See **border**.

frippery *noun* See **attire, trivia**.

frisk *verb* See **gambol, search**.

frisk *noun* See **shakedown**.

friskiness *noun* See **playfulness**.

frisky *adjective* See **playful**.

fritter away *verb* See **waste**.

frivolity *noun* See **trivia**.

frivolous *adjective* See **giddy**.

frock *noun* See **dress**.

frolic *verb* See **gambol, revel**.

frolic *noun* See **prank**[1].

frolicsome *adjective* See **playful**.

frolicsomeness *noun* See **playfulness**.

front *noun* The part of someone or something facing the viewer : fore,

forepart. See PRECEDE in Index.
— See also façade.

front verb See confront, defy, face.

frontage noun See façade.

frontal noun See façade.

frontier noun See border.

frontispiece noun See façade.

front-runner also **frontrunner**
noun See leader.

frore adjective See frigid.

frostiness noun See frigidness.

frosty adjective See cold, frigid.

froth noun See foam, trivia.

froth verb See foam.

frothy adjective Amusing but essentially empty and frivolous : light[2].
See SURFACE in Index. — See also
foamy, giddy.

froward adjective See contrary.

frown verb To wrinkle one's brow,
as in thought, puzzlement, or displeasure : glower, lower[1], scowl.
Idiom: look black. See EXPRESS in
Index.

frown on or **upon** verb See disapprove.

frown noun The act of wrinkling
the brow, as in thought, puzzlement,
or displeasure : black look, glower,
lower[1], scowl. See EXPRESS in Index.

frowzy also **frowsy** adjective See
moldy.

frugal adjective See economical.

frugality noun See economy.

fruit noun See effect, harvest.

fruitage noun See harvest.

fruitful adjective See fertile.

fruitfulness noun See fertility.

fruition noun See fulfillment.

fruitless adjective See futile.

fruitlessness noun See futility.

fruity adjective See insane.

frumpish adjective See tacky[2].

frustrate verb To prevent from
accomplishing a purpose : baffle,
balk, check, checkmate, defeat, foil,
stymie, thwart. *Informal:* cross,

stump. *Idiom:* cut the ground from
under. See ALLOW in Index.

fuddle verb See befuddle, confuse.

fuddy-duddy noun See square.

fudge verb See muddle.

fugacious adjective See transitory.

fugitive noun One who flees, as
from home, confinement, captivity,
or justice : escapee, refugee, runaway. See SEEK in Index.

fugitive adjective Fleeing or having fled, as from home, confinement,
captivity, or justice : escaped, runaway. See SEEK in Index. — See also
transitory.

führer also **fuehrer** noun See
dictator.

fulfill also **fulfil** verb To carry out
the functions, requirements, or
terms of : discharge, do, execute,
exercise, implement, keep, perform.
Idiom: live up to. See DO in Index.
— See also satisfy.

fulfilled adjective Having achieved
satisfaction, as of one's goal : content, gratified, happy, satisfied. See
HAPPY in Index.

fulfillment also **fulfilment** noun
The condition of being fulfilled :
consummation, culmination, fruition, materialization, realization.
See DO, HAPPY in Index.

full adjective **1.** Completely filled :
brimful, brimming, bursting, chockablock, packed, replete. See FULL in
Index. **2.** Of full measure; not narrow or restricted : ample, capacious, voluminous, wide. See
TIGHTEN in Index. — See also close,
complete, detailed, round.

full-blooded adjective See ruddy,
thoroughbred.

full-blown adjective See mature.

full-dress adjective See formal,
thorough.

full-fledged adjective See mature.

full-grown adjective See mature.

full-strength *adjective* See **straight.**

fully *adverb* See **completely.**

fulminate *verb* See **explode.**

fulmination *noun* See **blast, tirade.**

fulsome *adjective* See **unctuous.**

fumble *verb* See **botch, grope, muddle.**

fumble *noun* See **blunder.**

fume *verb* See **anger.**

fume *noun* See **state.**

fun *noun* See **gaiety, play.**

fun *verb* See **joke.**

function *noun* The proper activity of a person or thing : job, purpose, role, task. See DO in Index. — See also **party.**

function *verb* To react in a speci-fied way : act, behave, operate, per-form, work. See ACTION in Index. — See also **act, work.**

functional *adjective* See **practical.**

functioning *noun* See **behavior.**

functioning *adjective* See **active.**

fund *noun* The monetary resources of a government, organization, or individual. Used in plural : capital, finance (used in plural), money (often used in plural). See MONEY in Index.

fund *verb* See **finance.**

fundament *noun* See **base¹, basis.**

fundamental *adjective* See **elemen-tal, essential, radical.**

fundamental *noun* See **basis, ele-ment, law.**

fundamentally *adverb* See **essen-tially.**

funding *noun* See **capital.**

funk *noun* See **coward, cowardice, fear, gloom.**

funky *adjective* See **afraid.**

funniness *noun* See **humor.**

funny *adjective* Causing puzzle-ment; perplexing : curious, odd, peculiar, queer, strange, weird. See USUAL in Index. — See also **amusing, humorous, laughable, quaint.**

funny *noun* See **joke.**

funnyman *noun* See **joker.**

fur *noun* See **hide².**

furbish *verb* See **gloss, renew.**

furious *adjective* Full of or marked by extreme anger : irate, ireful, rabid, wrathful. *Idioms:* fit to be tied, foaming at the mouth, in a rage (or temper), in a towering rage. See FEELINGS in Index. — See also **high, intense.**

furiously *adverb* See **hard.**

furlough *noun* See **vacation.**

furnish *verb* To supply what is needed for some activity or pur-pose : accouter, appoint, equip, fit¹, fit out (or up), gear, outfit, rig, turn out. See GIVE in Index. — See also **give.**

furnishing *noun* A piece of equip-ment for comfort or convenience : appointment (used in plural), mova-ble. *Chiefly British:* fitting (used in plural). See MACHINE in Index.

furor *noun* See **fashion, fury.**

furrow *noun* See **line.**

furry *adjective* See **hairy.**

further *adjective* See **additional.**

further *verb* See **advance.**

further *adverb* See **additionally.**

furtherance *noun* See **advance.**

furthermore *adverb* See **addi-tionally.**

furthermost *adjective* See **extreme.**

furthest *adjective* See **extreme.**

furtive *adjective* See **sly, stealthy.**

furtiveness *noun* See **stealth.**

fury *noun* Violent or unrestrained anger : furor, irateness, ire, rage, wrath, wrathfulness. See FEELINGS in Index. — See also **intensity, scold.**

fuse *verb* See **melt, mix.**

fusillade *noun* See **barrage.**

fusillade *verb* See **barrage.**

fusion *noun* See **mixture.**

fuss *noun* Busy and useless activ-ity : ado. *Informal:* to-do. See

ACTION, CALM in Index. — See also
bother.

fuss *verb* **1.** To be nervously or
uselessly active : bustle, putter.
Informal: mess around. See
ACTION, CALM in Index. **2.** To
worry over trifles : chafe, pother.
Informal: take on. See CALM in
Index.

fuss at *verb* See **nag.**

fussy *adjective* See **busy, nice.**

fustian *adjective* See **sonorous.**

fustian *noun* See **bombast.**

fusty *adjective* See **moldy, old-
fashioned.**

futile *adjective* Having no useful
result : barren, bootless, fruitless,
unavailing, unprofitable, unsuccessful, useless, vain. *Idiom:* in vain. See
THRIVE, USED in Index.

futility *noun* The condition or quality of being useless or ineffective :
bootlessness, fruitlessness, unavailingness, unprofitableness, uselessness, vainness, vanity. See THRIVE,
USED in Index.

future *noun* **1.** Time that is yet to
be : by-and-by, hereafter. *Idiom:*
time to come. See PRECEDE, TIME
in Index. **2.** Chance of success or
advancement : outlook, prospect
(used in plural). See HOPE in Index.

future *adjective* Being or occurring
in the time ahead : coming, later,
subsequent. See PRECEDE, TIME in
Index.

fuzz *noun* See **policeman.**

fuzzy *adjective* See **hairy, unclear.**

G

gab *verb* See **chatter.**

gab *noun* See **chatter.**

gabble *verb* See **babble.**

gabble *noun* See **babble.**

gabby *adjective* See **talkative.**

gad *verb* See **rove.**

gadget *noun* A small specialized
mechanical device : concern, contraption, contrivance, gimmick, jigger, thing. *Informal:* doodad, doohickey, widget. *Slang:* gizmo. See
MACHINE in Index.

gag *noun* See **joke.**

gag *verb* See **repress.**

gaga *adjective* See **giddy, insane.**

gaiety *noun* **1.** A state of joyful exuberance : blitheness, blithesome-
ness, glee, gleefulness, hilarity,
jocoseness, jocosity, jocularity,
jocundity, jolliness, jollity, joviality,
lightheartedness, merriment, merriness, mirth, mirthfulness. See
LAUGHTER in Index. **2.** Joyful, exuberant activity : conviviality, festival, festiveness, festivity, fun, jollity,
merriment, merrymaking, revel
(often used in plural), revelry. See
LAUGHTER in Index.

gain *verb* To achieve an increase of
gradually : build up, develop. See
INCREASE in Index. — See also
accomplish, arrive at at **arrive,
benefit, capture, earn, get,
recover, return.**

gain *noun* Something earned,
won, or otherwise acquired : earnings, profit, return. See GET, MONEY
in Index. — See also **advantage.**

gainsay *verb* See **deny.**

gala *noun* See **party.**

gala *adjective* See **merry.**

gale *noun* See **wind**[1].

gall[1] *noun* See **impudence,
resentment.**

gall[2] *verb* See **annoy, chafe.**

gallant *adjective* Respectfully
attentive, especially to women :
chivalric, chivalrous. See ATTI-
TUDE, COURTESY in Index. — See
also **attentive, brave, gracious.**

gallant *noun* A man amorously attentive to women : amorist, Casanova, Don Juan, lady's man, Lothario, Romeo. See SEX in Index.

gallantry *noun* Respectful attention, especially toward women : chivalrousness, chivalry. See ATTITUDE, COURTESY in Index. ─ See also **courage, heroism.**

gallimaufry *noun* See **assortment.**

galling *adjective* See **vexatious.**

gallivant *verb* See **rove.**

galumph *verb* See **lump**[1]**.**

galvanize *verb* See **provoke.**

gamble *verb* **1.** To take a risk in the hope of gaining advantage : speculate, venture. *Idiom:* take a flyer. See GAMBLING in Index. **2.** To put up as a stake in a game or speculation : bet, lay[1] (down), post[2], put, risk, stake, venture, wager. *Informal:* go. See GAMBLING in Index. ─ See also **bet.**

gamble *noun* A venture depending on chance : bet, risk, speculation, wager. See GAMBLING in Index. ─ See also **risk.**

gambler *noun* See **bettor, speculator.**

gambol *verb* To leap and skip about playfully : caper, cavort, dance, frisk, frolic, rollick, romp. See WORK in Index.

game *verb* See **bet.**

game *noun* See **play.**

game *adjective* See **brave, willing.**

gameness *noun* See **courage.**

game plan *noun* See **design.**

gamester *noun* See **bettor.**

gander *noun* See **fool, glance.**

gang *noun* An organized group of criminals, hoodlums, or wrongdoers : band[2], pack, ring[1]. *Informal:* mob. See GROUP in Index. ─ See also **crowd, force.**

gang up *verb* See **band**[2]**.**

gangling *adjective* Tall, thin, and awkwardly built : gangly, lanky, rangy, spindling, spindly. See FAT in Index.

gangly *adjective* See **gangling.**

gap *noun* **1.** An interval during which continuity is suspended : break, hiatus, interim, lacuna, void. See CONTINUE in Index. **2.** A marked lack of correspondence or agreement : difference, disagreement, discrepance, discrepancy, disparity, incompatibility, incongruity, inconsistency. See AGREE in Index. **3.** A space or interval between objects or points : interspace, interstice, interval, separation. See OPEN in Index. ─ See also **breach.**

gap *verb* See **breach, yawn.**

gape *verb* See **gaze, yawn.**

gape *noun* See **gaze.**

gaping *adjective* See **yawning.**

garb *noun* See **dress.**

garb *verb* See **dress.**

garbage *noun* See **nonsense.**

garden *adjective* See **ordinary.**

garden-variety *adjective* See **ordinary.**

gargantuan *adjective* See **giant.**

garish *adjective* See **gaudy.**

garment *verb* See **dress.**

garment *noun* See **dress.**

garner *verb* See **accumulate, gather, glean.**

garnish *verb* See **adorn.**

garnishment *noun* See **adornment.**

garniture *noun* See **adornment.**

garrulous *adjective* See **talkative.**

gas *noun* See **chatter, scream.**

gas *verb* See **chatter.**

gasconade *verb* See **boast.**

gasconade *noun* See **boast.**

gash *verb* See **cut.**

gash *noun* See **cut.**

gasp *verb* To utter in a breathless manner : heave, pant. See BREATH, WORDS in Index. ─ See also **pant.**

gate *noun* See **take**.

gather *verb* To collect ripe crops : crop, garner, harvest, pick, reap. See COLLECT in Index. — See also **accumulate, assemble, glean, infer**.

gathering *noun* See **accumulation, assembly, junction**.

gauche *adjective* See **tactless, unskillful**.

gaudy *adjective* Tastelessly showy : brummagem, chintzy, flashy, garish, glaring, loud, meretricious, tawdry, tinsel. *Informal:* tacky². See STYLE in Index.

gauge also **gage** *noun* See **standard**.

gauge also **gage** *verb* See **estimate, measure**.

gaunt *adjective* See **haggard, thin, wasted**.

gauzy *adjective* See **filmy**.

gawk *noun* See **lump¹**.

gawk *verb* See **gaze**.

gawky *adjective* See **awkward**.

gay *adjective* **1.** Characterized by joyful exuberance : blithe, blithesome, boon², convivial, gleeful, jocund, jolly, jovial, merry, mirthful. See HAPPY in Index. **2.** Of, relating to, or having a sexual orientation to members of one's own sex : homophile, homosexual, lesbian. See SEX in Index. — See also **abandoned, colorful**.

gaze *verb* To look intently and fixedly : eye, gape, gawk, goggle, ogle, peer¹, stare. *Idioms:* gaze openmouthed, rivet the eyes on. See SEE in Index.

gaze *noun* An intent fixed look : gape, stare. See SEE in Index.

gear *noun* See **outfit**.

gear *verb* See **furnish**.

gelatinize *verb* See **coagulate**.

gelatinous *adjective* See **thick**.

geld *verb* See **sterilize**.

gelid *adjective* See **frigid**.

gelidity *noun* See **frigidness**.

gelidness *noun* See **frigidness**.

gelt *noun* See **money**.

gem *noun* See **treasure**.

geminate *adjective* See **double**.

geminate *verb* See **double**.

gendarme *noun* See **policeman**.

genealogy *noun* A written record of ancestry : family tree, pedigree. See KIN in Index. — See also **ancestry**.

general *adjective* **1.** Belonging or relating to the whole : common, generic, universal. See SPECIFIC in Index. **2.** Covering a wide scope : all-around, all-inclusive, all-round, broad, broad-spectrum, comprehensive, expansive, extended, extensive, far-ranging, far-reaching, global, inclusive, large, overall, sweeping, wide-ranging, wide-reaching, widespread. See SPECIFIC in Index. **3.** Not limited to a single class : diversified. See SPECIFIC in Index. — See also **common, popular**.

generalize *verb* See **universalize**.

generally *adverb* See **usually**.

generate *verb* See **cause, develop**.

generic *adjective* See **general**.

generosity *noun* The quality or state of being generous : bigheartedness, bounteousness, bountifulness, freehandedness, generousness, great-heartedness, large-heartedness, lavishness, liberality, magnanimity, magnanimousness, munificence, openhandedness, unselfishness, unsparingness. See GIVE in Index.

generous *adjective* **1.** Willing to give of oneself and one's possessions : big, big-hearted, great-hearted, large-hearted, magnanimous, unselfish. See GIVE in Index. **2.** Characterized by bounteous giving : free, freehanded, handsome, lavish, liberal, munificent, open-

handed, unsparing, unstinting. See
GIVE in Index. **3.** Characterized by
abundance : abundant, ample,
bounteous, bountiful, copious,
heavy, plenitudinous, plenteous,
plentiful, substantial, voluminous.
See BIG, GIVE, RICH in Index.

generousness *noun* See **generosity**.

genesis *noun* See **birth**.

genial *adjective* See **amiable**.

geniality *noun* See **amiability**.

genialness *noun* See **amiability**.

genius *noun* See **fire, talent**.

genteel *adjective* Marked by excessive concern for propriety and good
form : bluenosed, old-maidish, precise, priggish, prim, prissy, proper,
prudish, puritanical, strait-laced,
stuffy, Victorian. *Idiom:* prim and
proper. See PLAIN in Index. — See
also **courteous**.

genteelness *noun* See **courtesy**.

gentility *noun* See **courtesy, society**.

gentle *adjective* **1.** Of a kindly, considerate character : mild, soft, softhearted, tender[1], tenderhearted. See
KIND in Index. **2.** Free from severity
or violence, as in movement :
balmy[1], delicate, faint, mild,
smooth, soft. See CALM, STRONG
in Index. **3.** Easily managed or han-
dled : docile, meek, mild, tame. See
WILD in Index. — See also **gradual,
light[2]**.

gentle *verb* To make (an animal)
docile : break, bust, master, tame.
See WILD in Index. — See also
domesticate, pacify.

gentry *noun* See **society**.

genuflection *noun* See **bow[1]**.

genuine *adjective* Devoid of any
hypocrisy or pretense : heartfelt,
hearty, honest, natural, real, sincere,
true, unaffected, unfeigned, unmannered. See TRUE in Index. — See also
authentic.

genuinely *adverb* See **really**.

genuineness *noun* See **authenticity**.

germ *noun* **1.** A minute organism
usually producing disease : bug,
microbe, microorganism. See
BEINGS in Index. **2.** A source of further growth and development :
bud[1], embryo, kernel, nucleus, seed,
spark[1]. See START in Index.

germane *adjective* See **relevant**.

germaneness *noun* See **relevance**.

gest or **geste** *noun* See **feat**.

gestation *noun* See **pregnancy**.

gesticulate *verb* See **gesture**.

gesticulation *noun* See **gesture**.

gesture *noun* An expressive, meaningful bodily movement : gesticulation, indication, motion, sign, signal. *Informal:* high sign. See
EXPRESS in Index. — See also
expression.

gesture *verb* To make bodily
motions so as to convey an idea or
complement speech : gesticulate,
motion, sign, signal, signalize.
Idiom: give the high sign. See
EXPRESS in Index.

get *verb* **1.** To come into possession
of : acquire, come by, gain, obtain,
procure, secure, win. *Informal:* land,
pick up. See GET in Index. **2.** To
cause to be in a certain state or to
undergo a particular experience or
action : have, make. See CAUSE in
Index. — See also **affect[1], annoy,
become, capture, contract, derive,
earn, father, learn, persuade, reach,
run, take, understand**.

get across *verb* See **communicate**.

get ahead *verb* See **succeed**.

get along *verb* To live or act
together in harmony : get on, harmonize. *Informal:* cotton. *Idiom:* hit
it off. See AGREE in Index. — See also
age, come, manage.

get around *verb* To become
known far and wide : circulate, go
around, spread, travel. *Idiom:* go (or

make) the rounds. See KNOWLEDGE in Index. — See also **avoid**.

get away *verb* See **escape, go**.

get behind *verb* See **support**.

get by *verb* See **manage**.

get in *verb* See **arrive**.

get off *verb* See **go, start**.

get on *verb* See **age, don, get along** at **get, succeed**.

get out *verb* See **come out** at **come, run**.

get to *verb* See **arrive at** at **arrive**.

get together *verb* See **agree, assemble, meet**[1].

get up *verb* 1. To leave one's bed : arise, pile, rise, roll out. *Informal:* turn out. *Idiom:* rise and shine. See RISE in Index. 2. To adopt a standing posture : arise, rise, stand (up), uprise, upspring. *Idiom:* get to one's feet. See RISE in Index.

get *noun* See **progeny**.

getaway *noun* See **escape**.

gettable *adjective* See **available**.

get-together *noun* See **assembly**.

getup *noun* See **dress**.

get-up-and-go *noun* See **drive, energy**.

gewgaw *noun* See **novelty**.

ghastly *adjective* 1. Shockingly repellent : grim, grisly, gruesome, hideous, horrible, horrid, lurid, macabre. See BEAUTIFUL in Index. 2. Gruesomely suggestive of ghosts or death : cadaverous, deadly, deathlike, deathly, ghostlike, ghostly, spectral. See LIVE in Index. — See also **fearful, terrible**.

ghost *noun* A supernatural being, such as a ghost : apparition, bogey, bogeyman, bogle, eidolon, phantasm, phantasma, phantom, revenant, shade, shadow, specter, spirit, visitant, wraith. *Informal:* spook. *Regional:* haunt. See BEINGS, SUPERNATURAL in Index. — See also **shade**.

ghost *verb* To write for and credit authorship to another : *Informal:* ghost. See WORDS in Index.

ghostlike *adjective* See **ghastly**.

ghostly *adjective* See **ghastly**.

ghostwrite *verb* See **ghost**.

ghoul *noun* See **fiend**.

ghoulish *adjective* See **fiendish**.

giant *noun* One that is extraordinarily large and powerful : behemoth, Goliath, jumbo, leviathan, mammoth, monster, titan. *Slang:* whopper. See BEINGS, BIG in Index.

giant *adjective* Of extraordinary size and power : behemoth, Brobdingnagian, Bunyanesque, colossal, cyclopean, elephantine, enormous, gargantuan, gigantesque, gigantic, herculean, heroic, huge, immense, jumbo, mammoth, massive, massy, mastodonic, mighty, monster, monstrous, monumental, mountainous, prodigious, pythonic, stupendous, titanic, tremendous, vast. *Informal:* walloping. *Slang:* whopping. See BIG in Index.

gibber *verb* See **babble**.

gibberish *noun* 1. Unintelligible or nonsensical talk or language : abracadabra, double talk, gobbledygook, jabberwocky, mumbo jumbo. See CLEAR, WORDS in Index. 2. Esoteric, formulaic, and often incomprehensible speech relating to the occult : abracadabra, hocus-pocus, mumbo jumbo. See CLEAR, SUPERNATURAL, WORDS in Index. — See also **babble**.

gibbet *verb* See **hang**.

gibe also **jibe** *verb* See **ridicule**.

gibe *noun* See **taunt**.

giddiness *noun* See **dizziness**.

giddy *adjective* 1. Given to lighthearted silliness : empty-headed, featherbrained, flighty, frivolous, frothy, harebrained, lighthearted, scatterbrained, silly. *Informal:* gaga.

Slang: birdbrained, dizzy. See ABIL-
ITY in Index. **2.** Producing dizziness
or vertigo : dizzy, dizzying, vertiginous. See AWARENESS in Index.
— See also **dizzy.**

gift *noun* Something bestowed
freely : present[2], presentation.
Chiefly British: handsel. See GIVE in
Index. — See also **donation, talent.**

   gift *verb* To present with a quality,
   trait, or power : dower, endow,
   endue, gird, invest. See GIVE in
   Index.

gifted *adjective* Having talent :
endowed, talented. See ABILITY,
GIVE in Index.

gig *noun* See **booking, position.**

gigantesque *adjective* See **giant.**

gigantic *adjective* See **giant.**

giggle *verb* To laugh in a stifled
way : snicker, snigger, titter. See
LAUGHTER in Index.

   giggle *noun* A stifled laugh :
   snicker, snigger, titter. See LAUGH-
   TER in Index.

gild *verb* See **color, sweeten.**

gimcrack *noun* See **novelty.**

gimmick *noun* See **gadget, trick,
wrinkle.**

ginger *noun* See **spirit.**

gingerliness *noun* See **care,
caution.**

gingerly *adjective* See **wary.**

gird *verb* To prepare (oneself) for
action : brace, forearm, fortify,
ready, steel, strengthen. *Idiom:* gird
(or gird up) one's loins. See PRE-
PARED in Index. — See also **band[1],
gift, surround.**

girdle *verb* See **band[1], surround.**

girt *verb* See **band[1].**

gist *noun* See **heart.**

give *verb* **1.** To make a gift of. Also
used with *away* : bestow, hand out,
present[2]. See GIVE in Index. **2.** To
relinquish to the possession or control of another : deliver, furnish,

hand, hand over, provide, supply,
transfer, turn over. See GIVE in
Index. **3.** To mete out by means of
some action : administer, deal,
deliver. See GIVE in Index. — See also
**administer, allot, apply, bear, bend,
cave in** at **cave, communicate,
donate, emit, entrust, grant, have,
spend, stage.**

give away *verb* See **betray.**

give back *verb* See **restore,
return.**

give forth *verb* See **emit.**

give in *verb* To cease opposition :
concede, yield. See WIN in Index.

give off *verb* See **emit.**

give out *verb* See **collapse, dry up**
at **dry, emit, fail, run down** at **run.**

give over *verb* To yield (oneself)
unrestrainedly, as to a particular
impulse : abandon, give up, surrender. See RESIST in Index. — See also
drop.

give up *verb* See **abandon, break,
despair, drop, give over** at **give.**

give *noun* See **flexibility.**

give-and-take also **give and
take** *noun* See **compromise.**

given *adjective* See **inclined.**

giver *noun* See **donor.**

gizmo also **gismo** *noun* See
gadget.

glacial *adjective* See **cold, frigid.**

glad *adjective* **1.** Providing joy and
pleasure : cheerful, cheery, festive,
happy, joyful, joyous, pleasing. See
HAPPY in Index. **2.** Eagerly compliant : delighted, happy, pleased,
tickled. See HAPPY in Index. — See
also **merry.**

gladden *verb* See **delight.**

gladly *adverb* See **yes.**

gladness *noun* See **happiness.**

gladsome *adjective* See **merry.**

glamorous also **glamourous**
adjective See **attractive.**

glamour also **glamor** noun See **attraction**.

glance verb To strike a surface at such an angle as to be deflected : carom, dap, graze, ricochet, skim, skip. See STRIKE in Index. — See also **flash, glimpse.**

glance at or **over** or **through** verb See **browse**.

glance noun A quick look : blush, glimpse, peek, peep. *Informal:* gander. See SEE in Index. — See also **blink**.

glare verb **1.** To stare fixedly and angrily : glower, lower[1], scowl. *Idiom:* look daggers at. See EXPRESS, SEE in Index. **2.** To be projected with blinding intensity : beat down, blaze[1]. See LIGHT in Index. **3.** To be obtrusively conspicuous : stand out, stick out. *Idioms:* stare someone in the face, stick out like a sore thumb. See SEE in Index.

glare noun **1.** A fixed angry stare : glower, lower[1], scowl. See EXPRESS, SEE in Index. **2.** An intense blinding light : blaze[1], dazzle. See LIGHT in Index.

glaring adjective See **brilliant, flagrant, gaudy.**

glaringness noun See **flagrancy**.

glary adjective See **brilliant**.

glassy adjective See **glossy**.

glaze noun See **gloss**.

glaze verb See **gloss**.

gleam noun See **blink**.

gleam verb See **beam, flash, glow.**

gleaming adjective See **glossy**.

glean verb To collect (something) bit by bit : cull, extract, garner, gather, pick up. See COLLECT in Index.

glee noun See **gaiety**.

gleeful adjective See **gay**.

gleefulness noun See **gaiety**.

glib adjective Characterized by ready but often insincere or superfi-

cial discourse : facile, slick, smooth-tongued. See SURFACE, WORDS in Index.

glide verb To move smoothly, continuously, and effortlessly : glissade, lapse, slide, slip, slither. See MOVE in Index. See also **ease, flow, sneak.**

glimmer noun See **blink**.

glimmer verb See **blink, flash.**

glimpse verb To look briefly and quickly : glance, peek, peep. See SEE in Index. — See also **catch**.

glimpse noun See **glance**.

glint noun See **blink, glitter.**

glint verb See **flash**.

glissade verb See **glide**.

glisten verb See **flash**.

glisten noun See **glitter**.

glistening adjective See **glossy**.

glister verb See **flash**.

glister noun See **glitter**.

glitter noun **1.** Sparkling, brilliant light : flash, glint, glisten, glister, scintillation, shimmer, sparkle. See BEAUTIFUL, LIGHT in Index. **2.** Brilliant, showy splendor : brilliance, brilliancy, glory, gorgeousness, magnificence, resplendence, resplendency, sparkle, sumptuousness. *Informal:* glitz. See BEAUTIFUL in Index. **3.** A small sparkling decoration : sequin, spangle. See BEAUTIFUL in Index.

glitter verb See **flash**.

glitz noun See **glitter**.

gloaming noun See **evening**.

global adjective See **general, universal.**

globoid adjective See **round**.

globular adjective See **round**.

globule noun See **drop**.

gloom noun A feeling or spell of dismally low spirits : blues, dejection, depression, despondence, despondency, doldrums, dolefulness, downheartedness, dumps, dysphoria, funk, glumness, heavy-heartedness, melancholy, mope (used in plural), mournfulness, sadness, unhappiness. See FEELINGS, HAPPY in Index.

gloom *verb* See **obscure.**

gloomy *adjective* **1.** Dark and depressing : black, bleak, blue, cheerless, dark, desolate, dismal, dreary, glum, joyless, somber, tenebrific. See HAPPY, LIGHT in Index. **2.** Marked by little hopefulness : dark, dismal, pessimistic. See HAPPY, HOPE in Index. — See also **depressed, glum, sad.**

glorification *noun* See **exaltation, praise.**

glorify *verb* See **exalt, honor, praise.**

glorious *adjective* Marked by extraordinary elegance, beauty, and splendor : brilliant, gorgeous, magnificent, proud, resplendent, splendid, splendorous. See BEAUTIFUL in Index. — See also **marvelous.**

glory *noun* Something meriting the highest praise or regard : grandeur, grandiosity, grandness, greatness, majesty, splendor. See PRAISE in Index. — See also **eminence, glitter.**

glory *verb* See **exult.**

gloss *noun* A radiant brightness or glow, usually due to light reflected from a smooth surface : burnish, glaze, luster, polish, sheen, shine, sleekness. See LIGHT in Index. — See also **façade.**

gloss *verb* To give a gleaming luster to, usually through friction : buff[1], burnish, furbish, glaze, polish, shine, sleek. See LIGHT in Index. — See also **color.**

gloss over *verb* See **extenuate.**

glossary *noun* See **vocabulary.**

glossy *adjective* Having a high, radiant sheen : glassy, gleaming, glistening, lustrous, polished, shining, shiny. See LIGHT in Index.

glow *verb* To shine brightly and steadily but without a flame : gleam, incandesce, luminesce. See LIGHT in Index. — See also **beam, blush.**

glow *noun* A feeling of pervasive emotional warmth : flush. See FEELINGS in Index. — See also **bloom[1].**

glower *verb* See **frown, glare.**

glower *noun* See **frown, glare.**

glowing *adjective* See **fresh, passionate, ruddy.**

gloze *verb* See **color, extenuate.**

gluey *adjective* See **sticky.**

glum *adjective* Broodingly and sullenly unhappy : dour, gloomy, moody, morose, saturnine, sour, sulky, sullen, surly. See HAPPY in Index. — See also **gloomy.**

glumness *noun* See **gloom.**

glut *verb* See **satiate.**

glut *noun* See **surplus.**

glutinous *adjective* See **viscous.**

glutinousness *noun* See **viscosity.**

gluttonous *adjective* See **greedy, voracious.**

gnash *verb* See **bite, grind.**

gnaw *verb* See **bite.**

gnawing *adjective* See **sharp.**

go *verb* **1.** To move along a particular course : fare, journey, pass, proceed, push on, remove, travel, wend. *Idiom:* make one's way. See MOVE in Index. **2.** To move or proceed away from a place : depart, exit, get away, get off, go away, leave[1], pull out, quit, retire, run (along), withdraw. *Informal:* cut out, push off, shove off. *Slang:* blow[1], split, take off. *Idioms:* hit the road, take leave. See APPROACH in Index. **3.** To be depleted : consume, spend. *Idiom:* go down the drain. See INCREASE in Index. **4.** To move toward a termination : go away, pass, pass away. See APPROACH, INCREASE, TIME in

Index. **5.** To move past in time. Also used with *by* : elapse, lapse, pass. See TIME in Index. **6.** To change or fluctuate within limits : extend, range, run, vary. See CHANGE in Index. **7.** *Informal.* To make an offer of : bid, offer. See OFFER in Index. — See also **bear, belong, cave** in at **cave, die, endure, extend, gamble, prosper, resort, succeed, work.**

go along *verb* See **play along** at **play.**

go around *verb* See **get around** at **get, skirt.**

go at *verb* See **attack.**

go away *verb* See **go.**

go back *verb* See **return.**

go down *verb* See **fall, surrender.**

go far *verb* See **succeed.**

go for *verb* See **approve, cost, enjoy.**

go in *verb* See **enter.**

go off *verb* See **explode.**

go on *verb* See **carry on** at **carry, chatter, endure.**

go out *verb* See **see.**

go over *verb* See **examine, review, succeed.**

go through *verb* See **experience.**

go under *verb* See **collapse, surrender.**

go up *verb* See **ascend.**

go with *verb* See **fit**[1].

go *noun* See **attempt, energy, try, turn.**

go *adjective* See **ready.**

goad *verb* See **provoke.**

goad *noun* See **stimulus.**

goal *noun* See **intention.**

goat *noun* See **scapegoat.**

gob[1] *noun* See **heap, lump**[1].

gob[2] *noun* See **mouth.**

gob[3] *noun* See **sailor.**

gobble *verb* See **gulp.**

gobbledygook also **gobbledegook** *noun* See **gibberish.**

go-between *noun* Someone who acts as an intermediate agent in a transaction or helps to resolve differences : broker, interceder, intercessor, intermediary, intermediate, intermediator, mediator, middleman. See MEANS in Index.

go-by *noun* See **snub.**

godforsaken also **Godforsaken** *adjective* See **lonely.**

godlike *adjective* See **divine.**

godly *adjective* See **divine, holy.**

God's country *noun* See **country.**

go-getter *noun* See **eager beaver.**

goggle *verb* See **gaze.**

going *noun* See **departure.**

going *adjective* See **active.**

going-over *noun* See **examination.**

goldbrick *verb* See **idle.**

golden ager *noun* See **senior.**

Goliath *noun* See **giant.**

gone *adjective* See **absent, dead, infatuated, lost, pregnant.**

good *adjective* **1.** Well above average : high-grade, nice. See ABILITY, GOOD in Index. **2.** Having pleasant desirable qualities : nice. *Scots:* bonny, braw. See GOOD in Index. **3.** In excellent condition : entire, flawless, intact, perfect, sound[2], unblemished, unbroken, undamaged, unharmed, unhurt, unimpaired, uninjured, unmarred, whole. See THRIVE in Index. — See also **able, agreeable, authentic, beneficial, benevolent, big, convenient, exemplary, favorable, honest, round.**

good *noun* **1.** The quality or state of being morally sound : goodness, morality, probity, rectitude, righteousness, rightness, uprightness, virtue, virtuousness. See RIGHT in Index. **2.** A product or products bought and sold in commerce. Used in plural : commodity, line, merchandise, ware. See MATTER, TRANS-

ACTIONS in Index. — See also **effect, interest**.

good-bye or **goodbye** also **good-by** noun See **parting**.

good-bye or **goodbye** also **good-by** adjective See **parting**.

good form noun See **manner**.

good-for-nothing noun See **wastrel**.

good-for-nothing adjective See **worthless**.

goodhearted adjective See **benevolent**.

goodish adjective See **acceptable**.

good-looking adjective See **beautiful**.

goodly adjective See **sizable**.

good name noun See **honor**.

good-natured adjective See **amiable**.

goodness noun See **good**.

good report noun See **honor**.

good-tempered adjective See **amiable**.

good turn noun See **favor**.

goodwill also **good will** noun See **benevolence**.

goody noun See **delicacy**.

gooey adjective See **sentimental, sticky**.

goof noun See **blunder, fool**.

goof verb See **idle**.

goof up verb See **botch**.

goon noun See **thug**.

goose noun See **fool**.

gore noun See **blood**.

gorge verb See **satiate**.

gorgeous adjective See **beautiful, glorious**.

gorgeousness noun See **glitter**.

gorilla noun See **thug**.

gory adjective See **bloody**.

gossamer adjective See **filmy**.

gossamery adjective See **filmy**.

gossip noun **1.** Idle, often sensational and groundless talk about others : gossipry, hearsay, report, rumor, talebearing, tattle, tittle-tattle, word. *Slang:* scuttlebutt. See WORDS in Index. **2.** A person habitually engaged in idle talk about others : blab, gossiper, gossipmonger, newsmonger, rumormonger, scandalmonger, tabby, talebearer, taleteller, tattle, tattler, tattletale, telltale, whisperer. *Slang:* yenta. See WORDS in Index.

gossip verb To engage in or spread gossip : blab, noise, rumor, talk, tattle, tittle-tattle, whisper. *Idioms:* tell tales, tell tales out of school. See WORDS in Index.

gossiper noun See **gossip**.

gossipmonger noun See **gossip**.

gossipry noun See **gossip**.

gossipy adjective Inclined to gossip : blabby, talebearing, taletelling. See WORDS in Index.

gouge verb See **skin**.

govern verb **1.** To exercise the authority of a sovereign : reign, rule. *Archaic:* sway. *Idiom:* wear the crown (or purple). See OVER in Index. **2.** To keep the mechanical operation of (a device) within proper parameters : control, regulate. See CONTROL, MACHINE in Index. — See also **administer, control**.

governable adjective Capable of being governed : administrable, controllable, manageable, rulable. See CONTROL in Index.

governance noun See **government**.

governing adjective See **dominant**.

government noun **1.** A system by which a political unit is controlled : governance, regime, rule. See POLITICS in Index. **2.** The continuous exercise of authority over a political unit : administration, control, direction, governance, rule. See CONTROL, POLITICS in Index. — See also **administration**.

governmental *adjective* Of or relating to government : gubernatorial, regulatory. See POLITICS in Index.

gown *noun* See **dress.**

grab *verb* See **catch, grasp, grip, coize.**

grab *noun* See **catch.**

grab bag *noun* See **assortment.**

grabbiness *noun* See **greed.**

grabble *verb* See **grope.**

grabby *adjective* See **greedy.**

grace *noun* **1.** Kind, forgiving, or compassionate treatment of or disposition toward others : charity, clemency, lenience, leniency, lenity, mercifulness, mercy. See FORGIVENESS in Index. **2.** Temporary immunity from penalties : reprieve, respite. See CONTINUE in Index. **3.** A short prayer said at meals : benediction, blessing, thanks, thanksgiving. See GRATEFUL, RELIGION in Index. — See also **benevolence, decency, elegance, favor.**

grace *verb* **1.** To lend dignity or honor to by an act or favor : dignify, honor. See BEAUTIFUL in Index. **2.** To endow with beauty and elegance by way of a notable addition : adorn, beautify, embellish, enhance, set off. See BEAUTIFUL in Index.

graceful *adjective* See **elegant, smooth.**

graceless *adjective* See **awkward.**

gracious *adjective* **1.** Characterized by kindness and warm, unaffected courtesy : affable, hospitable. See KIND in Index. **2.** Characterized by elaborate but usually formal courtesy : chivalrous, courtly, gallant, knightly, stately. See ATTITUDE, COURTESY in Index.

gradation *noun* See **shade.**

gradational *adjective* See **gradual.**

grade *noun* See **class, degree, inclination, quality.**

grade *verb* See **class, score.**

gradient *noun* See **inclination.**

gradual *adjective* **1.** Proceeding very slowly by degrees : gradational, piecemeal, step-by-step. See FAST in Index. **2.** Not steep or abrupt : easy, gentle, moderate. See RISE in Index.

graft *noun* See **bribe.**

grain *noun* See **bit¹.**

grainy *adjective* See **coarse.**

grand *adjective* Large and impressive in size, scope, or extent : august, baronial, grandiose, imposing, lordly, magnific, magnificent, majestic, noble, princely, regal, royal, splendid, stately, sublime, superb. See BIG, GOOD in Index. — See also **elevated, exalted.**

grandeur *noun* See **glory.**

grandiloquence *noun* See **bombast.**

grandiloquent *adjective* See **sonorous.**

grandiose *adjective* See **grand, pompous.**

grandioseness *noun* See **pretentiousness.**

grandiosity *noun* See **glory, pretentiousness.**

grandness *noun* See **glory.**

grant *verb* To let have as a favor, prerogative, or privilege : accord, award, concede, give, vouchsafe. See GIVE in Index. — See also **acknowledge, confer, transfer.**

grant *noun* **1.** Something, as a gift, granted for a definite purpose : appropriation, subsidy, subvention. See GIVE in Index. **2.** *Law.* A making over of legal ownership or title : alienation, assignment, conveyance, transfer, transferal. See LAW in Index. — See also **conferment.**

granular *adjective* See **coarse.**

granulate *verb* See **crush.**

graphic *adjective* **1.** Of or relating to representation by means of writing : calligraphic, scriptural, written. See WORDS in Index. **2.** Of or relating to representation by drawings or pictures : hieroglyphic, illustrative, photographic, pictographic, pictorial. See SEE in Index. **3.** Described verbally in sharp and accurate detail : lifelike, photographic, pictorial, picturesque, realistic, vivid. See SPECIFIC, WORDS in Index. — See also **descriptive.**

grapple *noun* See **hold.**

grapple *verb* See **grasp, wrestle.**

grasp *verb* To take firmly with the hand and maintain a hold on : clasp, clench, clutch[1], grab, grapple, grip, seize. See KEEP in Index. — See also **know, understand.**

grasp *noun* **1.** The ability or power to seize or attain : capacity, compass, range, reach, scope. See ABILITY in Index. **2.** Intellectual hold : apprehension, comprehension, grip, hold, understanding. *Informal:* savvy. See KNOWLEDGE in Index. — See also **grip, hold.**

grasping *adjective* See **greedy.**

graspingness *noun* See **greed.**

grate *verb* See **scrape.**

grateful *adjective* Showing or feeling gratitude : appreciative, thankful. See GRATEFUL in Index. — See also **agreeable.**

gratefulness *noun* See **appreciation.**

gratified *adjective* See **fulfilled.**

gratify *verb* See **delight, humor, satisfy.**

gratifying *adjective* See **agreeable, enjoyable.**

grating *adjective* See **harsh.**

gratis *adjective* See **free.**

gratitude *noun* See **appreciation.**

gratuitous *adjective* See **free, wanton.**

gratuity *noun* A material favor or gift, usually money, given in return for service : cumshaw, largess, perquisite, tip[3]. See GIVE, TRANSACTIONS in Index.

gravamen *noun* See **heart.**

grave[1] *noun* A burial place or receptacle for human remains : catacomb, cinerarium, crypt, mausoleum, ossuary, sepulcher, sepulture, tomb, vault[1]. See KEEP, PLACE in Index.

grave[2] *adjective* **1.** Having great consequence or weight : earnest[1], heavy, momentous, serious, severe, weighty. See IMPORTANT in Index. **2.** Full of or marked by dignity and seriousness : earnest[1], sedate, serious, sober, solemn, somber, staid. See ATTITUDE, HEAVY in Index. — See also **fateful, grievous.**

grave[3] *verb* See **engrave.**

graveness *noun* See **gravity.**

gravid *adjective* See **pregnant.**

gravidity *noun* See **pregnancy.**

gravidness *noun* See **pregnancy.**

gravitate *verb* See **settle.**

gravity *noun* **1.** The condition of being grave and of involving serious consequences : graveness, momentousness, seriousness, weightiness. See IMPORTANT in Index. **2.** High seriousness of manner or bearing : graveness, sedateness, sobriety, solemnity, solemnness, staidness. See ATTITUDE, HEAVY, STYLE in Index.

gray matter *noun* See **head.**

graze *verb* See **brush**[1]**, glance.**

graze *noun* See **brush**[1]**.**

greasy *adjective* See **fatty.**

great *adjective* See **big, eminent, excellent, marvelous, pregnant.**

greater *adjective* See **best.**

great-hearted *adjective* See **generous.**

great-heartedness *noun* See **generosity.**

greatly *adverb* See **very.**

greatness *noun* See **glory, size.**

greed *noun* Excessive desire for more than one needs or deserves : acquisitiveness, avarice, avariciousness, avidity, covetousness, cupidity, graspingness. *Informal:* grabbiness. See DESIRE, GIVE in Index.

greedy *adjective* **1.** Having a strong urge to obtain or possess something, especially material wealth, in quantity : acquisitive, avaricious, avid, covetous, grasping, hungry. *Informal:* grabby. See DESIRE, GIVE in Index. **2.** Wanting to eat or drink more than one can reasonably consume : edacious, gluttonous, hoggish, piggish, ravenous, voracious. See DESIRE, INGESTION in Index.
— See also **voracious.**

green *adjective* See **inexperienced, young.**

green *noun* See **common, money.**

green-eyed *adjective* See **envious.**

greenhorn *noun* See **beginner.**

greenness *noun* See **inexperience, youth.**

greet *verb* **1.** To address in a friendly and respectful way : hail[2], salute, welcome. See GREETING in Index. **2.** To present with a specified reaction : meet[1], react, respond. See FEELINGS, GREETING in Index.
— See also **accost.**

greeting *noun* An expression, in words or gestures, marking a meeting of persons : hail[2], salutation, salute, welcome. See GREETING in Index.

gregarious *adjective* See **outgoing, social.**

gridlock *noun* See **tie-up.**

grief *noun* Mental anguish or pain caused by loss or despair : heartache, heartbreak, sorrow. See HAPPY in Index.

grievance *noun* See **complaint.**

grieve *verb* To feel, show, or express grief : lament, mourn, sorrow, suffer. See HAPPY in Index.
— See also **distress.**

grievous *adjective* Causing or marked by danger or pain, for example : dangerous, grave[2], serious, severe. See HELP in Index. — See also **sorrowful.**

grill *verb* See **interrogate.**

grim *adjective* See **bleak, ghastly, stubborn.**

grimace *noun* See **face.**

grimace *verb* To contort one's face to indicate displeasure, disgust, or pain, for example : mouth, mug. *Idioms:* make a face, make faces. See EXPRESS in Index.

grime *noun* See **filth.**

griminess *noun* See **dirtiness.**

grimness *noun* See **stubbornness.**

grimy *adjective* See **dirty.**

grin *verb* See **smile.**

grin *noun* See **smile.**

grind *verb* **1.** To rub together noisily : crunch, gnash. See SOUNDS in Index. **2.** *Informal.* To do tedious, laborious, and sometimes menial work : drudge, grub, plod, slave, slog. See WORK in Index. — See also **bone, crush, tyrannize.**

grind *noun* *Informal.* A habitual, laborious, often tiresome course of action : routine, rut[1], treadmill. *Slang:* groove. See USUAL in Index.
— See also **drudge.**

grip *noun* Firm control : grasp, hold. See CONTROL in Index. — See also **grasp, hold.**

grip *verb* To compel, as the attention, interest, or imagination, of : arrest, catch up, enthrall, fascinate, hold, mesmerize, rivet, spellbind, transfix. *Slang:* grab. See EXCITE in Index. — See also **grasp.**

gripe *verb* See **complain.**

 gripe *noun* See **complaint.**

griper *noun* See **grouch.**

grisly *adjective* See **ghastly.**

gritty *adjective* See **coarse.**

groom *verb* See **tidy.**

groove *noun* See **grind.**

 groove on *verb* See **adore.**

groovy *adjective* See **marvelous.**

grope *verb* To reach about or search blindly or uncertainly : feel, fumble, grabble, poke. See SEEK, TOUCH in Index.

gross *adjective* See **coarse, fat, flagrant, obscene, whole.**

 gross *noun* See **whole.**

 gross *verb* See **return.**

grossness *noun* See **flagrancy, obscenity.**

grotesque *adjective* See **fantastic, freakish.**

grotto *noun* See **cave.**

grouch *verb* See **complain.**

 grouch *noun* A person who habitually complains or grumbles : complainer, crab, faultfinder, growler, grumbler, grump, murmurer, mutterer, whiner. *Informal:* crank, griper, grouser. *Slang:* bellyacher, sorehead, sourpuss. See HAPPY in Index.

grouchy *adjective* See **ill-tempered.**

ground *noun* See **base¹, basis, cause, reason.**

 ground *verb* See **base¹, drop.**

groundless *adjective* See **baseless.**

groundlessly *adverb* See **unfoundedly.**

groundwork *noun* See **base¹, basis.**

group *noun* A number of individuals making up or considered a unit : array, band², batch, bevy, body, bunch, bundle, clump, cluster, clutch², collection, knot, lot, party, set². See GROUP in Index. — See also **assembly, circle.**

 group *verb* See **assemble, assort, class.**

grouping *noun* See **arrangement.**

grouse *verb* See **complain.**

 grouse *noun* See **complaint.**

grouser *noun* See **grouch.**

grovel *verb* See **fawn.**

grow *verb* To bring into existence and foster the development of : breed, cultivate, propagate, raise. See CARE FOR, REPRODUCTION in Index. — See also **become, increase, mature.**

growl *verb* See **rumble.**

growler *noun* See **grouch.**

grown *adjective* See **mature.**

grown-up *adjective* See **mature.**

growth *noun* See **development, increase.**

grub *verb* See **dig, grind.**

 grub *noun* See **drudge, food.**

grubbiness *noun* See **dirtiness.**

grubby *adjective* See **dirty.**

grubstake *verb* See **finance.**

 grubstake *noun* See **capital.**

grudge *verb* See **envy.**

gruesome *adjective* See **ghastly.**

gruff *adjective* See **abrupt, hoarse.**

grumble *verb* See **mutter, rumble.**

 grumble *noun* See **mutter.**

grumbler *noun* See **grouch.**

grump *noun* See **grouch.**

 grump *verb* See **complain.**

grumpy *adjective* See **ill-tempered.**

grunt *verb* See **mutter.**

 grunt *noun* See **mutter.**

guarantee *noun* An assumption of responsibility, as one given by a manufacturer, for the quality, worth, or durability of a product : guaranty, surety, warrant, warranty. See OBLIGATION in Index. — See also **promise.**

 guarantee *verb* **1.** To render certain : assure, ensure, insure,

secure, warrant. *Informal:* cinch. See
CERTAIN in Index. **2.** To assume
responsibility for the quality, worth,
or durability of : certify, guaranty,
warrant. See OBLIGATION in Index.
— See also **secure.**

guarantor *noun* See **sponsor.**

guaranty *noun* See **guarantee,
pawn[1], promise, sponsor.**

guaranty *verb* See **guarantee.**

guard *verb* See **defend.**

guard *noun* A person or special
body of persons assigned to provide
protection or keep watch over, for
example : lookout, picket, protector, sentinel, sentry, ward, watch.
See AWARENESS, SAFETY in Index.
— See also **defense.**

guardian *noun* A person who is
legally responsible for the person or
property of another considered by
law to be incompetent to manage his
or her affairs : caretaker, custodian,
keeper. *Law:* conservator. See LAW
in Index.

guardianship *noun* See **care.**

gubernatorial *adjective* See **governmental.**

gudgeon *noun* See **dupe.**

guerdon *noun* See **due, reward.**

guerdon *verb* See **reward.**

guess *verb* To draw an inference on
the basis of inconclusive evidence or
insufficient information : conjecture, infer, speculate, suppose, surmise. See OPINION in Index.

guess *noun* A judgment, estimate,
or opinion arrived at by guessing :
conjecture, guesswork, speculation,
supposition, surmise. See OPINION
in Index.

guesswork *noun* See **guess.**

guest *noun* See **company.**

guffaw *verb* See **break up** at **break,
laugh.**

guffaw *noun* See **laugh.**

guidance *noun* An act or instance
of guiding : direction, lead, leadership, management. See AFFECT in
Index.

guide *noun* Something or someone
that shows the way : conductor,
director, escort, lead, leader, pilot,
shepherd, usher. See SHOW in Index.

guide *verb* To show the way to :
conduct, direct, escort, lead, pilot,
route, shepherd, show, steer, usher.
See SHOW in Index. — See also
maneuver.

guild *noun* See **union.**

guile *noun* See **art, deceit.**

guileful *adjective* See **artful,
underhand.**

guileless *adjective* See **artless.**

guilt *noun* See **blame.**

guiltless *adjective* See **innocent.**

guilty *adjective* See **blameworthy.**

guise *noun* See **dress, façade.**

gulf *noun* See **deep.**

gull *noun* See **dupe.**

gull *verb* See **cheat.**

gullible *adjective* See **easy.**

gulp *verb* To swallow (food or
drink) greedily or rapidly in large
amounts : bolt, down, englut,
engorge, gobble, guzzle, ingurgitate,
swill, wolf. See INGESTION in Index.

gulp *noun* See **swallow.**

gummy *adjective* See **sticky.**

gumption *noun* See **common sense,
drive.**

gumshoe *noun* See **detective.**

gumshoe *verb* See **sneak.**

gum up *verb* See **botch.**

gun *verb* See **shoot.**

gung ho *adjective* See **enthusiastic.**

gurgle *verb* See **wash.**

gurgling *adjective* See **laughing.**

gush *verb* See **emotionalize, flow.**

gush *noun* See **spate.**

gushy *adjective* See **sentimental.**

gust *noun* See **outburst, wind[1].**

gusto *noun* See **zest.**

gusty *adjective* See **airy.**

gut *adjective* See **inner.**

 gut *noun* See **courage.**

gutless *adjective* See **cowardly.**

gutlessness *noun* See **cowardice.**

gutsiness *noun* See **courage.**

gutsy *adjective* See **brave.**

gutty *adjective* See **brave.**

guzzle *verb* See **drink, gulp.**

gyp also **gip** *verb* See **cheat.**

 gyp also **gip** *noun* See **cheat.**

gypper also **gypper** *noun* See **cheat.**

gyrate *verb* See **turn.**

gyration *noun* See **revolution.**

gyre *noun* See **circle.**

gyve *noun* See **bond.**

H

habiliment *noun* See **dress.**

habit *noun* Clothing worn by members of a religious order : robe, vestment. See PUT ON in Index. — See also **constitution, custom.**

habitable *adjective* See **livable.**

habitat *noun* See **home.**

habitation *noun* See **home.**

habitual *adjective* See **accustomed, chronic, customary.**

habitually *adverb* See **usually.**

habitualness *noun* See **usualness.**

habituate *verb* See **accustom.**

habituated *adjective* See **accustomed, chronic.**

habitude *noun* See **custom.**

habitus *noun* See **constitution.**

hackneyed *adjective* See **trite.**

hag *noun* See **witch.**

haggard *adjective* Pale and exhausted, as because of worry or sleeplessness : careworn, drawn, gaunt, hollow-eyed, wan, worn. See TIRED in Index.

haggle *verb* To argue about the terms, as of a sale : bargain, dicker, higgle, huckster, negotiate, palter. See AGREE in Index.

ha-ha *noun* See **joke.**

hail[1] *noun* See **barrage.**

hail[2] *verb* See **accost, come, greet, honor.**

 hail *noun* See **greeting.**

hair *noun* See **shade.**

hair-raising *adjective* See **horrible.**

hairy *adjective* Covered with hair : fleecy, furry, fuzzy, hirsute, pilose, woolly. See SMOOTH in Index. — See also **dangerous.**

halcyon *adjective* See **still.**

hale *adjective* See **healthy.**

haleness *noun* See **health.**

halfhearted *adjective* See **tepid.**

half-witted *adjective* See **backward.**

halloo also **halloa** *verb* See **roar.**

 halloo also **halloa** *noun* See **shout.**

hallow *verb* See **devote, sanctify.**

hallowed *adjective* See **holy, sacred.**

hallucination *noun* An illusion of perceiving something that does not really exist : phantasmagoria, phantasmagory. *Slang:* trip. See REAL in Index. — See also **illusion.**

hallucinatory *adjective* See **illusive.**

hallucinogen *noun* See **drug.**

halt[1] *verb* See **stop.**

 halt *noun* See **stop.**

halt[2] *verb* See **hesitate, limp.**

halting *adjective* See **hesitant.**

hammer *verb* See **beat.**

hamper *verb* To restrict the activity or free movement of : chain, fetter, hamstring, handcuff, hobble, leash, manacle, shackle, tie, trammel. *Informal:* hog-tie. See FREE, HELP in Index.

 hamper *noun* See **bar.**

hamstring *verb* See **hamper.**

hand *verb* See **give, pass.**

hand down *verb* To convey (something) from one generation to the next : bequeath, hand on, pass (along *or* on), transmit. See GIVE in Index. — See also **return.**

hand on *verb* See **hand down** at **hand.**

hand out *verb* See **distribute, donate, give.**

hand over *verb* See **abdicate, entrust, give.**

hand *noun* See **applause, help, laborer, phase, side.**

handcuff *verb* See **hamper.**

handcuff *noun* See **bond.**

handicap *noun* See **advantage, disadvantage.**

handle *verb* To use with or as if with the hands : manipulate, ply^2, wield. See CONTROL, USED in Index. — See also **deal with** at **deal, sell, touch.**

handle *noun* See **name.**

handout *noun* See **donation, relief.**

handsel *also* **hansel** *noun* See **gift.**

handsome *adjective* See **beautiful, generous.**

handy *adjective* See **convenient, dexterous, practical.**

hang *verb* **1.** To fasten or be fastened at one point with no support from below : dangle, depend, sling, suspend, swing. See HANG in Index. **2.** To execute by suspending by the neck : gibbet. *Informal:* string up. *Slang:* swing. See HELP in Index. **3.** To remain stationary over a place or object : hover, poise. See HANG in Index.

hang around *verb* See **associate, frequent.**

hang on *verb* See **carry on** at **carry, depend on** at **depend.**

hang out *verb* See **associate, frequent.**

hang over *verb* See **threaten.**

hang up *verb* See **delay.**

hang upon *verb* See **depend on** at **depend.**

hang *noun* *Informal.* The proper method for doing, using, or handling something : feel, knack, trick. See ABILITY in Index.

hanger-on *noun* See **parasite.**

hanging *adjective* Hung or appearing to be hung from a support : dangly, pendulous, pensile. See HANG in Index.

hangout *noun* See **haunt.**

hang-up *noun* See **complex.**

hanker *verb* See **desire.**

hap *verb* See **chance, come.**

hap *noun* See **chance.**

haphazard *adjective* See **random.**

hapless *adjective* See **unfortunate.**

haplessness *noun* See **misfortune.**

happen *verb* See **chance, come.**

happen on *or* **upon** *verb* See **come across** at **come.**

happenchance *noun* See **chance.**

happening *noun* See **circumstance, event.**

happenstance *noun* See **chance.**

happiness *noun* A condition of supreme well-being and good spirits : beatitude, blessedness, bliss, cheer, cheerfulness, felicity, gladness, joy, joyfulness. See HAPPY in Index.

happy *adjective* Characterized by luck or good fortune : fortunate, lucky, providential. See LUCK in Index. — See also **appropriate, cheerful, fulfilled, glad, merry.**

harangue *verb* See **rant.**

harangue *noun* See **tirade.**

harass *verb* See **annoy, besiege.**

harassment *noun* See **annoyance.**

harbinger *noun* See **precursor.**

harbor *noun* See **cover.**

harbor *verb* **1.** To give refuge to : haven, house, shelter. See PROTECTION in Index. **2.** To provide with often temporary lodging : accommodate, bed (down), berth, bestow, billet, board, bunk[1], domicile, house, lodge, put up, quarter, room. See PROTECTION in Index. — See also **bear.**

harborage *noun* See **refuge.**

hard *adjective* **1.** Physically toughened so as to have great endurance : hard-bitten, hard-handed, hardy, rugged, tough. *Idiom:* hard as nails. See CONTINUE, STRONG in Index. **2.** Containing alcohol : alcoholic, intoxicative, spirituous, strong. See INGESTION in Index. — See also **bitter, bleak, burdensome, certain, cold-blooded, difficult, factual, firm[1], heavy, realistic, resentful, severe.**

hard *adverb* **1.** With intense energy and force : energetically, forcefully, forcibly, powerfully, vigorously. *Idioms:* hammer and tongs, tooth and nail, with might and main. See STRONG in Index. **2.** In a violent, strenuous way : fiercely, frantically, frenziedly, furiously, strenuously. See STRONG in Index. **3.** With effort : arduously, difficultly, heavily, laboriously. See EASY in Index. — See also **close.**

hard-bitten *adjective* See **hard.**

hard-boiled *adjective* See **cold-blooded.**

harden *verb* **1.** To make or become physically hard : cake, concrete, congeal, dry, indurate, petrify, set[1], solidify. See SOLID in Index. **2.** To make resistant to hardship, especially through continued exposure : acclimate, acclimatize, caseharden, indurate, season, toughen. See CONTINUE, RESIST in Index. — See also **confirm.**

hardened *adjective* See **cold-blooded.**

hard-fisted *adjective* See **stingy.**

hard-handed *adjective* See **hard.**

hardheaded *adjective* See **obstinate, realistic.**

hardheadedness *noun* See **obstinacy.**

hardhearted *adjective* See **cold-blooded.**

hard-hitting *adjective* See **forceful.**

hardly *adverb* See **barely.**

hardness *noun* See **severity, stability.**

hard-shell *adjective* See **confirmed.**

hardship *noun* See **difficulty.**

hardy *adjective* See **brave, hard, strong.**

harebrained *adjective* See **foolish, giddy.**

hark *verb* See **hear, listen.**

harlot *noun* See **prostitute.**

harm *noun* The action or result of inflicting loss or pain : damage, detriment, hurt, injury, mischief. See HELP in Index.

harm *verb* See **injure.**

harmful *adjective* Causing harm or injury : bad, deleterious, detrimental, evil, hurtful, ill, injurious, mischievous. See HELP in Index.

harmless *adjective* Devoid of hurtful qualities : hurtless, innocent, innocuous, inoffensive, unoffensive. See HELP in Index. — See also **innocent.**

harmonic *adjective* See **harmonious.**

harmonious *adjective* Characterized by harmony of sound : consonant, harmonic, musical, symphonic, symphonious. See BEAUTIFUL, SOUNDS in Index. — See also **agreeable, symmetrical.**

harmonization *noun* See **agreement.**

harmonize *verb* **1.** To bring into accord : accommodate, attune, conform, coordinate, integrate, proportion, reconcile, tune. See AGREE in Index. **2.** To combine and adapt in order to attain a particular effect : arrange, blend, coordinate, integrate, orchestrate, synthesize, unify. See BEAUTIFUL in Index. — See also **agree, get along** at **get.**

harmony *noun* Pleasing agreement, as of musical sounds : accord, concert, concord, symphony, tune. *Music:* consonance. See BEAUTIFUL in Index. — See also **agreement, proportion.**

harpy *noun* See **scold.**

harrow *verb* See **sack².**

harrowing *adjective* See **tormenting.**

harry *verb* See **annoy, besiege, raid.**

harsh *adjective* Disagreeable to the sense of hearing : dry, grating, hoarse, jarring, rasping, raspy, raucous, rough, scratchy, squawky, strident. See SOUNDS in Index. — See also **bitter, bleak, rough, severe.**

harshness *noun* See **severity.**

harum-scarum *adjective* See **rash¹.**

haruspex also **aruspex** *noun* See **prophet.**

harvest *noun* The produce harvested from the land : crop, fruit, fruitage, yield. See INGESTION in Index. — See also **effect.**

harvest *verb* See **gather.**

hash *noun* See **botch.**

hash *verb* See **discuss.**

hassle *noun* See **argument.**

hassle *verb* See **argue.**

haste *noun* **1.** Rapidness of movement or activity : celerity, dispatch, expedition, expeditiousness, fleetness, hurry, hustle, quickness, rapidity, rapidness, speed, speediness, swiftness. See FAST in Index. **2.** Careless headlong action : hastiness, hurriedness, precipitance, precipitancy, precipitateness, precipitation, rashness, rush. See CAREFUL in Index.

haste *verb* See **rush.**

hasten *verb* See **rush, speed.**

hastiness *noun* See **haste.**

hasty *adjective* See **quick, rash¹.**

hatch *verb* See **invent, produce.**

hate *verb* To regard with extreme dislike and hostility : abhor, abominate, despise, detest, execrate, loathe. See LOVE in Index.

hate *noun* **1.** Extreme hostility and dislike : abhorrence, abomination, antipathy, aversion, detestation, hatred, horror, loathing, repellence, repellency, repugnance, repugnancy, repulsion, revulsion. See LOVE in Index. **2.** An object of extreme dislike : abhorrence, abomination, anathema, aversion, bête noire, bugbear, detestation, execration. *Informal:* horror. See LOVE in Index.

hateable *adjective* See **hateful.**

hateful *adjective* Eliciting or deserving hate : hateable. See LOVE in Index. — See also **malevolent.**

hatred *noun* See **hate.**

haughtiness *noun* See **arrogance.**

haughty *adjective* See **arrogant.**

haul *noun* See **burden¹, pull.**

haul *verb* See **pull.**

haunt *verb* To come to mind continually : obsess, torment, trouble, weigh on (*or* upon). See REPETITION in Index. — See also **frequent.**

haunt *noun* A frequently visited place : rendezvous, resort, stamping ground. *Slang:* hangout. See PLACE, REPETITION in Index. — See also **ghost, home.**

hauteur *noun* See **arrogance.**

have *verb* **1.** To keep at one's disposal : hold, own, possess, retain. See KEEP in Index. **2.** To organize and carry out (an activity) : give, hold, stage. See CONTROL, PLANNED in Index. — See also **bear, carry, command, contain, deceive,**

enjoy, experience, feel, get, participate, permit, receive, take.
have at *verb* See **attack.**
haven *noun* See **cover.**
haven *verb* See **harbor.**
have-not *noun* See **pauper.**
havoc *noun* See **destruction.**
havoc *verb* See **sack².**
hawk *verb* See **peddle.**
hazard *verb* To run the risk of :
adventure, chance, risk, venture.
See SAFETY in Index. — See also
presume, risk.
hazard *noun* See **chance, danger,**
risk.
hazardous *adjective* See
dangerous.
haze *noun* A thick, heavy atmospheric condition offering reduced
visibility because of the presence of
suspended particles : brume, fog,
mist, murk, smaze. See CLEAR in
Index.
hazy *adjective* See **filmy, turbid,**
unclear.
head *noun* **1.** The uppermost part of
the body : noddle, pate, poll. *Slang:*
bean, block, conk, dome, noggin,
noodle, nut. See BODY in Index.
2. The seat of the faculty of intelligence and reason : brain,
mind. *Informal:* gray matter. See
THOUGHTS in Index. **3.** A term or
terms in large type introducing a
text : heading, headline. See
WORDS in Index. — See also **boss,**
chief, crisis, foam, talent.
head *verb* See **administer, aim,**
bear.
head off *verb* To block the progress of and force to change direction : cut off, intercept. See ALLOW
in Index.
head *adjective* See **principal.**
headache *noun* See **burden¹.**
header *noun* See **fall, plunge.**
heading *noun* The compass direc-

tion in which a ship or an aircraft
moves : bearing, course, vector. See
APPROACH in Index. — See also
head.
headline *noun* See **head.**
headlong *adjective* See **rash¹.**
headman *noun* See **chief.**
headquarters *noun* See **base¹,**
center.
head start *noun* See **advantage.**
headstrong *adjective* See
obstinate.
headway *noun* See **advance.**
heal *verb* See **cure.**
health *noun* The condition of being
physically and mentally sound :
haleness, healthiness, heartiness,
soundness, wholeness. See HEALTH
in Index.
healthful *adjective* Promoting good
health : healthsome, healthy, hygienic, salubrious, salutary, wholesome. See HEALTH in Index. — See
also **healthy.**
healthiness *noun* See **health.**
healthsome *adjective* See **healthful.**
healthy *adjective* Having good
health : fit¹, hale, healthful,
hearty, right, sound², well², whole,
wholesome. *Idioms:* fit as a fiddle,
hale and hearty, in fine fettle. See
HEALTH in Index. — See also **big,**
healthful.
heap *noun* **1.** A group of things
gathered haphazardly : agglomeration, bank¹, cumulus, drift, hill,
mass, mess, mound, mountain, pile,
shock², stack, tumble. See ORDER in
Index. **2.** *Informal.* A great deal :
abundance, mass, mountain, much,
plenty, profusion, wealth, world.
Informal: barrel, lot, pack, peck²,
pile. *Regional:* power, sight. See BIG
in Index. **3.** *Informal.* An indeter-
minately great amount or number.
Often used in plural : jillion, million (often used in plural), multiplic-

ity, ream, trillion. *Informal:* bushel, gob¹ (often used in plural), load (often used in plural), lot, oodles, passel, peck², scad (often used in plural), slew, wad, zillion. See BIG in Index.

heap *verb* **1.** To put into a disordered pile : bank¹, drift, hill, lump¹, mound, pile (up), stack. See ORDER in Index. **2.** To fill to overflowing : lade, load, pile. See FULL in Index. — See also **fill, shower.**

hear *verb* To perceive by ear, usually attentively : attend, hark, heed, listen. *Archaic:* hearken. *Idiom:* give (or lend) one's ear. See SOUNDS in Index. — See also **discover.**

hear of *verb* To receive (an idea) and take it into consideration : consider, entertain, think of. See THOUGHTS in Index.

hearing *noun* **1.** The sense by which sound is perceived : audition, ear. See SOUNDS in Index. **2.** Range of audibility : earshot, sound¹. See SOUNDS in Index. **3.** A chance to be heard : audience, audition. See SOUNDS in Index. — See also **trial.**

hearken *also* **harken** *verb* See **hear, listen.**

hearsay *noun* See **gossip.**

heart *noun* **1.** The circulatory organ of the body : *Slang:* ticker. See BODY in Index. **2.** The seat of a person's innermost emotions and feelings : bosom, breast, soul. *Idioms:* bottom of one's heart, cockles of one's heart, one's heart of hearts. See FEELINGS in Index. **3.** The most central and material part : core, essence, gist, kernel, marrow, meat, nub, pith, quintessence, root¹, soul, spirit, stuff, substance. *Law:* gravamen. See BE in Index. — See also **center, courage.**

heartache *noun* See **grief.**

heartbreak *noun* See **grief.**

hearten *verb* See **encourage.**

heartening *adjective* See **encouraging.**

heartfelt *adjective* See **genuine.**

heartiness *noun* See **health.**

heartless *adjective* See **cold-blooded.**

hearty *adjective* See **genuine, healthy.**

heat *noun* **1.** Intense warmth : fervor, hotness, torridity, torridness. See HOT in Index. **2.** Intensity of feeling or reaction : excitation, excitement, warmth. See EXCITE, FEELINGS, HOT in Index. **3.** A regular period of sexual excitement in female mammals : estrus, rut², season. See SEX in Index. — See also **policeman.**

heated *adjective* See **fervid, hot, passionate.**

heave *verb* See **elevate, gasp, throw, toss, vomit.**

heave *noun* See **lift, throw.**

heaven *noun* A state of elated bliss : ecstasy, paradise, rapture, seventh heaven, transport. *Informal:* cloud nine. See HAPPY in Index. — See also **air.**

heavenly *adjective* **1.** Of or relating to heaven : celestial, divine, paradisaic, paradisaical, paradisal, paradisiac, paradisiacal. See RELIGION in Index. **2.** Of or relating to the heavens : celestial, empyreal. See PLACE in Index. — See also **delicious, delightful, divine.**

heavily *adverb* See **hard.**

heaviness *noun* The state or quality of being physically heavy : heftiness, massiveness, ponderosity, ponderousness, weight, weightiness. *Informal:* avoirdupois. See HEAVY in Index.

heavy *adjective* **1.** Having a relatively great weight : heavyweight, hefty, massive, ponderous, weighty. See HEAVY in Index. **2.** Intensely sustained, especially in activity : concentrated, fierce, heightened, intense, intensive. See STRONG in Index. **3.** Indulging in drink to an excessive degree : hard. *Informal:* two-fisted. See EXCESS in Index. **4.** Not readily digested because of richness : rich. See INGESTION in Index. **5.** Unwieldy or clumsy, especially due to excess weight : cumbersome, cumbrous, lumpish, lumpy, ponderous. See EASY, HEAVY in Index. **6.** Burdened by a weighty load : heavy-laden, laden, loaded. See FULL in Index. — See also **bulky, burdensome, deep, generous, grave², high, rough, severe, thick.**

heavy *noun Slang.* A mean, worthless character in a story or play : villain. See RIGHT in Index.

heavy-handed *adjective* See **ponderous, unskillful.**

heavy-hearted *adjective* See **depressed.**

heavy-heartedness *noun* See **gloom.**

heavy-laden *adjective* See **heavy.**

heavyset *adjective* See **stocky.**

heavyweight *adjective* See **bigleague, heavy.**

heavyweight *noun* See **dignitary.**

hebetate *verb* See **dull.**

hebetude *noun* See **lethargy.**

hebetudinous *adjective* See **lethargic, stupid.**

hecatomb *noun* See **sacrifice.**

heckle *verb* See **bait.**

hectic *adjective* See **fervid, hot.**

hector *verb* See **bait, intimidate.**

hector *noun* See **bully.**

hedge *verb* See **close in** at **close, equivocate, evade, surround.**

hedge *noun* See **equivocation.**

hedonic *adjective* See **sybaritic.**

hedonist *noun* See **sybarite.**

hedonistic *adjective* See **sybaritic.**

heebie-jeebies *noun* See **jitter.**

heed *noun* See **care, notice.**

heed *verb* See **hear.**

heedful *adjective* See **attentive, careful, mindful.**

heedfulness *noun* See **attention, care.**

heedless *adjective* See **careless, mindless.**

heedlessness *noun* See **abandon.**

heehaw *noun* See **laugh.**

heehaw *verb* See **laugh.**

heel¹ *verb* See **dog.**

heel² *verb* See **incline.**

heel *noun* See **inclination.**

heftiness *noun* See **heaviness.**

hefty *adjective* See **bulky, heavy, severe.**

height *noun* The highest point : apex, cap, crest, crown, peak, roof, summit, top, vertex. See HIGH in Index. — See also **climax, elevation.**

heighten *verb* See **elevate, intensify.**

heightened *adjective* See **elevated, heavy.**

heinous *adjective* See **outrageous.**

heinousness *noun* See **enormity.**

heist *verb* See **rob, steal.**

heist *noun* See **robbery.**

hell *noun* Excruciating punishment : living hell, persecution, torment, torture. *Idiom:* tortures of the damned. See REWARD in Index.

hell *verb* See **revel.**

hellfire *adjective* See **fateful.**

hell-for-leather *adjective* See **fast.**

hell-for-leather *adverb* See **fast.**

hellish *adjective* See **fiendish.**

helotry *noun* See **slavery.**

help *verb* To give support or assistance. Also used with *out* : abet, aid, assist, boost, relieve, succor. *Idioms:* give (or lend) a hand, give a leg up. See HELP in Index. — See also **improve.**

help *noun* The act or an instance of helping : abetment, aid, assist, assistance, hand, relief, succor, support. See HELP in Index. — See also **helper.**

helper *noun* A person who helps : abettor, aid, attendant, help, reliever, succorer. See HELP in Index. — See also **assistant.**

helpful *adjective* See **beneficial.**

helping *noun* See **serving.**

helpless *adjective* **1.** Lacking power or strength : impotent, powerless. See ABILITY, HELP in Index. **2.** Devoid of help or protection : defenseless, unprotected. See SAFETY in Index. — See also **ineffectual.**

helplessly *adverb* Without regard to desire or inclination : involuntarily, perforce, willy-nilly. See WILLING in Index.

helplessness *noun* See **ineffectuality.**

helter-skelter *adjective* See **confused.**

helter-skelter *noun* See **disturbance.**

hem *verb* See **close in** at **close, surround.**

henchman *noun* See **follower.**

henpeck *verb* See **nag.**

herald *verb* See **usher in** at **usher.**

herald *noun* See **precursor.**

herculean *adjective* See **giant.**

herd *verb* See **drive.**

hereafter *noun* See **future.**

hereditary *adjective* See **ancestral, innate.**

heretic *noun* See **separatist.**

heretofore *adverb* See **earlier.**

heritage *noun* Something immaterial, as a style or philosophy, that is passed from one generation to another : inheritance, legacy, tradi-

tion. See AFFECT in Index. — See also **birthright.**

hermeneutic *adjective* See **explanatory.**

hermeneutical *adjective* See **explanatory.**

hero *noun* A person revered especially for noble courage : paladin. See FEAR in Index. — See also **celebrity.**

heroic *adjective* See **brave, giant.**

heroism *noun* The quality or state of being heroic : gallantry, prowess, valiance, valiancy, valor. See FEAR in Index.

hesitancy *noun* See **hesitation.**

hesitant *adjective* Given to or exhibiting hesitation : halting, indecisive, irresolute, pendulous, shilly-shally, tentative, timid, vacillant, vacillatory. See DECIDE in Index.

hesitate *verb* To be irresolute in acting or doing : dither, falter, halt², pause, shilly-shally, stagger, vacillate, waver, wobble. See DECIDE in Index.

hesitation *noun* The act of hesitating or state of being hesitant : hesitancy, indecision, indecisiveness, irresoluteness, irresolution, pause, shilly-shally, tentativeness, timidity, timidness, to-and-fro, vacillation. See DECIDE in Index.

Hessian *noun* See **mercenary.**

heterogeneity *noun* See **variety.**

heterogeneous *adjective* See **various.**

heterogeneousness *noun* See **variety.**

hew *verb* See **cut.**

hex *noun* See **jinx.**

hex *verb* See **jinx.**

hiatus *noun* See **gap.**

hick *adjective* See **country.**

hidden *adjective* See **blind, secluded, ulterior.**

hide¹ *verb* To put or keep out of sight : bury, cache, conceal, ensconce, occult, secrete. *Slang:* plant, stash. See SHOW in Index.
— See also **block, cover, obscure.**

hide out *verb* See **hole up** at **hole.**

hide² *noun* The skin of an animal : fell³, fur, jacket, pelt¹. See SURFACE in Index.

hide *verb* See **beat.**

hideaway *noun* See **hide-out.**

hidebound *adjective* See **intolerant.**

hideous *adjective* See **ghastly, ugly.**

hideousness *noun* See **ugliness.**

hide-out *noun* A hiding place : covert, den, hideaway, lair. See PLACE, SHOW in Index.

hiding *noun* See **beating.**

hierarch *noun* See **chief.**

hieroglyphic *adjective* See **graphic.**

higgle *verb* See **haggle.**

higgledy-piggledy *adjective* See **confused.**

high *adjective* **1.** Having a rather great upward projection : long¹, tall. See HIGH in Index. **2.** Elevated in pitch : high-pitched, piercing, piping, shrieky, shrill, shrilly, treble. *Music:* acute. See HIGH, SOUNDS in Index. **3.** Long past : ancient, immemorial. See NEW in Index. **4.** Intensely violent in sustained velocity : fierce, furious, heavy, strong. See STRONG in Index. — See also **costly, drugged, drunk, elevated, tall.**

high *noun* See **thrill.**

high-and-mighty *adjective* See **arrogant.**

highball *verb* See **rush.**

highborn *adjective* See **noble.**

highbred *adjective* See **noble, thoroughbred.**

highbrow *adjective* See **intellectual.**

higher *adjective* **1.** Being at a rank above another : senior, superior. See OVER in Index. **2.** Being at a height or level above another : superior, upper. See HIGH in Index.

higher-up *noun* See **superior.**

highest *adjective* Preeminent in rank or position : top, top-drawer. See OVER in Index. — See also **top.**

highfalutin or **hifalutin** also **high-faluting** *adjective* See **pompous.**

high-flown *adjective* See **elevated, sonorous.**

high-grade *adjective* See **good.**

high-hat *adjective* See **snobbish.**

high-hat *verb* See **condescend.**

high jinks *noun* See **mischief.**

highlight *verb* See **emphasize.**

highly *adverb* See **very.**

high-minded *adjective* See **elevated.**

high-pitched *adjective* See **high.**

high-priced *adjective* See **costly.**

high-ranking *adjective* See **exalted.**

high sign *noun* See **gesture.**

high-sounding *adjective* See **sonorous.**

high-spirited *adjective* See **lively, spirited.**

hightail *verb* See **run.**

highway *noun* See **way.**

highwayman *noun* See **larcenist.**

hijack also **highjack** *verb* See **coerce.**

hike *noun* See **increase.**

hike *verb* To travel about or journey on foot : backpack, march¹, peregrinate, traipse, tramp, trek. See MOVE in Index. — See also **raise.**

hilarious *adjective* See **priceless.**

hilarity *noun* See **gaiety.**

hill *noun* A natural land elevation : eminence, prominence, rise. See HIGH in Index. — See also **heap.**

hill *verb* See **heap.**

hind *adjective* See **back.**

hinder *verb* To interfere with the progress of : bog (down), encumber,

hold back, impede, obstruct. *Idiom:* get in the way of. See HELP, OPEN in Index.
hindermost *adjective* See **last**[1].
hindmost *adjective* See **back, last**[1].
hindrance *noun* See **bar**.
hinge on or **upon** *verb* See **depend on** at **depend**.
hint *noun* **1.** A subtle pointing out : clue, cue, intimation, suggestion. See KNOWLEDGE, SUGGEST in Index. **2.** A subtle quality underlying or felt to underlie a situation, action, or person : implication, inkling, suspicion, undercurrent, undertone. See SHOW, SUGGEST in Index. — See also **shade**.

hint *verb* **1.** To convey an idea by indirect, subtle means : imply, insinuate, intimate[2], suggest. *Idiom:* drop a hint. See SHOW, SUGGEST in Index. **2.** To try to obtain something, usually by subtleness and cunning : angle[1], fish. See ASK in Index.
hip *adjective* See **aware**.
hire *verb* To engage the temporary use of (something) for a fee : charter, lease, rent[1]. See GET, TRANSACTIONS in Index. — See also **employ, lease**.

hire *noun* See **employee, employment, wage**.
hired *adjective* See **employed**.
hired hand *noun* See **employee**.
hireling *noun* See **employee**.
hirer *noun* See **employer**.
hirsute *adjective* See **hairy**.
hiss *verb* To make a sharp sibilant sound : fizz, fizzle, sibilate, sizzle, swish, whiz, whoosh. See SOUNDS in Index.

hiss *noun* Any of various derisive sounds of disapproval : boo, catcall, hoot. *Slang:* bird, Bronx cheer, raspberry, razz. See SOUNDS in Index.
historic *adjective* See **important**.

history *noun* **1.** A chronological record of past events : annals, chronicle. See HAPPEN, WORDS in Index. **2.** Past events surrounding a person or thing : background, past. See HAPPEN in Index. — See also **story**.
histrionic *adjective* See **dramatic**.
histrionical *adjective* See **dramatic**.
histrionics *noun* See **theatrics**.
hit *verb* To deliver a powerful blow to suddenly and sharply : bash, catch, clout, knock, pop[1], slam, slog, slug[3], smash, smite, sock, strike, swat, thwack, whack, wham, whop. *Informal:* biff, bop, clip[1], wallop. *Slang:* belt, conk, paste. *Idioms:* let someone have it, sock it to someone. See ATTACK, STRIKE in Index. — See also **occur, take**.

hit back *verb* See **retaliate**.
hit on or **upon** *verb* See **arrive at** at **arrive, take**.
hit *noun* A dazzling, often sudden instance of success : sleeper. *Informal:* smash, smash hit, tenstrike, wow. *Slang:* boff, boffo, boffola. See THRIVE in Index. — See also **blow**[2]**, murder, pull**.
hitch *verb* See **limp, marry**.
hitch *noun* See **time, turn**.
hit-or-miss *adjective* See **random**.
hive *verb* See **accumulate**.
hoard *verb* To store up (supplies or money), usually well beyond one's needs : squirrel (away), stockpile, treasure. *Slang:* stash. See COLLECT, GIVE in Index.

hoard *noun* A supply stored or hidden for future use : backlog, cache, inventory, nest egg, reserve, reservoir, stock, stockpile, store, treasure. *Slang:* stash. See COLLECT in Index.
hoarse *adjective* Low and grating in sound : croaking, croaky, gruff,

husky[1]. See SOUNDS in Index. —See also **harsh.**

hoary *adjective* See **old.**

hobble

hobble *noun* See **bond.** *verb* See **hamper, limp.**

hobnob *verb* See **associate.**

hock *verb* See **pawn[1].**

hocus-pocus *noun* See **gibberish.**

hodgepodge *noun* See **assortment.**

hoggish *adjective* See **greedy.**

hog-tie also **hogtie** *verb* See **hamper.**

hoi polloi *noun* See **commonalty.**

hoist *verb* See **elevate.**

hoist *noun* See **lift.**

hoity-toity *adjective* See **pompous.**

hold *verb* **1.** To have and maintain in one's possession : hold back, keep, keep back, reserve, retain, withhold. See KEEP in Index. **2.** To keep in custody : detain. See FREE, LAW in Index. —See also **accommodate, assert, believe, command, contain, embrace, enjoy, feel, grip, have, restrain, support, wash.**

hold back *verb* See **hinder, hold, repress, restrain.**

hold down *verb* See **repress, restrain.**

hold in *verb* See **restrain.**

hold off *verb* See **defer[1], refrain.**

hold out *verb* See **endure.**

hold up *verb* See **bear up** at **bear, defer[1], delay, rob.**

hold with *verb* See **approve.**

hold *noun* **1.** An act or means of holding something : clasp, clench, clutch[1], grasp, grip. *Sports:* grapple. See KEEP in Index. **2.** A strong or powerful influence : grasp, grip. See AFFECT in Index. —See also **grasp, grip.**

holder *noun* See **owner.**

holding *noun* Something, as land and assets, legally possessed. Often used in plural : estate, possession

(used in plural), property. See LAW, OWNED in Index.

holdup *noun* See **delay, robbery.**

hole *noun* **1.** A space in an otherwise solid mass : cavity, hollow, pocket, vacuity, void. See CONVEX in Index. **2.** An open space allowing passage : aperture, mouth, opening, orifice, outlet, vent. See OPEN in Index. **3.** A place used as an animal's dwelling : burrow, den, lair. See PROTECTION in Index. **4.** An ugly, squalid dwelling : hovel, hut, shack, shanty. See GOOD, RICH in Index. —See also **breach, predicament.**

hole *verb* See **breach.**

hole up *verb* *Informal.* To shut oneself up in secrecy : hide out. *Idioms:* go underground, lay (*or* lie) low. See SHOW in Index.

holiday *noun* See **vacation.**

holiness *noun* The quality of being holy or sacred : blessedness, sacredness, sacrosanctity, sanctity. See RELIGION in Index.

holler *verb* See **roar.**

holler *noun* See **shout.**

hollow *adjective* Curving inward : cavernous, concave, indented, sunken. See CONVEX in Index. —See also **empty.**

hollow *noun* See **depression, hole.**

hollow-eyed *adjective* See **haggard.**

hollowness *noun* See **emptiness.**

holy *adjective* **1.** Deeply concerned with God and the beliefs and practice of religion : devotional, devout, godly, pietistic, pietistical, pious, prayerful, religious, saintly. See RELIGION in Index. **2.** Regarded with particular reverence or respect : blessed, hallowed, sacred, sacrosanct. See RELIGION, RESPECT in Index. —See also **divine.**

homage *noun* See **honor.**

home *noun* **1.** A building or shelter where one lives : abode, domicile, dwelling, habitation, house, lodging (often used in plural), place, residence. *Chiefly British:* dig (used in plural). See PROTECTION in Index. **2.** The natural environment of an animal or plant : habitat, haunt, stamping ground. See TERRITORY in Index. **3.** An institution that provides care and shelter : asylum, hospice, hospital, shelter. See PROTECTION in Index.

home *adjective* See **domestic.**

homely *adjective* See **domestic, plain, rustic.**

homespun *adjective* See **rustic.**

homicidal *adjective* See **murderous.**

homicide *noun* See **murder, murderer.**

hominoid *adjective* See **manlike.**

homo *noun* See **human being.**

homophile *adjective* See **gay.**

Homo sapiens *noun* See **mankind.**

homosexual *adjective* See **gay.**

honcho *noun* See **chief.**

hone[1] *verb* See **sharpen.**

hone[2] *verb* See **desire.**

honest *adjective* Having or marked by uprightness in principle and action : good, honorable, incorruptible, righteous, true, upright, upstanding. *Informal:* straight-shooting. *Idiom:* on the up-and-up (or up and up). See HONEST in Index. — See also **frank, genuine.**

honesty *noun* The quality of being honest : honor, honorableness, incorruptibility, integrity, upstandingness. See HONEST in Index. — See also **character.**

honey *verb* See **coax, flatter, sweeten.**

honey *noun* See **darling.**

honky-tonk *noun* See **joint.**

honor *noun* **1.** Great respect or high public esteem accorded as a right or as due : deference, homage, obeisance. See RESPECT in Index. **2.** A person's high standing among others : dignity, good name, good report, prestige, reputation, repute, respect, status. See RESPECT in Index. — See also **distinction, esteem, honesty.**

honor *verb* To pay tribute or homage to : acclaim, celebrate, eulogize, exalt, extol, glorify, hail[2], laud, magnify, panegyrize, praise. *Idiom:* sing someone's praises. See PRAISE in Index. — See also **admire, distinguish, grace.**

honorable *adjective* See **admirable, honest.**

honorableness *noun* See **honesty.**

honorarium *noun* See **reward.**

hood *noun* See **thug, tough.**

hoodlum *noun* See **thug, tough.**

hoodoo *noun* See **jinx.**

hoodoo *verb* See **jinx.**

hoodwink *verb* See **deceive.**

hooey *noun* See **nonsense.**

hoof *verb* See **dance, walk.**

hoofer *noun* See **dancer.**

hoo-hah *noun* See **sensation.**

hook *verb* See **steal.**

hook *noun* See **catch.**

hooker *noun* See **prostitute.**

hookup *noun* See **relation.**

hooky *noun* See **cut.**

hooligan *noun* See **thug.**

hoosegow *noun* See **jail.**

hoot *noun* See **damn, hiss, scream.**

hop *noun* See **dance, skip.**

hop *verb* See **skip.**

hopeful *adjective* See **encouraging.**

hopeful *noun* See **applicant, aspirant.**

hopeless *adjective* Offering no hope or expectation of improvement : cureless, incurable, irremediable, irreparable. See HOPE in Index. — See also **despondent.**

hopelessness *noun* See **despair.**

hopped-up *adjective* See **drugged.**

horde *noun* See **crowd.**

horizon *noun* See **ken.**

horizontal *adjective* See **flat.**

hornets' nest *noun* See **problem.**

horn in *verb* See **intrude, meddle.**

horrendous *adjective* See **terrible.**

horrible *adjective* Causing great horror : bloodcurdling, hair-raising, horrid, horrific, terrific. See FEAR in Index. — See also **ghastly, terrible.**

horrid *adjective* See **ghastly, horrible, offensive.**

horrific *adjective* See **horrible.**

horrify *verb* See **dismay.**

horror *noun* See **fear, hate.**

horse around *verb* See **misbehave.**

horseplay *noun* See **misbehavior.**

horse sense *noun* See **common sense.**

hospice *noun* See **home.**

hospitable *adjective* See **gracious.**

hospital *noun* See **home.**

host *noun* See **crowd.**

hostile *adjective* Feeling or showing unfriendliness : inimical, unfriendly. See LOVE in Index. — See also **aggressive, belligerent.**

hostility *noun* See **aggression, belligerence, conflict, enmity.**

hot *adjective* **1.** Marked by much heat : ardent, baking, blistering, boiling, broiling, burning, fiery, heated, red-hot, roasting, scalding, scorching, searing, sizzling, sultry, sweltering, torrid. See HOT in Index. **2.** Being at a higher temperature than is normal or desirable : febrific, febrile, feverish, hectic, pyretic. See HOT in Index. **3.** *Informal.* Of great current interest : live[2], red-hot. See EXCITE in Index. — See also **marvelous.**

hot-blooded *adjective* See **passionate.**

hotfoot *verb* See **run, rush.**

hotheaded *adjective* See **rash[1].**

hotness *noun* See **heat.**

hot pursuit *noun* See **pursuit.**

hot spot *noun* See **predicament.**

hot water *noun* See **distress, predicament.**

hound *verb* See **bait, besiege.**

house *noun* See **company, family, home.**

house *verb* See **harbor, live[1].**

housebreaker *noun* See **larcenist.**

housecleaning *noun* See **shakeup.**

household *noun* See **family.**

household *adjective* See **domestic.**

house of correction *noun* See **jail.**

housing *noun* See **shelter.**

hovel *noun* See **hole.**

hover *verb* See **flutter, hang.**

however *adverb* See **still.**

howl *verb* To utter or emit a long, mournful, plaintive sound : bay[2], moan, ululate, wail, yowl. See SOUNDS in Index. — See also **bawl, break up** at **break, cry.**

howl *noun* A long, mournful cry : bay[2], moan, ululation, wail, yowl. See SOUNDS in Index. — See also **scream.**

hub *noun* See **center.**

hubbub *noun* See **noise.**

huckster *verb* See **haggle, peddle.**

huddle *verb* See **crouch.**

hue *noun* See **color, shade, tint.**

huff *noun* See **offense, temper.**

huff *verb* See **insult, pant.**

hug *verb* See **embrace.**

hug *noun* See **embrace.**

huge *adjective* See **giant.**

hugeness *noun* See **enormousness.**

huggermugger or **huggermugger** *adjective* See **secret.**

huggermugger or **huggermugger** *noun* See **secrecy.**

huggermugger or **huggermugger** *adverb* See **secretly.**

huggermuggery or **huggermuggery** *noun* See **secrecy.**

hulk *noun* See lump[1].
  hulk *verb* See lump[1].
hulking *adjective* See bulky.
hulky *adjective* See bulky.
hullabaloo also **hullaballoo**
  noun See noise, vociferation.
hum *verb* To make a continuous
  low-pitched droning sound : bumble[2], burr, buzz, drone[2], whir, whiz.
  See SOUNDS in Index.
  hum *noun* A continuous low-
  pitched droning sound : bumble[2],
  burr, buzz, drone[2], whir, whiz. See
  SOUNDS in Index.
human *adjective* Of or characteristic of human beings or mankind :
  mortal. See BEINGS in Index. — See
  also **humanitarian**.
  human *noun* See human being.
human being *noun* A member of
  the human race : being, body, creature, homo, human, individual, life,
  man, mortal, party, person, personage, soul. See BEINGS in Index.
humane *adjective* See humanitarian.
humanitarian *adjective* Concerned with human welfare and the
  alleviation of suffering : charitable,
  compassionate, human, humane,
  merciful. See ATTITUDE, KIND in
  Index.
humanity *noun* See mankind.
humanize *verb* See socialize.
humanizing *adjective* See cultural.
humankind *noun* See mankind.
humanoid *adjective* See manlike.
humble *adjective* **1.** Having or
  expressing feelings of humility :
  lowly, meek, modest. See ATTI-
  TUDE, BIG, SELF-LOVE in Index.
  2. Of little distinction : lowly,
  mean[2], simple. See PLAIN in Index.
  — See also **lowly**.
  humble *verb* To deprive of esteem,
  self-worth, or effectiveness : abase,
  degrade, demean[2], humiliate, mor-

tify. *Idioms:* bring low, take down a
  peg. See RESPECT, WIN in Index.
humbleness *noun* See modesty.
humbug *verb* See deceive.
  humbug *noun* See fake.
humdrum *adjective* See boring.
  humdrum *noun* See monotony.
humid *adjective* See sticky.
humiliate *verb* See humble.
humiliation *noun* See degradation,
  disgrace.
humility *noun* See modesty.
humor *noun* The quality of being
  laughable or comical : comedy,
  comicality, comicalness, drollery,
  drollness, farcicality, funniness,
  humorousness, jocoseness, jocosity,
  jocularity, ludicrousness, ridiculousness, wit, wittiness, zaniness. See
  LAUGHTER in Index. — See also **disposition, fancy, mood**.
  humor *verb* To comply with the
  wishes or ideas of (another) : cater,
  gratify, indulge. See RESIST in Index.
humorist *noun* See joker.
humorous *adjective* Intended to
  excite laughter or amusement :
  comedic, facetious, funny, jocose,
  jocular, witty. See LAUGHTER in
  Index. — See also **amusing**.
humorousness *noun* See humor.
hump *noun* See bump.
  hump *verb* See stoop.
hunch *verb* See crouch, stoop.
  hunch *noun* See feeling, lump[1].
hunger *noun* See appetite, desire.
  hunger *verb* See lust.
hungry *adjective* See greedy,
  ravenous.
hunk *noun* See beauty, lump[1].
hunker *verb* See crouch, squat.
hunt *verb* To look for and pursue
  (game) in order to capture or kill it :
  chase, drive, run, stalk. See SEEK in
  Index. — See also **seek**.
  hunt down *verb* See run down at
  run.

hurdle *noun* See **bar.**

hurdle *verb* See **clear, jump.**

hurl *verb* See **throw.**

hurl *noun* See **throw.**

hurried *adjective* See **abrupt, quick.**

hurriedness *noun* See **haste.**

hurry *verb* See **rush, speed.**

hurry *noun* See **haste.**

hurry-up *adjective* See **crash.**

hurt *verb* **1.** To cause physical damage to : injure, wound. See HELP in Index. **2.** To have or cause a feeling of physical pain or discomfort : ache, pain, pang, twinge. See PAIN in Index. — See also **distress, injure.**

hurt *noun* See **distress, harm.**

hurtful *adjective* See **harmful, painful.**

hurtle *verb* See **shoot, throw.**

hurtless *adjective* See **harmless.**

husband *verb* See **conserve.**

husbandry *noun* See **conservation.**

hush *verb* See **censor, cover, repress, silence.**

hush *noun* See **silence, stillness.**

hush *adjective* See **silent.**

hushed *adjective* See **silent, soft.**

hush-hush *adjective* See **confidential, secret.**

husky[1] *adjective* See **hoarse.**

husky[2] *adjective* See **bulky, muscular.**

hussy *noun* See **slut.**

hustle *noun* See **drive, haste.**

hustle *verb* See **rush, speed.**

hustler *noun* See **eager beaver.**

hut *noun* See **hole.**

hygienic *adjective* See **healthful.**

hymeneal *adjective* See **marital.**

hype *verb* See **promote.**

hype *noun* See **promotion.**

hyperbole *noun* See **exaggeration.**

hyperbolism *noun* See **exaggeration.**

hyperbolize *verb* See **exaggerate.**

hypercritic *noun* See **critic.**

hypercritical *adjective* See **critical.**

hypnotic *adjective* See **sleepy.**

hypnotic *noun* See **soporific.**

hypocrisy *noun* A show or expression of feelings or beliefs one does not actually hold or possess : pharisaism, phoniness, sanctimoniousness, sanctimony, tartuffery, two-facedness. See HONEST in Index.

hypocrite *noun* A person who practices hypocrisy : pharisee, phony, tartuffe. See HONEST in Index.

hypocritical *adjective* Of or practicing hypocrisy : Pecksniffian, pharisaic, pharisaical, phony, sanctimonious, two-faced. See HONEST in Index.

hypogeal *adjective* See **underground.**

hypogean *adjective* See **underground.**

hypogeous *adjective* See **underground.**

hypothecate *verb* See **pawn**[1].

hypothesis *noun* See **theory.**

hypothesize *verb* See **speculate.**

hypothetic *adjective* See **supposed, theoretical.**

hypothetical *adjective* See **supposed, theoretical.**

I

iciness *noun* See **frigidness.**

icky *adjective* See **unpleasant.**

icy *adjective* See **cold, frigid.**

idea *noun* **1.** That which exists in the mind as the product of careful mental activity : concept, conception, image, notion, perception, thought. See THOUGHTS in Index. **2.** The gist of a specific action or situation : import, meaning, point, purport, significance, significancy. See MEANING in Index. — See also **belief, design, feeling.**

ideal *noun* See **dream, model.**

ideal *adjective* Conforming to an ultimate form of perfection or excellence : exemplary, model, perfect, supreme. See GOOD in Index. — See also **theoretical.**

idealist *noun* See **dreamer.**

idealistic *adjective* 1. Showing a tendency to envision things in perfect but unrealistic form : utopian, visionary. See HOPE, REAL in Index. 2. Not compatible with reality : quixotic, romantic, starry-eyed, unrealistic, utopian, visionary. See HOPE, REAL in Index.

identic *adjective* See **same.**

identical *adjective* See **equal, same.**

identicalness *noun* See **sameness.**

identify *verb* To associate or affiliate oneself closely with a person or group : empathize, relate, sympathize. See SAME in Index. — See also **associate, liken, mark, place.**

identity *noun* The set of behavioral or personal characteristics by which an individual is recognizable : individualism, individuality, selfhood. See BE in Index. — See also **sameness.**

idiocy *noun* See **foolishness, nonsense.**

idiom *noun* See **language.**

idiosyncrasy *noun* See **eccentricity.**

idiosyncratic *adjective* See **eccentric.**

idiot *noun* See **fool.**

idiotic *adjective* See **foolish.**

idle *adjective* Not occupied or put to use : inactive, unemployed, unused, vacant. See USED in Index. — See also **baseless, empty, inactive, lazy.**

idle *verb* 1. To pass time without working or in avoiding work : bum[1] (around), laze, loaf, loiter, lounge, shirk. *Slang:* diddle[2], goldbrick, goof (off). See INDUSTRIOUS

in Index. 2. To pass (time) without working or in avoiding work. Also used with *away* : dawdle (away), fiddle away, kill[1], trifle away, waste, while (away), wile (away). See INDUSTRIOUS in Index. — See also **tie up** at **tie.**

idleness *noun* See **inaction, laziness.**

idler *noun* See **wastrel.**

idolization *noun* See **adoration.**

idolize *verb* See **adore.**

idyllic *adjective* See **pastoral.**

iffy *adjective* See **ambiguous.**

igg *verb* See **ignore.**

ignis fatuus *noun* See **illusion.**

ignite *verb* See **light[1].**

ignoble *adjective* See **lowly, sordid.**

ignominious *adjective* See **disgraceful.**

ignominiousness *noun* See **infamy.**

ignominy *noun* See **disgrace.**

ignorance *noun* 1. The condition of being ignorant; lack of knowledge or learning : benightedness, illiteracy, illiterateness, nescience. See KNOWLEDGE in Index. 2. The condition of being uninformed or unaware : innocence, nescience, obliviousness, unawareness, unconsciousness, unfamiliarity. See KNOWLEDGE in Index.

ignorant *adjective* 1. Without education or knowledge : illiterate, nescient, uneducated, uninstructed, unlearned, unschooled, untaught. See KNOWLEDGE in Index. 2. Exhibiting lack of education or knowledge : backward, benighted, primitive, unenlightened. See KNOWLEDGE in Index. 3. Not aware or informed : innocent, oblivious, unacquainted, unaware, unconscious, unenlightened, unfamiliar, uninformed, unknowing, unwitting. *Idiom:* in the dark. See KNOWLEDGE in Index.

ignore *verb* To refuse to pay attention to (a person); treat with contempt : disregard, neglect, slight. *Regional:* igg. See CONCERN, THOUGHTS in Index. — See also blink, neglect.

ilk *noun* See kind[2].

ill *adjective* See bad, harmful, sick.

ill *noun* See curse, disease, evil.

ill-advised *adjective* See unwise.

illation *noun* See deduction.

illative *noun* See deduction.

ill-behaved *adjective* See naughty.

ill-bred *adjective* See coarse, rude.

ill-chosen *adjective* See unfortunate.

ill-considered *adjective* See rash[1], unwise.

illegal *adjective* Prohibited by law : illegitimate, illicit, lawless, outlawed, unlawful, wrongful. See CRIMES, LAW in Index. — See also criminal.

illegality *noun* The state or quality of being illegal : illegitimacy, illicitness, unlawfulness. See CRIMES, LAW in Index. — See also crime.

illegitimacy *noun* The condition of being of illegitimate birth : bastardy. See KIN, LAW in Index. — See also illegality.

illegitimate *adjective* Born to parents who are not married to each other : baseborn, bastard, misbegotten, natural, spurious, unlawful. See KIN, LAW in Index. — See also criminal, illegal.

ill-fated *adjective* See unfortunate.

ill-favored *adjective* See objectionable, ugly.

illiberal *adjective* See intolerant.

illicit *adjective* See criminal, illegal, unlawful.

illicitness *noun* See illegality.

illimitable *adjective* See endless.

illiteracy *noun* See ignorance.

illiterate *adjective* See ignorant.

illiterateness *noun* See ignorance.

ill-mannered *adjective* See rude.

illness *noun* See disease, sickness.

illogical *adjective* See fallacious, unreasonable.

illogicality *noun* See unreason.

illogicalness *noun* See unreason.

ill repute *noun* See disgrace.

ill-starred *adjective* See unfortunate.

ill-suited *adjective* See unfit.

ill-tempered *adjective* Having or showing a bad temper : bad-tempered, cantankerous, crabbed, cranky, cross, disagreeable, fretful, grouchy, grumpy, irascible, irritable, nasty, peevish, petulant, querulous, snappish, snappy, surly, testy, ugly, waspish. *Informal:* crabby, mean[2]. *Idiom:* out of sorts. See ATTITUDE in Index.

ill-timed *adjective* See inconvenient.

ill-treat *verb* See abuse.

ill-treatment *noun* See abuse.

illume *verb* See illuminate.

illuminate *verb* **1.** To provide, cover, or fill with light : illume, illumine, light[1], lighten[1]. See LIGHT in Index. **2.** To enable (one) to understand, especially in a spiritual sense : edify, enlighten, illume, illumine. See TEACH in Index. — See also clarify.

illumination *noun* **1.** The act of physically illuminating or the condition of being filled with light : light[1], lighting. See LIGHT in Index. **2.** The condition of being informed spiritually : edification, enlightenment. See TEACH in Index. — See also explanation, light[1].

illuminative *adjective* See educational.

illumine *verb* See illuminate.

ill-use *verb* See abuse.

illusion *noun* **1.** An erroneous perception of reality : delusion, hallucination, ignis fatuus, mirage, phantasm, phantasma, will-o'-the-wisp. See REAL in Index. **2.** A fantastic, impracticable plan or desire : bubble, castle in the air, chimera, dream, fantasy, pipe dream, rainbow. See REAL in Index. — See also **dream.**

illusive *adjective* Of, relating to, or in the nature of an illusion; lacking reality : chimeric, chimerical, delusive, delusory, dreamlike, hallucinatory, illusory, phantasmagoric, phantasmal, phantasmic, visionary. See REAL in Index. — See also **fallacious, illusory.**

illusory *adjective* Tending to deceive; of the nature of an illusion : delusive, delusory, illusive. See REAL in Index. — See also **fallacious, illusive.**

illustratable *adjective* See **explainable.**

illustrate *verb* See **clarify, instance, represent.**

illustration *noun* See **example, explanation.**

illustrative *adjective* See **explanatory, graphic.**

illustrious *adjective* See **eminent.**

illustriousness *noun* See **eminence.**

ill will *noun* See **enmity, malevolence.**

image *noun* The character projected or given by someone to the public : appearance, impression. See SURFACE in Index. — See also **copy, double, idea, reflection.**

image *verb* See **echo, imagine, reflect, represent.**

imaginable *adjective* See **earthly.**

imaginary *adjective* Existing only in the imagination : chimeric, chimerical, conceptual, fanciful, fantastic, fantastical, notional, unreal, visionary. See REAL in Index.

imagination *noun* The power of the mind to form images : fancy, fantasy, imaginativeness. See REAL, THOUGHTS in Index.

imaginative *adjective* See **fanciful.**

imaginativeness *noun* See **imagination.**

imagine *verb* To form mental images of : conceive, envisage, envision, fancy, fantasize, image, picture, see, think, vision, visualize. *Informal:* feature. See THOUGHTS in Index.

imbecile *noun* See **fool.**

imbecilic *adjective* See **foolish.**

imbecility *noun* See **foolishness.**

imbibe *verb* See **absorb, drink.**

imbrue also **embrue** *verb* See **bloody.**

imbue *verb* See **charge.**

imitate *verb* To copy (the manner or expression of another), especially in an exaggerated or mocking way : ape, burlesque, caricature, mimic, mock, parody, travesty. *Idiom:* do a takeoff on. See SAME in Index. — See also **copy, echo, follow.**

imitation *noun* See **copy, echo, mimicry, takeoff.**

imitation *adjective* See **artificial.**

imitative *adjective* Copying another in an inferior or obsequious way : apish, emulative, slavish. See SAME in Index. — See also **echoic.**

imitator *noun* See **echo.**

immaculate *adjective* See **clean.**

immaterial *adjective* Having no body, form, or substance : bodiless, discarnate, disembodied, incorporeal, insubstantial, metaphysical, nonphysical, spiritual, unbodied, uncorporal, unsubstantial. See BODY in Index. — See also **irrelevant.**

immature *adjective* See **childish, young.**

immeasurability *noun* See **infinity.**

immeasurable *adjective* See **endless, incalculable.**

immeasurableness *noun* See
infinity.

immediate *adjective* Marked by
the absence of any intervention :
direct, firsthand, primary. See
CLEAR, NEAR in Index. — See also
close, instant.

immediately *adverb* Without intermediary : directly. See CLEAR,
NEAR in Index. — See also **directly.**

immemorial *adjective* See **high.**

immense *adjective* See **giant.**

immenseness *noun* See **enormousness.**

immensity *noun* See **enormousness.**

immerge *verb* See **dip.**

immerse *verb* See **absorb, dip.**

immersion *noun* See **absorption.**

immigrant *noun.* See **emigrant.**

immigrate *verb* See **emigrate.**

immigration *noun* See **emigration.**

imminence *noun* See **approach.**

imminent *adjective* See **momentary.**

immobile *adjective* See **fixed,
motionless.**

immobilization *noun* See **tie-up.**

immobilize *verb* See **disable, tie up**
at **tie.**

immoderate *adjective* See
excessive.

immodest *adjective* See **improper.**

immolate *verb* See **sacrifice.**

immolation *noun* See **sacrifice.**

immoral *adjective* See **evil, impure.**

immorality *noun* See **corruption,
crime.**

immortal *adjective* Not being subject to death : deathless, undying.
See CONTINUE, LIVE in Index. — See
also **endless.**

immortality *noun* Endless life after
death : afterlife, deathlessness,
eternity, everlasting life, everlastingness. See CONTINUE, LIVE in Index.

immortalize *verb* To cause to last
endlessly : eternalize, eternize, per-

petuate. See CONTINUE, REMEM-
BER in Index.

immovable *adjective* See **fixed.**

immune *adjective* See **resistant.**

immunity *noun* See **resistance.**

immure *verb* See **enclose, jail.**

immutable *adjective* See **inflexible.**

imp *noun* See **mischief.**

impact *noun* The strong effect
exerted by one person or thing on
another : force, impression, influence, repercussion. See AFFECT in
Index. — See also **collision, wallop.**

impair *verb* See **injure.**

impairment *noun* See **breakage.**

impalpable *adjective* See
imperceptible.

impart *verb* See **communicate.**

impartial *adjective* See **fair,
neutral.**

impartiality *noun* See **fairness.**

impartialness *noun* See **fairness.**

impassable *adjective* See
insuperable.

impassible *adjective* See
insensitive.

impassion *verb* See **fire.**

impassioned *adjective* See
passionate.

impassive *adjective* See **apathetic,
dry, insensitive.**

impassivity *noun* See **apathy.**

impatient *adjective* Being unable or
unwilling to endure irritation or
opposition, for example : fretful,
intolerant, unforbearing. See
ACCEPT, ATTITUDE, CALM in
Index. — See also **eager.**

impeccable *adjective* See **perfect.**

impecuniosity *noun* See **poverty.**

impecunious *adjective* See **poor.**

impecuniousness *noun* See
poverty.

impede *verb* See **hinder, obstruct.**

impediment *noun* See **bar.**

impel *verb* See **drive, provoke.**

impend *verb* See **threaten.**

impending *adjective* See **momentary.**

impenetrable *adjective* See **incomprehensible.**

impenitent *adjective* See **remorseless.**

imperative *adjective* See **burning, required.**

imperative *noun* See **duty.**

imperceptible *adjective* 1. Incapable of being apprehended by the mind or the senses : impalpable, imponderable, inappreciable, indiscernible, indistinguishable, insensible, intangible, invisible, unnoticeable, unobservable. See KNOWLEDGE in Index. 2. So minute as not to be discernible : infinitesimal, microscopic. See BIG in Index.

imperfect *adjective* See **defective.**

imperfection *noun* See **defect.**

imperil *verb* See **endanger.**

imperilment *noun* See **danger.**

imperious *adjective* See **dictatorial.**

impermanent *adjective* See **temporary.**

impermissible *adjective* See **forbidden.**

impersonal *adjective* See **neutral.**

impersonate *verb* See **act, pose.**

impersonator *noun* See **mimic.**

impertinence *noun* See **impudence.**

impertinent *adjective* See **impudent, irrelevant.**

imperturbability *noun* See **balance.**

imperturbable *adjective* See **cool.**

imperturbableness *noun* See **balance.**

impervious *adjective* See **resistant.**

imperviousness *noun* See **resistance.**

impetuous *adjective* See **rash¹.**

impetus *noun* See **stimulus.**

impingement *noun* See **trespass.**

impish *adjective* See **playful.**

impishness *noun* See **mischief.**

implacability *noun* See **stubbornness.**

implacable *adjective* See **stubborn.**

implacableness *noun* See **stubbornness.**

implant *verb* See **impress.**

implausible *adjective* Not plausible or believable : flimsy, improbable, inconceivable, incredible, shaky, thin, unbelievable, unconceivable, unconvincing, unsubstantial, weak. See LIKELY in Index.

implement *verb* See **enforce, fulfill, use.**

implement *noun* See **tool.**

implementation *noun* See **exercise.**

implicate *verb* To cause to appear involved in or guilty of a crime or fault : criminate, incriminate, inculpate. See ATTACK, CRIMES in Index. — See also **involve.**

implication *noun* See **hint.**

implicit *adjective* 1. Conveyed indirectly without words or speech : implied, inferred, tacit, understood, unsaid, unspoken, unuttered, wordless. *Idiom:* taken for granted. See SHOW in Index. 2. Involved in the essential nature of something but not shown or developed : practical, virtual. See BE, SHOW in Index. 3. Having no reservations : absolute, unconditional, undoubting, unfaltering, unhesitating, unquestioning, unreserved, wholehearted. See BIG, LIMITED in Index.

implied *adjective* See **implicit.**

imploration *noun* See **appeal.**

implore *verb* See **appeal.**

imply *verb* To lead to by logical inference : indicate, point to, suggest. See MEANING in Index. — See also **hint.**

impolite *adjective* See **rude.**

impolitic *adjective* See **tactless, unwise.**

imponderable *adjective* See
imperceptible.

import *noun* The general sense or
significance, as of an action or statement : amount, burden[2], drift, purport, substance, tenor. *Idioms:* sum
and substance, sum total. See MEAN-
ING in Index. — See also **idea, importance, meaning.**
   import *verb* See **count, mean[1].**

importance *noun* The quality or
state of being important : concern,
concernment, consequence, import,
moment, significance, significancy,
weight, weightiness. See IMPOR-
TANT in Index.

important *adjective* Having great
significance : big, consequential,
considerable, historic, large, material, meaningful, monumental, significant, substantial. See IMPOR-
TANT in Index. — See also **influential.**

importunate *adjective* See
insistent.

importune *verb* See **besiege.**
   importune *adjective* See **insistent.**

impose *verb* **1.** To establish and
apply as compulsory : assess, exact,
levy, put. See OBLIGATION, OVER,
WILLING in Index. **2.** To force
(another) to accept a burden : foist,
inflict, saddle. *Informal:* stick. See
GIVE, OVER, WILLING in Index.
   — See also **abuse, dictate, inflict.**

imposing *adjective* See **grand.**

imposition *noun* An excessive,
unwelcome burden : infliction,
intrusion. See LIKE, WILLING in
Index.

impossible *adjective* Not capable
of happening or being done :
impracticable, impractical, unattainable, unrealizable, unthinkable,
unworkable. *Idiom:* out of the question. See POSSIBLE in Index. — See
also **contrary, unbearable.**

impost *noun* See **burden[1], tax.**

impostor *noun* See **fake.**

imposture *noun* See **trick.**

impotence *noun* See **ineffectuality.**

impotent *adjective* See **barren,
helpless, ineffectual.**

impoverish *verb* See **deplete, ruin.**

impoverished *adjective* See
depressed, poor.

impoverishment *noun* See **debilitation, poverty.**

impracticable *adjective* Incapable
of being used or availed of to advantage : impractical, unnegotiable,
unserviceable, unusable, unworkable, useless. See USED in Index.
   — See also **impossible.**

impractical *adjective* Incapable of
dealing efficiently with practical
matters : ivory-tower. See THRIVE
in Index. — See also **impossible,
impracticable.**

imprecate *verb* See **curse.**

imprecation *noun* See **curse.**

impregnable *adjective* See
invincible.

impregnate *verb* See **charge.**

impress *verb* To fix (an idea, for
example) in someone's mind by
reemphasis and repetition : drill,
drive, implant, inculcate, instill,
pound. See TEACH in Index. — See
also **affect[1], engrave.**
   impress *noun* See **impression.**

impressible *adjective* See **sensitive.**

impression *noun* **1.** The visible
effect made on a surface by pressure : impress, imprint, indent,
indentation, mark, print, stamp. See
MARKS in Index. **2.** The entire number of copies of a publication printed
from a single typesetting : printing.
See WORDS in Index. — See also **feeling, image, impact.**

impressionable *adjective* See **flexible, sensitive.**

impressionistic *adjective* See
suggestive.

impressive *adjective* See **affecting**.
imprint *verb* See **engrave**.
 imprint *noun* See **impression**.
imprison *verb* To enclose so as to hinder or prohibit escape : closet, confine, shut up. See FREE in Index. — See also **jail**.
improbable *adjective* See **doubtful, implausible**.
improbity *noun* See **corruption, dishonesty**.
impromptu *adjective* See **extemporaneous**.
 impromptu *noun* See **improvisation**.
improper *adjective* **1.** Not suited to circumstances : inappropriate, inapt, incongruous, inept, malapropos, unapt, unbecoming, unbefitting, unfit, unseemly, unsuitable. *Idiom:* out of place. See AGREE, USUAL in Index. **2.** Not in keeping with conventional mores : immodest, indecent, indecorous, indelicate, naughty, unbecoming, unbefitting, unseemly, untoward. *Idiom:* out of line. See USUAL in Index.
improperness *noun* See **impropriety**.
impropriety *noun* **1.** The condition of being improper : improperness, inappropriateness, unbecomingness, unfitness, unseemliness, unsuitability, unsuitableness. See AGREE, USUAL in Index. **2.** An improper act or statement : indecency, indecorum, indelicacy. See USUAL in Index.
improve *verb* To advance to a more desirable state : ameliorate, amend, better, help, meliorate, upgrade. See HELP in Index. — See also **recover**.
improvement *noun* The act of making better or the condition of being made better : amelioration, amendment, betterment, melioration,

upgrade. See BETTER in Index. — See also **progress**.
improvident *adjective* Reckless, especially in the use of material resources : thriftless, unthrifty. See CAREFUL in Index. — See also **rash**[1].
improvisation *noun* Something improvised : ad-lib, extemporization, impromptu. See PLANNED, PREPARED in Index.
improvise *verb* To compose or recite without preparation : ad-lib, extemporize, fake, make up. *Idiom:* wing it. See PLANNED, PREPARED in Index.
improvised *adjective* See **extemporaneous**.
imprudent *adjective* See **unwise**.
impudence *noun* The state or quality of being impudent or arrogantly self-confident : assumption, audaciousness, audacity, boldness, brashness, brazenness, cheek, cheekiness, chutzpah, discourtesy, disrespect, effrontery, face, familiarity, forwardness, gall[1], impertinence, impudency, incivility, insolence, nerve, nerviness, overconfidence, pertness, presumptuousness, pushiness, rudeness, sassiness, sauciness. *Informal:* brass, crust, sauce, uppishness, uppityness. See ATTITUDE, COURTESY in Index.
impudency *noun* See **impudence**.
impudent *adjective* Rude and disrespectful : assuming, assumptive, audacious, bold, boldfaced, brash, brazen, cheeky, contumelious, familiar, forward, impertinent, insolent, malapert, nervy, overconfident, pert, presuming, presumptuous, pushy, sassy, saucy, smart. *Informal:* brassy, flip, fresh, smart-alecky, snippety, snippy, uppish, uppity. *Slang:* wise[1]. See ATTITUDE, COURTESY in Index.
impulse *noun* See **fancy, stimulus**.

impulsive *adjective* See **rash**[1], **spontaneous**.

impure *adjective* **1.** Ceremonially or religiously unfit : unclean. See CLEAN, RELIGION, SACRED in Index. **2.** Not chaste or moral : immoral, unchaste, unclean, uncleanly. See GOOD, RESTRAINT, SEX in Index. **3.** Mixed with other substances : adulterated, alloyed, doctored, loaded, sophisticated. See CLEAN in Index.

impurity *noun* Impure condition : defilement, dirtiness, foulness, pollution, uncleanness, unwholesomeness. See CLEAN in Index. — See also **contaminant**.

imputation *noun* See **accusation**, **attribution**.

impute *verb* See **attribute, fix**.

in *adjective* See **fashionable**.

inability *noun* Lack of ability or capacity : incapability, incapacity, incompetence, incompetency, powerlessness. See ABILITY in Index.

inaccessible *adjective* Unable to be reached : inapproachable, unapproachable, unattainable, unavailable, unreachable. *Idioms:* beyond reach, out of the way. See REACH in Index. — See also **inconvenient**.

inaccuracy *noun* See **error**.

inaccurate *adjective* See **erroneous**.

inaction *noun* A lack of action or activity : idleness, inactivity, inertness, inoperativeness, stagnation. See ACTION in Index.

inactive *adjective* Marked by a lack of action or activity : idle, inert, inoperative. See ACTION in Index. — See also **idle, latent**.

inactivity *noun* See **inaction**.

inadequacy *noun* See **ineffectuality, shortage**.

inadequate *adjective* Lacking capability : incapable, incompe-

tent, unequal, unfit, unqualified. See ABILITY, EXCESS in Index. — See also **ineffectual, insufficient**.

inadmissible *adjective* See **objectionable**.

inadvertent *adjective* See **accidental, unintentional**.

inalterable *adjective* See **inflexible**.

inane *adjective* See **vacant**.

inanimate *adjective* Completely lacking sensation or consciousness : dead, insensate, insentient. See LIVE in Index.

inanity *noun* See **emptiness**.

inapplicable *adjective* See **irrelevant**.

inappreciable *adjective* See **imperceptible**.

inapproachable *adjective* See **inaccessible**.

inappropriate *adjective* See **improper, unfit, unfortunate**.

inappropriateness *noun* See **impropriety**.

inapt *adjective* See **improper, inefficient, unfit**.

inarguable *adjective* See **certain**.

inarticulate *adjective* See **dumb, speechless**.

inattentive *adjective* See **absent-minded, careless**.

inaugural *noun* See **initiation**.

inaugurate *verb* See **initiate, start**.

inauguration *noun* See **beginning, initiation**.

inauspicious *adjective* See **bad**.

inborn *adjective* See **constitutional, innate**.

inbred *adjective* See **constitutional**.

incalculable *adjective* Too great to be calculated : countless, immeasurable, incomputable, inestimable, infinite, innumerable, measureless, uncountable. See BIG in Index.

incandesce *verb* See **beam, glow**.

incandescent *adjective* See **bright**.

incapability *noun* See **inability, ineffectuality**.

incapable *adjective* See **inadequate, ineffectual, inefficient**.

incapacitate *verb* See **disable**.

incapacity *noun* See **inability**.

incarcerate *verb* See **jail**.

incarnate *verb* See **embody**.

incarnation *noun* See **embodiment**.

incautious *adjective* See **rash[1]**.

incautiousness *noun* See **temerity**.

incense[1] *verb* See **anger**.

incense[2] *noun* See **flattery**.

incentive *noun* See **stimulus**.

inception *noun* See **beginning, birth**.

inceptive *adjective* See **beginning**.

incertitude *noun* See **doubt**.

incessant *adjective* See **continual**.

inch *verb* See **crawl**.

inchoate *adjective* See **shapeless**.

incident *noun* See **circumstance, event**.

incidental *adjective* Not part of the real or essential nature of a thing : adscititious, adventitious, supervenient. See SURFACE in Index.

incipience *noun* See **beginning**.

incipiency *noun* See **beginning**.

incipient *adjective* See **beginning**.

incise *verb* See **cut, engrave**.

incision *noun* See **cut**.

incisive *adjective* See **acute**.

incisiveness *noun* See **edge**.

incitation *noun* See **stimulus**.

incite *verb* See **provoke**.

incitement *noun* See **stimulus**.

inciter *noun* See **agitator**.

incivility *noun* See **impudence**.

inclination *noun* Deviation from a particular direction : cant[1], grade, gradient, heel[2], incline, lean[1], list[2], rake[2], slant, slope, tilt, tip[2]. See RISE, STRAIGHT in Index.

incline *verb* To depart or cause to depart from true vertical or horizontal : cant[1], heel[2], lean[1], list[2], rake[2], slant, slope, tilt, tip[2]. See STRAIGHT in Index. — See also **dispose, tend[1]**.

incline *noun* See **inclination**.

inclined *adjective* Having or showing a tendency or likelihood : apt, disposed, given, liable, likely, prone. See LIKELY in Index.

include *verb* See **contain**.

inclusive *adjective* See **general**.

incommode *verb* See **inconvenience**.

incommodious *adjective* See **inconvenient**.

incommodiousness *noun* See **inconvenience**.

incommodity *noun* See **inconvenience**.

incommunicable *adjective* See **taciturn, unspeakable**.

incommunicative *adjective* See **taciturn**.

incomparable *adjective* See **unique**.

incompatibility *noun* See **gap**.

incompatible *adjective* See **discrepant, incongruous**.

incompetence *noun* See **inability**.

incompetency *noun* See **inability**.

incompetent *adjective* Totally incapable of doing a job : unable, unfit, unqualified. See ABILITY in Index. — See also **inadequate, inefficient**.

incomplete *adjective* See **deficient**.

incompliance *noun* See **stubbornness**.

incompliancy *noun* See **stubbornness**.

incompliant *adjective* See **stubborn**.

incomprehensible *adjective* Incapable of being grasped by the intellect or understanding : impenetrable, inscrutable, uncomprehensible, unfathomable, unintelligible. See KNOWLEDGE in Index.

incompressible *adjective* See **firm¹**.

incomputable *adjective* See **incalculable**.

inconceivable *adjective* See **implausible, incredible**.

inconclusive *adjective* See **ambiguous**.

incongruent *adjective* See **discrepant, incongruous**.

incongruity *noun* See **gap**.

incongruous *adjective* Made up of parts or qualities that are disparate or otherwise markedly lacking in consistency : discordant, discrepant, dissonant, incompatible, incongruent, inconsistent. See AGREE in Index. — See also **discrepant, improper**.

inconsequence *noun* See **indifference**.

inconsequent *adjective* See **little**.

inconsequential *adjective* See **little**.

inconsequentiality *noun* See **indifference**.

inconsequentialness *noun* See **indifference**.

inconsiderable *adjective* See **petty**.

inconsiderableness *noun* See **pettiness**.

inconsiderate *adjective* See **thoughtless**.

inconsiderateness *noun* See **thoughtlessness**.

inconsideration *noun* See **thoughtlessness**.

inconsistency *noun* See **gap**.

inconsistent *adjective* See **capricious, discrepant, incongruous, uneven**.

inconsonant *adjective* See **inharmonious**.

inconspicuous *adjective* Not readily noticed or seen : obscure, unconspicuous, unnoticeable, unob-

trusive. *Idiom:* having (or keeping) a low profile. See SEE in Index.

inconstant *adjective* See **capricious, changeable**.

incontestable *adjective* See **certain**.

incontinence *noun* See **abandon**.

incontinent *adjective* See **abandoned**.

incontrovertible *adjective* See **certain**.

inconvenience *noun* **1.** The state or quality of being inconvenient : discomfort, incommodiousness, incommodity, trouble. See COMFORT in Index. **2.** Something that causes difficulty, trouble, or lack of ease : discomfort, incommodity. See COMFORT in Index.

inconvenience *verb* To cause inconvenience for : discomfort, discommode, incommode, put out, trouble. See COMFORT in Index.

inconvenient *adjective* **1.** Not accessible or handy : inaccessible. See REACH in Index. **2.** Causing difficulty, trouble, or discomfort : difficult, incommodious, troublesome. See COMFORT in Index. **3.** Not occurring at a favorable time : ill-timed, inopportune, untimely. See TIME in Index.

incorporate *verb* See **build in** at **build, embody**.

incorporated *adjective* See **built-in**.

incorporeal *adjective* See **immaterial**.

incorrect *adjective* See **erroneous**.

incorrectness *noun* See **error**.

incorruptibility *noun* See **honesty**.

incorruptible *adjective* See **honest**.

increase *verb* To make or become greater or larger : aggrandize, amplify, augment, boost, build, build up, burgeon, enlarge, escalate, expand, extend, grow, magnify, mount, multiply, proliferate, rise, run up, snowball, soar, swell, upsurge, wax. *Informal:* beef up. See INCREASE in Index. — See also **reproduce.**

increase *noun* **1.** The act of increasing or rising : aggrandizement, amplification, augment, augmentation, boost, buildup, enlargement, escalation, growth, hike, jump, multiplication, proliferation, raise, rise, swell, upsurge, upswing, upturn. See INCREASE in Index. **2.** The amount by which something is increased : advance, boost, hike, increment, jump, raise, rise. See INCREASE in Index. — See also **reproduction.**

incredible *adjective* Not to be believed : inconceivable, unbelievable, unimaginable, unthinkable. *Idioms:* beyond belief, contrary to all reason. See BELIEF in Index. — See also **fabulous, implausible.**

incredulity *noun* See **disbelief.**

incredulous *adjective* Refusing or reluctant to believe : disbelieving, questioning, skeptical, unbelieving. See BELIEF in Index.

incredulousness *noun* See **disbelief.**

increment *noun* See **increase.**

incriminate *verb* See **accuse, implicate.**

incrimination *noun* See **accusation.**

inculcate *verb* See **impress, indoctrinate.**

inculpate *verb* See **implicate.**

incumbency *noun* See **tenure.**

incur *verb* See **assume.**

incurable *adjective* See **hopeless.**

incuriosity *noun* See **apathy.**

incurious *adjective* See **apathetic, detached.**

incuriousness *noun* See **apathy.**

incursion *noun* See **invasion.**

indebted *adjective* See **obliged.**

indebtedness *noun* See **debt.**

indecency *noun* See **impropriety.**

indecent *adjective* See **improper.**

indecision *noun* See **hesitation.**

indecisive *adjective* See **ambiguous, hesitant.**

indecisiveness *noun* See **hesitation.**

indecorous *adjective* See **improper.**

indecorum *noun* See **impropriety.**

indeed *adverb* See **actually, even[1], really.**

indefatigable *adjective* See **tireless.**

indefectible *adjective* See **perfect.**

indefensible *adjective* See **inexcusable.**

indefinable *adjective* See **unspeakable.**

indefinite *adjective* **1.** Lacking precise limits : indeterminate, inexact, undetermined. See LIMITED in Index. **2.** Marked by lack of firm decision or commitment; of questionable outcome : open, uncertain, undecided, undetermined, unresolved, unsettled, unsure, vague. *Idiom:* up in the air. See CERTAIN in Index. — See also **unclear.**

indefiniteness *noun* See **vagueness.**

indelible *adjective* See **fast.**

indelicacy *noun* See **impropriety.**

indelicate *adjective* See **coarse, improper, tactless.**

indemnification *noun* See **compensation.**

indemnify *verb* See **compensate, reward.**

indemnity *noun* See **compensation.**

indent *noun* See **impression.**

indentation *noun* See **impression.**

indented *adjective* See **hollow.**

independence *noun* The capacity to manage one's own affairs, make one's own judgments, and provide for oneself : self-determination, self-reliance, self-sufficiency. See

DEPENDENCE in Index. — See also
freedom.

independency *noun* See **freedom.**

independent *adjective* 1. Free from
the influence, guidance, or control of
others : self-contained, self-reliant,
self-sufficient. See DEPENDENCE in
Index. 2. Able to support oneself
financially : self-sufficient, self-
supporting. See DEPENDENCE,
MONEY in Index. — See also **free.**

independently *adverb* See
separately.

indescribable *adjective* See
unspeakable.

indeterminate *adjective* See
ambiguous, indefinite.

index *noun* See **sign.**

indicate *verb* To give grounds for
believing in the existence or presence of : argue, attest, bespeak,
betoken, mark, point to, testify, witness. See SHOW in Index. — See also
designate, imply, show.

indication *noun* See **expression,
gesture, sign.**

indicative *adjective* See
designative.

indicator *noun* See **sign.**

indicatory *adjective* See
designative.

indict *verb* See **accuse.**

indicter or **indictor** *noun* See
accuser.

indictment *noun* See **accusation.**

indifference *noun* Lack of importance : inconsequence, inconsequentiality, inconsequentialness,
insignificance, insignificancy, unimportance. See CONCERN in Index.
— See also **apathy.**

indifferent *adjective* See **apathetic,
detached, fair, neutral, ordinary.**

indigence *noun* See **poverty.**

indigenous *adjective* Existing,
born, or produced in a land or
region : aboriginal, autochthonal,

autochthonic, autochthonous,
endemic, native. See NATIVE in
Index. — See also **constitutional.**

indigent *adjective* See **poor.**

indigent *noun* See **pauper.**

indigestible *adjective* See **bitter.**

indignant *adjective* See **angry.**

indignation *noun* See **anger.**

indignity *noun* An act that offends a
person's sense of pride or dignity :
affront, contumely, despite, insult,
offense, outrage, slight. *Idiom:* slap
in the face. See ATTACK in Index.

indirect *adjective* Not taking a
direct or straight line or course :
anfractuous, circuitous, circular,
devious, oblique, roundabout, tortuous. See STRAIGHT in Index. — See
also **underhand.**

indirection *noun* Lack of straight-
forwardness and honesty in action :
chicanery, craft, craftiness, deviousness, dishonesty, shadiness, shiftiness, slyness, sneakiness, trickery,
trickiness, underhandedness. See
HONEST in Index.

indiscernible *adjective* See
imperceptible.

indiscreet *adjective* See **unwise.**

indiscriminate *adjective* See
random.

indispensable *adjective* See
essential.

indisposed *adjective* Not inclined
or willing to do or undertake :
averse, disinclined, loath, reluctant,
unwilling. See WILLING in Index.
— See also **sickly.**

indisposition *noun* 1. A minor illness, especially one of a temporary
nature : ailment, bug, complaint,
malady. See HEALTH in Index.
2. The state of not being disposed or
inclined : averseness, disinclination, reluctance, unwillingness.
See WILLING in Index. — See also
sickness.

indisputable *adjective* See **certain.**

indistinct *adjective* See **unclear.**

indistinctive *adjective* See **neutral.**

indistinguishable *adjective* See **imperceptible.**

indite *verb* See **compose, write.**

individual *adjective* Being or related to a distinct entity : discrete, particular, separate, single, singular. See INCLUDE in Index.
— See also **distinctive, personal, special.**

individual *noun* See **human being, thing.**

individualism *noun* See **identity.**

individualistic *adjective* See **egocentric.**

individuality *noun* The quality of being individual : discreteness, distinctiveness, particularity, separateness, singularity. See INCLUDE in Index. — See also **identity.**

individualize *verb* See **distinguish.**

individually *adverb* See **separately.**

indocile *adjective* See **unruly.**

indocility *noun* See **unruliness.**

indoctrinate *verb* **1.** To instruct in a body of doctrine or belief : drill, inculcate. See TEACH in Index. **2.** To teach to accept a system of thought uncritically : brainwash, propagandize. See TEACH in Index.

indolence *noun* See **laziness.**

indolent *adjective* See **lazy.**

indomitable *adjective* See **invincible.**

indubitable *adjective* See **authentic, certain.**

indubitably *adverb* See **yes.**

induce *verb* See **cause, persuade.**

inducement *noun* See **lure, stimulus.**

induct *verb* See **draft, initiate.**

induction *noun* See **draft, initiation, introduction.**

inductive *adjective* See **preliminary.**

indulge *verb* See **baby, humor, luxuriate, participate, satisfy.**

indulgence *noun* See **favor, tolerance.**

indulgent *adjective* See **obliging, tolerant.**

indurate *verb* See **harden.**

industrious *adjective* See **diligent.**

industriousness *noun* See **diligence.**

industry *noun* See **business, diligence.**

indwelling *adjective* See **constitutional.**

inebriate *adjective* See **drunk.**

inebriate *noun* See **drunkard.**

inebriated *adjective* See **drunk.**

inebriation *noun* See **drunkenness.**

inebriety *noun* See **drunkenness.**

ineffable *adjective* See **unspeakable.**

ineffective *adjective* See **ineffectual.**

ineffectiveness *noun* See **ineffectuality.**

ineffectual *adjective* **1.** Not having the desired effect : ineffective, inefficacious, inefficient, useless. See AFFECT in Index. **2.** Not capable of accomplishing anything : helpless, impotent, inadequate, incapable, powerless, weak. See ABILITY, STRONG in Index. — See also **useless.**

ineffectuality *noun* The condition or state of being incapable of accomplishing or effecting anything : helplessness, impotence, inadequacy, incapability, ineffectiveness, ineffectualness, inefficacy, powerlessness, uselessness. See AFFECT, STRONG in Index.

ineffectualness *noun* See **ineffectuality.**

inefficacious *adjective* See **ineffectual.**

inefficacy *noun* See **ineffectuality.**

inefficient *adjective* Lacking the qualities, as efficiency or skill, required to produce desired results : inapt, incapable, incompetent, inept, inexpert, unskilled, unskillful, unworkmanlike. See ABILITY in Index. — See also **ineffectual.**

inelastic *adjective* See **rigid.**

inelegant *adjective* See **tacky².**

inept *adjective* See **awkward, improper, inefficient, unfortunate, unskillful.**

inequality *noun* The condition or fact of being unequal, as in age, rank, or degree : disparity, disproportion, disproportionateness. See SAME in Index. — See also **irregularity.**

inequitable *adjective* See **unfair.**

inequity *noun* See **injustice.**

ineradicable *adjective* See **confirmed.**

inert *adjective* See **inactive.**

inertness *noun* See **inaction.**

inescapable *adjective* See **certain.**

inessential *adjective* See **unnecessary.**

inestimable *adjective* See **incalculable, valuable.**

inevitable *adjective* See **certain.**

inexact *adjective* See **indefinite, loose.**

inexcusable *adjective* Impossible to excuse, pardon, or justify : indefensible, unforgivable, unjustifiable, unpardonable. See FORGIVENESS in Index.

inexhaustibility *noun* See **infinity.**

inexhaustible *adjective* See **tireless.**

inexhaustibleness *noun* See **infinity.**

inexorability *noun* See **stubbornness.**

inexorable *adjective* See **stubborn.**

inexorableness *noun* See **stubbornness.**

inexpensive *adjective* See **cheap.**

inexperience *noun* Lack of experience and the knowledge gained from it : greenness, inexpertness, rawness. See ABILITY in Index.

inexperienced *adjective* Lacking experience and the knowledge gained from it : green, inexpert, raw, uninitiate, uninitiated, unpracticed, unseasoned, untried, unversed. See ABILITY in Index.

inexpert *adjective* See **inefficient, inexperienced.**

inexpertness *noun* See **inexperience.**

inexplicable *adjective* That cannot be explained : unaccountable, unexplainable. See EXPLAIN in Index.

inexplicit *adjective* See **ambiguous.**

inexpressible *adjective* See **unspeakable.**

inexpressive *adjective* See **expressionless.**

infallible *adjective* See **sure.**

infamous *adjective* See **filthy, notorious.**

infamousness *noun* See **notoriety.**

infamy *noun* The condition of being infamous : disgracefulness, dishonorableness, disreputability, disreputableness, ignominiousness, shamefulness. See GOOD, RESPECT, RIGHT in Index. — See also **notoriety.**

infancy *noun* See **minority.**

infant *noun* See **baby, minor.**

infant *adjective* See **young.**

infantile *adjective* See **babyish, childish.**

infantine *adjective* See **babyish.**

infatuate *adjective* See **infatuated.**

infatuated *adjective* Affected with intense romantic attraction : enamored, infatuate, smitten. *Slang:* gone. See EXCITE, SEX in Index.

infatuation *noun* An extravagant, short-lived romantic attachment :

Informal: crush. See EXCITE, SEX in Index.

infect *verb* See **poison, taint.**

infectious *adjective* See **communicable.**

infelicitous *adjective* See **unfortunate.**

infer *verb* To arrive at (a conclusion) from evidence or reasoning : conclude, deduce, deduct, draw, gather, judge, understand. See REASON in Index. — See also **guess.**

inference *noun* See **deduction.**

inferential *adjective* See **supposed.**

inferior *adjective* Of low or lower quality : common, low-grade, low-quality, mean², mediocre, second-class, second-rate, shabby, substandard. See BETTER in Index. — See also **minor.**

inferior *noun* See **subordinate.**

infernal *adjective* See **damned, fiendish.**

inferred *adjective* See **implicit.**

infertile *adjective* See **barren.**

infertility *noun* See **sterility.**

infidelity *noun* See **faithlessness.**

infiltrate *verb* See **insinuate.**

infinite *adjective* See **endless, eternal, incalculable.**

infiniteness *noun* See **infinity.**

infinitesimal *adjective* See **imperceptible.**

infinity *noun* The state or quality of being infinite : boundlessness, immeasurability, immeasurableness, inexhaustibility, inexhaustibleness, infiniteness, limitlessness, measurelessness, unboundedness, unlimitedness. See LIMITED in Index. — See also **eternity.**

infirm *adjective* Not physically strong : decrepit, delicate, feeble, flimsy, fragile, frail, insubstantial, puny, unsound, unsubstantial, weak, weakly. See STRONG in Index. — See also **insecure.**

infirmity *noun* The condition of being infirm or physically weak : debility, decrepitude, delicacy, delicateness, feebleness, flimsiness, fragileness, fragility, frailness, frailty, insubstantiality, puniness, unsoundness, unsubstantiality, weakliness, weakness. See STRONG in Index. — See also **disease, sickness, weakness.**

infix *verb* See **fix.**

inflame *verb* See **irritate, provoke.**

inflammation *noun* See **irritation.**

inflate *verb* See **exaggerate.**

inflated *adjective* Filled up with or as if with something insubstantial : flatulent, overblown, tumescent, tumid, turgid, windy. See INCREASE, PLAIN in Index.

inflection *noun* See **tone.**

inflexibility *noun* See **stubbornness.**

inflexible *adjective* Incapable of changing or being modified : immutable, inalterable, invariable, ironclad, rigid, unalterable, unchangeable. See FLEXIBLE in Index. — See also **rigid, stubborn.**

inflexibleness *noun* See **stubbornness.**

inflict *verb* To cause to undergo or bear (something unwelcome or damaging, for example) : impose, play, visit, wreak. See GIVE, OVER, WILLING in Index. — See also **impose.**

infliction *noun* See **imposition.**

influence *noun* The power to produce an effect by indirect means : leverage, sway, weight. *Informal:* clout. *Slang:* pull. See AFFECT in Index. — See also **effect, impact.**

influence *verb* See **dispose.**

influential *adjective* Having or exercising influence : consequential, important, powerful, weighty. See AFFECT, IMPORTANT, STRONG in Index.

infold *verb* See **wrap.**

inform *verb* **1.** To impart information to : acquaint, advise, apprise, educate, enlighten, notify, tell. See KNOWLEDGE, TEACH in Index.
2. To give incriminating information about others, especially to the authorities : talk, tattle, tip³ (off). *Informal:* fink. *Slang:* rat, sing, snitch, squeal, stool. *Idiom:* blow the whistle. See KNOWLEDGE, LAW in Index.

informal *adjective* See **conversational, easygoing.**

informality *noun* See **ease.**

informant *noun* See **informer.**

information *noun* That which is known about a specific subject or situation : data, fact (used in plural), intelligence, knowledge, lore. See KNOWLEDGE in Index. — See also **knowledge.**

informative *adjective* See **educational.**

informed *adjective* Provided with information; made aware : acquainted, advised, educated, enlightened, instructed, knowledgeable. See KNOWLEDGE in Index. — See also **educated.**

informer *noun* One who gives incriminating information about others : informant, tattler, tattletale. *Informal:* rat, tipster. *Slang:* fink, snitch, snitcher, squealer, stoolie, stool pigeon. See KNOWLEDGE, LAW in Index.

infraction *noun* See **breach.**

infrequent *adjective* Rarely occurring or appearing : occasional, rare, scarce, sporadic, uncommon, unusual. *Idiom:* few and far between. See USUAL in Index.

infrequently *adverb* At rare intervals : little, occasionally, rarely, seldom, sporadically. *Idioms:* hardly (or scarcely) ever, once in a blue moon. See USUAL in Index.

infringe *verb* See **violate.**

infringement *noun* See **breach, trespass.**

infuriate *verb* See **anger.**

infuse *verb* See **steep².**

ingenerate *verb* See **cause.**

ingenious *adjective* See **inventive, resourceful.**

ingeniousness *noun* See **invention.**

ingénue *noun* See **innocent.**

ingenuity *noun* See **invention.**

ingenuous *adjective* See **artless, frank.**

ingest *verb* See **eat, swallow.**

ingestion *noun* See **swallow.**

ingrain *verb* See **fix.**

ingrained *adjective* See **confirmed, constitutional.**

ingratiating *adjective* See **insinuating.**

ingratiatory *adjective* See **insinuating.**

ingredient *noun* See **element.**

ingress *noun* See **admission, entrance¹.**

ingression *noun* See **admission.**

ingurgitate *verb* See **gulp.**

inhabit *verb* To live in (a place), as does a people : occupy, people, populate. See PLACE in Index.

inhabitable *adjective* See **livable.**

inhalation *noun* See **inspiration.**

inhale *verb* See **breathe.**

inharmonic *adjective* See **inharmonious.**

inharmonious *adjective*
1. Characterized by unpleasant discordance of sound : cacophonous, discordant, disharmonious, dissonant, inharmonic, rude, unharmonious, unmusical. See AGREE, SOUNDS in Index. **2.** Devoid of harmony and accord : discordant, inconsonant, uncongenial, unharmonious. See AGREE in Index.

inharmony *noun* See **conflict.**

inhere *verb* See **consist.**

inherent *adjective* See **constitutional.**

inherit *verb* To receive (property) from one who has died : come into. See GET, LAW in Index.

inheritance *noun* See **birthright, heritage.**

inherited *adjective* See **ancestral, innate.**

inhibit *verb* See **constrain, forbid, restrain.**

inhibited *adjective* See **frigid, reserved.**

inhibition *noun* See **forbiddance, restriction.**

inhospitable *adjective* See **forbidding.**

inhospitableness *noun* See **unwelcome.**

inhospitality *noun* See **unwelcome.**

inhuman *adjective* See **fierce.**

inhumanity *noun* See **cruelty.**

inhumation *noun* See **burial.**

inhume *verb* See **bury.**

inimical *adjective* See **hostile.**

iniquitous *adjective* See **evil.**

iniquity *noun* See **crime, evil, injustice.**

initial *adjective* See **beginning, early, first.**

initiate *verb* To admit formally into membership or office, as with ritual : inaugurate, induct, install, instate, invest. See ACCEPT in Index. — See also **start.**

initiate *noun* See **beginner.**

initiation *noun* The act or process of formally admitting a person to membership or office : inaugural, inauguration, induction, installation, instatement, investiture. See ACCEPT in Index. — See also **beginning.**

initiative *noun* See **drive.**

initiatory *adjective* See **beginning.**

inject *verb* See **introduce.**

injudicious *adjective* See **unwise.**

injunction *noun* See **command.**

injure *verb* To spoil the soundness or perfection of : blemish, damage, detract from, disserve, flaw, harm, hurt, impair, mar, prejudice, tarnish, vitiate. See BETTER, HELP in Index. — See also **distress, hurt.**

injurious *adjective* See **harmful, libelous.**

injury *noun* See **harm, injustice.**

injustice *noun* **1.** Lack of justice : inequity, iniquity, unfairness, unjustness, wrong. See LAW, RIGHT in Index. **2.** An act that is not just : disservice, inequity, raw deal, wrong. *Law:* injury. See LAW, RIGHT in Index.

inkhorn *adjective* See **pedantic.**

inkling *noun* See **hint.**

inky *adjective* See **black.**

inlet *noun* See **bay**[1]**.**

inlying *adjective* See **inner.**

innate *adjective* Possessed at birth : congenital, hereditary, inborn, inherited, native. See BE, NATIVE in Index. — See also **constitutional.**

inner *adjective* **1.** Located inside or farther in : inlying, inside, interior, internal. See EDGE in Index. **2.** Of, relating to, or arising from one's mental or spiritual being : interior, internal, intimate[1], inward, visceral. *Slang:* gut. See BODY in Index. **3.** Being closer to a center of power and influence : inside. See EDGE, POLITICS in Index.

innerving *adjective* See **tonic.**

inning *noun* See **turn.**

innocence *noun* See **chastity, ignorance.**

innocent *adjective* **1.** Free from evil and corruption : angelic, angelical, clean, lily-white, pure, sinless, unblemished, uncorrupted, undefiled, unstained, unsullied, untainted, virginal. *Idiom:* pure as the driven snow. See CLEAN, RIGHT, SEX in Index. **2.** Free from guilt or blame : blameless, faultless, guiltless, harmless, irreproachable, lily-white, unblamable. *Slang:* clean. *Idiom:* in the clear. See RIGHT in Index. — See also **artless, empty, harmless, ignorant, lawful.**

innocent *noun* **1.** A pure, uncorrupted person : angel, lamb, virgin. See CLEAN, RIGHT in Index. **2.** A guileless, unsophisticated person : babe, child, ingénue, naive. *Idiom:* babe in the woods. See KNOWLEDGE in Index. — See also **child.**

innocuous *adjective* See **harmless, insipid.**

innocuousness *noun* See **insipidity.**

innovation *noun* See **novelty.**

innovative *adjective* See **inventive, new.**

innovativeness *noun* See **novelty.**

innovatory *adjective* See **inventive.**

innuendo *noun* See **insinuation.**

innumerable *adjective* See **incalculable.**

inobtrusive *adjective* See **quiet.**

inoffensive *adjective* See **harmless.**

inoperative *adjective* See **inactive.**

inoperativeness *noun* See **inaction.**

inopportune *adjective* See **inconvenient.**

inordinate *adjective* See **excessive.**

inquest *noun* See **inquiry.**

inquietude *noun* See **restlessness.**

inquire also **enquire** *verb* See **ask, explore.**

inquirer also **enquirer** *noun* One who inquires : inquisitor, investigator, prober, querier, quester, questioner, researcher. See ASK, INVESTIGATE in Index.

inquiring also **enquiring** *adjective* See **curious.**

inquiry also **enquiry** *noun* **1.** A seeking of knowledge, data, or the truth about something : inquest,

inquisition, investigation, probe, research. See INVESTIGATE in Index. **2.** A request for data : interrogation, query, question. *Law:* interrogatory. See ASK, INVESTIGATE in Index.

inquisition *noun* See **inquiry.**

inquisitive *adjective* See **curious.**

inquisitiveness *noun* See **curiosity.**

inquisitor *noun* One who conducts an official inquiry, usually with no regard for human rights : interrogator, questioner. See ASK, INVESTIGATE in Index. — See also **inquirer.**

inquisitorial *adjective* See **curious.**

inroad *noun* See **invasion.**

insalubrious *adjective* See **unwholesome.**

insane *adjective* Afflicted with or exhibiting irrationality and mental unsoundness : brainsick, crazy, daft, demented, disordered, distraught, dotty, lunatic, mad, maniac, maniacal, mentally ill, moonstruck, off, touched, unbalanced, unsound, wrong. *Informal:* bonkers, cracked, daffy, gaga, loony. *Slang:* bananas, batty, buggy, cuckoo, fruity, loco, nuts, nutty, screwy, wacky. *Chiefly British:* crackers. *Law:* non compos mentis. *Idioms:* around the bend, crazy as a loon, mad as a hatter, not all there, nutty as a fruitcake, off (or out of) one's head, off one's rocker, of unsound mind, out of one's mind, sick in the head, stark raving mad. See SANE in Index. — See also **foolish.**

insaneness *noun* See **insanity.**

insanity *noun* Serious mental illness or disorder impairing a person's capacity to function normally and safely : brainsickness, craziness, dementia, derangement, disturbance, insaneness, lunacy, madness, mental illness, psychopathy, unbalance. *Psychiatry:* mania.

Psychology: aberration, alienation. See SANE in Index. — See also **foolishness**.

inscribe *verb* See **engrave, list[1], sign, write.**

inscrutable *adjective* See **incomprehensible.**

insecure *adjective* **1.** Inadequately protected : unguarded, unprotected, unsafe. See SAFETY in Index. **2.** Lacking stability : infirm, precarious, shaky, tottering, tottery, unstable, unsteady, unsure, weak, wobbly. See CHANGE, STRONG in Index.

insecureness *noun* See **instability.**

insecurity *noun* See **instability.**

insensate *adjective* See **inanimate, insensitive, mindless.**

insensibility *noun* See **apathy.**

insensible *adjective* See **apathetic, dead, dull, imperceptible, insensitive, unconscious.**

insensibleness *noun* See **apathy.**

insensitive *adjective* **1.** Lacking passion and emotion : anesthetic, bloodless, dull, insensate, insensible. See ATTITUDE, FEELINGS in Index. **2.** Not capable of being affected or impressed : impassible, impassive, insusceptible, unimpressionable, unsusceptible. See AFFECT in Index. — See also **dead, dull.**

insentient *adjective* See **inanimate.**

insert *verb* See **introduce, post[3].**

insertion *noun* See **entry.**

inside *adjective* See **confidential, inner, intimate[1].**

inside track *noun* See **advantage.**

insight *noun* See **instinct, wisdom.**

insignificance *noun* See **indifference.**

insignificancy *noun* See **indifference.**

insignificant *adjective* See **little.**

insincere *adjective* Not being what one purports to be : ambidextrous, disingenuous, left-handed, mala fide. See HONEST in Index. — See also **artificial.**

insincerity *noun* Lack of sincerity : ambidexterity, artificiality, disingenuousness, phoniness. See HONEST in Index.

insinuate *verb* To introduce gradually and slyly : edge, foist, infiltrate, wind[2], work, worm. See ENTER in Index. — See also **hint.**

insinuating *adjective* **1.** Provoking a change of outlook and especially gradual doubt and suspicion : insinuative, insinuatory, suggestive. See SUGGEST in Index. **2.** Purposefully contrived to gain favor : ingratiating, ingratiatory, saccharine, sugary. See PAIN in Index.

insinuation *noun* An artful, indirect, often derogatory hint : innuendo. See SUGGEST in Index.

insinuative *adjective* See **insinuating.**

insinuatory *adjective* See **insinuating.**

insipid *adjective* Lacking the qualities requisite for spiritedness and originality : bland, innocuous, jejune, namby-pamby, vapid, washy, waterish, watery. *Informal:* wishy-washy. See EXCITE, GOOD in Index. — See also **flat.**

insipidity *noun* The state or quality of being insipid : blandness, innocuousness, insipidness, jejuneness, vapidity, vapidness, washiness, wateriness. *Informal:* wishy-washiness. See EXCITE, TASTE in Index. — See also **dullness.**

insipidness *noun* See **dullness, insipidity.**

insist *verb* **1.** To take and maintain a stand obstinately : persevere, persist. See CONTINUE in Index. **2.** To solicit (something) insistently :

press, urge. See CONTINUE, SEEK in Index.

insist on or **upon** *verb* See **demand.**

insistence *noun* **1.** The state or quality of being insistent : insistency, perseverance, persistence, persistency. See CONTINUE in Index. **2.** Urgent solicitation : insistency, pressing. *Archaic:* instance. See CONTINUE, SEEK in Index.

insistency *noun* See **insistence.**

insistent *adjective* Firm or obstinate, as in making a demand or maintaining a stand : importunate, importune, persistent, urgent. See CONTINUE in Index. — See also **emphatic.**

insobriety *noun* See **drunkenness.**

insolence *noun* See **arrogance, impudence.**

insolent *adjective* See **arrogant, impudent.**

insolvency *noun* See **failure.**

inspect *verb* See **analyze, examine, search.**

inspection *noun* See **analysis, examination.**

inspiration *noun* **1.** Divine guidance and motivation imparted directly : afflatus. See RELIGION in Index. **2.** The act of breathing in : inhalation. See BREATH in Index. **3.** A sudden exciting thought : brainstorm. *Informal:* brain wave. See THOUGHTS in Index. — See also **elation, encouragement, fire.**

inspire *verb* See **breathe, elate, encourage, fire, provoke.**

inspirit *verb* See **elate, encourage.**

inspissate *verb* See **thicken.**

instability *noun* The quality or condition of being erratic and undependable : insecureness, insecurity, precariousness, shakiness, unstableness, unsteadiness, unsureness. See CHANGE, STRONG in Index. — See also **unstableness.**

install also **instal** *verb* See **establish, initiate, position.**

installation *noun* See **base¹, initiation.**

instance *verb* To demonstrate and clarify with examples : exemplify, illustrate. See SHOW in Index. — See also **name.**

instance *noun* See **example, insistence, lawsuit.**

instant *noun* A particular interval of time that is limited and often crucial : juncture, moment, point. See TIME in Index. — See also **flash.**

instant *adjective* Occurring at once : immediate, instantaneous. See TIME in Index. — See also **burning.**

instant *adverb* See **directly.**

instantaneous *adjective* See **instant.**

instantly *adverb* See **directly.**

instate *verb* See **initiate.**

instatement *noun* See **initiation.**

instigate *verb* See **provoke.**

instigation *noun* See **stimulus.**

instigator *noun* See **agitator.**

instill also **instil** *verb* See **impress.**

instinct *noun* The power to discern the true nature of a person or situation : insight, intuition, intuitiveness, penetration, sixth sense. See THOUGHTS in Index. — See also **talent.**

instinctive *adjective* Derived from or prompted by a natural tendency or impulse : instinctual, intuitive, visceral. See THOUGHTS in Index. — See also **spontaneous.**

instinctual *adjective* See **instinctive.**

institute *verb* See **found, start.**

institute *noun* See **law.**

institution *noun* See **foundation.**

institutionalize *verb* See **commit.**

instruct *verb* See **command, educate.**

instructed *adjective* See **informed.**

instruction *noun* See **command, education.**

instructional *adjective* See **educational.**

instructive *adjective* See **educational.**

instructor *noun* See **educator.**

instrument *noun* See **mean³, pawn², tool.**

instrumentality *noun* See **mean³.**

instrumentation *noun* See **mean³.**

insubordinate *adjective* See **disobedient.**

insubordination *noun* See **disobedience.**

insubstantial *adjective* See **immaterial, infirm, tenuous.**

insubstantiality *noun* See **infirmity.**

insufferable *adjective* See **unbearable.**

insufficiency *noun* See **shortage.**

insufficient *adjective* Not enough to meet a demand or requirement : deficient, inadequate, scarce, short, shy¹, under, wanting. See BIG, EXCESS in Index.

insular *adjective* See **local, remote.**

insulate *verb* See **isolate.**

insulation *noun* See **isolation.**

insult *verb* To cause resentment or hurt by callous, rude behavior : affront, huff, miff, offend, outrage, pique. *Idioms:* add insult to injury, give offense to. See ATTACK, PAIN in Index.

insult *noun* See **indignity, taunt.**

insuperable *adjective* Incapable of being negotiated or overcome : impassable, insurmountable. See DO in Index.

insupportable *adjective* See **unbearable.**

insure *verb* See **guarantee.**

insurgence *noun* See **rebellion.**

insurgency *noun* See **rebellion.**

insurgent *adjective* See **rebellious.**

insurgent *noun* See **rebel.**

insurmountable *adjective* See **insuperable.**

insurrection *noun* See **rebellion.**

insurrectionary *noun* See **rebel.**

insurrectionist *noun* See **rebel.**

insusceptibility *noun* See **resistance.**

insusceptible *adjective* See **insensitive, resistant.**

intact *adjective* See **complete, good.**

intangible *adjective* See **imperceptible.**

integral *adjective* See **complete, essential.**

integral *noun* See **system.**

integrant *noun* See **element.**

integrate *verb* **1.** To make into a whole by joining a system of parts : articulate, concatenate. See INCLUDE, PART in Index. **2.** To open to all people regardless of race : desegregate. See INCLUDE, SAME in Index. — See also **build in** at **build, embody, harmonize.**

integration *noun* The act, process, or result of abolishing racial segregation : desegregation. See INCLUDE, SAME in Index.

integrity *noun* See **character, completeness, honesty, soundness.**

integument *noun* See **skin.**

intellect *noun* See **intelligence, mind.**

intellective *adjective* See **mental.**

intellectual *adjective* Appealing to or engaging the intellect : cerebral, sophisticated, thoughtful. *Informal:* highbrow. See THOUGHTS in Index. — See also **intelligent, mental.**

intellectual *noun* See **mind.**

intelligence *noun* The faculty of thinking, reasoning, and acquiring and applying knowledge : brain (often used in plural), brainpower, intellect, mentality, mind, sense, understanding, wit. *Slang:* smart (used in plural). See ABILITY, THOUGHTS in Index. — See also **information, news.**

intelligent *adjective* Having or showing intelligence, often of a high order : brilliant, intellectual, knowing, knowledgeable. *Informal:* brainy. See ABILITY in Index. — See also **clever, logical.**

intelligible *adjective* See **understandable.**

intemperance *noun* See **excess.**

intend *verb* To have in mind as a goal or purpose : aim, contemplate, design, mean¹, plan, project, propose, purpose, target. *Regional:* mind. See PLANNED, PURPOSE in Index. — See also **mean¹.**

intended *noun* *Informal.* A person to whom one is engaged to be married : betrothed, fiancé, fiancée. See MARRIAGE in Index.

intended *adjective* See **deliberate, engaged.**

intense *adjective* Extreme in degree, strength, or effect : desperate, fierce, furious, terrible, vehement, violent. See BIG, STRONG in Index. — See also **deep, heavy.**

intensify *verb* To make greater in intensity or severity : aggravate, deepen, enhance, heighten, redouble. See INCREASE in Index.

intensity *noun* Exceptionally great concentration, power, or force, especially in activity : depth (often used in plural), ferociousness, ferocity, fierceness, fury, pitch, severity, vehemence, vehemency, violence. See BIG, STRONG in Index.

intensive *adjective* See **concentrated, heavy, thorough.**

intensively *adverb* See **completely.**

intent *noun* See **intention, meaning, thrust.**

intent *adjective* See **absorbed, attentive, set¹.**

intention *noun* What one intends to do or achieve : aim, ambition, design, end, goal, intent, mark, meaning, object, objective, point, purpose, target, view, why. *Idioms:* end in view, why and wherefore. See PLANNED, PURPOSE in Index.

intentional *adjective* See **calculated, deliberate.**

inter *verb* See **bury.**

interceder *noun* See **go-between.**

intercept *verb* See **head off** at **head.**

intercessor *noun* See **go-between.**

interchange *verb* See **change, exchange, rotate.**

interchange *noun* See **change, rotation.**

intercommunication *noun* See **communication, touch.**

interconnection *noun* See **relation.**

intercourse *noun* See **communication.**

interdependence *noun* See **relation.**

interdict *verb* See **forbid.**

interdict *noun* See **sanction.**

interdiction *noun* See **forbiddance, sanction.**

interest *noun* **1.** Something that contributes to or increases one's well-being. Often used in plural : advantage, benefit, good, profit. See HELP in Index. **2.** A right or legal share in something : claim, portion, stake, title. See PART in Index. — See also **concern, curiosity.**

interest *verb* To arouse the interest and attention of : attract, intrigue. *Slang:* turn on. See EXCITE in Index.

interested *adjective* See **concerned.**

interestedness *noun* See **concern.**

interfere *verb* See **meddle.**

interference *noun* See **meddling.**

interfering *adjective* See **meddling.**

interim *adjective* See **temporary.**

interim *noun* See **gap.**

interior *adjective* See **inner.**

interject *verb* See **introduce.**

interlard *verb* See **introduce.**

interlope *verb* See **meddle.**

interloper *noun* See **meddler.**

intermediary *noun* See **go-between, mean³.**

intermediate *adjective* See **middle.**

intermediate *noun* See **go-between.**

intermediator *noun* See **go-between.**

interment *noun* See **burial.**

interminable *adjective* See **continual.**

intermingle *verb* See **mix.**

intermission *noun* See **abeyance, break.**

intermittent *adjective* Happening or appearing now and then : fitful, occasional, periodic, periodical, sporadic. *Informal:* on-again, off-again. See CONTINUE in Index.

intermittently *adverb* Once in a while; at times : betimes, occasionally, periodically, sometimes, sporadically. *Idioms:* ever and again (or anon), now and again (or then). See CONTINUE in Index.

intermix *verb* See **mix.**

intern *verb* See **jail.**

internal *adjective* See **domestic, inner.**

interpolate *verb* See **introduce.**

interpose *verb* See **introduce.**

interpret *verb* **1.** To perform according to one's artistic conception : execute, play, render. See PERFORMING ARTS in Index. **2.** To understand in a particular way : construe, read, take. See UNDERSTAND in Index. — See also **explain.**

interpretable *adjective* See **explainable.**

interpretation *noun* One's artistic conception as shown by the way in which something such as a dramatic role or musical composition is rendered : execution, performance, reading, realization, rendering, rendition. See PERFORMING ARTS in Index. — See also **commentary, explanation.**

interpretative *adjective* See **explanatory.**

interpretive *adjective* See **explanatory.**

interrelationship *noun* See **relation.**

interrogate *verb* To question thoroughly and relentlessly to verify facts : cross-examine. *Informal:* grill. *Idiom:* give someone the third degree. See INVESTIGATE in Index.

interrogation *noun* See **inquiry.**

interrogator *noun* See **inquisitor.**

interrogatory *noun* See **inquiry.**

interrupt *verb* To interject remarks or questions into another's discourse : break in, chime in, chip in, cut in. See CONTINUE in Index. — See also **suspend.**

interruption *noun* See **break.**

intersect *verb* See **cross.**

interspace *noun* See **gap.**

interstice *noun* See **gap.**

interval *noun* See **gap.**

intervention *noun* See **meddling.**

intimacy *noun* See **friendship.**

intimate¹ *adjective* Characterized by a close and thorough acquaintance : inside, personal. See NEAR in Index. — See also **confidential, familiar, inner.**

intimate *noun* See **friend.**

intimate² *verb* See **hint.**

intimation *noun* See **hint, shade.**

intimidate *verb* To domineer or drive into compliance, as by the use of threats or force, for example : bludgeon, browbeat, bulldoze, bully, bullyrag, cow, hector, menace, threaten. *Informal:* strong-arm. See OVER in Index.

intimidation *noun* See **threat**.

intimidator *noun* See **bully**.

intolerable *adjective* See **unbearable**.

intolerance *noun* See **prejudice**.

intolerant *adjective* Not tolerant of the beliefs or opinions of others, for example : bigoted, close-minded, hidebound, illiberal, narrow-minded. See ACCEPT in Index. — See also **impatient**.

intonation *noun* See **tone**.

intoxicated *adjective* See **drunk**.

intoxicating *adjective* See **tonic**.

intoxication *noun* See **drunkenness**.

intoxicative *adjective* See **hard**.

intractability *noun* See **unruliness**.

intractable *adjective* See **unruly**.

intractableness *noun* See **unruliness**.

intransigence *noun* See **stubbornness**.

intransigency *noun* See **stubbornness**.

intransigent *adjective* See **stubborn**.

intrepid *adjective* See **brave**.

intrepidity *noun* See **courage**.

intrepidness *noun* See **courage**.

intricacy *noun* See **complexity**.

intricate *adjective* See **complex, elaborate**.

intrigue *noun* See **plot**.

intrigue *verb* See **interest, plot**.

intrinsic *adjective* See **constitutional**.

introduce *verb* **1.** To bring into currency, use, fashion, or practice : launch, originate. See START in Index. **2.** To put or set into, between, or among another or other things : inject, insert, interject, interlard, interpolate, interpose. See PUT IN in Index. **3.** To begin (something) with preliminary or prefatory material : lead, precede, preface, usher in. See START, WORDS in Index. — See also **acquaint, broach, usher in** at **usher**.

introduction *noun* A short section of preliminary remarks : foreword, induction, lead-in, overture, preamble, preface, prelude, prolegomenon, prologue. See START, WORDS in Index. — See also **admission**.

introductory *adjective* Serving to introduce a subject or person, for example : prefatory, preliminary, preparatory, prolegomenous. See START, WORDS in Index. — See also **beginning, preliminary**.

intromission *noun* See **admission**.

intromit *verb* See **admit**.

intrude *verb* To force or come in as an improper or unwanted element : cut in, horn in, obtrude. See ENTER in Index.

intrusion *noun* See **imposition, meddling, trespass**.

intrusive *adjective* See **disturbing, meddling**.

intuit *verb* See **perceive**.

intuition *noun* See **feeling, instinct**.

intuitive *adjective* See **instinctive**.

intuitiveness *noun* See **instinct**.

inundate *verb* See **flood**.

inundation *noun* See **flood**.

inure *verb* See **accustom**.

inutile *adjective* See **useless, worthless**.

invade *verb* To enter so as to attack, plunder, destroy, or conquer : foray, overrun, raid. See ATTACK, ENTER in Index.

invalid *adjective* See **fallacious**.

invalidate *verb* See **abolish**.

invalidation *noun* See **abolition**.

invaluable *adjective* See **valuable**.

invariable *adjective* See **consistent, even[1], inflexible**.

invariant *adjective* See **even[1]**.

invasion *noun* An act of invading, especially by military forces : foray, incursion, inroad, raid. See ATTACK, ENTER in Index.

invective *noun* See vituperation.

invective *adjective* See abusive.

inveigh *verb* See object.

inveigle *verb* See seduce.

inveiglement *noun* See lure.

inveigler *noun* See seducer.

inveigling *adjective* See seductive.

invent *verb* To use ingenuity in making, developing, or achieving : concoct, contrive, devise, dream up, fabricate, formulate, hatch, make up, think up. *Informal:* cook up. *Idiom:* come up with. See MAKE in Index.

invented *adjective* See fictitious.

invention *noun* **1.** Something invented : brainchild, contrivance, device. See MACHINE, MAKE in Index. **2.** The power or ability to invent : creativeness, creativity, ingeniousness, ingenuity, inventiveness, originality. See ABILITY, MAKE in Index. — See also myth.

inventive *adjective* Characterized by or productive of new things or new ideas : creative, ingenious, innovative, innovatory, original. See ABILITY in Index. — See also new, resourceful.

inventiveness *noun* See invention.

inventor *noun* See originator.

inventory *noun* See hoard.

inveracity *noun* See lie², mendacity.

inversion *noun* See reversal.

invert *verb* See reverse.

inverted *adjective* See upside-down.

invest *verb* See besiege, dress, gift, initiate, wrap.

investigate *verb* See analyze, explore.

investigation *noun* See analysis, exploration, inquiry.

investigative *adjective* See curious.

investigator *noun* See detective, inquirer.

investiture *noun* See initiation.

investment *noun* See siege.

inveterate *adjective* See chronic, confirmed.

invidious *adjective* See envious, libelous.

invigorate *verb* See energize.

invigorating *adjective* See tonic.

invincible *adjective* Incapable of being conquered, overrun, or subjugated : impregnable, indomitable, unconquerable. See DO, WIN in Index.

inviolability *noun* See sanctity.

inviolable *adjective* See sacred.

invisible *adjective* See imperceptible.

invitation *noun* A spoken or written request for someone to take part or be present : bid. *Informal:* invite. See WARN in Index. — See also lure.

invite *verb* To request that someone take part in or be present at a particular occasion : ask, bid. See WARN in Index. — See also court.

invite *noun* See invitation.

inviting *adjective* See seductive.

invocation *noun* See prayer¹.

invoice *noun* See account.

invoice *verb* See bill¹.

invoke *verb* See enforce.

involuntarily *adverb* See helplessly.

involuntary *adjective* See spontaneous.

involute *adjective* See complex.

involve *verb* To draw in so that extrication is difficult : catch up, embrangle, embroil, implicate, mix up, suck. See FREE, PARTICIPATE in Index. — See also carry, complicate, contain, demand, engage.

involved *adjective* See complex, concerned.

involvement *noun* See **entanglement, participation.**

inward *adjective* See **inner.**

iota *noun* See **bit¹, damn.**

irascibility *noun* See **temper.**

irascible *adjective* See **ill-tempered, testy.**

irascibleness *noun* See **temper.**

irate *adjective* See **furious.**

irateness *noun* See **anger, fury.**

ire *noun* See **anger, fury.**

ireful *adjective* See **furious.**

irenic *adjective* See **peaceable.**

irk *verb* See **annoy.**

irksome *adjective* See **boring, vexatious.**

iron *noun* See **bond.**

  iron *verb* See **press.**

  iron *adjective* See **lusty, stubborn.**

ironbound *adjective* See **rough.**

ironclad *adjective* See **inflexible.**

ironic *adjective* See **cynical.**

ironical *adjective* See **cynical.**

irradiant *adjective* See **bright.**

irradiate *verb* See **shed.**

irradicable *adjective* See **confirmed.**

irrational *adjective* See **unreasonable.**

irrationality *noun* See **unreason.**

irrefutable *adjective* See **certain.**

irregular *adjective* Not straight, uniform, or symmetrical : asymmetric, asymmetrical. See SMOOTH, STRAIGHT in Index. — See also **abnormal.**

irregularity *noun* Lack of smoothness or regularity : asymmetry, crookedness, inequality, jaggedness, roughness, unevenness. See SMOOTH, STRAIGHT in Index. — See also **abnormality.**

irrelevancy *noun* See **digression.**

irrelevant *adjective* Not relevant or pertinent to the subject; not applicable : extraneous, immaterial, impertinent, inapplicable. *Idioms:*

beside the point, neither here nor there. See RELEVANT in Index.

irremediable *adjective* See **hopeless.**

irreparable *adjective* See **hopeless.**

irreprehensible *adjective* See **exemplary.**

irreproachable *adjective* See **exemplary, innocent.**

irresolute *adjective* See **hesitant.**

irresoluteness *noun* See **hesitation.**

irresolution *noun* See **hesitation.**

irresponsible *adjective* See **careless.**

irreverence *noun* See **disrespect.**

irreverent *adjective* See **disrespectful.**

irreversible *adjective* See **irrevocable.**

irrevocable *adjective* That cannot be revoked or undone : irreversible, unalterable. *Idiom:* beyond recall. See CHANGE in Index.

irritable *adjective* See **ill-tempered.**

irritant *noun* See **annoyance.**

irritate *verb* To cause to become sore or inflamed : burn, inflame, sting. See HELP in Index. — See also annoy, chafe.

irritating *adjective* See **vexatious.**

irritation *noun* An instance of being irritated, as in a part of the body : inflammation, soreness. See HELP in Index. — See also **annoyance.**

isochronal *adjective* See **recurrent.**

isochronous *adjective* See **recurrent.**

isolate *verb* To set apart from a group : close off, cut off, insulate, seclude, segregate, separate, sequester. See INCLUDE in Index.

  isolate *adjective* See **solitary.**

isolated *adjective* See **remote, solitary.**

isolation *noun* The act or process of isolating : insulation, segregation, separation, sequestration. See

INCLUDE in Index. — See also aloneness.

issue verb See appear, descend, discharge, emit, publish, stem.

issue noun See effect, problem, progeny, publication.

italicize verb See emphasize.

itch noun See desire.

itch verb See lust.

item noun A usually brief detail of news or information : bit[1], paragraph, piece, squib, story. See WORDS in Index. — See also detail, element, object.

item adverb See additionally.

itemize verb See enumerate.

iterate verb See repeat.

iteration noun See repetition.

iterative adjective See repetitive.

itinerant adjective See migrant, nomadic.

ivory adjective See fair.

ivory-tower adjective See impractical.

J

jab verb See dig.

jab noun See dig.

jabber verb See babble, chatter.

jabber noun See babble, chatter.

jabberwocky noun See babble, gibberish.

jack noun See flag[1], money, sailor.

jack verb See raise.

jackass noun See fool.

jacket noun See hide[2].

jack-tar noun See sailor.

jade noun See slut.

jade verb See fatigue.

jag noun See bender, binge.

jagged adjective See rough.

jaggedness noun See irregularity.

jail noun A place for the confinement of persons in lawful detention : brig, house of correction, keep, penitentiary, prison. *Informal:* lockup, pen[3]. *Slang:* big house, can, clink, cooler, coop, hoosegow, joint, jug, pokey, slammer, stir[2]. *Chiefly Regional:* calaboose. See FREE in Index.

jail verb To put in jail : confine, detain, immure, imprison, incarcerate, intern, lock (up). See FREE in Index.

jailer also **jailor** noun A guard or keeper of a prison : turnkey, warden. *British:* warder. See FREE in Index.

jam verb See crowd.

jam noun See predicament, tie-up.

jam-pack verb See crowd.

jape noun See joke.

jar verb See conflict.

jar noun See collision.

jargon noun See babble, dialect, language.

jarring adjective See harsh.

jaundice verb See bias.

jaunt noun See trip.

jaunty adjective See airy.

jaw verb See chatter.

jaw noun See conversation.

jealous adjective Fearful of the loss of position or affection : clutching, possessive. See OWNED in Index. — See also envious.

jealousy noun See envy.

jeer verb See ridicule.

jeer noun See taunt.

jeering adjective See sarcastic.

jejune adjective See insipid.

jejuneness noun See dullness, insipidity.

jell verb See coagulate.

jelly verb See coagulate.

jeopardize verb See endanger.

jeopardous adjective See dangerous.

jeopardy noun See danger.

jeremiad *noun* See **tirade**.

jerk *verb* To move or cause to move with a sudden abrupt motion : lurch, snap, twitch, wrench, yank. See MOVE, PUSH in Index. — See also **bump**.

jerk *noun* A sudden motion, such as a pull : lurch, snap, tug, twitch, wrench, yank. See MOVE, PUSH in Index. — See also **drip, fool**.

jerky *adjective* See **foolish**.

jest *verb* See **joke, ridicule**.

jest *noun* See **joke**.

jester *noun* See **joker**.

jet¹ *adjective* See **black**.

jet² *noun* See **spurt**.

jet *verb* See **spurt**.

jettison *noun* See **disposal**.

jettison *verb* See **discard**.

jetty *adjective* See **black**.

jibe *verb* See **agree**.

jiff *noun* See **flash**.

jiffy *noun* See **flash**.

jig *noun* See **trick**.

jigger *noun* See **drop, gadget**.

jiggle *verb* See **shake**.

jillion *noun* See **heap**.

jim-jams *noun* See **jitter**.

jinx *noun* *Informal.* Something or someone believed to bring bad luck : curse, hex, hoodoo. See LUCK in Index.

jinx *verb* *Informal.* To bring bad luck or evil to : curse, hex, hoodoo. See LUCK in Index.

jitter *noun* A state of nervous restlessness or agitation. Used in plural : fidget (often used in plural), jump (used in plural), shiver¹ (used in plural), tremble (often used in plural). *Informal:* all-overs, shake (used in plural). *Slang:* heebie-jeebies, jimjams, willies. See CALM, FEAR in Index.

jittery *adjective* See **edgy**.

jive *verb* See **joke**.

job *noun* See **business, function, position, task**.

jobholder *noun* See **employee**.

jobholding *adjective* See employed.

jobless *adjective* See **workless**.

jockey *verb* See **maneuver**.

jocose *adjective* See **humorous**.

jocoseness *noun* See **gaiety, humor**.

jocosity *noun* See **gaiety, humor**.

jocular *adjective* See **humorous**.

jocularity *noun* See **gaiety, humor**.

jocund *adjective* See **gay**.

jocundity *noun* See **gaiety**.

jog *verb* See **dig, trot**.

jog *noun* See **dig, trot**.

joggle *verb* See **shake**.

join *verb* To become a member of : enlist, enroll, enter, muster in, sign up. *Informal:* sign on. See PARTICIPATE in Index. — See also **adjoin, associate, combine**.

joint *noun* **1.** A point or position at which two or more things are joined : connection, coupling, junction, juncture, seam, union. See CONNECT in Index. **2.** *Slang.* A disreputable or run-down bar or restaurant : dive, honky-tonk. See GOOD in Index. — See also **jail**.

joint *adjective* See **common**.

jointly *adverb* See **together**.

joke *noun* **1.** Words or actions intended to excite laughter or amusement : gag, jape, jest, quip, witticism. *Informal:* funny, gag. *Slang:* ha-ha. See LAUGHTER in Index. **2.** An object of amusement or laughter : butt³, jest, laughingstock, mockery. See RESPECT in Index. — See also **prank¹, scream**.

joke *verb* **1.** To make jokes; behave playfully : jest. *Informal:* clown (around), fool around, fun. See LAUGHTER in Index. **2.** To tease or mock good-humoredly : banter, chaff, josh. *Informal:* kid, rib, ride. *Slang:* jive, rag[2], razz. See LAUGHTER in Index.

joker *noun* A person whose words or actions provoke or are intended to provoke amusement or laughter : clown, comedian, comic, farceur, funnyman, humorist, jester, jokester, quipster, wag[2], wit, zany. *Informal:* card. See LAUGHTER in Index.

jokester *noun* See **joker.**

jolliness *noun* See **gaiety.**

jollity *noun* See **gaiety.**

jolly *adjective* See **gay.**

jolt *verb* See **bump, startle.**

jolt *noun* See **collision, shock**[1].

josh *verb* See **joke.**

jot *noun* See **bit**[1], **damn.**

journey *verb* To make or go on a journey : pass, peregrinate, travel, trek, trip. *Idiom:* hit the road. See MOVE in Index. — See also **go.**

joust *noun* See **tilt.**

jovial *adjective* See **gay.**

joviality *noun* See **gaiety.**

joy *noun* See **delight, happiness.**

joy *verb* See **delight, rejoice.**

joyful *adjective* See **glad, merry.**

joyfulness *noun* See **happiness.**

joyless *adjective* See **gloomy, sad.**

joyous *adjective* See **glad, merry.**

jubilance *noun* See **exultation.**

jubilant *adjective* See **exultant.**

jubilate *verb* See **exult.**

jubilation *noun* See **exultation.**

Judas *noun* See **betrayer.**

judge *verb* To make a decision about (a controversy or dispute, for example) after deliberation, as in a court of law : adjudge, adjudicate, arbitrate, decide, decree, determine, referee, rule, umpire. See DECIDE, LAW in Index. — See also **believe, estimate, infer.**

judge *noun* **1.** A public official who decides cases brought before a court of law in order to administer justice : jurisprudent, jurist, justice, justice of the peace, magistrate. See DECIDE, LAW in Index. **2.** A person, usually appointed, who decides the issues or results, or supervises the conduct, of a competition or conflict : arbiter, arbitrator, referee, umpire. *Sports:* ref, ump. See DECIDE in Index. — See also **critic.**

judgment also **judgement** *noun* See **common sense, deduction, estimate, ruling, sentence.**

judgmental *adjective* See **arbitrary.**

judicious *adjective* See **sane.**

jug *noun* See **jail.**

juju *noun* See **charm.**

jumble *verb* See **confuse, disorder, shuffle.**

jumble *noun* See **assortment, disorder.**

jumbo *noun* See **giant.**

jumbo *adjective* See **giant.**

jump *verb* **1.** To move off the ground by a muscular effort of the legs and feet : hurdle, leap, spring, vault[2]. See MOVE, RISE in Index. **2.** To move suddenly and involuntarily : bolt, start. See MOVE in Index. — See also **bounce, eject, promote, raise.**

jump *noun* **1.** The act of jumping : leap, spring, vault[2]. See MOVE, RISE in Index. **2.** A sudden and involuntary movement : bolt, start, startle. See MOVE in Index. — See also **advancement, advantage, bounce, increase, jitter.**

jumpy *adjective* See **edgy.**

junction *noun* The act or fact of coming together : concourse, confluence, convergence, gathering, meeting. See CONNECT in Index. — See also **joint.**

juncture *noun* See **crisis, instant, joint.**

jungle *noun* See **tangle.**

junior *noun* See **subordinate.**

junior *adjective* See **minor.**

junk *verb* See **discard.**

junket *noun* See **feast, trip.**

jurisdiction *noun* See **authority.**

jurisprudent *noun* See **judge.**

jurist *noun* See **judge.**

just *adjective* Consistent with pre-vailing or accepted standards or circumstances : appropriate, deserved, due, fit¹, fitting, merited, proper, right, rightful, suitable. See RIGHT in Index. — See also **fair, sound².**

just *adverb* Only a moment ago : newly, recently. See TIME in Index. — See also **barely, completely, directly, even¹, merely.**

justice *noun* The state, action, or principle of treating all persons equally in accordance with the law : due process, equity. See RIGHT in Index. — See also **fairness, judge.**

justice of the peace *noun* See **judge.**

justifiable *adjective* Capable of being justified : defensible, excusable, tenable. See FORGIVENESS, RIGHT in Index.

justification *noun* See **account, apology, basis, cause.**

justify *verb* To show to be just, right, or valid : excuse, rationalize, vindicate. *Idiom:* make a case for. See RIGHT in Index. — See also **account for** at **account, call for** at **call, confirm, defend.**

justness *noun* See **fairness.**

jut *verb* See **bulge.**

jut *noun* See **bulge.**

juvenescence *noun* See **youth.**

juvenile *adjective* See **childish, young.**

juvenile *noun* See **child, minor.**

juvenility *noun* See **youth.**

K

kaput *adjective* See **through.**

keel over *verb* See **black out** at **black.**

keen¹ *adjective* See **acute, clever, eager, enthusiastic, marvelous, sharp.**

keen² *verb* See **cry.**

keenness *noun* See **discernment, edge.**

keep *verb* **1.** To persevere in some condition, action, or belief : maintain, retain, stay with. See CONTINUE in Index. **2.** To have or put in a customary place : store. See PLACE in Index. **3.** To remain fresh and unspoiled : last². See CHANGE in Index. — See also **carry, celebrate, follow, fulfill, hold, refrain, restrain, save, support.**

keep back *verb* See **hold, restrain.**

keep off *verb* See **parry.**

keep on *verb* See **carry on** at **carry.**

keep out *verb* See **exclude.**

keep up *verb* See **maintain.**

keep *noun* See **jail, living.**

keeper *noun* See **guardian.**

keeping *noun* See **agreement, care.**

keepsake *noun* See **remembrance.**

ken *noun* The extent of one's perception, understanding, knowledge, or vision : horizon, purview, range, reach, scope. See ABILITY, KNOWLEDGE, SEE in Index.

ken *verb* See **know, see, understand.**

kernel *noun* See **germ, heart, seed.**

key *noun* See **ticket.**

key *adjective* See **pivotal, primary.**

kibitzer *noun* See **meddler.**

kick *verb* See **break, complain, object.**

kick around *verb* See **discuss.**

kick in *verb* See **contribute, die.**

kick off *verb* See **die, start.**

kick out *verb* See **eject.**

kick *noun* **1.** *Slang.* A temporary concentration of interest : **trip.** See EXCITE in Index. **2.** *Slang.* A stimulating or intoxicating effect : *Informal:* **punch, sting, wallop.** See DRUGS in Index. — See also **complaint, objection, thrill, wrinkle.**

kicker *noun* See **wrinkle.**

kickoff *noun* See **beginning.**

kid *noun* See **child.**

kid *verb* See **joke.**

kidnap *verb* To seize and detain (a person) unlawfully : **abduct, snatch, spirit away.** See CRIMES, FREE in Index.

kill[1] *verb* To cause the death of : **carry off, cut down, cut off, destroy, dispatch, finish (off), slay.** *Slang:* **waste, zap.** *Idioms:* **put an end to, put to sleep.** See HELP in Index. — See also **annihilate, idle, murder.**

kill[2] *noun* See **branch.**

killer *noun* See **murderer.**

killing *noun* See **murder.**

killing *adjective* See **priceless.**

kilter *noun* See **trim.**

kin *noun* One's relatives collectively : **family, kindred, kinfolk.** See KIN in Index. — See also **relative.**

kind[1] *adjective* See **benevolent.**

kind[2] *noun* A class that is defined by the common attribute or attributes possessed by all its members : **breed, cast, description, feather, ilk, lot, manner, mold, nature, order, sort, species, stamp, stripe, type, variety.** *Informal:* **persuasion.** See GROUP in Index.

kindhearted *adjective* See **benevolent.**

kindheartedness *noun* See **benevolence.**

kindle *verb* See **arouse, fire, light**[1].

kindliness *noun* See **benevolence.**

kindly *adjective* See **benevolent.**

kindness *noun* See **benevolence, favor.**

kindred *noun* See **family, kin.**

kindred *adjective* See **related.**

kinetic *adjective* See **energetic.**

kinfolk also **kinsfolk** or **kinfolks** *noun* See **kin.**

kinsman *noun* See **relative.**

kinswoman *noun* See **relative.**

kismet *noun* See **fate.**

kiss *verb* To touch or caress with the lips, especially as a sign of passion or affection : **buss, osculate, smack**[1]. *Informal:* **peck**[1]. *Slang:* **smooch.** See TOUCH in Index. — See also **brush**[1].

kiss *noun* The act or an instance of kissing : **buss, osculation, smack**[1], **smacker.** *Informal:* **peck**[1]. *Slang:* **smooch.** See TOUCH in Index.

kisser *noun* See **face.**

klutz *noun* See **lump**[1].

klutzy *adjective* See **awkward.**

knack *noun* See **ability, hang, talent.**

knead *verb* See **work.**

knell *verb* See **ring**[2].

knickknack *noun* See **novelty.**

knifelike *adjective* See **sharp.**

knightly *adjective* See **gracious.**

knob *noun* See **bulge, bump.**

knock *verb* See **blame, hit, tap**[1].

knock about or **around** *verb* See **batter, discuss, slap around** at **slap.**

knock down *verb* See **destroy, drop.**

knock off *verb* See **deduct, murder, rob.**

knock out *verb* See **disable, exhaust.**

knock over *verb* See **overturn.**

knock *noun* See **blame, tap**[1].

knockabout *adjective* See **rough.**

knockout *noun* See **beauty.**

knot *noun* See **bond, bulge, bump, group, tangle.**

knot *verb* See **tie.**

knotty *adjective* See **complex.**

know *verb* To perceive directly with the intellect : apprehend, compass, comprehend, fathom, grasp, understand. *Scots:* ken. See KNOWLEDGE in Index. — See also **distinguish, experience, feel, recognize.**

knowable *adjective* See **understandable.**

know-how *noun* See **ability.**

knowing *adjective* See **intelligent, shrewd, wise[1].**

know-it-all *noun* See **smart aleck.**

knowledge *noun* That which is known; the sum of what has been perceived, discovered, or inferred : information, lore, wisdom. See KNOWLEDGE in Index. — See also **education, information.**

knowledgeable *adjective* See **informed, intelligent.**

kook *noun* See **crackpot.**

kooky *adjective* See **eccentric.**

kowtow *noun* See **bow[1].**

 kowtow *verb* See **fawn.**

kosher *adjective* See **permissible.**

kudos *noun* See **distinction, praise.**

Kultur *noun* See **culture.**

L

label *noun* See **mark, ticket.**

 label *verb* See **call, mark, ticket.**

labor *noun* Physical exertion that is usually difficult and exhausting : drudgery, moil, toil, travail, work. *Informal:* sweat. *Chiefly British:* fag. *Idiom:* sweat of one's brow. See WORK in Index. — See also **birth.**

 labor *verb* To exert one's mental or physical powers, usually under difficulty and to the point of exhaustion : drive, fag, moil, strain[1], strive, sweat, toil, travail, tug, work. *Idiom:* break one's back (*or* neck).

See WORK in Index. — See also **elaborate.**

labored *adjective* See **forced, ponderous.**

laborer *noun* One who labors : hand, operative, roustabout, worker, working girl, workingman, workingwoman, workman, workwoman. See WORK in Index.

laborious *adjective* See **burdensome, difficult.**

laboriously *adverb* See **hard.**

labyrinth *noun* See **tangle.**

labyrinthine *adjective* See **complex.**

lachrymose *adjective* See **tearful.**

lack *verb* To be without what is needed, required, or essential : need, require, want. See OWNED in Index.

 lack *noun* See **absence, shortage.**

lackadaisical *adjective* See **languid.**

lacking *adjective* See **absent, deficient, empty.**

lackluster *adjective* See **dull.**

laconic *adjective* See **brief.**

lacuna *noun* See **gap.**

lade *verb* See **charge, dip, heap.**

laden *adjective* See **heavy.**

la-di-da *also* **la-de-da** *adjective* See **affected.**

ladle *verb* See **dip.**

lady-killer *noun* See **philanderer.**

lady's man *also* **ladies' man** *noun* See **gallant, philanderer.**

lag *verb* See **delay.**

 lag *noun* See **delay, laggard.**

laggard *noun* One that lags : dawdler, dilly-dallier, lag, lagger, lingerer, loiterer, poke, procrastinator, straggler, tarrier. *Informal:* slowpoke. See FAST in Index.

 laggard *adjective* See **slow.**

lagger *noun* See **laggard.**

lagging *adjective* See **backward.**

laid-back *adjective* See **easygoing.**

laid up *adjective* See **sick.**

lair *noun* See **hide-out, hole.**

lam *noun* See **escape.** *verb* See **escape.**

lamb *noun* See **dupe, innocent.**

lambaste *verb* See **beat, call down** at **call.**

lambent *adjective* See **bright.**

lament *verb* See **grieve.**

lamentable *adjective* See **sorrowful.**

lamia *noun* See **witch.**

lamina *noun* See **skin.**

lampoon *noun* See **satire.**

lampoonery *noun* See **satire.**

lancinating *adjective* See **sharp.**

land *noun* Usually extensive real estate : acre (often used in plural), estate, property. See OWNED in Index. — See also **state.**

land *verb* **1.** To come to rest on the ground : alight[1], light[2], set down, settle, touch down. See MOVE in Index. **2.** To come ashore from a seacraft : debark, disembark. See MOVE in Index. — See also **get.**

language *noun* **1.** A system of terms used by a people sharing a history and culture : dialect, speech, tongue, vernacular. *Linguistics:* langue. See WORDS in Index. **2.** Specialized expressions indigenous to a particular field, subject, trade, or subculture : argot, cant[2], dialect, idiom, jargon, lexicon, lingo, patois, terminology, vernacular, vocabulary. See WORDS in Index.

langue *noun* See **language.**

languid *adjective* Lacking energy and vitality or showing such a lack : lackadaisical, languorous, leaden, limp, listless, lymphatic, spiritless. See ACTION, TIRED in Index.

languidness *noun* See **lethargy.**

languish *verb* To waste away from longing or grief : pine (away), wither. See HEALTH in Index. — See also **fade.**

languor *noun* See **lethargy.**

languorous *adjective* See **languid.**

lank *adjective* See **thin.**

lanky *adjective* See **gangling, thin.**

lap *verb* See **wash.**

lapse *noun* **1.** A minor mistake : slip, slip up. *Informal:* fluff. See CORRECT in Index. **2.** A slipping from a higher or better condition to a lower or poorer one : backslide, backsliding, recidivation, recidivism, relapse. See BETTER, REPETITION in Index. — See also **error.**

lapse *verb* To become void, especially through passage of time or an omission : expire, run out. See CONTINUE, LAW in Index. — See also **glide, go, relapse, subside.**

larcener *noun* See **larcenist.**

larcenist *noun* A person who steals : bandit, burglar, highwayman, housebreaker, larcener, pilferer, purloiner, robber, stealer, thief. See CRIMES in Index.

larcenous *adjective* Tending to larceny : thievish. See CRIMES in Index.

larceny *noun* The crime of taking someone else's property without consent : pilferage, steal, theft, thievery. *Slang:* rip-off. See CRIMES in Index.

lares and penates *noun* See **effect.**

large *adjective* See **big, general, important.**

large-hearted *adjective* See **generous.**

large-heartedness *noun* See **generosity.**

largeness *noun* See **size.**

larger *adjective* See **best.**

large-scale *adjective* See **big.**

largess also **largesse** *noun* See **gratuity.**

largest *adjective* See **best.**

largish *adjective* See **sizable.**

lark *noun* See **prank[1].**

lascivious *adjective* See **erotic.**

lash *verb* See **beat, slam.**

lashing *noun* See **beating.**

lassitude *noun* See **apathy, lethargy.**

last[1] *adjective* **1.** Coming after all others : closing, concluding, final, terminal. See START in Index. **2.** Of or relating to a terminative condition, stage, or point : final, latter, terminal, ultimate. See START in Index. **3.** Bringing up the rear : endmost, hindermost, hindmost, lattermost, rearmost. See START in Index. **4.** Next before the present one : foregoing, latter, preceding, previous. See NEAR, PRECEDE in Index.

last *noun* See **end.**

last *adverb* In conclusion : conclusively, finally, lastly. See START in Index.

last[2] *verb* See **endure, keep, survive.**

lasting *adjective* See **continuing.**

lastly *adverb* See **last**[1].

late *adjective* **1.** Not being on time : behindhand, belated, overdue, tardy. See TIME in Index. **2.** Having been such previously : erstwhile, former, old, once, onetime, past, previous, quondam, sometime, whilom. See PRECEDE in Index. — See also **dead.**

late *adverb* **1.** Not on time : behind, behindhand, belatedly, tardily. See TIME in Index. **2.** Not long ago : lately, latterly, recently. *Idiom:* of late. See NEAR, PRECEDE, TIME in Index. — See also **slow.**

lately *adverb* See **late.**

latency *noun* See **abeyance.**

lateness *noun* The quality or condition of not being on time : belatedness, tardiness. See TIME in Index.

latent *adjective* Existing in a temporarily inactive form or state : abeyant, dormant, inactive, quiescent,

sleeping. See ACTION, SHOW in Index. — See also **potential.**

later *adjective* Following something else in time : after, posterior, subsequent, ulterior. See PRECEDE in Index. — See also **future.**

later *adverb* At a subsequent time : after, afterward, afterwards, latterly, next, subsequently, ulteriorly. *Idioms:* after a while, by and by, later on. See PRECEDE in Index.

lather *noun* See **agitation, foam, sweat.**

lather *verb* See **foam, sweat.**

lathery *adjective* See **foamy.**

latitude *noun* See **room.**

latter *adjective* See **last**[1].

latter-day *adjective* See **modern.**

latterly *adverb* See **late, later.**

lattermost *adjective* See **last**[1].

laud *verb* See **honor, praise.**

laudable *adjective* See **admirable.**

laudation *noun* See **praise.**

laudatory *adjective* See **complimentary.**

laugh *verb* To express amusement, mirth, or scorn by smiling and emitting loud, inarticulate sounds : cachinnate, cackle, guffaw. *Informal:* heehaw. *Idioms:* die laughing, laugh one's head off, roll in the aisles, split one's sides. See LAUGHTER, SOUNDS in Index. — See also **ridicule.**

laugh *noun* An act of laughing : cachinnation, cackle, guffaw, laughter. *Informal:* heehaw. See LAUGHTER, SOUNDS in Index. — See also **scream.**

laughable *adjective* Deserving laughter : comic, comical, farcical, funny, laughing, ludicrous, ridiculous, risible. See LAUGHTER in Index. — See also **amusing.**

laughing *adjective* Emitting a murmuring sound felt to resemble a laugh : babbling, bubbling, bur-

bling, gurgling, rippling. See LAUGH-
TER, SOUNDS in Index. — See also
laughable.

laughingstock noun See joke.

laughter noun See laugh.

launch verb See introduce, start,
throw.

launch noun See beginning, throw.

laurel noun See distinction.

lave verb See wash.

lavish adjective See extravagant,
generous, luxurious, profuse.

lavish verb See shower.

lavishness noun See extravagance,
generosity.

law noun 1. The formal product of a
legislative or judicial body : act,
assize, bill[1], enactment, legislation,
lex, measure, statute. See LAW in
Index. 2. A principle governing
affairs within or among political
units : canon, decree, edict, institute, ordinance, precept, prescription, regulation, rule. See LAW in
Index. 3. A broad and basic rule or
truth : axiom, fundamental, principle, theorem, universal. See ORDER
in Index. — See also policeman.

law verb See sue.

lawbreaker noun See criminal.

lawful adjective Within, allowed by,
or sanctioned by the law : innocent, legal, legitimate, licit. Slang:
legit. See LAW in Index.

lawfulness noun See legality.

lawless adjective See criminal, illegal, unruly.

lawlessness noun See disorder.

lawsuit noun A legal proceeding to
demand justice or enforce a right :
action, case, cause, instance, suit.
See LAW in Index.

lawyer noun A person who practices law : attorney, counsel, counselor. Slang: ambulance chaser.
Chiefly British: barrister. See LAW in
Index.

lax adjective See loose, negligent,
tolerant.

laxity noun See negligence.

laxness noun See negligence.

lay[1] verb To place (a story, for
example) in a designated setting :
set[1]. See PLACE in Index. See also
aim, attribute, bet, bury, design,
gamble, present[2], set[1].

lay aside verb See save.

lay away verb See bank[2], save.

lay by verb See save.

lay down verb See dictate,
relinquish.

lay for verb Informal. To wait
concealed in order to attack (someone) : Idioms: lay wait for, lie in
wait for. See ATTACK, SHOW in
Index.

lay in verb See save, stockpile.

lay into verb See beat.

lay off verb See abandon.

lay out verb See arrange, design,
plot, spend.

lay up verb See save, stockpile.

lay[2] adjective See profane.

layabout noun See wastrel.

layout noun See arrangement,
design.

laze verb See idle.

laziness noun The quality or state
of being lazy : idleness, indolence,
shiftlessness, sloth, slothfulness,
sluggardness, sluggishness.
Informal: do-nothingism. See
INDUSTRIOUS in Index.

lazy adjective Resistant to exertion
and activity : fainéant, idle, indolent, shiftless, slothful, sluggard,
sluggish. Informal: do-nothing.
Idiom: bone lazy. See ACTION,
INDUSTRIOUS in Index.

lazybones noun See wastrel.

leach verb See ooze.

lead verb 1. To have authoritative
charge of : captain, command. See
PRECEDE in Index. 2. To go through

(life) in a certain way : live[1], pass, pursue. See BE in Index. — See also extend, guide, introduce.

lead off *verb* See start.

lead to *verb* See cause.

lead *noun* **1.** A piece of information useful in a search : clue, scent. See SHOW in Index. **2.** The capacity to lead others : command, leadership. See PRECEDE in Index. **3.** The main performer in a theatrical production : principal, protagonist, star. See PERFORMING ARTS in Index. — See also feature, guidance, guide.

leaden *adjective* See languid.

leadenness *noun* See lethargy.

leader *noun* A leading contestant : front-runner, number one. See PRECEDE in Index. — See also boss, chief, dignitary, feature, guide.

leadership *noun* See guidance, lead.

lead-in *noun* See introduction.

leading *adjective* See famous, primary.

leadoff *noun* See beginning.

leadoff *adjective* See beginning.

leaf *verb* See browse.

league *noun* See alliance, class, conference, union.

league *verb* See ally, band[2].

leaguer *noun* See ally.

leak *verb* See come out at come.

lean[1] *verb* See incline, tend[1].

lean *noun* See inclination.

lean[2] *adjective* See brief, thin, tight.

leaning *noun* See bent.

leap *verb* See bounce, jump.

leap *noun* See bounce, jump.

learn *verb* To gain knowledge or mastery of by study : get, master. *Informal:* pick up. See TEACH in Index. — See also discover, memorize.

learned *adjective* Having or showing profound knowledge and scholar-

ship : erudite, lettered, scholarly, wise[1]. See KNOWLEDGE in Index.

learner *noun* See student.

learning *noun* See education.

lease *verb* To give temporary use of in return for payment : hire (out), let, rent[1]. See TRANSACTIONS in Index. — See also hire.

leash *verb* See hamper.

leash *noun* See bit[2].

leave[1] *verb* To give (property) to another person after one's death : will. *Law:* bequeath, devise. See GIVE, LAW in Index. — See also abandon, go, quit.

leave off *verb* See abandon, break, stop.

leave[2] *noun* See permission, vacation.

leaven *noun* See catalyst.

leavening *noun* See catalyst.

leave-taking *noun* See parting.

leavings *noun* See balance.

lech *noun* See lecher.

lecher *noun* An immoral or licentious man : roué, satyr. *Informal:* dirty old man. *Slang:* lech. See SEX in Index.

lecherous *adjective* See erotic.

lecture *verb* See address.

lecture *noun* See speech.

lecturer *noun* See speaker.

leech *noun* See parasite.

leech *verb* See freeload.

leeriness *noun* See distrust.

leery *adjective* See distrustful.

lees *noun* See deposit.

leeway *noun* See room.

left-handed *adjective* See insincere.

leftover *adjective* See remaining.

leftover *noun* See balance.

legacy *noun* See birthright, heritage.

legal *adjective* See lawful.

legality *noun* The state or quality of being within the law : lawfulness, legitimacy, legitimateness, licitness. See LAW in Index.

legalize *verb* To make lawful : legitimate, legitimatize, legitimize. See LAW in Index.

legation *noun* See **mission.**

legend *noun* See **lore, myth.**

legendary *adjective* See **mythical.**

legerdemain *noun* See **magic.**

legion *noun* See **crowd.**

legion *adjective* See **many.**

legislate *verb* See **establish.**

legislation *noun* See **law.**

legit *adjective* See **lawful.**

legitimacy *noun* See **legality.**

legitimate *adjective* See **lawful, true.**

legitimate *verb* See **legalize.**

legitimateness *noun* See **legality.**

legitimatize *verb* See **legalize.**

legitimize *verb* See **legalize.**

leisure *noun* See **rest[1].**

leisurely *adjective* See **deliberate.**

lemon *noun* See **failure.**

lend *verb* To supply (money), especially on credit : advance, loan. See GIVE in Index.

length *noun* The ultimate point to which an action, thought, discussion, or policy is carried : end, extreme, limit. See LIMITED in Index. — See also **distance, extent.**

lengthen *verb* To make or become longer : draw out, elongate, extend, prolong, prolongate, protract, spin (out), stretch (out). *Mathematics:* produce. See INCREASE, LONG in Index.

lengthy *adjective* See **long[1].**

lenience *noun* See **grace, tolerance.**

leniency *noun* See **grace, tolerance.**

lenient *adjective* See **tolerant.**

lenity *noun* See **grace, tolerance.**

lesbian *adjective* See **gay.**

lese majesty *also* **lèse majesté** *noun* See **disrespect.**

lessen *verb* See **decrease, relieve.**

le er *adjective* See **minor.**

lesson *noun* See **example, moral.**

let *verb* See **lease, permit.**

let down *verb* See **disappoint, lower[2].**

let in *verb* See **admit.**

let off *verb* See **emit, excuse.**

let out *verb* See **betray, drain, emit.**

let up *verb* See **decrease, ease, subside.**

letdown *noun* See **disappointment.**

lethal *adjective* See **deadly.**

lethality *noun* See **fatality.**

lethargic *adjective* Lacking mental and physical alertness and activity : hebetudinous, sluggish, stupid, stuporous, torpid. *Slang:* dopey. See ACTION in Index. — See also **apathetic.**

lethargy *noun* A deficiency in mental and physical alertness and activity : dullness, hebetude, languidness, languor, lassitude, leadenness, listlessness, sluggishness, stupor, torpidity, torpor. See ACTION in Index. — See also **apathy.**

letter *noun* A written communication directed to another : epistle, missive, note. See WORDS in Index.

lettered *adjective* See **educated, learned.**

lettuce *noun* See **money.**

letup *noun* See **wane.**

level *adjective* See **even[1].**

level *noun* See **degree.**

level *verb* See **aim, destroy, drop, equalize, even[1].**

levelheaded *adjective* See **sane.**

leverage *noun* See **influence.**

leviathan *noun* See **giant.**

levy *noun* See **draft, tax.**

levy *verb* See **draft, impose.**

lewd *adjective* See **erotic, obscene.**

lewdness *noun* See **obscenity.**

lex *noun* See **law.**

lexicon _noun_ See **language, vocabulary.**

liability _noun_ See **debt, exposure.**

liable _adjective_ **1.** Legally obligated : accountable, amenable, answerable, responsible. See LAW in Index. **2.** Tending to incur : open, prone, subject, susceptible, susceptive, vulnerable. See LIKELY in Index. — See also **inclined.**

liar _noun_ One who tells lies : fabricator, fabulist, falsifier, fibber, prevaricator. _Informal:_ storyteller. _Law:_ perjurer. See TRUE in Index.

libel _noun_ _Law._ The expression of injurious, malicious statements about someone : aspersion, calumniation, calumny, character assassination, defamation, denigration, detraction, scandal, slander, traducement, vilification. See ATTACK, CRIMES, LAW in Index.

libel _verb_ _Law._ To make defamatory statements about : asperse, backbite, calumniate, defame, malign, slander, slur, tear down, traduce, vilify. _Idiom:_ cast aspersions on. See ATTACK, CRIMES, LAW in Index.

libelous _adjective_ _Law._ Damaging to the reputation : calumnious, defamatory, detractive, injurious, invidious, scandalous, slanderous. See ATTACK, CRIMES, LAW in Index.

liberal _adjective_ Favoring civil liberties and social progress : liberalistic, progressive. See POLITICS in Index. — See also **broad, generous.**

liberal _noun_ A person with liberal political opinions : liberalist, progressive. See POLITICS in Index.

liberalist _noun_ See **liberal.**

liberalistic _adjective_ See **liberal.**

liberality _noun_ See **generosity.**

liberate _verb_ See **free.**

liberation _noun_ See **liberty.**

libertine _adjective_ See **wanton.**

libertine _noun_ See **wanton.**

libertinism _noun_ See **license.**

liberty _noun_ **1.** The state of not being in confinement or servitude : emancipation, freedom, liberation, manumission. See FREE in Index. **2.** Departure from normal rules or procedures : freedom, license. See RESTRAINT in Index. — See also **freedom.**

libidinous _adjective_ See **erotic.**

libidinousness _noun_ See **desire.**

license _noun_ **1.** Proof of legal permission to do something : permit, warrant. _Idiom:_ piece of paper. See ALLOW, LAW in Index. **2.** Excessive freedom; lack of restraint : dissoluteness, dissolution, libertinism, licentiousness, profligacy. See RESTRAINT in Index. — See also **liberty, permission.**

license _verb_ See **authorize.**

licentious _adjective_ See **abandoned.**

licentiousness _noun_ See **license.**

licit _adjective_ See **lawful.**

licitness _noun_ See **legality.**

lick _verb_ See **beat, defeat.**

lick _noun_ See **blow².**

lickety-split _adverb_ See **fast.**

licking _noun_ See **beating, defeat.**

lie¹ _verb_ To be or place oneself in a prostrate or recumbent position. Also used with _down_ : recline, repose, stretch (out). See HORIZONTAL in Index. — See also **consist, rest¹.**

lie² _noun_ An untrue declaration : canard, cock-and-bull story, falsehood, falsity, fib, fiction, inveracity, misrepresentation, misstatement, prevarication, story, tale, untruth. _Informal:_ fish story, tall tale. _Slang:_ whopper. See TRUE in Index.

lie _verb_ To make untrue declarations : falsify, fib, forswear, prevaricate. *Law:* perjure. See TRUE in Index.

liege *adjective* See **faithful.**

lieu *noun* See **place.**

lieutenant *noun* See **assistant.**

life *noun* The period during which someone or something exists : day (often used in plural), duration, existence, lifetime, span, term. See LIVE, TIME in Index. — See also **human being, spirit.**

life force *noun* See **spirit.**

lifeless *adjective* See **dead, dull.**

lifelessness *noun* See **dullness.**

lifelike *adjective* See **graphic, realistic.**

lifetime *noun* See **life.**

lift *verb* **1.** To disappear by or as if by rising : disperse, dissipate, scatter. See COLLECT, RISE in Index. **2.** To take back or remove : recall, repeal, rescind, reverse, revoke. See CONTINUE, LAW, MAKE in Index. — See also **elate, elevate, rise, steal, take off** at take off.

lift *noun* An instance of lifting or being lifted : boost, heave, hoist. See RISE in Index. — See also **elation, thrill.**

liftoff *noun* See **takeoff.**

ligament *noun* See **bond.**

ligature *noun* See **bond.**

light¹ *noun* Electromagnetic radiation that makes vision possible : illumination. See LIGHT in Index. — See also **illumination, phase, vision.**

light *verb* **1.** To cause to burn or undergo combustion : enkindle, fire, ignite, kindle. *Slang:* torch. *Idioms:* set afire (or on fire), set fire to. See HOT, START in Index. **2.** To make lively or animated : animate, brighten, enliven. See HAPPY in Index. — See also **illuminate.**

light *adjective* See **fair.**

light² *adjective* **1.** Having little weight; not heavy : lightweight, weightless. *Idiom:* light as a feather. See HEAVY in Index. **2.** Of small intensity : gentle, moderate, slight, soft. See STRONG in Index. **3.** Free from care or worry : blithe, carefree, debonair, lighthearted. See CAREFUL, HAPPY in Index. **4.** Requiring little effort or exertion : easy, moderate. See EASY in Index. — See also **frothy, wanton.**

light *verb* See **land.**

light into *verb* See **attack.**

light on or **upon** *verb* See **come across** at come.

lighten¹ *verb* See **clear, illuminate.**

lighten² *verb* See **relieve.**

lightheaded *adjective* See **dizzy.**

lightheadedness *noun* See **dizziness.**

lighthearted *adjective* See **cheerful, giddy, light².**

lightheartedness *noun* See **gaiety.**

lighting *noun* See **illumination.**

lightweight *adjective* See **light².**

like¹ *verb* To find agreeable : fancy, take to. *Chiefly British:* conceit. See LIKE in Index. — See also **choose, enjoy.**

like² *adjective* Possessing the same or almost the same characteristics : alike, analogous, comparable, corresponding, equivalent, parallel, similar, uniform. See SAME in Index.

likelihood *noun* See **chance.**

likely *adjective* See **earthly, encouraging, inclined, presumptive, probable.**

liken *verb* To represent as similar : analogize, assimilate, compare, equate, identify, match, parallel. See SAME in Index.

likeness *noun* The quality or state of being alike : affinity, alikeness, analogy, comparison, correspondence, parallelism, resemblance,

similarity, similitude, uniformity, uniformness. See SAME in Index.
— See also **copy.**

likewise *adverb* See **additionally.**

liking *noun* A desire for a particular thing or activity : fancy, mind, pleasure, will. See LIKE in Index.
— See also **attachment.**

Lilliputian also **lilliputian** *adjective* See **tiny.**

lily-livered *adjective* See **cowardly.**

lily-white *adjective* See **exemplary, innocent.**

limit *noun* **1.** The boundary surrounding a certain area. Used in plural : bound[2] (used in plural), confine (used in plural), precinct (often used in plural). See LIMITED in Index. **2.** The greatest amount or number allowed : ceiling, limitation, maximum. See LIMITED in Index. — See also **end, extreme, length, restriction.**

limit *verb* To place a limit on : circumscribe, confine, restrict. See LIMITED in Index. — See also **determine.**

limitation *noun* See **limit, restriction.**

limited *adjective* See **definite, local, narrow, qualified, restricted.**

limitless *adjective* See **endless.**

limitlessness *noun* See **infinity.**

limn *verb* See **represent.**

limp *verb* To walk in a lame way : halt[2], hitch, hobble. See MOVE in Index. — See also **muddle.**

limp *adjective* Lacking in stiffness or firmness : flabby, flaccid, floppy. See FLEXIBLE in Index. — See also **languid.**

limpid *adjective* See **clear, transparent.**

limpidity *noun* See **clarity.**

limpidness *noun* See **clarity.**

line *noun* **1.** A group of people or things arranged in a row : column,

file, queue, rank[1], row[1], string, tier. See GROUP in Index. **2.** An indentation or seam on the skin, especially on the face : crease, crinkle, furrow, wrinkle. See SMOOTH in Index. **3.** An official or prescribed plan or course of action : policy, procedure, program. See PLANNED in Index. — See also **ancestry, approach, business, good.**

line *verb* To place in or form a line or lines. Also used with *up* : align, range. See ORDER in Index.

lineage *noun* See **ancestry, family.**

lineal *adjective* See **direct.**

lineup also **line-up** *noun* See **arrangement, program, ticket.**

linger *verb* See **delay, pause, remain.**

lingerer *noun* See **laggard.**

lingering *adjective* See **chronic.**

lingo *noun* See **dialect, language.**

link *verb* See **associate, combine.**

link *noun* See **bond, relation.**

linkage *noun* See **relation.**

lion *noun* See **celebrity, dignitary.**

lip *verb* See **wash.**

liquefy *verb* See **melt.**

liquidate *verb* See **annihilate, eliminate, murder, settle.**

liquidation *noun* See **annihilation, elimination.**

liquor *noun* See **drink.**

list[1] *verb* To register in or as if in a book : book, catalog, enroll, inscribe, set down, write down. See REMEMBER in Index. — See also **enumerate.**

list *noun* A series, as of names or words, printed or written down : catalog, register, roll, roster, schedule. See REMEMBER in Index.

list[2] *verb* See **incline.**

list *noun* See **inclination.**

list[3] *verb* See **listen.**

listen *verb* To make an effort to hear something : hark, hearken.

Archaic: list³. **Idiom:** give (or lend) an ear. See SOUNDS in Index. — See also **hear.**

listless *adjective* See **apathetic, languid.**

listlessness *noun* See **apathy, lethargy.**

lit *adjective* See **drugged, drunk.**

litany *noun* See **prayer¹.**

literal *adjective* Employing the very same words as another : verbal, verbatim, word-for-word. See SAME in Index.

literary *adjective* See **pedantic.**

literate *adjective* See **educated.**

litigable *adjective* *Law.* Subject to legal proceedings : actionable, prosecutable, triable. See LAW in Index.

litigate *verb* See **sue.**

litigious *adjective* See **argumentative.**

litigiousness *noun* See **argumentativeness.**

litter *noun* See **young.**

little *adjective* **1.** Notably below average in amount, size, or scope : bantam, petite, small, smallish. See BIG in Index. **2.** Not of great importance : inconsequent, inconsequential, insignificant, trivial, unimportant. See BIG in Index. — See also **narrow, small.**

little *adverb* See **infrequently.**

littlest *adjective* See **minimal.**

liturgical *adjective* See **ritual.**

liturgy *noun* See **ceremony.**

livable also **liveable** *adjective* Fit to live in : habitable, inhabitable. See COMFORT in Index.

live¹ *verb* **1.** To have as one's domicile, usually for an extended period : abide, domicile, dwell, house, reside. See PLACE in Index. **2.** To maintain existence in a certain way : feed, subsist. See INGESTION in Index. — See also **be, lead.**

live² *adjective* See **alive, hot.**

livelihood *noun* See **living.**

liveliness *noun* See **spirit.**

lively *adjective* Very brisk, alert, and full of high spirits : animated, bouncy, chipper, dashing, high-spirited, pert, spirited, vivacious. *Informal:* peppy. **Idioms:** bright-eyed and bushy-tailed, full of life. See ACTION in Index. — See also **energetic, vigorous.**

live wire *noun* See **eager beaver.**

livid *adjective* See **pale.**

living *adjective* See **alive.**

living *noun* The means needed to support life : alimentation, alimony, bread, bread and butter, keep, livelihood, maintenance, subsistence, support, sustenance, upkeep. See MONEY in Index.

living hell *noun* See **hell.**

load *noun* A quantity of explosive put into a weapon : charge. See EXPLOSION in Index. — See also **burden¹, heap.**

load *verb* To put (explosive material) into a weapon : charge. See PUT IN in Index. — See also **adulterate, charge, crowd, distort, fill, heap.**

loaded *adjective* See **drunk, heavy, impure, rich.**

loaf *verb* See **idle.**

loafer *noun* See **wastrel.**

loan *verb* See **lend.**

loath also **loth** *adjective* See **indisposed.**

loathe *verb* See **hate.**

loathing *noun* See **hate.**

loathsome *adjective* See **filthy.**

local *adjective* **1.** Confined to a particular location or site : localized. See LIMITED in Index. **2.** Having the restricted outlook often characteristic of geographic isolation : insular, limited, narrow, narrow-minded, parochial, provincial, small-town. See LIMITED in Index.

locale *noun* See **environment, locality, scene.**

locality *noun* 1. A particular geographic area : locale, location, place. See PLACE in Index. 2. A surrounding site : area, neighborhood, vicinity. See NEAR, PLACE in Index. — See also **area, environment.**

localized *adjective* See **local.**

locate *verb* See **find, position.**

location *noun* See **bearing, locality, point, position.**

lock *verb* See **bar, jail.**

lockup *noun* See **jail.**

loco *adjective* See **insane.**

locus *noun* See **point, position.**

locution *noun* See **expression, term.**

lodge *verb* See **catch, fix, harbor, stay¹.**

lodging *noun* See **home, shelter.**

loftiest *adjective* See **top.**

loftiness *noun* See **arrogance.**

lofty *adjective* Imposingly high : aerial, airy, sky-high, soaring, towering. See HIGH in Index. — See also **arrogant, elevated, exalted.**

logic *noun* Exact, valid, and rational reasoning : ratiocination, rationality, reason. See REASON in Index. — See also **sense.**

logical *adjective* 1. Consistent with reason and intellect : consequent, intelligent, rational, reasonable. See REASON in Index. 2. Able to reason validly : analytic, analytical, ratiocinative, rational. See REASON in Index.

loiter *verb* See **delay, idle.**

loiterer *noun* See **laggard.**

loll *verb* See **slouch, sprawl.**

lone *adjective* Alone in a given category : one, only, particular, separate, single, singular, sole, solitary, unique. *Idioms:* first and last, one and only. See INCLUDE in Index. — See also **alone, single, solitary.**

loneliness *noun* See **aloneness.**

lonely *adjective* 1. Empty of people : deserted, desolate, forlorn, godforsaken, lonesome, unfrequented. See FULL in Index. 2. Dejected due to the awareness of being alone : desolate, forlorn, lonesome, lorn. See HAPPY in Index. — See also **alone, remote.**

lonesome *adjective* See **alone, lonely, remote.**

long¹ *adjective* 1. Having great physical length : elongate, elongated, extended, lengthy, prolonged. See LONG in Index. 2. Extending tediously beyond a standard duration : dragging, drawn-out, lengthy, long-drawn-out, overlong, prolonged, protracted. See EXCITE, LONG in Index. 3. Having many syllables : polysyllabic, sesquipedal, sesquipedalian. See LONG in Index. — See also **high.**

long *noun* See **age.**

long² *verb* See **desire.**

long-drawn-out *adjective* See **long¹.**

long green *noun* See **money.**

longing *noun* See **desire.**

long-lasting *adjective* See **continuing.**

long-lived *adjective* See **continuing.**

long-standing *adjective* See **continuing.**

long-suffering *adjective* See **patient.**

long-suffering *noun* See **patience.**

long suit *noun* See **forte.**

long-winded *adjective* See **wordy.**

long-windedness *noun* See **wordiness.**

look *verb* To direct the eyes on an object : consider, contemplate, eye, view. *Idiom:* clap (or lay or set) one's eyes on. See SEE in Index. — See also **appear, face, seek.**

look after *verb* See **tend².**

look for *verb* See **expect.**

look in *verb* See **visit.**

look into *verb* See **explore.**

look out *verb* To be careful : beware, mind, watch out. *Idioms:* be on guard, be on the lookout, keep an eye peeled, take care (or heed). See AWARENESS, CAREFUL in Index.

look over *verb* See **survey.**

look up *verb* See **visit.**

look *noun* An act of directing the eyes on an object : contemplation, regard, sight, view. See SEE in Index. — See also **appearance, expression, face.**

looker *noun* See **beauty.**

looker-on *noun* See **watcher.**

look-in *noun* See **visit.**

lookout *noun* **1.** The act of carefully watching : surveillance, vigil, vigilance, watch. *Idiom:* watch and ward. See AWARENESS in Index. **2.** A high structure or place commanding a wide view : observatory, outlook, overlook. See AWARENESS in Index. — See also **business, guard, view.**

loom *verb* See **appear, threaten.**

loon *noun* See **crackpot.**

loony or **looney** also **luny** *adjective* See **foolish, insane.**

loony or **looney** also **luny** *noun* See **crackpot.**

loop *noun* A length of line folded over and joined at the ends so as to form a curve or circle : eye, ring[1]. See STRAIGHT in Index. — See also **conference.**

looped *adjective* See **drunk.**

loopy *adjective* See **foolish.**

loose *adjective* **1.** Able to move about at will without bounds or restraint : free, unconfined, unrestrained. *Idioms:* at large, at liberty, free as a bird, on the loose. See FREE in Index. **2.** Not tautly bound, held, or fastened : lax, relaxed, slack. See TIGHTEN in Index. **3.** Lacking literal exactness : free, inexact. See PRECISE in Index. — See also **wanton.**

loose *verb* See **ease, free, shoot, undo.**

loosen *verb* See **ease, undo.**

loot *verb* See **sack**[2].

loot *noun* See **plunder.**

lop[1] *verb* See **cut back** at **cut.**

lop[2] *verb* See **slouch.**

lope *verb* See **trot.**

lope *noun* See **trot.**

loquacious *adjective* See **talkative.**

lordliness *noun* See **arrogance.**

lordly *adjective* See **arrogant, authoritative, grand.**

lore *noun* A body of traditional beliefs and notions accumulated about a particular subject : folklore, legend, myth, mythology, mythos, tradition. See KNOWLEDGE in Index. — See also **information, knowledge.**

lorn *adjective* See **abandoned, lonely.**

lose *verb* **1.** To be unable to find : mislay, misplace. See GET in Index. **2.** To fail to take advantage of : miss, waste. *Idioms:* let slip, let slip through one's fingers, lose out on. See USED in Index. **3.** To get away from (a pursuer) : elude, evade, shake off, slip, throw off. *Slang:* shake. *Idiom:* give someone the shake (or slip). See SEEK in Index. — See also **drop.**

loser *noun* See **failure, unfortunate.**

losing *noun* See **loss.**

loss *noun* The act or an instance of losing something : losing, misplacement. See GET in Index. — See also **deprivation.**

lost *adjective* No longer in one's possession : gone, missing. See

GET in Index. — See also **condemned, damned, stray, vanished.**

lot *noun* A piece of land : parcel, plot, tract. See TERRITORY in Index. — See also **allotment, deal, fate, group, heap, kind²**.

lot *verb* See **allot.**

Lothario also **lothario** *noun* See **gallant, seducer.**

loud *adjective* Marked by extremely high volume and intensity of sound : blaring, deafening, ear-splitting, roaring, stentorian. See SOUNDS in Index. — See also **gaudy.**

loudmouthed *adjective* See **vociferous.**

lounge *verb* See **idle.**

louse up *verb* See **botch.**

lousy *adjective* See **filthy, shoddy.**

lout *noun* See **lump¹.**

lovable *adjective* See **adorable.**

love *noun* **1.** The passionate affection and desire felt by lovers for each other : amorousness, fancy, passion, romance. See LOVE, SEX in Index. **2.** An intimate sexual relationship between two people : affair, amour, love affair, romance. See LOVE, SEX in Index. **3.** A strong, enthusiastic liking for something : love affair, passion, romance. See LOVE in Index. — See also **adoration, attachment, darling.**

love *verb* See **adore.**

love affair *noun* See **love.**

loved *adjective* See **darling.**

lovely *adjective* See **attractive, beautiful.**

lovely *noun* See **beauty.**

lover *noun* A person's regular sexual partner : paramour. See SEX in Index. — See also **admirer.**

loving *adjective* See **affectionate.**

low *adjective* **1.** Cut to reveal the wearer's neck, chest, and back : décolleté, low-cut, low-neck, low-necked, plunging. See HIGH in

Index. **2.** Being a sound produced by a relatively small frequency of vibrations : alto, bass, contralto, deep, low-pitched. See SOUNDS in Index. — See also **cheap, depressed, disparaging, filthy, minor, sickly, soft, sordid.**

low *noun* A very low level, position, or degree : bottom, rock bottom. See HIGH in Index.

low-cost *adjective* See **cheap.**

low-cut *adjective* See **low.**

low-down *adjective* See **sordid.**

lower¹ also **lour** *verb* See **frown, glare, threaten.**

lower also **lour** *noun* See **frown, glare.**

lower² *verb* To cause to descend : depress, drop, let down, take down. See RISE in Index. — See also **cut back** at **cut, depreciate, descend.**

lower *adjective* See **minor.**

lowermost *adjective* See **bottom.**

lowery also **loury** *adjective* See **dark.**

lowest *adjective* See **bottom.**

low-grade *adjective* See **inferior.**

low-key *adjective* See **soft.**

low-keyed *adjective* See **soft.**

lowliness *noun* See **modesty.**

lowly *adjective* Lacking high station or birth : baseborn, common, déclassé, declassed, humble, ignoble, mean², plebeian, unwashed, vulgar. *Archaic:* base². See OVER in Index. — See also **humble.**

low-neck *adjective* See **low.**

low-necked *adjective* See **low.**

low-pitched *adjective* See **low.**

low-priced *adjective* See **cheap.**

low-quality *adjective* See **inferior.**

loyal *adjective* See **faithful.**

loyalty *noun* See **attachment, fidelity.**

lubricious *adjective* See **slick, underhand.**

lucent *adjective* See **bright.**

lucid *adjective* See **clear, sane, transparent.**

lucidity *noun* See **clarity, sanity.**

lucidness *noun* See **clarity, sanity.**

luck *noun* Success attained as a result of chance : fortunateness, fortune, luckiness. *Idiom:* good fortune (or luck). See LUCK in Index. — See also **chance.**

luckiness *noun* See **luck.**

luckless *adjective* See **unfortunate.**

lucky *adjective* See **happy.**

lucrative *adjective* See **profitable.**

lucre *noun* See **money.**

lucubrate *verb* See **study.**

lucubration *noun* See **advisement.**

ludicrous *adjective* See **laughable.**

ludicrousness *noun* See **humor.**

lug¹ *noun* See **lump¹.**

lug² *verb* See **carry.**

lugubrious *adjective* See **sorrowful.**

lukewarm *adjective* See **tepid.**

lull *verb* See **calm.**

lull *noun* See **stillness.**

lumber *verb* See **lump¹.**

luminary *noun* See **celebrity.**

luminesce *verb* See **glow.**

luminosity *noun* See **fire.**

luminous *adjective* See **bright.**

lummox *noun* See **lump¹.**

lump¹ *noun* **1.** An irregularly shaped mass of indefinite size : chunk, clod, clump, gob¹, hunch, nugget, wad. *Informal:* hunk. See PART in Index. **2.** A large, ungainly, and dull-witted person : gawk, hulk, lout, oaf, ox. *Informal:* lummox. *Slang:* klutz, lug¹, meatball, meathead. See ABILITY in Index. — See also **bump, due.**

lump *verb* To move heavily : clump, galumph, hulk, lumber, stump. See MOVE in Index. — See also **heap.**

lump² *verb* See **endure.**

lumpenproletariat *noun* See **trash.**

lumpish *adjective* See **awkward, heavy.**

lumpy *adjective* See **heavy.**

lunacy *noun* See **foolishness, insanity.**

lunatic *adjective* See **foolish, insane.**

lunatic *noun* See **crackpot.**

lunge *verb* See **plunge.**

lurch *verb* **1.** To lean suddenly, unsteadily, and erratically from the vertical axis : pitch, roll, seesaw, yaw. See MOVE, STRAIGHT in Index. **2.** To walk unsteadily : falter, reel, stagger, stumble, teeter, totter, weave, wobble. See MOVE in Index. — See also **jerk.**

lurch *noun* See **jerk.**

lure *noun* **1.** Something that attracts, especially with the promise of pleasure or reward : allurement, bait, come-on, enticement, inducement, inveiglement, invitation, seduction, temptation. See LIKE in Index. **2.** Something that leads one into a place or situation from which escape is difficult : bait, snare, trap. See LIKE, SAFETY in Index. — See also **attraction.**

lure *verb* See **attract, seduce.**

lurer *noun* See **seducer.**

lurid *adjective* See **ghastly, pale.**

luring *adjective* See **seductive.**

lurk *verb* See **sneak.**

luscious *adjective* See **delicious, delightful.**

lush¹ *adjective* See **luxurious, profuse, thick.**

lush² *noun* See **drunkard.**

lush *verb* See **drink.**

lust *verb* To have a greedy, obsessive desire : crave, hunger, itch, thirst. See DESIRE in Index.

lust *noun* See **desire.**

luster *noun* See **eminence, gloss.**

lusterless *adjective* See **dull.**

lustful *adjective* See **erotic.**

lustfulness *noun* See **desire.**

lustral *adjective* See **purgative.**

lustrate *verb* See **purify.**

lustration *noun* See **purification.**

lustrative *adjective* See **purgative.**

lustrous *adjective* See **bright, glossy.**

lusty *adjective* Full of vigor : able-bodied, iron, red-blooded, robust, strapping, sturdy, vigorous, vital. See STRONG in Index. — See also **erotic.**

luxuriant *adjective* See **luxurious, profuse, thick.**

luxuriate *verb* To take extravagant pleasure : bask, indulge, revel, roll, rollick, wallow. See LIKE in Index.

luxurious *adjective* Characterized by extravagant, ostentatious magnificence : lavish, lush[1], luxuriant, opulent, palatial, plush, rich, sumptuous. *Informal:* plushy. See RICH in Index.

luxury *noun* Something costly and unnecessary : extravagance, extravagancy, frill. See SAVE in Index.

lying *adjective* See **dishonest.**

lying-in *noun* See **birth.**

lymphatic *adjective* See **languid.**

lyric *adjective* See **poetic.**

lyricism *noun* See **poetry.**

M

macabre *adjective* See **ghastly, morbid.**

machinate *verb* See **plot.**

machination *noun* See **plot.**

macho *adjective* See **manly.**

macrocosm *noun* See **universe.**

mad *adjective* See **angry, enthusiastic, foolish, frantic, insane.**

madcap *adjective* See **rash[1].**

madden *verb* See **anger, derange.**

madding *adjective* See **frantic.**

made-to-order *adjective* See **custom.**

made-up *adjective* See **assumed, fictitious.**

madness *noun* See **foolishness, insanity.**

magazine *noun* See **depository.**

magic *noun* **1.** The use of supernatural powers to influence or predict events : conjuration, sorcery, sortilege, thaumaturgy, theurgy, witchcraft, witchery, witching, wizardry. See SUPERNATURAL in Index. **2.** The use of skillful tricks and deceptions to produce entertainingly baffling effects : conjuration, legerdemain, prestidigitation, sleight of hand. See PERFORMING ARTS in Index. — See also **spell[2].**

magic also **magical** *adjective* Having, brought about by, or relating to supernatural powers or magic : fey, magical, talismanic, thaumaturgic, thaumaturgical, theurgic, theurgical, witching, wizardly. See SUPERNATURAL in Index.

magical *adjective* See **magic.**

magisterial *adjective* See **dictatorial.**

magistrate *noun* See **judge.**

magnanimity *noun* See **generosity.**

magnanimous *adjective* See **generous.**

magnanimousness *noun* See **generosity.**

magnetism *noun* See **attraction, force.**

magnetize *verb* See **attract.**

magnific *adjective* See **grand.**

magnification *noun* See **praise.**

magnificence *noun* See **glitter.**

magnificent *adjective* See **glorious, grand, rare.**

magnify *verb* See **exaggerate, exalt, honor, increase, praise.**

magniloquent *adjective* See **sonorous.**

magniloquence *noun* See **bombast.**

magnitude *noun* See **bulk, degree, size.**

magnum opus *noun* See **masterpiece.**

maiden *adjective* See **first.**

maim *verb* See **cripple.**

main *adjective* See **primary.**

maintain *verb* To keep in a condition of good repair, efficiency, or use : keep up, preserve, sustain. See KEEP in Index. — See also **assert, defend, keep, support.**

maintenance *noun* See **living.**

majestic *adjective* See **grand.**

majesty *noun* See **glory.**

major *adjective* See **big-league, primary.**

major-league *adjective* See **big-league.**

make *verb* To create by forming, combining, or altering materials : assemble, build, construct, fabricate, fashion, forge[1], frame, manufacture, mold, produce, put together, shape. See MAKE in Index. — See also **appoint, bear, cause, constitute, cover, earn, establish, force, get, prepare, produce.**

make out *verb* See **discern, manage, neck, understand.**

make over *verb* See **transfer.**

make up *verb* See **balance, improvise, invent, reconcile.**

make-believe *noun* See **pretense.**

maker *noun* See **builder, originator.**

makeshift *noun* Something used temporarily or reluctantly when other means are not available : expediency, expedient, shift, stopgap. See HELP, SUBSTITUTE in Index.

makeup or **make-up** *noun* See **character.**

maladroit *adjective* See **awkward, tactless, unskillful.**

malady *noun* See **disease, indisposition.**

mala fide *adjective* See **insincere.**

malapert *adjective* See **impudent.**
malapert *noun* See **smart aleck.**

malapropos *adjective* See **improper.**

malarkey also **malarky** *noun* See **nonsense.**

male *adjective* See **manly.**

maledict *verb* See **curse.**

malediction *noun* See **curse.**

malefactor *noun* See **criminal.**

malevolence *noun* A desire to harm others or to see others suffer : despitefulness, ill will, malice, maliciousness, malignancy, malignity, meanness, nastiness, poisonousness, spite, spitefulness, venomousness, viciousness. See ATTITUDE in Index.

malevolent *adjective* Characterized by intense ill will or spite : black, despiteful, evil, hateful, malicious, malign, malignant, mean[2], nasty, poisonous, spiteful, venomous, vicious, wicked. *Slang:* bitchy. See ATTITUDE in Index.

malformation *noun* See **deformity.**

malfunction *verb* To work improperly due to mechanical difficulties : act up, misbehave. See THRIVE in Index.

malice *noun* See **malevolence.**

malicious *adjective* See **malevolent.**

maliciousness *noun* See **malevolence.**

malign *verb* See **libel.**
malign *adjective* Strongly suggestive of great harm, menace, or evil : baleful, sinister. See WARN in Index. — See also **malevolent.**

malignancy *noun* See **malevolence.**

malignant *adjective* See **malevolent, virulent.**

malignity *noun* See **malevolence.**

malison *noun* See **curse.**

malleability *noun* See **flexibility.**

malleable *adjective* Capable of being shaped, bent, or drawn out, as

by hammering or pressure : ductile, flexible, flexile, flexuous, moldable, plastic, pliable, pliant, supple, workable. See FLEXIBLE in Index.
— See also **adaptable, flexible.**

malleableness *noun* See **flexibility.**

malodorous *adjective* See **smelly.**

maltreat *verb* See **abuse.**

maltreatment *noun* See **abuse.**

mammoth *noun* See **giant.**
　mammoth *adjective* See **giant.**

man *noun* See **human being, mankind, policeman.**

manacle *noun* See **bond.**
　manacle *verb* See **hamper.**

manage *verb* To progress or perform adequately, especially in difficult circumstances : do, fare, fend, get along, get by, muddle through, shift. *Informal:* make out. *Idioms:* make do, make shift. See THRIVE in Index. — See also **administer, conduct, operate.**

manageable *adjective* See **governable.**

management *noun* See **administration, conservation, guidance.**

manager *noun* See **boss, executive.**

managerial *adjective* See **administrative.**

mandate *noun* See **command, faculty.**

mandatory *adjective* See **required.**

maneuver *noun* See **move, movement, tactic, trick.**
　maneuver *verb* **1.** To direct the course of carefully : guide, jockey, navigate, pilot, steer. *Idiom:* back and fill. See CONTROL, MOVE in Index. **2.** To take clever or cunning steps to achieve one's goals : jockey. *Informal:* finagle. *Idiom:* pull strings (or wires). See CONTROL, MEANS in Index. — See also **manipulate, move.**

manful *adjective* See **manly.**

mangle¹ *verb* See **batter.**

mangle² *verb* See **press.**

mangy *adjective* See **shabby.**

manhandle *verb* See **slap around** at **slap.**

mania *noun* See **enthusiasm, insanity, thing.**

maniac *noun* See **enthusiast.**
　maniac *adjective* See **insane.**

maniacal *adjective* See **insane.**

manifest *verb* See **embody, express, show.**
　manifest *adjective* See **apparent.**

manifestation *noun* See **display, embodiment, sign.**

manifesto *noun* See **announcement.**

manipulate *verb* To control to one's own advantage by artful or indirect means : exploit, maneuver, play. See CONTROL, STRAIGHT in Index. — See also **handle, work.**

mankind *noun* The human race : earth, flesh, Homo sapiens, humanity, humankind, man, universe, world. See CULTURE in Index.

manlike *adjective* Resembling a human being : anthropoid, anthropomorphic, anthropomorphous, hominoid, humanoid. See CULTURE in Index. — See also **manly.**

manly *adjective* Of, characteristic of, or befitting the male sex : macho, male, manful, manlike, mannish, masculine, virile. See GENDER in Index.

manmade *adjective* See **artificial.**

manner *noun* Socially correct behavior. Used in plural : decorum, etiquette, good form, mores, propriety (also used in plural), p's and q's. See USUAL in Index. — See also **bearing, custom, kind², style, way.**

mannered *adjective* See **affected.**

mannerism *noun* See **affectation.**

mannerliness *noun* See **courtesy.**

mannerly *adjective* See **courteous.**

mannish *adjective* See **manly.**

man on horseback *noun* See **dictator.**

manslayer *noun* See **murderer.**

mantic *adjective* See **prophetic.**

mantle *verb* See **blush, clothe.**

man-to-man *adjective* See **frank.**

manufacture *verb* See **make.**

manufactured *adjective* See **artificial.**

manufacturer *noun* See **builder.**

manumission *noun* See **liberty.**

manumit *verb* See **free.**

many *adjective* Amounting to or consisting of a large, indefinite number : legion, multitudinous, myriad, numerous. *Idiom:* quite a few. See BIG in Index.

many-sided *adjective* See **versatile.**

map *noun* See **face.**

map *verb* See **design, plot.**

mar *verb* See **injure.**

maraud *verb* See **raid.**

marble *noun* See **sanity.**

march[1] *verb* See **come, hike, stride.**

march *noun* See **advance.**

march[2] *noun* See **border.**

marchland *noun* See **border.**

margin *noun* See **border, room.**

margin *verb* See **border.**

marine *adjective* Of or relating to the seas or oceans : maritime, oceanic, pelagic, thalassic. See SEA in Index. — See also **nautical.**

mariner *noun* See **sailor.**

marital *adjective* Of, relating to, or typical of marriage : conjugal, connubial, hymeneal, married, matrimonial, nuptial, spousal, wedded. See MARRIAGE in Index.

maritime *adjective* See **marine, nautical.**

mark *noun* A name or other device placed on merchandise to signify its ownership or manufacture : brand, colophon, label, trademark. See MARKS in Index. — See also **dupe, eminence, impression, intention,** notice, quality, sign, standard, target.

mark *verb* To set off by or as if by a mark indicating ownership or manufacture : brand, identify, label, tag, trademark. See MARKS in Index. — See also **designate, determine, distinguish, indicate, notice, score, show, target, ticket.**

mark down *verb* See **depreciate.**

markdown *noun* See **depreciation.**

marked *adjective* See **noticeable.**

market *verb* See **sell.**

marketability *noun* See **sell.**

marketableness *noun* See **sell.**

marriable *adjective* See **eligible.**

marriage *noun* The state of being united as husband and wife : conjugality, connubiality, matrimony, wedlock. See MARRIAGE in Index. — See also **wedding.**

marriageable *adjective* See **eligible.**

married *adjective* See **marital.**

marrow *noun* See **heart.**

marrowy *adjective* See **pithy.**

marry *verb* To join or be joined in marriage : espouse, mate, wed. *Slang:* hitch. *Idiom:* tie the knot. See MARRIAGE in Index. — See also **combine.**

marsh *noun* See **swamp.**

marshal *verb* See **arrange, mobilize.**

marshland *noun* See **swamp.**

martial *adjective* See **military.**

martinet *noun* See **authoritarian.**

marvel *noun* One that evokes great surprise and admiration : astonishment, miracle, phenomenon, prodigy, sensation, stunner, wonder, wonderment. *Idioms:* one for the books, the eighth wonder of the world. See GOOD in Index. — See also **wonder.**

marvel *verb* See **wonder.**

marvelous also **marvellous** *adjective* Particularly excellent :

divine, fabulous, fantastic, fantastical, glorious, sensational, splendid,
superb, terrific, wonderful. *Informal:*
dandy, dreamy, great, ripping, super,
swell, tremendous. *Slang:* cool,
groovy, hot, keen[1], neat, nifty.
Idiom: out of this world. See GOOD
in Index. — See also **fabulous.**

masculine *adjective* See **manly.**

mash *verb* See **crush.**

mask *noun* See **façade.**

　mask *verb* See **cover, disguise.**

masquerade *noun* See **act, façade.**

　masquerade *verb* See **disguise,
　pose.**

mass *noun* See **accumulation, body,
bulk, commonalty, crowd, heap,
weight.**

massacre *noun* The savage killing
of many victims : bloodbath,
bloodletting, bloodshed, butchery,
carnage, pogrom, slaughter. See
HELP in Index. — See also **defeat.**

　massacre *verb* See **annihilate,
　overwhelm.**

massacrer *noun* See **murderer.**

massive *adjective* See **bulky, giant,
heavy.**

massiveness *noun* See **heaviness.**

massy *adjective* See **giant.**

master *noun* See **chief, conqueror,
expert, original, owner.**

　master *verb* See **defeat, domesti-
　cate, gentle, learn.**

　master *adjective* See **expert.**

masterful *adjective* See **authoritative, dictatorial, expert.**

masterly *adjective* See **expert.**

masterpiece *noun* An outstanding
and ingenious work : chef-
d'oeuvre, magnum opus, masterwork. See GOOD in Index.

masterstroke *noun* See **feat.**

masterwork *noun* See **masterpiece.**

mastery *noun* See **ability, authority,
domination.**

masticate *verb* See **chew.**

mastodonic *adjective* See **giant.**

mat also **matte** *adjective* See **dull.**

match *noun* See **couple, mate,
parallel.**

　match *verb* See **agree, compare,
　equal, fit[1], liken, oppose.**

matchless *adjective* See **unique.**

mate *noun* One of a matched pair of
things : companion, counterpart,
double, duplicate, fellow, match,
twin. See SAME in Index. — See also
associate, friend, spouse.

　mate *verb* See **marry, take.**

material *noun* That from which
things are or can be made : matter,
stuff, substance. *Idiom:* grist for
one's mill. See MATTER in Index.
— See also **outfit, timber.**

　material *adjective* See **important,
　materialistic, physical, relevant.**

materialistic *adjective* Of or preoccupied with material rather than
spiritual or intellectual things :
material, sensual. See BODY in
Index.

materiality *noun* See **matter,
relevance.**

materialization *noun* See **effect,
embodiment, fulfillment.**

materialize *verb* See **appear,
embody, realize.**

materiel or **matériel** *noun* See
outfit.

matey *adjective* See **companionable.**

matrimonial *adjective* See **marital.**

matrimony *noun* See **marriage.**

matrix *noun* See **form.**

matter *noun* 1. That which occupies
space and can be perceived by the
senses : materiality, substance. See
BODY in Index. 2. Something to be
done, considered, or dealt with :
affair, business, thing. See THING in
Index. — See also **material, subject.**

　matter *verb* See **count.**

matter-of-fact *adjective* See **dry, dull, realistic.**

maturate *verb* See **mature.**

mature *adjective* Having reached full growth and development : adult, big, developed, full-blown, full-fledged, full-grown, grown, grown-up, ripe. *Idiom:* of age. See YOUTH in Index.

mature *verb* To bring or come to full development : age, develop, grow, maturate, mellow, ripen. See YOUTH in Index.

maudlin *adjective* See **sentimental.**

maudlinism *noun* See **sentimentality.**

maul *verb* See **batter.**

mausoleum *noun* See **grave¹.**

mawkish *adjective* See **sentimental.**

mawkishness *noun* See **sentimentality.**

maxim *noun* See **proverb.**

maximal *adjective* See **maximum.**

maximum *adjective* Greatest in quantity or highest in degree that has been or can be attained : maximal, top, topmost, ultimate, utmost, uttermost. See HIGH, LIMITED in Index.

maximum *noun* The greatest quantity or highest degree attainable : outside, top, ultimate, utmost, uttermost. *Idiom:* ne plus ultra. See HIGH, LIMITED in Index. — See also **limit.**

maybe *adverb* Possibly but not certainly : mayhap, perchance, perhaps. See CERTAIN in Index.

mayhap *adverb* See **maybe.**

maze *verb* See **daze.**

maze *noun* See **tangle.**

mazuma *noun* See **money.**

mea culpa *noun* See **apology.**

meager *adjective* Conspicuously deficient in quantity, fullness, or extent : exiguous, poor, puny, scant, scanty, skimpy, spare, sparse,

stingy, thin. *Slang:* measly. See BIG, EXCESS in Index. — See also **thin.**

mean¹ *verb* To have or convey a particular idea : connote, denote, import, intend, signify, spell¹. *Idiom:* add up to. See MEANING in Index. — See also **intend.**

mean² *adjective* See **filthy, humble, ill-tempered, inferior, lowly, malevolent, sickly, sordid, stingy, troublesome.**

mean³ *noun* That by which something is accomplished or some end achieved. Used in plural : agency, agent, instrument, instrumentality, instrumentation, intermediary, mechanism, medium, organ. See MEANS in Index. — See also **average, resource.**

mean *adjective* See **middle.**

meander *verb* See **rove, stroll, wind².**

meander *noun* See **walk.**

meandrous *adjective* See **winding.**

meaning *noun* That which is signified by a word or expression : acceptation, connotation, denotation, import, intent, message, purport, sense, significance, significancy, signification, value. See MEANING in Index. — See also **idea, intention, thrust.**

meaning *adjective* See **expressive.**

meaningful *adjective* See **expressive, important, pregnant.**

meaningless *adjective* See **mindless.**

meanness *noun* See **malevolence.**

measly *adjective* See **meager, petty.**

measure *noun* See **allotment, degree, law, measurement, moderation, move, rhythm, size, standard.**

measure *verb* To ascertain the dimensions, quantity, or capacity of : gauge. *Archaic:* mete. *Idiom:* take the measure of. See BIG in Index. — See also **determine.**

measure out *verb* See **allot.**

measure up *verb* See **compare.**

measured *adjective* See **deliberate, rhythmical.**

measureless *adjective* See **endless, incalculable.**

measurelessness *noun* See **infinity.**

measurement *noun* The act or process of ascertaining dimensions, quantity, or capacity : measure, mensuration, metrology. See BIG in Index.

meat *noun* See **food, heart.**

meatball *noun* See **lump¹.**

meathead *noun* See **lump¹.**

mechanical *adjective* See **perfunctory.**

mechanism *noun* See **mean³.**

medal *noun* See **decoration.**

meddle *verb* To intervene officiously or indiscreetly in the affairs of others : butt in, horn in, interfere, interlope. See PARTICIPATE in Index. — See also **tamper.**

meddler *noun* A person given to intruding in other people's affairs : busybody, interloper, quidnunc. *Informal:* kibitzer. *Slang:* buttinsky. *Archaic:* pragmatic. See PARTICIPATE in Index.

meddlesome *adjective* See **meddling.**

meddling *noun* The act or an instance of interfering or intruding : interference, intervention, intrusion, obtrusion. See PARTICIPATE in Index.

meddling *adjective* Given to intruding in other people's affairs : interfering, intrusive, meddlesome, obtrusive, officious. See PARTICIPATE in Index.

medial *adjective* See **central, middle.**

median *noun* See **average, center.**

median *adjective* See **central, middle.**

mediator *noun* See **go-between.**

medicament *noun* See **cure, drug.**

medicate *verb* See **drug.**

medication *noun* See **cure, drug.**

medicine *noun* See **cure, drug.**

mediocre *adjective* See **inferior, ordinary.**

meditate *verb* See **ponder.**

meditation *noun* See **thought.**

meditative *adjective* See **thoughtful.**

medium *noun* See **average, compromise, environment, mean³, press.**

medley *noun* See **assortment.**

meek *adjective* See **gentle, humble.**

meekness *noun* See **modesty.**

meet¹ *verb* To come together face-to-face by arrangement : get together, rendezvous. See MEET in Index. — See also **adjoin, close, encounter, engage, equal, experience, greet, satisfy.**

meet *noun* See **competition.**

meet² *adjective* See **appropriate, convenient.**

meeting *noun* See **assembly, convention, junction.**

megrim *noun* See **fancy.**

melancholic *adjective* See **depressed.**

melancholy *adjective* See **depressed, sad.**

melancholy *noun* See **gloom.**

mélange also **melange** *noun* See **assortment.**

meld *verb* See **combine.**

melee also **mêlée** *noun* See **brawl.**

meliorate *verb* See **improve.**

melioration *noun* See **improvement, progress.**

mellow *adjective* See **aged, resonant.**

mellow *verb* See **mature.**

melodic *adjective* See **melodious.**

melodious *adjective* **1.** Having or producing a pleasing melody : melodic, musical, tuneful. See

SOUNDS in Index. **2.** Resembling or having the effect of music, especially pleasing music : dulcet, euphonic, euphonious, melodic, musical, tuneful. See SOUNDS in Index.

melodramatic *adjective* See **dramatic.**

melodramatics *noun* See **theatrics.**

melody *noun* A pleasing succession of musical tones forming a usually brief aesthetic unit : air, aria, strain², tune. *Obsolete:* note. See SOUNDS in Index.

melt *verb* To change from a solid to a liquid : deliquesce, dissolve, flux, fuse, liquefy, run, thaw. See SOLID in Index. — See also **fade.**

member *noun* See **division.**

membrane *noun* See **skin.**

memento *noun* See **remembrance.**

memo *noun* See **note.**

memoir *noun* See **commentary.**

memorandum *noun* See **note.**

memorial *noun* Something, as a structure or custom, serving to honor or keep alive a memory : commemoration, monument, remembrance. See REMEMBER in Index.

memorial *adjective* Serving to honor or keep alive a memory : commemorative. See REMEMBER in Index.

memorialize *verb* To honor or keep alive the memory of : commemorate. See REMEMBER in Index.

memorize *verb* To commit to memory : con, learn. See REMEMBER in Index.

memory *noun* **1.** The power of retaining and recalling past experience : recall, recollection, remembrance, reminiscence. See REMEMBER in Index. **2.** An act or instance of remembering : recollection, remembrance, reminiscence. See REMEMBER in Index.

menace *verb* See **endanger, intimidate, threaten.**

menace *noun* See **threat.**

ménage *noun* See **family.**

mend *verb* See **correct, fix, recover.**

mendacious *adjective* See **dishonest.**

mendacity *noun* The practice of lying : falsehood, inveracity, perjury, truthlessness, untruthfulness. See TRUE in Index.

mendicancy *noun* See **beggary.**

mendicant *noun* See **beggar.**

mendicity *noun* See **beggary.**

menial *adjective* See **servile.**

mensuration *noun* See **measurement.**

mental *adjective* Relating to or performed by the mind : cerebral, intellective, intellectual, psychic, psychical, psychological. See THOUGHTS in Index.

mental illness *noun* See **insanity.**

mentality *noun* See **intelligence, psychology.**

mentally ill *adjective* See **insane.**

mention *verb* See **name, refer.**

mentor *noun* See **adviser.**

mentor *verb* See **advise.**

mephitic *adjective* See **poisonous, smelly.**

mephitical *adjective* See **poisonous.**

mercenary *adjective* See **corrupt.**

mercenary *noun* A freelance fighter : adventurer, Hessian, soldier of fortune. See GET in Index.

merchandise *noun* See **good.**

merchandise *verb* See **sell.**

merchandiser *noun* See **dealer.**

merchant *noun* See **dealer.**

merchant *verb* See **sell.**

merciful *adjective* See **humanitarian, tolerant.**

mercifulness *noun* See **grace.**

merciless *adjective* Having or showing no mercy : pitiless,

remorseless, unmerciful. See KIND
in Index.

mercurial *adjective* See **capricious.**

mercy *noun* See **grace.**

mere *adjective* Considered apart
from anything else : very. See
INCLUDE, SPECIFIC in Index.

merely *adverb* Nothing more
than : just, only. See INCLUDE,
SPECIFIC in Index.

meretricious *adjective* See **gaudy.**

merge *verb* See **mix.**

merger *noun* See **mixture.**

meridian *noun* See **climax.**

merit *noun* A level of superiority
that is usually high : caliber, quality, stature, value, virtue, worth. See
GOOD, VALUE in Index. — See also
virtue.

merit *verb* See **earn.**

merited *adjective* See **just.**

meritorious *adjective* See
admirable.

merriment *noun* See **gaiety.**

merriness *noun* See **gaiety.**

merry *adjective* Marked by festal
celebration : festive, gala, glad,
gladsome, happy, joyful, joyous. See
HAPPY in Index. — See also **gay.**

merrymaking *noun* See **celebration, gaiety.**

mesh *noun* See **tangle, web.**

mesh *verb* See **engage.**

mesmerize *verb* See **grip.**

mess *noun* An unsightly object :
monstrosity, ugliness. *Informal:*
fright, sight, ugly. See BEAUTIFUL in
Index. — See also **botch, disorder,
heap, serving.**

mess *verb* See **tamper, tousle.**

mess around *verb* *Informal.* To
waste time by engaging in aimless
activity : doodle, fool, putter.
Informal: fool around. See THRIVE in
Index. — See also **fuss, philander.**

mess up *verb* See **botch, confuse,
disorder, slap around** at **slap.**

message *noun* See **communication,
meaning.**

messenger *noun* See **bearer.**

messiness *noun* See **disorderliness.**

messy *adjective* Marked by an
absence of cleanliness and order :
disheveled, mussy, slipshod, sloppy,
slovenly, unkempt, untidy. See
ORDER in Index. — See also **careless,
disorderly.**

metamorphose *verb* See **convert,
revolutionize.**

metamorphosis *noun* See **change.**

metanoia *noun* See **conversion.**

metaphysical *adjective* See **immaterial, supernatural.**

mete *verb* See **allot, measure.**

meter *noun* See **rhythm.**

method *noun* Systematic arrangement and design : order, orderliness, organization, pattern, plan,
system, systematization,
systemization. See ORDER in Index.
— See also **way.**

methodic *adjective* See **methodical.**

methodical *adjective* Arranged or
proceeding in a set, systematized
pattern : methodic, orderly, regular, systematic, systematical. See
ABILITY, ORDER in Index.

methodize *verb* To arrange in an
orderly manner : order, organize,
systematize, systemize. See ORDER
in Index.

meticulous *adjective* See **careful,
nice.**

meticulousness *noun* See
thoroughness.

métier *noun* See **business, forte.**

metrical *adjective* See **rhythmical.**

metrology *noun* See **measurement.**

metropolis *noun* See **city.**

metropolitan *adjective* See **city.**

metropolitanize *verb* See **citify.**

mettle *noun* See **courage.**

mettlesome *adjective* See **brave,
spirited.**

mew *verb* See enclose.

microbe *noun* See germ.

microorganism also **micro-organism** *noun* See germ.

microscopic *adjective* See imperceptible.

mid *adjective* See central, middle.

middle *adjective* Not extreme : central, intermediate, mean[3], medial, median, mid, middle-of-the-road, midway. See EDGE in Index. — See also central.

middle *noun* See center.

middleman *noun* See go-between.

middle-of-the-road *adjective* See middle.

midget *adjective* See tiny.

midpoint *noun* See center.

midst *noun* See center, thick.

midway *adjective* See middle.

mien *noun* See appearance, bearing.

miff *noun* See offense.

miff *verb* See insult.

might *noun* See ability, authority, energy, strength.

mighty *adjective* See giant, powerful, strong.

mighty *adverb* See very.

migrant *noun* See emigrant.

migrant *adjective* Moving from one area to another in search of work : itinerant, migratory. See MOVE in Index. — See also migratory.

migrate *verb* To change habitat seasonally : transmigrate. See MOVE in Index. — See also emigrate.

migration *noun* See emigration.

migrational *adjective* See migratory.

migratory *adjective* Moving from one habitat to another on a seasonal basis : migrant, migrational, transmigratory. See MOVE in Index. — See also migrant.

mild *adjective* Free from extremes in temperature : moderate, temperate. See EDGE in Index. — See also gentle.

milieu *noun* See environment.

militance *noun* See aggression, belligerence.

militancy *noun* See aggression, belligerence.

militant *adjective* See aggressive, belligerent.

militaristic *adjective* See military.

militarize *verb* To assemble, equip, and train for war : mobilize. See PEACE in Index.

military *adjective* **1.** Relating to, characteristic of, or performed by troops : martial, soldierly. See PEACE in Index. **2.** Of, relating to, or inclined toward war : bellicose, martial, militaristic, warlike. See PEACE in Index.

milksop *noun* See baby.

mill *noun* See work.

mill *verb* See crush.

million *noun* See heap.

millstone *noun* See burden[1].

milquetoast *noun* See baby.

mime *noun* See mimic.

mimic *noun* A performer skilled at copying the manner or expression of another : impersonator, mime. See PERFORMING ARTS, SAME in Index. — See also echo.

mimic *verb* See echo, imitate.

mimicry *noun* The act, practice, or art of copying the manner or expression of another : aping, imitation. See SAME in Index.

minacious *adjective* See threatening.

minatory *adjective* See threatening.

mind *noun* A person of great mental ability : brain, intellect, intellectual, thinker. See ABILITY in Index. — See also belief, head, intelligence, liking, psychology, sanity.

mind *verb* See **care, follow, intend, look out** at **look, notice, remember, tend²**.

mind-blowing *adjective* See **staggering**.

mind-boggling *adjective* See **staggering**.

minded *adjective* See **willing**.

mindful *adjective* Tending toward awareness and appreciation : conscious, heedful, observant. See AWARENESS in Index. — See also **careful**.

mindfulness *noun* See **care**.

mindless *adjective* 1. Displaying a complete lack of forethought and good sense : brainless, fatuous, foolish, insensate, senseless, silly, unintelligent, weak-minded, witless. See ABILITY, PLANNED in Index. 2. Lacking rational direction or purpose : meaningless, pointless, purposeless, senseless. *Idiom:* without rhyme or reason. See PURPOSE in Index. 3. Showing no concern, attention, or regard : careless, forgetful, heedless, unconcerned, unheeding, unmindful, unobservant, unthinking. See CAREFUL in Index.

mindset or **mind-set** *noun* See **psychology**.

mingle *verb* See **mix, socialize**.

miniature *noun* See **model**.

miniature *adjective* See **tiny**.

minim *noun* See **bit¹**.

minimal *adjective* Comprising the least possible : littlest, minimum, smallest. See BIG in Index.

minimization *noun* See **belittlement**.

minimize *verb* See **belittle**.

minimum *adjective* See **minimal**.

minion *noun* See **darling, follower**.

minister *noun* See **preacher**.

minister to *verb* See **serve, tend²**.

ministerial *adjective* See **administrative**.

minor *adjective* 1. Below another in standing or importance : inferior, junior, lesser, low, lower², minor-league, petty, secondary, small, subaltern, subordinate, under. *Informal:* smalltime. See OVER in Index. 2. *Law.* Not yet a legal adult : underage². See LAW, YOUTH in Index.

minor *noun* *Law.* One who is not yet legally of age : child, juvenile. *Law:* infant. See LAW, YOUTH in Index.

minority *noun* The state or period of being under legal age : nonage. *Law:* infancy. See LAW, YOUTH in Index.

minor-league *adjective* See **minor**.

mint *noun* See **fortune**.

minus *noun* See **disadvantage**.

minuscule also **miniscule** *adjective* See **tiny**.

minute¹ *noun* See **flash**.

minute² *adjective* See **detailed, tiny**.

minutia *noun* See **trivia**.

miracle *noun* An event inexplicable by the laws of nature : wonder. See SUPERNATURAL in Index. — See also **marvel**.

miraculous *adjective* See **fabulous, supernatural**.

mirage *noun* See **illusion**.

mire *noun* See **slime, swamp**.

mire *verb* See **muddy**.

mirror *noun* See **model**.

mirror *verb* See **echo, reflect**.

mirth *noun* See **gaiety**.

mirthful *adjective* See **gay**.

mirthfulness *noun* See **gaiety**.

miry *adjective* See **muddy, slimy**.

misadventure *noun* See **accident**.

misanthrope *noun* See **cynic**.

misanthropist *noun* See **cynic**.

misapplication *noun* See **abuse**.

misapply *verb* See **abuse**.

misapprehend *verb* See **misunderstand**.

misapprehension *noun* See **misunderstanding.**

misappropriate *verb* See **abuse.**

misappropriation *noun* See **abuse.**

misbegotten *adjective* See **illegitimate.**

misbehave *verb* To behave in a rowdy, improper, or unruly fashion : act up, carry on. *Informal:* cut up, horse around. See GOOD in Index. — See also **malfunction.**

misbehavior *noun* Improper, often rude behavior : horseplay, misconduct, misdoing, naughtiness, wrongdoing. See GOOD in Index.

miscalculate *verb* To calculate wrongly : misestimate, misjudge, misreckon. See CORRECT in Index.

miscalculation *noun* A wrong calculation : misestimate, misestimation, misjudgment, misreckoning. See CORRECT in Index.

miscarry *verb* 1. To go wrong, be unsuccessful, or fail to attain a goal : misfire, miss. *Idioms:* fall short, miss fire, miss the mark. See THRIVE in Index. 2. To bring forth a nonviable fetus prematurely : abort, slip. See REPRODUCTION in Index.

miscellaneous *adjective* See **various.**

miscellaneousness *noun* See **variety.**

miscellany *noun* See **assortment.**

mischance *noun* See **accident.**

mischief *noun* 1. Annoying yet harmless, usually playful acts : devilry, deviltry, diablerie, high jinks, impishness, mischievousness, prankishness, rascality, roguery, roguishness, tomfoolery. *Informal:* shenanigan (often used in plural). See GOOD in Index. 2. One who causes minor trouble or damage : devil, imp, prankster, rascal, rogue, scamp.

Informal: cutup. See GOOD in Index. — See also **harm.**

mischievous *adjective* See **harmful, playful.**

mischievousness *noun* See **mischief.**

misconceive *verb* See **misunderstand.**

misconception *noun* See **misunderstanding.**

misconduct *noun* See **misbehavior.**

misconstrue *verb* See **misunderstand.**

miscreant *adjective* See **corrupt.**

miscue *noun* See **error.**

miscue *verb* See **err.**

misdeed *noun* See **crime.**

misdoing *noun* See **misbehavior.**

misdoubt *verb* See **distrust, doubt.**

mise en scène *noun* See **environment, scene.**

miser *noun* A stingy person : niggard, Scrooge, skinflint. *Informal:* penny pincher. *Slang:* cheapskate, stiff, tightwad. See GIVE in Index.

miserable *adjective* 1. Suffering from usually prolonged anguish : woebegone, woeful, wretched. See HAPPY in Index. 2. Having a painful ailment : afflicted, suffering, wretched. See HAPPY in Index. — See also **shoddy.**

miserable *noun* See **unfortunate.**

miserly *adjective* See **stingy.**

misery *noun* A state of prolonged anguish and privation : suffering, woe, wretchedness. See HAPPY in Index. — See also **distress, pain.**

misestimate *verb* See **miscalculate, misjudge.**

misestimate *noun* See **miscalculation.**

misestimation *noun* See **miscalculation.**

misfire *verb* See **miscarry.**

misfortune *noun* Bad fortune : adversity, haplessness, unfortunate-

ness, unluckiness, untowardness.
See LUCK in Index. — See also
accident.

misgiving *noun* See qualm.

mishandle *verb* See abuse, botch.

mishandling *noun* See abuse.

mishap *noun* See accident.

mishmash *noun* See assortment.

misinterpret *verb* See misunderstand.

misinterpretation *noun* See misunderstanding.

misjudge *verb* To make a mistake in judging : misestimate. See CORRECT in Index. — See also miscalculate.

misjudgment *noun* See miscalculation.

mislay *verb* See lose.

mislead *verb* See deceive.

misleading *adjective* See fallacious.

mislike *verb* See dislike.

  mislike *noun* See dislike.

mismanage *verb* See botch.

misplace *verb* See lose.

misplacement *noun* See loss.

misread *verb* See misunderstand.

misreckon *verb* See miscalculate.

misreckoning *noun* See miscalculation.

misrepresent *verb* See distort.

misrepresentation *noun* See lie².

misrule *noun* See disorder.

miss *verb* See lose, miscarry.

misshape *verb* See deform.

missing *adjective* See absent, lost.

mission *noun* **1.** An assignment one is sent to carry out : commission, errand. See WORK in Index. **2.** A diplomatic office or headquarters in a foreign country : legation. See POLITICS in Index. — See also vocation.

missionary *noun* A person doing religious or charitable work in a foreign country : apostle, evangelist, missioner. See RELIGION in Index.

missionary *adjective* Of missionaries or their work : apostolic. See RELIGION in Index.

missioner *noun* See missionary.

missive *noun* See letter.

misstate *verb* See distort.

misstatement *noun* See lie².

misstep *noun* See error.

mist *noun* See haze.

  mist *verb* See obscure.

mistake *noun* See error.

  mistake *verb* See confuse, err, misunderstand.

mistaken *adjective* See erroneous.

mistreat *verb* See abuse.

mistreatment *noun* See abuse.

mistrust *noun* See distrust, doubt.

  mistrust *verb* See distrust, doubt.

mistrustful *adjective* See distrustful.

misty *adjective* See filmy, unclear.

misunderstand *verb* To understand incorrectly : misapprehend, misconceive, misconstrue, misinterpret, misread, mistake. See UNDERSTAND in Index.

misunderstanding *noun* A failure to understand correctly : false impression, misapprehension, misconception, misinterpretation. See UNDERSTAND in Index.

misusage *noun* See abuse.

misuse *verb* See abuse.

  misuse *noun* See abuse.

mite *noun* See bit¹.

mitigate *verb* See relieve.

mitigation *noun* See relief.

mix *verb* To put together into one mass so that the constituent parts are more or less homogeneous : admix, amalgamate, blend, commingle, commix, fuse, intermingle, intermix, merge, mingle, stir¹. See ASSEMBLE in Index. — See also socialize.

mix up *verb* See confuse, disorder, involve.

mix *noun* See mixture.

mixed *adjective* See **various.**

mixed bag *noun* See **assortment.**

mixed-up *adjective* See **confused.**

mixture *noun* Something produced by mixing : admixture, amalgam, amalgamation, blend, commixture, fusion, merger, mix. See ASSEMBLE in Index. — See also **assortment.**

mix-up also **mixup** *noun* See **disorder.**

moan *noun* See **howl.**

moan *verb* See **howl.**

mob *noun* See **commonalty, crowd, gang.**

mob *verb* See **crowd.**

mobile *adjective* **1.** Capable of moving or being moved from place to place : movable, moving, transportable, traveling. See MOVE in Index. **2.** Changing easily, as in expression : changeable, fluid, plastic. See CHANGE in Index.

mobilize *verb* To assemble, prepare, or put into operation, as for war or a similar emergency : marshal, muster, organize, rally. See MOVE in Index. — See also **drive, militarize.**

mock *verb* See **imitate, ridicule.**

mock *noun* See **mockery.**

mock *adjective* See **artificial.**

mockery *noun* A false, derisive, or impudent imitation of something : burlesque, caricature, farce, mock, parody, sham, travesty. See RESPECT, SAME in Index. — See also **joke, ridicule.**

mocking *adjective* See **sarcastic.**

mod *adjective* See **contemporary, fashionable.**

mode *noun* See **condition, fashion, style, way.**

model *noun* **1.** A small-scale representation of something : miniature. See SAME in Index. **2.** One that is worthy of imitation or duplication : beau ideal, example, exem-

plar, ideal, mirror, paradigm, pattern, standard. See GOOD in Index.

model *verb* See **follow, form.**

model *adjective* See **ideal, typical.**

moderate *adjective* Not excessive or extreme in amount, degree, or force : modest, reasonable, temperate. See BIG, EDGE in Index. — See also **acceptable, conservative, gradual, light², mild, popular.**

moderate *verb* To make or become less severe or extreme : mute, qualify, soften, subdue, tame, temper, tone down. See INCREASE in Index. — See also **subside.**

moderateness *noun* See **moderation.**

moderation *noun* Avoidance of extremes of opinion, feeling, or personal conduct : measure, moderateness, temperance. See EDGE in Index.

modern *adjective* Of or relating to the present or times close to the present : latter-day, recent. See NEW, TIME in Index. — See also **contemporary.**

modern *noun* See **contemporary.**

modernize *verb* To make modern in appearance or style : update. See NEW in Index.

modest *adjective* **1.** Not forward but reticent or reserved in manner : backward, bashful, coy, demure, diffident, retiring, self-effacing, shy¹, timid. See RESTRAINT in Index. **2.** Not elaborate or showy, as in appearance or style : plain, simple, unassuming, unostentatious, unpretentious. See PLAIN in Index. — See also **chaste, clean, humble, moderate, popular.**

modesty *noun* **1.** Reserve in speech, behavior, or dress : demureness, diffidence, reticence, self-effacement. See RESTRAINT in Index. **2.** Lack of vanity or self-

importance : humbleness, humility, lowliness, meekness. See ATTI-
TUDE, BIG, SELF-LOVE in Index.
3. Lack of ostentation or pretension : plainness, simpleness, simplicity, unassumingness, unostentatiousness, unpretentiousness. See
PLAIN in Index. — See also **chastity.**

modicum *noun* See **bit**[1].

modification *noun* See **change.**

modified *adjective* See **qualified.**

modify *verb* See **change.**

modish *adjective* See **fashionable.**

modus operandi *noun* See
approach, way.

moil *verb* See **labor.**

  moil *noun* See **labor.**

moist *adjective* See **damp.**

moisten *verb* See **wash.**

moistureless *adjective* See **dry.**

mold *noun* See **form, kind**[2].

  mold *verb* See **form, make.**

moldable *adjective* See **malleable.**

molder *verb* See **decay.**

moldy *adjective* Smelling of mildew
or decay : frowzy, fusty, musty,
putrid, rancid, rank[2], rotten. See
SMELLS in Index.

molecule *noun* See **bit**[1].

moll *noun* See **prostitute.**

mollify *verb* See **pacify.**

mollycoddle *noun* See **baby.**

  mollycoddle *verb* See **baby.**

molt *verb* See **shed.**

moment *noun* See **flash, importance, instant.**

momentary *adjective* About to
occur at any moment : imminent,
impending, proximate. See NEAR in
Index. — See also **transitory.**

momentous *adjective* See **fateful,
grave**[2].

momentousness *noun* See **gravity.**

monetary *adjective* See **financial.**

money *noun* Something, such as
coins or printed bills, used as a
medium of exchange : cash, currency, lucre. *Informal:* wampum.
Slang: bread, cabbage, dough, gelt,
green, jack, lettuce, long green,
mazuma, moola, scratch. *Chiefly
British:* brass. See MONEY in Index.
— See also **fund.**

moneyed *adjective* See **rich.**

moneymaking *adjective* See
profitable.

moneyman *noun* See **financier.**

moniker or **monicker** *noun* See
name.

monition *noun* See **warning.**

monitory *adjective* See **cautionary.**

monkey *noun* See **dupe.**

  monkey *verb* See **fiddle, tamper.**

monkeyshine *noun* See **prank**[1].

monocracy *noun* See **absolutism.**

monocratic *adjective* See **absolute.**

monopolize *verb* See **absorb, tie up
at tie.**

monopoly *noun* Exclusive control
or possession : corner. See CON-
TROL, OWNED in Index.

monotone *noun* See **monotony.**

monotonous *adjective* See **boring.**

monotonousness *noun* See
monotony.

monotony *noun* A tiresome lack of
variety : humdrum, monotone,
monotonousness, sameness. See
CHANGE, EXCITE in Index.

monster *noun* See **fiend, freak,
giant.**

  monster *adjective* See **giant.**

monstrosity *noun* See **freak, mess,
outrage.**

monstrous *adjective* See **freakish,
giant, outrageous.**

monstrousness *noun* See **enormity.**

monument *noun* See **memorial.**

monumental *adjective* See **giant,
important.**

mooch *verb* See **beg.**

moocher *noun* See **beggar.**

mood *noun* A temporary state of
mind or feeling : frame of mind,

humor, spirit (used in plural), temper, vein. See FEELINGS in Index.
— See also **air, temper.**

moody *adjective* Given to changeable emotional states, especially of anger or gloom ; temperamental. See FEELINGS in Index. — See also **glum.**

moola or **moolah** *noun* See **money.**

mooncalf *noun* See **fool.**

moonstruck also **moonstricken** *adjective* See **insane.**

moony *adjective* See **dreamy.**

moor *verb* See **attach, fasten.**

moot *verb* See **argue, broach, discuss.**

moot *adjective* See **debatable.**

mootable *adjective* See **debatable.**

mope *verb* See **brood, sulk.**

mope *noun* See **gloom.**

moppet *noun* See **child.**

moral *adjective* Teaching morality : didactic, didactical, moralizing. See TEACH in Index. — See also **elevated, ethical.**

moral *noun* The principle taught by a fable or parable, for example : lesson. See MEANING in Index. — See also **ethic.**

morale *noun* A strong sense of enthusiasm and dedication to a common goal that unites a group : esprit, esprit de corps. See CONCERN, FEELINGS in Index.

morality *noun* See **ethic, good.**

moralize *verb* To indulge in moral reflection, usually pompously : preach, sermonize. See TEACH in Index.

moralizing *adjective* See **moral.**

morass *noun* See **swamp, tangle.**

morbid *adjective* Susceptible to or marked by preoccupation with unwholesome matters : macabre, sick, unhealthy, unwholesome. See GOOD in Index.

mordacious *adjective* See **biting.**

mordacity *noun* See **sarcasm.**

mordancy *noun* See **sarcasm.**

mordant *adjective* See **biting.**

more *adjective* See **additional.**

more *adverb* See **additionally, better.**

moreover *adverb* See **additionally.**

mores *noun* See **manner.**

morn *noun* See **dawn.**

morning *noun* The time of day from sunrise to noon : forenoon. See TIME in Index. — See also **dawn.**

moron *noun* See **fool.**

moronic *adjective* See **foolish.**

morose *adjective* See **glum.**

morsel *noun* See **bit[1], bite, delicacy.**

mortal *adjective* See **deadly, earthly, human.**

mortal *noun* See **human being.**

mortgage *verb* See **pawn[1].**

mortification *noun* See **degradation.**

mortify *verb* See **embarrass, humble.**

mosey *verb* See **stroll.**

mossback *noun* See **reactionary, square.**

mossbacked *adjective* See **reactionary.**

most *adverb* See **very.**

most *adjective* See **best.**

mother *noun* See **ancestor, origin.**

motif *noun* See **figure.**

motion *noun* The act or process of moving : move, movement, stir[1]. See MOVE in Index. — See also **gesture.**

motion *verb* See **gesture.**

motionless *adjective* Not moving : immobile, stationary, still, stockstill, unmoving. See MOVE in Index.

motivate *verb* See **encourage, provoke.**

motivation *noun* See **cause, encouragement, stimulus.**

motive *noun* See **cause, figure.**

motley *adjective* See **multicolor, various.**

motor *verb* See **drive.**

motorist *noun* See **driver.**

mottle *verb* See **speckle.**

motto *noun* See **cry, proverb.**

moue *noun* See **face.**

mound *noun* See **heap.**

  mound *verb* See **heap.**

mount *verb* See **ascend, increase, rise.**

mountain *noun* See **heap.**

mountainous *adjective* See **giant.**

mountebank *noun* See **fake.**

mourn *verb* See **grieve.**

mournful *adjective* See **sorrowful.**

mournfulness *noun* See **gloom.**

mouse *noun* See **black eye.**

  mouse *verb* See **sneak.**

mouth *noun* The opening in the body through which food is ingested : *Slang:* gob[2], puss, trap. See MOUTH in Index. — See also **face, hole, speaker.**

  mouth *verb* See **grimace, rant.**

mouthful *noun* See **bit[1].**

mouthpiece *noun* See **speaker.**

movable also **moveable** *adjective* See **mobile.**

  movable also **moveable** *noun* See **effect, furnishing.**

move *verb* **1.** To go or cause to go from one place to another : maneuver, remove, shift, transfer. See MOVE in Index. **2.** To change one's residence or place of business, for example : relocate, remove, transfer. See MOVE in Index. — See also **affect[1], come, disturb, drive, provoke, stir[1].**

  move *noun* An action calculated to achieve an end : maneuver, measure (often used in plural), procedure, step, tactic. See ACTION in Index. — See also **displacement, motion, movement, removal.**

movement *noun* A calculated change in position : evolution, maneuver, move, turn. See MOVE in Index. — See also **displacement, drive, motion.**

moving *adjective* See **affecting, mobile.**

moxie *noun* See **courage.**

Mrs. Grundy *noun* See **prude.**

much *noun* See **heap.**

  much *adverb* See **considerably.**

mucilaginous *adjective* See **viscous.**

muck *noun* See **filth, slime.**

  muck *verb* See **muddy.**

  muck up *verb* See **botch.**

muckamuck *noun* See **dignitary.**

mucky *adjective* See **slimy.**

mucro *noun* See **point.**

mucronate *adjective* See **pointed.**

mucronation *noun* See **point.**

mud *verb* See **muddy.**

muddle *verb* To proceed or perform in an unsteady, faltering manner : blunder, bumble[1], bungle, flounder, fudge, fumble, limp, shuffle, stagger, stumble. See THRIVE in Index. — See also **botch, confuse, disorder.**

  muddle through *verb* See **manage.**

  muddle *noun* See **botch, daze, disorder.**

muddle-headed *adjective* See **confused.**

muddy *adjective* Covered or soiled with mud : miry. See CLEAN in Index. — See also **dull, turbid.**

  muddy *verb* To soil with mud : bemire, mire, muck (up), mud, slush. See CLEAN in Index.

mudslinging *noun* See **smear.**

muff *verb* See **botch.**

  muff *noun* See **blunder.**

muffle *verb* To decrease or dull the sound of : dampen, deaden, mute, stifle. See INCREASE, SOUNDS in Index. — See also **repress.**

mug *noun* See **dupe, face, tough.**
  mug *verb* See **grimace.**
muggy *adjective* See **sticky.**
mulct *verb* See **cheat, fine².**
  mulct *noun* See **fine².**
muliebrity *noun* See **femininity.**
mulish *adjective* See **obstinate.**
mulishness *noun* See **obstinacy.**
mull *verb* See **ponder.**
multicolor *adjective* Having many
  different colors : motley, multicolored, polychromatic, polychrome,
  polychromic, polychromous, varicolored, variegated, versicolor, versicolored. See COLORS in Index.
multicolored *adjective* See
  multicolor.
multifaceted *adjective* See
  versatile.
multifarious *adjective* See **various.**
multifariousness *noun* See **variety.**
multiform *adjective* See **various.**
multiformity *noun* See **variety.**
multiplication *noun* See **buildup,**
  increase, reproduction.
multiplicity *noun* See **heap, variety.**
multiply *verb* See **increase,**
  reproduce.
multitude *noun* See **crowd.**
multitudinous *adjective* See **many.**
mum *adjective* See **speechless.**
mumble *verb* See **mutter.**
  mumble *noun* See **murmur.**
mumbo jumbo *noun* See **gibberish.**
mummify *verb* See **dry up** at **dry.**
munch *verb* See **chew.**
mundane *adjective* See **earthly.**
municipal *adjective* See **city.**
municipality *noun* See **city.**
munificence *noun* See **generosity.**
munificent *adjective* See **generous.**
murder *verb* To take the life of (a
  person or persons) unlawfully :
  destroy, finish (off), kill¹, liquidate,
  slay. *Informal:* put away. *Slang:*
  bump off, do in, knock off, off, rub

out, waste, wipe out, zap. See HELP
in Index.
  murder *noun* The crime of mur-
  dering someone : blood, homicide,
  killing. *Slang:* hit. See HELP in
  Index.
murderer *noun* One who murders
  another : butcher, cutthroat, homicide, killer, manslayer, massacrer,
  murderess, slaughterer, slayer, triggerman. See HELP in Index.
murderess *noun* See **murderer.**
murderous *adjective* Eager for
  bloodshed : bloodthirsty, bloody,
  bloody-minded, cutthroat, homicidal, sanguinary, sanguineous,
  slaughterous. See HELP in Index.
murk also **mirk** *noun* See **haze.**
murkiness *noun* See **dark.**
murky also **mirky** *adjective* See
  dark, dull, turbid.
murmur *noun* A low, indistinct, and
  often continuous sound : mumble,
  sigh, sough, susurration, susurrus,
  whisper. See SOUNDS in Index.
  – See also **mutter.**
  murmur *verb* To make a low, continuous, and indistinct sound :
  sigh, sough, whisper. See SOUNDS
  in Index. — See also **mutter.**
murmurer *noun* See **grouch.**
muscle *noun* *Informal.* Effective
  means of influencing, compelling, or
  punishing : force, power, weight.
  Informal: clout. See OVER, STRONG in
  Index. — See also **strength.**
  muscle *verb* *Informal.* To force
  one's way into a place or situation :
  push, shove. See ENTER, PUSH in
  Index.
muscular *adjective* Characterized
  by marked muscular development;
  powerfully built : athletic, brawny,
  burly, husky², robust, sinewy,
  sturdy. See STRONG in Index.
muscularity *noun* See **brawn.**
muse¹ *verb* See **dream, ponder.**

muse² *noun* See **poet, trance.**

mush *verb* See **crush.**

  mush *noun* See **sentimentality.**

mushiness *noun* See **sentimentality.**

mushroom *verb* See **explode.**

mushy *adjective* See **sentimental, soft.**

musical *adjective* See **harmonious, melodious.**

musician *noun* See **player.**

muskeg *noun* See **swamp.**

muss *verb* See **tousle.**

  muss *noun* See **disorder.**

mussy *adjective* See **messy.**

must *verb* To be required or compelled to do : **need.** *Idioms:* have got to, have to, must needs. See NECESSARY in Index.

  must *noun* See **condition, duty.**

muster *verb* See **assemble, call, mobilize.**

  muster in *verb* See **join.**

  muster out *verb* See **discharge.**

  muster *noun* See **assembly.**

musty *adjective* See **moldy, trite.**

mutable *adjective* See **changeable.**

mutate *verb* See **change, convert.**

mutation *noun* See **change.**

mute *adjective* See **dumb, speechless.**

  mute *verb* See **moderate, muffle.**

muteness *noun* See **silence.**

mutilate *verb* See **cripple.**

mutineer *noun* See **rebel.**

mutinous *adjective* See **rebellious.**

mutiny *noun* See **rebellion.**

  mutiny *verb* See **rebel.**

mutter *verb* **1.** To speak or utter indistinctly, as by lowering the voice or partially closing the mouth : mumble, murmur, whisper. See SOUNDS in Index. **2.** To complain in low indistinct tones : grumble, grunt, murmur. See HAPPY, SOUNDS in Index.

  mutter *noun* A low indistinct utterance of complaint : grumble, grunt, murmur. See HAPPY, SOUNDS in Index.

mutterer *noun* See **grouch.**

mutual *adjective* Having the same relationship each to the other : reciprocal, reciprocative. See CONNECT in Index. — See also **common.**

muzzle *noun* See **face.**

myriad *adjective* See **many.**

mysterious *adjective* Difficult to explain or understand : arcane, cabalistic, cryptic, enigmatic, mystic, mystical, mystifying, occult, puzzling. See EXPLAIN, KNOWLEDGE in Index.

mystery *noun* Anything that arouses curiosity or perplexes because it is unexplained, inexplicable, or secret : conundrum, enigma, perplexity, puzzle, puzzler, riddle. See SHOW in Index.

mystic *adjective* See **mysterious.**

mystical *adjective* See **mysterious.**

mystification *noun* See **daze.**

mystify *verb* See **confuse.**

mystifying *adjective* See **mysterious.**

myth *noun* **1.** A traditional story or tale that has no proven factual basis : fable, legend. See BELIEF, REAL, RELIGION in Index. **2.** Any fictitious idea accepted as part of an ideology by an uncritical group; a received idea : creation, fantasy, fiction, figment, invention. See BELIEF, REAL in Index. — See also **lore.**

mythic *adjective* See **mythical.**

mythical *adjective* Of or existing only in myths : fabulous, legendary, mythic, mythologic, mythological. See REAL in Index.

mythologic *adjective* See **mythical.**

mythological *adjective* See **mythical.**

mythology *noun* See **lore.**

mythos *noun* See **lore.**

N

nab *verb* See **arrest, catch.**

nabob *noun* See **dignitary.**

nag *verb* To scold or find fault with constantly : carp at, fuss at, peck at, pick on. *Informal:* henpeck. See PRAISE in Index.

nagging *adjective* See **painful.**

nail *verb* See **take.**

naive or **naïve** also **naif** or **naïf** *adjective* See **artless, easy.**
   naive or **naïve** also **naif** or **naïf** *noun* See **innocent.**

naked *adjective* See **bare, nude.**

nakedness *noun* See **nudity.**

namby-pamby *adjective* See **insipid.**

name *noun* The word or words by which one is called and identified : appellation, appellative, cognomen, denomination, designation, epithet, nickname, style, tag, title. *Slang:* handle, moniker. See SPECIFIC, WORDS in Index. — See also **celebrity, reputation.**
   name *verb* **1.** To give a name or title to : baptize, call, christen, denominate, designate, dub, entitle, style, term, title. See SPECIFIC, WORDS in Index. **2.** To refer to by name : cite, instance, mention, specify. See SPECIFIC in Index. — See also **appoint, call.**

nameless *adjective* See **anonymous, obscure.**

namelessness *noun* See **obscurity.**

namely *adverb* That is to say : scilicet, specifically, videlicet. *Idiom:* to wit. See SPECIFIC in Index.

nap *noun* A brief sleep : catnap, doze, siesta, snooze. See AWARENESS in Index.
   nap *verb* To sleep for a brief period : catnap, doze (off), nod (off),

siesta, snooze. *Idiom:* catch (or grab or take) forty winks. See AWARENESS in Index.

narcissism also **narcism** *noun* See **egotism.**

narcissist *noun* See **egotist.**

narcissistic *adjective* See **egotistic, vain.**

narcotic *noun* See **drug, soporific.**
   narcotic *adjective* See **sleepy.**

narcotize *verb* See **drug.**

narrate *verb* See **describe.**

narration *noun* See **story.**

narrative *noun* See **story.**

narrow *adjective* Not broad or elevated in scope or understanding : limited, little, narrow-minded, petty, small, small-minded. See LIMITED, WIDE in Index. — See also **local, tight.**
   narrow *verb* See **constrict.**

narrow-minded *adjective* See **intolerant, local, narrow.**

nascence *noun* See **birth.**

nascency *noun* See **birth.**

nastiness *noun* See **malevolence.**

nasty *adjective* See **filthy, ill-tempered, malevolent, obscene, offensive.**

nation *noun* See **state.**

national *noun* See **citizen.**
   national *adjective* See **domestic, public.**

nationalize *verb* See **socialize.**

native *adjective* See **constitutional, crude, domestic, indigenous, innate, wild.**

natural *adjective* Produced by nature; not artificial or manmade : organic, unadulterated. *Idiom:* pure as the driven snow. See CULTURE in Index. — See also **artless, constitutional, easygoing, genuine, illegitimate, realistic, rustic, wild.**

naturalistic *adjective* See **realistic.**

naturally *adverb* See **usually.**

naturalness *noun* See **ease.**

nature *noun* See **character, disposition, essence, kind²**, **universe**.

naughtiness *noun* See **misbehavior**.

naughty *adjective* Misbehaving, often in a troublesome way : bad, ill-behaved. See CONTROL, GOOD in Index. — See also **improper**.

nausea *noun* See **disgust**.

nauseate *verb* See **disgust**.

nauseating *adjective* See **offensive**.

nautical *adjective* Of or relating to sea navigation : marine, maritime, navigational. See SEA in Index.

navigable *adjective* See **passable**.

navigate *verb* See **maneuver**.

navigational *adjective* See **nautical**.

navigator *noun* See **sailor**.

nay *noun* See **no**.

nay *adverb* See **no**.

near *adjective* See **close**.

near *verb* See **approach**.

near *adverb* See **close**.

nearby *adjective* See **close, convenient**.

nearby *adverb* See **close**.

nearly *adverb* See **approximately**.

nearness *noun* See **approach**.

neat *adjective* 1. In good order or clean condition : orderly, shipshape, snug, spick-and-span, spruce, taut, tidy, trig, trim, well-groomed. *Chiefly British:* tight. *Idiom:* neat as a pin. See CLEAN, ORDER in Index. 2. Well done or executed : adroit, clean, deft, skillful. See ABILITY, GOOD in Index. — See also **marvelous, straight**.

neaten *verb* See **tidy**.

nebbish *noun* See **nonentity**.

nebulous *adjective* See **ambiguous**.

nebulousness *noun* See **vagueness**.

necessary *adjective* See **essential, required**.

necessitate *verb* See **demand**.

necessitous *adjective* See **poor**.

necessity *noun* See **cause, condition, need**.

neck *verb* *Informal.* To engage in kissing, caressing, and other amorous behavior : fool around, pet¹, spoon. *Slang:* make out. See SEX in Index.

neck and neck *adjective* See **close**.

neck of the woods *noun* See **area**.

need *noun* A condition in which something necessary or desirable is required or wanted : exigence, exigency, necessity. See NECESSARY in Index. — See also **condition, demand, duty, poverty**.

need *verb* See **lack, must**.

needful *adjective* See **essential**.

neediness *noun* See **poverty**.

needle *noun* See **prick**.

needle *verb* See **bait**.

needless *adjective* See **unnecessary**.

needy *adjective* See **poor**.

ne'er-do-well *noun* See **wastrel**.

nefarious *adjective* See **filthy**.

negate *verb* See **abolish, cancel, deny**.

negation *noun* See **abolition, denial**.

negative *adjective* See **unfavorable**.

negative *verb* See **deny, veto**.

neglect *verb* 1. To fail to care for or give proper attention to : disregard, ignore, slight. See CARE FOR, CONCERN in Index. 2. To avoid the fulfillment of : disregard, shirk, slack. *Idiom:* let slide. See DO in Index. — See also **fail, ignore**.

neglect *noun* An act or instance of neglecting : disregard, oversight, slight. See CARE FOR, CONCERN in Index. — See also **failure**.

neglectful *adjective* See **negligent**.

negligence *noun* The state or quality of being negligent : laxity, laxness, remissness, slackness. See CAREFUL in Index.

negligent *adjective* Guilty of neglect; lacking due care or concern : derelict, lax, neglectful, remiss, slack. See CAREFUL in Index.

negligibility *noun* See **pettiness.**

negligible *adjective* See **petty, remote.**

negligibleness *noun* See **pettiness.**

negotiable *adjective* See **passable.**

negotiate *verb* See **arrange, clear, haggle.**

negotiation *noun* See **talk.**

neighbor *verb* See **adjoin.**

neighborhood *noun* **1.** A rather small part of a geographic unit considered in regard to its inhabitants or distinctive characteristics : area, district, quarter (often uppercase). See TERRITORY in Index. **2.** *Informal.* Approximate size or amount : range, vicinity. See NEAR in Index. — See also **area, environment, locality.**

neighborly *adjective* See **friendly.**

nemesis *noun* See **enemy.**

neonate *noun* See **baby.**

neophyte *noun* See **beginner.**

nerd also **nurd** *noun* See **drip, fool.**

nerve *noun* See **courage, impudence.**

nerve *verb* See **encourage.**

nerviness *noun* See **impudence.**

nervous *adjective* See **anxious, edgy.**

nervousness *noun* See **anxiety.**

nervy *adjective* See **impudent.**

nescience *noun* See **ignorance.**

nescient *adjective* See **ignorant.**

nest egg *noun* See **hoard.**

nestle *verb* See **snuggle.**

net[1] *verb* See **take.**

net *noun* See **web.**

net[2] *verb* See **return.**

nethermost *adjective* See **bottom.**

netting *noun* See **web.**

nettle *verb* See **annoy.**

nettlesome *adjective* See **thorny, vexatious.**

network *noun* See **web.**

neuter *verb* See **sterilize.**

neuter *adjective* See **neutral.**

neutral *adjective* **1.** Not inclining toward or actively taking either side in a matter under dispute : impartial, neuter, nonaligned, nonpartisan, unbiased, uncommitted, uninvolved, unprejudiced. *Idiom:* on the fence. See FAIR in Index. **2.** Without definite or distinctive characteristics : bland, colorless, indistinctive. See STRONG in Index. **3.** Feeling or showing no strong emotional involvement : detached, disinterested, dispassionate, impersonal, indifferent. See FEELINGS in Index.

neutralize *verb* See **cancel, compensate.**

never-ending *adjective* See **endless.**

nevertheless *adverb* See **still.**

new *adjective* Not the same as what was previously known or done : different, fresh, innovative, inventive, newfangled, novel, original, unfamiliar, unprecedented. See NEW in Index. — See also **additional, fresh, present[1].**

newborn *noun* See **baby.**

newcomer *noun* See **foreigner.**

newfangled *adjective* See **new.**

newfangledness *noun* See **novelty.**

newly *adverb* See **just.**

newness *noun* See **novelty.**

news *noun* New information, especially about recent events and happenings : advice (often used in plural), intelligence, tiding (often used in plural), word. *Informal:* scoop. See KNOWLEDGE, WORDS in Index. — See also **event.**

newsmonger *noun* See **gossip.**

next *adjective* See **adjoining, following.**

next adverb See **later.**

nexus noun See **bond.**

Niagara noun See **flood.**

nice adjective Very difficult to please : choosy, dainty, exacting, fastidious, finical, finicky, fussy, meticulous, particular, persnickety, squeamish. Informal: picky. See ACCEPT in Index. — See also **agreeable, chaste, correct, delicate, fine¹, good.**

niche noun See **place.**

nick verb See **skin.**

nickname noun See **name.**

nictate verb See **blink.**

nictation noun See **blink.**

nictitate verb See **blink.**

nictitation noun See **blink.**

nifty adjective See **marvelous.**

niggard noun See **miser.**

niggard adjective See **stingy.**

niggardly adjective See **stingy.**

niggle verb See **quibble.**

niggler noun See **critic.**

niggling adjective See **petty.**

nigh adverb See **close.**

nigh adjective See **close.**

night noun The period of time between sunset and sunrise : nighttime. See LIGHT in Index.

night adjective See **nightly.**

nightfall noun See **evening.**

nightly adjective Of or occurring during the night : night, nocturnal. See LIGHT in Index.

nighttime noun See **night.**

nihility noun See **nothingness.**

nil noun See **nothing.**

nimble adjective Moving or performing quickly, lightly, and easily : agile, brisk, facile, quick, spry. See ABILITY in Index. — See also **dexterous.**

nimbleness noun See **agility.**

nincompoop noun See **fool.**

ninny noun See **fool.**

nip¹ verb See **blast, rush, snap, steal.**

nip² noun See **drop.**

nip verb See **drink.**

nip and tuck adjective See **close.**

nippy adjective See **cold.**

nitpick verb See **quibble.**

nitpicker noun See **critic.**

nitwit noun See **fool.**

nix verb See **decline, veto.**

nix noun See **nothing.**

nix adverb See **no.**

no noun 1. A negative response : nay, refusal, rejection. See AFFIRM in Index. 2. A negative vote or voter : nay. See AFFIRM in Index.

no adverb Not so : nay, nix. Informal: nope. Idiom: nothing doing. See AFFIRM in Index.

no-account adjective See **worthless.**

nobility noun Noble rank or status by birth : birth, blood, blue blood, noblesse. See KIN, OVER in Index. — See also **society.**

noble adjective Of high birth or social position : aristocratic, blue-blooded, elite, highborn, highbred, patrician, thoroughbred, upper-class, wellborn. Informal: upper-crust. See OVER in Index. — See also **elevated, grand.**

noblesse noun See **nobility.**

nobody pronoun No person : none, no one. See ABSENCE in Index.

nobody noun See **nonentity.**

nocturnal adjective See **nightly.**

nod noun See **acceptance, bow¹.**

nod verb See **assent, nap.**

nodding adjective See **sleepy.**

noddle noun See **head.**

noggin noun See **head.**

no-good noun See **wastrel.**

no-good adjective See **worthless.**

noise noun Sounds or a sound, especially when loud, confused, or disagreeable : babel, clamor, din, hubbub, hullabaloo, pandemonium, racket, rumpus, tumult, uproar. See SOUNDS in Index. — See also **sound**[1].

noise verb See **advertise, gossip**.

noiseless adjective See **silent**.

noiselessness noun See **silence**.

noisome adjective See **smelly**.

nomadic adjective Leading the life of a person without a fixed domicile; moving from place to place : itinerant, peripatetic, vagabond, vagrant. See MOVE in Index.

nominate verb See **appoint**.

nomination noun See **appointment**.

nominee noun See **appointee**.

nonage noun See **minority**.

nonaligned adjective See **neutral**.

nonappearance noun See **absence**.

nonattendance noun See **absence**.

nonbeliever noun See **skeptic**.

nonchalance noun See **balance**.

nonchalant adjective See **cool**.

noncommittal adjective See **reserved**.

noncompliance noun See **disobedience**.

noncompliant adjective See **disobedient**.

non compos mentis adjective See **insane**.

nonconformist noun See **separatist**.

none pronoun See **nobody**.

nonentity noun A totally insignificant person : cipher, nebbish, nobody, nothing. Informal: pipsqueak, zero. Slang: shrimp, zilch. See IMPORTANT in Index.

nonessential adjective See **unnecessary**.

nonesuch noun See **nonpareil**.

nonetheless adverb See **still**.

nonexistence noun See **nothingness**.

nonfeasance noun See **failure**.

no-nonsense adjective See **serious**.

nonpareil noun A person or thing so excellent as to have no equal or match : nonesuch, paragon, phoenix. See GOOD in Index.

nonpareil adjective See **unique**.

nonpartisan adjective See **fair, neutral**.

nonpartisanship noun See **fairness**.

nonphysical adjective See **immaterial**.

nonplus verb To make incapable of finding something to think, do, or say : confound. Informal: flummox, stick, stump, throw. Slang: beat. Idiom: put someone at a loss. See AFFECT, KNOWLEDGE in Index.

nonprofessional noun See **amateur**.

nonprofessional adjective See **amateurish**.

nonresistant adjective See **passive**.

nonsense noun Something that does not have or make sense : balderdash, blather, bunkum, claptrap, drivel, garbage, idiocy, piffle, poppycock, rigmarole, rubbish, tomfoolery, trash, twaddle. Informal: tommyrot. Slang: applesauce, baloney, bilge, bull[1], bunk[2], crap, hooey, malarkey. See KNOWLEDGE in Index. — See also **babble, foolishness, trivia**.

nonsensical adjective See **foolish**.

nonstop adjective See **continual**.

noodle noun See **head**.

no one pronoun See **nobody**.

nope adverb See **no**.

norm noun See **average, usual**.

normal adjective See **common**.

normalcy noun See **usualness**.

normality noun See **usualness**.

normally adverb See **usually**.

nose noun The structure on the human face that contains the nostrils and organs of smell and forms the beginning of the respiratory tract : proboscis. *Informal:* beak, snoot. *Slang:* nozzle, schnoz, schnozzle, snout. See BODY, CONVEX in Index. — See also **discernment, smell.**

nose *verb* See **smell, snoop.**

nose out *verb* See **run down** at **run.**

nosedive *noun* See **fall, plunge.**

nose-dive *verb* See **fall.**

nosegay *noun* See **bouquet.**

nosiness *noun* See **curiosity.**

nostrum *noun* See **cure.**

nosy or **nosey** *adjective* See **curious.**

notability *noun* See **dignitary, eminence.**

notable *adjective* See **eminent.**

notable *noun* See **celebrity, dignitary.**

notably *adverb* See **very.**

notation *noun* See **note.**

notch *verb* See **score.**

notch *noun* See **degree.**

note *noun* A brief record written as an aid to the memory : memorandum, notation. *Informal:* memo. See WORDS in Index. — See also **comment, commentary, eminence, letter, melody, notice, sign.**

note *verb* See **comment, notice.**

noted *adjective* See **eminent.**

nothing *noun* No thing; not anything : nil, null. *Informal:* zero. *Slang:* nix, zilch. *Archaic:* aught. See ABSENCE in Index. — See also **nonentity, nothingness.**

nothing *adjective* See **worthless.**

nothingness *noun* **1.** The condition of not existing : nihility, nonexistence, nothing. See ABSENCE in Index. **2.** Empty, unfilled space : barrenness, emptiness, vacancy, vacuity, vacuum, void. See FULL in Index.

notice *noun* The act of noting,

observing, or taking into account : attention, cognizance, espial, heed, mark, note, observance, observation, regard, remark. See KNOWLEDGE, SEE in Index. — See also **announcement, review, sign.**

notice *verb* To perceive with a special effort of the senses or the mind : descry, detect, discern, distinguish, mark, mind, note, observe, remark, see. See KNOWLEDGE, SEE in Index.

noticeable *adjective* Readily attracting notice : arresting, bold, conspicuous, eye-catching, marked, observable, outstanding, pointed, prominent, pronounced, remarkable, salient, signal, striking. *Idiom:* sticking out like a sore thumb. See SEE in Index. — See also **apparent, perceptible.**

notify *verb* See **inform.**

notion *noun* See **belief, fancy, idea.**

notional *adjective* See **imaginary.**

notoriety *noun* Unfavorable, usually unsavory renown : infamousness, infamy, notoriousness. See KNOWLEDGE in Index. — See also **fame.**

notorious *adjective* Known widely and unfavorably : common, infamous. See KNOWLEDGE in Index. — See also **famous.**

notoriousness *noun* See **notoriety.**

nourish *verb* To sustain (a living organism) with food : feed. See INGESTION in Index. — See also **bear, nurse.**

nourishing *adjective* See **nutritious.**

nourishment *noun* See **food.**

novel *adjective* See **new, unusual.**

novelty *noun* **1.** The quality of being novel : freshness, innovativeness, newfangledness, newness, originality. See NEW in Index. **2.** A new and unusual thing : innovation. See

NEW in Index. **3.** A small showy article : bauble, bibelot, gewgaw, gimcrack, knickknack, toy, trifle, trinket, whatnot. See THING in Index.

novice *noun* An entrant who has not yet taken the final vows of a religious order : novitiate. See RELIGION in Index. — See also **beginner.**

novitiate also **noviciate** *noun* See **beginner, novice.**

now *noun* The current time : nowadays, present[1], today. See TIME in Index.

now *adjective* See **present[1].**

now *adverb* **1.** At the present; these days : nowadays, today. See TIME in Index. **2.** At this moment : actually, currently. *Idiom:* even (or just or right) now. See TIME in Index. **3.** At times : sometimes. See TIME in Index. — See also **directly.**

nowadays *noun* See **now.**

nowadays *adverb* See **now.**

noxious *adjective* See **virulent.**

nozzle *noun* See **nose.**

nuance *noun* See **shade.**

nub *noun* See **bump, heart.**

nucleus *noun* See **germ.**

nude *adjective* Not wearing any clothes : au naturel, bare, naked, unclad. *Chiefly British:* starkers. *Idioms:* in one's birthday suit, in the altogether (or buff or raw), naked as a jaybird, stark naked, without a stitch. See PUT ON, SHOW in Index. — See also **bare.**

nudeness *noun* See **nudity.**

nudge *verb* See **dig.**

nudge *noun* See **dig.**

nudity *noun* The state of being without clothes : bareness, nakedness, nudeness, undress. See PUT ON, SHOW in Index.

nugatory *adjective* See **petty.**

nugget *noun* See **lump[1].**

nuisance *noun* See **annoyance.**

null *noun* See **nothing.**

nullification *noun* See **abolition.**

nullify *verb* See **abolish, cancel.**

numb *verb* See **deaden, paralyze.**

numb *adjective* See **dead, dull.**

number *verb* See **amount, count.**

number *noun* See **figure.**

number one *adjective* See **primary.**

number one *noun* See **leader.**

numerate *verb* See **count, enumerate.**

numeration *noun* See **count.**

numerous *adjective* See **many.**

numinous *adjective* See **spiritual.**

numskull also **numbskull** *noun* See **dullard.**

nuptial *noun* See **wedding.**

nuptial *adjective* See **marital.**

nurse *verb* To promote and sustain the development of : cultivate, foster, nourish, nurture. See CARE FOR in Index. — See also **bear.**

nursling *noun* See **baby.**

nurture *verb* See **nurse.**

nurture *noun* See **food.**

nut *noun* See **crackpot, enthusiast, head.**

nutrient *adjective* See **nutritious.**

nutriment *noun* See **food.**

nutrition *noun* See **food.**

nutritional *adjective* See **nutritive.**

nutritious *adjective* Providing nourishment : alimentary, nourishing, nutrient, nutritive. See INGESTION in Index.

nutritive *adjective* Of or relating to food or nutrition : alimentary, nutritional. See INGESTION in Index. — See also **nutritious.**

nuts *adjective* See **enthusiastic, insane.**

nutty *adjective* See **insane.**

nuzzle *verb* See **snuggle.**

O

oaf *noun* See **lump¹**.

oath *noun* See **swearword**.

obduracy *noun* See **stubbornness**.

obdurate *adjective* See **cold-blooded, stubborn**.

obdurateness *noun* See **stubbornness**.

obedience *noun* **1.** The quality or state of willingly carrying out the wishes of others : acquiescence, amenability, amenableness, compliance, compliancy, deference, submission, submissiveness, tractability, tractableness. See RESIST in Index. **2.** An act of willingly carrying out the wishes of others : compliance, observance. See RESIST in Index.

obedient *adjective* Willing to carry out the wishes of others : amenable, biddable, compliant, conformable, docile, submissive, supple, tractable. See RESIST in Index.

obeisance *noun* See **bow¹, honor**.

obeisant *adjective* See **deferential**.

obese *adjective* See **fat**.

obey *verb* See **follow**.

obfuscate *verb* See **obscure**.

obiter dictum *noun* See **comment**.

object *noun* Something having material existence : article, item, thing. See THING in Index. — See also **body, intention, thing**.

object *verb* To express opposition, often by argument : challenge, demur, except, expostulate, inveigh, protest, remonstrate. *Informal:* kick, squawk. *Idioms:* set up a squawk, take exception. See SUPPORT in Index. — See also **care, disapprove**.

objectification *noun* See **embodiment**.

objectify *verb* See **embody**.

objection *noun* The act of expressing strong or reasoned opposition : challenge, demur, exception, expostulation, protest, protestation, remonstrance, remonstration, squawk. *Slang:* kick. See SUPPORT in Index.

objectionable *adjective* Arousing disapproval : exceptionable, ill-favored, inadmissible, unacceptable, undesirable, unwanted, unwelcome. See LIKE in Index.

objective *noun* See **intention**.

objective *adjective* See **fair, physical, real, realistic**.

objectiveness *noun* See **fairness**.

objectivity *noun* See **fairness**.

oblation *noun* See **benevolence, offering**.

obligate *verb* See **commit, force**.

obligated *adjective* See **obliged**.

obligation *noun* See **debt, duty**.

obligatory *adjective* See **required**.

oblige *verb* To perform a service or a courteous act for : accommodate, favor. See HELP in Index. — See also **force**.

obliged *adjective* Owing something, such as gratitude or appreciation, to another : beholden, bound³, indebted, obligated. *Archaic:* bounden. *Idiom:* under obligation. See OBLIGATION in Index.

obliging *adjective* Ready to do favors for another : accommodating, agreeable, complaisant, indulgent. See HELP, WILLING in Index.

oblique *adjective* See **bias, indirect**.

obliterate *verb* See **annihilate, cancel**.

obliteration *noun* See **annihilation, erasure**.

oblivion *noun* See **escape**.

oblivious *adjective* See **forgetful, ignorant**.

obliviousness *noun* See **escape, ignorance.**

obloquy *noun* See **disgrace, vituperation.**

obnoxious *adjective* See **filthy.**

obscene *adjective* Offensive to accepted standards of decency : barnyard, bawdy, broad, coarse, dirty, Fescennine, filthy, foul, gross, lewd, nasty, profane, ribald, scatologic, scatological, scurrilous, smutty, vulgar. *Slang:* raunchy. See DECENT in Index. — See also **outrageous.**

obscenity *noun* **1.** The quality or state of being obscene : bawdiness, coarseness, dirtiness, filthiness, foulness, grossness, lewdness, profaneness, profanity, scurrility, scurrilousness, smuttiness, vulgarity, vulgarness. *Slang:* raunch, raunchiness. See DECENT in Index. **2.** Something that is offensive to accepted standards of decency : bawdry, dirt, filth, profanity, ribaldry, scatology, smut, vulgarity. *Slang:* raunch. See DECENT in Index.

obscure *verb* **1.** To make dim or indistinct : becloud, bedim, befog, blear, blur, cloud, dim, dull, eclipse, fog, gloom, mist, obfuscate, overcast, overshadow, shadow. See CLEAR in Index. **2.** To conceal in obscurity : hide[1], submerge. See SHOW in Index. — See also **block.**

obscure *adjective* Not known or not widely known by name : nameless, unheard-of, unknown. See KNOWLEDGE in Index. — See also **ambiguous, dark, inconspicuous, remote, unclear.**

obscured *adjective* See **ulterior.**

obscureness *noun* See **dark, vagueness.**

obscurity *noun* The quality or state of being obscure : anonymity, namelessness. See KNOWLEDGE in Index. — See also **dark, vagueness.**

obsequious *adjective* See **servile.**

observable *adjective* See **apparent, noticeable, perceptible.**

observance *noun* See **celebration, ceremony, notice, obedience, watch.**

observant *adjective* See **alert, careful, mindful.**

observation *noun* See **comment, notice, watch.**

observatory *noun* See **lookout.**

observe *verb* See **celebrate, comment, follow, notice, watch.**

observer *noun* See **watcher.**

obsess *verb* See **haunt, possess.**

obsession *noun* See **thing.**

obsolesce *verb* To make or become obsolete : obsolete, outdate, superannuate. See NEW, USED in Index.

obsolete *adjective* No longer in use : superseded. *Idioms:* in mothballs, on the shelf. See NEW, USED in Index.

obsolete *verb* See **obsolesce.**

obsolete *noun* See **obsoletism.**

obsoleteness *noun* The quality or state of being obsolete : desuetude, disuse, obsoletism. See NEW, USED in Index.

obsoletism *noun* Something that is obsolete : obsolete. See NEW, USED in Index. — See also **obsoleteness.**

obstacle *noun* See **bar.**

obstinacy *noun* The quality or state of being stubbornly unyielding : bullheadedness, doggedness, hardheadedness, mulishness, obstinateness, pertinaciousness, pertinacity, perverseness, perversity, pigheadedness, tenaciousness, tenacity, willfulness. See RESIST in Index. — See also **unruliness.**

obstinate *adjective* Tenaciously unwilling to yield : bullheaded, dogged, hardheaded, headstrong, mulish, pertinacious, perverse, pigheaded, stiff-necked, tenacious, will-

ful. See RESIST in Index. — See also
stubborn, unruly.

obstinateness *noun* See **obstinacy,
unruliness.**

obstreperous *adjective* See **unruly,
vociferous.**

obstreperousness *noun* See
unruliness.

obstruct *verb* To stop or prevent
passage of : bar, block, dam,
impede. *Idiom:* be (or stand) in the
way of. See OPEN in Index. — See
also **block, hinder.**

obstruction *noun* See **bar.**

obtain *verb* See **get.**

obtainable *adjective* See **available.**

obtrude *verb* See **intrude.**

obtrusion *noun* See **meddling,
trespass.**

obtrusive *adjective* See **meddling.**

obtuse *adjective* See **stupid.**

obviate *verb* See **prevent.**

obviation *noun* See **prevention.**

obvious *adjective* See **apparent,
unsubtle.**

occasion *noun* The general point at
which an event occurs : time.
Idiom: point in time. See TIME in
Index. — See also **cause, circumstance, event, opportunity, party.**
occasion *verb* See **call for** at **call,
cause.**

occasional *adjective* See **infrequent, intermittent.**

occasionally *adverb* See **infrequently, intermittently.**

occult *verb* See **hide**[1].
occult *adjective* See **mysterious.**

occupancy *noun* See **tenure.**

occupation *noun* See **business,
tenure.**

occupied *adjective* See **busy.**

occupy *verb* To seize and move into
by force : take over. See ATTACK in
Index. — See also **busy, engage,
inhabit, tie up** at **tie.**

occur *verb* To enter a person's
mind : hit, strike. *Idiom:* cross
one's mind. See HAPPEN in Index.
— See also **come.**

occurrence *noun* See **circumstance,
event, presence.**

oceanic *adjective* See **marine.**

odd *adjective* See **accidental, eccentric, funny, quaint.**

oddball *noun* See **character.**

oddity *noun* See **character.**

oddment *noun* See **odds and ends.**

odds *noun* See **advantage, chance.**

odds and ends *noun* Articles too
small or numerous to be specified :
etcetera (used in plural), oddment
(used in plural), sundries. See THING
in Index.

odious *adjective* See **filthy.**

odium *noun* See **disgrace.**

odor *noun* See **smell.**

off *adjective* See **erroneous, insane,
slow.**
off *verb* See **murder.**

offbeat *adjective* See **unusual.**

off-color *adjective* See **racy, sickly.**

offend *verb* **1.** To be very disagreeable to : displease. *Slang:* turn off.
Idioms: give offense to, not set right
(or well) with. See LIKE, PAIN in
Index. **2.** To violate a moral or
divine law : err, sin, transgress,
trespass. See RIGHT in Index. — See
also **insult.**

offender *noun* See **criminal.**

offense *noun* Extreme displeasure
caused by an insult or slight : dudgeon, huff, miff, pique, resentment,
ruffled feathers, umbrage. See LIKE,
PAIN in Index. — See also **attack,
crime, indignity.**

offensive *adjective* Extremely
unpleasant to the senses or feelings : atrocious, disgusting, foul,
horrid, nasty, nauseating, repellent,
repulsive, revolting, sickening, ugly,

unwholesome, vile. See LIKE, PAIN in Index. — See also **unpleasant.**

offensive noun See **attack.**

offer verb **1.** To put before another for acceptance : extend, present[2], proffer, tender[2], volunteer. *Idioms:* come forward with, lay at someone's feet, lay before. See OFFER in Index. **2.** To make (something) readily available : afford, extend, provide. *Idiom:* place (or put) at one's disposal. See OFFER in Index. — See also **go, propose.**

offer noun Something offered : bid, proffer, proposal, tender[2]. See OFFER in Index. — See also **attempt.**

offering noun A presentation made to a deity as an act of worship : oblation. See OFFER, RELIGION in Index. — See also **donation, sacrifice.**

offhand adjective See **extemporaneous.**

office noun See **benevolence, ceremony, position, task.**

officer noun See **executive, policeman.**

official adjective See **authoritative.**

official noun See **authority, executive.**

officiate verb See **act.**

officious adjective See **meddling.**

offish adjective See **cool.**

offset verb See **balance, compensate.**

offset noun See **compensation.**

offshoot noun See **branch, derivative, shoot.**

offspring noun See **descendant, progeny.**

off-the-cuff adjective See **extemporaneous.**

often adverb See **usually.**

ogle verb See **gaze.**

ogre noun See **fiend.**

ogreish adjective See **fiendish.**

oil noun See **flattery.**

oily adjective See **fatty, unctuous.**

OK or **O.K.** or **okay** adjective See **acceptable.**

OK or **O.K.** or **okay** adverb See **yes.**

OK or **O.K.** or **okay** verb See **permit.**

OK or **O.K.** or **okay** noun See **acceptance, permission.**

old adjective **1.** Far along in life or time : advanced, aged, elderly, senior. *Idiom:* getting along (or on) in years. See NEW in Index. **2.** Belonging to, existing, or occurring in times long past : age-old, ancient, antediluvian, antiquated, antique, archaic, hoary, olden, old-time, timeworn, venerable. *Idioms:* old as Methuselah, old as the hills. See NEW in Index. — See also **continuing, experienced, late, old-fashioned.**

olden adjective See **old.**

older adjective See **senior.**

old-fashioned adjective Of a style or method formerly in vogue : antiquated, antique, archaic, bygone, dated, dowdy, fusty, old, old-time, outdated, outmoded, out-of-date, passé, vintage. See NEW in Index.

old hand noun See **veteran.**

old maid noun See **prude.**

old-maidish adjective See **genteel.**

old man noun See **father.**

oldster noun See **senior.**

old-time adjective See **old, old-fashioned.**

old-timer noun See **senior, veteran.**

oleaginous adjective See **fatty, unctuous.**

olfaction noun See **smell.**

olio noun See **assortment.**

omen noun A phenomenon that serves as a sign or warning of some future good or evil : augury, forerunner, foretoken, portent, prefigurement, presage, prognostic, prognostication, sign. *Idiom:* writing (or

handwriting) on the wall. See FORE-
SIGHT, WARN in Index.

ominous *adjective* See **fateful.**

omission *noun* See **failure.**

omit *verb* See **drop, fail.**

omnipresent *adjective* See
universal.

omnivorous *adjective* See
voracious.

omnivorousness *noun* See
voracity.

on-again, off-again *adjective* See
intermittent.

once *adjective* See **late.**

once *adverb* See **earlier.**

one *adjective* See **lone.**

one-dimensional *adjective* See
superficial.

oneness *noun* See **completeness,
sameness, uniqueness, unity.**

onerous *adjective* See **burdensome.**

one-sided *adjective* See **biased.**

one-sidedness *noun* See **bias.**

onetime *adjective* See **late.**

one-up *verb* See **trump.**

ongoing *adjective* See **continual.**

onlooker *noun* See **watcher.**

only *adjective* See **lone, unique.**

only *adverb* See **merely, solely.**

onomatopoeia *noun* See **echoism.**

onomatopoeic *adjective* See
echoic.

onomatopoetic *adjective* See
echoic.

onrush *noun* See **attack.**

onset *noun* See **attack, birth.**

onslaught *noun* See **attack.**

onus *noun* See **blame, burden¹,
stain.**

onyx *adjective* See **black.**

oodles *noun* See **heap.**

oomph *noun* See **spirit.**

ooze *verb* To flow or leak out or
emit something slowly : bleed,
exude, leach, percolate, seep, transpire, transude, weep. See MOVE,
SOLID in Index.

ooze *noun* See **slime.**

oozy *adjective* See **slimy.**

open *adjective* **1.** Having no pro-
tecting or concealing cover :
exposed, uncovered, unprotected.
See PROTECTION in Index. **2.** Not
restricted or confined to few :
open-door, public, unrestricted. See
OPEN in Index. **3.** Available for
use : accessible, employable, operable, operative, practicable, usable,
utilizable. See POSSIBLE in Index.
— See also **clear, frank, indefinite,
liable, receptive, unreserved.**

open *verb* To become or cause to
become open : unclose, undo. See
OPEN in Index. — See also **clear,
spread, start.**

open-door *adjective* See **open.**

open-eyed *adjective* See **alert.**

openhanded *adjective* See
generous.

openhandedness *noun* See
generosity.

opening *noun* See **beginning, birth,
hole, opportunity.**

open-minded *adjective* See **broad,
receptive.**

open-mindedness *noun* See
openness.

openness *noun* Ready acceptance
of often new suggestions, ideas,
influences, or opinions : open-
mindedness, receptiveness, receptivity, responsiveness. See ACCEPT in
Index. — See also **exposure.**

operable *adjective* See **open.**

operate *verb* To control or direct
the functioning of : manage, run,
use, work. See CONTROL in Index.
— See also **conduct, function, work.**

operating *adjective* See **active.**

operation *noun* See **behavior,
exercise.**

operational *adjective* See **effective.**

operative *noun* See **laborer, spy.**

operative *adjective* See **active, effective, open.**

operator *noun* See **driver, speculator.**

opiate *noun* See **drug, soporific.**

opiate *adjective* See **sleepy.**

opiate *verb* See **drug.**

opine *verb* See **believe.**

opinion *noun* See **belief.**

opponent *noun* One that opposes another in a battle, contest, controversy, or debate : adversary, antagonist, opposer, opposition, oppositionist, resister. See RESIST, SUPPORT in Index. — See also **competitor.**

opportune *adjective* Occurring at a fitting or advantageous time : auspicious, favorable, propitious, prosperous, seasonable, timely, well-timed. See LUCK in Index.

opportunity *noun* A favorable or advantageous combination of circumstances : break, chance, occasion, opening. *Informal:* shot. See LUCK in Index.

oppose *verb* To place in opposition or be in opposition to : counter, match, pit[1], play off. *Idioms:* bump heads with, meet head-on, set (or be) at odds, set (or be) at someone's throat, trade blows (or punches). See SUPPORT in Index. — See also **contest.**

opposed *adjective* See **opposing.**

opposer *noun* See **opponent.**

opposing *adjective* Acting against or in opposition : adversarial, adverse, antagonistic, antipathetic, opposed, oppositional. See SUPPORT in Index. — See also **opposite.**

opposite *adjective* Diametrically opposed : antipodal, antipodean, antithetical, antonymic, antonymous, contradictory, contrary, converse[2], counter, diametric, diametri-cal, opposing, polar, reverse. See SUPPORT in Index.

opposite *noun* That which is diametrically opposed to another : antipode, antipodes, antithesis, antonym, contrary, converse[2], counter, reverse. *Logic:* contradictory, contrapositive. See SUPPORT in Index.

opposite number *noun* See **counterpart.**

opposition *noun* The condition of being in conflict : antagonism, antithesis, contradiction, contradistinction, contraposition, contrariety, contrariness, polarity. See SUPPORT in Index. — See also **opponent, resistance.**

oppositional *adjective* See **opposing.**

oppositionist *noun* See **opponent.**

oppress *verb* See **depress, wrong.**

oppressive *adjective* See **burdensome.**

oppressor *noun* See **dictator.**

opprobrious *adjective* See **abusive, disgraceful.**

opprobrium *noun* See **disgrace.**

oppugn *verb* See **deny.**

opt *verb* See **choose.**

optic *adjective* See **visual.**

optical *adjective* See **visual.**

optimal *adjective* See **best.**

optimism *noun* A tendency to expect a favorable outcome or to dwell on hopeful aspects : sanguineness, sanguinity. See HOPE in Index.

optimist *noun* One who expects a favorable outcome or dwells on hopeful aspects : Pollyanna. See HOPE in Index.

optimistic *adjective* Expecting a favorable outcome or dwelling on hopeful aspects : Panglossian, roseate, rose-colored, rosy, sanguine. *Informal:* upbeat. *Idioms:* looking on the bright side, looking through rose-colored glasses. See HOPE in Index.

optimum *adjective* See **best.**

option *noun* See **choice.**

optional *adjective* Not compulsory or automatic : discretionary, elective, facultative. See CHOICE in Index.

opulent *adjective* See **luxurious, profuse.**

opus *noun* See **composition, publication.**

oracle *noun* See **prophecy.**

oracular *adjective* See **prophetic.**

oral *adjective* Expressed or transmitted in speech : spoken, unwritten, verbal, word-of-mouth. See WORDS in Index. — See also **vocal.**

oration *noun* See **speech.**

orator *noun* A public speaker : rhetorician. See WORDS in Index.

oratorical *adjective* Of or relating to the art of public speaking : declamatory, elocutionary, rhetorical. See WORDS in Index.

oratory *noun* The art of public speaking : declamation, elocution, rhetoric. See WORDS in Index.

orb *noun* See **circle, eye.**

orbit *noun* See **area, circle, range.**

orbit *verb* See **turn.**

orchestrate *verb* See **harmonize.**

ordain *verb* See **dictate.**

ordeal *noun* See **trial.**

order *noun* A way in which things follow each other in space or time : consecution, procession, sequence, succession. See ORDER, PRECEDE in Index. — See also **arrangement, class, command, kind², method, series, trim, union.**

order *verb* See **arrange, boss, command, methodize.**

orderliness *noun* See **method.**

orderly *adjective* See **methodical, neat.**

order of the day *noun* See **program.**

ordinance *noun* See **law.**

ordinariness *noun* See **usualness.**

ordinary *adjective* Being of no special quality or type : average, common, commonplace, cut-and-dried, formulaic, garden, garden-variety, indifferent, mediocre, plain, routine, run-of-the-mill, standard, stock, undistinguished, unexceptional, unremarkable. See GOOD, USUAL in Index. — See also **common.**

ordinary *noun* See **usual.**

organ *noun* See **branch, mean³.**

organic *adjective* See **natural.**

organization *noun* See **alliance, arrangement, foundation, method, union.**

organize *verb* See **arrange, found, methodize, mobilize.**

orgy *noun* See **binge.**

orientation *noun* See **bearing.**

orifice *noun* See **hole.**

oriflamme *noun* See **flag¹.**

origin *noun* A point of origination : beginning, derivation, fount, fountain, fountainhead, mother, parent, provenance, provenience, root¹, rootstock, source, spring, well¹. See START in Index. — See also **ancestry, birth.**

original *adjective* Not derived from something else : primary, prime, primitive. See START in Index. — See also **authentic, first, inventive, new, radical.**

original *noun* A first form from which varieties arise or imitations are made : archetype, father, master, protoplast, prototype. See START in Index. — See also **character.**

originality *noun* See **invention, novelty.**

originate *verb* See **begin, come, dawn, found, introduce, produce, stem.**

origination noun See **beginning, foundation.**

originator noun One that creates, founds, or originates : architect, author, creator, entrepreneur, father, founder², inventor, maker, parent, patriarch. See START in Index.

orison noun See **prayer¹.**

ornament verb See **adorn.**

ornament noun See **adornment.**

ornamentation noun See **adornment.**

ornate adjective Elaborately and heavily ornamented : baroque, flamboyant, florid, rococo. See PLAIN in Index.

ornery adjective See **contrary.**

orotund adjective See **resonant, sonorous.**

orotundity noun See **bombast.**

ort noun See **bit¹, end.**

orthodox adjective Adhering to beliefs or practices approved by authority or tradition : canonical, received, sanctioned, time-honored. See USUAL in Index. — See also **accepted, conservative, conventional.**

orthodox noun See **conservative.**

oscillate verb See **swing.**

osculate verb See **kiss.**

osculation noun See **kiss.**

ossuary noun See **grave¹.**

ostensible adjective See **apparent.**

ostensibly adverb See **apparently.**

ostensive adjective See **apparent.**

ostensively adverb See **apparently.**

ostentation noun See **pretentiousness.**

ostentatious adjective See **showy.**

ostracism noun See **exile.**

ostracize verb See **banish, blackball.**

other adjective See **additional.**

otherworldly adjective See **spiritual.**

otiose adjective See **empty.**

ounce noun See **bit¹, damn.**

oust verb See **eject.**

ouster noun See **ejection.**

out verb See **come out** at **come.**

outage noun See **failure.**

out-and-out adjective See **utter².**

outbreak noun A sudden increase in something, as the occurrence of a disease : epidemic, plague, rash². See INCREASE in Index. — See also **eruption, outburst.**

outburst noun A sudden violent expression, as of emotion : access, blowup, burst, eruption, explosion, fit², flare-up, gust, outbreak. See EXPLOSION in Index. — See also **eruption.**

outcome noun See **effect.**

outcry noun See **exclamation, vociferation.**

outdate verb See **obsolesce.**

outdated adjective See **old-fashioned.**

outdo verb See **surpass.**

outermost adjective See **extreme.**

outfit noun Things needed for a task, journey, or other purpose : accouterment (often used in plural), apparatus, equipment, gear, material (used in plural), materiel, paraphernalia, rig, tackle, thing (used in plural), turnout. See MEANS in Index. — See also **company, dress.**

outfit verb See **furnish.**

outflow noun See **spate.**

outgoing adjective Disposed to be open, sociable, and talkative : communicable, communicative, expansive, extraverted, extroverted, gregarious, unreserved. See ATTITUDE in Index.

outgrowth noun See **derivative.**

outing noun See **trip.**

outlander noun See **foreigner.**

outlandish adjective See **eccentric, foreign.**

outlast *verb* To live, exist, or remain longer than : outlive, outwear, survive. See CONTINUE in Index.

outlaw *verb* See forbid.

outlawed *adjective* See illegal.

outlay *noun* See cost.

    outlay *verb* See spend.

outlet *noun* See hole, store.

outline *noun* A line marking and shaping the outer form of an object : contour, delineation, profile, silhouette. See EDGE, SURFACE in Index. — See also **draft**.

    outline *verb* See draft.

outlive *verb* See outlast.

outlook *noun* See future, lookout, point of view, posture, prediction, view.

outlying *adjective* See remote.

outmaneuver *verb* See outwit.

outmatch *verb* See surpass.

outmoded *adjective* See old-fashioned.

outmost *adjective* See extreme.

out-of-date *adjective* See old-fashioned.

out of sight *adjective* See rare.

out-of-the-way *adjective* See remote.

outpour *noun* See spate.

outpouring *noun* See spate.

output *noun* See yield.

outrage *noun* A monstrous offense or evil : atrocity, enormity, monstrosity. See RIGHT in Index. — See also **crime, indignity.**

    outrage *verb* See insult, wrong.

outrageous *adjective* **1.** Disgracefully and grossly offensive : atrocious, heinous, monstrous, scandalous, shocking. *Archaic:* enormous. See RIGHT in Index. **2.** Beyond all reason : obscene, preposterous, ridiculous, shocking, unconscionable, unreasonable. *Idioms:* out of bounds, out of sight. See USUAL in Index.

outrageousness *noun* See flagrancy.

outright *adjective* See utter².

outrun *verb* See surpass.

outset *noun* See birth.

outshine *verb* See surpass.

outside *adjective* See remote.

    outside *noun* See maximum.

outsider *noun* See foreigner.

outskirt *noun* See skirt.

outsmart *verb* See outwit.

outspoken *adjective* Speaking or spoken without reserve : free, free-spoken, vocal. See RESTRAINT in Index.

outstanding *adjective* See due, noticeable, rare.

outstretch *verb* See reach, spread.

outstrip *verb* See surpass.

outthink *verb* See outwit.

outward *adjective* See apparent.

outwardly *adverb* See apparently.

outwear *verb* See outlast.

outweigh *verb* See compensate.

outwit *verb* To get the better of by cleverness or cunning : outmaneuver, outsmart, outthink, overreach. See WIN in Index.

oval *adjective* Resembling an egg in shape : ovate, oviform, ovoid, ovoidal. See GEOMETRY in Index.

ovate *adjective* See oval.

ovation *noun* See applause.

over *adverb* See through.

overabundance *noun* See excess.

overabundant *adjective* See excessive.

overage *noun* See surplus.

overall *adjective* See general.

overbearing *adjective* See arrogant, dictatorial.

overbearingness *noun* See arrogance.

overblown *adjective* See fat, inflated, sonorous.

overcast *verb* See **obscure**.

overcharge *verb* See **exaggerate, skin**.

overcome *verb* See **defeat, overwhelm**.

overconfidence *noun* See **impudence**.

overconfident *adjective* See **impudent**.

overcritical *adjective* See **critical**.

overdue *adjective* See **late**.

overflow *verb* See **flood, teem**.

overflow *noun* See **flood, surplus**.

overflowing *adjective* See **big**.

overhang *verb* See **bulge, threaten**.

overhang *noun* See **bulge**.

overhaul *verb* See **fix, pass**.

overhaul *noun* See **shakeup**.

overindulge *verb* See **baby**.

overindulgence *noun* See **excess**.

overjoy *verb* See **delight**.

overjoyed *adjective* See **elated**.

overlay *verb* See **cover**.

overlong *adjective* See **long¹**.

overlook *verb* See **dominate, supervise, survey**.

overlook *noun* See **lookout**.

overly *adverb* See **unduly**.

overmuch *adjective* See **excessive**.

overmuch *noun* See **surplus**.

overmuch *adverb* See **unduly**.

overpower *verb* See **overwhelm**.

overpowering *adjective* See **towering**.

overreach *verb* See **exceed, outwit**.

overrun *verb* See **exceed, invade**.

overrun *noun* See **surplus**.

oversee *verb* See **supervise**.

overseer *noun* See **boss**.

overshadow *verb* See **obscure**.

oversight *noun* See **neglect**.

oversize *adjective* See **bulky**.

oversized *adjective* See **bulky**.

oversleep *verb* See **sleep in** at **sleep**.

overstate *verb* See **exaggerate**.

overstatement *noun* See **exaggeration**.

overstep *verb* See **exceed**.

overstock *noun* See **surplus**.

oversupply *noun* See **surplus**.

overtake *verb* See **catch up** at **catch, puss**.

overthrow *verb* To bring about the downfall of : bring down, overturn, subvert, topple, tumble, unhorse. See HELP in Index. — See also **overturn**.

overthrow *noun* See **defeat**.

overture *noun* See **advance, introduction**.

overturn *verb* To turn or cause to turn from a vertical or horizontal position : capsize, knock over, overthrow, topple, turn over, upset. See CHANGE, HORIZONTAL, MOVE in Index. — See also **overthrow**.

overturned *adjective* See **upside-down**.

overused *adjective* See **trite**.

overview *noun* See **survey**.

overweening *adjective* See **arrogant**.

overweight *adjective* See **fat**.

overwhelm *verb* **1.** To render totally ineffective by decisive defeat : annihilate, crush, drub, overpower, smash, steamroller, thrash, trounce, vanquish. *Informal:* massacre, wallop. *Slang:* clobber, cream, shellac, smear. See WIN in Index. **2.** To affect deeply or completely, as with emotion : crush, engulf, overcome, overpower, prostrate. See AFFECT in Index. — See also **break, flood**.

overwhelming *adjective* See **towering**.

overworked *adjective* See **trite**.

oviform *adjective* See **oval**.

ovoid *adjective* See **oval**.

ovoidal *adjective* See **oval**.

owed *adjective* See **due**.

owing *adjective* See **due.**

own *verb* See **acknowledge, have.**

owner *noun* A person who has legal title to property : holder, master, possessor, proprietor. See OWNED in Index.

ownership *noun* The fact of possessing or the legal right to possess something : dominion, possession, proprietorship, title. See OWNED in Index.

ox *noun* See **lump**[1].

P

pa *noun* See **father.**

pabulum *noun* See **food.**

pace *noun* See **speed.**

　pace *verb* See **walk.**

pacific *adjective* See **peaceable.**

pacifical *adjective* See **peaceable.**

pacifist *adjective* See **peaceable.**

pacifistic *adjective* See **peaceable.**

pacify *verb* To ease the anger or agitation of : appease, assuage, calm (down), conciliate, dulcify, gentle, mollify, placate, propitiate, soften, soothe, sweeten. *Idiom:* pour oil on troubled water. See CALM in Index.

pack *verb* See **carry, crowd, fill.**

　pack *noun* See **gang, heap.**

package *verb* See **wrap.**

packed *adjective* See **full, thick.**

pact *noun* See **agreement, treaty.**

pain *noun* A sensation of physical discomfort occurring as the result of disease or injury : ache, pang, prick, prickle, smart, soreness, stab, sting, stitch, throe, twinge. *Informal:* misery. See PAIN in Index. — See also **distress, effort, thorn, thoroughness.**

　pain *verb* See **distress, hurt.**

painful *adjective* Marked by, causing, or experiencing physical pain :

aching, achy, afflictive, hurtful, nagging, smarting, sore. See PAIN in Index. — See also **bitter.**

painstaking *adjective* See **careful.**

　painstaking *noun* See **thoroughness.**

pair *noun* Two persons united, as by marriage : couple, duo, twosome. See GROUP in Index. — See also **couple.**

paired *adjective* See **twin.**

pal *noun* See **associate, friend.**

paladin *noun* See **hero.**

palatial *adjective* See **luxurious.**

palaver *noun* See **chatter.**

　palaver *verb* See **chatter.**

pale *adjective* **1.** Lacking color : ashen, ashy, bloodless, cadaverous, colorless, livid, lurid, pallid, pasty, sallow, wan, waxen. See COLORS in Index. **2.** Being weak in quality or substance : anemic, bloodless, pallid, waterish, watery. See STRONG in Index. — See also **fair.**

　pale *verb* To lose normal coloration; turn pale : blanch, bleach, etiolate, wan. See COLORS in Index.

palinode *noun* See **retraction.**

pall *verb* See **satiate.**

palliate *verb* See **extenuate, relieve.**

palliation *noun* See **relief.**

pallid *adjective* See **pale.**

palm off *verb* See **foist.**

palpability *noun* See **tangibility.**

palpable *adjective* See **perceptible, tangible.**

palpate *verb* See **touch.**

palpation *noun* See **touch.**

palpitate *verb* See **beat.**

palpitation *noun* See **beat.**

palter *verb* See **equivocate, haggle.**

paltriness *noun* See **pettiness.**

paltry *adjective* See **petty, shoddy.**

pamper *verb* See **baby.**

pan *verb* See **blame.**

　pan out *verb* See **succeed.**

　pan *noun* See **blame, face.**

panacea *noun* Something believed to cure all human disorders : catholicon, cure-all. See HELP in Index.

pandemic *adjective* See **universal**.

pandemonium *noun* See **noise**.

panegyric *noun* See **praise**.

panegyrize *verb* See **honor**.

pang *noun* See **pain**.

pang *verb* See **hurt**.

Panglossian *adjective* See **optimistic**.

panhandle *verb* See **beg**.

panhandler *noun* See **beggar**.

panic *noun* See **fear, scream**.

panic *verb* See **frighten**.

panicky *adjective* See **afraid**.

panoply *noun* See **display**.

panorama *noun* See **view**.

pant *verb* To breathe hard : blow[1], gasp, huff, puff. See BREATH in Index. — See also **desire, gasp**.

pap *noun* See **food**.

papa *noun* See **father**.

paper *noun* See **composition**.

pappy[1] *adjective* See **soft**.

pappy[2] *noun* See **father**.

par *noun* See **average, equivalence**.

parade *noun* See **display, review**.

parade *verb* See **display**.

paradigm *noun* See **model**.

paradigmatic *adjective* See **typical**.

paradisaic *adjective* See **heavenly**.

paradisaical *adjective* See **heavenly**.

paradisal *adjective* See **heavenly**.

paradise *noun* See **heaven**.

paradisiac *adjective* See **heavenly**.

paradisiacal *adjective* See **heavenly**.

paragon *noun* See **nonpareil**.

paragraph *noun* See **item**.

parallel *adjective* Lying in the same plane and not intersecting ; collateral. *Idiom:* side by side. See GEOMETRY in Index. — See also **like[2]**.

parallel *noun* Something closely resembling or analogous to something else : analogue, congener, correlate, correlative, correspondent, counterpart, match. See SAME in Index.

parallel *verb* See **compare, liken**.

parallelism *noun* See **likeness**.

paralyze *verb* To render helpless, as by emotion : benumb, numb, petrify, stun, stupefy, wither. See AFFECT in Index. — See also **disable**.

paramount *adjective* See **dominant, primary**.

paramountcy *noun* See **dominance**.

paramour *noun* See **lover**.

paraphernalia *noun* See **outfit**.

paraphrase *noun* A restating of something in other, especially simpler, words : rendering, restatement, translation, version. See WORDS in Index.

paraphrase *verb* To express the meaning of in other, especially simpler, words : render, rephrase, restate, reword, translate. See WORDS in Index.

parasite *noun* One who depends on another for support without reciprocating : bloodsucker, hanger-on, leech, sponge. *Slang:* freeloader. See DEPENDENCE in Index.

parasitic *adjective* Of or characteristic of a parasite : bloodsucking, parasitical. *Slang:* freeloading. See DEPENDENCE in Index.

parasitical *adjective* See **parasitic**.

parboil *verb* See **boil**.

parcel *noun* See **lot**.

parcel out *verb* See **distribute**.

parch *verb* See **dry**.

parched *adjective* See **thirsty**.

pardon *verb* See **forgive**.

pardon *noun* See **forgiveness**.

pardonable *adjective* Admitting of forgiveness or pardon : excusable, forgivable, venial. See FORGIVENESS in Index.

pare *verb* See **cut back** at **cut, skin.**

parent *verb* See **produce.**
　parent *noun* See **ancestor, origin, originator.**

parentage *noun* See **ancestry.**

parenthesis *noun* See **digression.**

parenthetic *adjective* See **digressive.**

parenthetical *adjective* See **digressive.**

parity *noun* See **equivalence.**

parlance *noun* See **wording.**

parley *noun* See **conference, deliberation, talk.**
　parley *verb* See **confer.**

parlous *adjective* See **dangerous.**

parochial *adjective* See **local.**

parody *noun* See **mockery, takeoff.**
　parody *verb* See **imitate.**

paroxysm *noun* See **throe.**

parrot *noun* See **echo.**
　parrot *verb* See **echo.**

parry *verb* To turn or drive away : beat off, fend (off), keep off, repel, repulse, ward off. See ALLOW, STRIKE in Index.

parsimonious *adjective* See **stingy.**

parson *noun* See **preacher.**

part *noun* One's proper or expected function in a common effort : piece, role, share. See DO, PARTICIPATE in Index. — See also **allotment, division, element, section, side.**
　part *verb* See **divide, separate.**
　part *adjective* See **partial.**

partake *verb* See **contribute, eat, participate.**

partial *adjective* Relating to or affecting only a part; not total : fractional, fragmentary, part. See PART in Index. — See also **biased, favorable.**

partiality *noun* See **bent, bias, favor, taste.**

partialness *noun* See **favor.**

participant *noun* One who participates : actor, party, player. See PARTICIPATE in Index.

participate *verb* To involve oneself in (an activity) : carry on, engage, have, indulge, partake. *Idiom:* take part. See PARTICIPATE in Index. — See also **contribute.**

participation *noun* The act or fact of participating : involvement, sharing. See PARTICIPATE in Index.

particle *noun* See **bit**[1].

particular *noun* See **circumstance, detail, element.**
　particular *adjective* See **detailed, individual, lone, nice, special, specific.**

particularity *noun* See **individuality.**

particularize *verb* See **stipulate.**

parting *noun* A separation of two or more people : adieu, farewell, goodbye, leave-taking, valediction. See APPROACH in Index. — See also **division.**
　parting *adjective* Of, done, given, or said on departing : departing, farewell, good-bye, valedictory. See APPROACH in Index.

partisan *noun* See **follower.**
　partisan *adjective* See **biased.**

partisanship *noun* See **bias.**

partition *noun* See **division, wall.**
　partition *verb* See **divide, wall.**

partner *noun* See **associate, spouse.**

partnership *noun* See **association.**

parturiency *noun* See **pregnancy.**

parturient *adjective* See **pregnant.**

parturition *noun* See **birth.**

party *noun* A large or important social gathering : affair, celebration, festivity, fete, function, gala, occasion, soiree. *Informal:* do. *Slang:* bash. See GROUP, WORK in Index. — See also **band**[2], **combine, group, human being, participant.**

pass *verb* **1.** To catch up with and move past : overhaul, overtake. See APPROACH in Index. **2.** To cause to be transferred from one to another : convey, hand (over), transmit. See GIVE in Index. **3.** To be accepted or approved : carry, clear. See ACCEPT in Index. — See also **come, communicate, confirm, cross, die, fall, go, hand down** at hand, **journey, lead, pose, spend, surpass.**

pass away *verb* See **die, go.**

pass off *verb* See **foist.**

pass out *verb* See **black out** at black.

pass over *verb* See **blink.**

pass *noun* A free ticket entitling one to transportation or admission : *Informal:* comp. *Slang:* freebie. See ENTER, TRANSACTIONS in Index. — See also **crisis.**

passable *adjective* Capable of being passed, traversed, or crossed : navigable, negotiable. See OPEN in Index. — See also **acceptable.**

passage *noun* See **section, transition.**

passé *adjective* See **old-fashioned.**

passel *noun* See **heap.**

passing *adjective* See **transitory.**

passing *noun* See **death.**

passion *noun* Powerful, intense emotion : ardor, fervency, fervor, fire. See FEELINGS in Index. — See also **desire, enthusiasm, love, temper.**

passionate *adjective* Fired with intense feeling : ardent, blazing, burning, dithyrambic, fervent, fervid, fiery, flaming, glowing, heated, hot-blooded, impassioned, perfervid, red-hot, scorching, torrid. See FEELINGS in Index. — See also **erotic.**

passionless *adjective* See **frigid.**

passive *adjective* Submitting without objection or resistance : acqui-escent, nonresistant, resigned, submissive. See RESIST in Index.

past *adjective* Just gone by or elapsed : antecedent, anterior, earlier, foregoing, former, precedent, preceding, previous, prior. See TIME in Index. — See also **late.**

past *noun* A former period of time or of one's life : yesterday, yesteryear, yore. *Idioms:* bygone days, days gone by, the good old days, the old days. See TIME in Index. — See also **history.**

past master *noun* See **expert.**

paste *verb* See **hit.**

paste *noun* See **blow².**

pastoral *adjective* Charmingly simple and carefree : idyllic. See CALM, SIMPLE in Index. — See also **country.**

pasty *adjective* See **pale.**

pat *verb* See **caress.**

patch *verb* See **fix.**

patchwork *noun* See **assortment.**

patchy *adjective* See **uneven.**

pate *noun* See **head.**

patent *adjective* See **apparent, unsubtle.**

paternal *adjective* See **fatherly.**

path *noun* See **way.**

pathetic *adjective* See **pitiful.**

patience *noun* The capacity of enduring hardship or inconvenience without complaint : forbearance, long-suffering, resignation, tolerance. See ACCEPT in Index.

patient *adjective* Enduring or capable of enduring hardship or inconvenience without complaint : forbearing, long-suffering, resigned. See ACCEPT in Index.

patois *noun* See **dialect, language.**

patriarch *noun* See **originator.**

patrician *adjective* See **noble.**

patriciate *noun* See **society.**

patrimonial *adjective* See **ancestral.**

patrimony *noun* See **birthright.**

patrol *verb* See **police.**

patrolman *noun* See **policeman.**

patrolwoman *noun* See **policeman.**

patron *noun* **1.** A person who supports or champions an activity, cause, or institution, for example : backer, benefactor, contributor, friend, sponsor, supporter. *Informal:* angel. See HELP in Index. **2.** One who buys goods or services : buyer, client, customer, purchaser. See TRANSACTIONS in Index.

patronage *noun* **1.** Aid or support given by a patron : aegis, auspice (often used in plural), backing, patronization, sponsorship. See HELP in Index. **2.** The commercial transactions of customers with a supplier : business, custom, trade, traffic. See TRANSACTIONS in Index. **3.** Customers or patrons collectively : clientele. See TRANSACTIONS in Index. **4.** The political appointments or jobs that are at the disposal of those in power : spoil (used in plural). *Slang:* pork. See POLITICS in Index.

patronization *noun* See **condescension, patronage.**

patronize *verb* To act as a patron to : sponsor, support. See HELP in Index. — See also **condescend.**

patsy *noun* See **dupe, scapegoat.**

pattern *noun* See **figure, form, method, model.**

pattern *verb* See **follow, form.**

paucity *noun* See **shortage.**

pauper *noun* An impoverished person : beggar, down-and-out, down-and-outer, have-not, indigent. See RICH in Index.

pauperize *verb* See **ruin.**

pause *verb* To stop temporarily and remain, as if reluctant to leave : abide, bide, linger, stay[1], tarry, wait.

See CONTINUE in Index. — See also **hesitate.**

pause *noun* See **break, hesitation.**

pawn[1] *noun* Something given to guarantee the repayment of a loan or the fulfillment of an obligation : earnest[2], guaranty, pledge, security, token, warrant. See TRANSACTIONS in Index.

pawn *verb* To give or deposit as a pawn : hypothecate, mortgage, pledge. *Slang:* hock. See TRANSACTIONS in Index.

pawn[2] *noun* A person used or controlled by others : cat's-paw, dupe, instrument, puppet, stooge, tool. See OVER in Index.

pay *verb* To give payment to in return for goods or services rendered : compensate, recompense, remunerate. See PAY in Index. — See also **compensate, return, reward, settle, spend.**

pay back *verb* See **avenge.**

pay off *verb* See **avenge, bribe.**

pay *noun* See **wage.**

payable *adjective* See **due.**

payment *noun* Something given in exchange for goods or services rendered : compensation, consideration, recompense, remuneration. See PAY in Index.

payoff *noun* See **bribe, climax.**

payola *noun* See **bribe.**

peace *noun* See **calm, stillness.**

peaceable *adjective* Inclined or disposed to peace; not quarrelsome or unruly : irenic, pacific, pacifical, pacifist, pacifistic, peaceful. See PEACE in Index.

peaceful *adjective* See **calm, peaceable, still.**

peacefulness *noun* See **calm, stillness.**

peace officer *noun* See **policeman.**

peaches-and-cream *adjective* See **fresh.**

peacock *verb* See **strut.**

peak *noun* See **bill², climax, height.**

 peak *adjective* See **climactic.**

 peak *verb* See **climax.**

peaked *adjective* See **sickly.**

peal *verb* See **ring².**

peanut *noun* *Informal.* A small or trifling amount of money. Used in plural : small change. *Slang:* chicken feed, two bits. See BIG, MONEY in Index.

pearl *noun* See **treasure.**

peccancy *noun* See **crime, evil.**

peccant *adjective* See **evil.**

peck¹ *noun* See **kiss.**

 peck *verb* See **kiss.**

 peck at *verb* See **nag.**

peck² *noun* See **heap.**

Pecksniffian *adjective* See **hypocritical.**

peculiar *adjective* See **distinctive, eccentric, funny.**

peculiarity *noun* See **eccentricity, quality.**

pecuniary *adjective* See **financial.**

pedagogics *noun* See **education.**

pedagogue *noun* See **educator.**

pedagogy *noun* See **education.**

pedantic *adjective* Characterized by a narrow concern for book learning and formal rules, without knowledge or experience of practical matters : academic, bookish, donnish, formalistic, inkhorn, literary, pedantical, scholastic. See ATTITUDE, FLEXIBLE, TEACH in Index.

pedantical *adjective* See **pedantic.**

peddle *verb* To travel about selling goods : hawk, huckster, vend. See TRANSACTIONS in Index. — See also **push, sell.**

peddler *noun* See **pusher.**

pedestrian *adjective* See **dull.**

pedigree *noun* See **ancestry, genealogy.**

peek *verb* See **glimpse.**

 peek *noun* See **glance.**

peel *noun* See **skin.**

 peel *verb* See **skin.**

peeler *noun* See **policeman.**

peep *verb* See **glimpse.**

 peep *noun* See **glance.**

peer¹ *verb* See **gaze.**

peer² *noun* One that is very similar to another in rank or position : coequal, colleague, compeer, equal, equivalent, fellow. See SAME in Index.

peerless *adjective* See **unique.**

peeve *verb* See **annoy.**

 peeve *noun* See **annoyance.**

peevish *adjective* See **ill-tempered.**

peewee *adjective* See **tiny.**

peg *noun* See **degree.**

pejorative *adjective* See **disparaging.**

pelagic *adjective* See **marine.**

pelf *noun* See **riches.**

pellucid *adjective* See **clear, transparent.**

pellucidity *noun* See **clarity.**

pellucidness *noun* See **clarity.**

pelt¹ *noun* See **hide².**

pelt² *verb* See **rush.**

pen¹ *verb* See **publish.**

pen² *verb* See **enclose.**

pen³ *noun* See **jail.**

penalize *verb* See **fine², punish.**

penalty *noun* See **fine², punishment, sanction.**

penchant *noun* See **bent.**

pendulous *adjective* See **hanging, hesitant.**

penetrate *verb* To pass into or through by overcoming resistance : break (through), enter, perforate, pierce, puncture. See ENTER in Index. — See also **enter.**

penetrating *adjective* See **acute.**

penetration *noun* See **discernment, instinct.**

penitence *noun* A feeling of regret for one's sins or misdeeds : compunction, contriteness, contrition, penitency, remorse, remorsefulness, repentance, rue. *Theology:* attrition. See REGRET in Index.

penitency *noun* See **penitence**.

penitent *adjective* See **apologetic, remorseful**.

penitential *adjective* See **remorseful**.

penitentiary *noun* See **jail**.

pennant *noun* See **flag**[1].

penniless *adjective* See **poor**.

pennilessness *noun* See **poverty**.

pennon *noun* See **flag**[1].

penny pincher *noun* See **miser**.

penny-pinching *adjective* See **stingy**.

pensile *adjective* See **hanging**.

pension *verb* See **retire**.

pensive *adjective* See **thoughtful**.

penumbra *noun* See **shade**.

penurious *adjective* See **poor, stingy**.

penuriousness *noun* See **poverty**.

penury *noun* See **poverty**.

people *noun* See **public**.

people *verb* See **inhabit**.

pep *noun* See **energy, spirit**.

pepper *verb* See **barrage, speckle**.

peppery *adjective* See **spirited, testy**.

peppiness *noun* See **energy, spirit**.

peppy *adjective* See **energetic, lively, vigorous**.

perambulate *verb* See **stroll**.

perambulation *noun* See **walk**.

perceivable *adjective* See **perceptible, visible**.

perceive *verb* To be intuitively aware of : apprehend, feel, intuit, sense. *Idioms:* feel in one's bones, get vibrations. See KNOWLEDGE in Index. — See also **see**.

perceptibility *noun* See **visibility**.

perceptible *adjective* Capable of being noticed or apprehended mentally : appreciable, detectable, discernible, distinguishable, noticeable,

observable, palpable, perceivable, ponderable, sensible. See KNOWLEDGE in Index. — See also **visible**.

perception *noun* See **awareness, idea**.

perceptive *adjective* See **acute**.

perceptiveness *noun* See **discernment**.

perch *verb* See **balance**.

perchance *adverb* See **maybe**.

percipience *noun* See **discernment**.

percipiency *noun* See **discernment**.

percolate *verb* See **ooze**.

percussion *noun* See **collision**.

perdurable *adjective* See **continuing**.

peregrinate *verb* See **hike, journey, rove**.

peremptory *adjective* See **dictatorial**.

perennial *adjective* See **continuing**.

perfect *adjective* Supremely excellent in quality or nature : absolute, consummate, faultless, flawless, impeccable, indefectible, unflawed. See GOOD in Index. — See also **clean, complete, good, ideal, pure, round, utter**[2].

perfect *verb* To bring to perfection or completion : polish, refine, smooth. *Idiom:* smooth off the rough edges. See BETTER in Index.

perfection *noun* See **virtue**.

perfectly *adverb* See **completely**.

perfervid *adjective* See **passionate**.

perfidious *adjective* See **faithless**.

perfidiousness *noun* See **faithlessness**.

perfidy *noun* See **faithlessness, treachery**.

perforate *verb* See **breach, penetrate**.

perforation *noun* See **breach, prick**.

perforce *adverb* See **helplessly**.

perform *verb* To begin and carry through to completion : do, exe-

cute, prosecute. *Informal:* pull off.
See DO in Index. — See also **act, ful-fill, function, play, stage.**

performance *noun* The act of
beginning and carrying through to
completion : discharge, effectuation, execution, prosecution. See DO
in Index. — See also **behavior,
interpretation.**

performer *noun* See **player.**

perfume *noun* See **fragrance.**
perfume *verb* See **scent.**

perfunctory *adjective* Performed or
performing automatically and imper-
sonally : automatic, mechanical.
See CONCERN in Index.

perhaps *adverb* See **maybe.**

periapt *noun* See **charm.**

peril *noun* See **danger.**
peril *verb* See **endanger.**

perilous *adjective* See **dangerous.**

perimeter *noun* See **border,
circumference.**

period *noun* **1.** A specific length of
time characterized by the occurrence
of certain conditions or events :
season, span, stretch, term. See TIME
in Index. **2.** An interval regarded as
a distinct evolutionary or developmental unit : phase, stage. See
TIME in Index. — See also **age, end,
time.**

periodic *adjective* See **intermittent,
recurrent.**

periodical *adjective* See **intermittent, recurrent.**

periodically *adverb* See **intermittently.**

peripatetic *adjective* See **nomadic.**

periphery *noun* See **border,
circumference.**

periphrastic *adjective* See **wordy.**

perish *verb* See **die.**

perjure *verb* See **lie².**

perjured *adjective* See **perjurious.**

perjurer *noun* See **liar.**

perjurious *adjective* Marked by
lying under oath : forsworn, perjured. See TRUE in Index.

perjury *noun* See **mendacity.**

perk up *verb* See **encourage,
recover.**

permanent *adjective* See
continuing.

permeate *verb* See **charge.**

permissible *adjective* Capable of
being allowed : admissible, allowable. *Slang:* kosher. See ALLOW in
Index.

permission *noun* The approving of
an action, especially when done by
one in authority : allowance,
approbation, approval, authorization, consent, endorsement, leave²,
license, permit, sanction. *Informal:*
OK. See ALLOW in Index.

permit *verb* **1.** To neither forbid nor
prevent : allow, have, let, suffer,
tolerate. See ALLOW in Index. **2.** To
give one's consent to : allow,
approbate, approve, authorize,
consent, endorse, let, sanction.
Informal: OK. See ALLOW in Index.
3. To afford an opportunity for :
admit, allow, let. See ALLOW in
Index. — See also **enable.**
permit *noun* See **license,
permission.**

permutation *noun* See **change.**

pernicious *adjective* See **destructive, virulent.**

perorate *verb* See **rant.**

perpendicular *adjective* See
vertical.

perpetrate *verb* See **commit.**

perpetual *adjective* See **continual,
endless.**

perpetuate *verb* See **immortalize.**

perpetuity *noun* See **endlessness,
eternity.**

perplex *verb* See **complicate,
confuse.**

perplexed *adjective* See **confused.**

perplexity noun See **daze, mystery.**

perquisite noun See **birthright, gratuity.**

persecute verb See **wrong.**

persecution noun See **hell.**

perseverance noun See **insistence.**

persevere verb See **carry on at carry, insist.**

persist verb See **carry on at carry, endure, insist, survive.**

persistence noun See **continuation, insistence.**

persistency noun See **continuation, insistence.**

persistent adjective See **chronic, continual, continuing, insistent, stubborn.**

persnickety adjective See **nice.**

person noun See **human being.**

persona noun See **character.**

personage noun See **celebrity, character, dignitary, human being.**

personal adjective Belonging to, relating to, or affecting a particular person : individual, private. See SPECIFIC in Index. — See also arbitrary, bodily, intimate1, private.

personal effects noun See **effect.**

personality noun See **celebrity, character.**

personalization noun See **embodiment.**

personalize verb See **embody.**

personal property noun See **effect.**

personification noun See **embodiment.**

personify verb See **embody.**

perspective noun See **view.**

perspicacious adjective See **shrewd.**

perspicacity noun See **discernment.**

perspicuity noun See **clarity.**

perspicuousness noun See **clarity.**

perspiration noun See **sweat.**

perspire verb See **sweat.**

perspiring adjective See **sweaty.**

persuade verb To succeed in causing (a person) to act in a certain way : argue into, bring, bring around (or round), convince, get, induce, prevail on (or upon), sell (on), talk into. See PERSUASION in Index. — See also convince.

persuasion noun See **belief, faith, kind2, religion.**

persuasive adjective See **convincing.**

pert adjective See **impudent, lively.**

pertain verb See **apply.**

pertinacious adjective See **obstinate, stubborn.**

pertinaciousness noun See **obstinacy.**

pertinacity noun See **obstinacy.**

pertinence noun See **relevance.**

pertinency noun See **relevance.**

pertinent adjective See **relevant.**

pertness noun See **impudence, spirit.**

perturb verb See **agitate.**

perturbation noun See **agitation.**

perturbing adjective See **disturbing.**

perusal noun See **examination.**

peruse verb See **examine.**

pervade verb See **charge.**

perverse adjective See **contrary, corrupt, obstinate.**

perverseness noun See **obstinacy.**

perversion noun See **abuse, corruption.**

perversity noun See **obstinacy.**

pervert verb See **abuse, corrupt, distort.**

pervert noun See **deviant.**

pesky adjective See **troublesome.**

pessimist noun A prophet of misfortune or disaster : Cassandra, doomsayer, worrywart. See HOPE in Index.

pessimistic adjective See **gloomy.**

pester verb See **annoy, besiege.**

pestering noun See **annoyance.**

pestilent adjective See **virulent.**

pestilential *adjective* See **virulent.**
pet¹ *verb* See **caress, neck.**
 pet *noun* See **favorite.**
 pet *adjective* See **favorite.**
pet² *verb* See **sulk.**
petechia *noun* See **stigma.**
peter *verb* See **decrease.**
petite *adjective* See **little.**
petition *noun* See **appeal.**
 petition *verb* To make application
 to a higher authority, as to a court of
 law : *Law:* appeal, sue. See LAW in
 Index. — See also **address, apply.**
petitioner *noun* See **appealer,
 applicant.**
petrify *verb* See **harden, paralyze.**
pettifog *verb* See **quibble.**
pettiness *noun* Contemptible
 unimportance : inconsiderableness, negligibility, negligibleness,
 paltriness, smallness, triviality,
 trivialness. See IMPORTANT in
 Index.
 petty *adjective* Contemptibly unimportant : inconsiderable, negligible,
 niggling, nugatory, paltry, picayune,
 piddling, small, small-minded, trifling. *Slang:* measly. *Idiom:* of no
 account. See IMPORTANT in Index.
 — See also **minor, narrow, stingy.**
petulant *adjective* See **ill-tempered.**
phantasm *noun* See **dream, ghost,
 illusion.**
phantasma *noun* See **dream, ghost,
 illusion.**
phantasmagoria *noun* See
 hallucination.
phantasmagoric *adjective* See
 illusive.
phantasmagory *noun* See
 hallucination.
phantasmal *adjective* See **illusive.**
phantasmic *adjective* See **illusive.**
phantom *noun* See **ghost.**
pharisaic *adjective* See **hypocritical.**

pharisaical *adjective* See **hypocritical.**
pharisaism *noun* See **hypocrisy.**
pharisee *noun* See **hypocrite.**
pharmaceutical *noun* See **drug.**
phase *noun* The particular angle
 from which something is considered : angle², aspect, facet, frame
 of reference, hand, light¹, regard,
 respect, side. See PERSPECTIVE in
 Index. — See also **period.**
phenomenal *adjective* See **fabulous, physical.**
phenomenon *noun* See **fact,
 marvel.**
philander *verb* To be sexually
 unfaithful to another : womanize.
 Informal: cheat, fool around, mess
 around, play around. See SEX in
 Index.
philanderer *noun* A man who phi-
 landers : Casanova, Don Juan,
 lady's man, womanizer. *Slang:* lady-
 killer, wolf. *Idioms:* man on the
 make, skirt chaser. See SEX in Index.
philanthropic *adjective* See
 benevolent.
philanthropical *adjective* See
 benevolent.
philanthropy *noun* See
 benevolence.
philippic *noun* See **tirade.**
Philistine also **philistine** *noun* See
 boor.
 philistine also **Philistine** *adjective* See **coarse.**
philosopher *noun* See **thinker.**
phlegm *noun* See **apathy.**
phlegmatic *adjective* See
 apathetic.
phoenix *noun* See **nonpareil.**
phone *verb* See **telephone.**
phoniness *noun* See **hypocrisy,
 insincerity.**
phony also **phoney** *adjective* See
 artificial, counterfeit, hypocritical.

phony also **phoney** noun See counterfeit, fake, hypocrite.

photographic adjective See graphic.

phrase verb To convey in language or words of a particular form : couch, express, formulate, put, word. See WORDS in Index.

phrase noun See expression, wording.

phraseology noun See wording.

phrasing noun See wording.

phthisic adjective See tubercular.

phthisic noun See tuberculosis.

phthisical adjective See tubercular.

phthisis noun See tuberculosis.

phylactery noun See charm.

physic noun See cure.

physic verb See drug.

physical adjective **1.** Composed of or relating to things that occupy space and can be perceived by the senses : concrete, corporeal, material, objective, phenomenal, sensible, substantial, tangible. See BODY, MATTER in Index. **2.** Relating to the desires and appetites of the body : animal, carnal, fleshly, sensual. See BODY in Index. ─ See also bodily.

physicality noun A preoccupation with the body and satisfaction of its desires : animalism, animality, carnality, fleshliness, sensuality. See BODY in Index.

physiognomy noun See face.

physique noun See constitution.

picayune adjective See petty.

pick noun See best, elect.

pick verb See choose, gather.

pick off verb See shoot.

pick on verb See nag.

pick out verb See discern.

pick up verb See arrest, continue, elevate, get, glean, learn.

picket noun See guard.

pickle noun See predicament.

pickled adjective See drunk.

pick-me-up noun See tonic.

pickup noun See arrest.

picky adjective See nice.

pictographic adjective See graphic.

pictorial adjective See graphic.

picture verb See imagine, represent.

picture noun See double.

picturesque adjective See colorful, graphic.

piddling adjective See petty.

piece noun See bit¹, composition, cut, distance, division, item, part.

piecemeal adjective See gradual.

pierce verb See breach, cut, penetrate.

piercing adjective See high, sharp.

pietism noun See devotion.

pietistic adjective See holy.

pietistical adjective See holy.

piety noun See devotion.

piffle noun See nonsense.

pigeon noun See dupe.

pigeonhole verb See assort, class.

piggish adjective See greedy.

pigheaded adjective See obstinate.

pigheadedness noun See obstinacy.

pigment noun See color.

pile noun See building, fortune, heap.

pile verb See fill, get up at get, heap.

pile up verb See accumulate, crash.

pileup or **pile-up** noun See crash.

pilfer verb See steal.

pilferage noun See larceny.

pilferer noun See larcenist.

pilgrimage noun See expedition.

pill noun See drip.

pillage verb See sack².

pillage noun See plunder.

pilose adjective See hairy.

pilot noun See guide.

pilot verb See drive, guide, maneuver.

pilot *adjective* Constituting a tentative model for future experiment or development : experimental, test, trial. See START in Index.

pinch *verb* See **arrest, scrimp, steal.**

pinch *noun* See **arrest.**

pinchbeck *noun* See **copy.**

pinch-hit *verb* See **substitute.**

pinch hitter *noun* See **substitute.**

pinching *adjective* See **stingy.**

pine *verb* See **desire, languish.**

pink-slip *verb* See **dismiss.**

pinnacle *noun* See **climax.**

pin on *verb* See **fix.**

pinpoint *noun* See **point.**

pinpoint *verb* See **find, place.**

pintsize *adjective* See **tiny.**

pintsized *adjective* See **tiny.**

pioneer *noun* See **builder.**

pioneer *adjective* See **first.**

pious *adjective* See **holy.**

piousness *noun* See **devotion.**

pip *noun* See **seed.**

pipe dream *noun* See **illusion.**

piping *adjective* See **high.**

pip-squeak *noun* See **nonentity.**

piquant *adjective* See **pungent.**

pique *noun* See **offense.**

pique *verb* See **insult, provoke.**

pirate *noun* One who illicitly reproduces the artistic work, for example, of another : cribber, plagiarist, plagiarizer. See GIVE, WORDS in Index.

pirate *verb* To reproduce (the artistic work of another, for example) illicitly : crib, plagiarize. See GIVE, WORDS in Index.

pit[1] *noun* A place known for its great filth or corruption : cesspit, cesspool, sink. *Slang:* armpit. See CLEAN, RIGHT in Index. — See also **depression.**

pit *verb* See **oppose.**

pit[2] *noun* See **seed.**

pitch *verb* See **advertise, drop, erect, fall, lurch, throw, toss.**

pitch into *verb* See **attack.**

pitch *noun* See **drop, fall, intensity, promotion, throw.**

pitch-black *adjective* See **black.**

pitch-dark *adjective* See **black.**

pitchy *adjective* See **black.**

piteous *adjective* See **pitiful, pitying.**

pitfall *noun* A source of danger or difficulty not easily foreseen and avoided : booby trap, trap. See SAFETY in Index.

pith *noun* See **heart.**

pithy *adjective* Precisely meaningful and tersely cogent : aphoristic, compact[1], epigrammatic, epigrammatical, marrowy. *Informal:* brasstacks. *Idioms:* down to brass tacks, to the point. See MEANING, STYLE in Index.

pitiable *adjective* See **pitiful.**

pitiful *adjective* Arousing or deserving pity : pathetic, piteous, pitiable, poor, rueful, ruthful. See PITY in Index. — See also **pitying.**

pitiless *adjective* See **merciless.**

pity *noun* Sympathetic, sad concern for someone in misfortune : commiseration, compassion, condolence, empathy, sympathy. See PITY in Index. — See also **shame.**

pity *verb* See **feel.**

pitying *adjective* Feeling or expressing pity : commiserative, compassionate, condolatory, sympathetic. *Archaic:* piteous, pitiful. See FEELINGS, PITY in Index.

pivot *verb* See **swing, traverse, turn.**

pivotal *adjective* Dominant in importance or influence : central, key. See IMPORTANT in Index.

pixilated *adjective* See **drunk.**

placard *noun* See **sign.**

placate *verb* See **pacify.**

place *noun* **1.** The function or position customarily occupied by another : stead. *Archaic:* lieu. See PLACE, SUBSTITUTE in Index. **2.** Positioning of one individual vis-à-vis others : footing, position, rank[1], situation, standing, station, status. See PLACE in Index. **3.** The proper or designated location : niche. See PLACE in Index. — See also **home, locality, point, position.**

place verb To establish the identification of : identify, pinpoint, recognize. Slang: finger. Idiom: put one's finger on. See KNOWLEDGE in Index. — See also **class, estimate, fix, position, run, set[1].**

placement noun See **arrangement, position.**

placid adjective See **calm, still.**

placidity noun See **calm, stillness.**

placidness noun See **calm, stillness.**

plagiarist noun See **pirate.**

plagiarize verb See **pirate.**

plagiarizer noun See **pirate.**

plague noun See **annoyance, curse, outbreak.**

plague verb See **afflict, annoy, besiege.**

plaguy also **plaguey** adjective See **vexatious.**

plain adjective Not handsome or beautiful : homely, unattractive, uncomely, unlovely. Idioms: not much for looks, not much to look at, short on looks. See BEAUTIFUL in Index. — See also **apparent, bare, modest, ordinary, pure, straight, unsubtle, utter[2].**

plainness noun See **clarity, modesty.**

plainspoken adjective See **frank.**

plaintiff noun See **complainant.**

plaintive adjective See **sorrowful.**

plan noun See **approach, design, method.**

plan verb See **design, intend, time.**

planar adjective See **even[1].**

plane[1] adjective See **even[1].**

plane[2] verb See **even[1].**

planetary adjective See **universal.**

plangent adjective See **resonant.**

plant verb See **hide[1], seed.**

plant noun See **work.**

plaster verb See **smear.**

plastered adjective See **drunk.**

plastic adjective Marked by unnaturalness, pretension, and often a slavish love of fads : artificial, factitious, synthetic, unnatural. See HONEST in Index. — See also **flexible, malleable, mobile.**

plasticity noun See **flexibility.**

platform noun See **stage.**

platitude noun See **cliché.**

platitudinal adjective See **trite.**

platitudinous adjective See **trite.**

plaudit noun See **applause, praise.**

plausibility noun See **verisimilitude.**

plausible adjective See **believable.**

plausibleness noun See **verisimilitude.**

play verb **1.** To occupy oneself with amusement or diversion : disport, recreate, sport. See WORK in Index. **2.** To be performed : run, show. See PERFORMING ARTS in Index. **3.** To make music : perform. See PERFORMING ARTS in Index. — See also **act, bet, fiddle, flirt, inflict, interpret, manipulate.**

play along verb Informal. To agree to cooperate or participate : go along. See PARTICIPATE in Index.

play around verb See **philander.**

play down verb See **soft-pedal.**

play off verb See **oppose.**

play out verb To cause (a line) to become longer and less taut : unreel, unroll, unwind. See GIVE in Index. — See also **dry up at dry, exhaust.**

play up verb See **emphasize.**

play noun **1.** Activity engaged in for relaxation and amusement : disport, diversion, fun, recreation, sport. See WORK in Index. **2.** Actions taken as a joke : fun, game, sport. See WORK in Index.

— See also **exercise, freedom, room.**

play-act *verb* See **act.**

player *noun* One who plays a musical instrument : musician, performer. See PERFORMING ARTS in Index. — See also **actor, bettor, participant.**

playful *adjective* Full of high-spirited fun : frisky, frolicsome, impish, mischievous, sportive, waggish. See WORK in Index.

playfulness *noun* The state of being full of high-spirited fun : friskiness, frolicsomeness, sportiveness, waggishness. See WORK in Index.

plaything *noun* See **toy.**

plea *noun* See **appeal, excuse.**

plead *verb* See **appeal.**

pleasant *adjective* See **agreeable, amiable, enjoyable.**

pleasantness *noun* See **amiability.**

pleasantry *noun* See **amenity.**

please *verb* To be satisfactory to : satisfy, suit. See PAIN in Index.
— See also **choose, delight.**

pleased *adjective* See **glad.**

pleasing *adjective* See **agreeable, enjoyable, glad.**

pleasurable *adjective* See **agreeable, enjoyable.**

pleasure *noun* See **delight, enjoyment, liking, will.**

pleasure *verb* See **delight, rejoice.**

pleat *noun* See **fold.**

pleat *verb* See **fold.**

pleb *noun* See **commonalty.**

plebeian *adjective* See **lowly.**

plebeian *noun* See **commonalty.**

pledge *verb* 1. To guarantee by a solemn promise : covenant, plight[2], promise, swear, vow. *Idiom:* give one's word of honor. See AGREE, OBLIGATION in Index.
2. To assume an obligation : contract, engage, promise, undertake. See AGREE, OBLIGATION in Index.
— See also **commit, drink, pawn**[1].

pledge *noun* See **pawn**[1], **promise, toast.**

plenitude *noun* See **plenty.**

plenitudinous *adjective* See **generous.**

plenteous *adjective* See **generous.**

plenteousness *noun* See **plenty.**

plentiful *adjective* See **generous.**

plenty *noun* Prosperity and a sufficiency of life's necessities : abundance, bounteousness, bountifulness, plenitude, plenteousness. See RICH in Index. — See also **heap.**

pleonasm *noun* See **wordiness.**

pleonastic *adjective* See **wordy.**

plethora *noun* See **excess.**

pliability *noun* See **flexibility.**

pliable *adjective* See **adaptable, flexible, malleable.**

pliableness *noun* See **flexibility.**

pliancy *noun* See **flexibility.**

pliant *adjective* See **adaptable, flexible, malleable.**

pliantness *noun* See **flexibility.**

plica *noun* See **fold.**

plication *noun* See **fold.**

plight[1] *noun* See **predicament.**

plight[2] *verb* See **pledge.**

plight *noun* See **promise.**

plighted *adjective* See **engaged.**

plod *verb* To walk heavily, slowly, and with difficulty : slog, slop, toil, trudge, wade. See MOVE in Index.
— See also **grind.**

plodder *noun* See **drudge.**

plop *verb* See **flop.**

plot *noun* 1. The series of events and relationships forming the basis of a composition : story, story line. See HAPPEN, WORDS in Index. 2. A secret plan to achieve an evil or illegal end : cabal, collusion, connivance, conspiracy, intrigue, machination, scheme. See CRIMES, PLANNED in Index. — See also **lot.**

plot *verb* 1. To show graphically the direction or location of, as by using coordinates : chart, lay out, map (out). See SHOW in Index.

2. To work out a secret plan to achieve an evil or illegal end : collude, connive, conspire, intrigue, machinate, scheme. See CRIMES, PLANNED in Index.

plow *verb* See **turn.**

ploy *noun* See **trick.**

pluck *noun* See **courage.**

  pluck *verb* See **pull.**

pluckiness *noun* See **courage.**

plucky *adjective* See **brave.**

plug *verb* See **advertise, fill, promote, shoot.**

  plug *noun* Something used to fill a hole, space, or container : choke, cork, fill, stop, stopper. See FULL in Index. — See also **promotion.**

plum *noun* See **catch, reward.**

plumb *adjective* See **vertical.**

plume *verb* See **pride.**

plummet *verb* See **fall.**

plump[1] *adjective* Well-rounded and full in form : chubby, plumpish, pudgy, roly-poly, rotund, round, tubby, zaftig. See FAT in Index.

plump[2] *verb* See **flop.**

  plump for *verb* See **support.**

plumpish *adjective* See **plump**[1].

plunder *noun* Goods or property seized unlawfully, especially by a victor in wartime : booty, loot, pillage, spoil (used in plural). *Slang:* boodle. *Nautical:* prize[2]. See CRIMES, GIVE in Index.

  plunder *verb* See **sack**[2].

plunge *verb* **1.** To move or thrust at, under, or into the midst of with sudden force : dive, lunge, wade in (*or* into). See ENTER in Index. **2.** To move or advance against strong resistance : drive, forge[2], lunge. See MOVE in Index. — See also **fall, ram.**

  plunge *noun* **1.** The act of plunging suddenly downward into or as if

into water : dive, nosedive, swoop. *Informal:* header. See ENTER in Index. **2.** The act of swimming : dip, duck, dunk, swim. See WORK in Index. — See also **fall.**

plunging *adjective* See **low.**

plunk *verb* See **flop.**

plush *adjective* See **luxurious.**

plushy *adjective* See **luxurious.**

ply[1] *verb* See **fold.**

ply[2] *verb* See **exercise, handle.**

pneumatic *adjective* See **airy.**

pocket *noun* See **hole.**

poem *noun* A poetic work or poetic works : poesy, poetry, rhyme, verse. See WORDS in Index. — See also **poetry.**

poesy *noun* See **poem.**

poet *noun* One who writes poetry : bard, muse[2], poetaster, poetess, rhymer, rhymester, versifier. See WORDS in Index.

poetaster *noun* See **poet.**

poetess *noun* See **poet.**

poetic *adjective* Of, relating to, or having the characteristics of poetry : lyric, poetical. See WORDS in Index.

poetical *adjective* See **poetic.**

poetry *noun* Something likened to poetry, as in form or style : lyricism, poem. See STYLE, WORDS in Index. — See also **poem.**

pogrom *noun* See **massacre.**

poignant *adjective* See **affecting, pungent.**

point *noun* **1.** A sharp or tapered end : acicula, acumination, apex, cusp, mucro, mucronation, tip[1]. See SHARP in Index. **2.** A very small mark : dash, dot, fleck, pinpoint, speck, spot. See MARKS in Index. **3.** A particular portion of space chosen for something : location, locus, place, spot. See PLACE in Index.

— See also **argument, degree, ele-**

ment, idea, instant, intention, subject, verge.

point *verb* To mark with punctua-
tion : punctuate. See MARKS in
Index. — See also **aim, refer.**

point out *verb* See **designate,
refer.**

point to *verb* See **imply, indicate.**

point up *verb* See **emphasize.**

pointed *adjective* Having an end
that tapers to a point : acicular,
aciculate, aciculated, acuminate,
acute, cuspate, cuspated, cuspidate,
cuspidated, mucronate, pointy,
sharp. See SHARP in Index. — See
also **noticeable.**

pointer *noun* See **tip³.**

pointless *adjective* See **aimless,
mindless.**

point of view *noun* The position
from which something is observed or
considered : angle², eye, outlook,
slant, standpoint, vantage, viewpoint. See PERSPECTIVE in Index.

pointy *adjective* See **pointed.**

poise *noun* See **balance, ease.**

poise *verb* See **balance, hang.**

poison *noun* Anything that is injurious, destructive, or fatal : bane,
canker, contagion, toxin, venom,
virus. See HELP in Index. — See also
contaminant.

poison *verb* To have a destructive
effect on : canker, envenom, infect.
Archaic: empoison. See HELP in
Index. — See also **contaminate.**

poison *adjective* See **poisonous.**

poisonous *adjective* Capable of
injuring or killing by poison :
mephitic, mephitical, poison, toxic,
toxicant, venomous, virulent. See
HELP in Index. — See also
malevolent.

poisonousness *noun* See
malevolence.

poke *verb* To cause to stick out :
push, shove, thrust. See CONVEX in

Index. — See also **delay, dig, grope,
snoop.**

poke *noun* See **dig, laggard.**

pokerfaced *adjective* See **expressionless.**

pokey also **poky** *noun* See **jail.**

poky also **pokey** *adjective* See
slow.

polar *adjective* See **frigid, opposite.**

polarity *noun* See **opposition.**

polemic *noun* See **argument.**

polemic *adjective* See
argumentative.

polemical *adjective* See
argumentative.

police *verb* To maintain or keep in
order with or as if with police :
patrol. See LAW in Index. — See also
tidy.

police *noun* See **policeman.**

policeman *noun* A member of a
law-enforcement agency : bluecoat, finest, officer, patrolman,
patrolwoman, peace officer, police,
police officer, policewoman.
Informal: cop, law. *Slang:* bull¹, copper, flatfoot, fuzz, gendarme, heat,
man (often uppercase). *Chiefly
British:* bobby, constable, peeler. See
LAW in Index.

police officer *noun* See **policeman.**

policewoman *noun* See **policeman.**

policy *noun* See **line.**

polish *verb* See **gloss, perfect, touch
up** at **touch.**

polish off *verb* See **consume,
exhaust.**

polish *noun* See **elegance, gloss.**

polished *adjective* See **cultured,
glossy.**

polite *adjective* See **attentive,
courteous.**

politeness *noun* See **amenity,
courtesy.**

politesse *noun* See **courtesy.**

politic *adjective* See **delicate.**

polity *noun* See **state.**

poll *noun* See **head.**

pollutant *noun* See **contaminant.**

pollute *verb* See **contaminate, taint, violate.**

pollution *noun* See **contamination, impurity.**

Pollyanna *noun* See **optimist.**

poltroon *noun* See **coward.**

polychromatic *adjective* See **multicolor.**

polychrome *adjective* See **multicolor.**

polychromic *adjective* See **multicolor.**

polychromous *adjective* See **multicolor.**

polymorphic *adjective* See **various.**

polymorphism *noun* See **variety.**

polymorphous *adjective* See **various.**

polysyllabic *adjective* See **long**[1].

pomp *noun* See **display.**

pomposity *noun* See **pretentiousness.**

pompous *adjective* Characterized by an exaggerated show of dignity or self-importance : grandiose, hoity-toity, pretentious, puffed-up, self-important. *Informal:* highfalutin. See PLAIN in Index.

pompousness *noun* See **pretentiousness.**

ponder *verb* To think or think about carefully and at length : chew on (or over), cogitate, consider, contemplate, deliberate, entertain, excogitate, meditate, mull, muse[1], reflect, revolve, ruminate, study, think, think out, think over, think through, turn over, weigh. *Idioms:* cudgel one's brains, put on one's thinking cap, rack one's brain. See THOUGHTS in Index.

ponderable *adjective* See **perceptible.**

ponderosity *noun* See **heaviness.**

ponderous *adjective* Lacking fluency or gracefulness : elephantine, heavy-handed, labored. See GOOD in Index. — See also **heavy.**

ponderousness *noun* See **heaviness.**

pool *noun* See **combine.**

poop[1] *verb* See **exhaust.**
  poop out

poop[2] *noun* See **drip.**

pooped *adjective* See **exhausted.**

poor *adjective* Having little or no money or wealth : beggarly, destitute, down-and-out, impecunious, impoverished, indigent, necessitous, needy, penniless, penurious, poverty-stricken. *Informal:* broke, strapped. *Idioms:* hard up, on one's uppers. See RICH in Index. — See also **bad, meager, pitiful, shoddy.**

poorly *adjective* See **sick.**

pop[1] *verb* See **burst, crack, hit.**
  pop in *verb* See **visit.**
  pop off *verb* See **die.**
  pop *noun* See **report.**

pop[2] *noun* See **father.**

poppycock *noun* See **nonsense.**

populace *noun* See **commonalty.**

popular *adjective* **1.** Of, representing, or carried on by people at large : democratic, general, public. See POLITICS, SPECIFIC in Index.
2. Suited to or within the means of ordinary people : moderate, modest, reasonable. See MONEY in Index. — See also **famous, favorite.**

popularize *verb* See **advertise.**

popularity *noun* See **fame.**

populate *verb* See **inhabit.**

porcine *adjective* See **fat.**

pork *noun* See **patronage.**

port *noun* See **bearing.**

portend *verb* See **adumbrate.**

portent *noun* See **omen.**

portentous *adjective* See **fateful.**

portion *verb* See **distribute.**

portion *noun* See **allotment, cut, division, fate, interest, serving.**

portly *adjective* See **fat.**

portrait *noun* See **double.**

portray *verb* See **act, represent.**

portrayal *noun* See **representation.**

pose *verb* **1.** To assume a particular position, as for a portrait : posture, sit. See POSTURE in Index. **2.** To represent oneself in a given character or as other than what one is : attitudinize, impersonate, masquerade, pass, posture. *Idiom:* pass oneself off as. See HONEST in Index. — See also **act, ask, posture, propose.**

pose *noun* See **affectation, position, posture.**

posh *adjective* See **exclusive, fashionable.**

posit *verb* See **suppose.**

position *noun* **1.** The place where a person or thing is located : emplacement, location, locus, placement, site, situation. See PLACE in Index. **2.** The way in which one is placed or arranged : attitude, pose, posture. See POSTURE in Index. **3.** A post of employment : appointment, berth, billet, job, office, place, situation, slot, spot. *Slang:* gig. See PLACE in Index. — See also **bearing, belief, place, posture.**

position *verb* To put in or assign to a certain position or location : emplace, install, locate, place, set[1], site, situate, spot. See PLACE in Index.

positive *adjective* Of a constructive nature : affirmative. *Informal:* upbeat. See HELP in Index. — See also **certain, definite, favorable, sure, utter[2].**

positiveness *noun* See **sureness.**

positively *adverb* See **absolutely, flatly, really.**

possess *verb* To dominate the mind or thoughts of : obsess. See CON-TROL in Index. — See also **bear, carry, command, enjoy, have.**

possessed *adjective* See **cool.**

possession *noun* An area subject to rule by an outside power : colony, dependency, province, territory. See POLITICS in Index. — See also **effect, holding, ownership.**

possessive *adjective* See **jealous.**

possessor *noun* See **owner.**

possibility *noun* Something that may occur or be done : contingency, eventuality. See POSSIBLE in Index. — See also **chance.**

possible *adjective* **1.** Capable of occurring or being done : feasible, practicable, viable, workable. *Idiom:* within reach. See POSSIBLE in Index. **2.** Capable of favorable development : potential. See POSSIBLE in Index. — See also **earthly, potential, probable.**

post[1] *verb* See **score.**

post[2] *verb* See **gamble, station.**

post *noun* See **station.**

post[3] *verb* To place on a list or in a record : enter, insert, record, register. See REMEMBER in Index.

poster *noun* See **sign.**

posterior *adjective* See **back, later.**

posterior *noun* See **bottom.**

posterity *noun* See **progeny.**

postern *adjective* See **back.**

posthaste *adverb* See **fast.**

posthumous *adjective* Occurring or done after death : postmortem. See TIME in Index.

posting *noun* See **entry.**

postmortem *adjective* See **posthumous.**

postpone *verb* See **defer**[1].

postponement *noun* See **delay.**

postulate *verb* See **suppose.**

postulate *noun* See **assumption.**

postulation *noun* See **assumption.**

posture *noun* **1.** The way in which a person holds or carries his or her body : attitude, carriage, pose, stance. See POSTURE in Index. **2.** A frame of mind affecting one's thoughts or behavior : attitude, outlook, position, stance. See ATTITUDE in Index. — See also **position.**

posture *verb* To assume an exaggerated or unnatural attitude or pose : attitudinize, pose. *Idiom:* strike an attitude. See POSTURE in Index. — See also **pose.**

posy *noun* See **bouquet.**

pot *noun* See **bet.**

potable *noun* See **drink.**

potation *noun* See **drink.**

potence *noun* See **strength.**

potency *noun* See **effect, energy, strength.**

potent *adjective* See **powerful, strong.**

potential *adjective* Capable of being but not yet in existence : eventual, latent, possible. See POSSIBLE in Index. — See also **possible.**

potential *noun* The inherent capacity for growth or development : potentiality. See POSSIBLE in Index.

potentiality *noun* See **potential.**

pother *noun* See **bother.**

pother *verb* See **fuss.**

potpourri *noun* See **assortment.**

potted *adjective* See **drugged, drunk.**

pouch *verb* See **bulge.**

pound *verb* See **beat, impress.**

pound *noun* See **beat, blow².**

pour *verb* **1.** To cause (a liquid) to flow in a steady stream : decant, draw (off), effuse. See MOVE in Index. **2.** To rain heavily : *Idioms:* come down in buckets (*or* sheets *or* torrents), rain cats and dogs. See DRY in Index. **3.** To come or go in large numbers : flood, swarm, throng, troop. See BIG, MOVE in Index. — See also **flow.**

pout *verb* See **sulk.**

pout *noun* See **face.**

poverty *noun* The condition of being extremely poor : beggary, destitution, impecuniosity, impecuniousness, impoverishment, indigence, need, neediness, pennilessness, penuriousness, penury, privation, want. See RICH in Index. — See also **shortage.**

poverty-stricken *adjective* See **poor.**

powder *verb* See **crush, sprinkle.**

powdery *adjective* See **fine¹.**

power *noun* See **authority, energy, force, heap, muscle, strength.**

powerful *adjective* Having or able to exert great power : mighty, potent, puissant. See STRONG in Index. — See also **forceful, influential, severe, strong.**

powerfully *adverb* See **hard.**

powerfulness *noun* See **strength.**

powerless *adjective* See **helpless, ineffectual.**

powerlessness *noun* See **inability, ineffectuality.**

powwow *noun* See **conference.**

powwow *verb* See **confer.**

practicable *adjective* See **open, possible, practical.**

practical *adjective* **1.** Serving or capable of serving a useful purpose : functional, handy, practicable, serviceable, useful, utilitarian. See USED in Index. **2.** Resulting from experience or practice : practiced. See KNOWLEDGE in Index. — See also **implicit, realistic.**

practice *verb* **1.** To do or perform repeatedly so as to master : rehearse. See WORK in Index. **2.** To work at, especially as a profession : pursue. See DO, WORK in Index. — See also **exercise, use.**

practice *noun* **1.** Repetition of an action so as to develop or maintain one's skill : drill, exercise, rehearsal, study, training. See WORK in Index. **2.** A working at a profession or occupation : pursuit. See DO, WORK in Index. — See also **custom.**

practiced *adjective* See **accomplished, experienced, practical.**

praetorian *adjective* See **corrupt.**

pragmatic *noun* See **meddler.**

pragmatic *adjective* See **realistic.**

pragmatical *adjective* See **realistic.**

praise *noun* **1.** An expression of warm approval : acclaim, acclamation, applause, celebration, commendation, compliment, encomium, eulogy, kudos, laudation, panegyric, plaudit. See PRAISE in Index. **2.** The honoring of a deity, as in worship : exaltation, extolment, glorification, laudation, magnification. See RELIGION in Index. — See also **compliment.**

praise *verb* **1.** To express warm approval of : acclaim, applaud, commend, compliment, laud. See PRAISE in Index. **2.** To honor (a deity) in religious worship : exalt, extol, glorify, laud, magnify. See RELIGION in Index. — See also **compliment, honor.**

praiseworthy *adjective* See **admirable.**

prance *verb* See **strut.**

prank¹ *noun* A mischievous act : antic, caper, frolic, joke, lark, trick. *Informal:* shenanigan. *Slang:* monkeyshine (often used in plural). See GOOD, WORK in Index.

prank² *verb* See **dress up** at **dress.**

prankishness *noun* See **mischief.**

prankster *noun* See **mischief.**

prate *verb* See **babble, chatter.**

prate *noun* See **babble, chatter.**

prattle *verb* See **babble, chatter.**

prattle *noun* See **babble, chatter.**

praxis *noun* See **custom.**

pray *verb* To offer a reverent petition to God or a god : supplicate. See RELIGION in Index. — See also **appeal.**

prayer¹ *noun* **1.** The act of praying : invocation, supplication. See RELIGION in Index. **2.** A formula of words used in praying : collect², litany, orison, rogation (often used in plural). See RELIGION in Index. — See also **appeal.**

prayer² *noun* See **supplicant.**

prayerful *adjective* See **holy.**

preach *verb* To deliver a sermon, especially as a vocation : evangelize, sermonize. See RELIGION in Index. — See also **moralize.**

preacher *noun* A person ordained for service in a Christian church : churchman, churchwoman, clergyman, clergywoman, cleric, clerical, clerk, divine, ecclesiastic, minister, parson. *Informal:* reverend. See RELIGION in Index.

preachy *adjective* See **didactic.**

preamble *noun* See **introduction.**

precarious *adjective* See **insecure, unstable.**

precariousness *noun* See **instability, unstableness.**

precaution *noun* See **caution, prudence.**

precede *verb* To come, exist, or occur before in time : antecede, antedate, predate. See PRECEDE in Index. — See also **introduce.**

precedence *noun* The act, condition, or right of preceding : antecedence, precedency, priority, right of way. See PRECEDE in Index.

precedency *noun* See **precedence.**

precedent *noun* A closely similar case in existence or in the past : example. See SAME in Index.

precedent *adjective* See **advance, past.**

preceding *adjective* See **advance, last[1], past.**

precept *noun* See **law.**

precinct *noun* See **environment, limit.**

precious *adjective* See **affected, darling, valuable.**

precious *noun* See **darling.**

precipitance *noun* See **haste.**

precipitancy *noun* See **haste.**

precipitant *adjective* See **abrupt, rash[1].**

precipitate *verb* See **deposit.**

precipitate *adjective* See **abrupt, rash[1].**

precipitate *noun* See **deposit, effect.**

precipitateness *noun* See **haste.**

precipitation *noun* See **deposit, haste.**

precipitous *adjective* See **steep[1].**

precise *adjective* Strictly distinguished from others : exact, very. See PRECISE in Index. — See also **accurate, definite, genteel.**

precisely *adverb* See **directly, even[1].**

preciseness *noun* See **accuracy.**

precision *noun* See **accuracy.**

preclude *verb* See **prevent.**

preclusion *noun* See **prevention.**

preclusive *adjective* See **preventive.**

precocious *adjective* See **advanced, early.**

precondition *noun* See **condition.**

precursor *noun* One that indicates or announces someone or something to come : forerunner, foreshadower, harbinger, herald, presager. See FORESIGHT, SHOW in Index. — See also **ancestor.**

predate *verb* See **precede.**

predecessor *noun* See **ancestor.**

predestinate *verb* See **fate.**

predestination *noun* See **fate.**

predestine *verb* See **fate.**

predetermine *verb* See **fate, premeditate.**

predicament *noun* A difficult, often embarrassing situation or condition : box[1], corner, deep water, difficulty, dilemma, Dutch, fix, hole, hot spot, hot water, jam, plight[1], quagmire, scrape, soup, trouble. *Informal:* bind, pickle, spot. See EASY in Index.

predicate *verb* See **base[1].**

predict *verb* To tell about or make known (future events) in advance, especially by means of special knowledge or inference : call, forecast, foretell, prognosticate, project. See FORESIGHT in Index.

prediction *noun* The act of predicting : forecast, outlook, prognosis, prognostication, projection. See FORESIGHT in Index.

predictive *adjective* Of or relating to prediction : prognostic, prognosticative. See FORESIGHT in Index.

predilection *noun* See **bent.**

predispose *verb* See **dispose.**

predisposition *noun* See **bent.**

predominance *noun* See **dominance.**

predominant *adjective* See **prevailing, ruling.**

predominate *verb* See **dominate.**

preeminence or **pre-eminence** *noun* See **dominance, eminence.**

preeminent or **pre-eminent** *adjective* See **eminent, rare.**

preempt or **pre-empt** *verb* See **assume, tie up** at **tie.**

preemption or **pre-emption** *noun* See **usurpation.**

preen *verb* See **pride.**

preface *noun* See **introduction.**

preface *verb* See **introduce.**

prefatory *adjective* See **introductory, preliminary.**

prefer *verb* See **favor.**

preferable *adjective* See **better.**

preference *noun* See **choice, favor, taste.**

preferential *adjective* See **favorable.**

preferred *adjective* See **favorite.**

prefigure *verb* See **adumbrate.**

prefigurement *noun* See **omen.**

pregnable *adjective* See **vulnerable.**

pregnancy *noun* The condition of carrying a developing fetus within the uterus : gestation, gravidity, gravidness, parturiency. See REPRODUCTION in Index.

pregnant *adjective* **1.** Carrying a developing fetus within the uterus : big, enceinte, expectant, expecting, gravid, parturient. *Slang:* gone. *Archaic:* great. *Idioms:* in a family way, with child. See REPRODUCTION in Index. **2.** Conveying hidden or unexpressed meaning : meaningful, significant, suggestive. See MEANING in Index.

prejudice *noun* Irrational suspicion or hatred of a particular group, race, or religion : bigotry, intolerance. See LIKE in Index. — See also **bias.**

prejudice *verb* See **bias, injure.**

prejudiced *adjective* See **biased.**

prejudicial *adjective* See **biased.**

prelect *verb* See **address.**

prelection *noun* See **speech.**

preliminary *adjective* Before or in preparation for the main matter, action, or business : inductive, introductory, prefatory, preparatory, prolegomenous. See START in Index. — See also **introductory, rough.**

prelude *noun* See **introduction.**

premature *adjective* See **early.**

premeditate *verb* To consider and plan in advance : predetermine. See PLANNED in Index.

premeditated *adjective* See **calculated.**

premier *adjective* See **primary.**

premise *noun* See **assumption.**

premise *verb* See **suppose.**

premium *noun* See **reward.**

preoccupation *noun* See **absorption.**

preoccupied *adjective* See **absent-minded, absorbed.**

preoccupy *verb* See **absorb.**

preordain *verb* See **fate.**

preparation *noun* The condition of being made ready beforehand : preparedness, readiness. See PREPARED in Index. — See also **arrangement.**

preparatory *adjective* See **introductory, preliminary.**

prepare *verb* To cause to be ready, as for use, consumption, or a special purpose : fit[1], fix, make, prime, ready. See PREPARED in Index. — See also **arrange.**

preparedness *noun* See **preparation.**

preponderance *noun* See **dominance, weight.**

preponderancy *noun* See **dominance, weight.**

preponderant *adjective* See **dominant.**

preponderate *verb* See **dominate.**

prepossess *verb* See **bias.**

prepossessed *adjective* See **biased.**

prepossessing *adjective* See **attractive.**

prepossession *noun* See **absorption, bias.**

preposterous *adjective* See **foolish, outrageous.**

preposterousness *noun* See **foolishness.**

prepotency *noun* See **dominance.**

prepotent *adjective* See **ruling.**

prerequisite *noun* See **condition.**

prerogative *noun* See **authority, birthright.**

presage *verb* See **adumbrate.**

presage *noun* See **omen.**

presager *noun* See **precursor**.

prescience *noun* See **vision**.

prescient *adjective* See **visionary**.

prescribe *verb* See **dictate**.

prescript *noun* See **rule**.

prescription *noun* See **law**.

presence *noun* The condition or fact of being present : occurrence. See BE in Index. — See also **bearing**.

present[1] *noun* See **now**.

present *adjective* In existence now : contemporary, current, existent, existing, new, now, present-day. See TIME in Index.

present[2] *verb* To bring forward for formal consideration : adduce, cite, lay[1]. *Archaic:* allege. See LAW, WORDS in Index. — See also **acquaint, confer, give, offer, stage**.

present *noun* See **gift**.

presentable *adjective* See **decent**.

presentation *noun* The instance or occasion of being presented for the first time to society : coming-out, debut. See KNOWLEDGE in Index. — See also **conferment, gift**.

present-day *adjective* See **present**[1].

preservation *noun* See **conservation, defense**.

preservative *adjective* Able to preserve : conservative, protective. See HELP in Index.

preserve *verb* See **conserve, defend, maintain**.

preserve *noun* See **reservation**.

press *verb* To smooth by applying heat and pressure : iron, mangle[2]. See SMOOTH in Index. — See also **bear, crowd, embrace, insist, push, squeeze, urge**.

press *noun* Journalists and journalism in general : fourth estate, medium (used in plural **media**). *British:* Fleet Street. See WORDS in Index. — See also **crowd**.

pressing *adjective* See **burning**.

pressing *noun* See **insistence**.

pressure *noun* The act, condition, or effect of exerting force on someone or something : strain[1], stress, tension. See PUSH in Index. — See also **force**.

pressure *verb* See **force, pressurize**.

pressurize *verb* To maintain normal air pressure in : pressure. See PUSH in Index.

prestidigitation *noun* See **magic**.

prestige *noun* See **eminence, face, honor**.

prestigious *adjective* See **eminent**.

presumable *adjective* See **presumptive**.

presume *verb* To have the courage to put forward, as an idea, especially when rebuff or criticism is likely : dare, hazard, pretend, venture. See TRY in Index. — See also **abuse, suppose**.

presuming *adjective* See **impudent**.

presumption *noun* See **arrogance**.

presumptive *adjective* Based on probability or presumption : assumptive, likely, presumable, probable, prospective. *Idiom:* taken for granted. See BELIEF, LIKELY in Index. — See also **supposed**.

presumptuous *adjective* See **impudent**.

presumptuousness *noun* See **impudence**.

presuppose *verb* See **suppose**.

presupposition *noun* See **assumption**.

pretend *verb* To claim or allege insincerely or falsely : feign, profess. See TRUE in Index. — See also **act, assume, fake, presume**.

pretend *adjective* See **artificial**.

pretended *adjective* See **artificial**.

pretender *noun* See **claimant, fake**.

pretense *noun* 1. The presentation of something false as true : charade, make-believe. See HONEST, TRUE in Index. **2.** A professed rather than a real reason : pretension, pretext. See HONEST in Index. — See also **act, affectation, claim, façade.**

pretension *noun* See **claim, pretense, pretentiousness.**

pretentious *adjective* See **pompous, showy.**

pretentiousness *noun* Boastful self-importance or display : grandioseness, grandiosity, ostentation, pomposity, pompousness, pretension. See PLAIN in Index.

preternatural *adjective* Greatly exceeding or departing from the normal course of nature : supernatural, unnatural. See USUAL in Index. — See also **abnormal, supernatural.**

preternaturalness *noun* See **abnormality.**

pretext *noun* See **excuse, façade, pretense.**

pretty *adjective* See **attractive, beautiful.**

pretty *adverb* See **fairly.**

pretty penny *noun* See **fortune.**

prevail *verb* See **dominate.**

prevail against or **over** *verb* See **defeat.**

prevail on or **upon** *verb* See **persuade.**

prevailing *adjective* Most generally existing or encountered at a given time : current, predominant, prevalent, regnant, rife, widespread. See SPECIFIC in Index. — See also **ruling.**

prevalence *noun* See **usualness.**

prevalent *adjective* See **prevailing.**

prevaricate *verb* See **equivocate, lie².**

prevarication *noun* See **equivocation, lie².**

prevaricator *noun* See **liar.**

prevent *verb* To prohibit from occurring by advance planning or action : avert, forestall, forfend,

obviate, preclude, rule out, stave off, ward (off). *Idiom:* nip in the bud. See ALLOW in Index.

preventative *adjective* See **preventive.**

prevention *noun* The act of preventing : determent, deterrence, forestallment, obviation, preclusion. See ALLOW in Index.

preventive *adjective* **1.** Intended to prevent : deterrent, preclusive, preventative. See ALLOW in Index. **2.** Defending against disease : preventative, prophylactic, protective. See ALLOW in Index.

previous *adjective* See **advance, last¹, late, past.**

previously *adverb* See **earlier.**

prey *noun* See **victim.**

price *noun* See **cost.**

priceless *adjective* Extremely funny : hilarious, sidesplitting. *Informal:* killing, rich. See LAUGHTER in Index. — See also **valuable.**

prick *noun* **1.** A small mark or hole made by a sharp, pointed object : perforation, puncture, stab. See MARKS, OPEN in Index. **2.** A sharp, pointed object : needle, prickle, spine, thorn. See SHARP in Index. — See also **pain.**

prick *verb* See **provoke.**

prickle *noun* See **pain, prick.**

prickly *adjective* See **thorny.**

pricky *adjective* See **thorny.**

pride *noun* A sense of one's own dignity or worth : amour-propre, ego, self-esteem, self-regard, self-respect. See RESPECT in Index. — See also **arrogance, egotism.**

pride *verb* To be proud of (oneself), as for an accomplishment or achievement : congratulate, plume, preen. See RESPECT in Index.

prideful *adjective* See **arrogant, proud.**

pridefulness *noun* See **arrogance.**

prier also **pryer** noun See **snoop**.

priggish adjective See **genteel**.

prim adjective See **genteel**.

primary adjective Most important, influential, or significant : capital, cardinal, chief, first, foremost, key, leading, main, major, number one, paramount, premier, prime, principal, top. See IMPORTANT in Index. — See also **first, immediate, original, radical**.

prime noun See **bloom**[1].

prime adjective See **choice, excellent, first, original, primary**.

prime verb See **prepare**.

primeval adjective See **primitive**.

primitive adjective Of or relating to early stages in the evolution of human culture : primeval. See START in Index. — See also **early, elemental, ignorant, original, rude, uncivilized**.

primordial adjective See **first**.

princely adjective See **grand**.

principal adjective Having or exercising authority : chief, head. See OVER in Index. — See also **primary**.

principal noun See **lead**.

principle noun See **character, law**.

principled adjective See **ethical**.

print noun See **impression, track**.

printing noun See **impression, publication**.

prior adjective See **advance, past**.

priority noun See **precedence**.

prison noun See **jail**.

prissy adjective See **genteel**.

private adjective Belonging or confined to a particular person or group as opposed to the public or the government : personal, privy. See SPECIFIC in Index. — See also **confidential, personal**.

privation noun See **deprivation, poverty**.

privileged adjective See **confidential**.

privy adjective See **private**.

prize[1] noun See **best, catch, reward, treasure, trophy**.

prize verb See **appreciate, cherish**.

prize[2] noun See **plunder**.

probability noun See **chance**.

probable adjective Having a chance of happening or being true : contingent, likely, possible. See LIKELY in Index. — See also **presumptive**.

probe noun See **exploration, feeler, inquiry**.

probe verb See **explore, feel out** at **feel**.

prober noun See **inquirer**.

probing adjective See **acute**.

probity noun See **good**.

problem noun A situation that presents difficulty, uncertainty, or perplexity : hornets' nest, issue, question. *Informal:* can of worms. See EASY in Index.

problematic adjective See **ambiguous, debatable**.

problematical adjective See **ambiguous, debatable**.

proboscis noun See **nose**.

procedure noun See **approach, line, move**.

proceed verb See **come, go, stem**.

procession noun See **order, series**.

proclaim verb See **announce, show, usher in** at **usher**.

proclamation noun See **announcement**.

proclivity noun See **bent**.

procrastinate verb See **delay**.

procrastinator noun See **laggard**.

procreant adjective See **reproductive**.

procreate verb See **father, produce, reproduce**.

procreation noun See **reproduction**.

procreative adjective See **reproductive**.

procumbent *adjective* See **flat**.

procurable *adjective* See **available**.

procure *verb* See **get**.

prod *verb* See **dig, provoke**.

prod *noun* See **stimulus**.

prodigal *adjective* See **extravagant, profuse**.

prodigal *noun* See **wastrel**.

prodigality *noun* See **extravagance**.

prodigious *adjective* See **fabulous, giant**.

prodigiousness *noun* See **enormousness**.

prodigy *noun* See **marvel**.

produce *verb* To cause to come into existence : beget, breed, create, engender, father, hatch, make, originate, parent, procreate, sire, spawn. *Idiom:* give birth (or rise) to. See MAKE in Index. — See also **bear, compose, develop, lengthen, make, return**.

producer *noun* See **builder**.

product *noun* Something produced by human effort : production. See MAKE in Index.

production *noun* See **composition, product, yield**.

productive *adjective* See **effective, efficient, fertile**.

productiveness *noun* See **fertility**.

productivity *noun* See **efficiency, fertility**.

profanation *noun* See **sacrilege**.

profane *adjective* Not religious in subject matter, form, or use : lay[2], secular, temporal, worldly. See SACRED in Index. — See also **obscene, sacrilegious**.

profane *verb* See **violate**.

profaneness *noun* See **obscenity**.

profanity *noun* See **obscenity**.

profess *verb* See **pretend**.

profession *noun* See **business**.

professional *noun* See **expert**.

adjective See **expert**.

proffer *verb* See **offer**.

proffer *noun* See **offer**.

proficiency *noun* See **ability**.

proficient *adjective* See **expert**.

proficient *noun* See **expert**.

profile *noun* See **outline**.

profit *verb* To be an advantage to : advantage, avail, benefit, serve. *Archaic:* boot[2]. *Idiom:* stand someone in good stead. See HELP in Index. — See also **benefit, clean up at clean**.

profit *noun* See **advantage, gain, interest, use**.

profitable *adjective* Affording profit : advantageous, fat, lucrative, moneymaking, remunerative, rewarding. See GET in Index. — See also **beneficial**.

profligacy *noun* See **extravagance, license**.

profligate *adjective* See **abandoned, extravagant**.

profligate *noun* See **wanton, wastrel**.

profound *adjective* See **deep**.

profoundness *noun* See **depth**.

profundity *noun* See **depth, wisdom**.

profuse *adjective* Given to or marked by unrestrained abundance : extravagant, exuberant, lavish, lush[1], luxuriant, opulent, prodigal, riotous, superabundant. See BIG, EXCESS in Index. — See also **extravagant, thick**.

profuseness *noun* See **extravagance**.

profusion *noun* See **extravagance, heap**.

progenitor *noun* See **ancestor**.

progeny *noun* A group consisting of those descended directly from the same parents or ancestors : brood, get, issue, offspring, posterity, seed. See KIN in Index. — See also **descendant**.

prognosis *noun* See **prediction**.

prognostic *adjective* See predictive.

  prognostic *noun* See omen.

prognosticate *verb* See adumbrate, predict.

prognostication *noun* See omen, prediction.

prognosticative *adjective* See predictive.

program *noun* 1. An organized list, as of procedures, activities, or events : agenda, calendar, docket, lineup, order of the day (often used in plural), schedule, timetable. See PLANNED in Index. 2. A document, such as a list or an outline, that gives, for example, the order of events in a public performance or the chief features of a stock offering : bill¹, prospectus, syllabus. See PLANNED, WORDS in Index. — See also line.

  program *verb* See schedule.

progress *noun* Steady improvement, as of an individual or a society : amelioration, betterment, development, improvement, melioration. See BETTER in Index. — See also advance, development.

  progress *verb* See come.

progression *noun* See advance, series.

progressive *adjective* See advanced, broad, liberal.

  progressive *noun* See liberal.

prohibit *verb* See forbid.

prohibition *noun* See forbiddance.

project *noun* Something undertaken, especially something requiring extensive planning and work : enterprise, undertaking, venture. See WORK in Index. — See also design.

  project *verb* See bulge, design, intend, predict, shed, shoot.

projection *noun* See bulge, prediction.

prolegomenon *noun* See introduction.

prolegomenous *adjective* See introductory, preliminary.

proliferate *verb* See increase, reproduce.

proliferation *noun* See buildup, increase, reproduction.

proliferous *adjective* See fertile.

prolific *adjective* See fertile.

prolificacy *noun* See fertility.

prolificness *noun* See fertility.

prolix *adjective* See wordy.

prolixity *noun* See wordiness.

prologue *noun* See introduction.

prolong *verb* See lengthen.

prolongate *verb* See lengthen.

prolongation *noun* See extension.

prolonged *adjective* See chronic, long¹.

promenade *verb* See stroll.

  promenade *noun* See walk.

prominence *noun* See eminence, hill.

prominency *noun* See eminence.

prominent *adjective* See eminent, noticeable.

promise *noun* A declaration that one will or will not do a certain thing : assurance, covenant, engagement, guarantee, guaranty, pledge, plight², solemn word, vow, warrant, word, word of honor. See OBLIGATION in Index.

  promise *verb* See pledge.

promising *adjective* See coming, encouraging.

promote *verb* 1. To raise in rank : advance, elevate, jump, raise, upgrade. See RISE in Index. 2. To help bring about : encourage, feed, foster. See HELP in Index. 3. To increase or seek to increase the importance or reputation of by favorable publicity : ballyhoo, boost, build up, enhance, publicize, puff, talk up, tout. *Informal:* plug. *Slang:*

hype. See KNOWLEDGE in Index.
— See also **advance, advertise.**

promotion *noun* A systematic effort or part of this effort to increase the importance or reputation of by favorable publicity : advertisement, ballyhoo, buildup, publicity, puffery. *Informal:* pitch, plug. *Slang:* hype. See KNOWLEDGE in Index.
— See also **advancement, advertising.**

prompt *adjective* See **punctual.**

prompt *verb* See **provoke.**

promulgate *verb* See **advertise, announce, establish.**

promulgation *noun* See **announcement.**

prone *adjective* See **flat, inclined, liable.**

proneness *noun* See **bent.**

pronounce *verb* To produce or make (speech sounds) : articulate, enunciate, say, utter[1], vocalize. See WORDS in Index.

pronounced *adjective* See **apparent, decided, noticeable.**

pronouncement *noun* See **announcement, ruling.**

pronto *adverb* See **fast.**

proof *noun* See **confirmation, reason, test.**

proof *adjective* See **resistant.**

prop *noun* See **support.**

prop *verb* See **sustain.**

propagandize *verb* See **indoctrinate.**

propagate *verb* See **advertise, grow, reproduce.**

propagation *noun* See **reproduction.**

propel *verb* See **drive, provoke, shoot.**

propensity *noun* See **bent.**

proper *adjective* See **appropriate, convenient, correct, ethical, genteel, just.**

properly *adverb* See **fair.**

properness *noun* See **decency.**

property *noun* See **effect, holding, land, quality.**

prophecy *noun* Something that is foretold by or as if by supernatural means : divination, oracle, soothsaying, vaticination, vision. See FORESIGHT in Index.

prophesier *noun* See **prophet.**

prophesy *verb* To tell about or make known (future events) by or as if by supernatural means : augur, divine, foretell, soothsay, vaticinate. See FORESIGHT in Index.

prophet *noun* A person who foretells future events by or as if by supernatural means : augur, auspex, diviner, foreteller, haruspex, prophesier, prophetess, seer, sibyl, soothsayer, vaticinator. See FORESIGHT in Index.

prophetess *noun* See **prophet.**

prophetic *also* **prophetical** *adjective* Of or relating to the foretelling of events by or as if by supernatural means : augural, divinitory, fatidic, fatidical, mantic, oracular, sibylline, vatic, vatical, vaticinal, visionary. See FORESIGHT in Index.

prophylactic *adjective* See **preventive.**

propitiate *verb* See **pacify.**

propitious *adjective* See **beneficial, favorable, opportune.**

proportion *noun* Satisfying arrangement marked by even distribution of elements, as in a design : balance, harmony, symmetry. See BEAUTIFUL in Index. — See also **degree, size.**

proportion *verb* See **harmonize.**

proportional *adjective* Properly or correspondingly related in size, amount, or scale : commensurable, commensurate, proportionate. *Idiom:* in proportion. See BIG in Index. — See also **symmetrical.**

proportionate *adjective* See **proportional, symmetrical.**

proposal *noun* Something that is put forward for consideration : proposition, submission, suggestion. See OFFER in Index. — See also **offer.**

propose *verb* To state, as an idea, for consideration : advance, offer, pose, propound, put forward, set forth, submit, suggest. See OFFER in Index. — See also **intend.**

proposition *noun* See **proposal.**

propound *verb* See **propose.**

proprietor *noun* See **owner.**

proprietorship *noun* See **ownership.**

propriety *noun* See **amenity, decency, ethic, manner.**

prosaic *adjective* See **dull, realistic.**

proscenium *noun* See **stage.**

proscribe *verb* See **forbid.**

proscription *noun* See **forbiddance.**

prosecutable *adjective* See **litigable.**

prosecute *verb* See **perform, sue.**

prosecution *noun* See **performance.**

prosopopeia also **prosopopoeia** *noun* See **embodiment.**

prospect *noun* See **chance, expectation, future, view.**

prospective *adjective* See **presumptive.**

prospectus *noun* See **program.**

prosper *verb* To do or fare well : boom, flourish, go, thrive. *Slang:* score. *Idioms:* get (or go) somewhere, go great guns, go strong. See THRIVE in Index.

prospering *adjective* See **flourishing.**

prosperity *noun* Steady good fortune or financial security : comfort, ease, prosperousness. *Informal:* easy street. *Idioms:* comfortable (or easy) circumstances, the good life.

See RICH, THRIVE in Index. — See also **welfare.**

prosperous *adjective* Enjoying steady good fortune or financial security : comfortable, easy, well-heeled, well-off, well-to-do. *Informal:* well-fixed. *Idioms:* comfortably off, in clover, on easy street. See RICH, THRIVE in Index. — See also **flourishing, opportune.**

prosperousness *noun* See **prosperity.**

prostitute *noun* A woman who engages in sexual intercourse for payment : bawd, call girl, camp follower, courtesan, harlot, scarlet woman, streetwalker, strumpet, tart[2], whore. *Slang:* hooker, moll. *Idioms:* lady of easy virtue, lady of pleasure, lady of the night. See SEX in Index.

prostrate *verb* See **drop, overwhelm.**

prostrate *adjective* See **flat.**

protagonist *noun* See **lead.**

protean *adjective* See **versatile.**

protect *verb* See **defend.**

protection *noun* See **cover, defense.**

protective *adjective* See **preservative, preventive.**

protector *noun* See **defense, guard.**

pro tem *adjective* See **temporary.**

protest *verb* See **object.**

protest *noun* See **objection.**

protestation *noun* See **objection.**

protocol *noun* See **ceremony.**

protoplast *noun* See **original.**

prototypal *adjective* See **typical.**

prototype *noun* See **original.**

prototypic *adjective* See **typical.**

prototypical *adjective* See **typical.**

protract *verb* See **lengthen.**

protracted *adjective* See **chronic, long[1].**

protractile *adjective* See **extensible.**

protraction noun See **extension**.

protrude verb See **bulge**.

protrusion noun See **bulge**.

protuberance noun See **bulge**, **bump**.

protuberate verb See **bulge**.

proud adjective Properly valuing oneself, one's honor, or one's dignity : prideful, self-respecting. See RESPECT in Index. — See also **arrogant, glorious**.

proudness noun See **arrogance**.

prove verb To establish as true or genuine : authenticate, bear out, confirm, corroborate, demonstrate, endorse, establish, evidence, show, substantiate, validate, verify. See SHOW, SUPPORT in Index. — See also **experience, test**.

provenance noun See **origin**.

provender noun See **food**.

provenience noun See **origin**.

prove out verb verb See **wash**.

proverb noun A usually pithy and familiar statement expressing an observation or principle generally accepted as wise or true : adage, aphorism, byword, maxim, motto, saw, saying. See WORDS in Index.

provide verb See **give, offer**.

provide for verb See **support**.

providence noun See **economy**.

provident adjective See **economical**.

providential adjective See **happy**.

province noun See **area, possession**.

provincial adjective See **country, local**.

provision noun A restricting or modifying element : condition, proviso, qualification, reservation, specification, stipulation, term (often used in plural). Informal: string (often used in plural). See

LIMITED in Index. — See also **arrangement, food**.

provisional adjective See **conditional, temporary**.

proviso noun See **provision**.

provisory adjective See **conditional**.

provocation noun See **annoyance, defiance, stimulus**.

provocative adjective See **racy**.

provoke verb To stir to action or feeling : egg on, excite, foment, galvanize, goad, impel, incite, inflame, inspire, instigate, motivate, move, pique, prick, prod, prompt, propel, set off, spur, stimulate, touch off, trigger, work up. See CAUSE, EXCITE in Index. — See also **anger, annoy, court**.

provoking adjective See **vexatious**.

prowess noun See **dexterity, heroism**.

prowl verb See **sneak**.

prowler noun See **sneak**.

proximate adjective See **close, momentary**.

prude noun A person who is too much concerned with being proper, modest, or righteous : bluenose, Mrs. Grundy, puritan, Victorian. Informal: old maid. See SEX in Index.

prudence noun The exercise of good judgment or common sense in practical matters : caution, circumspection, discretion, forehandedness, foresight, foresightedness, forethought, forethoughtfulness, precaution. See CAREFUL in Index. — See also **economy**.

prudent adjective See **economical, sane, wary**.

prudish adjective See **genteel**.

prune verb See **cut back** at **cut**.

prurience noun See **desire**.

pruriency noun See **desire**.

prurient adjective See **erotic**.

pry verb See **snoop**.

pry *noun* See **snoop.**

p's and q's *noun* See **manner.**

pseudonymous *adjective* See assumed.

psyche *noun* See **psychology, spirit.**

psyched *adjective* See **thrilled.**

psychic *adjective* See **mental.**

psychical *adjective* See **mental.**

psychological *adjective* See mental.

psychology *noun* The thought processes characteristic of an individual or group : ethos, mentality, mind, mindset, psyche. *Idiom:* what makes someone tick. See THOUGHTS in Index.

psychopathy *noun* See **insanity.**

puberty *noun* See **youth.**

public *adjective* Of, concerning, or affecting the community or the people : civic, civil, national. See SPECIFIC in Index. — See also **common, open, popular.**

public *noun* 1. Persons as an organized body : community, people, society. See SPECIFIC in Index. 2. The body of persons who admire a public personality, especially an entertainer : audience, following. See LIKE in Index. — See also **commonalty.**

public assistance *noun* See **relief.**

publication *noun* 1. The act or process of publishing printed matter : issue, printing, publishing. See WORDS in Index. 2. An issue of printed material offered for sale or distribution : opus, title, volume, work. See WORDS in Index. — See also **announcement.**

publicity *noun* See **advertising, promotion.**

publicize *verb* See **advertise, promote.**

publish *verb* 1. To present for circulation, exhibit, or sale : bring out, issue, put out. See WORDS in Index.

2. To be the author of (a published work or works) : pen[1], write. See WORDS in Index. — See also announce.

publishing *noun* See **publication.**

pucker *noun* See **fold.**

pudgy *adjective* See **plump[1].**

puerile *adjective* See **childish.**

puff *verb* See **blow[1], pant, promote.**

puff *noun* See **pull.**

puffed-up *adjective* See **pompous.**

puffery *noun* See **promotion.**

puffy *adjective* See **pompous.**

pugnacious *adjective* See belligerent.

pugnaciousness *noun* See **belligerence, fight.**

pugnacity *noun* See **belligerence, fight.**

puissance *noun* See **energy, strength.**

puissant *adjective* See **powerful, strong.**

puke *verb* See **vomit.**

pulchritudinous *adjective* See beautiful.

pule *verb* See **whine.**

pull *verb* 1. To exert force so as to move (something) toward the source of the force : drag, draw, haul, tow, tug. See PUSH in Index. 2. To remove from a fixed position : extract, pluck, tear[1]. See PUT IN Index. — See also **attract.**

pull back *verb* See **retreat.**

pull down *verb* See **destroy, earn.**

pull in *verb* See **arrive, restrain.**

pull off *verb* See **commit, perform.**

pull on *verb* See **don, drink.**

pull out *verb* See **go, retreat.**

pull through *verb* See **survive.**

pull *noun* 1. The act of drawing or pulling a load : draft, drag, draw, haul, traction. See PUSH in Index. 2. An inhalation, as of a cigar, pipe, or cigarette : drag, draw, puff. *Slang:* hit. See BREATH in Index.

— See also **attraction, drink, influence.**

pullback *noun* See **retreat.**

pullout *noun* See **retreat.**

pullulate *verb* See **teem.**

pulp *verb* See **crush.**

pulpous *adjective* See **soft.**

pulpy *adjective* See **soft.**

pulsate *verb* See **beat.**

pulsation *noun* See **beat.**

pulse *noun* See **beat.**

  pulse *verb* See **beat.**

pulverize *verb* See **crush, destroy.**

pulverous *adjective* See **fine¹.**

pulverulent *adjective* See **fine¹.**

pummel *verb* See **beat.**

pump *verb* See **drain.**

punch *noun* See **drive, kick, slap, vigor, wallop.**

  punch *verb* See **slap.**

punctilious *adjective* See **careful, ceremonious.**

punctiliousness *noun* See **ceremony, thoroughness.**

punctual *adjective* Occurring, acting, or performed exactly at the time appointed : prompt, timely. *Idioms:* at (or on) the dot, on time. See TIME in Index.

punctuate *verb* See **point.**

puncture *verb* See **breach, discredit, penetrate.**

  puncture *noun* See **prick.**

pundit *noun* See **sage.**

pungent *adjective* Affecting the organs of taste or smell with a strong and often harsh sensation : piquant, sharp, spicy, zesty. *Archaic:* poignant. See SMELLS, TASTE in Index. — See also **biting.**

puniness *noun* See **infirmity.**

punish *verb* To subject (one) to a penalty for a wrong : castigate, chastise, correct, discipline, penalize. See REWARD in Index.

punishing *adjective* Inflicting or aiming to inflict punishment : dis-

ciplinary, punitive, punitory. See REWARD in Index.

punishment *noun* Something, such as loss, pain, or confinement, imposed for wrongdoing : castigation, chastisement, correction, discipline, penalty. See REWARD in Index.

punitive *adjective* See **punishing.**

punitory *adjective* See **punishing.**

punk *noun* See **tough.**

puny *adjective* See **infirm, meager.**

pup *noun* See **squirt.**

pupil *noun* See **student.**

puppet *noun* See **pawn².**

puppy *noun* See **squirt.**

purblind *adjective* See **blind.**

purchasable *adjective* See **corruptible.**

purchase *verb* See **buy.**

  purchase *noun* See **buy.**

purchaser *noun* See **patron.**

pure *adjective* Free from extraneous elements : absolute, perfect, plain, sheer², simple, unadulterated, undiluted, unmixed. See CLEAN in Index. — See also **chaste, innocent, straight, utter².**

pureblood *adjective* See **thoroughbred.**

pureblooded *adjective* See **thoroughbred.**

purebred *adjective* See **thoroughbred.**

pureness *noun* See **purity.**

purgation *noun* See **elimination, purification.**

purgative *adjective* Serving to purify of sin : expiatory, lustral, lustrative, purgatorial, purificatory. See CLEAN, RELIGION in Index. — See also **eliminative.**

purgatorial *adjective* See **purgative.**

purge *verb* See **clear, eliminate, purify.**

  purge *noun* See **elimination.**

purification *noun* **1.** The act or process of removing physical impurities : clarification, refinement. See CLEAN in Index. **2.** A freeing from sin, guilt, or defilement : lustration, purgation. See CLEAN, RELIGION in Index.

purificatory *adjective* See **purgative.**

purifier *noun* Something that purifies or cleans : clarifier, cleaner, cleanser, refiner, refinery. See CLEAN in Index.

purify *verb* To free from sin, guilt, or defilement : cleanse, lustrate, purge. See CLEAN, RELIGION in Index. — See also **refine.**

puritan *noun* See **prude.**

puritanical *adjective* See **genteel.**

purity *noun* The condition of being clean and free of contaminants : clarity, cleanliness, cleanness, pureness, taintlessness. See CLEAN in Index. — See also **chastity.**

purloin *verb* See **steal.**

purloiner *noun* See **larcenist.**

purport *noun* See **idea, import, meaning, thrust.**

purpose *noun* See **decision, function, intention.**

  purpose *verb* See **intend.**

purposeful *adjective* See **deliberate.**

purposefulness *noun* See **decision.**

purposeless *adjective* See **aimless, mindless.**

pursue *verb* To follow (another) with the intent of overtaking and capturing : chase, run after. *Idioms:* be (or go) in pursuit, give chase. See SEEK in Index. — See also **court, follow up** at **follow, lead, practice.**

pursuing *noun* See **pursuit.**

pursuit *noun* **1.** The following of another in an attempt to overtake and capture : chase, hot pursuit. See SEEK in Index. **2.** An attempting to accomplish or attain : pursuing, quest, search. See SEEK in Index. — See also **business, practice.**

purview *noun* See **ken, range.**

push *verb* **1.** To do or achieve by forcing obstacles out of one's way : press, ram, shove. See PUSH in Index. **2.** *Slang.* To engage in the illicit sale of (narcotics) : deal, peddle. See TRANSACTIONS in Index. — See also **advertise, bear, drive, muscle, poke.**

  push off *verb* See **go.**

  push on *verb* See **go.**

  push *noun* An act or instance of using force so as to propel ahead : butt[1], shove, thrust. See PUSH in Index. — See also **drive, stimulus.**

pusher *noun* *Slang.* A person who sells narcotics illegally : dealer, peddler. See TRANSACTIONS in Index.

pushiness *noun* See **impudence.**

pushover *noun* See **breeze, dupe.**

pushy *adjective* See **impudent.**

pusillanimity *noun* See **cowardice.**

pusillanimous *adjective* See **cowardly.**

puss *noun* See **face, mouth.**

pussyfoot *verb* See **equivocate, sneak.**

put *verb* See **air, ask, estimate, gamble, impose, phrase, set[1], translate.**

  put away *verb* See **consume, murder.**

  put by *verb* See **save.**

  put down *verb* See **suppress.**

  put forth *verb* See **broach.**

  put forward *verb* See **propose.**

  put in *verb* See **apply, enter, serve, spend.**

  put off *verb* See **foist.**

  put on *verb* See **act, assume, don, stage.**

put out *verb* See **annoy, exercise, extinguish, inconvenience, publish.**
put through *verb* See **effect.**
put together *verb* See **make.**
put up *verb* See **build, conserve, erect, harbor.**
putative *adjective* See **reputed.**
put-on *noun* See **façade.**
putrefaction *noun* See **decay.**
putrefy *verb* See **decay.**
putrescence *noun* See **decay.**
putrid *adjective* See **bad, moldy.**
putridness *noun* See **decay.**
putter *verb* See **fiddle, fuss, mess around** at **mess.**
puzzle *noun* See **mystery.**
puzzle *verb* See **confuse.**
puzzle out *verb* See **break.**
puzzlement *noun* See **daze.**
puzzler *noun* See **mystery.**
puzzling *adjective* See **mysterious.**
pygmy also **pigmy** *adjective* See **tiny.**
pyretic *adjective* See **hot.**
pythonic *adjective* See **giant.**

Q

quack *noun* See **fake.**
quad *noun* See **court.**
quadrangle *noun* See **court.**
quadrate *adjective* See **square.**
quadrate *verb* See **agree.**
quaff *verb* See **drink.**
quaff *noun* See **drink.**
quag *noun* See **swamp.**
quaggy *adjective* See **soft.**
quagmire *noun* See **predicament, swamp.**
quail *verb* See **flinch.**
quaint *adjective* Agreeably curious, especially in an old-fashioned or unusual way : funny, odd. See USUAL in Index. — See also **eccentric.**

quake *verb* See **shake.**
quake *noun* See **tremor.**
quaky *adjective* See **tremulous.**
qualification *noun* The quality or state of being eligible : eligibility, fitness, suitability, suitableness, worthiness. See ABILITY in Index. — See also **provision.**
qualified *adjective* Not total, unlimited, or wholehearted : limited, modified, reserved, restricted. See BIG, LIMITED in Index. — See also **eligible.**
qualify *verb* See **authorize, moderate.**
quality *noun* **1.** A distinctive element : attribute, character, characteristic, feature, mark, peculiarity, property, savor, trait. See BE in Index. **2.** Degree of excellence : caliber, class, grade. See BE, VALUE in Index. — See also **class, merit, society.**
quality *adjective* See **excellent.**
qualm *noun* A feeling of uncertainty about the fitness or correctness of an action : compunction, misgiving, reservation, scruple. See CERTAIN in Index.
quantity *noun* A measurable whole : amount, body, budget, bulk, corpus, quantum. See BIG in Index. — See also **deal.**
quantum *noun* See **allotment, quantity.**
quarrel *noun* See **argument.**
quarrel *verb* See **argue.**
quarrelsome *adjective* See **argumentative, belligerent.**
quarter *noun* One of four equal parts of something : quartern. See PART in Index. — See also **area, neighborhood.**
quarter *verb* See **harbor.**
quartern *noun* See **quarter.**
quash *verb* See **suppress.**

quaver *verb* See **shake.**

queer *adjective* See **eccentric, funny.**

quell *verb* See **suppress.**

quench *verb* See **extinguish, repress, suppress.**

querier *noun* See **inquirer.**

querulous *adjective* See **ill-tempered.**

query *noun* See **inquiry.**
 query *verb* See **ask.**

quest *noun* See **pursuit.**
 quest *verb* See **seek.**

quester *noun* See **inquirer.**

question *noun* See **doubt, inquiry, problem.**
 question *verb* See **ask, doubt.**

questionable *adjective* See **ambiguous, debatable, doubtful, shady.**

questioner *noun* See **inquirer, inquisitor.**

questioning *adjective* See **curious, incredulous.**

questioningly *adverb* See **skeptically.**

queue *noun* See **line.**

quibble *verb* To raise unnecessary or trivial objections : carp, cavil, niggle, nitpick, pettifog. *Idiom:* pick to pieces. See SUPPORT in Index. — See also **argue.**

quibbler *noun* See **critic.**

quick *adjective* Accomplished in very little time : brief, expeditious, fast, flying, hasty, hurried, rapid, short, speedy, swift. See FAST in Index. — See also **clever, fast, nimble.**
 quick *noun* See **center.**
 quick *adverb* See **fast.**

quicken *verb* To make alive : animate, vitalize, vivify. See LIVE in Index. — See also **speed.**

quickening *adjective* See **stimulating.**

quickly *adverb* See **fast.**

quickness *noun* See **agility, haste.**

quick-tempered *adjective* See **testy.**

quick-witted *adjective* See **clever.**

quidnunc *noun* See **meddler.**

quiescence *noun* See **abeyance.**

quiescent *adjective* See **latent.**

quiet *adjective* Not showy or obtrusive : inobtrusive, restrained, subdued, tasteful, unobtrusive. See PLAIN in Index. — See also **silent, soft, still.**
 quiet *noun* See **silence, stillness.**
 quiet *verb* See **calm, silence.**

quieten *verb* See **silence.**

quietness *noun* See **silence, stillness.**

quietude *noun* See **calm.**

quietus *noun* See **death.**

quintessence *noun* See **essence, heart.**

quintessential *adjective* See **typical.**

quip *noun* See **crack, joke.**

quipster *noun* See **joker.**

quirk *noun* See **eccentricity.**

quirkiness *noun* See **eccentricity.**

quirky *adjective* See **eccentric.**

quit *verb* To relinquish one's engagement in or occupation with : demit, leave[1], resign, terminate. See CONTINUE in Index. — See also **abandon, act, go, stop.**
 quit *adjective* See **even[1].**

quitclaim *noun* See **abdication.**
 quitclaim *verb* See **abdicate.**

quite *adverb* See **completely, considerably.**

quits *adjective* See **even[1].**

quittance *noun* See **compensation.**

quiver *verb* See **shake.**
 quiver *noun* See **tremor.**

quivery *adjective* See **tremulous.**

quixotic *adjective* See **idealistic.**

quiz *verb* See **ask, ridicule, test.**
 quiz *noun* See **test.**

quondam *adjective* See **late.**

quota *noun* See **allotment.**

quotidian *adjective* See **everyday.**

R

rabble *noun* See **trash.**

rabid *adjective* See **enthusiastic, extreme, furious.**

race *noun* See **competition.**

race *verb* See **rush.**

rack *verb* See **afflict, torture.**

racket *noun* See **business, noise.**

racy *adjective* Bordering on indelicacy or impropriety : blue, earthy, off-color, provocative, risqué, salty, scabrous, spicy, suggestive. See DECENT in Index.

radiance *noun* See **fire.**

radiant *adjective* See **bright.**

radiate *verb* See **beam, shed, spread.**

radical *adjective* Arising from or going to the root or source : basal, basic, foundational, fundamental, original, primary, underlying. See SURFACE in Index. — See also **extreme.**

radical *noun* See **extremist.**

rafter *noun* See **beam.**

rag[1] *noun* See **tatter.**

rag[2] *verb* See **joke.**

ragamuffin *noun* See **tatterdemalion.**

rage *noun* See **enthusiasm, fashion, fury.**

rage *verb* See **anger.**

ragged *adjective* See **rough, tattered.**

raggedy *adjective* See **tattered.**

raging *adjective* See **rough.**

ragtag and bobtail *noun* See **trash.**

raid *noun* See **invasion.**

raid *verb* To make a surprise attack on : harry, maraud. See ATTACK in Index. — See also **invade.**

rail against or **at** *verb* See **revile.**

railing *noun* See **vituperation.**

raillery *noun* See **ribbing.**

raiment *noun* See **dress.**

rain *verb* See **shower.**

rainbow *noun* See **illusion.**

rainless *adjective* See **dry.**

raise *verb* To increase in amount : boost, hike, jack (up), jump, up. See INCREASE in Index. — See also **arouse, ask, bring up** at **bring, broach, build, elevate, erect, grow, promote.**

raise *noun* See **increase.**

raised *adjective* See **elevated, erect.**

rake[1] *noun* See **wanton.**

rake[2] *verb* See **incline.**

rake *noun* See **inclination.**

rakish *adjective* See **abandoned.**

rally *verb* See **mobilize, recover.**

rally *noun* See **recovery.**

rallying cry *noun* See **cry.**

ram *verb* To cause to penetrate with force : dig, drive, plunge, run, sink, stab, stick, thrust. See PUT IN in Index. — See also **drive, push.**

ramble *verb* See **digress, rove, stroll.**

ramble *noun* See **walk.**

rambling *adjective* See **digressive.**

ramification *noun* See **effect.**

ramify *verb* See **branch.**

rampage *noun* See **binge.**

ramshackle *adjective* See **ruinous.**

rancid *adjective* See **moldy.**

rancor *noun* See **resentment.**

rancorous *adjective* See **resentful.**

rancorousness *noun* See **resentment.**

random *adjective* Having no particular pattern, purpose, organization, or structure : chance, desultory, haphazard, hit-or-miss, indiscriminate, spot, unplanned. See PLANNED in Index.

range *noun* An area within which something or someone exists, acts, or has influence or power : ambit, compass, extension, extent, orbit, purview, reach, realm, scope, sphere, sweep, swing. See TERRITORY in Index. — See also **grasp, ken, neighborhood.**

range *verb* See **arrange, class, go, line, rove.**

rangy *adjective* See **gangling.**

rank¹ *noun* See **class, line, place.**

rank *verb* See **class.**

rank² *adjective* See **flagrant, moldy, thick.**

rankness *noun* See **flagrancy.**

ransack *verb* See **sack², scour¹.**

rant *verb* To speak in a loud, pompous, or prolonged manner : declaim, harangue, mouth, perorate, rave. See WORDS in Index.

rant *noun* See **bombast.**

rap¹ *verb* See **blame, call down** at **call, tap¹.**

rap out *verb* See **exclaim.**

rap *noun* See **rebuke, sentence, tap¹.**

rap² *noun* See **damn.**

rap³ *noun* See **conference.** *verb* See **discuss.**

rapacious *adjective* See **voracious.**

rapaciousness *noun* See **voracity.**

rapacity *noun* See **voracity.**

rape *verb* To compel (another) to participate in or submit to a sexual act : assault, force, ravish, violate. See SEX in Index. — See also **sack².**

rapid *adjective* See **fast, quick.**

rapidity *noun* See **haste.**

rapidness *noun* See **haste.**

rapport *noun* See **agreement.**

rapprochement *noun* See **reconciliation.**

rap session *noun* See **conference.**

rapt *adjective* See **absorbed.**

rapture *noun* See **heaven.**

rare *adjective* Far beyond what is usual, normal, or customary : exceptional, extraordinary, magnificent, outstanding, preeminent, remarkable, singular, towering, uncommon, unusual. *Informal:*

standout. *Slang:* awesome, out of sight. See BETTER, USUAL in Index. — See also **infrequent, thin.**

rarefied *adjective* See **thin.**

rarefy *verb* See **thin.**

rarely *adverb* See **infrequently.**

raring *adjective* See **eager.**

rascal *noun* See **mischief.**

rascality *noun* See **mischief.**

rash¹ *adjective* Characterized by unthinking boldness and haste : brash, foolhardy, harum-scarum, hasty, headlong, hotheaded, ill-considered, impetuous, improvident, impulsive, incautious, madcap, precipitant, precipitate, reckless, slapdash, temerarious, unconsidered. See CAREFUL in Index.

rash² *noun* See **outbreak.**

rashness *noun* See **haste, temerity.**

rasp *verb* See **scrape.**

raspberry *noun* See **hiss.**

rasping *adjective* See **harsh.**

raspy *adjective* See **harsh.**

rat *verb* See **betray, defect, inform.**

rat *noun* See **betrayer, defector, informer.**

rat-a-tat-tat *noun* See **report.**

rate¹ *verb* See **class, earn, estimate.**

rate² *verb* See **bawl out** at **bawl.**

rather *adverb* See **fairly.**

ratification *noun* See **confirmation.**

ratify *verb* See **confirm.**

ratiocinate *verb* See **think.**

ratiocination *noun* See **logic.**

ratiocinative *adjective* See **logical.**

ration *noun* See **allotment.**

ration *verb* See **distribute.**

rational *adjective* See **logical, sane.**

rationale *noun* See **account, sense.**

rationality *noun* See **logic, sense.**

rationalization *noun* See **account.**

rationalize *verb* See **account for** at **account, justify.**

rationalness *noun* See **sense.**

rattle *verb* To make or cause to make a succession of short, sharp sounds : brattle, chatter, clack, clatter. See SOUNDS in Index. — See also **agitate, chatter.**

ratty *adjective* See **shabby.**

raucous *adjective* See **harsh.**

raunch *noun* See **obscenity.**

raunchiness *noun* See **obscenity.**

raunchy *adjective* See **obscene.**

ravage *verb* See **devastate, sack².**

rave *verb* To show enthusiasm : carry on, rhapsodize. See FEELINGS in Index. — See also **rant.**

ravel *verb* See **complicate.**

ravenous *adjective* Desiring or craving food : famished, hungry, starving, voracious. See INGESTION in Index. — See also **greedy, voracious.**

ravenousness *noun* See **voracity.**

ravish *verb* See **rape.**

ravishing *adjective* See **beautiful.**

raw *adjective* Not cooked : uncooked. See INGESTION in Index. — See also **crude, inexperienced, rude.**

rawboned *adjective* See **thin.**

raw deal *noun* See **injustice.**

rawness *noun* See **inexperience.**

ray *noun* See **beam.**

raze *verb* See **destroy.**

razz *noun* See **hiss.**

razz *verb* See **joke.**

reach *verb* **1.** To extend, especially an appendage : outstretch, stretch (out). See REACH in Index. **2.** To succeed in communicating with : contact, get. *Idioms:* catch up with, get hold of, get in touch with, get through to, get to. See REACH in Index. — See also **accomplish, amount, arrive, extend.**

reach *noun* See **expanse, extent, grasp, ken, range.**

react *verb* See **greet, respond.**

reaction *noun* See **behavior, response.**

reactionary *adjective* Vehemently, often fanatically opposing progress or reform : die-hard, mossbacked, ultraconservative. See POLITICS in Index. — See also **unprogressive.**

reactionary *noun* A person who vehemently, often fanatically opposes progress and favors return to a previous condition : die-hard, mossback, ultraconservative. See POLITICS in Index.

reactivate *verb* See **revive.**

reactivation *noun* See **revival.**

read *verb* See **interpret, show, understand.**

readiness *noun* See **ease, preparation.**

reading *noun* See **interpretation.**

ready *adjective* In a state of preparedness : set¹. *Informal:* go. *Slang:* together. *Idioms:* all set, in working order. See PREPARED in Index. — See also **willing.**

ready *verb* See **gird, prepare.**

real *adjective* Having verifiable existence : concrete, objective, substantial, substantive, tangible. See REAL in Index. — See also **actual, authentic, genuine.**

realistic *adjective* **1.** Accurately representing what is depicted or described : lifelike, natural, naturalistic, true, true-life, truthful. See REAL in Index. **2.** Having or indicating an awareness of things as they really are : down-to-earth, hard, hardheaded, matter-of-fact, objective, practical, pragmatic, pragmatical, prosaic, sober, tough-minded, unromantic. See EXCITE, REAL in Index. — See also **graphic.**

reality *noun* See **actuality, existence, fact.**

realization *noun* See **effect, fulfillment, interpretation.**

realize *verb* To make real or actual : actualize, materialize. *Idioms:* bring to pass, carry into effect. See DO in Index. — See also **accomplish, bring, return.**

really *adverb* In truth : actually, fairly, genuinely, indeed, positively, truly, truthfully, verily. *Idiom:* for fair. See REAL, TRUE in Index. — See also **actually.**

realm *noun* See **area, range.**

realness *noun* See **authenticity.**

ream *noun* See **heap.**

reanimate *verb* See **revive.**

reap *verb* See **gather.**

reappear *verb* See **recur.**

reappearance *noun* See **recurrence.**

rear[1] *noun* See **back, bottom, tail.**
  rear *adjective* See **back.**

rear[2] *verb* See **bring up** at **bring, build, elevate, erect.**

rearmost *adjective* See **last**[1].

rearrangement *noun* See **displacement.**

rearward *adverb* See **back, backward.**
  rearward *noun* See **back.**

reason *noun* A fact or circumstance that gives logical support to an assertion, claim, or proposal : argument, ground (often used in plural), proof, wherefore, why. *Idiom:* why and wherefore. See REASON in Index. — See also **account, basis, cause, logic, sanity, sense.**

reasonable *adjective* See **conservative, logical, moderate, popular, sane.**

reassume *verb* See **resume.**

reawaken *verb* See **revive.**

rebate *noun* See **deduction.**
  rebate *verb* See **decrease, deduct.**

rebel *verb* To refuse allegiance to and oppose by force a government or ruling authority : mutiny, revolt, rise (up). See RESIST in Index.

rebel *noun* A person who rebels : insurgent, insurrectionary, insurrectionist, mutineer, revolutionary, revolutionist. See RESIST in Index.

rebellion *noun* Organized opposition intended to change or overthrow existing authority : insurgence, insurgency, insurrection, mutiny, revolt, revolution, sedition, uprising. See RESIST in Index.

rebellious *adjective* Participating in open revolt against a government or ruling authority : insurgent, mutinous, revolutionary. See RESIST in Index.

rebirth *noun* See **conversion, revival.**

rebound *verb* See **bounce, echo, recoil.**
  rebound *noun* See **bounce.**

rebuff *noun* See **snub.**
  rebuff *verb* See **snub.**

rebuild *verb* See **restore.**

rebuke *noun* Words expressive of strong disapproval : admonishment, admonition, reprimand, reproach, reproof, scolding. *Slang:* rap[1]. See PRAISE in Index.
  rebuke *verb* See **call down** at **call.**

rebut *verb* See **refute.**

recalcitrance *noun* See **defiance, unruliness.**

recalcitrancy *noun* See **defiance, unruliness.**

recalcitrant *adjective* See **defiant, unruly.**

recall *verb* See **lift, remember, retract.**
  recall *noun* See **memory, reversal.**

recant *verb* See **retract.**

recantation *noun* See **retraction.**

recap *noun* See **summary.**
  recap *verb* See **review.**

recapitulate *verb* See **review.**

recapitulation *noun* See **summary.**

recede *verb* To move back or away from a point, limit, or mark : ebb, retract, retreat, retrocede, retrograde, retrogress. See APPROACH in Index.

receivable *adjective* See **due.**

receive *verb* To admit to one's possession, presence, or awareness : accept, have, take. See ACCEPT in Index. — See also **accept.**

received *adjective* See **accepted, orthodox.**

recent *adjective* See **modern.**

recently *adverb* See **just, late.**

receptive *adjective* Ready and willing to receive favorably, as new ideas : acceptant, amenable, open, open-minded, responsive. See ACCEPT in Index.

receptiveness *noun* See **openness.**

receptivity *noun* See **openness.**

recess *noun* See **break.**
  recess *verb* See **break.**

recession *noun* See **depression.**

recidivation *noun* See **lapse.**

recidivism *noun* See **lapse.**

reciprocal *adjective* See **mutual.**

reciprocate *verb* To give or take mutually : requite, return. See CONNECT in Index. — See also **retaliate.**

reciprocation *noun* See **retaliation.**

reciprocative *adjective* See **mutual.**

recite *verb* See **describe.**

reckless *adjective* See **careless, rash[1].**

recklessness *noun* See **temerity.**

reckon *verb* See **calculate, count, estimate, regard, suppose.**
  reckon on or **upon** *verb* See **depend on** at **depend.**

reckoning *noun* See **account, calculation, count.**

reclaim *verb* See **rescue, restore.**

re-claim *verb* See **resume.**

recline *verb* See **lie[1], rest[1].**

recluse *adjective* See **secluded.**

reclusion *noun* See **seclusion.**

recognition *noun* Favorable notice, as of an achievement : acknowl-edgment, credit. See KNOWLEDGE in Index.

recognize *verb* To perceive to be identical with something held in the memory : know. See KNOWLEDGE, REMEMBER in Index. — See also **acknowledge, place.**

recognized *adjective* See **accepted.**

recoil *verb* To jerk backward, as a gun upon firing : rebound. See FORWARD in Index. — See also **flinch.**

recoil *noun* An act of drawing back in an involuntary or instinctive fashion : cringe, flinch, shrink, wince. See APPROACH, SEEK in Index.

recollect *verb* See **remember.**

recollection *noun* See **memory.**

recommend *verb* See **advise, support.**

recommendable *adjective* See **advisable.**

recommendation *noun* See **advice, endorsement, reference.**

recompense *verb* See **compensate, pay, reward.**
  recompense *noun* See **compensation, due, payment.**

reconcile *verb* **1.** To reestablish friendship between : conciliate, make up, reunite. See LOVE in Index. **2.** To bring (oneself) to accept : resign. See ACCEPT in Index. — See also **adapt, harmonize, settle.**

reconcilement *noun* See **reconciliation.**

reconciliation *noun* A reestablishment of friendship or harmony : conciliation, rapprochement, reconcilement. See LOVE in Index.

recondite *adjective* See **deep.**

recondition *verb* See **renew, restore.**

reconnaissance *noun* See **exploration.**

reconnoiter *verb* See **explore.**

reconsider *verb* To consider again, especially with the possibility of change : reevaluate, reexamine, rethink, review. See THOUGHTS in Index.

reconstruct *verb* See **restore**.

record *verb* See **post³, show**.

recount *verb* See **describe**.

recoup *verb* See **recover**.

recoup *noun* See **recovery**.

recourse *noun* See **resort**.

recover *verb* **1.** To get back : recoup, regain, repossess, retrieve. See GET in Index. **2.** To regain one's health : come around (*or* round), convalesce, gain, improve, mend, perk up, rally, recuperate. See HEALTH in Index. — See also **rescue**.

recovery *noun* **1.** A return to normal health : rally, recuperation. See HEALTH in Index. **2.** The act of getting back or regaining : recoup, repossession, retrieval. See GET in Index. — See also **comeback**.

recreance *noun* See **defection**.

recreancy *noun* See **defection**.

recreant *adjective* See **faithless**.

recreant *noun* See **defector**.

recreate *verb* See **amuse, play**.

re-create *verb* See **renew**.

recreation *noun* See **amusement, play**.

recrudesce *verb* See **return**.

rectify *verb* See **correct, settle**.

rectitude *noun* See **good**.

recumbent *adjective* See **flat**.

recuperate *verb* See **recover**.

recuperation *noun* See **recovery**.

recur *verb* To happen again or repeatedly : reappear, reoccur. See REPETITION in Index. — See also **return**.

recurrence *noun* A repeated occurrence : reappearance, reoccurrence, return. See REPETITION in Index.

recurrent *adjective* Happening or appearing at regular intervals :

cyclic, cyclical, isochronal, isochronous, periodic, periodical. *Idiom:* like clockwork. See REPETITION in Index.

red-blooded *adjective* See **lusty**.

redden *verb* See **blush**.

redeem *verb* See **compensate, rescue**.

red-hot *adjective* See **hot, passionate**.

redo *verb* See **repeat**.

redolence *noun* See **fragrance**.

redolent *adjective* See **fragrant**.

redouble *verb* See **double, intensify**.

redoubtable *adjective* See **eminent, fearful**.

redress *verb* See **avenge, compensate, correct**.

redress *noun* See **compensation**.

reduce *verb* To lose body weight, as by dieting : slim (down), trim down. See FAT, INCREASE in Index. — See also **decrease, demote, depreciate, shorten**.

reduction *noun* See **decrease, deduction, demotion, depreciation**.

redundancy *noun* See **wordiness**.

redundant *adjective* See **wordy**.

reduplication *noun* See **copy**.

reecho *verb* See **echo**.

reek *verb* See **smell**.

reeky *adjective* See **smelly**.

reel *verb* See **lurch, spin**.

reeling *adjective* See **dizzy**.

reestablish *verb* See **restore**.

reevaluate *verb* See **reconsider**.

reexamine *verb* See **reconsider**.

ref *noun* See **judge**.

refer *verb* **1.** To direct (a person) elsewhere for help or information : send, transfer, turn over. See MOVE in Index. **2.** To call or direct attention to something : advert, bring up, mention, point, point out, touch (on *or* upon). See WORDS in Index. — See also **apply, attribute, resort**.

referee *noun* See **judge**.

referee *verb* See **judge.**

reference *noun* A statement attesting to personal qualifications, character, and dependability : character, recommendation, testimonial. See SUPPORT in Index.

refine *verb* To make or become clear by the removal of impurities : clarify, clean, cleanse, purify. See CLEAN in Index. — See also **perfect.**

refined *adjective* See **cultured, delicate.**

refinement *noun* See **class, culture, discrimination, purification.**

refiner *noun* See **purifier.**

refinery *noun* See **purifier.**

refining *adjective* See **cultural.**

reflect *verb* To send back or form an image of : image, mirror. See SHOW in Index. — See also **echo, ponder, think.**

reflection *noun* 1. Something that is reflected : image. See SHOW in Index. 2. An implied criticism : reproach, slur. See PRAISE in Index. — See also **echo, thought.**

reflective *adjective* See **thoughtful.**

reflex *adjective* See **spontaneous.**

reflex *noun* See **echo.**

reform *verb* See **correct.**

reformative *adjective* See **corrective.**

reformatory *adjective* See **corrective.**

refract *verb* See **bend.**

refractoriness *noun* See **unruliness.**

refractory *adjective* See **unruly.**

refrain *verb* To hold oneself back : abstain, forbear, hold off, keep, withhold. See RESTRAINT in Index.

refresh *verb* To impart renewed energy and strength to (a person) : freshen, reinvigorate, rejuvenate, renew, restore, revitalize, revivify. See HELP, STRONG in Index. — See also **renew.**

refreshing *adjective* See **tonic.**

refuge *noun* The state of being protected or safeguarded, as from danger or hardship : asylum, harborage, sanctuary, shelter. See SAFETY in Index. — See also **cover, resort.**

refugee *noun* See **fugitive.**

refulgent *adjective* See **bright.**

refund *verb* To give back, especially money : reimburse, repay, restitute. See PAY in Index.

refurbish *verb* See **renew.**

refurbishment *noun* See **renewal.**

refusal *noun* A turning down of a request : denial, disallowance, rejection, turndown. See ACCEPT in Index. — See also **no.**

refuse *verb* To be unwilling to grant : deny, disallow, turn down, withhold. See ACCEPT in Index. — See also **decline.**

refute *verb* To prove or show to be false : belie, confute, discredit, disprove, rebut. See AFFIRM in Index.

regain *verb* See **recover.**

regal *adjective* See **grand.**

regale *verb* See **amuse.**

regalia *noun* See **attire.**

regard *verb* To look upon in a particular way : account, consider, deem, esteem, reckon, see, view. See PERSPECTIVE in Index. — See also **admire, watch.**

regard *noun* Friendly greetings. Used in plural : best, respect (used in plural). See GREETING in Index. — See also **care, concern, consideration, esteem, look, notice, phase.**

regardful *adjective* See **attentive.**

regardfulness *noun* See **attention.**

regeneration *noun* See **conversion.**

regime *noun* See **government.**

regimen *noun* See **treatment.**

region *noun* See **area, territory.**

regional *adjective* See **territorial.**

register *verb* To come as a realization : dawn on (or upon), sink in,

soak in. See KNOWLEDGE in Index.
— See also post³, show.

register noun See list¹.

regnant adjective See **dominant, prevailing, ruling.**

regress verb See **relapse.**

regression noun See **reversion.**

regret verb To feel or express sorrow for : deplore, repent, rue. See REGRET in Index.

regret noun See **apology, disappointment.**

regretful adjective See **apologetic, remorseful.**

regrettable adjective See **sorrowful.**

regular adjective See **clean, common, customary, even¹, methodical, symmetrical.**

regularity noun See **usualness.**

regularly adverb See **usually.**

regulate verb See **adjust, govern.**

regulation noun See **law, rule.**

regulatory adjective See **governmental.**

rehab noun See **treatment.**

rehabilitate verb See **restore.**

rehabilitation noun See **treatment.**

rehearsal noun See **practice.**

rehearse verb See **describe, practice.**

reign verb See **dominate, govern.**

reign noun See **domination.**

reigning adjective See **dominant.**

reimburse verb See **compensate, refund.**

reimbursement noun See **compensation.**

rein verb See **restrain.**

reinforce verb See **tighten.**

reinstate verb See **restore.**

reintroduce verb See **restore.**

reinvigorate verb See **refresh.**

reinvigorating adjective See **tonic.**

reiterate verb See **repeat.**

reiteration noun See **repetition.**

reiterative adjective See **repetitive.**

reject verb See **decline, repudiate.**

rejection noun See **denial, no, refusal.**

rejoice verb To feel or take joy or pleasure : delight, exult, joy, pleasure. See HAPPY in Index. — See also celebrate.

rejoicing noun See **celebration.**

rejoin verb See **answer.**

rejoinder noun See **answer.**

rejuvenate verb See **refresh, renew, restore.**

rejuvenation noun See **renewal.**

rekindle verb See **revive.**

relapse verb To slip from a higher or better condition to a former, usually lower or poorer one : backslide, lapse, regress, retrogress, revert. See BETTER, REPETITION in Index.

relapse noun See **lapse.**

relate verb To interact with another or others in a meaningful fashion : communicate, connect. *Slang:* click. *Idioms:* be on the same wavelength, hit it off. See CONNECT in Index. — See also **apply, associate, describe, identify.**

related adjective Connected by or as if by kinship or common origin : agnate, akin, allied, cognate, connate, connatural, consanguine, consanguineous, kindred. See KIN in Index.

relation noun A logical or natural association between two or more things : connection, correlation, interconnection, interdependence, interrelationship, link, linkage, relationship, tie-in. *Informal:* hookup. See CONNECT in Index. — See also **relative.**

relationship noun See **relation.**

relative adjective See **comparative, dependent.**

relative noun A person connected to another person by blood or marriage : kin, kinsman, kinswoman, relation. See KIN in Index.

relax verb See **ease, rest¹**.

relaxation noun See **rest¹**.

relaxed adjective See **easygoing, loose**.

release verb See **dismiss, emit, free, rid**.

relegate verb See **entrust**.

relent verb See **weaken**.

relentless adjective See **continual, stubborn**.

relentlessness noun See **stubbornness**.

relevance noun The fact of being related to the matter at hand : applicability, application, appositeness, bearing, concernment, germaneness, materiality, pertinence, pertinency, relevancy. See RELEVANT in Index.

relevancy noun See **relevance**.

relevant adjective Related to the matter at hand : applicable, apposite, apropos, germane, material, pertinent. *Idiom:* to the point. See RELEVANT in Index.

reliable adjective See **dependable**.

reliance noun See **confidence**.

reliant adjective See **dependent**.

relic noun See **trace**.

relief noun 1. Assistance, especially money, food, and other necessities, given to the needy or dispossessed : aid, dole, handout, public assistance, welfare. See HELP in Index. 2. Freedom, especially from pain : alleviation, assuagement, ease, mitigation, palliation. See INCREASE in Index. 3. A person or persons taking over the duties of another : replacement. See SUBSTITUTE in Index. — See also **help**.

relieve verb 1. To make less severe or more bearable : allay, alleviate, assuage, comfort, ease, lessen, lighten², mitigate, palliate. See

INCREASE in Index. 2. To free from a specific duty by acting as a substitute : spell³, take over. See SUBSTITUTE in Index. — See also **excuse, help, rid**.

reliever noun See **helper**.

religion noun A system of religious belief : confession, creed, denomination, faith, persuasion, sect. See RELIGION in Index.

religionism noun See **devotion**.

religiosity noun See **devotion**.

religious adjective See **divine, holy, spiritual**.

religiousness noun See **devotion**.

relinquish verb To let (something) go : abandon, cede, forgo, lay down, surrender, yield. See KEEP in Index. — See also **abandon, abdicate**.

relinquishment noun See **abdication**.

relish verb See **eat up** at eat, **enjoy**.

relish noun See **flavor, taste, zest**.

relocate verb See **move**.

relocation noun See **removal**.

reluctance noun See **indisposition**.

reluctant adjective See **indisposed**.

rely on or **upon** verb See **depend on** at depend.

remain verb To continue to be in a place : abide, bide, linger, stay¹, tarry, wait. *Informal:* stick around. *Idiom:* stay put. See CONTINUE in Index. — See also **endure**.

remainder noun See **balance**.

remaining adjective Being what remains, especially after a part has been removed : leftover. See LEFTOVER in Index.

remains noun See **balance, body, trace**.

remark verb See **comment, notice**.

remark noun See **comment, notice**.

remarkable adjective See **noticeable, rare**.

remarkably adverb See **unusually**.

remedial *adjective* See **corrective, curative.**

remedy *noun* Something that corrects or counteracts : antidote, corrective, countermeasure, curative, cure. See BETTER in Index. — See also **cure.**

remedy *verb* See **correct, cure.**

remember *verb* **1.** To renew an image or thought in the mind : bethink, mind, recall, recollect, reminisce, retain, revive, think. *Idiom:* bring to mind. See REMEMBER in Index. **2.** To care enough to keep (someone) in mind : think about, think of. See REMEMBER in Index.

remembrance *noun* Something that causes one to remember : keepsake, memento, reminder, souvenir, token, trophy. See REMEMBER in Index. — See also **memorial, memory.**

reminder *noun* See **remembrance.**

reminisce *verb* See **remember.**

reminiscence *noun* See **commentary, memory.**

reminiscent *adjective* See **suggestive.**

remiss *adjective* See **negligent.**

remission *noun* See **forgiveness, wane.**

remissness *noun* See **negligence.**

remit *verb* See **abandon, defer¹, forgive, subside.**

remnant *noun* See **balance.**

remonstrance *noun* See **objection.**

remonstrate *verb* See **object.**

remonstration *noun* See **objection.**

remorse *noun* See **penitence.**

remorseful *adjective* Feeling or expressing regret for one's sins or misdeeds : compunctious, contrite, penitent, penitential, regretful, repentant, sorry. See REGRET in Index.

remorsefulness *noun* See **penitence.**

remorseless *adjective* Devoid of remorse : impenitent, unrepentant. See REGRET in Index. — See also **merciless, stubborn.**

remorselessness *noun* See **stubbornness.**

remote *adjective* **1.** Small in degree, especially of probability : faint, negligible, outside, slender, slight, slim. See BIG in Index. **2.** Far from centers of human population : back, insular, isolated, lonely, lonesome, obscure, outlying, out-of-the-way, removed, secluded, solitary. *Idiom:* off the beaten path (or track). See NEAR in Index. — See also **cool, distant.**

remoteness *noun* See **detachment, distance.**

remotion *noun* See **removal.**

removal *noun* The act or process of moving from one place to another : move, relocation, remotion. See MOVE in Index. — See also **elimination.**

remove *verb* **1.** To move (something) from a position occupied : take, take away, take off, take out, withdraw. See MOVE in Index. **2.** To take from one's own person : doff, take off. See PUT ON in Index. — See also **annihilate, drop, eliminate, go, move.**

remove *noun* Degree of separation, especially in time : distance. See NEAR in Index.

removed *adjective* See **distant, remote, solitary.**

remunerate *verb* See **compensate, pay, reward.**

remuneration *noun* See **compensation, payment, wage.**

remunerative *adjective* See **compensatory, profitable.**

renaissance *noun* See **revival.**

renascence *noun* See **revival.**

rend *verb* See **tear¹.**

render *verb* See **abdicate, interpret, paraphrase, represent, return, translate.**

rendering *noun* See **interpretation, paraphrase.**

rendezvous *noun* See **engagement, haunt.**

rendezvous *verb* See **meet¹.**

rendition *noun* See **interpretation.**

renege *verb* See **back down** at **back.**

renegade *noun* See **defector.**

renegade *verb* See **defect.**

renew *verb* **1.** To make new or as if new again : furbish, recondition, re-create, refresh, refurbish, rejuvenate, renovate, restore, revamp. *Idiom:* give a new look to. See HELP, NEW in Index. **2.** To arrange for the extension of : extend. See CONTINUE in Index. — See also **continue, refresh, restore, revive.**

renewal *noun* **1.** The act of making new or as if new again : face-lift, facelifting, refurbishment, rejuvenation, renovation, restoration, revampment. See HELP, NEW in Index. **2.** A continuing after interruption : continuation, resumption, resurgence, revival. See CONTINUE in Index. — See also **revival.**

renewing *adjective* See **tonic.**

renitence *noun* See **resistance.**

renitency *noun* See **resistance.**

renitent *adjective* See **resistant.**

renounce *verb* See **abdicate, repudiate.**

renovate *verb* See **renew, restore.**

renovation *noun* See **renewal.**

renown *noun* See **eminence, fame.**

renowned *adjective* See **eminent.**

rent¹ *verb* See **hire, lease.**

rent² *noun* See **breach, tear¹.**

renunciation *noun* See **abdication.**

reoccupy *verb* See **resume.**

reoccur *verb* See **recur, return.**

reoccurrence *noun* See **recurrence.**

reopen *verb* See **continue.**

rep *noun* See **reputation.**

repair¹ *verb* See **fix.**

repair² *verb* See **frequent, resort.**

reparation *noun* See **compensation.**

repartee *noun* See **retort.**

repay *verb* See **avenge, compensate, refund, return, reward.**

repayment *noun* See **compensation.**

repeal *verb* See **lift.**

repeal *noun* See **reversal.**

repeat *verb* **1.** To state again : iterate, reiterate, restate. See REPETITION in Index. **2.** To do or perform (an act) again : duplicate, redo. See REPETITION in Index. — See also **echo.**

repel *verb* See **disgust, parry.**

repellence *noun* See **hate.**

repellency *noun* See **hate.**

repellent *adjective* See **offensive.**

repent *verb* See **regret.**

repentance *noun* See **penitence.**

repentant *adjective* See **apologetic, remorseful.**

repercussion *noun* See **echo, impact.**

repetition *noun* The act or process of repeating : iteration, reiteration, restatement. See REPETITION in Index. — See also **echo.**

repetitious *adjective* See **repetitive.**

repetitive *adjective* Characterized by repetition : iterative, reiterative, repetitious. See REPETITION in Index.

rephrase *verb* See **paraphrase.**

replace *verb* To substitute for or fill the place of : supersede, supplant, surrogate. See SUBSTITUTE in Index. — See also **restore.**

replacement *noun* See **relief, substitute.**

replete *adjective* See **alive, full.**

repletion *noun* See **satiation.**

replica *noun* See **copy.**

replicate *verb* See **copy.**

replication *noun* See **copy.**

reply *verb* See **answer.**

reply *noun* See **answer.**

report *noun* A sudden sharp, explosive noise : bang, bark, clap, crack, explosion, pop[1], rat-a-tat-tat, snap. See SOUNDS in Index. — See also **gossip, reputation, story.**

report *verb* See **communicate, cover, describe.**

reportage *noun* See **coverage.**

repose *verb* See **consist, lie[1], rest[1].**

repose *noun* See **rest[1].**

repository *noun* See **confidant, depository.**

repossess *verb* See **recover, resume.**

repossession *noun* See **recovery.**

reprehend *verb* See **deplore.**

reprehensible *adjective* See **blameworthy.**

reprehension *noun* See **blame.**

represent *verb* **1.** To serve as an example, image, or symbol of : epitomize, exemplify, illustrate, stand for, symbol, symbolize, typify. See SUBSTITUTE in Index. **2.** To present a lifelike image of : delineate, depict, describe, express, image, limn, picture, portray, render, show. See SHOW in Index. **3.** To serve as an official delegate of : speak for, stand for. See SUBSTITUTE in Index. — See also **act.**

representation *noun* The act or process of describing in lifelike imagery : delineation, depiction, description, expression, portrayal. See SHOW in Index.

representative *noun* One who stands for another : delegate, deputy. See SUBSTITUTE in Index. — See also **example.**

representative *adjective* See **descriptive, symbolic, typical.**

repress *verb* To hold (something requiring an outlet) in check : burke, choke (back), gag, hold back, hold down, hush (up), muffle, quench, smother, squelch, stifle, strangle, suppress, throttle. *Informal:* sit on (or upon). See RESTRAINT in Index.

repression *noun* See **suppression.**

repressive *adjective* Serving to restrain forcefully : suppressive. See ATTACK, RESTRAINT in Index.

reprieve *noun* See **grace.**

reprimand *verb* See **call down** at **call.**

reprimand *noun* See **rebuke.**

reprisal *noun* See **retaliation.**

reproach *verb* See **call down** at **call, shame.**

reproach *noun* See **rebuke, reflection.**

reprobate *adjective* See **evil.**

reprobate *verb* See **deplore.**

reprobation *noun* See **blame.**

reproduce *verb* To produce sexually or asexually others of one's kind : breed, increase, multiply, procreate, proliferate, propagate, spawn. See REPRODUCTION in Index. — See also **copy.**

reproduction *noun* The process by which an organism produces others of its kind : breeding, multiplication, procreation, proliferation, propagation, spawning. *Obsolete:* increase. See REPRODUCTION in Index. — See also **copy.**

reproductive *adjective* **1.** Of or relating to reproduction : procreant, procreative. See REPRODUCTION in Index. **2.** Employed in reproduction : sexual. See REPRODUCTION in Index.

reproof *noun* See **rebuke.**

reprove *verb* See **call down** at **call.**

repudiate *verb* To refuse to recognize or acknowledge : deny, disacknowledge, disavow, disclaim, disown, reject, renounce. *Idiom:* turn one's back on. See ACCEPT in Index.

repugnance *noun* See **hate.**

repugnancy *noun* See **hate.**

repugnant *adjective* See **discrepant, filthy.**

repulse *verb* See **parry.**

repulsion *noun* See **hate.**

repulsive *adjective* See **offensive.**

reputable *adjective* See **admirable.**

reputation *noun* Public estimation of someone : character, name, report, repute. *Informal:* rep. See RESPECT in Index. — See also **fame, honor.**

repute *verb* To regard in an appraising way : believe, suppose, think. See BELIEF in Index.

repute *noun* See **fame, honor, reputation.**

reputed *adjective* Assumed to be such : putative, supposed. See BELIEF in Index.

request *verb* To endeavor to obtain (something) by expressing one's needs or desires : ask (for), seek, solicit. See REQUEST in Index.

require *verb* To oblige to do or not do by force of authority, propriety, or custom : expect, suppose. See OBLIGATION in Index. — See also **demand, lack.**

required *adjective* Imposed on one by authority, command, or convention : compulsory, imperative, mandatory, necessary, obligatory, requisite. See OBLIGATION in Index. — See also **essential.**

requirement *noun* See **condition.**

requisite *adjective* See **essential, required.**

requisite *noun* See **condition.**

requisition *verb* See **demand.**

requisition *noun* See **demand.**

requital *noun* See **compensation, retaliation.**

requite *verb* See **avenge, compensate, reciprocate, reward.**

rescind *verb* See **lift.**

rescission *noun* See **reversal.**

rescue *verb* **1.** To extricate, as from danger or confinement : deliver, save. *Idiom:* come to the rescue of. See HELP in Index. **2.** To extricate from an undesirable state : reclaim, recover, redeem, salvage. See HELP in Index.

rescue *noun* Extrication from danger or confinement : deliverance, delivery, salvage, salvation. See HELP in Index.

research *noun* See **inquiry.**

researcher *noun* See **inquirer.**

resemblance *noun* See **likeness.**

resemble *verb* See **favor.**

resentful *adjective* Bitingly hostile : acrimonious, bitter, embittered, hard, rancorous, virulent. See ATTITUDE, LOVE in Index.

resentfulness *noun* See **resentment.**

resentment *noun* The quality or state of feeling bitter : acrimony, bitterness, embitterment, gall[1], rancor, rancorousness, resentfulness, virulence, virulency. See FEELINGS in Index. — See also **offense.**

reservation *noun* Public land kept for a special purpose : preserve, reserve. See TERRITORY in Index. — See also **provision, qualm.**

reserve *noun* The keeping of one's thoughts and emotions to oneself : control, restraint, reticence, self-control, self-restraint, taciturnity, uncommunicativeness. See RESTRAINT in Index. — See also **hoard, reservation.**

reserve *verb* See **book, hold.**

reserve *adjective* See **auxiliary.**

reserved *adjective* Tending to keep one's thoughts and emotions to oneself : controlled, inhibited, noncommittal, restrained, self-

controlled, self-restrained. See
RESTRAINT in Index. — See also
cool, qualified, taciturn.

reservoir *noun* See **hoard.**

reside *verb* See **consist, live¹.**

residence *noun* See **home.**

residue *noun* See **balance.**

resign *verb* See **abdicate, quit,
reconcile.**

resignation *noun* See **abdication,
patience.**

resigned *adjective* See **passive,
patient.**

resilience *noun* The ability to
recover quickly from depression or
discouragement : bounce, buoyancy, elasticity, resiliency. See ABIL-
ITY in Index. — See also **flexibility.**

resiliency *noun* See **flexibility,
resilience.**

resilient *adjective* See **flexible.**

resist *verb* To oppose actively and
with force : withstand. *Idioms:*
mount (or offer) resistance, put up a
fight, stand up to (or against). See
RESIST in Index. — See also **contest.**

resistance *noun* **1.** The capacity to
withstand : immunity, imperviousness, insusceptibility, unsusceptibility. See RESIST in Index. **2.** The
act of resisting : opposition, renitence, renitency. See RESIST in
Index. **3.** A clandestine organization
of freedom fighters in an oppressed
land : underground. See RESIST in
Index.

resistant *adjective* **1.** Having the
capacity to withstand : immune,
impervious, insusceptible, proof,
resistive, unsusceptible. See RESIST
in Index. **2.** Tending to resist, as an
influence or idea : renitent, resisting, resistive. See RESIST in Index.

resister *noun* See **opponent.**

resisting *adjective* See **resistant.**

resistive *adjective* See **resistant.**

resolute *adjective* See **decisive,
firm¹, set¹.**

resoluteness *noun* See **decision.**

resolution *noun* See **decision.**

resolve *verb* To find a solution for :
clear up, decipher, explain, solve,
unravel. *Informal:* dope out, figure
out. *Idiom:* get to the bottom of. See
ASK, REASON in Index. — See also
analyze, decide, settle.

resolve *noun* See **decision.**

resonant *adjective* Having or producing a full, deep, or rich sound :
mellow, orotund, plangent, resounding, ringing, rotund, round, sonorous, vibrant. See SOUNDS in Index.

resort *noun* That to which one
turns for help when in desperation :
recourse, refuge, resource. See HELP
in Index. — See also **haunt.**

resort *verb* To look to when in
need : apply, go, refer, repair², run,
turn. *Idioms:* fall back on (or upon),
have recourse to. See USED in Index.
— See also **frequent.**

resound *verb* See **echo.**

resounding *adjective* See **emphatic,
resonant.**

resource *noun* **1.** The ability and
the means to meet situations effectively. Often used in plural :
resourcefulness, wherewithal. See
ABILITY in Index. **2.** All things,
such as money, property, or goods,
having economic value. Used in plural : asset (used in plural), capital,
fortune, mean³ (used in plural),
wealth, wherewithal. See OWNED in
Index. — See also **resort.**

resourceful *adjective* Able to use
the means at one's disposal to meet
situations effectively : ingenious,
inventive. See ABILITY in Index.

resourcefulness *noun* See
resource.

respect *verb* See **admire,
appreciate.**

respect *noun* See **esteem, honor, phase, regard.**

respectability *noun* See **decency.**

respectable *adjective* See **acceptable, admirable, correct, decent, sizable.**

respectableness *noun* See **decency.**

respectful *adjective* See **deferential.**

respiration *noun* See **breath.**

respire *verb* See **breathe.**

respite *noun* See **break, grace.**

resplendence *noun* See **glitter.**

resplendency *noun* See **glitter.**

resplendent *adjective* See **glorious.**

respond *verb* To act in return to something, as a stimulus : react. See ACTION in Index. — See also **answer, greet.**

respondent *noun* See **accused.**

response *noun* An action elicited by a stimulus : reaction, retroaction. See ACTION in Index. — See also **answer.**

responsibility *noun* See **duty.**

responsible *adjective* See **dependable, liable.**

responsive *adjective* See **approachable, receptive, sensitive.**

responsiveness *noun* See **openness.**

rest¹ *noun* Freedom from labor, responsibility, or strain : ease, leisure, relaxation, repose. See CONTINUE in Index. — See also **break, death.**

rest *verb* **1.** To take repose, as by sleeping or lying quietly : lie¹ (down), recline, repose, stretch (out). See CONTINUE in Index. **2.** To take repose by ceasing work or other effort for an interval of time : relax, unbend, unwind. *Idioms:* lead (or live) the life of Riley, take it easy. See CONTINUE in Index. — See also **base¹, consist.**

rest on or **upon** *verb* See **depend on** at **depend.**

rest² *noun* See **balance.**

restart *verb* See **continue.**

restate *verb* See **paraphrase, repeat.**

restatement *noun* See **paraphrase, repetition.**

restitute *verb* See **refund, restore.**

restitution *noun* See **compensation.**

restive *adjective* See **edgy.**

restiveness *noun* See **restlessness.**

restless *adjective* Affording no quiet, repose, or rest : uneasy, unquiet, unsettled. See CALM, TIRED in Index. — See also **edgy.**

restlessness *noun* An uneasy or nervous state : disquiet, disquietude, inquietude, restiveness, unease, uneasiness, unrest. See CALM in Index.

restoration *noun* See **renewal.**

restorative *adjective* See **curative, tonic.**

restorative *noun* See **tonic.**

restore *verb* **1.** To bring back into existence or use : reestablish, reinstate, reintroduce, renew, return, revive. See INCREASE, KEEP in Index. **2.** To bring back to a previous normal condition : rebuild, reclaim, recondition, reconstruct, rehabilitate, reinstate, rejuvenate, renovate, restitute. See HELP in Index. **3.** To put (someone) in the possession of a prior position or office : give back, reinstate, replace, return. See INCREASE, KEEP in Index. — See also **refresh, renew, return, revive.**

restrain *verb* To control, restrict, or arrest : bit², brake, bridle, check, constrain, curb, hold, hold back, hold down, hold in, inhibit, keep, keep back, pull in, rein (back, in, or up). See RESTRAINT in Index.

restrained *adjective* See **conservative, quiet, reserved.**

restraint *noun* See **bit², bond, reserve, restriction.**

restrict *verb* See **limit.**

restricted *adjective* **1.** Kept within certain limits : limited. See LIMITED in Index. **2.** Excluding or unavailable to certain minorities : segregated. See INCLUDE, LIMITED in Index. — See also **confidential, qualified.**

restriction *noun* **1.** The act of limiting or condition of being limited : circumscription, confinement, constraint, limitation, restraint. See LIMITED in Index. **2.** Something that limits or restricts : check, circumscription, constraint, cramp², curb, inhibition, limit, limitation, restraint, stricture, trammel. See LIMITED in Index.

result *noun* See **answer, effect.**

result *verb* See **follow.**

result in *verb* See **cause.**

resultant *noun* See **effect.**

resume *verb* To occupy or take again : reassume, re-claim, reoccupy, repossess, retake, take back. See GIVE in Index. — See also **continue.**

resumption *noun* See **renewal.**

resurgence *noun* See **renewal, revival.**

resurrect *verb* See **revive.**

resurrection *noun* See **revival.**

resuscitate *verb* See **revive.**

resuscitation *noun* See **revival.**

retail *verb* See **sell.**

retain *verb* See **employ, have, hold, keep, remember.**

retained *adjective* See **employed.**

retake *verb* See **resume.**

retaliate *verb* To return like for like, especially to return an unfriendly or hostile action with a similar one : counter, hit back,

reciprocate, retort, strike back. See ATTACK, FORGIVENESS in Index.

retaliation *noun* The act of retaliating : counteraction, counterattack, counterblow, reciprocation, reprisal, requital, retribution, revenge, tit for tat, vengeance. *Idioms:* an eye for an eye, a tooth for a tooth, like for like, measure for measure. See ATTACK, FORGIVENESS in Index.

retard *verb* See **delay.**

retardation *noun* See **delay.**

retarded *adjective* See **backward.**

rethink *verb* See **reconsider.**

reticence *noun* See **modesty, reserve.**

reticent *adjective* See **cool, taciturn.**

retinue *noun* A group of attendants or followers : entourage, following, suite, train. See OVER in Index.

retire *verb* **1.** To go to bed : bed (down). *Informal:* turn in. *Slang:* crash, flop. *Idioms:* call it a night, hit the hay (or sack). See AWARENESS in Index. **2.** To withdraw from business or active life : step down. *Idioms:* call it quits, hang up one's spurs, turn in one's badge. See CONTINUE in Index. **3.** To remove from active service : pension (off), superannuate. *Idiom:* put out to pasture. See KEEP in Index. — See also **go, retreat.**

retirement *noun* See **retreat, seclusion.**

retiring *adjective* See **modest.**

retiringness *noun* See **shyness.**

retort *noun* A spirited, incisive reply : comeback, repartee, riposte. See ASK in Index.

retort *verb* See **answer, retaliate.**

retouch *verb* See **touch up at touch.**

retract *verb* To disavow (something previously written or said) irrevocably and usually formally : abjure, recall, recant, take back, withdraw.

See ACCEPT in Index. — See also
recede, withdraw.

retractation *noun* See **retraction.**

retraction *noun* A formal statement of disavowal : abjuration, palinode, recantation, retractation,
withdrawal. See ACCEPT in Index.

retreat *noun* The moving back of a
military force in the face of enemy
attack or after a defeat : fallback,
pullback, pullout, retirement, withdrawal. See FORWARD in Index.
— See also **cover.**

  retreat *verb* To move back in the
  face of enemy attack or after a
  defeat : draw back, fall back, pull
  back, pull out, retire, withdraw.
  Idioms: beat a retreat, give ground
  (*or* way). See FORWARD in Index.
  — See also **back, back down** at **back,
  recede.**

retribution *noun* See **retaliation.**

retrieval *noun* See **recovery.**

retrieve *verb* See **recover.**

retroaction *noun* See **response.**

retrocede *verb* See **back, recede.**

retrogradation *noun* See
reversion.

retrograde *adjective* See
backward.

  retrograde *verb* See **back, deteriorate, recede.**

retrogress *verb* See **back, recede,
relapse.**

retrogression *noun* See **reversion.**

retrogressive *adjective* See
backward.

return *verb* **1.** To go again to a former place : come back, go back,
revisit. See APPROACH in Index.
2. To come back to a former condition : recrudesce, recur, reoccur,
revert. See REPETITION in Index.
3. To send, put, or carry back to a former location : give back, restore,
take back. See INCREASE, KEEP in
Index. **4.** To make as income or

profit : bring in, clear, draw, earn,
gain, gross, net[2], pay, produce, realize, repay, yield. See MONEY in
Index. **5.** To deliver (an indictment
or verdict, for example) : hand
down, render. See LAW in Index.
— See also **answer, reciprocate,
restore.**

return *noun* See **gain, recurrence.**

reunite *verb* See **reconcile.**

revamp *verb* See **fix, renew, revise.**

revampment *noun* See **renewal.**

reveal *verb* To make visible; bring
to view : bare, disclose, display,
expose, show, unclothe, uncover,
unmask, unveil. *Archaic:* discover.
Idioms: bring to light, lay open,
make plain. See SHOW in Index.
— See also **betray, show.**

revel *verb* To behave riotously :
carouse, frolic, riot, roister.
Informal: hell (around). *Idioms:*
blow off steam, cut loose, kick over
the traces, kick up one's heels, let
go, let loose, make merry, make
whoopee, paint the town red, raise
Cain (*or* the devil *or* hell), whoop it
up. See RESTRAINT in Index. — See
also **celebrate, luxuriate.**

revel *noun* See **celebration, gaiety.**

revelation *noun* Something disclosed, especially something not previously known or realized : apocalypse, disclosure, exposé, exposure.
Informal: eye opener. See SHOW in
Index.

revelry *noun* See **celebration,
gaiety.**

revenant *noun* See **ghost.**

revenge *noun* See **retaliation,
vindictiveness.**

revengeful *adjective* See **vindictive.**

reverberate *verb* See **echo.**

reverberation *noun* See **echo.**

revere *verb* See **adore.**

reverence *noun* See **adoration.**

  reverence *verb* See **adore.**

reverend *noun* See **preacher.**

reverent *adjective* Feeling or showing reverence : reverential, venerational, worshipful. See RESPECT in Index.

reverential *adjective* See **reverent.**

reverie *noun* See **dream, trance.**

reversal *noun* **1.** The act of reversing or annulling : recall, repeal, rescission, revocation. See CONTINUE, LAW in Index. **2.** The act of changing or being changed from one position, direction, or course to the opposite : inversion, transposition, turnabout, turnaround. See CHANGE in Index. — See also **reverse.**

reverse *noun* A change from better to worse : backset, reversal, setback. See BETTER in Index. — See also **opposite.**

reverse *adjective* See **opposite.**

reverse *verb* To change to the opposite position, direction, or course : invert, transpose, turn (about, around, over, or round). See CHANGE in Index. — See also **double, lift.**

reversion *noun* A return to a former, usually worse condition : regression, retrogradation, retrogression. See FORWARD, REPETITION in Index.

revert *verb* See **relapse, return.**

review *verb* **1.** To write a critical report on : criticize. See OPINION, WORDS in Index. **2.** To give a recapitulation of the salient facts of : abstract, epitomize, go over, recapitulate, run down, run through, summarize, sum up, synopsize, wrap up. *Informal:* recap. See THOUGHTS in Index. — See also **reconsider.**

review *noun* **1.** A formal military inspection : parade. See INVESTIGATE in Index. **2.** Evaluative and critical discourse : criticism, critique, notice. See OPINION, WORDS in Index. — See also **analysis.**

reviewer *noun* See **critic.**

revile *verb* To attack with harsh, often insulting language : abuse, assail, rail against (or at), vituperate. See PRAISE in Index.

revilement *noun* See **vituperation.**

reviling *noun* See **vituperation.**

revise *verb* To prepare a new version of : amend, emend, emendate, revamp, rework, rewrite. See CHANGE in Index.

revision *noun* The act or process of revising : amendment, emendation, rewrite. See CHANGE in Index.

revisit *verb* See **return.**

revitalization *noun* See **revival.**

revitalize *verb* See **refresh, revive.**

revival *noun* The act of reviving or condition of being revived : reactivation, rebirth, renaissance, renascence, renewal, resurgence, resurrection, resuscitation, revitalization, revivification. See AWARENESS in Index. — See also **renewal.**

revive *verb* **1.** To cause to come back to life or consciousness : bring around (or round), restore, resuscitate, revivify. See LIVE in Index. **2.** To rouse from a state of inactivity or quiescence : reactivate, reanimate, reawaken, rekindle, renew, resurrect, resuscitate, revitalize, revivify. See AWARENESS in Index. — See also **remember, restore.**

revivification *noun* See **revival.**

revivify *verb* See **refresh, revive.**

revocation *noun* See **reversal.**

revoke *verb* See **lift.**

revolt *verb* See **disgust, rebel.**

revolt *noun* See **rebellion.**

revolting *adjective* See **offensive.**

revolution *noun* **1.** A momentous or sweeping change : cataclysm, convulsion, upheaval. See CHANGE in Index. **2.** Circular movement

around a point or about an axis :
circuit, circulation, circumvolution,
gyration, rotation, turn, wheel,
whirl. See GEOMETRY, REPETITION
in Index. — See also **rebellion.**
revolutionary *noun* See **extremist,
rebel.**
   revolutionary *adjective* See
extreme, rebellious.
revolutionist *noun* See **extremist,
rebel.**
revolutionize *verb* To bring about a
radical change in : metamorphose,
transform. See CHANGE in Index.
revolve *verb* See **ponder, turn.**
revulsion *noun* See **hate.**
reward *noun* **1.** Something given in
return for a service or accomplishment : accolade, award, guerdon,
honorarium, plum, premium, prize[1].
Idiom: token of appreciation (or
esteem). See REWARD in Index.
2. A sum of money offered for a special service, such as the apprehension of a criminal : bonus, bounty.
See LAW, REWARD in Index. — See
also **due.**
   reward *verb* **1.** To bestow a
reward on : guerdon. See REWARD
in Index. **2.** To give a satisfactory
return to : compensate, indemnify,
pay, recompense, remunerate, repay,
requite. See PAY in Index.
rewarding *adjective* See **profitable.**
reword *verb* See **paraphrase.**
rework *verb* See **revise.**
rewrite *verb* See **revise.**
   rewrite *noun* See **revision.**
rhapsodize *verb* See **rave.**
rhetoric *noun* See **oratory.**
rhetorical *adjective* See **oratorical,
sonorous.**
rhetorician *noun* See **orator.**
rhubarb *noun* See **argument.**
rhyme *noun* See **poem.**
rhymer also **rimer** *noun* See **poet.**

rhymester also **rimester** *noun* See
poet.
rhythm *noun* The patterned, recurring alternation of contrasting
elements, such as stressed and
unstressed notes in music : beat,
cadence, cadency, measure, meter,
swing. See REPETITION in Index.
rhythmic *adjective* See **rhythmical.**
rhythmical *adjective* Marked by a
regular rhythm : cadenced, measured, metrical, rhythmic. See
REPETITION in Index.
rib *verb* See **joke.**
ribald *adjective* See **obscene.**
ribaldry *noun* See **obscenity.**
ribbing *noun* *Informal.* Good-
natured teasing : badinage, banter,
chaff, raillery, taunt. See LAUGHTER
in Index.
rich *adjective* Possessing a large
amount of money, land, or other
material possessions : affluent,
flush, moneyed, wealthy. *Slang:*
loaded. *Idioms:* having money to
burn, in the money, made of money,
rolling in money. See RICH in Index.
— See also **colorful, fertile, heavy,
luxurious, priceless.**
riches *noun* A great amount of accumulated money and precious possessions : affluence, fortune, pelf,
treasure, wealth. See OWNED, RICH
in Index.
richness *noun* See **fertility.**
ricketiness *noun* See **unstableness.**
rickety *adjective* See **unstable.**
ricochet *verb* See **glance.**
rid *verb* To free from or cast out
something objectionable or undesirable : clear, disburden, disembarrass, disencumber, release, relieve,
shake off, throw off, unburden.
Slang: shake. See KEEP in Index.
riddance *noun* See **disposal,
elimination.**
riddle *noun* See **mystery.**

ride *verb* See **bait, joke.**
  ride out *verb* See **survive.**
  ride *noun* See **drive.**
ridicule *verb* To make fun or make
  fun of : deride, gibe, jeer, jest,
  laugh, mock, scoff, scout[2], twit.
  Chiefly British: quiz. *Idiom:* poke
  fun at. See LAUGHTER, RESPECT in
  Index.
  ridicule *noun* Words or actions
  intended to evoke contemptuous
  laughter : derision, mockery. See
  LAUGHTER, RESPECT in Index.
ridiculous *adjective* See **laughable,
  outrageous.**
ridiculousness *noun* See **humor.**
rife *adjective* See **alive, prevailing.**
riffle *verb* See **browse, shuffle.**
riffraff *noun* See **trash.**
rift *noun* See **breach, crack.**
  rift *verb* See **break.**
rig *noun* See **dress, outfit.**
  rig *verb* See **furnish.**
right *adjective* See **accurate, appropriate, conservative, correct, ethical,
  healthy, just.**
  right *noun* See **birthright, faculty.**
  right *adverb* See **directly.**
  right *verb* To restore to or place in
  an upright or proper position :
  stand (up). See HORIZONTAL in
  Index. — See also **correct, fix.**
right away *adverb* See **directly.**
righteous *adjective* See **ethical,
  honest.**
righteousness *noun* See **ethic,
  good.**
rightful *adjective* See **ethical, just,
  true.**
rightfulness *noun* See **ethic.**
rightist *noun* See **conservative.**
  rightist *adjective* See **conservative.**
right-minded *adjective* See **ethical.**
rightness *noun* See **accuracy, ethic,
  good.**
right off *adverb* See **directly.**

right of way *noun* See **precedence.**
right on *adverb* See **yes.**
right-wing *adjective* See **conservative.**
right-winger *noun* See **conservative.**
rigid *adjective* Not changing shape
  or bending : inelastic, inflexible,
  stiff, unbending, unyielding. See
  FLEXIBLE in Index. — See also **inflexible, severe, stubborn.**
rigidity *noun* See **severity,
  stubbornness.**
rigidness *noun* See **stubbornness.**
rigmarole *also* **rigamarole** *noun*
  See **nonsense.**
rigor *noun* See **difficulty, severity.**
rigorous *adjective* See **accurate,
  burdensome, close, strict.**
rigorousness *noun* See **severity.**
rile *verb* See **annoy.**
rim *noun* See **border.**
  rim *verb* See **border.**
rimple *noun* See **fold.**
  rimple *verb* See **wrinkle.**
rind *noun* See **skin.**
ring[1] *noun* See **circle, combine,
  gang, loop.**
  ring *verb* See **band**[1]**, surround.**
ring[2] *verb* To give forth or cause to
  give forth a clear, resonant sound :
  bong, chime, knell, peal, strike,
  toll[2]. See SOUNDS in Index. — See
  also **telephone.**
  ring *noun* See **call.**
ringer *noun* See **double.**
ringing *adjective* See **resonant.**
riot *noun* See **brawl, scream.**
  riot *verb* See **revel.**
  riot away *verb* See **waste.**
riotous *adjective* See **disorderly,
  profuse.**
rip *verb* See **rush, tear**[1]**.**
  rip into *verb* See **slam.**
  rip off *verb* See **skin, steal.**
  rip *noun* See **tear**[1]**.**
ripe *adjective* See **aged, mature.**

ripen *verb* See **mature.**
rip-off *noun* See **larceny.**
riposte *noun* See **retort.**
 riposte *verb* See **answer.**
ripping *adjective* See **marvelous.**
rippling *adjective* See **laughing.**
rise *verb* **1.** To move from a lower to a higher position : arise, ascend, climb, lift, mount, soar. See RISE in Index. **2.** To attain a higher status, rank, or condition : advance, ascend, climb, mount. *Idiom:* go up the ladder. See INCREASE, RISE in Index. — See also **get up** at **get, increase, rebel, stem, succeed.**
 rise *noun* The act of rising or moving upward : ascension, ascent, rising. See RISE in Index. — See also **advancement, ascent, hill, increase.**
risible *adjective* See **amusing, laughable.**
rising *noun* See **rise.**
rising star *noun* See **comer.**
risk *verb* To expose to possible loss or damage : adventure, compromise, hazard, venture. See SAFETY in Index. — See also **endanger, gamble, hazard.**
 risk *noun* A possibility of danger or harm : chance, gamble, hazard. See SAFETY in Index. — See also **danger, gamble.**
risky *adjective* See **dangerous.**
risqué *adjective* See **racy.**
rite *noun* See **ceremony.**
ritual *noun* A conventional social gesture or act without intrinsic purpose : ceremony, form, formality. See RITUAL, USUAL in Index. — See also **ceremony.**
 ritual *adjective* Of or characterized by ceremony : ceremonial, ceremonious, formal, liturgical, ritualistic. See RITUAL in Index.
ritualistic *adjective* See **ritual.**
ritzy *adjective* See **exclusive.**

rival *verb* To come near, as in quality or amount : approach, approximate, border on (or upon), challenge, verge on. See SAME in Index. — See also **compete.**
 rival *noun* See **competitor.**
rivalry *noun* See **competition.**
rive *verb* See **break, tear**[1]**.**
rivet *verb* See **grip.**
road *noun* See **way.**
roadway *noun* See **way.**
roam *verb* See **rove.**
roaming *adjective* See **errant.**
roar *verb* To speak or say very loudly or with a shout : bawl, bellow, bluster, call, clamor, cry, halloo, holler, shout, vociferate, whoop, yawp, yell. See SOUNDS in Index. — See also **blast, break up** at **break.**
 roar *noun* A loud, deep, prolonged sound : bawl, bellow, clamor. See SOUNDS in Index. — See also **blast.**
roaring *adjective* See **flourishing, loud.**
roast *verb* See **burn, slam.**
roasting *adjective* See **hot.**
rob *verb* To take property or possessions from (a person or company, for example) unlawfully and usually forcibly : hold up, stick up. *Slang:* heist, knock off. See CRIMES, GIVE in Index. — See also **deprive.**
robber *noun* See **larcenist.**
robbery *noun* The act or crime of taking another's property unlawfully and by force : holdup. *Slang:* heist, stickup. See CRIMES, GIVE in Index.
robe *verb* See **clothe.**
 robe *noun* See **habit.**
roborant *adjective* See **tonic.**
 roborant *noun* See **tonic.**
robust *adjective* See **lusty, muscular.**
rock *verb* See **agitate, shake, toss.**
rock bottom *noun* See **low.**
rocket *verb* See **rush, soar.**
rocky *adjective* See **sickly.**
rococo *adjective* See **ornate.**

rod *noun* See **stick.**
rodomontade also **rhodomontade** *noun* See **boast.**
  rodomontade also **rhodomontade** *adjective* See **boastful.**
  rodomontade also **rhodomontade** *verb* See **boast.**
rogation *noun* See **prayer**[1].
roger *adverb* See **yes.**
rogue *noun* See **mischief.**
roguery *noun* See **mischief.**
roguishness *noun* See **mischief.**
roiled *adjective* See **rough, turbid.**
roily *adjective* See **rough, turbid.**
roister *verb* See **revel.**
role also **rôle** *noun* See **function, part.**
roll *verb* See **flow, lurch, luxuriate, rumble, toss, wrap.**
  roll out *verb* See **get up** at **get.**
  roll up *verb* See **accumulate.**
  roll *noun* See **list**[1].
rollick *verb* See **gambol, luxuriate.**
roly-poly *adjective* See **plump**[1].
romance *verb* See **court.**
  romance *noun* See **love.**
romantic *adjective* See **idealistic, sentimental.**
romanticize *verb* See **sentimentalize.**
Romeo *noun* See **gallant.**
romp *verb* See **gambol.**
  romp *noun* See **runaway.**
roof *noun* See **height.**
rook *verb* See **cheat.**
  rook *noun* See **cheat.**
rookie *noun* See **beginner.**
room *noun* Suitable opportunity to accept or allow something : elbowroom, latitude, leeway, margin, play, scope. See PLACE, RESTRAINT in Index.
  room *verb* See **harbor.**
roomy *adjective* Having plenty of room : ample, capacious, commodious, spacious. See BIG in Index.

root[1] *noun* See **basis, center, heart, origin, theme.**
  root *verb* See **annihilate, base**[1]**, fix.**
root[2] *verb* See **applaud.**
rootstock *noun* See **origin.**
roseate *adjective* See **optimistic.**
rose-colored *adjective* See **optimistic.**
roster *noun* See **list**[1].
rosy *adjective* See **optimistic, ruddy.**
rot *verb* See **decay.**
  rot *noun* See **decay.**
rotate *verb* To do, use, or occur in successive turns : alternate, interchange. See CHANGE in Index. — See also **turn.**
rotation *noun* Occurrence in successive turns : alternation, interchange. See CHANGE in Index. — See also **revolution.**
rotten *adjective* See **bad, corrupt, filthy, moldy, shoddy.**
rottenness *noun* See **decay.**
rotund *adjective* See **plump**[1]**, resonant.**
roué *noun* See **lecher.**
rough *adjective* **1.** Having a surface that is not smooth : coarse, cragged, craggy, harsh, ironbound, jagged, ragged, rugged, scabrous, uneven. See SMOOTH in Index. **2.** Marked by vigorous physical exertion : knockabout, rough-and-tumble, rugged, strenuous, tough. See ACTION in Index. **3.** Violently disturbed or agitated, as by storms : dirty, heavy, raging, roiled, roily, rugged, stormy, tempestuous, tumultuous, turbulent, ugly, violent, wild. See CALM in Index. **4.** Not perfected, elaborated, or completed : preliminary, sketchy, tentative, unfinished, unperfected, unpolished. See START in Index.
  — See also **bitter, burdensome, coarse, harsh, rude, tight, wild.**

rough *verb* See **slap around** at **slap.**

rough in or **out** *verb* See **draft.**

rough up *verb* See **batter.**

rough *noun* See **draft.**

rough-and-tumble *adjective* See **rough.**

roughly *adverb* See **approximately.**

roughneck *noun* See **tough.**

roughness *noun* See **irregularity.**

round *adjective* **1.** Having the shape of a curve everywhere equidistant from a fixed point : annular, circular, globoid, globular, spheric, spherical. See GEOMETRY in Index. **2.** Not more or less : complete, entire, full, good, perfect, whole. See PART, PRECISE in Index. — See also **plump¹, resonant.**

round *noun* See **beat, bend, circle, routine, series.**

round *adverb* See **back, through.**

round *verb* See **bend, complement.**

round up *verb* See **assemble.**

roundabout *adjective* See **indirect, tautological.**

rounded *adjective* See **bent.**

round-the-clock *adjective* See **continual.**

rouse *verb* See **arouse, wake¹.**

rousing *adjective* See **stimulating.**

roustabout *noun* See **laborer.**

rout *verb* See **defeat.**

rout *noun* See **defeat.**

route *verb* See **guide, send.**

route *noun* See **beat, ticket, way.**

routine *noun* A course of action to be followed regularly : round (often used in plural), track. See USUAL in Index. — See also **bit¹, grind.**

routine *adjective* See **accustomed, common, ordinary.**

routinely *adverb* See **usually.**

routineness *noun* See **usualness.**

rove *verb* To move about at random, especially over a wide area : drift, gad, gallivant, meander, peregrinate, ramble, range, roam, stray, traipse, wander. See MOVE in Index.

roving *adjective* See **errant.**

row¹ *noun* See **line.**

row² *noun* See **brawl.**

row *verb* See **brawl.**

rowdy *adjective* See **disorderly.**

rowdy *noun* See **tough.**

royal *adjective* See **grand.**

rub *noun* See **catch.**

rub *verb* See **cancel.**

rub out *verb* See **annihilate, murder.**

rubbish *noun* See **nonsense.**

rubble *noun* See **ruin.**

rubicund *adjective* See **ruddy.**

rubric *noun* See **rule.**

ruck¹ *noun* See **commonalty, crowd.**

ruck² *verb* See **fold.**

ruck *noun* See **fold.**

ruction *noun* See **brawl.**

ruddy *adjective* Of a healthy reddish color : blooming, florid, flush, flushed, full-blooded, glowing, rosy, rubicund, sanguine. See COLORS in Index. — See also **damned.**

rude *adjective* **1.** Lacking good manners : discourteous, disrespectful, ill-bred, ill-mannered, impolite, uncivil, ungracious, unmannerly, unpolished. See COURTESY in Index. **2.** Lacking expert, careful craftsmanship : crude, primitive, raw, rough, unpolished. See GOOD in Index. — See also **coarse, inharmonious, uncivilized.**

rudeness *noun* See **impudence.**

rudiment *noun* See **basis, element.**

rudimental *adjective* See **elementary.**

rudimentary *adjective* See **elementary.**

rue *noun* See **penitence.**

rue *verb* See **regret.**

rueful *adjective* See **pitiful, sorrowful.**

ruffian *noun* See **thug, tough.**

ruffle *verb* See **agitate, annoy.**

ruffled feathers *noun* See **offense.**

rugged *adjective* See **hard, rough.**

ruin *noun* **1.** Something that causes total loss or severe impairment, as of one's health, fortune, honor, or hopes : bane, destroyer, destruction, downfall, ruination, undoing, wrecker. See HELP in Index. **2.** The remains of something destroyed, disintegrated, or decayed : debris, rubble, wrack[2], wreck, wreckage. See LEFTOVER in Index. — See also **destruction.**

ruin *verb* To reduce to financial insolvency : bankrupt, break, bust, impoverish, pauperize. *Slang:* clean out. See MONEY in Index. — See also **break, destroy.**

ruination *noun* See **destruction, ruin.**

ruinous *adjective* Falling to ruin : dilapidated, ramshackle, rundown, tumbledown. See BETTER in Index. — See also **destructive, fatal.**

rulable *adjective* See **governable.**

rule *noun* A code or set of codes governing action or procedure, for example : dictate, prescript, regulation, rubric. See ORDER in Index. — See also **domination, government, law, usual.**

rule *verb* See **boss, control, dominate, govern, judge.**

rule out *verb* See **exclude, prevent.**

ruling *noun* An authoritative or official decision, especially one made by a court : decree, determination, edict, judgment, pronouncement. See LAW in Index.

ruling *adjective* Having preeminent significance : ascendant, dominant, predominant, prepotent, prevailing, regnant, supreme. See IMPORTANT in Index. — See also **dominant.**

rum *adjective* See **eccentric.**

rumble *verb* To make a continuous deep reverberating sound : boom, growl, grumble, roll. See SOUNDS in Index.

rumble *noun* See **brawl, fight.**

ruminate *verb* See **ponder.**

rumination *noun* See **thought.**

ruminative *adjective* See **thoughtful.**

rummage *verb* See **scour**[1].

rummy[1] *noun* See **drunkard.**

rummy[2] *adjective* See **eccentric.**

rumor *noun* See **gossip.**

rumor *verb* See **gossip.**

rumormonger *noun* See **gossip.**

rump *noun* See **bottom.**

rumple *verb* See **tousle, wrinkle.**

rumple *noun* See **fold.**

rumpus *noun* See **noise, vociferation.**

run *verb* **1.** To move swiftly on foot so that both feet leave the ground during each stride : scamper, scurry, sprint. See MOVE in Index. **2.** To leave hastily : bolt, get out. *Informal:* clear out, get, hotfoot, skedaddle. *Slang:* hightail, scram, vamoose. *Idioms:* beat it, hightail it, hotfoot it, make tracks. See APPROACH in Index. **3.** To complete a race or competition in a specified position : come in, finish, place. See BE in Index. — See also **administer, associate, conduct, drive, extend, flow, go, hunt, melt, operate, play, ram, resort, rush, smuggle, tear**[1], **work.**

run across *verb* See **come across** at **come.**

run after *verb* See **pursue.**

run away *verb* See **escape.**

run down *verb* **1.** To lose so much strength and power as to become ineffective or motionless : burn out, give out. *Slang:* poop out. See TIRED in Index. **2.** To pursue and locate : hunt down, nose out, trace,

track down. *Idiom:* run to earth (or
ground). See GET in Index. — See also
belittle, review.

run in *verb* See arrest, visit.

run into *verb* See amount, come
across at come, encounter.

run on *verb* See chatter.

run out *verb* See dry up at dry,
fail, lapse.

run through *verb* See browse,
exhaust, review.

run up *verb* See increase.

run *noun* See branch, drive, series,
tear[1].

runagate *noun* See defector.

runaway *noun* *Informal.* An easy
victory : walkaway, walkover.
Slang: romp. See EASY, WIN in
Index. — See also fugitive.

runaway *adjective* Out of control : amuck, uncontrolled. *Idioms:*
out of hand, running wild. See CON-
TROL in Index. — See also fugitive.

rundown *noun* See summary.

rundown also **run-down** *adjective* See exhausted, ruinous, shabby.

rung *noun* See degree.

run-in *noun* See argument, brush[2].

runner *noun* See bearer, shoot,
smuggler.

running *adjective* See active.

run-of-the-mill *adjective* See
ordinary.

run-through *noun* See summary.

rupture *noun* See breach.

rupture *verb* See crack.

rural *adjective* See country.

ruse *noun* See trick.

rush *verb* To move swiftly : bolt,
bucket, bustle, dart, dash, festinate,
flash, fleet, flit, fly, haste, hasten,
hurry, hustle, pelt[2], race, rocket,
run, sail, scoot, scour[2], shoot, speed,
sprint, tear[1], trot, whirl, whisk,
whiz, wing, zip, zoom. *Informal:*
hotfoot, rip. *Slang:* barrel, highball.
Chiefly British: nip[1]. *Idioms:* get a
move on, get cracking, go like lightning, go like the wind, hotfoot it,
make haste, make time, make
tracks, run like the wind, shake a
leg, step (or jump) on it. See MOVE in
Index. — See also flow.

rush *noun* See charge, flow, haste.

rush *adjective* See crash.

rustic *adjective* Of a plain and unsophisticated nature : artless,
homely, homespun, natural, unadorned, unpolished. See PLAIN in
Index. — See also country.

rustic *noun* See clodhopper.

rut[1] *noun* See grind.

rut[2] *noun* See heat.

ruthful *adjective* See pitiful.

ruthless *adjective* See unscrupulous.

S

sable *adjective* See black.

sabotage *noun* A deliberate and
underhanded effort to defeat or do
harm to an endeavor : subversion,
undermining. See ATTACK in Index.

sabotage *verb* To damage, destroy, or defeat by sabotage : subvert, undermine. See ATTACK in
Index.

saccharine *adjective* See insinuating, sweet.

sack[1] *noun* See dismissal.

sack *verb* See dismiss.

sack[2] *verb* To rob of goods by force,
especially in time of war : depredate, despoil, havoc, loot, pillage,
plunder, ransack, rape, ravage, spoliate, strip[1]. *Archaic:* harrow, spoil.
See CRIMES, GIVE in Index.

sacrarium *noun* See sanctuary.

sacred *adjective* **1.** Given over
exclusively to a single use or purpose : consecrated, dedicated,
devoted, hallowed. See GIVE,

INCLUDE in Index. **2.** Protected from violation or abuse by custom, law, or feelings of reverence : inviolable, sacrosanct. See SACRED in Index. — See also **divine, holy.**

sacredness *noun* See **holiness, sanctity.**

sacrifice *noun* One or more living creatures slain and offered to a deity as part of a religious rite : hecatomb, immolation, offering, victim. See RELIGION in Index. — See also **cost.**

sacrifice *verb* To offer as a sacrifice : immolate, victimize. See GIVE, RELIGION in Index.

sacrilege *noun* An act of disrespect or impiety toward something regarded as sacred : blasphemy, desecration, profanation, violation. See SACRED in Index.

sacrilegious *adjective* Showing irreverence and contempt for something sacred : blasphemous, profane. See SACRED in Index.

sacrosanct *adjective* See **holy, sacred.**

sacrosanctity *noun* See **holiness, sanctity.**

sad *adjective* Tending to cause sadness or low spirits : blue, cheerless, depressing, dismal, dispiriting, gloomy, joyless, melancholy. See HAPPY in Index. — See also **depressed, sorrowful.**

sadden *verb* See **depress.**

saddle *verb* See **charge, impose.**

sadness *noun* See **gloom.**

safari *noun* See **expedition.**

safe *adjective* **1.** Free from danger, injury, or the threat of harm : unharmed, unhurt, uninjured, unscathed. *Idiom:* safe and sound. See SAFETY in Index. **2.** Affording protection : secure. See SAFETY in Index.

safeguard *verb* See **defend.**

safeguard *noun* See **defense.**

safeness *noun* See **safety.**

safety *noun* The quality or state of being safe : assurance, safeness, security. See SAFETY in Index.

sag *verb* See **slip, slouch, wilt.**

sag *noun* See **depression.**

sagacious *adjective* See **sane, wise**[1].

sagaciousness *noun* See **wisdom.**

sagacity *noun* See **discernment, wisdom.**

sage *noun* A usually elderly person noted for wisdom, knowledge, and judgment : pundit, savant, scholar. See WISE in Index.

sage *adjective* See **sane, wise**[1].

sageness *noun* See **discernment, wisdom.**

sail *verb* See **flow, fly, rush.**

sail in *verb* See **attack.**

sail into *verb* See **attack.**

sailor *noun* A person engaged in sailing or working on a ship : jack (uppercase), jack-tar, mariner, navigator, sea dog, seafarer, seaman. *Informal:* salt, tar. *Slang:* gob[3]. See SEA in Index.

saintly *adjective* See **holy.**

salability *noun* See **sell.**

salableness *noun* See **sell.**

salacious *adjective* See **erotic.**

salad days *noun* See **youth.**

salary *noun* See **wage.**

salesclerk *noun* See **seller.**

salesgirl *noun* See **seller.**

salesman *noun* See **seller.**

salesperson *noun* See **seller.**

saleswoman *noun* See **seller.**

salient *adjective* See **noticeable.**

salivate *verb* See **drool.**

salivation *noun* See **drool.**

sallow *adjective* See **pale.**

salmagundi *noun* See **assortment.**

salt *noun* See **sailor.**

salt away *verb* See **bank**[2], **save.**

salty *adjective* See **racy.**

salubrious *adjective* See **healthful.**

salutary *adjective* See **beneficial, healthful.**

salutation *noun* See **greeting.**

salute *verb* See **accost, greet.**

  salute *noun* See **greeting, testimonial.**

salvage *verb* See **rescue.**

  salvage *noun* See **rescue.**

salvation *noun* See **rescue.**

salvo *noun* See **barrage, testimonial.**

same *adjective* Being one and not another or others; not different in nature or identity : **identic, identical, selfsame, very.** See SAME in Index. — See also **consistent, equal, even**[1].

sameness *noun* The quality or condition of being exactly the same as something else : **identicalness, identity, oneness, selfsameness.** See SAME in Index. — See also **equivalence, monotony.**

sample *noun* See **example, taste.**

sanctify *verb* To make sacred by a religious rite : **bless, consecrate, hallow.** See RELIGION in Index.

sanctimonious *adjective* See **hypocritical.**

sanctimoniousness *noun* See **hypocrisy.**

sanctimony *noun* See **hypocrisy.**

sanction *verb* See **confirm, permit.**

  sanction *noun* A coercive measure intended to ensure compliance or conformity : **interdict, interdiction, penalty.** See REWARD in Index. — See also **confirmation, permission.**

sanctioned *adjective* See **accepted, authoritative, orthodox.**

sanctity *noun* The quality or condition of being safe from assault, trespass, or violation : **inviolability, sacredness, sacrosanctity.** See SAFETY in Index. — See also **holiness.**

sanctorium *noun* See **sanctuary.**

sanctuary *noun* A sacred or holy place : **sacrarium, sanctorium, sanctum, shrine.** See SACRED in Index. — See also **cover, refuge.**

sanctum *noun* See **sanctuary.**

sane *adjective* **1.** Mentally healthy : **compos mentis, lucid, rational.** *Idioms:* all there, in one's right mind, of sound mind. See SANE in Index. **2.** Possessing, proceeding from, or exhibiting good judgment and prudence : **balanced, commonsensible, commonsensical, judicious, levelheaded, prudent, rational, reasonable, sagacious, sage, sapient, sensible, sound**[2]**, well-founded, well-grounded, wise**[1]**.** See REASON, SANE in Index.

saneness *noun* See **sanity.**

sang-froid *noun* See **balance.**

sanguinary *adjective* See **bloody, murderous.**

sanguine *adjective* See **optimistic, ruddy.**

sanguineness *noun* See **optimism.**

sanguineous *adjective* See **bloody, murderous.**

sanguinity *noun* See **optimism.**

sanitize *verb* See **sterilize.**

sanitized *adjective* See **sterile.**

sanity *noun* A healthy mental state : **lucidity, lucidness, mind, reason, saneness, sense** (often used in plural), **soundness, wit** (used in plural). *Slang:* marble (used in plural). See SANE in Index.

sap[1] *noun* See **dupe.**

sap[2] *verb* See **deplete, enervate.**

sapience *noun* See **wisdom.**

sapient *adjective* See **sane, wise**[1]**.**

sapor *noun* See **flavor.**

sappiness *noun* See **sentimentality.**

sappy *adjective* See **foolish, sentimental.**

sarcasm *noun* Irony or bitterness, as of tone : **acerbity, acidity, acridity, causticity, corrosiveness, mor-**

dacity, mordancy, trenchancy. See
LAUGHTER, RESPECT in Index.

sarcastic *adjective* Contemptuous
or ironic in manner or wit : derisive, jeering, mocking, satiric, satirical, scoffing, sneering. See LAUGH-
TER, RESPECT in Index.

sardonic *adjective* See **cynical.**

sashay *verb* See **strut.**

sass *verb* See **talk back** at **talk.**

sassiness *noun* See **impudence.**

sassy *adjective* See **impudent.**

satanic *adjective* See **fiendish.**

satanical *adjective* See **fiendish.**

sate *verb* See **satiate.**

satellite *noun* See **follower.**

satiate *verb* To satisfy to the full or
to excess : cloy, engorge, glut,
gorge, pall, sate, surfeit. See EXCESS,
FULL in Index.

satiation *noun* The condition of
being full to or beyond satisfaction :
engorgement, repletion, satiety, surfeit. See EXCESS, FULL in Index.

satiety *noun* See **satiation.**

satiny *adjective* See **sleek.**

satire *noun* A work, as a novel or
play, that exposes folly by the use of
humor or irony : lampoon, lampoonery. See LAUGHTER, RESPECT
in Index.

satiric *adjective* See **sarcastic.**

satirical *adjective* See **sarcastic.**

satisfaction *noun* See **compensation.**

satisfactory *adjective* See **acceptable, convincing, sufficient.**

satisfied *adjective* See **fulfilled.**

satisfy *verb* **1.** To grant or have what
is demanded by (a need or desire) :
appease, content, fulfill, gratify,
indulge. See GIVE in Index. **2.** To
supply fully or completely :
answer, fill, fulfill, meet¹. See DO
in Index. — See also **convince,
please, settle.**

satisfying *adjective* See **agreeable.**

saturate *verb* See **charge, wet.**

saturnine *adjective* See **glum.**

satyr *noun* See **lecher.**

sauce *noun* See **impudence.**

sauce *verb* See **talk back** at **talk.**

saucebox *noun* See **smart aleck.**

sauciness *noun* See **impudence.**

saucy *adjective* See **impudent.**

saunter *verb* See **stroll.**

saunter *noun* See **walk.**

savage *adjective* Of or relating to
wild animals : feral, wild. See
WILD in Index. — See also **cruel,
fierce, uncivilized.**

savagery *noun* See **cruelty.**

savant *noun* See **sage.**

save *verb* To reserve for the future.
Also used with *up* : keep, lay aside,
lay away, lay by, lay in, lay up, put
by, salt away, set by. See KEEP, SAVE
in Index. — See also **conserve, economize, rescue, stockpile.**

saving *adjective* See **economical.**

savoir-faire *noun* See **tact.**

savor *noun* See **flavor, quality.**

savor *verb* See **enjoy, feel, smack².**

savory *adjective* See **delicious.**

savvy *noun* See **grasp.**

savvy *adjective* See **shrewd.**

savvy *verb* See **understand.**

saw *noun* See **proverb.**

say *verb* To put into words : articulate, communicate, convey,
declare, express, state, talk, tell,
utter¹, vent, verbalize, vocalize,
voice. *Idiom:* give tongue (or vent or
voice) to. See WORDS in Index. — See
also **assert, pronounce.**

say *noun* See **voice.**

saying *noun* See **proverb, word.**

say-so *noun* See **authority, voice.**

scabrous *adjective* See **racy, rough.**

scad *noun* See **heap.**

scaffold *noun* See **stage.**

scaffolding *noun* See **stage.**

scalding *adjective* See **hot.**

scale¹ *verb* See **skin.**

scale² *verb* See **ascend**.

scalp *verb* See **skin**.

scamp *noun* See **mischief**.

scamper *verb* See **run**.

scan *verb* See **browse, survey**.

scandal *noun* See **libel**.

scandalize *verb* See **shock¹**.

scandalmonger *noun* See **gossip**.

scandalous *adjective* See **libelous, outrageous**.

scant *adjective* See **bare, meager**.

scantiness *noun* See **shortage**.

scantness *noun* See **shortage**.

scanty *adjective* See **meager**.

scapegoat *noun* One who is made an object of blame : goat, whipping boy. *Slang:* fall guy, patsy. See PRAISE in Index.

scarce *adjective* See **infrequent, insufficient**.

scarce *adverb* See **barely**.

scarcely *adverb* See **barely**.

scarceness *noun* See **shortage**.

scarcity *noun* See **shortage**.

scare *verb* See **frighten**.

scarecrow *noun* See **tatterdemalion**.

scaremonger *noun* See **alarmist**.

scarify¹ *verb* See **slam**.

scarify² *verb* See **frighten**.

scarlet woman *noun* See **prostitute**.

scary *adjective* See **fearful**.

scathe *verb* See **slam**.

scathing *adjective* See **biting**.

scatologic *adjective* See **obscene**.

scatological *adjective* See **obscene**.

scatology *noun* See **obscenity**.

scatter *verb* To cause to separate and go in various directions : dispel, disperse, dissipate. See COLLECT in Index. — See also **lift, spread**.

scatterbrained *adjective* See **giddy**.

scattergood *noun* See **wastrel**.

scene *noun* **1.** The place where an action or event occurs : locale, setting, site, stage. See PLACE in Index. **2.** The properties, backdrops, and other objects arranged for a dramatic presentation : mise en scène, scenery, set², setting. See PERFORMING ARTS in Index. — See also **area, condition, view**.

scenery *noun* See **scene**.

scent *noun* See **fragrance, lead, smell, trail**.

scent *verb* To fill with a pleasant odor : aromatize, perfume. See SMELLS in Index. — See also **smell**.

schedule *noun* See **list¹, program**.

schedule *verb* To enter on a schedule : program, slate. See REMEMBER in Index. — See also **arrange, time**.

scheduled *adjective* See **due**.

schema *noun* See **design**.

scheme *noun* See **design, plot**.

scheme *verb* See **design, plot**.

scheming *adjective* See **artful, calculating**.

schism *noun* See **breach, conflict, division**.

schismatic *noun* See **separatist**.

schlep *verb* See **carry**.

schlocky *adjective* See **shoddy**.

schmaltz *also* **schmalz** *noun* See **sentimentality**.

schmaltziness *noun* See **sentimentality**.

schmaltzy *adjective* See **sentimental**.

schmo *noun* See **fool**.

schmuck *noun* See **fool**.

schnoz *noun* See **nose**.

schnozzle *noun* See **nose**.

scholar *noun* See **sage, student**.

scholarly *adjective* See **learned, studious**.

scholarship *noun* See **education**.

scholastic *adjective* See **pedantic**.

school *verb* See **educate**.

schooling *noun* See **education.**

science *noun* See **education.**

scilicet *adverb* See **namely.**

scintillate *verb* See **flash.**

scintillating *adjective* See **clever.**

scintillation *noun* See **glitter.**

scion *noun* See **descendant.**

scoff *verb* See **ridicule.**

scoff *noun* See **taunt.**

scoffing *adjective* See **sarcastic.**

scold *verb* See **call down** at **call.**

scold *noun* A person, traditionally a woman, who persistently nags or criticizes : fishwife, fury, harpy, shrew, termagant, virago, vixen. *Informal:* battle-ax. See PRAISE in Index.

scolding *noun* See **rebuke.**

scoop *verb* See **dig, dip.**

scoop *noun* See **news.**

scoot *verb* See **rush.**

scope *noun* See **grasp, ken, range, room.**

scorch *verb* See **burn, slam.**

scorch *noun* See **burn.**

scorching *adjective* See **hot, passionate.**

score *noun* 1. An incision, a notch, or a slight cut made with or as if with a knife : scotch, scratch, slash. See MARKS in Index. 2. The total number of points made by a contestant, side, or team in a game or contest : tally. See COUNT in Index. — See also **crowd.**

score *verb* 1. To gain (a point or points) in a game or contest : post¹, tally. *Informal:* notch. See DO in Index. 2. To evaluate and assign a grade to : grade, mark. See VALUE in Index. — See also **accomplish, prosper, slam.**

scorn *noun* See **despisal.**

scorn *verb* See **despise.**

scornful *adjective* See **disdainful.**

scotch *noun* See **score.**

Scotch *adjective* See **economical.**

scour¹ *verb* To make a thorough search of : comb, forage, ransack, rummage. *Slang:* shake down. *Idioms:* beat the bushes, leave no stone unturned, look (or search) high and low, look (or search) up and down, turn inside out, turn upside down. See INVESTIGATE in Index. — See also **scrape, scrub.**

scour² *verb* See **rush.**

scourge *noun* See **curse.**

scourge *verb* See **afflict, slam.**

scout¹ *verb* See **explore.**

scout² *verb* See **despise, ridicule.**

scowl *noun* See **frown, glare.**

scowl *verb* See **frown, glare.**

scram *verb* See **run.**

scramble *verb* To move or climb hurriedly, especially on all fours : clamber. See MOVE in Index. — See also **confuse, shuffle.**

scramble *noun* See **disorder.**

scrap¹ *noun* See **bit¹, end.**

scrap *verb* See **discard.**

scrap² *noun* See **fight.**

scrape *verb* 1. To remove (an outer layer or adherent matter) by rubbing a surface with considerable pressure : scour¹, scrub. See PUT ON in Index. 2. To bring or come into abrasive contact, often with a harsh grating sound : grate, rasp, scratch. See SOUNDS in Index. — See also **scrimp.**

scrape *noun* See **predicament.**

scrappiness *noun* See **argumentativeness.**

scrappy *adjective* See **argumentative, belligerent.**

scratch *noun* See **money, score.**

scratch *verb* See **cancel, scrape.**

scratchy *adjective* See **harsh.**

scrawny *adjective* See **thin.**

screak *noun* See **scream.**

screak *verb* See **scream.**

scream *verb* 1. To utter a long, loud, piercing cry, as of pain or fright :

screak, screech, shriek, shrill. See
SOUNDS in Index. **2.** To proclaim in
a blatantly startling way : blare,
shout, shriek. See SHOW in Index.
scream *noun* **1.** A long, loud,
piercing cry or sound : screak,
screech, shriek. See SOUNDS in
Index. **2.** *Informal.* Something or
someone uproariously funny or
absurd : absurdity. *Informal:* hoot,
joke, laugh. *Slang:* gas, howl, panic,
riot. *Idiom:* a laugh a minute. See
LAUGHTER in Index.
screech *noun* See **scream.**
  screech *verb* See **scream.**
screen *verb* See **block, censor,
shade.**
screened *adjective* See **secluded.**
screwball *noun* See **crackpot.**
  screwball *adjective* See **eccentric.**
screwup also **screw-up** *noun* See
blunderer, botch.
screw up *verb* See **botch.**
screwy *adjective* See **insane.**
scribe *verb* See **write.**
scrimp *verb* To be severely sparing
in order to economize : pinch,
scrape, skimp, stint. *Idioms:* pinch
pennies, tighten (one's) belt. See
SAVE in Index.
scriptural *adjective* See **graphic.**
Scrooge also **scrooge** *noun* See
miser.
scrub *verb* To rub hard in order to
clean : scour[1]. See CLEAN, PUT ON
in Index. — See also **cancel, scrape.**
scrubby *adjective* See **shabby.**
scruffy *adjective* See **shabby.**
scrumptious *adjective* See
delicious.
scrunch *verb* See **stoop.**
scruple *noun* See **bit[1], qualm.**
scrupulous *adjective* See **careful.**
scrupulousness *noun* See
thoroughness.
scrutinize *verb* See **examine, watch.**

scrutiny *noun* See **examination,
watch.**
scuff *verb* See **shuffle.**
scuffle *noun* See **fight.**
  scuffle *verb* See **shuffle, wrestle.**
scum *noun* See **trash.**
scurrility *noun* See **obscenity,
vituperation.**
scurrilous *adjective* See **abusive,
obscene.**
scurrilousness *noun* See **obscenity,
vituperation.**
scurry *verb* See **run.**
scuttlebutt *noun* See **gossip.**
sea dog *noun* See **sailor.**
seafarer *noun* See **sailor.**
seam *noun* See **joint.**
seaman *noun* See **sailor.**
sear *verb* See **burn, dry up** at **dry.**
  sear *noun* See **burn.**
search *verb* To examine the person
or personal effects of in order to find
something lost or concealed : frisk,
inspect. *Slang:* shake down. See
INVESTIGATE in Index. — See also
seek.
  search *noun* See **pursuit,
shakedown.**
searing *adjective* See **hot.**
season *verb* See **flavor, harden.**
  season *noun* See **heat, period,
time.**
seasonable *adjective* See
opportune.
seasoned *adjective* See
experienced.
seasoner *noun* See **flavoring.**
seasoning *noun* See **flavoring.**
seat *noun* See **base[1], bottom,
center.**
  seat *verb* To cause to take a sitting
position : sit (down). See RISE in
Index. — See also **establish.**
secede *verb* To break away or withdraw from membership in an association or a federation : splinter (off).

Informal: split. See PARTICIPATE, POLITICS in Index.

seclude *verb* To put into solitude : cloister, sequester, sequestrate. See INCLUDE in Index. — See also **isolate**.

secluded *adjective* **1.** Solitary and shut off from society : recluse. See INCLUDE in Index. **2.** Concealed from view : hidden, screened, secret. See SHOW in Index. — See also **remote**.

seclusion *noun* The act of secluding or the state of being secluded : reclusion, retirement, sequestration. See INCLUDE in Index.

second[1] *noun* See **flash**.

second[2] *noun* See **assistant**.

secondary *adjective* See **auxiliary, derivative, minor**.

secondary *noun* See **subordinate**.

second-class *adjective* See **inferior**.

second-rate *adjective* See **inferior**.

secrecy *noun* The habit, practice, or policy of keeping secrets : clandestineness, clandestinity, concealment, covertness, huggermugger, huggermuggery, secretiveness, secretness. See SHOW in Index.

secret *adjective* Existing or operating in a way so as to ensure complete concealment and confidentiality : clandestine, cloak-and-dagger, covert, huggermugger, sub-rosa, undercover. *Informal:* hush-hush. *Idiom:* under wraps. See SHOW in Index. — See also **confidential, secluded**.

secret *noun* See **ticket**.

secrete *verb* See **hide**[1].

secretive *adjective* See **sly**.

secretiveness *noun* See **secrecy**.

secretly *adverb* In a secret way : clandestinely, covertly, huggermugger, sub rosa. *Idioms:* by stealth, on the sly, under cover. See SHOW in Index.

secretness *noun* See **secrecy**.

sect *noun* See **faith, religion**.

sectarian *noun* See **separatist**.

sectary *noun* See **devotee, separatist**.

section *noun* **1.** A particular subdivision of a written work : part, passage, segment. See PART in Index. **2.** A thin piece, especially of tissue, suitable for microscopic examination : slice. See PART in Index. — See also **cut, division**.

section *verb* See **divide**.

sectional *adjective* See **territorial**.

secular *adjective* See **earthly, profane**.

secure *verb* To give a promise of payment of : guarantee. See MONEY, OBLIGATION in Index. — See also **attach, cause, defend, fasten, get, guarantee, take, tie**.

secure *adjective* See **confident, safe, sound**[2]**, sure, tight**.

security *noun* See **defense, pawn**[1]**, safety, stability**.

sedate *adjective* See **grave**[2].

sedateness *noun* See **gravity**.

sedative *noun* See **soporific**. *adjective* See **sleepy**.

sediment *noun* See **deposit**.

sedition *noun* See **rebellion, treason**.

seditious *adjective* See **treasonous**.

seditiousness *noun* See **treason**.

seduce *verb* **1.** To lure or persuade into a sexual relationship or a sexual act : debauch, undo. See SEX in Index. **2.** To beguile or draw into a wrong or foolish course of action : allure, entice, inveigle, lure, tempt. *Idiom:* lead astray. See PERSUASION in Index.

seducer *noun* **1.** One that seduces : allurer, charmer, enticer, inveigler, lurer, tempter. See PERSUASION in Index. **2.** A man who seduces women : debaucher, Don Juan, Lothario. See SEX in Index.

seduction *noun* See **lure**.

seductive *adjective* Tending to seduce : alluring, bewitching, come-hither, enticing, inveigling, inviting, luring, siren, tempting, witching. See LIKE, PERSUASION, SEX in Index.

seductress *noun* A usually unscrupulous woman who seduces or exploits men : enchantress, femme fatale, siren, temptress. *Informal:* vamp, witch. See SEX in Index.

sedulous *adjective* See **diligent**.

sedulousness *noun* See **diligence**.

see *verb* **1.** To apprehend (images) by use of the eyes : behold, perceive. *Scots:* ken. See SEE in Index. **2.** To be with another person socially on a regular basis : date, go out. *Informal:* take out. See CONNECT in Index. — See also **experience, foresee, imagine, notice, regard, understand, visit**.

see to *verb* See **tend²**.

seeable *adjective* See **visible**.

seed *noun* **1.** A fertilized plant ovule capable of germinating : kernel, pip, pit². See START in Index. **2.** A propagative part of a plant : spore, tuber. See START in Index. **3.** The male fluid of fertilization : semen, sperm. See START in Index. — See also **ancestry, germ, progeny**.

seed *verb* To put (seeds) into the ground for growth : plant, sow. See START in Index.

seedtime *noun* See **spring**.

seedy *adjective* See **shabby**.

seeing *noun* See **vision**.

seek *verb* To try to find something : cast about, hunt, look, quest, search. See SEEK in Index. — See also **aim, attempt, request**.

seeker *noun* See **applicant**.

seem *verb* See **appear**.

seeming *adjective* See **apparent**.

seemingly *adverb* See **apparently**.

seemliness *noun* See **decency**.

seemly *adjective* See **correct**.

seep *verb* See **ooze**.

seer *noun* See **prophet, witness**.

seesaw *verb* See **lurch**.

seethe *verb* See **anger, boil**.

see-through *adjective* See **clear, transparent**.

segment *noun* See **cut, division, section**.

segment *verb* See **divide**.

segregate *verb* See **isolate**.

segregated *adjective* See **restricted**.

segregation *noun* The policy or practice of political, legal, economic, or social discrimination, as against the members of a minority group : apartheid, separatism. See INCLUDE in Index. — See also **isolation**.

seism *noun* See **tremor**.

seize *verb* **1.** To take quick and forcible possession of : commandeer, confiscate, expropriate, grab, snatch. *Idiom:* help oneself to. See GIVE in Index. **2.** To have a sudden overwhelming effect on : catch, strike, take. See ATTACK, OVER in Index. — See also **arrest, assume, catch, grasp**.

seizure *noun* **1.** The act of taking quick and forcible possession of : confiscation, expropriation. See GIVE in Index. **2.** A sudden and often acute manifestation of a disease : access, attack, fit². *Informal:* spell³. See HEALTH in Index. — See also **arrest, catch, usurpation**.

seldom *adverb* See **infrequently**.

select *verb* See **choose**.

select *noun* See **elect**.

select *adjective* Singled out in preference : choice, chosen, elect, exclusive. See CHOICE, INCLUDE in Index. — See also **choice, discriminating**.

selection *noun* See **choice**.

selective *adjective* See **discriminating.**

selectiveness *noun* See **discrimination.**

selectivity *noun* See **discrimination.**

self *noun* An individual's awareness of what constitutes his or her essential nature and distinguishes him or her from all others : ego. See BE, SELF in Index.

self-absorbed *adjective* See **egotistic.**

self-absorption *noun* See **egoism.**

self-assurance *noun* See **confidence.**

self-assured *adjective* See **confident.**

self-centered *adjective* See **egotistic.**

self-centeredness *noun* See **egoism.**

self-confidence *noun* See **confidence.**

self-confident *adjective* See **confident.**

self-contained *adjective* See **independent.**

self-control *noun* See **reserve.**

self-controlled *adjective* See **reserved.**

self-denying *adjective* See **selfless.**

self-determination *noun* See **independence.**

self-effacement *noun* See **modesty.**

self-effacing *adjective* See **modest.**

self-esteem *noun* See **pride.**

self-forgetful *adjective* See **selfless.**

self-forgetting *adjective* See **selfless.**

self-governing *adjective* See **free.**

self-government *noun* See **freedom.**

selfhood *noun* See **identity.**

self-importance *noun* See **egotism.**

self-important *adjective* See **pompous.**

self-involved *adjective* See **egotistic.**

self-involvement *noun* See **egoism.**

selfish *adjective* See **egotistic.**

selfishness *noun* See **egoism.**

selfless *adjective* Without concern for oneself : self-denying, self-forgetful, self-forgetting, unselfish. See SELF in Index.

self-possessed *adjective* See **confident.**

self-possession *noun* See **balance, confidence.**

self-regard *noun* See **pride.**

self-reliance *noun* See **independence.**

self-reliant *adjective* See **independent.**

self-respect *noun* See **pride.**

self-respecting *adjective* See **proud.**

self-restrained *adjective* See **reserved.**

self-restraint *noun* See **reserve.**

selfsame *adjective* See **same.**

selfsameness *noun* See **sameness.**

self-seeking *adjective* See **egotistic.**

self-serving *adjective* See **egotistic.**

self-sufficiency *noun* See **independence.**

self-sufficient *adjective* See **independent.**

self-supporting *adjective* See **independent.**

sell *noun* *Slang.* Market appeal : marketability, marketableness, salability, salableness. See DESIRE in Index.

sell *verb* To offer for sale : deal (in), handle, market, merchandise, merchant, peddle, retail, trade (in), vend. See TRANSACTIONS in Index.
— See also **persuade.**

sell for *verb* See **bring, cost.**

sell off *verb* To get rid of completely by selling, especially in quantity or at a discount : close out, dump, sell out, unload. See TRANSACTIONS in Index.

sell out *verb* See **betray, sell off** at **sell.**

seller *noun* One who sells : clerk, salesclerk, salesgirl, salesman, salesperson, saleswoman, vender. See TRANSACTIONS in Index.

sellout *noun* See **betrayal.**

semaphore *verb* See **signal.**

semblance *noun* See **façade, shade.**

semen *noun* See **seed.**

seminar *noun* See **conference.**

sempiternal *adjective* See **eternal.**

sempiternity *noun* See **eternity.**

send *verb* To cause (something) to be conveyed to a destination : address, consign, dispatch, forward, route, ship, transmit. See MOVE in Index. — See also **carry away** at **carry, dismiss, refer.**

send for *verb* See **call.**

send forth *verb* See **emit.**

send up *verb* See **commit.**

senectitude *noun* See **age.**

senescence *noun* See **age.**

senile *adjective* Exhibiting the mental and physical deterioration often accompanying old age : doddering, doting. See YOUTH in Index.

senility *noun* The condition of being senile : caducity, dotage. See YOUTH in Index.

senior *adjective* Of greater age than another : elder, older. See YOUTH in Index. — See also **higher, old.**

senior *noun* **1.** A person who is older than another : elder. See YOUTH in Index. **2.** An elderly person : ancient, elder, golden ager, senior citizen. *Informal:* oldster, oldtimer. See YOUTH in Index. — See also **superior.**

senior citizen *noun* See **senior.**

sensation *noun* **1.** The capacity for or an act of responding to a stimulus : feeling, sense, sensibility, sensitiveness, sensitivity, sentiment. See AWARENESS in Index. **2.** A condition of intense public interest or excitement : brouhaha, stir[1], uproar. *Informal:* to-do. *Slang:* hoohah. See EXCITE in Index. — See also **marvel.**

sensational *adjective* Of or relating to sensation or the senses : sensitive, sensorial, sensory, sensual[1], sensuous. See AWARENESS, BODY in Index. — See also **dramatic, marvelous.**

sense *noun* What is sound or reasonable : logic, rationale, rationality, rationalness, reason. *Idiom:* rhyme or reason. See REASON in Index. — See also **awareness, common sense, intelligence, meaning, sanity, sensation.**

sense *verb* See **feel, perceive, understand.**

senseless *adjective* See **mindless, unconscious.**

senselessness *noun* See **foolishness.**

sensibility *noun* See **sensation, sensitiveness.**

sensible *adjective* See **aware, perceptible, physical, sane, sensitive.**

sensitive *adjective* Able to receive and respond to external stimuli : impressible, impressionable, responsive, sensible, sentient, susceptible, susceptive. See AWARENESS in Index. — See also **acute, delicate, emotional, sensational.**

sensitiveness *noun* The quality or condition of being emotionally and intuitively sensitive : feeling, sensibility, sensitivity. See AWARENESS in Index. — See also **sensation.**

sensitivity *noun* See **sensation, sensitiveness.**

sensorial *adjective* See **sensational.**

sensory *adjective* Transmitting impulses from sense organs to nerve centers : afferent. See BODY in Index. — See also **sensational.**

sensual *adjective* Suggesting sexuality : sexual, sexy, suggestive, voluptuous. See SEX in Index. — See also **materialistic, physical, sensational, sensuous.**

sensualism *noun* See **sensuousness.**

sensualist *noun* See **sybarite.**

sensualistic *adjective* See **sensuous.**

sensuality *noun* The quality or condition of being sensual : sexiness, sexuality, suggestiveness, voluptuousness. See SEX in Index. — See also **physicality, sensuousness.**

sensuous *adjective* Relating to, suggestive of, or appealing to sense gratification : epicurean, sensual, sensualistic, voluptuous. See PAIN in Index. — See also **sensational.**

sensuousness *noun* The quality or condition of being sensuous : sensualism, sensuality, voluptuousness. See PAIN in Index.

sentence *noun* A judicial decision, especially one setting the punishment to be inflicted on a convicted person : judgment. *Slang:* rap[1]. See LAW in Index.

sentence *verb* See **condemn.**

sentient *adjective* See **aware, sensitive.**

sentiment *noun* A general cast of mind with regard to something : attitude, feeling. See ATTITUDE in Index. — See also **belief, emotion, sensation.**

sentimental *adjective* Affectedly or extravagantly emotional : bathetic, gushy, maudlin, mawkish, romantic, slushy, sobby, soft, soppy. *Informal:* gooey, mushy, schmaltzy, sloppy, soupy. *Slang:* drippy, sappy, tearjerking. See FEELINGS in Index.

sentimentalism *noun* See **sentimentality.**

sentimentality *noun* The quality or condition of being affectedly or overly emotional : bathos, maudlinism, mawkishness, sentimentalism. *Informal:* mush, mushiness, schmaltz, schmaltziness, sloppiness. *Slang:* sappiness. See FEELINGS in Index.

sentimentalize *verb* To regard or imbue with affected or exaggerated emotion : romanticize. See FEELINGS, REAL in Index.

sentinel *noun* See **guard.**

sentry *noun* See **guard.**

separate *verb* To terminate a relationship or an association by or as if by leaving one another : break off, break up, part. *Informal:* split (up). *Idioms:* call it quits, come to a parting of the ways, part company. See ASSEMBLE, CONTINUE in Index. — See also **assort, discharge, distinguish, divide, isolate, sort.**

separate *adjective* See **distinct, individual, lone.**

separately *adverb* As a separate unit : apart, discretely, independently, individually, singly. *Idioms:* one at a time, one by one. See INCLUDE in Index.

separateness *noun* See **individuality.**

separation *noun* See **detachment, distinction, division, gap, isolation.**

separationist *noun* See **separatist.**

separatism *noun* See **segregation.**

separatist *noun* A person who dissents from the doctrine of an established church : dissenter, dissident, heretic, nonconformist, schismatic, sectarian, sectary, separationist. See RELIGION in Index.

sepulcher *noun* See **grave**[1].

sepulture *noun* See **grave**[1].

sequel *noun* See **effect.**

sequence *noun* See **arrangement, effect, order, series.**

sequent *adjective* See **consecutive.**
sequent *noun* See **effect.**

sequential *adjective* See **consecutive.**

sequester *verb* See **isolate, seclude.**

sequestrate *verb* See **seclude.**

sequestration *noun* See **isolation, seclusion.**

sequin *noun* See **glitter.**

sere *adjective* See **dry.**

serene *adjective* See **calm, still.**

serenity *noun* See **calm, stillness.**

serfdom *noun* See **slavery.**

serial *adjective* See **consecutive.**

series *noun* A number of things placed or occurring one after the other : chain, consecution, course, order, procession, progression, round, run, sequence, string, succession, suite, train. *Informal:* streak. See ORDER in Index.

serious *adjective* Marked by sober sincerity : businesslike, earnest[1], no-nonsense, sobersided. *Idiom:* in earnest. See HEAVY, WORK in Index. — See also **difficult, grave[2], grievous.**

seriousness *noun* Sober sincerity : earnestness, sobersidedness. See HEAVY, WORK in Index. — See also **gravity.**

sermonize *verb* See **moralize, preach.**

serpentine *adjective* See **winding.**

serve *verb* 1. To work and care for : attend, do for, minister to, wait on (or upon). See CARE FOR in Index. 2. To place food before (someone) : wait on (or upon). See INGESTION in Index. 3. To spend or complete (time), as a prison term : put in. *Informal:* do. See TIME in Index. 4. To meet a need or requirement : answer, do, suffice, suit. See EXCESS, HELP in Index. — See also **act, profit.**

service *noun* See **ceremony, duty, favor.**

serviceable *adjective* See **practical, usable.**

servile *adjective* Excessively eager to serve or obey : menial, obsequious, slavish, subservient. See OVER in Index.

servileness *noun* See **slavery.**

servility *noun* See **slavery.**

serving *noun* An individual quantity of food : helping, mess, portion. See INGESTION in Index.

servitude *noun* See **slavery.**

sesquipedal *adjective* See **long[1].**

sesquipedalian *adjective* See **long[1].**

set[1] *verb* 1. To deposit in a specified place : lay[1], place, put, stick. See PLACE, RISE in Index. 2. To arrange tableware upon (a table) in preparation for a meal : lay[1], spread. See ORDER in Index. — See also **adjust, aim, arrange, coagulate, estimate, harden, lay[1], position, station.**

set about *verb* See **start.**
set apart *verb* See **distinguish.**
set aside *verb* See **abolish.**
set back *verb* See **delay.**
set by *verb* See **save.**
set down *verb* See **land, list[1].**
set forth *verb* See **propose.**
set off *verb* See **balance, cause, compensate, grace, provoke.**
set out *verb* See **bear, design, start.**
set to *verb* See **start.**
set up *verb* See **erect, found, treat.**
set *adjective* On an unwavering course of action : bent, decided, determined, fixed, intent, resolute. See DECIDE in Index. — See also **confirmed, firm[1], ready, specific.**

set[2] *noun* See **circle, class, crowd, group, scene.**

setback *noun* See **reverse.**

setoff *noun* See **compensation.**

setting *noun* See **scene**.

settle *verb* **1.** To fall or drift down to the bottom : gravitate, sink. See RISE in Index. **2.** To put into correct or conclusive form : arrange, conclude, dispose of, fix. See DO in Index. **3.** To bring (something) into a state of agreement or accord : reconcile, rectify, resolve, smooth over, straighten out. See AGREE in Index. **4.** To set right by giving what is due : clear, discharge, liquidate, pay (off *or* up), satisfy, square. See PAY in Index. — See also **arrange, calm, decide, establish, land**.

settled *adjective* See **confirmed**.

settlement *noun* See **compromise**.

seventh heaven *noun* See **heaven**.

sever *verb* See **cut**.

several *adjective* Consisting of a number more than two or three but less than many : divers, some, sundry, various. See BIG in Index. — See also **distinct**.

severance *noun* See **division**.

severe *adjective* **1.** Rigorous and unsparing in treating others : demanding, exacting, hard, harsh, rigid, stern, strict, tough, unyielding. See EASY in Index. **2.** Conveying great physical force : hard, heavy, hefty, powerful. See BIG in Index. — See also **bitter, bleak, burdensome, grave², grievous**.

severity *noun* The fact or condition of being rigorous and unsparing : austerity, hardness, harshness, rigidity, rigor, rigorousness, sternness, strictness, stringency, toughness. See EASY in Index. — See also **intensity**.

sexiness *noun* See **sensuality**.

sexual *adjective* See **erotic, reproductive, sensual**.

sexuality *noun* See **sensuality**.

sexy *adjective* See **desirable, erotic, sensual**.

shabby *adjective* Showing signs of wear and tear or neglect : bedraggled, broken-down, decaying, decrepit, dilapidated, dingy, downat-heel, faded, mangy, rundown, scrubby, scruffy, seedy, shoddy, sleazy, tattered, tatty, threadbare. *Informal:* tacky². *Slang:* ratty. *Idioms:* all the worse for wear, gone to pot (*or* seed), past cure (*or* hope). See BETTER in Index. — See also **filthy, inferior**.

shack *noun* See **hole**.

shackle *noun* See **bond**.

shackle *verb* See **hamper**.

shade *noun* **1.** Comparative darkness that results from the blocking of light rays : penumbra, shadow, umbra, umbrage. See LIGHT in Index. **2.** The degree of vividness of a color, as when modified by the addition of black or white pigment : gradation, hue, tinge, tint. See COLORS in Index. **3.** A slight variation between nearly identical entities : gradation, nuance. See BIG in Index. **4.** A slight amount or indication : breath, dash, ghost, hair, hint, intimation, semblance, shadow, soupçon, streak, suggestion, suspicion, taste, tinge, touch, trace, whiff, whisper. *Informal:* whisker. See BIG, SHOW in Index. — See also **color, ghost**.

shade *verb* **1.** To shelter, especially from light : screen, shadow. See PROTECTION in Index. **2.** To make dark or darker : adumbrate, darken, shadow. See LIGHT in Index. **3.** To make a slight reduction in (a price) : shave, trim. See INCREASE in Index.

shaded *adjective* See **shady**.

shadiness *noun* See **indirection**.

shadow *noun* See **ghost, shade, tail**.

shadow *verb* See **follow, obscure, shade**.

shadowy *adjective* See **shady, unclear.**

shady *adjective* 1. Full of shade : shaded, shadowy. See LIGHT in Index. 2. Casting shade : umbrageous. See LIGHT in Index. 3. Of dubious character : doubtful, equivocal, questionable, suspect, suspicious, uncertain. *Informal:* fishy. See HONEST in Index.

shaft *noun* See **beam, stick.**

shake *verb* 1. To cause to move to and fro with short, jerky movements : jiggle, joggle. See REPETITION in Index. 2. To move to and fro in short, jerky movements : quake, quaver, quiver, shiver[1], shudder, tremble, twitter, vibrate. See REPETITION in Index. 3. To move to and fro violently : quake, rock, tremble, vibrate. See REPETITION in Index. — See also **agitate, dismay, disturb, lose, rid.**

shake down *verb* See **extort, scour[1], search.**

shake off *verb* See **lose, rid.**

shake *noun* See **jitter, tremor.**

shakedown *noun* *Slang.* A thorough search of a place or persons : frisk, search. See INVESTIGATE in Index.

shakeup *noun* A thorough or drastic reorganization : overhaul. *Informal:* housecleaning. See CHANGE in Index.

shakiness *noun* See **instability, unstableness.**

shaky *adjective* See **implausible, insecure, tremulous, unstable.**

shallow *adjective* Measuring little from bottom to top or surface : shoal. See SURFACE in Index. — See also **superficial.**

shallow *noun* See **shoal.**

sham *noun* See **act, counterfeit, mockery.**

sham *verb* See **act, assume.**

sham *adjective* See **counterfeit.**

shamble *verb* See **shuffle.**

shambles *noun* See **botch.**

shame *noun* A great disappointment or regrettable fact : crime, pity. *Slang:* bummer. *Idiom:* a crying shame. See GOOD in Index. — See also **disgrace.**

shame *verb* To cause to feel embarrassment, dishonor, and often guilt : reproach. *Idioms:* put to shame, put to the blush. See RESPECT in Index. — See also **disgrace.**

shameful *adjective* See **deplorable, disgraceful.**

shamefulness *noun* See **infamy.**

shameless *adjective* Characterized by or done without shame : baldfaced, barefaced, blatant, brazen, brazenfaced, unabashed, unblushing. *Informal:* brassy. See COURTESY, RESPECT, RIGHT in Index.

shanty *noun* See **hole.**

shape *noun* See **form, trim.**

shape *verb* See **form, make.**

shapeless *adjective* Having no distinct shape : amorphous, formless, inchoate, unformed, unshaped. See ORDER in Index.

shapely *adjective* Having a full, voluptuous figure : buxom, curvaceous, curvy, well-developed. *Informal:* built. *Slang:* stacked. See BEAUTIFUL in Index.

shard *noun* See **end.**

share *noun* See **allotment, part.**

share *verb* See **contribute, distribute.**

sharing *noun* See **participation.**

sharp *adjective* 1. Having a fine edge, as for cutting : keen[1]. See SHARP in Index. 2. Clearly defined; not ambiguous : clear, distinct, unambiguous, unequivocal, unmistakable. See CLEAR in Index.

3. Marked by severity or intensity : acute, gnawing, knifelike, lancinating, piercing, shooting, stabbing. See BIG in Index. — See also **acute, artful, biting, clever, fashionable, pointed, pungent.**

sharpen verb To give a sharp edge to : acuminate, edge, hone[1], whet. See SHARP in Index.

sharper noun See **cheat.**

sharpness noun See **edge.**

sharp-witted adjective See **clever.**

shatter verb See **break, destroy.**

shave verb See **brush[1], shade.**

shawl noun See **wrap.**

shear verb See **cut back** at **cut.**

sheath noun See **skin.**

sheathe verb See **face.**

sheathing noun See **skin.**

shed verb **1.** To send out heat, light, or energy : cast, emit, irradiate, project, radiate, throw. See MOVE in Index. **2.** To cast off by a natural process : exuviate, molt, slough[2], throw off. See PUT ON in Index.

sheen noun See **gloss.**

sheer[1] verb See **swerve.**

sheer[2] adjective See **filmy, pure, steep[1], utter[2].**

shellac verb See **overwhelm.**

shell out verb See **spend.**

shelter noun Dwellings in general : housing, lodging. *Idiom:* a roof over one's head. See PROTECTION in Index. — See also **cover, home, refuge.**
  shelter verb See **harbor.**

shelve verb See **defer[1].**

shenanigan noun See **mischief, prank[1], trick.**

shepherd verb See **guide.**
  shepherd noun See **guide.**

shield noun See **defense.**
  shield verb See **defend.**

shift verb See **change, disturb, manage, move, turn.**

shift noun See **change, displacement, makeshift, transition, turn.**

shiftiness noun See **deceit, indirection.**

shiftless adjective See **lazy.**

shiftlessness noun See **laziness.**

shifty adjective See **underhand.**

shilly-shally verb See **hesitate.**
  shilly-shally noun See **hesitation.**
  shilly-shally adjective See **hesitant.**

shimmer verb See **flash.**
  shimmer noun See **glitter.**

shindig noun See **blast.**

shindy noun See **blast.**

shine verb See **beam, flourish, gloss.**
  shine noun See **gloss.**

shiner noun See **black eye.**

shining adjective See **glossy.**

shiny adjective See **bright, glossy.**

ship verb See **send.**

shipshape adjective See **neat.**

shipwreck verb See **wreck.**

shirk verb See **idle, neglect.**

shiver[1] verb See **shake.**
  shiver noun See **jitter, tremor.**

shiver[2] verb See **break.**

shivery adjective See **cold, tremulous.**

shoal noun A shallow part of a body of water : shallow (often used in plural). See SURFACE in Index.
  shoal adjective See **shallow.**

shock[1] noun Something that jars the mind or emotions : blow[2], jolt. *Psychiatry:* trauma. See STRIKE in Index. — See also **collision.**
  shock verb To affect with a strong feeling of moral aversion : scandalize. See RIGHT in Index. — See also **dismay, startle, traumatize.**

shock[2] noun See **heap.**

shocking adjective See **outrageous, terrible.**

shoddy adjective Of decidedly inferior quality : base[2], cheap, lousy, miserable, paltry, poor, rotten, sleazy, trashy. *Informal:* cheesy. *Slang:* crummy, schlocky. See GOOD in Index. —See also **shabby.**

shoo-in *noun* See **favorite.**

shoot *noun* A young stemlike growth arising from a plant : bine, offshoot, runner, sprig, sprout, tendril. See KIN in Index. —See also **throe.**

shoot *verb* **1.** To discharge a gun or firearm : fire. *Idiom:* take a shot at. See ACTION in Index. **2.** To wound or kill with a firearm : gun (down), pick off. *Slang:* plug. See HELP in Index. **3.** To launch with great force : fire, hurtle, loose, project, propel. *Idiom:* let fly. See MOVE in Index. —See also **fly, rush, throw.**

shoot down *verb* See **discredit.**

shoot up *verb* See **soar.**

shooting *adjective* See **sharp.**

shop *noun* See **store.**

shopworn *adjective* See **trite.**

shore *noun* See **support.**

short *adjective* See **abrupt, brief, insufficient, quick.**

short *adverb* Without any warning : abruptly, suddenly. *Idiom:* all of a sudden. See FAST in Index. —See also **unawares.**

shortage *noun* The condition or fact of being deficient : defect, deficiency, deficit, inadequacy, insufficiency, lack, paucity, poverty, scantiness, scantness, scarceness, scarcity, shortcoming, shortfall, underage[1]. See EXCESS in Index.

shortcoming *noun* See **defect, shortage, weakness.**

shorten *verb* To make short or shorter the duration or extent of : abbreviate, abridge, condense, curtail, reduce. See INCREASE, LONG in Index.

shortfall *noun* See **shortage.**

short fuse *noun* See **temper.**

shorthanded *adjective* See **undermanned.**

short-lived *adjective* See **transitory.**

short-range *adjective* See **tactical, temporary.**

short-spoken *adjective* See **abrupt.**

short-term *adjective* See **temporary.**

shot *noun* See **attempt, drop, opportunity, try.**

shoulder *verb* See **assume.**

shout *noun* A loud cry : call, halloo, holler, yell. See SOUNDS in Index.

shout *verb* See **roar, scream.**

shove *verb* See **drive, muscle, poke, push.**

shove off *verb* See **go.**

shove *noun* See **push.**

shovel *verb* See **dig.**

show *verb* **1.** To make manifest or apparent : demonstrate, display, evidence, evince, exhibit, manifest, proclaim, reveal. See SHOW in Index. **2.** To give a precise indication of, as on a register or scale : indicate, mark, read, record, register. See SHOW in Index. —See also **appear, designate, display, guide, play, prove, represent, reveal.**

show up *verb* See **arrive.**

show *noun* See **act, display, exhibition, façade.**

shower *noun* See **barrage.**

shower *verb* To give in great abundance : heap, lavish, rain. See BIG, GIVE in Index. —See also **barrage.**

showy *adjective* Marked by outward, often extravagant display : flamboyant, ostentatious, pretentious, splashy, splurgy. See PLAIN in Index.

shred *noun* See **bit[1], damn.**

shrew *noun* See **scold.**

shrewd *adjective* Having or showing a clever awareness and resourcefulness in practical matters : astute, cagey, canny, knowing, perspicacious, slick, smart, wise[1]. *Informal:* savvy. See ABILITY, CAREFUL in Index.

shrewdness *noun* See **discernment**.

shriek *noun* See **scream**.

  shriek *verb* See **scream**.

shrieky *adjective* See **high**.

shrill *adjective* See **high**.

  shrill *verb* See **scream**.

shrilly *adjective* See **high**.

shrimp *noun* See **nonentity**.

shrine *noun* See **sanctuary**.

shrink *verb* See **contract, flinch**.

  shrink *noun* See **recoil**.

shrivel *verb* See **dry up** at **dry**.

shroud *verb* See **block, cover, wrap**.

shrunken *adjective* See **wasted**.

shuck *verb* See **discard**.

shudder *verb* See **shake**.

  shudder *noun* See **tremor**.

shuffle *verb* **1.** To drag (the feet) along the floor or ground while walking : scuff, scuffle, shamble. See MOVE in Index. **2.** To mix together so as to change the order of arrangement : jumble, scramble. *Games:* riffle. See CHANGE, ORDER in Index. — See also **equivocate, muddle**.

  shuffle *noun* See **equivocation**.

shun *verb* See **avoid, snub**.

shush *verb* See **silence**.

shut *verb* See **close**.

  shut in *verb* See **enclose**.

  shut off or **out** *verb* See **block**.

  shut out *verb* See **blackball, dismiss, exclude**.

  shut up *verb* See **enclose, imprison, silence**.

shuteye *noun* See **sleep**.

shy[1] *adjective* See **insufficient, modest**.

  shy *verb* See **flinch**.

shy[2] *verb* See **throw**.

  shy *noun* See **throw**.

shyness *noun* An awkwardness or lack of self-confidence in the presence of others : backwardness, bashfulness, coyness, retiringness, timidity, timidness. See RESTRAINT in Index.

sibilate *verb* See **hiss**.

sibyl *noun* See **prophet**.

sibylline *adjective* See **prophetic**.

sick *adjective* **1.** Suffering from or affected with an illness : down, ill, unwell. *Informal:* laid up. *Chiefly Regional:* poorly. See HEALTH in Index. **2.** Out of patience with : disgusted, fed up, tired, weary. *Idiom:* sick and tired. See TIRED in Index. — See also **morbid, sickly**.

sicken *verb* See **contract, disgust**.

sickening *adjective* See **offensive**.

sickly *adjective* **1.** Affected or tending to be affected with minor health problems : ailing, indisposed, low, mean[2], off-color, rocky. *Idiom:* under the weather. See HEALTH in Index. **2.** Of or associated with sickness : anemic, peaked, sick. See HEALTH in Index.

sickness *noun* The condition of being sick : affliction, disorder, illness, indisposition, infirmity. See HEALTH in Index. — See also **disease**.

side *noun* **1.** One of two or more contrasted parts or places identified by its location with respect to a center : flank, hand. See PLACE in Index. **2.** One of two or more opposing opinions, actions, or attitudes, as in a disagreement : part. See PERSPECTIVE in Index. — See also **phase**.

  side *verb* See **face**.

  side with *verb* See **support**.

sidekick *noun* See **friend**.

sidesplitting *adjective* See **priceless**.

sidestep *verb* See **evade**.

sidle *verb* See **edge**.

siege *noun* **1.** A prolonged surrounding of an objective by hostile troops : beleaguerment, besiegement, blockade, investment. See ATTACK in Index. **2.** An often prolonged period, as of illness : bout. See TIME in Index.

siege *verb* See **besiege**.

siesta *noun* See **nap**.

siesta *verb* See **nap**.

sift *verb* See **sort**.

sigh *verb* See **murmur**.

sigh *noun* See **murmur**.

sight *noun* See **heap, look, mess, view, vision**.

sightless *adjective* See **blind**.

sightlessness *noun* See **blindness**.

sightly *adjective* See **beautiful**.

sightseer *noun* See **tourist**.

sign *noun* **1.** Something visible or evident that gives grounds for believing in the existence or presence of something else : badge, evidence, index, indication, indicator, manifestation, mark, note, signification, stamp, symptom, token, witness. See SHOW in Index. **2.** A usually public posting that conveys a message : bill[1], billboard, notice, placard, poster. See SHOW in Index. — See also **character, expression, gesture, omen**.

sign *verb* To affix one's signature to : autograph, endorse, inscribe, subscribe, undersign. *Idioms:* put one's John Hancock on, set one's hand to. See LAW in Index. — See also **gesture**.

sign on *verb* See **join**.

sign over *verb* See **transfer**.

sign up *verb* See **join**.

signal *noun* See **gesture**.

signal *verb* To communicate by means of such devices as lights or signs : flag[1], semaphore. See EXPRESS, WORDS in Index. — See also **gesture**.

signal *adjective* See **noticeable**.

signalize *verb* See **distinguish, gesture**.

significance *noun* See **idea, importance, meaning**.

significancy *noun* See **idea, importance, meaning**.

significant *adjective* See **expressive, important, pregnant**.

signification *noun* See **meaning, sign**.

signify *verb* See **count, mean**[1].

silence *noun* **1.** The absence of sound or noise : hush, noiselessness, quiet, quietness, soundlessness, still, stillness. See SOUNDS in Index. **2.** The avoidance of speech : dumbness, muteness, speechlessness, wordlessness. See WORDS in Index.

silence *verb* To cause to become silent : hush, quiet, quieten, shush, shut up, still. See SOUNDS in Index.

silent *adjective* **1.** Marked by, done with, or making no sound or noise : hushed, noiseless, quiet, soundless, still, stilly. *Archaic:* hush. See SOUNDS in Index. **2.** Not voiced or expressed : tacit, undeclared, unexpressed, unsaid, unspoken, unuttered, unvoiced, wordless. See WORDS in Index. — See also **speechless, taciturn**.

silhouette *noun* See **outline**.

silken *adjective* See **sleek**.

silky *adjective* See **sleek**.

silliness *noun* See **foolishness**.

silly *adjective* See **foolish, giddy, mindless**.

silver-tongued *adjective* See **eloquent**.

similar *adjective* See **like**[2].

similarity *noun* See **likeness**.

similitude *noun* See **likeness**.

simmer *verb* See **boil**.

simmer down *verb* See **compose.**

simper *verb* See **smirk.**

simper *noun* See **smirk.**

simple *adjective* See **artless, backward, bare, easy, humble, modest, pure.**

simple *noun* See **fool.**

simple-minded or **simpleminded** *adjective* See **backward.**

simpleness *noun* See **modesty.**

simpleton *noun* See **fool.**

simplicity *noun* See **modesty.**

simplify *verb* See **boil down** at **boil.**

simulacre *noun* See **copy.**

simulacrum *noun* See **copy.**

simulate *verb* See **act, assume, copy, fake.**

simulated *adjective* See **artificial.**

simulation *noun* See **act, copy.**

simultaneous *adjective* Existing or occurring at the same moment : coincident, contemporary. See TIME in Index.

simultaneously *adverb* See **together.**

sin *noun* See **crime, evil.**

sin *verb* See **offend.**

sincere *adjective* See **genuine.**

sine qua non *noun* See **condition.**

sinew *noun* See **strength.**

sinewy *adjective* See **muscular.**

sinful *adjective* See **evil.**

sing *verb* To utter words or sounds in musical tones : carol, chant, vocalize. *Archaic:* tune. See SOUNDS in Index. — See also **inform.**

singe *verb* See **burn.**

singe *noun* See **burn.**

singer *noun* See **vocalist.**

single *adjective* Without a spouse : fancy-free, footloose, lone, sole, spouseless, unattached, unmarried, unwed. *Idiom:* footloose and fancy-free. See MARRIAGE in Index. — See also **alone, exclusive, individual, lone.**

single *verb* See **choose.**

single-handedly *adverb* See **alone.**

singleness *noun* See **aloneness, uniqueness, unity.**

singly *adverb* See **alone, separately.**

singular *adjective* See **eccentric, individual, lone, rare, unique.**

singularity *noun* See **eccentricity, individuality, uniqueness, unity.**

singularize *verb* See **distinguish.**

singularly *adverb* See **unusually.**

sinister *adjective* See **malign.**

sink *noun* See **depression, pit**[1]**.**

sink *verb* To go beneath the surface or to the bottom of a liquid : founder[1], submerge, submerse. See RISE in Index. — See also **descend, destroy, deteriorate, drop, fade, fall, ram, settle.**

sink in *verb* See **register.**

sinkhole *noun* See **depression.**

sinless *adjective* See **innocent.**

sinuate *verb* See **slither.**

sinuous *adjective* See **winding.**

sip *verb* See **drink.**

sip *noun* See **drink, drop.**

sire *noun* See **father.**

sire *verb* See **father, produce.**

siren *noun* See **seductress.**

siren *adjective* See **seductive.**

sissified *adjective* See **effeminate.**

sissiness or **sissyness** *noun* See **effeminacy.**

sissyish *adjective* See **effeminate.**

sit *verb* See **pose, seat.**

sit on or **upon** *verb* See **repress.**

site *noun* See **position, scene.**

site *verb* See **position.**

situate *verb* See **position.**

situation *noun* See **bearing, condition, place, position.**

sixth sense *noun* See **instinct.**

sizable also **sizeable** *adjective* Somewhat big : biggish, goodly, largish, respectable. See BIG in Index. — See also **big.**

sizableness also **sizeableness** *noun* See **size.**

size *noun* **1.** The amount of space occupied by something : dimension, extent, magnitude, measure, proportion (often used in plural). See BIG in Index. **2.** The quality or state of being large in amount, extent, or importance : amplitude, bigness, greatness, largeness, magnitude, sizableness. See BIG in Index. — See also **bulk.**

size up *verb* See **estimate.**

sizzle *verb* See **hiss.**

sizzling *adjective* See **hot.**

skedaddle *verb* See **run.**

skein *noun* See **tangle, thread.**

skeletal *adjective* See **wasted.**

skeleton *noun* See **draft.**

skeptic also **sceptic** *noun* One who habitually or instinctively doubts or questions : doubter, doubting Thomas, nonbeliever, unbeliever. See BELIEF in Index.

skeptical also **sceptical** *adjective* See **doubtful, incredulous.**

skeptically also **sceptically** *adverb* With skepticism : askance, doubtfully, dubiously, questioningly. *Idiom:* with a grain of salt. See BELIEF in Index.

skepticism also **scepticism** *noun* See **doubt.**

sketch *noun* A short theatrical piece within a larger production : act, skit. See PERFORMING ARTS in Index. — See also **draft.**

sketch *verb* See **draft.**

sketchy *adjective* See **rough, superficial.**

skew *verb* See **bias, swerve.**

skid *verb* See **fall, slide.**

skid *noun* See **fall.**

skill *noun* See **ability, dexterity.**

skilled *adjective* See **able, expert.**

skillful also **skilful** *adjective* See **able, artful, expert, neat.**

skim *verb* See **browse, brush¹, fly, glance.**

skim *noun* See **brush¹.**

skimp *verb* See **scrimp.**

skimpy *adjective* See **meager.**

skin *noun* **1.** The tissue forming the external covering of the body : epidermis, integument. See SURFACE in Index. **2.** The outer covering of a fruit : peel, rind. See SURFACE in Index. **3.** A thin outer covering of an object : lamina, membrane, sheath, sheathing. See SURFACE in Index.

skin *verb* **1.** To remove the skin of : decorticate, pare, peel, scale¹, strip¹. See PUT ON in Index. **2.** *Slang.* To exploit (another) by charging too much for something : fleece, overcharge. *Slang:* clip¹, gouge, nick, rip off, scalp, soak. *Idioms:* make someone pay through the nose, take someone for a ride, take someone to the cleaners. See HONEST in Index. — See also **face.**

skin-deep *adjective* See **superficial.**

skinflint *noun* See **miser.**

skinny *adjective* See **thin.**

skip *verb* To bound lightly : hop, skitter, spring, trip. See MOVE in Index. — See also **cut, drop, escape, glance.**

skip *noun* A light bounding movement : hop, spring. See MOVE in Index.

skirmish *noun* See **brush².**

skirt *verb* To pass around but not through : bypass, circumnavigate, circumvent, detour, go around. See SEEK in Index. — See also **border, evade.**

skirt *noun* The periphery of a city or town. Used in plural : edge, environs, fringe, outskirt (often used in plural), suburb (used in plural). See EDGE in Index.

skit *noun* See **sketch.**

skitter *verb* See **skip.**

skittish *adjective* See **edgy.**

skulk *verb* See **sneak.**

sky *noun* See **air.**

sky *verb* See **soar.**

sky-high *adjective* See **lofty, steep**[1].

skyrocket *verb* See **soar.**

slab *noun* See **stick.**

slack *adjective* See **loose, negligent, slow.**

slack *verb* See **ease, neglect.**

slack off *verb* See **subside.**

slacken *verb* See **ease, subside, weaken.**

slackening *noun* See **wane.**

slackness *noun* See **negligence.**

slam *noun* A forceful movement causing a loud noise : bang, crash, smash, wham. See STRIKE in Index.

slam *verb* *Slang.* To criticize harshly and devastatingly : blister, drub, excoriate, flay, lash, rip into, scarify[1], scathe, scorch, score, scourge, slap, slash. *Informal:* roast. *Idioms:* burn someone's ears, crawl all over, pin someone's ears back, put someone on the griddle, put someone on the hot seat, rake over the coals, read the riot act to. See PRAISE in Index. — See also **bang, hit.**

slammer *noun* See **jail.**

slander *noun* See **libel.**

slander *verb* See **libel.**

slanderous *adjective* See **libelous.**

slant *verb* See **bias, incline, tend**[1].

slant *noun* See **inclination, point of view.**

slanted *adjective* See **bias.**

slanting *adjective* See **bias.**

slap *noun* A quick, sharp blow, especially with the hand : box[2], buffet, bust, chop[1], cuff, punch, smack[1], smacker, spank, swat, whack. *Informal:* clip[1], spat. See ATTACK, STRIKE in Index.

slap *verb* To hit with a quick, sharp blow of the hand. : box[2], buffet, bust, cuff, punch, smack[1], spank, swat, whack. *Informal:* clip[1], spat. See ATTACK, STRIKE in Index. — See also **slam.**

slap around *verb* To be rough or brutal with : knock about (or around), manhandle, rough (up). *Slang:* mess up. See ATTACK, STRIKE in Index.

slapdash *adjective* See **careless, rash**[1].

slash *verb* See **cut, cut back** at **cut, slam.**

slash *noun* See **cut, decrease, score.**

slashing *adjective* See **biting.**

slate *noun* See **ticket.**

slate *verb* See **schedule.**

slattern *noun* See **slut.**

slaughter *verb* See **annihilate.**

slaughter *noun* See **massacre.**

slaughterer *noun* See **murderer.**

slaughterous *adjective* See **murderous.**

slave *verb* See **grind.**

slave *noun* See **drudge.**

slaver *verb* See **drool, fawn, flatter.**

slaver *noun* See **drool, flattery.**

slavery *noun* A state of subjugation to an owner or master : bondage, enslavement, helotry, serfdom, servileness, servility, servitude, thrall, thralldom, villeinage, yoke. See OVER in Index.

slavish *adjective* See **imitative, servile.**

slay *verb* See **kill**[1], **murder.**

slayer *noun* See **murderer.**

sleazy *adjective* See **shabby, shoddy.**

sled *verb* See **slide.**

sledge *verb* See **slide.**

sleek *adjective* **1.** Smooth and lustrous as if polished : satiny, silken, silky. See SMOOTH in Index. **2.** Having slender and graceful lines : streamlined, trim. See BEAUTIFUL in Index. — See also **unctuous.**

sleek *verb* See **gloss.**

sleek over *verb* See **extenuate**.
sleekness *noun* See **gloss**.
sleep *noun* The natural recurring condition of suspended consciousness by which the body rests : slumber. *Slang:* shuteye. *Idioms:* land of Nod, the arms of Morpheus. See AWARENESS in Index.
sleep *verb* To be asleep : slumber. *Idioms:* be in the land of Nod, catch some shuteye, sleep like a log (or rock or top), sleep tight. See AWARENESS in Index.
sleep in *verb* To sleep longer than intended : oversleep. See AWARENESS in Index.
sleep with *verb* See **take**.
sleeper *noun* See **hit**.
sleeping *adjective* In a state of sleep : asleep, unawake. *Idioms:* dead to the world, fast (or sound) asleep, in a sound (or wakeless) sleep, out like a light. See AWARENESS in Index. — See also **latent**.
sleepless *adjective* See **wakeful**.
sleepy *adjective* **1.** Ready for or needing sleep : dozy, drowsy, nodding, slumberous, slumbery, somnolent, soporific. See AWARENESS in Index. **2.** Inducing sleep or sedation : hypnotic, narcotic, opiate, sedative, slumberous, somnifacient, somniferous, somnific, somnolent, soporific. See AWARENESS in Index.
sleight *noun* See **dexterity, trick**.
sleight of hand *noun* See **magic**.
slender *adjective* See **remote, thin**.
sleuth *noun* See **detective**.
slew also **slue** *noun* See **heap**.
slice *verb* See **cut**.
slice *noun* See **cut, section**.
slick *adjective* So smooth and glassy as to offer insecure hold or footing : lubricious, slippery, slithery. *Idiom:* slippery as an eel. See SMOOTH in Index. — See also **dexterous, glib, shrewd**.

slick up *verb* See **tidy**.
slide *verb* **1.** To pass smoothly, quietly, and undisturbed on or as if on a slippery surface : coast, drift. See MOVE in Index. **2.** To lose one's balance and fall or almost fall : skid, slip, slither. *Idiom:* take a skid (or slide). See MOVE in Index. **3.** To ride on a sled in the snow : sled, sledge. See MOVE in Index. — See also **crawl, ease, glide, slip, sneak**.
slide *noun* See **fall**.
slight *adjective* See **light², remote**.
slight *verb* See **belittle, ignore, neglect**.
slight *noun* See **indignity, neglect**.
slighting *adjective* See **disparaging**.
slim *adjective* See **remote, thin**.
slim *verb* See **reduce, thin**.
slime *noun* A viscous, usually offensively dirty substance : mire, muck, ooze, slop, sludge, slush. See CLEAN in Index.
slimy *adjective* Of, relating to, or covered with slime : miry, mucky, oozy, sludgy, slushy. See CLEAN in Index.
sling *verb* See **hang, throw**.
sling *noun* See **throw**.
slink *verb* See **sneak**.
slinkiness *noun* See **stealth**.
slinky *adjective* See **stealthy**.
slip *noun* See **error, lapse**.
slip *verb* **1.** To shift or be shifted out of place : slide. See MOVE in Index. **2.** To decline, as in value or quantity, very gradually : drop off, fall off, sag. See INCREASE in Index. **3.** To displace (a bone) from a socket or joint : dislocate, throw out. *Idiom:* throw out of joint. See HELP in Index. — See also **ease, err, fall, glide, lose, miscarry, slide, sneak, undo**.
slip into *verb* See **don**.
slip on *verb* See **don**.

slip up verb See **err.**

slippery adjective See **evasive, slick.**

slipshod adjective See **careless, messy.**

slip-up noun See **error, lapse.**

slit verb See **cut.**

slit noun See **cut.**

slither verb To move sinuously : sinuate, snake, undulate. See MOVE in Index. — See also **glide, slide.**

slithery adjective See **slick.**

slobber verb See **drool.**

slobber noun See **drool.**

slog verb See **grind, hit, plod.**

slop verb See **plod, splash.**

slop noun See **slime.**

slope verb See **incline.**

slope noun See **inclination.**

sloppiness noun See **disorderliness, sentimentality.**

sloppy adjective See **careless, messy, sentimental.**

slosh verb See **splash.**

sloshed adjective See **drunk.**

slot noun See **position.**

sloth noun See **laziness.**

slothful adjective See **lazy.**

slothfulness noun See **laziness.**

slouch verb **1.** To have an awkward, slovenly posture : loll, slump. See MOVE, POSTURE in Index. **2.** To hang limply, loosely, and carelessly : droop, flop, loll, lop[2], sag, wilt. See HANG in Index.

slouch noun See **wastrel.**

slough[1] noun See **swamp.**

slough[2] verb See **shed.**

slovenliness noun See **disorderliness.**

slovenly adjective See **careless, messy.**

slow adjective **1.** Proceeding at a rate less than usual or desired : dilatory, laggard, slow-footed, slow-going, slow-paced, tardy. *Informal:* poky. *Idiom:* slow as molasses in January. See FAST in Index.

2. Characterized by reduced economic activity : down, dull, off, slack, sluggish, soft. See INCREASE in Index. — See also **backward.**

slow verb See **delay.**

slow adverb So as to fall behind schedule : behind, behindhand, late. *Idiom:* behind time. See TIME in Index.

slowdown noun See **decrease.**

slow-footed adjective See **slow.**

slow-going adjective See **slow.**

slow-paced adjective See **slow.**

slowpoke noun See **laggard.**

slow-witted or **slowwitted** adjective See **backward.**

sludge noun See **slime.**

sludgy adjective See **slimy.**

slue verb See **swerve.**

slug[1] noun See **drop.**

slug[2] noun See **wastrel.**

slug[3] verb See **hit.**

slug noun See **blow**[2].

slugabed noun See **wastrel.**

sluggard noun See **wastrel.**

sluggard adjective See **lazy.**

sluggardness noun See **laziness.**

sluggish adjective See **lazy, lethargic, slow.**

sluggishness noun See **laziness, lethargy.**

slumber verb See **sleep.**

slumber noun See **sleep.**

slumberless adjective See **wakeful.**

slumberous or **slumbrous** adjective See **sleepy.**

slumbery adjective See **sleepy.**

slump noun See **depression, fall.**

slump verb See **drop, fall, slouch.**

slur verb See **libel.**

slur noun See **reflection.**

slush noun See **slime.**

slush verb See **muddy.**

slushy adjective See **sentimental, slimy.**

slut noun A vulgar promiscuous woman who flouts propriety : baggage, hussy, jade, slattern, tart[2], tramp, wanton, wench, whore. *Slang:* floozy. See SEX in Index.

sly *adjective* Trickily secret : furtive, secretive, sneaking, sneaky, surreptitious. See HONEST in Index. — See also **artful.**

slyness *noun* See **art, indirection.**

smack[1] *verb* See **kiss, slap.**

  smack *noun* See **kiss, slap.**

  smack *adverb* See **directly.**

smack[2] *verb* To have a particular flavor or suggestion of something : savor, smell, suggest, taste. See SUGGEST in Index.

  smack *noun* See **flavor.**

smack-dab *adverb* See **directly.**

smacker *noun* See **kiss, slap.**

small *adjective* Not yet large in size because of incomplete growth : little. See YOUTH in Index. — See also **little, minor, narrow, petty, soft.**

small change *noun* See **peanut, trivia.**

smallest *adjective* See **minimal.**

smallish *adjective* See **little.**

small-minded *adjective* See **narrow, petty.**

smallness *noun* See **pettiness.**

small potatoes *noun* See **trivia.**

small talk *noun* See **chatter.**

smalltime or **small-time** *adjective* See **minor.**

small-town *adjective* See **local.**

smarmy *adjective* See **unctuous.**

smart *verb* See **sting.**

  smart *noun* See **intelligence, pain.**

  smart *adjective* See **clever, fashionable, impudent, shrewd.**

smart aleck *noun* *Informal.* One who is obnoxiously self-assertive and arrogant : malapert, witling. *Informal:* know-it-all, saucebox, smarty, smarty-pants, wisenheimer. *Slang:* wiseacre, wisecracker, wise guy. See GOOD in Index.

smart-alecky *adjective* See **impudent.**

smarten *verb* See **fix up** at **fix.**

smarting *adjective* See **painful.**

smarty *noun* See **smart aleck.**

smarty-pants *noun* See **smart aleck.**

smash *verb* See **beat, break, clash, crash, destroy, hit, overwhelm.**

  smash *noun* See **clash, collapse, collision, crash, hit, slam.**

smashed *adjective* See **drunk.**

smash hit *noun* See **hit.**

smashup *noun* See **collapse, crash.**

smatterer *noun* See **amateur.**

smaze *noun* See **haze.**

smear *verb* To spread with a greasy, sticky, or dirty substance : bedaub, besmear, dab[1], daub, plaster, smirch, smudge. See PUT ON in Index. — See also **blacken, overwhelm.**

  smear *noun* **1.** A discolored mark made by smearing : blot, blotch, daub, smirch, smudge, smutch, splotch, stain. See MARKS in Index. **2.** An attempt to destroy someone's reputation : mudslinging, smear campaign. See PRAISE in Index.

smear campaign *noun* See **smear.**

smell *noun* **1.** The sense by which odors are perceived : nose, olfaction, scent. See SMELLS in Index. **2.** The quality of something that may be perceived by the olfactory sense : aroma, odor, scent. See SMELLS in Index. — See also **air.**

smell *verb* **1.** To perceive with the olfactory sense : nose, scent, sniff, snuff, whiff. *Idiom:* catch (or get) a whiff of. See SMELLS in Index. **2.** To have or give off a foul odor : reek, stink. *Idiom:* smell to high heaven. See SMELLS in Index. — See also **smack**[2]**.**

smelly *adjective* *Informal.* Having an unpleasant odor : fetid, foul, foul-smelling, malodorous,

mephitic, noisome, reeky, stinking.
See SMELLS in Index.

smidgen also **smidgeon** or **smidgin** noun See bit[1].

smile noun A facial expression marked by an upward curving of the lips : grin. See EXPRESS in Index.

smile verb To curve the lips upward in expressing amusement, pleasure, or happiness : beam, grin. *Idioms:* break into a smile, crack a smile. See EXPRESS in Index.

smile on or **upon** verb See encourage.

smirch noun See smear.

smirch verb See smear.

smirk verb To smile in an affected, knowing way : simper. See EXPRESS in Index.

smirk noun An affected, knowing smile : simper. See EXPRESS in Index.

smite verb See afflict, hit.

smitten adjective See infatuated.

smoggy adjective See turbid.

smolder verb See boil.

smooch noun See kiss.

smooch verb See kiss.

smooth adjective Marked by facility, especially of expression : easy, effortless, flowing, fluent, fluid, graceful. See STYLE in Index. — See also easy, even[1], gentle, suave.

smooth verb See even[1], perfect.

smooth over verb See settle.

smooth-spoken adjective See eloquent.

smooth-tongued adjective See glib.

smother verb See choke, repress.

smudge verb See blacken, dirty, smear.

smudge noun See smear.

smuggle verb 1. To import or export secretly and illegally : bootleg, run. *Idiom:* run contraband. See CRIMES, MOVE in Index. 2. To

bring in or take out secretly : sneak, spirit. See MOVE in Index.

smuggler noun A person who engages in smuggling : bootlegger, contrabandist, runner. See CRIMES, MOVE in Index.

smut noun See obscenity.

smut verb See blacken, stain.

smutch verb See dirty.

smutch noun See smear.

smuttiness noun See dirtiness, obscenity.

smutty adjective See dirty, obscene.

snack noun See bite.

snaffle noun See bit[2].

snafu noun See botch, disorder.

verb See botch, confuse.

snag noun See bar, catch.

snail's pace noun See crawl.

snake verb See crawl, slither, sneak, wind[2].

snaky adjective See winding.

snap verb 1. To make a light, sharp noise : clack, click. See SOUNDS in Index. 2. To grasp at (something) eagerly, forcibly, and abruptly with the jaws : catch, nip[1], snatch, strike. See REACH in Index. 3. To speak abruptly and sharply : bark, snarl[1]. *Idioms:* bite someone's head off, snap someone's head (or nose) off. See WORDS in Index. — See also break, crack, jerk.

snap noun A light, sharp noise : clack, click. See SOUNDS in Index. — See also breeze, jerk, report, vigor.

snap adjective See easy, extemporaneous.

snappish adjective See ill-tempered.

snappy adjective See fashionable, ill-tempered, spirited, vigorous.

snare verb See catch.

snare noun See lure.

snarl[1] verb See snap.

snarl[2] noun See tangle.

snarl *verb* See **complicate, confuse, entangle.**

snatch *verb* See **catch, kidnap, seize, snap, steal.**

snatch *noun* See **catch.**

sneak *verb* To move silently and furtively : creep, glide, lurk, mouse, prowl, pussyfoot, skulk, slide, slink, slip, snake, steal. *Slang:* gumshoe. See MOVE in Index. — See also **smuggle.**

sneak *noun* One who behaves in a stealthy, furtive way : prowler, sneaker, weasel. See MOVE in Index.

sneaker *noun* See **sneak.**

sneakiness *noun* See **indirection, stealth.**

sneaking *adjective* See **sly, stealthy.**

sneaky *adjective* See **sly, stealthy, underhand.**

sneer *noun* A facial expression or laugh conveying scorn or derision : fleer, snicker, snigger. See EXPRESS, LAUGHTER, RESPECT in Index.

sneer *verb* To smile or laugh scornfully or derisively : fleer, snicker, snigger. *Idiom:* curl one's lip. See EXPRESS, LAUGHTER, RESPECT in Index.

sneering *adjective* See **sarcastic.**

snicker *verb* See **giggle, sneer.**

snicker *noun* See **giggle, sneer.**

sniff *verb* See **smell.**

snigger *verb* See **giggle, sneer.**

snigger *noun* See **giggle, sneer.**

snippety *adjective* See **impudent.**

snippy *adjective* See **impudent.**

snit *noun* See **state.**

snitch *verb* See **inform, steal.**

snitch *noun* See **informer.**

snitcher *noun* See **informer.**

snob *noun* One who despises people or things regarded as inferior, especially because of social or intellectual pretension : elitist. *Informal:* snoot. See ATTITUDE, SELF-LOVE in Index.

snobbish *adjective* Characteristic of or resembling a snob : elitist, snobby. *Informal:* high-hat, snooty, stuck-up, uppish, uppity. See ATTITUDE, SELF-LOVE in Index.

snobby *adjective* See **snobbish.**

snoop *verb* To look into or inquire about curiously, inquisitively, or in a meddlesome fashion : poke, pry. *Informal:* nose (around). *Idiom:* stick one's nose into. See INVESTIGATE, PARTICIPATE in Index.

snoop *noun* A person who snoops : prier, pry, snooper. See INVESTIGATE, PARTICIPATE in Index.

snooper *noun* See **snoop.**

snoopiness *noun* See **curiosity.**

snoopy *adjective* See **curious.**

snoot *noun* See **nose, snob.**

snooty *adjective* See **snobbish.**

snooze *verb* See **nap.**

snooze *noun* See **nap.**

snort *noun* See **drop.**

snout *noun* See **nose.**

snowball *verb* See **explode, increase.**

snub *verb* To slight (someone) deliberately : cut, rebuff, shun, spurn. *Informal:* coldshoulder. *Idioms:* close (or shut) the door on, give someone the cold shoulder, give someone the go-by, turn one's back on. See ACCEPT in Index.

snub *noun* A deliberate slight : cut, rebuff, spurn. *Informal:* cold shoulder, go-by. See ACCEPT in Index.

snuff *verb* See **smell.**

snuff out *verb* See **annihilate, extinguish.**

snug *adjective* See **comfortable, neat, tight.**

snug *verb* See **snuggle.**

snuggle *verb* To lie or press close together, usually with another per-

son or thing : cuddle, nestle, nuzzle, snug. See NEAR in Index.

soak noun See **drunkard**.

    soak verb See **absorb, drink, skin,
steep², wet**.

    soak in verb See **register**.

soar verb To rise abruptly and pre-
cipitously : rocket, sky, skyrocket.
Informal: shoot up. See INCREASE in
Index. — See also **increase, rise**.

soaring adjective See **lofty**.

sob verb See **cry**.

sobbing noun See **cry**.

sobby adjective See **sentimental**.

sober adjective See **grave², realistic, temperate**.

soberness noun See **temperance**.

sobersided adjective See **serious**.

sobersidedness noun See
seriousness.

sobriety noun See **gravity,
temperance**.

sociability noun See **amiability**.

sociable adjective See **amiable,
companionable, social**.

sociableness noun See **amiability**.

social adjective 1. Of, characterized
by, or inclined to living together in
communities : gregarious. See
CONNECT, GROUP in Index. 2.
Spent, marked by, or enjoyed in
the company of others : companionable, convivial, sociable. See
ATTITUDE, PARTICIPATE in Index.
— See also **companionable, societal**.

socialize verb 1. To place under
government or group ownership or
control : communalize, nationalize. See POLITICS, SPECIFIC in
Index. 2. To fit for companionship
with others, especially in attitude or
manners : acculturate, civilize,
humanize. See TEACH in Index.
3. To take part in social activities :
mingle, mix. See GROUP in Index.

societal adjective Of or relating to
the structure, organization, or func-

tioning of society : social. See
GROUP in Index.

society noun People of the highest
social level : aristocracy, blue
blood, crème de la crème, elite,
flower, gentility, gentry, nobility,
patriciate, quality, upper class,
who's who. *Informal:* upper crust.
See OVER in Index. — See also **company, public, union**.

sock noun See **blow²**.

    sock verb See **hit**.

sock away verb See **bank²**.

sodden verb See **wet**.

sodden adjective See **drunk, wet**.

soft adjective 1. Yielding easily to
pressure or weight; not firm :
mushy, pappy¹, pulpous, pulpy,
quaggy, spongy, squashy, squishy,
yielding. See RESIST in Index.
2. Not irritating, strident, or loud :
hushed, low, low-key, low-keyed,
quiet, small, subdued, whispery. See
SOUNDS in Index. — See also **backward, comfortable, gentle, light²,
sentimental, slow, tolerant**.

soften verb See **moderate, pacify,
weaken**.

softhead noun See **fool**.

softheaded adjective See **foolish**.

softhearted adjective See **gentle**.

soft-pedal verb *Informal.* To
make less emphatic or obvious :
de-emphasize, play down, tone
down. See SHOW in Index.

soft soap noun See **flattery**.

    soft-soap verb See **coax, flatter**.

soggy adjective See **sticky, wet**.

soil verb See **blacken, dirty, taint**.

soiled adjective See **dirty**.

soiree also **soirée** noun See **party**.

sojourn verb See **stay¹**.

    sojourn noun See **stay¹**.

solace verb See **comfort**.

    solace noun See **comfort**.

soldier noun See **fighter**.

soldierly adjective See **military**.

soldier of fortune *noun* See **mercenary.**

sole *adjective* See **exclusive, lone, single.**

solecism *noun* See **corruption.**

solely *adverb* To the exclusion of anyone or anything else : **alone, but, entirely, exclusively, only.** See INCLUDE in Index. — See also **alone.**

solemn *adjective* See **grave².**

solemnity *noun* See **gravity.**

solemnize *verb* See **celebrate.**

solemnness *noun* See **gravity.**

solemn word *noun* See **promise.**

solicit *verb* See **besiege, request.**

solicitous *adjective* See **anxious, attentive, eager.**

solicitude *noun* See **anxiety, consideration.**

solid *adjective* See **dependable, firm¹, sound², unanimous.**

solidarity *noun* See **unity.**

solidify *verb* See **harden.**

solidity *noun* See **soundness, thickness.**

solitarily *adverb* See **alone.**

solitariness *noun* See **aloneness.**

solitary *adjective* Set away from all others : **alone, apart, detached, isolate, isolated, lone, removed.** See INCLUDE in Index. — See also **alone, cool, lone, remote.**

solitude *noun* See **aloneness.**

solo *adverb* See **alone.**

solution *noun* See **answer.**

solve *verb* See **resolve, work.**

somatic *adjective* See **bodily.**

somber *adjective* See **gloomy, grave².**

some *adjective* See **several.**

somebody *noun* See **dignitary.**

someone *noun* See **dignitary.**

something *noun* See **thing.**

sometime *adjective* See **late.**

sometimes *adverb* See **intermittently, now.**

somnifacient *adjective* See **sleepy.**

somnifacient *noun* See **soporific.**

somniferous *adjective* See **sleepy.**

somnific *adjective* See **sleepy.**

somnolent *adjective* See **sleepy.**

sonance *noun* See **sound¹.**

sonant *adjective* See **vocal.**

songster *noun* See **vocalist.**

songstress *noun* See **vocalist.**

sonorous *adjective* Characterized by language that is elevated and sometimes pompous in style : **aureate, bombastic, declamatory, flowery, fustian, grandiloquent, high-flown, high-sounding, magniloquent, orotund, overblown, rhetorical, swollen.** See PLAIN, STYLE, WORDS in Index. — See also **resonant.**

soothe *verb* See **comfort, pacify.**

soothsay *verb* See **prophesy.**

soothsayer *noun* See **prophet.**

soothsaying *noun* See **prophecy.**

sooty *adjective* See **black.**

sop *verb* See **wet.**

sop up *verb* See **drink.**

sophism *noun* See **fallacy.**

sophistic *adjective* See **fallacious.**

sophisticate *verb* See **adulterate.**

sophisticated *adjective* Experienced in the ways of the world; lacking natural simplicity : **cosmopolitan, worldly, worldly-wise.** See KNOWLEDGE in Index. — See also **impure, intellectual.**

sophistication *noun* See **contamination.**

sophistry *noun* See **fallacy.**

soporific *noun* Something that induces sleep or sedation : **hypnotic, narcotic, opiate, sedative, somnifacient.** See AWARENESS in Index.

soporific *adjective* See **sleepy.**

sopping *adjective* See **wet.**

soppy *adjective* See **sentimental, wet.**

sorceress *noun* See **witch.**

sorcery *noun* See **magic.**

sordid *adjective* Having or proceeding from low moral standards : base[2], ignoble, low, low-down, mean[2], squalid, vile. See RIGHT in Index.

sore *adjective* See **angry, painful.**

sorehead *noun* See **grouch.**

soreness *noun* See **irritation, pain.**

sorority *noun* See **union.**

sorrow *noun* See **grief.**

sorrow *verb* See **grieve.**

sorrowful *adjective* **1.** Causing sorrow or regret : deplorable, doleful, dolorous, grievous, lamentable, mournful, regrettable, rueful, sad, woeful. See HAPPY in Index. **2.** Full of or expressive of sorrow : doleful, dolorous, lugubrious, mournful, plaintive, rueful, sad, woebegone, woeful. See HAPPY in Index.

sorry *adjective* See **apologetic, disappointing, remorseful.**

sort *noun* See **kind**[2].

sort *verb* To set apart (one kind or type) from others : separate, sift, winnow. See INCLUDE in Index.
— See also **arrange, assort.**

sortilege *noun* See **magic.**

sot *noun* See **drunkard.**

sough *verb* See **murmur.**

sough *noun* See **murmur.**

soul *noun* The essential being of a person, regarded as immaterial and immortal : spirit. See BE in Index.
— See also **heart, human being, spirit.**

sound[1] *noun* The sensation caused by vibrating wave motion that is perceived by the organs of hearing : noise, sonance. See SOUNDS in Index. — See also **hearing.**

sound *verb* See **appear.**

sound[2] *adjective* **1.** Not easily moved or shaken : firm[1], secure, solid, stable, strong, sturdy, substantial, sure, unshakable. See CONTINUE, STRONG in Index. **2.** Based

on good judgment, reasoning, or evidence : cogent, just, solid, tight, valid, well-founded, well-grounded. See GOOD, REASON in Index. — See also **dependable, good, healthy, sane.**

sound[3] *verb* See **feel out** at **feel.**

soundless *adjective* See **silent.**

soundlessness *noun* See **silence.**

soundness *noun* The condition of being free from defects or flaws : durability, firmness, integrity, solidity, stability, strength, wholeness. See BETTER in Index. — See also **health, sanity, stability.**

soup *noun* See **predicament.**

soupçon *noun* See **shade.**

soupy *adjective* See **sentimental.**

sour *adjective* Having a taste characteristic of that produced by acids : acerb, acerbic, acetous, acid, acidulous, dry, tangy, tart[1]. See TASTE in Index. — See also **amiss, bitter, glum.**

sour *verb* See **embitter.**

source *noun* See **contact, origin.**

sourpuss *noun* See **grouch.**

souse *noun* See **drunkard.**

souse *verb* See **dip, wet.**

soused *adjective* See **drunk.**

souvenir *noun* See **remembrance.**

sovereign *adjective* See **free.**

sovereignty *noun* See **authority, freedom.**

sow *verb* See **seed.**

space *noun* See **bit**[1], **distance, expanse.**

spaced-out *adjective* See **drugged.**

spacious *adjective* See **broad, roomy.**

spade *verb* See **dig.**

span *noun* See **extent, life, period, term.**

spangle *verb* See **flash.**

spangle *noun* See **glitter.**

spank *verb* See **slap.**

spank *noun* See **slap.**

spanner *noun* See **wrench.**

spare *verb* See **economize, excuse, favor.**

spare *adjective* See **meager, superfluous, thin, tight.**

sparing *adjective* See **economical.**

spark[1] *noun* See **blink, germ.**

spark[2] *verb* See **court.**

sparkle *verb* See **flash.**

sparkle *noun* See **glitter, spirit.**

sparkling *adjective* See **clever, exuberant.**

sparse *adjective* See **meager.**

spasm *noun* See **throe.**

spat *noun* See **argument, slap.**

spat *verb* See **argue, slap.**

spate *noun* A sudden or rapid flowing outward : efflux, gush, outflow, outpour, outpouring. See MOVE in Index. — See also **flood, flow.**

spatter *verb* See **blacken, splash, spot.**

spawn *verb* See **produce, reproduce.**

spawning *noun* See **reproduction.**

spay *verb* See **sterilize.**

speak *verb* To express oneself in speech : talk, verbalize, vocalize. *Idioms:* open one's mouth (*or* lips), put in (*or* into) words, wag one's tongue. See WORDS in Index. — See also **address, converse**[1].

speak for *verb* See **represent.**

speaker *noun* **1.** One who delivers a public speech : declaimer, lecturer, speechifier, speechmaker. See WORDS in Index. **2.** A person who speaks on behalf of another or others : mouth, spokesman, spokesperson, spokeswoman. *Informal:* mouthpiece. See SUBSTITUTE in Index.

special *adjective* Of, relating to, or intended for a distinctive thing or group : especial, individual, particular, specific. — See also **specific.**

specialty *noun* See **branch, forte.**

species *noun* See **kind**[2].

specific *adjective* Fixed and distinct from others : express, particular, set[1], special. See SPECIFIC in Index. — See also **definite, special.**

specifically *adverb* See **namely.**

specification *noun* See **provision.**

specify *verb* See **designate, name, stipulate.**

specimen *noun* See **example.**

specious *adjective* See **fallacious, false.**

speciousness *noun* See **fallacy.**

speck *noun* See **bit**[1], **point.**

speck *verb* See **speckle.**

speckle *verb* To mark with many small spots : bespeckle, besprinkle, dapple, dot, fleck, freckle, mottle, pepper, speck, sprinkle, stipple. See MARKS in Index.

spectacle *noun* See **display.**

spectacular *adjective* See **dramatic.**

spectator *noun* See **watcher.**

specter *noun* See **ghost.**

spectral *adjective* See **ghastly.**

speculate *verb* To formulate or assert as a tentative explanation : hypothesize, theorize. See BELIEF, THOUGHTS in Index. — See also **gamble, guess, think.**

speculation *noun* See **gamble, guess, theory, thought.**

speculative *adjective* See **theoretical, thoughtful.**

speculator *noun* One who speculates for quick profits : adventurer, gambler, operator. See GAMBLING, MONEY in Index. — See also **dealer.**

speech *noun* **1.** The faculty, act, or product of speaking : discourse, talk, utterance, verbalization, vocalization. See WORDS in Index. **2.** A usually formal oral communication to an audience : address, allocution, declamation, lecture, oration, prelection, talk. See WORDS in

Index. —See also **conversation, language.**

speechifier *noun* See **speaker.**

speechless *adjective* Temporarily unable or unwilling to speak, as from shock or fear : dumb, inarticulate, mum, mute, silent, voiceless, wordless. See WORDS in Index. —See also **dumb.**

speechlessness *noun* See **silence.**

speechmaker *noun* See **speaker.**

speed *noun* Rate of motion or performance : pace, tempo, velocity. *Informal:* clip[1]. See FAST in Index. —See also **haste.**

speed *verb* To increase the speed of. Also used with *up* : accelerate, expedite, hasten, hurry, hustle, quicken, step up. See FAST in Index. —See also **rush.**

speediness *noun* See **haste.**

speedy *adjective* See **fast, quick.**

spell[1] *verb* See **mean**[1].

spell out *verb* See **explain.**

spell[2] *verb* See **charm.**

spell *noun* An object or power that one uses to cause often evil events : charm, evil eye, magic. *Slang:* whammy. See SUPERNATURAL in Index.

spell[3] *noun* See **bit**[1], **seizure, turn.**

spell *verb* See **relieve.**

spellbind *verb* See **charm, grip.**

spend *verb* 1. To distribute (money) as payment : disburse, expend, give, lay out, outlay, pay (out). *Informal:* fork out (or over or up), shell out. See SAVE in Index. 2. To use time in a particular way : pass, put in. See TIME in Index. —See also **exhaust, go.**

spendthrift *adjective* See **extravagant.**

spendthrift *noun* See **wastrel.**

spent *adjective* See **exhausted.**

sperm *noun* See **seed.**

spew *verb* See **erupt.**

sphere *noun* See **range.**

spheric *adjective* See **round.**

spherical *adjective* See **round.**

spice *noun* See **flavoring.**

spick-and-span also **spic-and-span** *adjective* See **neat.**

spicy *adjective* See **pungent, racy.**

spiel *verb* See **chatter.**

spill *verb* See **betray, fall, sprawl.**

spill *noun* See **fall.**

spin *noun* See **drive.**

spin *verb* 1. To rotate rapidly : swirl, twirl, whirl. See REPETITION in Index. 2. To have the sensation of turning in circles : reel, swim, swirl, whirl. See REPETITION in Index. —See also **lengthen.**

spindling *adjective* See **gangling.**

spindly *adjective* See **gangling.**

spine *noun* See **prick.**

spinoff or **spin-off** *noun* See **derivative.**

spiny *adjective* See **thorny.**

spiral *verb* See **wind**[2].

spirit *noun* 1. The vital principle or animating force within living beings : breath, divine spark, élan vital, life force, psyche, soul, vital force, vitality. See BODY in Index. 2. A lively, emphatic, eager quality or manner : animation, bounce, brio, dash, élan, esprit, life, liveliness, pertness, sparkle, verve, vigor, vim, vivaciousness, vivacity, zip. *Informal:* ginger, pep, peppiness. *Slang:* oomph. See ACTION in Index. —See also **courage, ghost, heart, mood, soul, temper.**

spirit *verb* See **smuggle.**

spirit away *verb* See **kidnap.**

spirited *adjective* Full of or characterized by a lively, emphatic, eager quality : fiery, high-spirited, mettlesome, peppery, vibrant. *Informal:* snappy. See ACTION, FEELINGS in Index. —See also **lively.**

spiritless *adjective* See **depressed, dull, languid.**

spiritual *adjective* **1.** Of or concerned with the spirit rather than the body or material things : numinous, otherworldly, unworldly. See BODY in Index. **2.** Of or relating to a church or to an established religion : church, churchly, ecclesiastical, religious. See RELIGION in Index. — See also **immaterial.**

spirituous *adjective* See **hard.**

spite *noun* See **malevolence, vindictiveness.**

spiteful *adjective* See **malevolent, vindictive.**

spitefulness *noun* See **malevolence, vindictiveness.**

spitting image *noun* See **double.**

splash *verb* To hurl or scatter liquid upon : bespatter, dash, slop, slosh, spatter, splatter, spray, swash. See STRIKE in Index. — See also **wash.**

splashy *adjective* See **showy.**

splatter *verb* See **splash, spot.**

spleen *noun* See **temper.**

splendid *adjective* See **excellent, glorious, grand, marvelous.**

splendor *noun* See **glory.**

splendorous or **splendrous** *adjective* See **glorious.**

splinter *verb* See **break, secede.**

split *noun* See **allotment, breach, crack, cut, division.**

split *verb* See **crack, cut, divide, go, secede, separate, tear¹.**

splotch *noun* See **smear.**

splotch *verb* See **spot.**

splurgy *adjective* See **showy.**

splutter *verb* See **crackle.**

spoil *verb* See **baby, botch, decay, destroy, sack².**

spoil *noun* See **patronage, plunder.**

spoilage *noun* See **decay.**

spoken *adjective* See **oral, vocal.**

spokesman *noun* See **speaker.**

spokesperson *noun* See **speaker.**

spokeswoman *noun* See **speaker.**

spoliate *verb* See **sack².**

sponge *noun* See **drunkard, parasite.**

sponge *verb* See **freeload.**

spongy *adjective* See **soft.**

sponsor *noun* One who assumes financial responsibility for another : backer, guarantor, guaranty, surety, underwriter. *Informal:* angel. See LAW, SUPPORT in Index. — See also **patron.**

sponsor *verb* See **patronize.**

sponsorship *noun* See **patronage.**

spontaneity *noun* See **ease.**

spontaneous *adjective* Acting or happening without apparent forethought, prompting, or planning : automatic, impulsive, instinctive, involuntary, reflex, unpremeditated. See PLANNED in Index. — See also **easygoing, voluntary.**

spontaneously *adverb* See **voluntarily.**

spook *noun* See **ghost, spy.**

spooky *adjective* See **weird.**

spoon *verb* See **neck.**

spoor *noun* See **trail.**

sporadic *adjective* See **infrequent, intermittent.**

sporadically *adverb* See **infrequently, intermittently.**

spore *noun* See **seed.**

sport *noun* See **play.**

sport *verb* See **display, play.**

sporting *adjective* See **sportsmanlike.**

sportive *adjective* See **playful.**

sportiveness *noun* See **playfulness.**

sportsmanlike *adjective* According to the rules : clean, fair, sporting, sportsmanly. See FAIR in Index.

sportsmanly *adjective* See **sportsmanlike.**

spot *noun* See **bit¹, point, position, predicament, stain.**

spot *verb* To mark or soil with spots : bespatter, blotch, spatter, splatter, splotch. See MARKS in Index. — See also **catch, discern, find, position.**

spot *adjective* See **random.**

spotless *adjective* See **clean.**

spotty *adjective* See **uneven.**

spousal *adjective* See **marital.**

spousal *noun* See **wedding.**

spouse *noun* A husband or wife : consort, mate, partner. *Informal:* better half. See MARRIAGE in Index.

spouseless *adjective* See **single.**

spout *noun* See **spurt.**

spout *verb* See **spurt.**

sprain *verb* See **turn.**

sprawl *verb* **1.** To sit or lie with the limbs spread out awkwardly : drape, loll, spread-eagle, straddle. See POSTURE in Index. **2.** To grow or spread in a disorderly or planless fashion : spill, straggle. See ORDER in Index.

spray *noun* See **spurt.**

spray *verb* See **splash, spurt.**

spread *verb* **1.** To extend over a wide area : circulate, diffuse, disperse, disseminate, distribute, radiate, scatter, strew. See MOVE, WIDE in Index. **2.** To move or arrange so as to cover a larger area : expand, extend, fan[1] (out), open (out *or* up), outstretch, stretch, unfold, unroll. See MOVE in Index. — See also **advertise, communicate, cover, get around** at get, set[1].

spread *noun* See **expanse, expansion, feast.**

spread-eagle *verb* See **sprawl.**

spree *noun* See **bender, binge.**

sprig *noun* See **shoot.**

sprightliness *noun* See **energy.**

sprightly *adjective* See **energetic, vigorous.**

spring *verb* See **bounce, descend, free, jump, skip, stem.**

spring *noun* The season of the year during which the weather becomes warmer and plants revive : seedtime, springtide, springtime. See TIME in Index. — See also **birth, bounce, cause, flexibility, jump, origin, skip, youth.**

spring *adjective* Of, occurring in, or characteristic of the season of spring : vernal. See TIME in Index.

springiness *noun* See **flexibility.**

springtide *noun* See **spring.**

springtime *noun* See **spring.**

springy *adjective* See **flexible.**

sprinkle *verb* To scatter or release in drops or small particles : besprinkle, dust, powder. See STRIKE in Index. — See also **speckle.**

sprint *verb* See **run, rush.**

sprout *noun* See **shoot.**

spruce *verb* See **fix up** at fix, tidy.

spruce *adjective* See **neat.**

spry *adjective* See **nimble, vigorous.**

spume *noun* See **foam.**

spume *verb* See **foam.**

spumous *adjective* See **foamy.**

spumy *adjective* See **foamy.**

spunk *noun* See **courage.**

spunkiness *noun* See **courage.**

spunky *adjective* See **brave.**

spur *verb* See **provoke.**

spur *noun* See **stimulus.**

spurious *adjective* See **counterfeit, fallacious, false, illegitimate.**

spuriousness *noun* See **fallacy.**

spurn *verb* See **decline, snub.**

spurn *noun* See **snub.**

spur-of-the-moment *adjective* See **extemporaneous.**

spurt *noun* A sudden swift stream of ejected liquid : jet[2], spout, spray, squirt. See MOVE in Index.

spurt *verb* To eject or be ejected in a sudden thin, swift stream : jet[2], spout, spray, squirt. See MOVE in Index.

sputter *verb* See **crackle.**

spy *noun* A person who secretly observes others to obtain information : agent, operative. *Informal:* spook. *Idiom:* secret (or undercover) agent. See INVESTIGATE in Index.

spy *verb* To observe or listen in secret to obtain information : eavesdrop. See INVESTIGATE in Index. — See also **catch**.

squabble *noun* See **argument**.

squabble *verb* See **argue**.

squalid *adjective* See **filthy, sordid**.

squalor *noun* See **dirtiness**.

squander *verb* See **waste**.

squander *noun* See **extravagance**.

square *noun* *Slang.* An old-fashioned person who is reluctant to change or innovate : fogy, fossil, fuddy-duddy, mossback. *Informal:* stick-in-the-mud. See NEW in Index.

square *adjective* Having four equal sides and four right angles : quadrate. See GEOMETRY in Index. — See also **conventional, even[1], fair**.

square *verb* See **adapt, agree, equalize, settle**.

square *adverb* See **directly**.

squarely *adverb* See **directly**.

squash *verb* See **crush, suppress**.

squashy *adjective* See **soft**.

squat *verb* To sit on one's heels : hunker (down). See POSTURE in Index. — See also **crouch**.

squat *adjective* See **stocky**.

squawk *verb* See **object**.

squawk *noun* See **objection**.

squawky *adjective* See **harsh**.

squeal *verb* See **inform, yelp**.

squeal *noun* See **yelp**.

squealer *noun* See **informer**.

squeamish *adjective* See **nice**.

squeeze *verb* **1.** To subject to compression : compact[1], compress, constrict, constringe. See TIGHTEN in Index. **2.** To extract from by applying pressure : crush, express,

press. See TIGHTEN in Index. — See also **embrace, extort**.

squeeze *noun* See **constriction, embrace**.

squelch *verb* See **repress, suppress**.

squib *noun* See **item**.

squiggle *verb* See **wiggle**.

squinch *verb* See **squint**.

squint *verb* To peer with the eyes partly closed : squinch. *Idiom:* screw up one's eyes. See SEE in Index. — See also **tend[1]**.

squint *noun* The condition of not having the visual axes parallel : cross-eye, strabismus. See SEE in Index. — See also **bent**.

squint-eyed *adjective* See **squinty**.

squinty *adjective* Marked by or affected with a squint : cross-eyed, squint-eyed, strabismal, strabismic. See SEE in Index.

squirm *verb* See **wiggle, writhe**.

squirrel *verb* See **hoard**.

squirt *verb* See **spurt**.

squirt *noun* *Informal.* An insignificant but arrogant and obnoxious young person : pup, puppy. *Slang:* twerp. See YOUTH in Index. — See also **spurt**.

squishy *adjective* See **soft**.

stab *verb* See **ram**.

stab *noun* See **attempt, pain, prick, try**.

stabbing *adjective* See **sharp**.

stability *noun* Reliability in withstanding pressure, force, or stress : fastness, firmness, hardness, security, soundness, stableness, steadiness, strength, sturdiness, sureness. See BETTER, CHANGE, CONTINUE in Index. — See also **soundness**.

stabilize *verb* To make stable : steady. See CHANGE in Index. — See also **balance**.

stable *adjective* See **sound[2], steady, sure**.

stableness *noun* See **stability**.

stack *noun* See **heap.**
  stack *verb* See **heap.**
  stack up *verb* See **compare.**
stacked *adjective* See **shapely.**
staff *noun* See **stick.**
stage *noun* **1.** A temporary framework with a floor, used by workers : platform, scaffold, scaffolding. See MACHINE in Index. **2.** A raised platform on which theatrical performances are given : board (used in plural), proscenium. See PERFORMING ARTS in Index. — See also **acting, degree, period, scene.**
  stage *verb* To produce on the stage : act (out), do, dramatize, enact, give, perform, present², put on. See PERFORMING ARTS in Index. — See also **have.**
stagger *verb* To overwhelm with surprise, wonder, or bewilderment : boggle, bowl over, dumbfound, flabbergast, floor. See EXCITE, SURPRISE in Index. — See also **hesitate, lurch, muddle.**
staggering *adjective* Of such a character as to overwhelm : *Informal:* mind-blowing, mind-boggling. See BIG, EXCITE, SURPRISE in Index. — See also **towering.**
staginess *noun* See **theatricalism.**
stagnation *noun* See **inaction.**
staid *adjective* See **grave².**
staidness *noun* See **gravity.**
stain *verb* To soil with foreign matter : bestain, discolor, smut. See CLEAN, MARKS in Index. — See also **blacken, color, corrupt.**
  stain *noun* A mark of discredit or disgrace : black eye, blemish, blot, onus, spot, stigma, taint, tarnish. *Archaic:* attaint. *Idiom:* a blot on one's escutcheon. See MARKS, RESPECT in Index. — See also **color, smear.**
stainless *adjective* See **clean.**
stake *noun* See **bet, capital, interest.**

stake *verb* See **finance, gamble.**
stale *adjective* See **flat, trite.**
stalemate *noun* See **tie.**
stalk *verb* See **hunt, stride.**
stall¹ *verb* See **stop.**
stall² *verb* See **delay.**
stalwart *adjective* See **strong.**
stamina *noun* See **endurance.**
stammer *verb* To introduce involuntary repetitions and pauses into one's speech : stutter. See WORDS in Index.
  stammer *noun* A speech impediment marked by involuntary repetitions and pauses : stammering, stutter, stuttering. See WORDS in Index.
stammering *noun* See **stammer.**
stamp *noun* See **impression, kind², sign.**
  stamp *verb* See **engrave, tramp, trample.**
  stamp out *verb* See **annihilate.**
stamping ground *noun* See **haunt, home.**
stance *noun* See **posture.**
stand *verb* See **endure, get up** at **get, right, treat.**
  stand behind *verb* See **support.**
  stand by *verb* See **support.**
  stand for *verb* See **represent.**
  stand in *verb* See **substitute.**
  stand out *verb* See **bulge, glare.**
  stand up *verb* See **bear up** at **bear, wash.**
standard *noun* A means by which individuals are compared and judged : benchmark, criterion, gauge, mark, measure, test, touchstone, yardstick. See USUAL in Index. — See also **flag¹, model.**
  standard *adjective* See **authoritative, ordinary.**
standby *adjective* See **auxiliary.**
stand-in *noun* See **substitute.**
standing *noun* See **face, place.**
standoff *noun* See **tie.**

standoffish *adjective* See **cool.**

standout *adjective* See **rare.**

standpoint *noun* See **point of view.**

standstill *noun* See **stop.**

star *noun* See **lead.**

starch *noun* See **vigor.**

starch *verb* See **stiffen.**

starchy *adjective* See **stiff.**

star-crossed *adjective* See **unfortunate.**

stare *verb* See **gaze.**

stare *noun* See **gaze.**

stark *adjective* See **bleak.**

starkers *adjective* See **nude.**

starry-eyed *adjective* See **idealistic.**

start *verb* To go about the initial step in doing (something) : approach, begin, commence, embark, enter, get off, inaugurate, initiate, institute, launch, lead off, open, set about, set out, set to, take on, take up, undertake. *Informal:* kick off. *Idioms:* get cracking, get going, get the show on the road. See START in Index. — See also **begin, flinch, found, jump.**

start *noun* See **advantage, beginning, birth, jump.**

startle *verb* To cause to experience a sudden momentary shock : electrify, jolt, shock[1]. See EXCITE, SURPRISE in Index. — See also **frighten, surprise.**

startle *noun* See **jump.**

start-up or **startup** *noun* See **foundation.**

starving *adjective* See **ravenous.**

stash *verb* See **hide[1], hoard.**

stash *noun* See **hoard.**

stasis *noun* See **balance.**

state *noun* 1. An organized geopolitical unit : body politic, country, land, nation, polity. See POLITICS, TERRITORY in Index. 2. *Informal.* A condition of excited distress : fume. *Informal:* snit, sweat, swivet.

Slang: tizzy. See CALM in Index. — See also **condition.**

state *verb* To declare by way of a systematic statement : enounce, enunciate. See WORDS in Index. — See also **air, assert, say.**

stately *adjective* See **gracious, grand.**

statement *noun* See **account, assertion, expression, story, word.**

station *noun* An assigned position : post[2]. See PLACE in Index. — See also **base[1], place.**

station *verb* To appoint and send to a particular place : assign, post[2], set[1]. See PLACE in Index.

stationary *adjective* See **fixed, motionless.**

stature *noun* See **merit.**

status *noun* See **basis, condition, face, honor, place.**

statute *noun* See **law.**

staunch *adjective* See **faithful.**

stave *noun* See **stick.**

stave off *verb* See **prevent.**

stay[1] *verb* To remain as a guest or lodger : lodge, sojourn, visit. See PLACE in Index. — See also **defer[1], endure, pause, remain, stop.**

stay with *verb* See **keep.**

stay *noun* A remaining in a place as a guest or lodger : sojourn, visit. See PLACE in Index. — See also **delay, stop.**

stay[2] *noun* See **support.**

staying power *noun* See **endurance.**

stead *noun* See **place.**

steadfast *adjective* See **faithful, firm[1], fixed, steady.**

steadfastness *noun* See **fidelity.**

steadiness *noun* See **stability.**

steady *adjective* Consistently reliable, especially because of resistance to outside pressures : stable, steadfast, steady-going. See CONTINUE in

Index. — See also **even**[1], **firm**[1], **fixed**, **sure**.

steady *verb* See **balance, stabilize**.
steady-going *adjective* See **steady**.
steal *verb* To take (another's property) without permission : filch, pilfer, purloin, snatch, thieve. *Informal:* lift, swipe. *Slang:* cop, heist, hook, nip[1], pinch, rip off, snitch. *Idiom:* make (or walk) off with. See CRIMES, GIVE in Index. — See also **sneak**.
steal *noun* See **bargain, larceny**.
stealer *noun* See **larcenist**.
stealth *noun* The act of proceeding slowly, deliberately, and secretly to escape observation : furtiveness, slinkiness, sneakiness, stealthiness. See MOVE in Index.
stealthiness *noun* See **stealth**.
stealthy *adjective* So slow, deliberate, and secret as to escape observation : catlike, feline, furtive, slinky, sneaking, sneaky. See MOVE in Index.
steam *noun* See **energy**.
steam *verb* See **anger**.
steamroller *verb* See **overwhelm**.
steel *verb* See **gird**.
steep[1] *adjective* 1. So sharply inclined as to be almost perpendicular : abrupt, bold, precipitous, sheer[2]. See HORIZONTAL in Index. 2. Vastly exceeding a normal limit, as in cost : sky-high, stiff, stratospheric, unconscionable. See BIG, USUAL in Index.
steep[2] *verb* To saturate (something) with a liquid : soak. *Chemistry:* infuse. See DRY in Index.
steer *verb* See **conduct, guide, maneuver**.
steer *noun* See **tip**[3].
stem *verb* To have as a source : arise, come, derive, emanate, flow, issue, originate, proceed, rise, spring, upspring. See START in Index.

stem *noun* See **theme**.
stentorian *adjective* See **loud**.
step *verb* See **dance, walk**.
step down *verb* See **retire**.
step up *verb* See **speed**.
step *noun* See **degree, move, tread**.
step-by-step *adjective* See **gradual**.
stereotype *noun* See **cliché**.
stereotyped *adjective* See **trite**.
stereotypic *adjective* See **trite**.
stereotypical *adjective* See **trite**.
sterile *adjective* 1. Free or freed from microorganisms : sanitized, sterilized. See CLEAN in Index. 2. Lacking originality : uncreative, unimaginative, uninspired, uninventive, unoriginal. See RICH in Index. — See also **barren, dull**.
sterileness *noun* See **dullness**.
sterility *noun* 1. The state or condition of being unable to reproduce sexually : barrenness, infertility, sterilization. See REPRODUCTION, RICH in Index. 2. The state or condition of being free from microorganisms : sterilization. See CLEAN in Index. — See also **dullness**.
sterilization *noun* The act or an instance of making one incapable of reproducing sexually : castration. See REPRODUCTION, RICH in Index. — See also **sterility**.
sterilize *verb* 1. To render incapable of reproducing sexually : alter, castrate, fix, geld, neuter, spay, unsex. See REPRODUCTION, RICH in Index. 2. To render free of microorganisms : decontaminate, disinfect, sanitize. See CLEAN in Index.
sterilized *adjective* See **sterile**.
stern *adjective* See **severe**.
sternness *noun* See **severity**.
stew *verb* See **boil, brood**.
stew *noun* See **agitation**.
stewed *adjective* See **drunk**.

stick *noun* **1.** A fairly long straight piece of solid material used especially as a support in walking : cane, staff, stave, walking stick. See MACHINE in Index. **2.** A relatively long, straight, rigid piece of metal or other solid material : bar, bloom², rod, shaft, slab. See THING in Index.

stick *verb* See **bond, catch, cheat, impose, nonplus, ram, set¹.**

stick around *verb* See **remain.**

stick out *verb* See **bulge, glare.**

stick up *verb* See **rob.**

stick-in-the-mud *noun* See **square.**

stickup *noun* See **robbery.**

sticky *adjective* **1.** Having the property of adhering : adhesive, gluey, gooey, gummy, tacky¹. See CLEAN, KEEP in Index. **2.** Damp and warm : humid, muggy, soggy, sultry. See DRY, HOT in Index. — See also **tight.**

stiff *adjective* So rigidly constrained, formal, or awkward as to lack all grace and spontaneity : buckram, starchy, stilted, wooden. See FLEXIBLE in Index. — See also **firm¹, rigid, steep¹, strong, taut.**

stiff *noun* See **body, drunkard, miser.**

stiffen *verb* To make stiff or stiffer : starch. See FLEXIBLE in Index. — See also **tense.**

stiff-necked *adjective* See **obstinate.**

stifle *verb* See **censor, choke, muffle, repress.**

stifling *adjective* See **airless.**

stigma *noun* A mark on the skin indicative of a disease, as typhus : petechia. See MARKS in Index. — See also **stain.**

stigmatize *verb* To mark with disgrace or infamy : brand. *Idiom:* give someone a bad name. See MARKS, RESPECT in Index.

still *adverb* In spite of a preceding event or consideration : all the same, however, nevertheless, nonetheless, yet. *Informal:* still and all. *Idiom:* be that as it may. See AFFIRM in Index. — See also **additionally, even¹.**

still *adjective* Motionless and undisturbed : calm, halcyon, peaceful, placid, quiet, serene, stilly, tranquil, untroubled. See CALM in Index. — See also **airless, motionless, silent.**

still *verb* See **calm, silence.**

still *noun* See **silence.**

still and all *adverb* See **still.**

stillness *noun* An absence of motion or disturbance : calm, calmness, hush, lull, peace, peacefulness, placidity, placidness, quiet, quietness, serenity, tranquillity, untroubledness. See CALM in Index. — See also **silence.**

stilly *adjective* See **silent, still.**

stilted *adjective* See **stiff.**

stimulant *noun* See **stimulus.**

stimulate *verb* See **energize, provoke.**

stimulating *adjective* Serving to enliven : animating, enlivening, quickening, rousing, vitalizing, vivifying. See EXCITE in Index. — See also **tonic.**

stimulation *noun* See **encouragement, stimulus.**

stimulator *noun* See **stimulus.**

stimulus *noun* **1.** Something that causes and encourages a given response : encouragement, fillip, impetus, impulse, incentive, inducement, motivation, prod, push, spur, stimulant, stimulation, stimulator. See CAUSE in Index. **2.** Something that incites especially a violent response : goad, incitation, incitement, instigation, provocation, trigger. See CAUSE in Index.

sting *noun* See **edge, kick, pain.**

sting *verb* To feel or cause to feel a sensation of heat or discomfort :

bite, burn, smart. See PAIN in Index.
— See also **cheat, irritate.**

stinging *adjective* See **biting.**

stingy *adjective* Ungenerously or
pettily reluctant to spend money :
cheap, close, close-fisted, costive,
hard-fisted, mean[2], miserly, niggard,
niggardly, parsimonious, penny-
pinching, penurious, petty, pinching,
tight, tightfisted. See GIVE in Index.
— See also **meager.**

stink *verb* See **smell.**

stinking *adjective* See **drunk, smelly.**

stinko *adjective* See **drunk.**

stint *verb* See **scrimp.**

   stint *noun* See **task, turn.**

stipend *noun* See **wage.**

stipple *verb* See **speckle.**

stipulate *verb* To make specific :
detail, particularize, specify. See SPE-
CIFIC in Index.

stipulation *noun* See **provision.**

stir[1] *verb* **1.** To impart slight movement to : budge, move. See MOVE
in Index. **2.** To make a slight movement : budge, move. See MOVE in
Index. — See also **arouse, cause, fire,
mix, wake**[1]**.**

   stir *noun* Agitated, excited movement and activity : bustle, flurry,
whirl, whirlpool. See CALM in Index.
— See also **disturbance, motion,
sensation.**

stir[2] *noun* See **jail.**

stirring *adjective* See **affecting.**

stitch *noun* See **pain.**

stock *adjective* See **ordinary.**

   stock *verb* See **carry.**

   stock *noun* See **ancestry, family,
hoard.**

stockpile *verb* To accumulate and
set aside for future use : lay in, lay
up, save (up), store (up). See KEEP in
Index. — See also **hoard.**

   stockpile *noun* See **hoard.**

stock-still *adjective* See **motionless.**

stocky *adjective* Short, heavy, and
solidly built : blocky, chunky,
compact[1], dumpy, heavyset, squat,
stodgy, stubby, stumpy, thick, thickset. See FAT in Index.

stodginess *noun* See **dullness.**

stodgy *adjective* See **dull, stocky,
thick.**

stoked *adjective* See **thrilled.**

stole *noun* See **wrap.**

stolid *adjective* See **apathetic.**

stolidity *noun* See **apathy.**

stolidness *noun* See **apathy.**

stomach *noun* See **appetite.**

   stomach *verb* See **endure.**

stomp *verb* See **tramp, trample.**

stoned *adjective* See **drugged,
drunk.**

stonyhearted *adjective* See **cold-
blooded.**

stooge *noun* See **pawn**[2]**.**

stool *verb* See **inform.**

stoolie *noun* See **informer.**

stool pigeon *noun* See **informer.**

stoop *verb* To incline the body :
arch, bend, bow[1], hump, hunch,
scrunch. See POSTURE in Index.
— See also **condescend, descend.**

stop *verb* **1.** To prevent the occurrence or continuation of a move-
ment, action, or operation : arrest,
belay, cease, check, discontinue,
halt[1], stall[1], stay[1], surcease. *Idioms:*
bring to a standstill, call a halt to,
put a stop to. See CONTINUE in
Index. **2.** To come to a cessation :
arrest, belay, cease, check, discontinue, halt[1], leave off, quit, stall[1],
surcease. *Idiom:* come to a halt (*or*
standstill *or* stop). See CONTINUE in
Index. — See also **abandon, break,
fill, tie up at tie, visit.**

   stop *noun* **1.** The act of stopping :
cessation, check, cut-off, halt[1], stay[1],
stoppage, surcease. See CONTINUE
in Index. **2.** The condition of being

stopped : cessation, discontinuance, discontinuation, halt[1], standstill, stoppage, surcease. See CONTINUE in Index. — See also **bar, end, plug.**

stopgap *noun* See **makeshift.**

stoppage *noun* See **stop, tie-up.**

stopper *noun* See **plug.**

stopping point *noun* See **end.**

store *noun* A retail establishment where merchandise is sold : boutique, emporium, outlet, shop. See TRANSACTIONS in Index. — See also **depository, hoard.**

store *verb* See **keep, stockpile.**

storehouse *noun* See **depository.**

storm *verb* See **attack.**

storm *noun* See **barrage.**

stormy *adjective* See **rough, turbulent.**

story *noun* A recounting of past events : account, chronicle, description, history, narration, narrative, report, statement, version. See WORDS in Index. — See also **fiction, item, lie[2], plot, yarn.**

story line *noun* See **plot.**

storyteller *noun* See **liar.**

stout *adjective* See **brave, bulky, fat, strong.**

stouthearted *adjective* See **brave.**

stoutheartedness *noun* See **courage.**

strabismal *adjective* See **squinty.**

strabismic *adjective* See **squinty.**

strabismus *noun* See **squint.**

straddle *verb* See **sprawl, stride.**

straggle *verb* See **sprawl.**

straggler *noun* See **laggard.**

straight *adjective* Not diluted or mixed with other substances : full-strength, neat, plain, pure, unblended, undiluted, unmixed. See CLEAN, STRONG in Index. — See also **conventional, direct, even[1], frank.**

straight *adverb* See **directly.**

straightaway *adverb* See **directly.**

straighten *verb* See **even[1], tidy.**

straighten out *verb* See **settle.**

straightforward *adjective* See **direct, frank.**

straight-from-the-shoulder *adjective* See **frank.**

straight off *adverb* See **directly.**

straight-out *adjective* See **frank.**

straight-shooting *adjective* See **frank, honest.**

strain[1] *verb* See **labor.**

strain *noun* See **effort, pressure.**

strain[2] *noun* See **melody, streak.**

strained *adjective* See **forced.**

strait-laced *adjective* See **genteel.**

strand *noun* See **thread.**

strange *adjective* See **eccentric, foreign, funny.**

stranger *noun* See **foreigner.**

strangle *verb* See **choke, repress.**

strapped *adjective* See **poor.**

strapping *adjective* See **lusty.**

stratagem *noun* See **tactic, trick.**

strategize *verb* See **design.**

strategy *noun* See **design.**

stratospheric *adjective* See **steep[1].**

straw boss *noun* See **boss.**

stray *verb* See **deviate, digress, rove.**

stray *adjective* Unable to find the correct way or place to go : astray, disoriented, lost. See SEEK in Index. — See also **erratic.**

streak *noun* An intermixture of a contrasting or unexpected quality, especially in a person's character : strain[2], vein. See BE in Index. — See also **series, shade.**

streak *verb* To mark with a line or band, as of different color or texture : striate, stripe, variegate. See MARKS in Index.

stream *noun* See **flow.**

stream *verb* See **flow.**

streamer *noun* See **flag[1].**

streamlined *adjective* See **sleek.**

street *noun* See **way.**

streetwalker *noun* See **prostitute**.

strength *noun* The state or quality of being physically strong : brawn, might, muscle, potence, potency, power, powerfulness, puissance, sinew, thew (often used in plural). See STRONG in Index. — See also **energy, force, soundness, stability**.

strengthen *verb* See **confirm, gird, tighten, toughen**.

strenuous *adjective* See **energetic, rough**.

strenuously *adverb* See **hard**.

stress *noun* See **emphasis, pressure**.

stress *verb* See **emphasize**.

stretch *verb* See **extend, lengthen, lie¹, reach, rest¹, spread**.

stretch *noun* See **distance, expanse, extent, period, term, time, turn**.

stretch *adjective* See **extensible**.

stretchable *adjective* See **extensible**.

strew *verb* See **spread**.

striate *verb* See **streak**.

strict *adjective* Conforming completely to established rule : exact, rigorous, uncompromising. See USUAL in Index. — See also **close, severe**.

strictness *noun* See **severity**.

stricture *noun* See **constriction, restriction**.

stride *verb* 1. To walk with long steps, especially in a vigorous manner : march¹, stalk. See MOVE in Index. 2. To sit or stand with a leg on each side of : bestride, straddle. See POSTURE in Index.

strident *adjective* See **harsh, vociferous**.

strife *noun* See **competition, conflict**.

strike *verb* To cease working in support of demands made upon an employer : walk out. *Idiom:* go on strike. See CONTINUE in Index. — See also **affect¹, afflict, attack,**

cancel, hit, occur, ring², seize, snap.

strike back *verb* See **retaliate**.

strike down *verb* See **drop**.

strike out *verb* See **bear**.

strike *noun* See **attack, discovery**.

striking *adjective* See **noticeable**.

string *noun* See **line, provision, series**.

string *verb* See **thread**.

string up *verb* See **hang**.

stringency *noun* See **severity**.

strip¹ *verb* To remove all the clothing from : disrobe, unclothe, undress. See PUT ON, SHOW in Index. — See also **bare, deprive, sack², skin**.

strip² *noun* See **band¹**.

stripe *noun* See **band¹, kind²**.

stripe *verb* See **streak**.

strive *verb* See **attempt, labor**.

striving *noun* See **competition, effort**.

stroll *verb* To walk at a leisurely pace : amble, meander, perambulate, promenade, ramble, saunter, wander. *Informal:* mosey. See MOVE in Index.

stroll *noun* See **walk**.

strong *adjective* 1. Having great physical strength : mighty, potent, powerful, puissant. See STRONG in Index. 2. Capable of exerting considerable effort or of withstanding considerable stress or hardship : hardy, stalwart, stout, sturdy, tough. See STRONG in Index. 3. Having a high concentration of the distinguishing ingredient : concentrated, potent, stiff. See STRONG in Index. — See also **deep, forceful, hard, high, sound², sure**.

strong-arm *verb* See **coerce, intimidate**.

strong-arm *adjective* See **forcible**.

strongman *noun* See **dictator**.

strong point *noun* See **forte**.

strong suit noun See **forte.**
structure noun See **building.**
  structure verb See **form.**
struggle verb See **contend.**
  struggle noun See **competition, conflict, effort.**
strumpet noun See **prostitute.**
strut verb To walk with exaggerated or unnatural motions expressive of self-importance or self-display : flounce, peacock, prance, swagger, swank, swash. *Informal:* sashay. See MOVE, SELF-LOVE in Index.
stub noun See **end.**
stubborn adjective **1.** Firmly, often unreasonably immovable in purpose or will : adamant, adamantine, brassbound, die-hard, grim, implacable, incompliant, inexorable, inflexible, intransigent, iron, obdurate, relentless, remorseless, rigid, unbendable, unbending, uncompliant, uncompromising, unrelenting, unyielding. *Idiom:* stubborn as a mule (*or* ox). See RESIST in Index. **2.** Difficult to alleviate or cure : obstinate, persistent, pertinacious. See CONTINUE in Index.
stubbornness noun The quality or state of being stubbornly inflexible : die-hardism, grimness, implacability, implacableness, incompliance, incompliancy, inexorability, inexorableness, inflexibility, inflexibleness, intransigence, intransigency, obduracy, obdurateness, relentlessness, remorselessness, rigidity, rigidness. See RESIST in Index.
stubby adjective See **stocky.**
stuck-up adjective See **egotistic, snobbish.**
stud noun See **beauty.**
student noun One who is being educated : learner, pupil, scholar. See TEACH in Index.
studied adjective See **advised.**

studious adjective Devoted to study or reading : bookish, scholarly. See TEACH in Index. — See also **advised, diligent.**
study noun See **advisement, examination, practice, trance.**
  study verb To apply one's mind to the acquisition or production of knowledge : con, lucubrate. See TEACH in Index. — See also **examine, ponder.**
stuff noun See **effect, heart, material, timber.**
  stuff verb See **crowd.**
stuffy adjective See **airless, boring, genteel.**
stumble verb To catch the foot against something and lose one's balance : trip. *Idioms:* lose one's footing, make a false step. See MOVE in Index. — See also **blunder, err, lurch, muddle.**
  stumble on or **upon** verb See **come across** at **come.**
  stumble noun See **blunder.**
stump verb See **frustrate, lump[1], nonplus.**
stumpy adjective See **stocky.**
stun verb See **daze, paralyze.**
stunner noun See **beauty, marvel.**
stunning adjective See **beautiful.**
stunt noun See **feat, trick.**
stupefaction noun See **daze.**
stupefy verb See **daze, dull, paralyze.**
stupendous adjective See **fabulous, giant.**
stupendousness noun See **enormousness.**
stupid adjective Lacking in intelligence : blockheaded, dense, doltish, dumb, hebetudinous, obtuse, thickheaded, thick-witted. *Informal:* thick. *Slang:* dimwitted, dopey. See ABILITY in Index. — See also **lethargic.**
stupor noun See **daze, lethargy.**

stuporous *adjective* See **dull, lethargic.**

sturdiness *noun* See **stability.**

sturdy *adjective* See **lusty, muscular, sound[2], strong.**

Sturm und Drang *noun* See **unrest.**

stutter *verb* See **stammer.**

stutter *noun* See **stammer.**

stuttering *noun* See **stammer.**

style *noun* A distinctive way of expressing oneself : fashion, manner, mode, tone, vein. See STYLE in Index. — See also **bearing, fashion, name, way.**

style *verb* See **call, name.**

stylish *adjective* See **fashionable.**

stylize *verb* See **conventionalize.**

stymie *verb* See **frustrate.**

suave *adjective* Effortlessly gracious and tactful in social manner : bland, smooth, urbane. See STYLE in Index.

sub *noun* See **substitute.**

sub *verb* See **substitute.**

subaltern *noun* See **subordinate.**

subaltern *adjective* See **minor.**

subdivide *verb* See **branch.**

subdivision *noun* See **branch, division.**

subdue *verb* See **defeat, moderate.**

subdued *adjective* See **quiet, soft.**

subject *adjective* See **dependent, liable, subordinate.**

subject *noun* What a speech, piece of writing, or artistic work is about : argument, matter, point, subject matter, text, theme, topic. See MEANING in Index. — See also **area, citizen.**

subject *verb* See **enslave, expose.**

subjective *adjective* See **arbitrary.**

subject matter *noun* See **subject.**

subjoin *verb* See **attach.**

subjugate *verb* See **defeat, enslave.**

sublime *adjective* See **grand.**

submerge *verb* See **dip, flood, obscure, sink.**

submerse *verb* See **dip, sink.**

submission *noun* See **obedience, proposal, surrender.**

submissive *adjective* See **obedient, passive.**

submissiveness *noun* See **obedience.**

submit *verb* To commit to the consideration or judgment of another : turn in. See GIVE in Index. — See also **defer[2], propose, succumb.**

subordinate *noun* One belonging to a lower class or rank : inferior, junior, secondary, subaltern, underling. See OVER in Index.

subordinate *adjective* In a position of subordination : collateral, dependent, subject, subservient. See OVER, PART in Index. — See also **minor.**

sub rosa *adverb* See **secretly.**

sub-rosa *adjective* See **secret.**

subscribe *verb* See **assent, contribute, sign.**

subscription *noun* See **donation.**

subsequent *adjective* See **consecutive, future, later.**

subsequently *adverb* See **later.**

subservient *adjective* See **servile, subordinate.**

subside *verb* To become or cause to become less active or intense : abate, bate, die (away, down, off, or out), ease (off or up), ebb, fall, fall off, lapse, let up, moderate, remit, slacken, slack off, wane. See INCREASE in Index.

subsidence *noun* See **wane.**

subsidiary *noun* A local unit of a business or an auxiliary controlled by such a business : affiliate, branch, division. See PART in Index.

subsidiary *adjective* See **auxiliary.**

subsidization *noun* See **capital.**

subsidize *verb* See **finance.**

subsidy *noun* See **grant.**

subsist *verb* See **be, exist, live[1].**

subsistence *noun* See **living**.

substance *noun* See **essence, heart, import, material, matter, thrust**.

substandard *adjective* See **inferior**.

substantial *adjective* See **generous, important, physical, real, sound²**.

substantiate *verb* See **back, confirm, embody, prove**.

substantiation *noun* See **confirmation, embodiment**.

substantive *adjective* See **real**.

substitute *noun* One that takes the place of another : alternate, replacement, stand-in, surrogate. *Informal:* fill-in, pinch hitter, sub. See **SUBSTITUTE** in Index.

substitute *verb* To act as a substitute : fill in, stand in, supply. *Informal:* pinch-hit, sub. See **SUBSTITUTE** in Index. — See also **change**.

substitution *noun* See **change**.

substratum *noun* See **base¹**.

subsume *verb* See **contain**.

subterfuge *noun* See **trick**.

subterranean *adjective* See **underground**.

subterrestrial *adjective* See **underground**.

subtle *adjective* See **delicate, fine¹**.

subtract *verb* See **deduct**.

suburb *noun* See **skirt**.

subvention *noun* See **grant**.

subversion *noun* See **sabotage**.

subvert *verb* See **overthrow, sabotage**.

succeed *verb* **1.** To turn out well : come off, go, go over, pan out, work, work out. *Slang:* click. See **THRIVE** in Index. **2.** To gain success : arrive, get ahead, get on, go far, rise. *Idioms:* go places, make good, make it. See **THRIVE** in Index. — See also **follow**.

success *noun* The achievement of something desired, planned, or attempted : arrival, successfulness. See **THRIVE** in Index.

successfulness *noun* See **success**.

succession *noun* See **order, series**.

successional *adjective* See **consecutive**.

successive *adjective* See **consecutive**.

succinct *adjective* See **brief**.

succor *verb* See **help**.

succor *noun* See **help**.

succorer *noun* See **helper**.

succumb *verb* To give in from or as if from a gradual loss of strength : bow¹, buckle, capitulate, submit, surrender, yield. *Informal:* fold. See **RESIST** in Index. — See also **collapse, die**.

suck *verb* See **involve**.

suck up *verb* See **fawn**.

sucker *noun* See **dupe**.

sudden *adjective* See **abrupt**.

suddenly *adverb* See **short**.

sudoriferous *adjective* See **sweaty**.

suds *noun* See **foam**.

suds *verb* See **foam**.

sudsy *adjective* See **foamy**.

sue *verb* To institute or subject to legal proceedings : law, litigate, prosecute. *Idiom:* bring suit. See **LAW** in Index. — See also **address, appeal, petition**.

suet *noun* See **fat**.

suffer *verb* See **endure, experience, grieve, permit**.

sufferable *adjective* See **bearable**.

suffering *noun* See **misery**.

suffering *adjective* See **miserable**.

suffice *verb* See **serve**.

sufficiency *noun* See **enough**.

sufficient *adjective* Being what is needed without being in excess : adequate, comfortable, competent, decent, enough, satisfactory. See **EXCESS** in Index. — See also **acceptable**.

suffocate *verb* See **choke**.

suffrage *noun* See **voice**.

suffuse *verb* See **charge**.

sugar *verb* See **sweeten.**

sugarcoat *verb* See **color, sweeten.**

sugary *adjective* See **insinuating, sweet.**

suggest *verb* See **hint, imply, propose, smack².**

suggestible *adjective* See **flexible.**

suggestion *noun* Something, such as a feeling, thought, or idea, associated in one's mind or imagination with a specific person or thing : association, connection, connotation. See SUGGEST in Index. — See also **hint, proposal, shade.**

suggestive *adjective* Tending to bring a memory, mood, or image, for example, subtly or indirectly to mind : allusive, connotative, evocative, impressionistic, reminiscent. See SUGGEST in Index. — See also **insinuating, pregnant, racy, sensual.**

suggestiveness *noun* See **sensuality.**

suit *noun* See **courtship, lawsuit.**

suit *verb* To be appropriate or suitable to : become, befit, behoove. *Archaic:* beseem. See AGREE in Index. — See also **adapt, fit¹, flatter, please, serve.**

suitability *noun* See **qualification.**

suitable *adjective* See **convenient, eligible, just.**

suitableness *noun* See **qualification.**

suite *noun* See **retinue, series.**

suitor *noun* See **appealer, beau, supplicant.**

sulk *verb* To be sullenly aloof or withdrawn, as in silent resentment or protest : mope, pet², pout. See HAPPY in Index.

sulky *adjective* See **glum.**

sullen *adjective* See **dark, glum.**

sully *verb* See **blacken, dirty.**

sultry *adjective* See **hot, sticky.**

sum *verb* See **add.**

sum up *verb* See **review.**

sum *noun* See **summary, system, total, whole.**

summarize *verb* See **review.**

summary *noun* A condensation of the essential or main points of something : recapitulation, rundown, run-through, sum, summation, summing-up, wrap-up. *Informal:* recap. See WORDS in Index.

summary *adjective* See **brief.**

summation *noun* See **addition, summary, total.**

summer *noun* The season occurring between spring and autumn : summertime. See TIME in Index.

summertime *noun* See **summer.**

summing-up *noun* See **summary.**

summit *noun* See **climax, height.**

summon *verb* See **assemble, call, evoke.**

sumptuous *adjective* See **luxurious.**

sumptuousness *noun* See **glitter.**

sum total *noun* See **total.**

sunder *verb* See **break.**

sundries *noun* See **odds and ends.**

sundry *adjective* See **several, various.**

sunken *adjective* See **hollow.**

sunny *adjective* See **cheerful, clear.**

sunrise *noun* See **dawn.**

sunup *noun* See **dawn.**

sup *verb* See **drink.**

sup *noun* See **drink.**

super *adjective* See **marvelous.**

super *adverb* See **unduly.**

superabundance *noun* See **excess.**

superabundant *adjective* See **profuse.**

superannuate *verb* See **obsolesce, retire.**

superb *adjective* See **excellent, grand, marvelous.**

superbness *noun* See **excellence.**

supercilious *adjective* See **arrogant.**

superciliousness *noun* See **arrogance.**

supererogative *adjective* See
wanton.

supererogatory *adjective* See
superfluous, wanton.

superficial *adjective* Lacking in
intellectual depth or thoroughness :
cursory, one-dimensional, shallow,
sketchy, skin-deep, uncritical.
See SURFACE in Index. — See also
apparent.

superficially *adverb* See apparently.

superfluity *noun* See excess,
surplus.

superfluous *adjective* Being more
than is needed, desired, or appropriate : de trop, excess, extra, spare,
supererogatory, supernumerary, surplus. See EXCESS in Index.

superfluousness *noun* See excess.

superhighway *noun* See way.

superhuman *adjective* See
supernatural.

superintend *verb* See administer,
supervise.

superintendence *noun* See administration, care.

superintendent *noun* See boss.

superior *adjective* See arrogant,
better, choice, excellent, higher.

superior *noun* One who stands
above another in rank : better,
elder, senior. *Informal:* higher-up.
See OVER in Index.

superiority *noun* See advantage,
arrogance, excellence.

superlative *adjective* See best.

supernatural *adjective* Of, coming from, or relating to forces or beings that exist outside the natural
world : extramundane, extrasensory, metaphysical, miraculous, preternatural, superhuman, superphysical, supersensible, transcendental,
unearthly. See SUPERNATURAL in
Index. — See also preternatural.

supernumerary *adjective* See
superfluous.

superphysical *adjective* See
supernatural.

superscribe *verb* See address.

supersede *verb* See replace.

superseded *adjective* See obsolete.

supersensible *adjective* See
supernatural.

supervene *verb* See follow.

supervenient *adjective* See
incidental.

supervise *verb* To direct and watch
over the work and performance of
others : boss, overlook, oversee,
superintend, watch over. See OVER
in Index. — See also administer.

supervision *noun* See administration, care.

supervisor *noun* See boss.

supervisory *adjective* See administrative.

supplant *verb* To take the place of
(another) against the other's will :
cut out, displace. See SUBSTITUTE
in Index. — See also replace.

supple *adjective* See adaptable,
flexible, malleable, obedient.

supplement *noun* See attachment,
complement.

supplement *verb* See complement.

supplemental *adjective* See auxiliary, complementary.

supplementary *adjective* See
auxiliary.

suppleness *noun* See flexibility.

suppliant *noun* See supplicant.

supplicant *noun* One who humbly
entreats : beggar, prayer[2], suitor,
suppliant. See REQUEST in Index.

supplicate *verb* See appeal, pray.

supplication *noun* See appeal,
prayer[1].

supply *verb* See give, substitute.

support *verb* **1.** To aid the cause of
by approving or favoring : advo-

cate, back, champion, endorse, get
behind, plump for, recommend, side
with, stand behind, stand by, uphold.
Idioms: align oneself with, go to bat
for, take the part of. See SUPPORT in
Index. **2.** To sustain the weight of :
bear, carry, hold, uphold. See SUP-
PORT in Index. **3.** To supply with
the necessities of life : keep, maintain, provide for. *Idiom:* take care of.
See CARE FOR in Index. — See also
bear, endure, patronize, sustain.

support *noun* A means or device
that keeps something erect, stable,
or secure : brace, buttress, crutch,
prop, shore, stay[2], underpinning. See
SUPPORT in Index. — See also
endorsement, help, living.

supporter *noun* See **follower,
patron.**

supportive *adjective* See **auxiliary.**

suppose *verb* To take for granted
without proof : assume, posit, postulate, premise, presume, presuppose. *Informal:* reckon. See BELIEF
in Index. — See also **guess, repute,
require.**

supposed *adjective* Presumed to be
true, real, or genuine, especially on
inconclusive grounds : conjectural,
hypothetic, hypothetical, inferential,
presumptive, suppositional, suppositious, supposititious, suppositive.
See BELIEF in Index. — See also
reputed.

supposition *noun* See **assumption,
guess.**

suppositional *adjective* See
supposed.

suppositious *adjective* See **counterfeit, supposed.**

supposititious *adjective* See **counterfeit, supposed.**

suppositive *adjective* See
supposed.

suppress *verb* To bring to an end
forcibly as if by imposing a heavy

weight : choke off, crush, extinguish, put down, quash, quell,
quench, squash, squelch. *Idiom:* put
the lid on. See CONTINUE, WIN in
Index. — See also **censor, repress.**

suppression *noun* Sudden punitive
action : clampdown, crackdown,
repression. See CONTINUE, WIN in
Index.

suppressive *adjective* See
repressive.

supremacy *noun* See **dominance.**

supreme *adjective* See **ideal, ruling,
ultimate.**

surcease *verb* See **stop.**

surcease *noun* See **stop.**

sure *adjective* **1.** Having no doubt :
assured, certain, confident, positive,
undoubting. See CERTAIN in Index.
2. Such as could not possibly fail
or disappoint : certain, infallible, secure, unerring, unfailing.
Informal: sure-fire. See CERTAIN in
Index. **3.** Firmly settled or positioned : fast, firm[1], secure, stable,
steady, strong. See CONTINUE in
Index. — See also **certain, definite,
sound[2].**

sure-fire *adjective* See **sure.**

sureness *noun* The fact or condition
of being without doubt : assurance,
assuredness, certainty, certitude,
confidence, conviction, positiveness,
surety. See CERTAIN in Index. — See
also **stability.**

sure thing *noun* See **certainty.**

surety *noun* See **guarantee, sponsor, sureness.**

surface *noun* See **face.**

surfeit *noun* See **excess, satiation.**

surfeit *verb* See **satiate.**

surge *verb* See **flow.**

surge *noun* See **flow.**

surly *adjective* See **glum, ill-
tempered.**

surmise *verb* See **guess.**

surmise *noun* See **guess.**

surmount *verb* See **clear, defeat.**

surpass *verb* To be greater or better than : best, better, exceed, excel, outdo, outmatch, outrun, outshine, outstrip, pass, top, transcend. *Informal:* beat. *Idioms:* go beyond, go one better. See BIG in Index.
— See also **exceed.**

surplus *noun* An amount or quantity beyond what is needed, desired, or appropriate : excess, fat, glut, overage, overflow, overmuch, overrun, overstock, oversupply, superfluity, surplusage. See EXCESS in Index.

surplus *adjective* See **superfluous.**

surplusage *noun* See **surplus.**

surprise *verb* To impress strongly by what is unexpected or unusual : amaze, astonish, astound, awe, startle. *Idioms:* catch (or take) unawares, take aback. See SURPRISE in Index.
— See also **ambush, take.**

surrender *verb* To undergo capture, defeat, or ruin : collapse, fall, go down, go under, topple. See RESIST, WIN in Index. — See also **abdicate, give over** at **give, relinquish, succumb.**

surrender *noun* The act of submitting or surrendering to the power of another : capitulation, submission. See RESIST, WIN in Index.
— See also **abdication, delivery.**

surreptitious *adjective* See **sly.**

surrogate *noun* See **substitute.**

surrogate *verb* See **replace.**

surround *verb* To shut in on all sides : begird, beset, circle, compass, encircle, encompass, environ, gird, girdle, hedge, hem, ring[1]. See OPEN in Index.

surroundings *noun* See **environment.**

surveillance *noun* See **lookout.**

survey *verb* To view broadly or from a height : look over, overlook, scan.

See SEE in Index. — See also **examine, watch.**

survey *noun* A general or comprehensive view or treatment : overview. See THOUGHTS in Index.
— See also **analysis.**

survive *verb* To exist in spite of adversity : come through, last[2], persist, pull through, ride out, weather. See LIVE in Index. — See also **outlast.**

susceptibility *noun* See **exposure.**

susceptible *adjective* See **easy, liable, sensitive.**

susceptibleness *noun* See **exposure.**

susceptive *adjective* See **liable, sensitive.**

suspect *verb* See **distrust.**

suspect *adjective* See **shady.**

suspend *verb* To stop suddenly, as a conversation, activity, or relationship : break off, cease, discontinue, interrupt, terminate. See CONTINUE in Index. — See also **defer[1], hang.**

suspension *noun* See **abeyance, break, delay.**

suspicion *noun* See **distrust, doubt, feeling, hint, shade.**

suspicious *adjective* See **distrustful, shady.**

sustain *verb* To keep from yielding or failing during stress or difficulty : bolster, buoy (up), prop, support, uphold. See HELP in Index. — See also **bear, endure, maintain.**

sustenance *noun* See **food, living.**

susurration *noun* See **murmur.**

susurrus *noun* See **murmur.**

swaddle *verb* See **wrap.**

swagger *verb* See **strut.**

swain *noun* See **beau.**

swallow *verb* To cause to pass from the mouth into the stomach : ingest, take. See MOUTH in Index.
— See also **believe, consume, endure.**

swallow *noun* An act of swallowing : gulp, ingestion. See MOUTH in Index.

swamp *noun* A usually low-lying area of soft waterlogged ground and standing water : bog, fen, marsh, marshland, mire, morass, muskeg, quag, quagmire, slough[1], swampland, wetland. See DRY in Index.

swamp *verb* See **flood.**

swampland *noun* See **swamp.**

swank *verb* See **strut.**

swank *adjective* See **exclusive, fashionable.**

swanky *adjective* See **exclusive, fashionable.**

swap also **swop** *verb* See **change.**

swap also **swop** *noun* See **change.**

swarm *verb* See **pour, teem.**

swarm *noun* See **crowd.**

swarthy *adjective* See **dark.**

swash *verb* See **splash, strut, wash.**

swat *noun* See **blow[2], slap.**

swat *verb* See **hit, slap.**

swathe *verb* See **wrap.**

sway *verb* To move back and forth or from side to side, as if about to fall : teeter, totter, vacillate, waver, weave, wobble. See REPETITION in Index. — See also **dispose, govern, swing.**

sway *noun* See **authority, domination, influence.**

swear *verb* To use profane or obscene language : blaspheme, curse, damn. *Informal:* cuss. See DECENT, SACRED, WORDS in Index. — See also **pledge, testify.**

swear off *verb* See **abandon.**

swearword *noun* A profane or obscene term : blasphemy, curse, epithet, expletive, oath. *Informal:* cuss. See DECENT, SACRED, WORDS in Index.

sweat *verb* To excrete moisture through the pores of the skin : lather, perspire. See DRY in Index. — See also **labor.**

sweat out *verb* See **endure.**

sweat *noun* Moisture excreted through the pores of the skin : lather, perspiration. See DRY in Index. — See also **labor, state.**

sweating *adjective* See **sweaty.**

sweaty *adjective* Producing or covered with sweat : perspiring, sudoriferous, sweating. See DRY in Index.

sweep *noun* See **expanse, range.**

sweep *verb* See **flourish.**

sweeping *adjective* See **general.**

sweet *adjective* Having or suggesting the taste of sugar : saccharine, sugary. See TASTE in Index. — See also **adorable, attractive.**

sweet *noun* See **darling.**

sweeten *verb* To make superficially more acceptable or appealing : candy, gild, honey, sugar, sugarcoat. See LIKE in Index. — See also **pacify.**

sweetheart *noun* See **darling.**

sweetie *noun* See **darling.**

sweet-talk *verb* See **coax, flatter.**

swell *verb* See **increase.**

swell *adjective* See **excellent, marvelous.**

swell *noun* See **increase.**

swelled head *noun* See **egotism.**

swellhead *noun* See **egotist.**

swellheaded *adjective* See **egotistic.**

swelling *noun* See **bump.**

swelter *verb* See **burn.**

sweltering *adjective* See **hot.**

swerve *verb* To turn aside sharply from a straight course : chop[2], cut, sheer[1], skew, slue, veer. *Nautical:* yaw. See CHANGE in Index. — See also **deviate.**

swift *adjective* See **fast, quick.**

swiftness *noun* See **haste.**

swig *verb* See **drink.**

swig *noun* See **drink.**

swill *verb* See **gulp.**

swill *noun* See **drink**.

swim *noun* See **plunge**.

swim *verb* See **spin**.

swindle *verb* See **cheat**.

swindle *noun* See **cheat**.

swindler *noun* See **cheat**.

swing *verb* **1.** To move rhythmically back and forth suspended or as if suspended from above : oscillate, sway. See MOVE, REPETITION in Index. **2.** To turn or cause to turn in place, as on a hinge or fixed point, tracing an arclike path : pivot, wheel. See MOVE in Index. **3.** To change one's attitudes or policies, for example : vacillate, waver. See CHANGE, DECIDE in Index. — See also **effect, hang, turn**.

swing *noun* See **range, rhythm**.

swipe *verb* See **steal**.

swirl *verb* To move or cause to move like a rapid rotary current of liquid : eddy, whirl. See MOVE, REPETITION in Index. — See also **spin**.

swish *verb* See **hiss**.

swish *adjective* See **fashionable**.

switch *verb* See **change, wag¹**.

switch *noun* See **change**.

swivel *verb* See **traverse**.

swivet *noun* See **state**.

swollen *adjective* See **sonorous**.

swoon *verb* See **black out** at **black**.

swoon *noun* See **blackout**.

swoop *noun* See **plunge**.

sword of Damocles *noun* See **threat**.

sybarite *also* **Sybarite** *noun* A person devoted to pleasure and luxury : epicure, epicurean, hedonist, sensualist, voluptuary. See PAIN in Index.

sybaritic *adjective* Characterized by or devoted to pleasure and luxury as a lifestyle : epicurean, hedonic, hedonistic, voluptuary, voluptuous. See PAIN in Index.

sycophant *noun* One who flatters another excessively : adulator, courtier, flatterer, toady. *Informal:* apple-polisher. See OVER, PRAISE in Index.

syllabus *noun* See **program**.

symbol *noun* An object associated with and serving to identify something else : attribute, emblem. See SUBSTITUTE in Index. — See also **character**.

symbol *verb* See **represent**.

symbolic *adjective* Serving as a symbol : emblematic, emblematical, representative, symbolical. See SUBSTITUTE in Index.

symbolical *adjective* See **symbolic**.

symbolize *verb* See **represent**.

symmetric *adjective* See **symmetrical**.

symmetrical *adjective*

1. Characterized by or displaying symmetry, especially correspondence in scale or measure : balanced, proportional, proportionate, regular, symmetric. See SAME in Index. **2.** Having components pleasingly combined : balanced, congruous, harmonious. See BEAUTIFUL in Index.

symmetry *noun* See **proportion**.

sympathetic *adjective* See **pitying, understanding**.

sympathize *verb* To understand or be sensitive to another's feelings or ideas : empathize. See UNDERSTAND in Index. — See also **feel, identify**.

sympathy *noun* A very close understanding between persons : empathy. See CONNECT, LOVE, UNDERSTAND in Index. — See also **pity**.

symphonic *adjective* See **harmonious**.

symphonious *adjective* See **harmonious**.

symphony *noun* See **harmony**.

symptom *noun* See **sign**.

synchronic *adjective* See **contemporary.**

synchronize *verb* See **coincide.**

synchronous *adjective* See **contemporary.**

synchronously *adverb* See **together.**

syncope *noun* See **blackout.**

syndicate *noun* See **combine.**

synergetic *adjective* See **cooperative.**

synergic *adjective* See **cooperative.**

synergistic *adjective* See **cooperative.**

synergy *noun* See **cooperation.**

synopsis *noun* A short summary or version prepared by cutting down a larger work : abridgment, abstract, brief, condensation, epitome. See WORDS in Index.

synopsize *verb* See **review.**

synthesize *verb* See **harmonize.**

synthetic *adjective* See **artificial, plastic.**

system *noun* An organized array of individual elements and parts forming and working as a unit : entity, integral, sum, totality, whole. See PART in Index. — See also **complex, method, way.**

systematic *adjective* See **methodical.**

systematical *adjective* See **methodical.**

systematization *noun* See **method.**

systematize *verb* See **arrange, methodize.**

systemization *noun* See **method.**

systemize *verb* See **methodize.**

T

tab *noun* See **account, cost.**

tabby *noun* See **gossip.**

table *noun* An orderly columnar display of data : chart, tabulation. See KNOWLEDGE in Index.

table *verb* See **defer¹.**

taboo also **tabu** *noun* See **forbiddance.**

taboo also **tabu** *adjective* See **forbidden.**

taboo also **tabu** *verb* See **forbid.**

tabulation *noun* See **table.**

tacit *adjective* See **implicit, silent.**

taciturn *adjective* Not speaking freely or openly : close, close-mouthed, incommunicable, incommunicative, reserved, reticent, silent, tightlipped, uncommunicable, uncommunicative. See RESTRAINT, SOUNDS in Index.

taciturnity *noun* See **reserve.**

tack *noun* See **approach, turn.**

tackle *noun* See **outfit.**

tackle *verb* See **assume, attack.**

tacky¹ *adjective* See **sticky.**

tacky² *adjective* **1.** *Informal.* Lacking style and good taste : inelegant, tasteless, unbecoming. See STYLE in Index. **2.** *Informal.* Quite outmoded or unfashionable : dowdy, frumpish. See NEW in Index. — See also **gaudy, shabby.**

tact *noun* The ability to say and do the right thing at the right time : address, diplomacy, savoir-faire, tactfulness. See ABILITY, COURTESY in Index.

tactful *adjective* See **delicate.**

tactfulness *noun* See **tact.**

tactic *noun* A method of deploying troops and equipment in combat : maneuver, stratagem. See MEANS in Index. — See also **move.**

tactical *adjective* Designed or implemented so as to gain a temporary limited advantage : short-range. See NEAR in Index.

tactile *adjective* Of, relating to, or arising from the sense of touch : tactual. See TOUCH in Index. — See also **tangible**.

tactility *noun* See **tangibility, touch**.

tactless *adjective* Lacking sensitivity and skill in dealing with others : brash, clumsy, gauche, impolitic, indelicate, maladroit, undiplomatic, unpolitic, untactful. See ABILITY, COURTESY in Index.

tactual *adjective* See **tactile**.

tag *verb* See **call, dog, mark, ticket**.

tag *noun* See **name, ticket**.

tag end *noun* See **tail**.

tail *noun* **1.** The hindmost part of something : end, rear[1], tag end, tail end. See PRECEDE in Index. **2.** *Informal.* An agent assigned to observe and report on another : shadow, watcher. See INVESTIGATE in Index. — See also **train**.

tail *verb* See **follow**.

tail away or **off** *verb* See **decrease**.

tail end *noun* See **tail**.

tailor *verb* See **adapt**.

tailor-made *adjective* See **appropriate, convenient, custom**.

taint *verb* To make morally impure : contaminate, corrupt, defile, infect, pollute, soil. See CLEAN in Index. — See also **blacken, decay**.

taint *noun* See **stain**.

taintlessness *noun* See **purity**.

take *verb* **1.** To go aboard (a means of transport) : board, catch. See USED in Index. **2.** To gain possession of, especially after a struggle or chase : capture, catch, get, net[1], secure. *Informal:* bag. *Slang:* nail. See GET in Index. **3.** To come upon,

especially suddenly or unexpectedly : catch, hit on (or upon), surprise. *Informal:* hit. See SURPRISE in Index. **4.** To engage in sexual relations with : bed, copulate, couple, have, mate, sleep with. *Idioms:* go to bed with, make love, make whoopee, roll in the hay. See SEX in Index.
— See also **accept, assume, attract, bring, capture, cheat, contract, deduct, demand, derive, endure, interpret, receive, remove, seize, swallow, understand, work**.

take after *verb* See **favor**.

take away *verb* See **remove**.

take back *verb* See **resume, retract, return**.

take down *verb* To take (something) apart : break down, disassemble, dismantle, dismount. See ASSEMBLE in Index. — See also **lower**[2].

take in *verb* See **accept, contain, deceive, understand**.

take off *verb* To rise up in flight : lift (off). See RISE in Index. — See also **go, remove**.

take on *verb* See **adopt, assume, employ, engage, fuss, start**.

take out *verb* See **remove, see**.

take over *verb* See **assume, occupy, relieve**.

take to *verb* See **like**[1].

take up *verb* See **absorb, adopt, continue, deal with** at **deal, drink, elevate, start**.

take *noun* The amount of money collected as admission, especially to a sporting event : box office, gate. See MONEY in Index. — See also **attempt**.

take-in *noun* See **trick**.

takeoff *noun* **1.** The act of rising in flight : liftoff. See RISE in Index. **2.** *Informal.* A usually amusing caricature of another : imitation, parody. See LAUGHTER, RESPECT, SAME in Index.

taking adjective See **attractive, communicable.**

tale noun See **count, lie², total, yarn.**

talebearer noun See **gossip.**

talebearing adjective See **gossipy.**

talebearing noun See **gossip.**

talent noun An innate capability : aptitude, aptness, bent, faculty, flair, genius, gift, head, instinct, knack, turn. See ABILITY, APPROACH in Index.

talented adjective See **gifted.**

taleteller noun See **gossip.**

taletelling adjective See **gossipy.**

talisman noun See **charm.**

talismanic adjective See **magic.**

talk verb See **address, confer, converse¹, gossip, inform, say, speak.**

talk back verb To utter an impertinent rejoinder : talk up. Informal: sass, sauce. Idiom: give someone lip. See RESIST, WORDS in Index.

talk down verb See **belittle.**

talk into verb See **persuade.**

talk over verb See **discuss.**

talk up verb See **advertise, promote, talk back** at **talk.**

talk noun The act or process of dealing with another to reach an agreement. Often used in plural : negotiation, parley. See WORDS in Index. — See also **conversation, speech.**

talkative adjective Given to conversation : chatty, conversational, garrulous, loquacious, talky, voluble. Slang: gabby. See WORDS in Index.

talker noun See **conversationalist.**

talky adjective See **talkative.**

tall adjective Extending to a great height : high. See HIGH in Index. — See also **difficult, high.**

tall tale noun See **lie², yarn.**

tall talk noun See **exaggeration.**

tally verb See **agree, count, score.**

tally noun See **count, score.**

tame adjective See **domestic, gentle.**

tame verb See **domesticate, gentle, moderate.**

tamper verb To handle something idly, ignorantly, or destructively : fiddle, fool, meddle, mess, tinker. Informal: monkey. See HELP, TOUCH in Index. — See also **fix.**

tang noun See **flavor.**

tangent noun See **digression.**

tangential adjective See **digressive.**

tangibility noun The quality or condition of being discernible by touch : palpability, tactility, tangibleness, touchableness. See TOUCH in Index.

tangible adjective Discernible by touch : palpable, tactile, touchable. See TOUCH in Index. — See also **physical, real.**

tangibleness noun See **tangibility.**

tangle noun Something that is intricately and often bewilderingly complex : cat's cradle, entanglement, jungle, knot, labyrinth, maze, mesh (often used in plural), morass, skein, snarl², web. See SIMPLE in Index. — See also **argument.**

tangle verb See **argue, catch, complicate, entangle.**

tangled adjective See **complex.**

tangy adjective See **sour.**

tank up verb See **drink.**

tantalize verb To excite (another) by exposing something desirable while keeping it out of reach : bait, tease. See EXCITE in Index.

tantamount adjective See **equal.**

tantrum noun See **temper.**

tap¹ verb To make a noise by striking : knock, rap¹. See SOUNDS in Index. — See also **appoint.**

tap noun The sound made by a light blow : knock, rap¹. See SOUNDS in Index.

tap² *verb* To monitor (telephone calls) with a concealed listening device connected to the circuit : bug, wiretap. See INVESTIGATE in Index. — See also **drain**.

taper *verb* See **decrease**.
   taper *noun* See **decrease**.

tar *noun* See **sailor**.

tardily *adverb* See **late**.

tardiness *noun* See **lateness**.

tardy *adjective* See **late, slow**.

target *noun* One that is fired at, attacked, or abused : butt³, mark. See SEEK in Index. — See also **intention**.
   target *verb* To make a target of : mark. *Idiom:* draw (or get) a bead on. See SEEK in Index. — See also **intend**.

tariff *noun* See **tax**.

tarnish *verb* See **blacken, injure**.
   tarnish *noun* See **stain**.

tarrier *noun* See **laggard**.

tarry *verb* See **delay, pause, remain**.

tart¹ *adjective* See **sour**.

tart² *noun* See **prostitute, slut**.

tartuffe also **tartufe** *noun* See **hypocrite**.

tartuffery *noun* See **hypocrisy**.

task *noun* **1.** A piece of work that has been assigned : assignment, chore, duty, job, office, stint. See WORK in Index. **2.** A difficult or tedious undertaking : chore, effort. *Informal:* job. See HEAVY, WORK in Index. — See also **function**.
   task *verb* See **work**.

taskmaster *noun* See **boss**.

taskmistress *noun* See **boss**.

taste *verb* See **experience, feel, smack²**.
   taste *noun* **1.** A limited or anticipatory experience : foretaste, sample. See FORESIGHT in Index. **2.** A liking for something : appetite, fondness, partiality, preference, relish, weakness. See LIKE in Index. **3.** The faculty or sense of discerning what is aesthetically pleasing or appropriate : tastefulness. See STYLE in Index. — See also **appetite, flavor, shade**.

tasteful *adjective* Showing good taste : artistic, tasty. *Informal:* aesthetic. See STYLE in Index. — See also **delicious, quiet**.

tastefulness *noun* See **taste**.

tasteless *adjective* See **coarse, flat, tacky²**.

tasty *adjective* See **delicious, tasteful**.

tatter *noun* Torn and ragged clothing. Used in plural : rag¹ (used in plural). See BETTER, PUT ON in Index.

tatterdemalion *noun* A person wearing ragged or tattered clothing : ragamuffin, scarecrow. See BETTER, RICH in Index.
   tatterdemalion *adjective* See **tattered**.

tattered *adjective* Torn into or marked by shreds or tatters : ragged, raggedy, tatterdemalion. See BETTER in Index. — See also **shabby**.

tattle *verb* See **gossip, inform**.
   tattle *noun* See **gossip**.

tattler *noun* See **gossip, informer**.

tattletale *noun* See **gossip, informer**.

tatty *adjective* See **shabby**.

taunt *verb* See **bait**.
   taunt *noun* An instance of mockery or derision : gibe, insult, jeer, scoff, twit. See LAUGHTER, RESPECT in Index. — See also **ribbing**.

taut *adjective* Stretched tightly : stiff, tense, tight. See TIGHTEN in Index. — See also **neat**.

tauten *verb* See **tense**.

tautological *adjective* Characterized by repetition and excessive wordiness : circumlocutionary, roundabout. See REPETITION, WORDS in Index.

tawdry *adjective* See **gaudy.**

tax *noun* A compulsory contribution, usually of money, that is required for the support of a government : assessment, duty, impost, levy, tariff. See MONEY, PAY, POLITICS in Index. — See also **burden**[1].

   tax *verb* See **accuse, call down** at **call, charge, work.**

taxing *adjective* See **burdensome.**

teach *verb* See **educate.**

teachable *adjective* See **educable.**

teacher *noun* See **educator.**

teaching *noun* See **doctrine, education.**

team *noun* See **force.**

teamwork *noun* See **cooperation.**

tear[1] *verb* To separate or pull apart by force : rend, rip, rive, run, split. See ASSEMBLE, HELP in Index. — See also **pull, rush.**

   tear down *verb* See **destroy, libel.**

   tear *noun* A hole made by tearing : rent[2], rip, run. See HELP in Index. — See also **bender.**

tear[2] *noun* A drop of the clear liquid secreted by the glands of the eyes : teardrop. See DRY in Index. — See also **cry.**

   tear *verb* To fill with tears : water. See DRY in Index.

teardrop *noun* See **tear**[2].

tearful *adjective* Filled with or shedding tears : lachrymose, teary, weeping, weepy. *Idiom:* in tears. See HAPPY in Index.

tear-jerking *adjective* See **sentimental.**

teary *adjective* See **tearful.**

tease *verb* See **annoy, tantalize.**

technicality *noun* See **detail.**

technique *noun* See **ability, approach.**

tedious *adjective* See **boring.**

teem *verb* To be abundantly filled or richly supplied : abound, bristle, crawl, flow, overflow, pullulate, swarm. See BIG, RICH in Index.

teen *noun* See **teenager.**

teenager *noun* A young person, usually between the ages of 13 and 19 : adolescent, teen, youth. *Informal:* teener. See YOUTH in Index.

teener *noun* See **teenager.**

teensy *adjective* See **tiny.**

teensy-weensy *adjective* See **tiny.**

teeny *adjective* See **tiny.**

teeny-weeny *adjective* See **tiny.**

teeter *verb* See **lurch, sway.**

teetotalism *noun* See **temperance.**

telephone *verb* To communicate with (someone) by telephone : buzz, call, ring[2]. *Informal:* dial, phone. *Idioms:* get someone on the horn, give someone a buzz (or call or ring). See WORDS in Index.

tell *verb* See **betray, command, communicate, count, describe, distinguish, inform, say.**

   tell off *verb* See **bawl out** at **bawl.**

telling *adjective* See **convincing.**

telltale *noun* See **gossip.**

tellurian *adjective* See **earthly.**

telluric *adjective* See **earthly.**

temerarious *adjective* See **rash**[1].

temerariousness *noun* See **temerity.**

temblor *noun* See **tremor.**

temerity *noun* Foolhardy boldness or disregard of danger : brashness, foolhardiness, incautiousness, rashness, recklessness, temerariousness. See CAREFUL in Index.

temper *noun* 1. A tendency to become angry or irritable : irascibility, irascibleness, spleen, temperament, tetchiness. *Informal:* dander. *Slang:* short fuse. *Idiom:* low boiling point. See FEELINGS in Index. 2. An angry outburst : fit[2], huff, passion,

tantrum. *Informal:* conniption, conniption fit. See FEELINGS in Index.
3. A prevailing quality, as of thought, behavior, or attitude : climate, mood, spirit, tone. See ATTITUDE in Index. — See also **disposition, mood.**

temper *verb* See **moderate.**

temperament *noun* See **disposition, temper.**

temperamental *adjective* See **capricious, moody.**

temperance *noun* The practice of refraining from use of alcoholic liquors : abstinence, dryness, soberness, sobriety, teetotalism. See DRUGS, RESTRAINT, USED in Index. — See also **moderation.**

temperate *adjective* Exercising moderation and self-restraint in appetites and behavior : abstemious, continent, sober. See RESTRAINT in Index. — See also **conservative, mild, moderate.**

tempestuous *adjective* See **rough, turbulent.**

tempo *noun* See **speed.**

temporal *adjective* See **earthly, profane, transitory.**

temporary *adjective* **1.** Intended, used, or present for a limited time : impermanent, interim, provisional, short-range, short-term. See CONTINUE in Index. **2.** Temporarily assuming the duties of another : acting, ad interim, interim, pro tem, provisional. See CONTINUE, SUBSTITUTE in Index. — See also **transitory.**

tempt *verb* See **court, seduce.**

temptation *noun* See **lure.**

tempter *noun* See **seducer.**

tempting *adjective* See **attractive, seductive.**

temptress *noun* See **seductress.**

tenable *adjective* Capable of being defended against armed attack : defendable, defensible. See ATTACK in Index. — See also **justifiable.**

tenacious *adjective* See **obstinate, tight.**

tenaciousness *noun* See **obstinacy.**

tenacity *noun* See **obstinacy.**

tend[1] *verb* To have a tendency or inclination : incline, lean[1], slant, squint, trend. See LIKELY in Index.

tend[2] *verb* To have the care and supervision of : attend, care for, look after, mind, minister to, see to, watch. *Idioms:* keep an eye on, look out for, take care (or charge) of, take under one's wing. See CARE FOR in Index. — See also **till.**

tendency *noun* See **bent, thrust.**

tendentious *adjective* See **biased.**

tendentiousness *noun* See **bias.**

tender[1] *adjective* See **gentle.**

tender[2] *noun* See **offer.**

tender *verb* See **offer.**

tenderfoot *noun* See **beginner.**

tenderhearted *adjective* See **gentle.**

tendril *noun* See **shoot.**

tenebrific *adjective* See **gloomy.**

tenet *noun* See **doctrine.**

tenor *noun* See **import, thrust.**

tense *verb* To make or become tense : stiffen, tauten, tighten. See TIGHTEN in Index.

tense *adjective* See **edgy, taut.**

tension *noun* See **pressure.**

ten-strike *noun* See **hit.**

tentative *adjective* See **conditional, hesitant, rough.**

tentativeness *noun* See **hesitation.**

tenuous *adjective* Having little substance or significance; not solidly based : feeble, flimsy, insubstantial, unsubstantial. See STRONG in Index.

tenure *noun* The holding of something, such as a position : incumbency, occupancy, occupation. See PLACE in Index.

tepid *adjective* Lacking warmth, interest, enthusiasm, or involvement : halfhearted, lukewarm, unenthusiastic. See ATTITUDE, HOT in Index.

tergiversate *verb* See **defect, equivocate.**

tergiversation *noun* See **ambiguity, defection, equivocation.**

tergiversator *noun* See **defector.**

term *noun* 1. A limited or specific period of time during which something happens, lasts, or extends : duration, span, stretch, time. See TIME in Index. 2. A sound or combination of sounds that symbolizes and communicates a meaning : expression, locution, word. See WORDS in Index. — See also **basis, life, period, provision.**

term *verb* See **call, name.**

termagant *noun* See **scold.**

terminal *adjective* See **last**[1].

terminate *verb* See **close, dismiss, quit, suspend.**

termination *noun* See **dismissal, end.**

terminology *noun* See **language.**

terminus *noun* See **end.**

terpsichorean *noun* See **dancer.**

terrain *noun* The character, natural features, and configuration of land : topography. *Idiom:* the lay of the land. See SURFACE in Index. — See also **area, territory.**

terrene *adjective* See **earthly.**

terrestrial *adjective* See **earthly, earthly.**

terrible *adjective* Very bad : appalling, awful, dreadful, fearful, frightful, ghastly, horrendous, horrible, shocking. See GOOD in Index. — See also **fearful, intense.**

terrific *adjective* See **excellent, horrible, marvelous.**

terrify *verb* See **frighten.**

territorial *adjective* Relating to or restricted to a particular territory :

regional, sectional. See TERRITORY in Index.

territory *noun* A particular area used for or associated with a specific individual or activity : country, district, region, terrain. *Slang:* turf. See TERRITORY in Index. — See also **area, possession.**

terror *noun* See **fear.**

terrorize *verb* See **frighten.**

terse *adjective* See **brief.**

test *noun* 1. A set of questions or exercises designed to determine knowledge or skill : catechism, catechization, exam, examination, quiz. See INVESTIGATE in Index. 2. An operation employed to resolve an uncertainty : experiment, experimentation, trial. See INVESTIGATE in Index. 3. A procedure that ascertains effectiveness, value, proper function, or other quality : assay, essay, proof, trial, tryout. See INVESTIGATE in Index. — See also **standard.**

test *verb* 1. To subject to a test of knowledge or skill : check, examine, quiz. See INVESTIGATE in Index. 2. To subject to a procedure that ascertains effectiveness, value, proper function, or other quality : assay, check, essay, examine, prove, try, try out. *Idioms:* bring to the test, make trial of, put to the proof (or test). See INVESTIGATE in Index. 3. To engage in experiments : experiment. See INVESTIGATE in Index.

test *adjective* See **pilot.**

testament *noun* See **confirmation.**

testifier *noun* See **witness.**

testify *verb* To give evidence or testimony under oath : attest, swear, witness. *Law:* depone, depose. *Idioms:* bear witness, take the stand. See LAW in Index. — See also **certify, confirm, indicate.**

testimonial *noun* A formal token of appreciation and admiration for a person's high achievements : salute, salvo, tribute. See PRAISE in Index. — See also **confirmation, reference.**

testimony *noun* A formal declaration of truth or fact given under oath : witness. *Law:* deposition. See LAW in Index. — See also **confirmation.**

testy *adjective* Easily annoyed : choleric, irascible, peppery, quick-tempered, tetchy, touchy. See FEELINGS in Index. — See also **ill-tempered.**

tetchiness or **techiness** *noun* See **temper.**

tetchy also **techy** *adjective* See **testy.**

text *noun* See **subject.**

texture *noun* A distinctive, complex underlying pattern or structure : contexture, fabric, fiber, warp and woof, web. See BE in Index. — See also **essence.**

thalassic *adjective* See **marine.**

thankful *adjective* See **grateful.**

thankfulness *noun* See **appreciation.**

thankless *adjective* 1. Not showing or feeling gratitude : unappreciative, ungrateful, unthankful, unthanking. See GRATEFUL in Index. 2. Not apt to be appreciated : unappreciated, ungrateful, unthankful. See GRATEFUL in Index.

thanks *noun* See **appreciation, grace.**

thanksgiving *noun* See **grace.**

thaumaturgic *adjective* See **magic.**

thaumaturgical *adjective* See **magic.**

thaumaturgy *noun* See **magic.**

thaw *verb* See **melt.**

theatric *adjective* See **dramatic.**

theatrical *adjective* See **dramatic.**

theatrical *noun* See **theatrics.**

theatricalism *noun* Showy mannerisms and behavior : exhibitionism, staginess, theatricality, theatricalness. See PLAIN, STYLE in Index.

theatricality *noun* See **theatricalism.**

theatricalness *noun* See **theatricalism.**

theatrics *noun* Overemotional exaggerated behavior calculated for effect : dramatics, histrionics, melodramatics, theatrical (used in plural). See FEELINGS, STYLE in Index.

theft *noun* See **larceny.**

thematic *adjective* Of, constituting, or relating to a theme or themes : topical. See MEANING in Index.

theme *noun* The main part of a word to which affixes are attached : base[1], root[1], stem. See WORDS in Index. — See also **composition, subject.**

theorem *noun* See **law.**

theoretic *adjective* See **theoretical.**

theoretical *adjective* 1. Concerned primarily with theories rather than practical matters : abstract, academic, speculative, theoretic. See THOUGHTS in Index. 2. Existing only in concept and not in reality : abstract, hypothetic, hypothetical, ideal, theoretic, transcendent, transcendental. See REAL in Index.

theorize *verb* See **speculate.**

theory *noun* 1. A belief used as the basis for action : hypothesis. See BELIEF, THOUGHTS in Index. 2. Abstract reasoning : conjecture, speculation. See BELIEF, THOUGHTS in Index. — See also **assumption.**

therapeutic *adjective* See **curative.**

therapy *noun* See **treatment.**

thesis *noun* 1. A thorough, written presentation of an original point of view : dissertation. See WORDS in Index. 2. A hypothetical controver-

sial proposition : contention, contestation. See OPINION in Index.
— See also **assumption**.
thespian *noun* See **actor**.
   thespian *adjective* See **dramatic**.
theurgic *adjective* See **magic**.
theurgical *adjective* See **magic**.
theurgy *noun* See **magic**.
thew *noun* See **strength**.
thick *adjective* **1.** Relatively great in extent from one surface to the opposite : fat. See THICK in Index.
2. Having all parts near to each other : close, compact[1], crowded, dense, packed, tight. See TIGHTEN in Index. **3.** Having a dense or viscous consistency : gelatinous, heavy, stodgy. See SOLID in Index.
4. Growing profusely : dense, heavy, lush[1], luxuriant, profuse, rank[2]. See BIG in Index. — See also **familiar, stocky, stupid**.
   thick *noun* The most intensely active central part : eye, midst. See EDGE in Index.
thicken *verb* To make thick or thicker, especially through evaporation or condensation : condense, inspissate. See SOLID in Index.
thickhead *noun* See **dullard**.
thickheaded *adjective* See **stupid**.
thickness *noun* The quality, condition, or degree of being thick : compactness, density, solidity. See THICK in Index.
thickset *adjective* See **stocky**.
thick-witted *adjective* See **stupid**.
thief *noun* See **larcenist**.
thieve *verb* See **steal**.
thievery *noun* See **larceny**.
thievish *adjective* See **larcenous**.
thin *adjective* **1.** Having little flesh or fat on the body : angular, bony, fleshless, gaunt, lank, lanky, lean[2], meager, rawboned, scrawny, skinny, slender, slim, spare, twiggy, weedy. *Idioms:* all skin and bones, thin as a

rail. See FAT in Index. **2.** Marked by great diffusion of component particles : rare, rarefied. See TIGHTEN in Index. — See also **dilute, implausible, meager**.
   thin *verb* **1.** To make physically thin or thinner : slim. *Archaic:* extenuate. See FAT, INCREASE in Index. **2.** To become diffuse : attenuate, rarefy. See TIGHTEN in Index. — See also **dilute**.
thing *noun* **1.** One that exists independently : being, entity, existence, existent, individual, object, something. See BE, THING in Index. **2.** *Informal.* An irrational preoccupation : fetish, fixation, mania, obsession. See CONCERN in Index. — See also **act, circumstance, effect, event, fashion, forte, gadget, matter, object, outfit**.
think *verb* To use the powers of the mind, as in conceiving ideas, drawing inferences, and making judgments : cerebrate, cogitate, deliberate, ratiocinate, reflect, speculate. *Idioms:* put on one's thinking cap, use one's head. See THOUGHTS in Index. — See also **believe, feel, imagine, ponder, remember, repute**.
   think about *verb* See **remember**.
   think of *verb* See **hear of** at **hear, remember**.
   think out *verb* See **ponder**.
   think over *verb* See **ponder**.
   think through *verb* See **ponder**.
   think up *verb* See **invent**.
thinkable *adjective* See **earthly**.
thinker *noun* A person who seeks reason and truth by thinking and meditation : philosopher. See THOUGHTS in Index. — See also **mind**.
thinking *adjective* See **thoughtful**.
third estate *noun* See **commonalty**.
thirst *noun* See **appetite, desire**.
   thirst *verb* See **lust**.

thirsting *adjective* See **eager.**

thirsty *adjective* Needing or desiring drink : dry, parched. *Archaic:* athirst. See DRY in Index. — See also **dry, eager.**

thistly *adjective* See **thorny.**

thorn *noun* One that makes another totally miserable by causing sharp pain and irritation : trial. *Informal:* pain. *Idioms:* pain in the neck, thorn in the flesh (or side). See PAIN in Index. — See also **prick.**

thorny *adjective* **1.** Full of sharp needlelike protuberances : briery, echinate, prickly, pricky, spiny, thistly. See SHARP in Index. **2.** So replete with interlocking points and complications as to be painfully irritating : nettlesome, prickly, spiny. See EASY, PAIN in Index.

thorough *adjective* Covering all aspects with painstaking accuracy : all-out, complete, exhaustive, full-dress, intensive, thoroughgoing, thoroughpaced. See BIG, CAREFUL in Index. — See also **detailed, utter².**

thoroughbred *adjective* Of pure breeding stock : full-blooded, high-bred, pureblood, pureblooded, purebred. See CLEAN in Index. — See also **noble.**

thoroughfare *noun* See **way.**

thoroughgoing *adjective* See **thorough, utter².**

thoroughly *adverb* See **completely.**

thoroughness *noun* Attentiveness to detail : care, carefulness, fastidiousness, meticulousness, pain (used in plural), painstaking, punctiliousness, scrupulousness. See CAREFUL in Index.

thoroughpaced *adjective* See **thorough.**

thought *noun* The act or process of thinking : brainwork, cerebration, cogitation, contemplation, deliberation, excogitation, meditation, reflection, rumination, speculation. See THOUGHTS in Index. — See also **idea.**

thoughtful *adjective* Of, characterized by, or disposed to thought : cogitative, contemplative, deliberative, excogitative, meditative, pensive, reflective, ruminative, speculative, thinking. *Idiom:* in a brown study. See THOUGHTS in Index. — See also **attentive, intellectual.**

thoughtfulness *noun* See **consideration.**

thoughtless *adjective* Devoid of consideration for others' feelings : disregardful, inconsiderate, unthinking, unthoughtful. See CAREFUL, COURTESY in Index. — See also **careless.**

thoughtlessness *noun* A lack of consideration for others' feelings : disregard, inconsiderateness, inconsideration, unthoughtfulness. See COURTESY in Index. — See also **abandon.**

thrall *noun* See **slavery.**

thralldom or **thraldom** *noun* See **slavery.**

thrash *verb* **1.** To swing about or strike at wildly : flail, thresh, toss. *Idiom:* toss and turn. See ATTACK, MOVE, STRIKE in Index. **2.** To beat (plants) with a machine or by hand to separate the grain from the straw : flail, thresh. See ATTACK, STRIKE in Index. — See also **beat, overwhelm.**

thrash out or **over** *verb* See **discuss.**

thrashing *noun* See **beating, defeat.**

thread *noun* **1.** A very fine continuous strand : fiber, fibril, filament. See THING in Index. **2.** Something that suggests the continuousness of a fine continuous filament : skein, strand. See CONTINUE in Index. — See also **dress.**

thread *verb* To put (objects) onto a fine continuous filament : string. See ORDER in Index.

threadbare *adjective* See **shabby, trite.**

threat *noun* **1.** An expression of the intent to hurt or punish another : intimidation, menace. See WARN in Index. **2.** An indication of impending danger or harm : foreboding, forewarning, thundercloud. *Idioms:* gathering clouds, storm clouds. See FORESIGHT in Index. **3.** One regarded as an imminent danger : menace, sword of Damocles. *Idiom:* clear and present danger. See SAFETY in Index.

threaten *verb* **1.** To give warning signs of (impending peril) : forebode, forewarn. See FORESIGHT in Index. **2.** To be imminent : brew, hang over, impend, loom, lower[1], menace, overhang. See NEAR in Index. — See also **endanger, intimidate.**

threatening *adjective* Expressing, indicating, or warning of an impending danger or misfortune : minacious, minatory. See FORESIGHT, NEAR in Index.

three *noun* See **trio.**

threesome *noun* See **trio.**

thresh *verb* See **beat, thrash.**

thresh out or **over** *verb* See **discuss.**

threshold *noun* See **verge.**

thrift *noun* See **economy.**

thriftiness *noun* See **economy.**

thriftless *adjective* See **improvident.**

thrifty *adjective* See **economical, flourishing.**

thrill *noun* A strong, pleasant feeling of excitement or stimulation : lift. *Informal:* wallop. *Slang:* bang, boot[1], high, kick. See EXCITE in Index. — See also **tremor.**

thrill *verb* See **carry away** at **carry.**

thrilled *adjective* Feeling a very strong emotion : atingle, excited, fired up, worked up. *Informal:* psyched. *Slang:* stoked, turned-on. See EXCITE in Index.

thrive *verb* See **flourish, prosper.**

thriving *adjective* See **flourishing.**

throb *verb* See **beat.**

throb *noun* See **beat.**

throe *noun* **1.** A violent, excruciating seizure of pain : cramp[1], paroxysm, shoot, spasm. See PAIN in Index. **2.** A condition of anguished struggle and disorder. Used in plural : convulsion, paroxysm. See CALM in Index. — See also **pain.**

throng *noun* See **crowd.**

throng *verb* See **crowd, pour.**

throttle *verb* See **choke, repress.**

through *adverb* **1.** From one end to the other : around, over, round, throughout. See PART in Index. **2.** To an end or conclusion : over. See START in Index.

through *adjective* **1.** No longer effective, capable, or valuable : done, done for, finished, washed-up. *Informal:* kaput. *Idioms:* at the end of the line (or road), over the hill, past one's prime. See ABILITY, START in Index. **2.** Having no further relationship : done, finished. See START in Index. — See also **complete, direct.**

throughout *adverb* See **through.**

throw *verb* To send through the air with a motion of the hand or arm : cast, dart, dash, fling, heave, hurl, hurtle, launch, pitch, shoot, shy[2], sling, toss. *Informal:* fire. See MOVE in Index. — See also **confuse, drop, exercise, nonplus, shed, trip.**

throw away *verb* See **discard, waste.**

throw off *verb* See **emit, lose, rid, shed.**

throw out *verb* See **discard, eject, slip.**

throw over *verb* See **abandon.**

throw up *verb* See **vomit.**

throw *noun* An act of throwing : cast, fling, heave, hurl, launch, pitch, sling², sling, toss. See MOVE in Index.

thrust *noun* The thread or current of thought uniting or occurring in all the elements of a text or discourse : aim, burden², drift, intent, meaning, purport, substance, tendency, tenor. See MEANING in Index. — See also **push.**

thrust *verb* See **drive, poke, ram.**

thruway *noun* See **way.**

thud *verb* To make a dull sound by or as if by striking a surface with a heavy object : clomp, clump, clunk. See SOUNDS in Index.

thud *noun* See **beat.**

thug *noun* A person who treats others violently and roughly, especially for hire : hoodlum, ruffian, tough. *Informal:* hooligan. *Slang:* goon, gorilla, hood. See ATTACK, CRIMES in Index.

thumb *verb* See **browse.**

thump *noun* See **beat.**

thunder *noun* See **blast.**

thunder *verb* See **blast.**

thundercloud *noun* See **threat.**

thwack *noun* See **blow².**

thwack *verb* See **hit.**

thwart *verb* See **frustrate.**

thwart *adjective* See **transverse.**

tic *noun* See **tremor.**

tick *noun* See **flash.**

tick off *verb* See **enumerate.**

ticker *noun* See **heart.**

ticket *noun* **1.** An identifying or descriptive slip : label, tag. See MARKS in Index. **2.** A list of candidates proposed or endorsed by a political party : lineup, slate. See POLITICS in Index. **3.** *Informal.* A means or method of entering into or achieving something desirable : formula, key, route, secret. See MEANS in Index.

ticket *verb* To attach a ticket to : label, mark, tag. See MARKS in Index.

tickle *verb* See **delight.**

tickled *adjective* See **glad.**

ticklish *adjective* See **capricious, delicate.**

tidbit *noun* See **delicacy.**

tide *noun* See **flow.**

tiding *noun* See **news.**

tidy *verb* **1.** To make or keep (an area) clean and orderly. Also used with *up* : clean (up), clear (up), neaten (up), police, spruce (up), straighten (up). See ORDER in Index. **2.** To make neat and trim; make presentable. Also used with *up* : clean (up), freshen (up), groom, neaten (up), slick up, spruce (up), trig (out), trim. See ORDER in Index.

tidy *adjective* See **acceptable, big, neat.**

tidy sum *noun* See **fortune.**

tie *verb* To make fast or firmly fixed, as by means of a cord or rope : bind, fasten, knot, secure, tie up. See KEEP, TIGHTEN in Index. — See also **equal, hamper.**

tie up *verb* **1.** To cause to cease regular activity : idle, immobilize, stop. *Idiom:* bring to a screeching halt. See CONTINUE in Index. **2.** To cause to be busy or in use : engage, monopolize, occupy, preempt. See ACTION, USED in Index. — See also **tie.**

tie *noun* An equality of scores, votes, or performances in a contest : dead heat, deadlock, draw, stalemate, standoff. See SAME in Index. — See also **bond.**

tie-in *noun* See **relation.**

tier *noun* See **class, line.**

tie-up *noun* A cessation of normal activity, caused by an accident or strike, for example : gridlock, immobilization, jam, stoppage. See CONTINUE in Index.

tiff *noun* See **argument**.
tiff *verb* See **argue**.

tiger *noun* See **fiend**.

tight *adjective* **1.** Hard to deal with or get out of : rough, tricky. *Informal:* sticky. See EASY in Index. **2.** Affording little room for movement : close, confining, cramped, crowded, narrow, snug. See TIGHTEN in Index. **3.** Persistently holding to something : clinging, fast, firm¹, secure, tenacious. See FREE, TIGHTEN in Index. **4.** Characterized by an economy of artistic expression : lean², spare. See STYLE in Index. — See also **close, drunk, familiar, neat, sound², stingy, taut, thick**.

tighten *verb* To make or become tight or tighter : reinforce, strengthen. See TIGHTEN in Index. — See also **tense**.

tightfisted *adjective* See **stingy**.

tightlipped also **tight-lipped** *adjective* See **taciturn**.

tightwad *noun* See **miser**.

till *verb* To prepare (soil) for the planting and raising of crops : cultivate, culture, dress, tend², work. See PREPARED, TOUCH in Index.

tilt *noun* Any competition or test of opposing wills likened to the sport in which knights fought with lances : joust, tournament, tourney. See CONFLICT in Index. — See also **inclination**.

tilt *verb* See **contend, incline**.

timber *noun* The basic substance or essential elements of character that qualify a person for a specified role : material, stuff. See BE in Index. — See also **beam**.

timbre *noun* See **tone**.

time *noun* **1.** A term of service, as in the military or in prison : hitch, stretch, tour. See TIME in Index. **2.** A span designated for a given activity : period, season. See TIME in Index. — See also **age, bit¹, occasion, term, turn**.

time *verb* **1.** To set the time for (an event or occasion) : plan, schedule. See TIME in Index. **2.** To record the speed or duration of : clock. See REMEMBER, TIME in Index.

time-honored *adjective* See **orthodox**.

timeless *adjective* See **ageless, continual**.

timely *adjective* See **opportune, punctual**.

time-out *noun* See **break**.

timetable *noun* See **program**.

timeworn *adjective* See **old, trite**.

timid *adjective* See **hesitant, modest**.

timidity *noun* See **hesitation, shyness**.

timidness *noun* See **hesitation, shyness**.

tincture *noun* See **color**.
tincture *verb* See **color**.

tinge *noun* See **shade, tint**.

tinker *verb* See **fiddle, tamper**.

tinsel *adjective* See **gaudy**.

tint *noun* A shade of a color, especially a pale or delicate variation : cast, hue, tinge, tone. See COLORS in Index. — See also **color, shade**.
tint *verb* See **color**.

tiny *adjective* Extremely small : diminutive, dwarf, Lilliputian, midget, miniature, minuscule, minute², pygmy, wee. *Informal:* peewee, pintsize, pintsized, teensy-weensy, teensy, teeny, teeny-weeny, weeny. See BIG in Index.

tip¹ *noun* See **point**.
tip² *verb* See **incline**.

tip *noun* See **inclination**.

tip³ *noun* An item of advance or inside information given as a guide to action : pointer, steer. *Informal:* tip-off. See KNOWLEDGE in Index. — See also **gratuity**.

tip *verb* See **inform**.

tip-off *noun* See **tip³**.

tipple *verb* See **drink**.

tippler *noun* See **drunkard**.

tipsiness *noun* See **drunkenness**.

tipster *noun* See **informer**.

tipsy *adjective* See **drunk**.

tiptop *adjective* See **excellent**.

tirade *noun* A long, violent, or blustering speech, usually of censure or denunciation : diatribe, fulmination, harangue, jeremiad, philippic. See PRAISE in Index.

tire *verb* See **bore, fatigue**.

tired *adjective* See **sick, trite**.

tiredness *noun* See **exhaustion**.

tired out *adjective* See **exhausted**.

tireless *adjective* Having or showing a capacity for protracted effort, regardless of difficulty or frustration : indefatigable, inexhaustible, unfailing, unflagging, untiring, unwearied, weariless. See CONTINUE, TIRED in Index.

tire out *verb* See **exhaust**.

tiresome *adjective* See **boring**.

tiring *adjective* Causing fatigue : draining, exhausting, fatiguing, wearing, wearying. See TIRED in Index.

tissue *noun* See **web**.

titan *noun* See **giant**.

titanic *adjective* See **giant**.

tit for tat *noun* See **retaliation**.

title *noun* See **claim, interest, name, ownership, publication**.

title *verb* See **name**.

titter *verb* See **giggle**.

titter *noun* See **giggle**.

tittle *noun* See **bit¹**.

tittle-tattle *noun* See **gossip**.

tittle-tattle *verb* See **gossip**.

tizzy *noun* See **state**.

toady *verb* See **fawn**.

toady *noun* See **sycophant**.

to-and-fro *noun* See **hesitation**.

toast *noun* The act of drinking to someone : pledge. See DESIRE, REMEMBER in Index.

toast *verb* See **drink**.

tocsin *noun* See **alarm**.

today *adverb* See **now**.

today *noun* See **now**.

to-do *noun* See **disturbance, fuss, sensation**.

tog *verb* See **dress**. *noun* See **dress**.

together *adverb* **1.** In, into, or as a single body : jointly. *Idioms:* as one, in one breath, in the same breath, in unison, with one accord, with one voice. See ACCOMPANIED in Index. **2.** At the same time : concurrently, simultaneously, synchronously. *Idioms:* all at once, all together. See ACCOMPANIED, TIME in Index.

together *adjective* See **ready**.

toil *verb* See **labor, plod**.

toil *noun* See **labor**.

token *noun* See **expression, pawn¹, remembrance, sign**.

tolerable *adjective* See **acceptable, bearable**.

tolerance *noun* Forbearing or lenient treatment : charitableness, charity, forbearance, indulgence, lenience, leniency, lenity, toleration. See ACCEPT in Index. — See also **patience**.

tolerant *adjective* Not strict or severe : charitable, clement, easy, forbearing, indulgent, lax, lenient, merciful, soft. See ACCEPT in Index. — See also **broad**.

tolerate *verb* See **endure, permit**.

toleration *noun* See **tolerance**.

toll¹ *noun* A fixed amount of money charged for a privilege or service :

charge, exaction, fee. See MONEY,
PAY, TRANSACTIONS in Index.
— See also **cost.**

toll² *verb* See **ring².**

tomb *noun* See **grave¹.**

tome *noun* See **book.**

tomfool *noun* See **fool.**

tomfool *adjective* See **foolish.**

tomfoolery *noun* See **foolishness,
mischief, nonsense.**

tommyrot *noun* See **nonsense.**

tonality *noun* See **tone.**

tone *noun* **1.** A sound of distinct
pitch and quality : timbre, tonality,
tone color. See SOUNDS in Index.
2. A particular vocal quality that
indicates some emotion or feeling :
accent, inflection, intonation.
Idiom: tone of voice. See SOUNDS in
Index. — See also **air, color, style,
temper, tint.**

tone down *verb* See **moderate,
soft-pedal.**

tone color *noun* See **tone.**

tongue *noun* See **language.**

tonic *noun* A medicine that restores
or increases vigor : restorative, roborant. *Informal:* bracer, pick-me-up.
See HELP in Index.

tonic *adjective* Producing or stimulating physical, mental, or emotional vigor : bracing, energizing,
exhilarant, exhilarating, innerving,
intoxicating, invigorating, refreshing, reinvigorating, renewing, restorative, roborant, stimulating. See
HELP in Index.

tony also **toney** *adjective* See
fashionable.

too *adverb* See **additionally.**

tool *noun* A device used to do work
or perform a task : implement,
instrument, utensil. See MACHINE,
MEANS in Index. — See also **pawn².**

tool *verb* See **drive.**

toothsome *adjective* See **delicious.**

top *noun* See **best, climax, face,
height, maximum.**

top *adjective* Of, being, located at,
or forming the top : highest, loftiest, topmost, upmost, uppermost.
See HIGH in Index. — See also **excellent, highest, maximum, primary.**

top *verb* To put a topping on :
cap, crown, top off. See OVER, PUT
ON in Index. — See also **climax,
surpass.**

top off *verb* See **top.**

top-drawer *adjective* See **highest.**

topflight *adjective* See **excellent.**

tophole *adjective* See **excellent.**

topic *noun* See **subject.**

topical *adjective* See **thematic.**

topmost *adjective* See **maximum,
top.**

topnotch *adjective* See **excellent.**

topography *noun* See **terrain.**

topple *verb* See **fall, overthrow,
overturn, surrender.**

topsy-turviness *noun* See **disorder.**

topsy-turvy *adjective* See **confused.**

torch *verb* See **light¹.**

torment *verb* See **afflict, annoy,
haunt, torture.**

torment *noun* See **annoyance, distress, hell.**

tormenting *adjective* Extraordinarily painful or distressing : agonizing, anguishing, excruciating, harrowing, torturous. See PAIN in
Index.

torpedo *verb* See **destroy.**

torpid *adjective* See **dull, lethargic.**

torpidity *noun* See **lethargy.**

torpor *noun* See **lethargy.**

torrent *noun* See **flood.**

torrid *adjective* See **hot, passionate.**

torridity *noun* See **heat.**

torridness *noun* See **heat.**

tortuous *adjective* See **indirect,
winding.**

torture *verb* To subject (another) to
extreme physical cruelty, as in pun-

ishing : crucify, rack, torment.
Idiom: put on the rack (or wheel).
See PAIN, REWARD in Index. — See
also **afflict.**

torture *noun* See **distress, hell.**

torturous *adjective* See **tormenting.**

Tory *noun* See **conservative.**

Tory *adjective* See **conservative.**

toss *verb* **1.** To move vigorously
from side to side or up and down :
heave, pitch, rock, roll. See REPETI-
TION in Index. **2.** To throw (a coin)
in order to decide something : flip.
Idiom: call heads or tails. See LUCK,
MOVE in Index. — See also **agitate,
thrash, throw, writhe.**

toss around *verb* See **discuss.**

toss down or **off** *verb* See **drink.**

toss *noun* See **throw.**

tot¹ *noun* See **child, drop.**

tot² *verb* See **add.**

total *noun* A number or quantity
obtained as a result of addition :
aggregate, amount, sum, summation, sum total, totality. *Archaic:*
tale. See COUNT in Index. — See also
whole.

total *adjective* See **utter², whole.**

total *verb* See **add, amount,
destroy.**

totalitarian *noun* See **authoritarian,
dictator.**

totalitarian *adjective* See **absolute, authoritarian.**

totalitarianism *noun* See **absolutism, tyranny.**

totality *noun* See **completeness, system, total, whole.**

totalization *noun* See **addition.**

totalize *verb* See **add.**

totally *adverb* See **completely.**

tote *verb* See **carry.**

totter *verb* See **lurch, sway.**

tottering *adjective* See **insecure,
unstable.**

tottery *adjective* See **insecure,
unstable.**

touch *verb* To bring the hands or
fingers, for example, into contact
with so as to give or receive a physical sensation : feel, finger, handle,
palpate. See TOUCH in Index. — See
also **adjoin, affect¹, compare, contact, refer.**

touch down *verb* See **land.**

touch off *verb* See **cause, explode,
provoke.**

touch up *verb* To improve by
making minor changes or additions : polish, retouch. See BETTER
in Index.

touch *noun* **1.** An act of touching : feeling, palpation. See TOUCH
in Index. **2.** The faculty or ability to
perceive tactile stimulation : feel,
feeling, tactility. See TOUCH in
Index. **3.** A particular sensation conveyed by means of physical contact : feel, feeling. See TOUCH in
Index. **4.** A situation allowing
exchange of ideas or messages :
communication, contact, intercommunication. See CONNECT, TOUCH
in Index. — See also **contact, shade.**

touchable *adjective* See **tangible.**

touchableness *noun* See
tangibility.

touch-and-go *adjective* See
delicate.

touched *adjective* See **insane.**

touching *adjective* See **affecting.**

touchstone *noun* See **standard.**

touchy *adjective* See **delicate, testy.**

tough *adjective* See **burdensome,
difficult, firm¹, hard, rough, severe,
strong.**

tough *noun* A rough, violent person who engages in destructive
actions : hoodlum, mug, roughneck, rowdy, ruffian. *Informal:*
toughie. *Slang:* hood, punk. See
ATTACK, CRIMES in Index. — See
also **thug.**

tough out *verb* See **endure.**

toughen *verb* To become or cause to become tough or strong : strengthen. See STRONG in Index. — See also **harden.**

toughie *noun* See **tough.**

tough-minded *adjective* See **realistic.**

toughness *noun* See **decision, severity.**

tour *noun* See **circle, expedition, time, turn.**

tour de force *noun* See **feat.**

tourist *noun* One who travels for pleasure : excursionist, sightseer. *Chiefly British:* tripper. See MOVE in Index.

tournament *noun* See **tilt.**

tourney *noun* See **tilt.**

tousle *verb* To put (the hair or clothes) into a state of disarray : disarrange, dishevel, disorder, mess (up), muss (up), rumple. See ORDER in Index.

tout *verb* See **promote.**

tow *verb* See **pull.**

toward *adjective* See **beneficial.**

tower above or **over** *verb* See **dominate.**

towering *adjective* Awesomely or forbiddingly intense : overpowering, overwhelming, staggering. See BIG in Index. — See also **lofty, rare.**

towheaded *adjective* See **fair.**

town *noun* See **city.**

toxic *adjective* See **poisonous.**

toxicant *adjective* See **poisonous.**

toxin *noun* See **poison.**

toy *noun* An object for children to play with : plaything. See WORK in Index. — See also **novelty.**

toy *verb* See **fiddle, flirt.**

trace *noun* A mark or remnant that indicates the former presence of something : relic, remains, vestige. See LEFTOVER, MARKS in Index. — See also **shade, track.**

trace *verb* See **run down** at **run, track.**

track *noun* A visible sign or mark of the passage of someone or something : print, trace, trail. See MARKS in Index. — See also **routine, trail.**

track *verb* To follow the traces or scent of, as in hunting : trace, trail. See MARKS, SEEK in Index. — See also **cross, follow.**

track down *verb* See **run down** at **run.**

tract *noun* See **area, lot.**

tractability *noun* See **obedience.**

tractable *adjective* See **obedient.**

tractableness *noun* See **obedience.**

traction *noun* See **pull.**

trade *noun* See **business, change, patronage.**

trade *verb* See **change, sell.**

trademark *noun* See **mark.**

trademark *verb* See **mark.**

trader *noun* See **dealer.**

tradesman *noun* See **dealer.**

trading *noun* See **business.**

tradition *noun* See **heritage, lore.**

traditional *adjective* See **conventional.**

traditionalist *adjective* See **conservative.**

traditionalist *noun* See **conservative.**

traditionalistic *adjective* See **conservative.**

traduce *verb* See **libel.**

traducement *noun* See **libel.**

traffic *noun* See **business, patronage.**

trafficker *noun* See **dealer.**

tragedy *noun* See **disaster.**

trail *verb* To hang or cause to hang down and be pulled along behind : drag, draggle, train. See HANG in Index. — See also **delay, dog, follow, track.**

trail *noun* Evidence of passage left along a course followed by a hunted animal or fugitive : scent, spoor, track. See MARKS, SMELLS in Index. — See also **track, train.**

train *noun* Something that follows or is drawn along behind : tail, trail, wake². See PRECEDE in Index. — See also **retinue, series.**

train *verb* See **aim, educate, exercise, trail.**

trainable *adjective* See **educable.**

trainer *noun* See **educator.**

training *noun* See **education, practice.**

traipse *verb* See **hike, rove.**

trait *noun* See **quality.**

traitor *noun* See **betrayer.**

traitorous *adjective* See **faithless, treasonous.**

traitorousness *noun* See **faithlessness, treason.**

trammel *noun* See **restriction.**

trammel *verb* See **catch, hamper.**

tramp *verb* To walk with loud, heavy steps : stamp, stomp, trample. *Informal:* tromp. See MOVE, SOUNDS in Index. — See also **hike, trample.**

tramp *noun* See **slut.**

trample *verb* To step on heavily and repeatedly so as to crush, injure, or destroy : stamp, stomp, tramp, tread, tromp. See HELP in Index. — See also **tramp, tyrannize.**

trance *noun* The condition of being so lost in solitary thought as to be unaware of one's surroundings : absent-mindedness, abstraction, bemusement, brown study, daydreaming, muse², reverie, study. See AWARENESS in Index. — See also **daze.**

tranquil *adjective* See **calm, still.**

tranquilize also **tranquillize** *verb* See **calm.**

tranquillity or **tranquility** *noun* See **calm, stillness.**

transaction *noun* See **bargain.**

transcend *verb* See **exceed, surpass.**

transcendent *adjective* See **theoretical, ultimate.**

transcendental *adjective* See **supernatural, theoretical.**

transfer *verb* *Law.* To change the ownership of (property) by means of a legal document : cede, deed, grant, make over, sign over. *Law:* alien, alienate, assign, convey. See GIVE, LAW in Index. — See also **give, move, refer.**

transfer *noun* See **delivery, grant.**

transferal *noun* See **grant.**

transfiguration *noun* See **change.**

transfigure *verb* See **convert.**

transfix *verb* See **grip.**

transform *verb* See **convert, revolutionize.**

transformation *noun* See **change.**

transfuse *verb* See **charge.**

transgress *verb* See **disobey, offend, violate.**

transgression *noun* See **breach.**

transient *adjective* See **transitory.**

transit *noun* See **transition, transportation.**

transit *verb* See **cross.**

transition *noun* The process or an instance of passing from one form, state, or stage to another : change, passage, shift, transit. See CHANGE in Index.

transitory *adjective* Lasting or existing only for a short time : ephemeral, evanescent, fleet, fleeting, fugacious, fugitive, momentary, passing, short-lived, temporal, temporary, transient. See CONTINUE, TIME in Index.

translate *verb* To express in another language, while systematically retaining the original sense :

construe, put, render. See WORDS in Index. — See also **convert, paraphrase.**

translation *noun* See **change, paraphrase.**

translucent *adjective* See **transparent.**

transmigrant *noun* See **emigrant.**

transmigrate *verb* See **emigrate, migrate.**

transmigration *noun* See **emigration.**

transmigratory *adjective* See **migratory.**

transmit *verb* See **communicate, conduct, hand down** at **hand, pass, send.**

transmogrification *noun* See **change.**

transmogrify *verb* See **convert.**

transmutation *noun* See **change.**

transmute *verb* See **convert.**

transparent *adjective* Admitting light so that objects beyond can be seen : clear, crystal clear, crystalline, limpid, lucid, pellucid, seethrough, translucent. See CLEAR in Index. — See also **clear, filmy.**

transpire *verb* See **come, come out** at **come, ooze.**

transport *verb* See **banish, bring, carry, carry away** at **carry.**

transport *noun* See **heaven, transportation.**

transportable *adjective* See **mobile.**

transportation *noun* The moving of persons or goods from one place to another : carriage, conveyance, transit, transport. See MOVE in Index. — See also **exile.**

transporter *noun* See **bearer.**

transpose *verb* See **convert, reverse.**

transposition *noun* See **change, reversal.**

transubstantiate *verb* See **convert.**

transubstantiation *noun* See **change.**

transude *verb* See **ooze.**

transversal *adjective* See **transverse.**

transverse *adjective* Situated or lying across : crossing, crosswise, thwart, transversal, traverse. See HORIZONTAL in Index.

trap *noun* See **ambush, lure, mouth, pitfall.**

trap *verb* See **catch.**

trash *noun* A group of persons regarded as the lowest class : dreg (often used in plural), lumpenproletariat, rabble, ragtag and bobtail, riffraff. *Slang:* scum. *Idioms:* scum of the earth, tag and rag, the great unwashed. See OVER, RICH in Index. — See also **nonsense.**

trash *verb* *Slang.* To injure or destroy (property) maliciously : vandalize. See HELP in Index.

trashy *adjective* See **shoddy.**

trauma *noun* Marked tissue damage, especially when produced by physical injury : traumatism, wound. See HELP in Index. — See also **shock**[1].

traumatism *noun* See **trauma.**

traumatize *verb* To inflict physical or mental injury or distress on : shock[1], wound. See HELP in Index.

travail *noun* See **birth, labor.**

travail *verb* See **labor.**

travel *verb* See **get around** at **get, go, journey.**

traveling *adjective* See **mobile.**

traversal *noun* See **denial.**

traverse *verb* **1.** To move in a zigzag manner, as on a ski slope : zigzag. See MOVE, RISE in Index. **2.** To move, as a gun, laterally : pivot, swivel. See MOVE in Index. — See also **contest, cross, deny, examine.**

traverse *adjective* See **transverse.**

traverse *noun* See **bar.**

travesty *noun* See **mockery**.
travesty *verb* See **imitate**.

treacherous *adjective* See **dangerous, faithless**.

treacherousness *noun* See **faithlessness, treachery**.

treachery *noun* Willful betrayal of fidelity, confidence, or trust : perfidy, treacherousness, treason. See TRUST in Index. — See also **betrayal, faithlessness**.

tread *noun* The act or manner of going on foot : footfall, footstep, step. See MOVE, SOUNDS in Index.
tread *verb* See **trample, walk**.

treadmill *noun* See **grind**.

treason *noun* Willful violation of allegiance to one's country : sedition, seditiousness, traitorousness. See TRUST in Index. — See also **treachery**.

treasonable *adjective* See **treasonous**.

treasonous *adjective* Involving or constituting treason : seditious, traitorous, treasonable. See TRUST in Index.

treasure *noun* Someone or something considered exceptionally precious : gem, pearl, prize[1]. See VALUE in Index. — See also **hoard, riches**.
treasure *verb* See **appreciate, cherish, hoard**.

treasure house *noun* See **treasury**.

treasury *noun* A place where one keeps one's valuables : treasure house. See KEEP in Index.

treat *verb* 1. To pay for the food, drink, or entertainment of (another) : *Informal:* set up, stand. *Slang:* blow[1]. *Idiom:* stand treat. See PAY in Index. 2. To give medical aid to : *Informal:* doctor. See HEALTH, HELP in Index. — See also **deal with** at **deal**.
treat *noun* See **delicacy**.

treatise *noun* See **discourse**.

treatment *noun* The systematic application of remedies to effect a cure : care, regimen, rehabilitation, therapy. *Informal:* rehab. See HEALTH, HELP in Index.

treaty *noun* A formal, usually written settlement between nations : accord, agreement, concord, convention, pact. See AGREE, POLITICS in Index.

treble *adjective* See **high**.

trek *verb* See **hike, journey**.
trek *noun* See **expedition**.

tremble *verb* See **shake**.
tremble *noun* See **jitter**.

tremblor *noun* See **tremor**.

tremendous *adjective* See **fearful, giant, marvelous**.

tremendousness *noun* See **enormousness**.

tremor *noun* 1. A shaking of the earth : earthquake, quake, seism, temblor, tremblor. *Informal:* shake. See MOVE, REPETITION in Index. 2. A nervous shaking of the body : quake, quiver, shake, shiver[1], shudder, thrill, tic, twitch. See REPETITION in Index.

tremulant *adjective* See **tremulous**.

tremulous *adjective* Marked by or affected with tremors : aquiver, quaky, quivery, shaky, shivery, tremulant, twittery. See REPETITION in Index.

trenchancy *noun* See **sarcasm**.

trenchant *adjective* See **acute, biting**.

trend *noun* See **bent, fashion**.
trend *verb* See **tend**[1].

trendy *adjective* See **fashionable**.

trepidation *noun* See **fear**.

trespass *verb* See **break in** at **break, offend**.
trespass *noun* 1. The act of entering a building or room with the intent to commit theft : break-in,

burglary. See CRIMES in Index.
2. An advance beyond proper or legal limits : encroachment, entrenchment, impingement, infringement, intrusion, obtrusion. See ENTER in Index. — See also **breach.**

triable *adjective* See **litigable.**

triad *noun* See **trio.**

trial *noun* **1.** The examination and deciding upon evidence, charges, and claims in court : hearing. See LAW in Index. **2.** A state of pain or anguish that tests one's resiliency and character : crucible, ordeal, tribulation, visitation. See EASY in Index. — See also **attempt, burden**[1], **test, thorn.**

trial *adjective* See **pilot.**

tribe *noun* See **family.**

tribulation *noun* See **burden**[1], **trial.**

tribunal *noun* See **court.**

tribute *noun* See **compliment, testimonial.**

trice *noun* See **flash.**

trick *noun* **1.** An indirect, usually cunning means of gaining an end : artifice, deception, device, dodge, feint, gimmick, imposture, jig, maneuver, ploy, ruse, sleight, stratagem, subterfuge, wile. *Informal:* shenanigan, take-in. See HONEST, MEANS in Index. **2.** A clever, dexterous act : feat, stunt. See ABILITY, EXCITE, GOOD in Index. — See also **hang, prank**[1], **turn.**

trick *adjective* So weak or defective as to be liable to fail : undependable, unreliable. See STRONG in Index.

trick *verb* See **deceive.**

trick out or **up** *verb* See **dress up** at **dress.**

trickery *noun* See **indirection.**

trickiness *noun* See **indirection.**

trickle *verb* See **drip.**

trickle *noun* See **drip.**

trickster *noun* See **cheat.**

tricky *adjective* See **artful, delicate, tight.**

trifle *noun* See **bit**[1], **novelty, trivia.**

trifle *verb* See **fiddle, flirt.**

trifle away *verb* See **idle, waste.**

trifling *adjective* See **petty.**

trig *adjective* See **fashionable, neat.**

trig *verb* See **tidy.**

trigger *noun* See **stimulus.**

trigger *verb* See **cause, provoke.**

triggerman *noun* See **murderer.**

trillion *noun* See **heap.**

trim *verb* See **adorn, beat, cheat, cut back** at **cut, defeat, shade, tidy.**

trim down *verb* See **reduce.**

trim *adjective* See **neat, sleek.**

trim *noun* A state of sound readiness : condition, fettle, fitness, form, kilter, order, shape. See BETTER in Index. — See also **adornment.**

trimming *noun* See **adornment, beating, defeat.**

trine *noun* See **trio.**

trinity *noun* See **trio.**

trinket *noun* See **novelty.**

trio *noun* A group of three individuals : three, threesome, triad, trine, trinity, triple, triumvirate, triune, triunity, troika. See GROUP in Index.

trip *verb* To release or move (a switch, for example) in order to activate, deactivate, or control a device : throw. See MOVE in Index. — See also **journey, skip, stumble.**

trip up *verb* See **err.**

trip *noun* A usually short journey taken for pleasure : excursion, jaunt, junket, outing. See MOVE in Index. — See also **error, hallucination, kick.**

triple *noun* See **trio.**

tripper *noun* See **tourist.**

tristful *adjective* See **depressed.**

trite *adjective* Without freshness or appeal because of overuse : banal, bromidic, clichéd, commonplace, corny, hackneyed, musty, overused, overworked, platitudinal, platitudinous, shopworn, stale, stereotyped, stereotypic, stereotypical, threadbare, timeworn, tired, warmed-over, well-worn, worn-out. See EXCITE, USUAL in Index.

triturate *verb* See **crush**.

triumph *verb* See **exult**.

   triumph over *verb* See **defeat**.

   triumph *noun* See **conquest, exultation**.

triumphal *adjective* See **victorious**.

triumphant *adjective* See **exultant, victorious**.

triumvirate *noun* See **trio**.

triune *noun* See **trio**.

triunity *noun* See **trio**.

trivia *noun* Something or things that are unimportant : fiddle-faddle, frippery, frivolity, froth, minutia, nonsense, small change, small potatoes, trifle, triviality. See IMPORTANT, SURFACE in Index.

trivial *adjective* See **little**.

triviality *noun* See **pettiness, trivia**.

trivialness *noun* See **pettiness**.

troika *noun* See **trio**.

tromp *verb* See **tramp, trample**.

troop *verb* See **associate, pour**.

   troop *noun* See **assembly, band²**.

trophy *noun* A memento received as a symbol of excellence or victory : accolade, award, prize¹. See RESPECT in Index. — See also **remembrance**.

tropic *adjective* See **tropical**.

tropical *adjective* Of or relating to the Tropics : tropic. See HOT in Index.

trot *noun* A person's steady easy gait that is faster than a walk but slower than a run : jog, lope. See MOVE in Index. — See also **witch**.

   trot *verb* To move with a steady easy gait faster than a walk but slower than a run : jog, lope. See MOVE in Index. — See also **rush**.

troth *noun* See **engagement**.

trouble *noun* See **care, distress, effort, inconvenience, predicament**.

   trouble *verb* See **haunt, inconvenience, worry**.

troublesome *adjective* Hard to treat, manage, or cope with : wicked. *Informal:* pesky. *Slang:* mean². See EASY in Index. — See also **disturbing, inconvenient, vexatious**.

troublous *adjective* See **disturbing**.

trounce *verb* See **overwhelm**.

troupe *noun* See **band²**.

truancy *noun* See **cut**.

truant *verb* See **cut**.

truantry *noun* See **cut**.

truce *noun* A temporary cessation of hostilities by mutual consent of the contending parties : armistice, cease-fire. See CONTINUE in Index.

truckle *verb* See **fawn**.

truculence *noun* See **belligerence, cruelty, fight**.

truculency *noun* See **belligerence, cruelty, fight**.

truculent *adjective* See **belligerent, biting, fierce**.

trudge *verb* See **plod**.

true *adjective* Being so legitimately : legitimate, rightful. See TRUE in Index. — See also **accurate, actual, authentic, faithful, genuine, honest, realistic**.

true-life *adjective* See **realistic**.

truelove *noun* See **darling**.

truism *noun* See **cliché**.

truly *adverb* See **really**.

trump *noun* Something, especially something held in reserve, that gives one a decisive advantage : trump card. *Informal:* clincher. **Idiom:** ace in the hole. See HELP, WIN in Index.

   trump *verb* To outmaneuver (an opponent), especially with the aid of some extra resource : finesse.

Informal: one-up. See WIN in Index.

trump card *noun* See **trump.**

truncate *verb* See **cut back** at **cut.**

trust *noun* See **care, combine, confidence.**

trust *verb* See **believe, depend on** at **depend, entrust.**

trustworthy *adjective* See **authentic, dependable.**

trusty *adjective* See **dependable.**

truth *noun* Freedom from deceit or falseness : truthfulness, veracity. See TRUE in Index. — See also **actuality, veracity.**

truthful *adjective* Consistently telling the truth : veracious, veridical. See TRUE in Index. — See also **realistic.**

truthfully *adverb* See **really.**

truthfulness *noun* See **authenticity, truth.**

truthless *adjective* See **false.**

truthlessness *noun* See **mendacity.**

try *noun* A brief trial : crack, go, stab. *Informal:* fling, shot, whack, whirl. See TRY in Index. — See also **attempt.**

try *verb* See **attempt, test.**

try out *verb* See **test.**

trying *adjective* See **burdensome.**

tryout *noun* See **test.**

tryst *noun* See **engagement.**

tubby *adjective* See **plump¹.**

tuber *noun* See **seed.**

tubercular *adjective* Relating to or afflicted with tuberculosis : consumptive (no longer in scientific use), phthisic (no longer in scientific use), phthisical (no longer in scientific use), tuberculate, tuberculous. See HEALTH in Index.

tuberculate *adjective* See **tubercular.**

tuberculosis *noun* An infectious disease producing lesions especially of the lungs : consumption (no longer in scientific use), phthisic (no longer in scientific use), phthisis (no longer in scientific use), white plague. See HEALTH in Index.

tuberculous *adjective* See **tubercular.**

tucker *verb* See **exhaust.**

tuckered *adjective* See **exhausted.**

tug *verb* See **labor, pull.**

tug *noun* See **jerk.**

tug of war *noun* See **competition.**

tuition *noun* See **education.**

tumble *verb* See **disorder, fall, overthrow.**

tumble on *verb* See **come across** at **come.**

tumble *noun* See **disorder, fall, heap.**

tumbledown *adjective* See **ruinous.**

tumescent *adjective* See **inflated.**

tumid *adjective* See **inflated.**

tumult *noun* See **agitation, brawl, disturbance, noise.**

tumultuous *adjective* See **rough, turbulent.**

tune *noun* See **agreement, harmony, melody.**

tune *verb* See **adjust, harmonize, sing.**

tuneful *adjective* See **melodious.**

turbid *adjective* **1.** Having sediment or foreign particles stirred up or suspended : cloudy, muddy, murky, roiled, roily. See CLEAR in Index. **2.** Heavy, dark, or dense, especially with impurities : hazy, murky, smoggy. See CLEAR in Index. — See also **confused.**

turbulence *noun* See **agitation, disturbance.**

turbulent *adjective* Marked by unrest or disturbance : stormy, tempestuous, tumultuous. See CALM in Index. — See also **rough.**

turf *noun* See **territory.**

turgid *adjective* See **inflated.**

turgidity *noun* See **bombast.**

turkey *noun* See **fool**.

turmoil *noun* See **agitation, disturbance, unrest**.

turn *verb* **1.** To move or cause to move in circles or around an axis : circle, circumvolve, gyrate, orbit, revolve, rotate, wheel. See MOVE, REPETITION in Index. **2.** To spade or dig (soil) to bring the undersoil to the surface : plow, turn over. See MOVE in Index. **3.** To injure a (bodily part) by twisting : sprain, wrench. See HEALTH in Index. **4.** To change the direction or course of : avert, deflect, deviate, divert, pivot, shift, swing, veer. See CHANGE in Index. — See also **aim, apply, become, bend, change, decay, defect, dull, resort, reverse, upset, writhe**.

turn down *verb* See **decline, refuse, veto**.

turn in *verb* See **retire, submit**.

turn off *verb* See **offend**.

turn on *verb* See **depend on** at **depend, interest**.

turn out *verb* See **furnish, get up** at **get**.

turn over *verb* See **entrust, give, overturn, ponder, refer, turn**.

turn up *verb* See **arrive, uncover**.

turn upon *verb* See **depend on** at **depend**.

turn *noun* **1.** An often sudden change or departure, as in a trend : shift, tack, twist. See CHANGE in Index. **2.** A limited, often assigned period of activity, duty, or opportunity : bout, go, hitch, inning (often used in plural), shift, spell³, stint, stretch, time, tour, trick, watch. See TIME in Index. — See also **bend, bent, circle, constitutional, movement, revolution, talent**.

turnabout *noun* See **reversal**.

turnaround *noun* See **reversal**.

turncoat *noun* See **defector**.

turndown *noun* See **refusal**.

turned-on *adjective* See **drugged, thrilled**.

turning point *noun* See **crisis**.

turnkey *noun* See **jailer**.

turnout *noun* See **dress, outfit**.

turnpike *noun* See **way**.

turpitude *noun* See **corruption**.

tush *noun* See **bottom**.

tussle *noun* See **fight**.

tussle *verb* See **wrestle**.

tutelage *noun* See **education**.

tutor *verb* See **educate**. *noun* See **educator**.

tutoring *noun* See **education**.

twaddle *noun* See **babble, nonsense**.

twelvemonth *noun* See **year**.

twerp also **twirp** *noun* See **squirt**.

twiddle *verb* See **fiddle**.

twig *verb* See **understand**.

twiggy *adjective* See **thin**.

twilight *noun* See **evening**.

twin *adjective* Consisting of two identical or similar related things, parts, or elements : double, dual, paired. See SAME in Index.

twin *noun* See **mate**.

twin *verb* See **double**.

twine *verb* See **wind²**.

twinge *noun* See **pain**.

twinge *verb* See **hurt**.

twinkle *verb* See **blink, flash**.

twinkle *noun* See **blink, flash**.

twinkling *noun* See **flash**.

twirl *verb* See **spin**.

twist *verb* See **deform, distort, wind²**.

twist *noun* See **turn, wrinkle**.

twit *verb* See **ridicule**.

twit *noun* See **taunt**.

twitch *verb* See **jerk**.

twitch *noun* See **jerk, tremor**.

twitchy *adjective* See **edgy**.

twitter *verb* See **shake**.

twittery *adjective* See **tremulous**.

two *noun* See **couple**.

two bits *noun* See **peanut.**

two-faced *adjective* See **double, hypocritical.**

two-facedness *noun* See **hypocrisy.**

two-fisted *adjective* See **heavy.**

twofold *adjective* See **double.**

twosome *noun* See **couple, pair.**

type *noun* See **embodiment, kind[2].**

typic *adjective* See **typical.**

typical *adjective* Having the nature of, constituting, or serving as a type : archetypal, archetypic, archetypical, classic, classical, model, paradigmatic, prototypal, prototypic, prototypical, quintessential, representative, typic. See SAME, USUAL in Index. — See also **common, distinctive.**

typically *adverb* See **usually.**

typify *verb* See **represent.**

tyrannic *adjective* See **absolute, authoritarian.**

tyrannical also **tyrannic** *adjective* See **absolute, authoritarian.**

tyrannize *verb* To treat arbitrarily or cruelly : grind, trample. See OVER in Index. — See also **boss.**

tyrannous *adjective* See **absolute.**

tyranny *noun* Absolute power, especially when exercised unjustly or cruelly : autocracy, despotism, dictatorship, totalitarianism. See OVER, POLITICS in Index. — See also **absolutism.**

tyrant *noun* See **authoritarian, dictator.**

tyro also **tiro** *noun* See **beginner.**

U

ubiquitous *adjective* See **universal.**

ugliness *noun* The quality or condition of being ugly : hideousness, unsightliness. See BEAUTIFUL in Index. — See also **mess.**

ugly *adjective* Extremely displeasing to the eye : hideous, ill-favored, unsightly. *Idiom:* ugly as sin. See BEAUTIFUL in Index. — See also **ill-tempered, offensive, rough.**

ugly *noun* See **mess.**

uh-huh *adverb* See **yes.**

ulterior *adjective* Lying beyond what is obvious or avowed : buried, concealed, covert, hidden, obscured. *Idiom:* under cover (or wraps). See SHOW in Index. — See also **later.**

ulteriorly *adverb* See **later.**

ultimate *adjective* Of the greatest possible degree, quality, or intensity : extreme, supreme, transcendent, unsurpassable, utmost, uttermost. See BETTER, BIG in Index. — See also **elemental, extreme, last[1], maximum.**

ultimate *noun* See **maximum.**

ultimately *adverb* After a considerable length of time, usually after a delay : finally. *Idioms:* at last, at long last, in the end. See START, TIME in Index.

ultra *adjective* See **extreme.**

ultra *noun* See **extremist.**

ultraconservative *adjective* See **reactionary.**

ultraconservative *noun* See **reactionary.**

ululate *verb* See **howl.**

ululation *noun* See **howl.**

umbra *noun* See **shade.**

umbrage *noun* See **offense, shade.**

umbrageous *adjective* See **shady.**

ump *noun* See **judge.**

umpire *verb* See **judge.**

umpire *noun* See **judge.**

unabashed *adjective* See **shameless.**

unabbreviated *adjective* See **complete.**

unable *adjective* See **incompetent.**

unabridged *adjective* See **complete.**

unacceptable *adjective* See objectionable.

unaccompanied *adjective* See alone.

unaccountable *adjective* See inexplicable.

unacquainted *adjective* See ignorant.

unadorned *adjective* See bare, rustic.

unadulterated *adjective* See natural, pure.

unadvantageous *adjective* See unfavorable.

unaffected *adjective* See artless, cold, genuine.

unafraid *adjective* See brave.

unalterable *adjective* See inflexible, irrevocable.

unambiguous *adjective* See definite, sharp.

unanimity *noun* The quality or condition of being in complete agreement or harmony : consensus, unanimousness. See AGREE in Index.

unanimous *adjective* Being in or characterized by complete agreement : solid. *Idioms:* as one, at one, of one mind, with one voice. See AGREE in Index.

unanimousness *noun* See unanimity.

unappeasable *adjective* See voracious.

unappetizing *adjective* See unpalatable.

unappreciated *adjective* See thankless.

unappreciative *adjective* See thankless.

unapproachable *adjective* See cool, inaccessible.

unapt *adjective* See doubtful, improper.

unassailable *adjective* See certain.

unassuming *adjective* See modest.

unassumingness *noun* See modesty.

unattached *adjective* See single.

unattainable *adjective* See impossible, inaccessible.

unattractive *adjective* See plain.

unavailable *adjective* See inaccessible.

unavailing *adjective* See futile.

unavailingness *noun* See futility.

unavoidable *adjective* See certain.

unawake *adjective* See sleeping.

unaware *adjective* See ignorant.

unawarely *adverb* See unawares.

unawareness *noun* See ignorance.

unawares *adverb* Without adequate preparation : aback, short, unawarely. *Idiom:* by surprise. See PREPARED in Index.

unbalance *verb* See derange.

unbalance *noun* See insanity.

unbalanced *adjective* See insane.

unbearable *adjective* So unpleasant or painful as not to be endured or tolerated : impossible, insufferable, insupportable, intolerable, unendurable, unsufferable, unsupportable. See PAIN in Index.

unbecoming *adjective* See improper, tacky[2].

unbecomingness *noun* See impropriety.

unbefitting *adjective* See improper.

unbelief *noun* See disbelief.

unbelievable *adjective* See fabulous, implausible, incredible.

unbeliever *noun* See skeptic.

unbelieving *adjective* See incredulous.

unbend *verb* See rest[1].

unbendable *adjective* See stubborn.

unbending *adjective* See firm[1], rigid, stubborn.

unbiased *adjective* See fair, neutral.

unbind *verb* See undo.

unblamable also **unblameable** *adjective* See **exemplary, innocent.**

unblemished *adjective* See **clear, good, innocent.**

unblended or **unblent** *adjective* See **straight.**

unblock *verb* See **clear.**

unblocked *adjective* See **clear.**

unblushing *adjective* See **shameless.**

unbodied *adjective* See **immaterial.**

unbounded *adjective* See **endless, utter**[2].

unboundedness *noun* See **infinity.**

unbridled *adjective* See **abandoned.**

unbroken *adjective* See **good.**

unburden *verb* See **rid.**

uncalled-for *adjective* See **unnecessary, wanton.**

uncanny *adjective* See **weird.**

uncaring *adjective* See **unsympathetic.**

unceasing *adjective* See **continual.**

uncensored *adjective* See **complete.**

unceremonious *adjective* See **easygoing.**

unceremoniousness *noun* See **ease.**

uncertain *adjective* See **ambiguous, capricious, changeable, debatable, doubtful, indefinite, shady.**

uncertainty *noun* See **doubt, vagueness.**

unchangeable *adjective* See **inflexible.**

unchanging *adjective* See **consistent, even**[1].

uncharitable *adjective* See **unsympathetic.**

unchaste *adjective* See **impure.**

uncivil *adjective* See **rude, uncivilized.**

uncivilized *adjective* Not civilized : barbarian, barbaric, barbarous, primitive, rude, savage, uncultivated, uncultured, wild. *Archaic:* uncivil. See CULTURE, WILD in Index. — See also **coarse.**

unclad *adjective* See **nude.**

unclasp *verb* See **undo.**

unclean *adjective* See **dirty, impure.**

uncleanliness *noun* See **dirtiness.**

uncleanly *adjective* See **dirty, impure.**

uncleanness *noun* See **dirtiness, impurity.**

unclear *adjective* Not clearly perceived or perceptible : blear, bleary, cloudy, dim, faint, foggy, fuzzy, hazy, indefinite, indistinct, misty, obscure, shadowy, undistinct, vague. See CLEAR in Index. — See also **ambiguous.**

unclearness *noun* See **vagueness.**

unclose *verb* See **open.**

unclothe *verb* See **reveal, strip**[1].

unclouded *adjective* See **clear.**

uncomely *adjective* See **plain.**

uncomfortable *adjective* Causing discomfort : comfortless, uncomforting. *Informal:* uncomfy. See COMFORT in Index. — See also **awkward.**

uncomforting *adjective* See **uncomfortable.**

uncomfy *adjective* See **uncomfortable.**

uncommitted *adjective* See **neutral.**

uncommon *adjective* See **infrequent, rare.**

uncommonly *adverb* See **unusually.**

uncommunicable *adjective* See **taciturn.**

uncommunicative *adjective* See **cool, taciturn.**

uncommunicativeness *noun* See **reserve.**

uncompassionate *adjective* See **unsympathetic.**

uncompelled *adjective* See **voluntary.**

uncompensated *adjective* See
unpaid.

uncompliant *adjective* See
stubborn.

uncomplimentary *adjective* See
disparaging.

uncomprehending *adjective* See
blind.

uncomprehensible *adjective* See
incomprehensible.

uncompromising *adjective* See
firm[1], strict, stubborn.

unconceivable *adjective* See
implausible.

unconcern *noun* See apathy.

unconcerned *adjective* See apathetic, careless, detached, mindless.

unconditional *adjective* Without
limitations or mitigating conditions : absolute, unconditioned,
unqualified, unreserved. See LIMITED in Index. — See also implicit.

unconditioned *adjective* See
unconditional.

unconfined *adjective* See loose.

uncongenial *adjective* See inharmonious, unpleasant.

unconquerable *adjective* See
invincible.

unconscionable *adjective* See outrageous, steep[1], unscrupulous.

unconscious *adjective* Lacking
consciousness : cold, insensible,
senseless. *Idioms:* out cold, out like
a light. See AWARENESS in Index.
— See also ignorant.

unconsciousness *noun* See
ignorance.

unconsidered *adjective* See rash[1].

unconspicuous *adjective* See
inconspicuous.

unconstrained *adjective* See
abandoned.

uncontrollability *noun* See
unruliness.

uncontrollable *adjective* See
unruly.

uncontrollableness *noun* See
unruliness.

uncontrolled *adjective* See abandoned, runaway.

unconventional *adjective* See
unusual.

unconvincing *adjective* See
implausible.

uncooked *adjective* See raw.

uncorporal *adjective* See
immaterial.

uncorrupted *adjective* See
innocent.

uncountable *adjective* See
incalculable.

uncouple *verb* See detach.

uncoupling *noun* See detachment.

uncouth *adjective* See coarse.

uncover *verb* To find by investigation : dig (out or up), turn up,
unearth. See SHOW in Index. — See
also bare, betray, reveal.

uncovered *adjective* See open.

uncreative *adjective* See sterile.

uncritical *adjective* See superficial.

unctuous *adjective* Affectedly and
self-servingly earnest : fulsome,
oily, oleaginous, sleek, smarmy. See
ATTITUDE, HONEST in Index. — See
also fatty.

uncultivated *adjective* See coarse,
uncivilized, wild.

uncultured *adjective* See coarse,
uncivilized.

uncut *adjective* See complete.

undamaged *adjective* See good.

undaunted *adjective* See brave.

undauntedness *noun* See courage.

undecided *adjective* See doubtful,
indefinite.

undeclared *adjective* See silent.

undefiled *adjective* See innocent.

undemonstrated *adjective* See
untried.

undemonstrative *adjective* See
cool.

undeniable *adjective* See certain.

undependable *adjective* Not to be depended on : unreliable, untrustworthy. See TRUST in Index. — See also **trick**.

under *adjective* See **insufficient, minor**.

underage[1] *noun* See **shortage**.

underage[2] *adjective* See **minor**.

undercover *adjective* See **secret**.

undercurrent *noun* See **hint**.

underdeveloped *adjective* See **backward**.

underdog *noun* See **unfortunate**.

undergo *verb* See **experience**.

underground *adjective* Located or operating beneath the earth's surface : hypogeal, hypogean, hypogeous, subterranean, subterrestrial. See SURFACE in Index.

underground *noun* See **resistance**.

underhand *adjective* Marked by treachery or deceit : devious, disingenuous, duplicitous, guileful, indirect, lubricious, shifty, sneaky, underhanded. See HONEST in Index.

underhanded *adjective* See **underhand**.

underhandedness *noun* See **indirection**.

underline *verb* See **emphasize**.

underling *noun* See **subordinate**.

underlying *adjective* See **elemental, radical**.

undermanned *adjective* Lacking the requisite workers or players : shorthanded. See EXCESS in Index.

undermine *verb* See **enervate, sabotage**.

undermining *noun* See **sabotage**.

undermost *adjective* See **bottom**.

underneath *noun* See **bottom**.

underpin *verb* See **base**[1].

underpinning *noun* See **base**[1], **basis, support**.

underprivileged *adjective* See **depressed**.

underprivileged *noun* See **unfortunate**.

underscore *verb* See **emphasize**.

underside *noun* See **bottom**.

undersign *verb* See **sign**.

understand *verb* To perceive and recognize the meaning of : accept, apprehend, catch (on), compass, comprehend, conceive, fathom, follow, get, grasp, make out, read, see, sense, take, take in. *Informal:* savvy. *Slang:* dig. *Chiefly British:* twig. *Scots:* ken. *Idioms:* get (or have) a handle on, get the picture. See UNDERSTAND in Index. — See also **infer, know**.

understandable *adjective* Capable of being readily understood : comprehensible, fathomable, intelligible, knowable. See KNOWLEDGE in Index.

understanding *adjective* Cognizant of and comprehending the needs, feelings, problems, and views of others : empathetic, empathic, feeling, sympathetic. See UNDERSTAND in Index.

understanding *noun* See **agreement, grasp, intelligence**.

understood *adjective* See **implicit**.

undersurface *noun* See **bottom**.

undertake *verb* See **assume, pledge, start**.

undertaking *noun* See **project**.

undertone *noun* See **hint**.

underwriter *noun* See **sponsor**.

undescribable *adjective* See **unspeakable**.

undesigned *adjective* See **unintentional**.

undesirable *adjective* See **objectionable, unwelcome**.

undesired *adjective* See **unwelcome**.

undetected *adjective* See **unfound**.

undetermined *adjective* See **indefinite**.

undeveloped *adjective* See backward.

undevised *adjective* See unintentional.

undiluted *adjective* See pure, straight.

undiplomatic *adjective* See tactless.

undisciplined *adjective* See unruly.

undiscovered *adjective* See unfound.

undisputable *adjective* See certain.

undistinct *adjective* See unclear.

undistinguished *adjective* See ordinary.

undivided *adjective* See concentrated.

undo *verb* To free from ties or fasteners : disengage, loose, loosen, slip, unbind, unclasp, unfasten, unloose, unloosen, untie. See TIGHTEN in Index. — See also cancel, destroy, enervate, open, seduce.

undoing *noun* See destruction, ruin.

undomesticated *adjective* See wild.

undoubted *adjective* See authentic.

undoubtedly *adverb* See absolutely, yes.

undoubting *adjective* See implicit, sure.

undress *noun* See nudity.

undress *verb* See strip[1].

undue *adjective* See excessive.

undulate *verb* See slither, wave.

unduly *adverb* Too much : overly, overmuch. *Informal:* super. See EXCESS in Index.

undying *adjective* See immortal.

unearth *verb* See uncover.

unearthly *adjective* See foolish, supernatural, weird.

unease *noun* See anxiety, restlessness.

uneasiness *noun* See anxiety, restlessness.

uneasy *adjective* See anxious, awkward, restless.

uneducated *adjective* See ignorant.

unemotional *adjective* See cold, dry.

unemployed *adjective* See idle, workless.

unending *adjective* See continual, endless.

unendurable *adjective* See unbearable.

unenlightened *adjective* See ignorant.

unenthusiastic *adjective* See tepid.

unequal *adjective* See inadequate, unfair.

unequaled *also* **unequalled** *adjective* See unique.

unequivocal *adjective* See definite, sharp, utter[2].

unerring *adjective* See sure.

unessential *adjective* See unnecessary.

unethical *adjective* See unscrupulous.

uneven *adjective* Lacking consistency or regularity in quality or performance : erratic, inconsistent, patchy, spotty, unsteady, variable. See CONTINUE, SAME in Index. — See also rough.

unevenness *noun* See irregularity.

unexampled *adjective* See unique.

unexceptional *adjective* See ordinary.

unexplainable *adjective* See inexplicable.

unexposed *adjective* See unfound.

unexpressed *adjective* See silent.

unexpurgated *adjective* See complete.

unfailing *adjective* See consistent, continual, sure, tireless.

unfair *adjective* Not fair, right, or just : inequitable, unequal, unjust. See FAIR in Index.

unfairness *noun* See injustice.

unfaithful *adjective* See **faithless.**

unfaithfulness *noun* See **faithlessness.**

unfaltering *adjective* See **implicit.**

unfamiliar *adjective* See **ignorant, new.**

unfamiliarity *noun* See **ignorance.**

unfasten *verb* See **undo.**

unfathomable *adjective* See **incomprehensible.**

unfavorable *adjective* Tending to discourage, retard, or make more difficult : adverse, disadvantageous, negative, unadvantageous, unsatisfactory, untoward. See HELP in Index. — See also **bad.**

unfeeling *adjective* See **cold-blooded, dead.**

unfeigned *adjective* See **genuine.**

unfinished *adjective* See **rough.**

unfit *adjective* Not suited to a given purpose : ill-suited, inappropriate, inapt, unsuitable, unsuited. See ABILITY in Index. — See also **improper, inadequate, incompetent.**

unfit *verb* To make incapable, as of doing a job : disable, disqualify. See ABILITY in Index.

unfitness *noun* See **impropriety.**

unflagging *adjective* See **tireless.**

unflappability *noun* See **balance.**

unflappable *adjective* See **cool.**

unflawed *adjective* See **perfect.**

unflinching *adjective* See **firm¹.**

unfold *verb* See **develop, spread.**

unfolding *noun* See **development.**

unforbearing *adjective* See **impatient.**

unforced *adjective* See **voluntary.**

unforgivable *adjective* See **inexcusable.**

unformed *adjective* See **shapeless.**

unfortunate *adjective* **1.** Involving or undergoing chance misfortune : hapless, ill-fated, ill-starred, luckless, star-crossed, unhappy, unlucky, untoward. See LUCK in Index.

2. Characterized by inappropriateness and gracelessness, especially in expression : awkward, ill-chosen, inappropriate, inept, infelicitous, unhappy. See ABILITY, GOOD in Index. — See also **deplorable.**

unfortunate *noun* A person living under very unhappy circumstances : loser, miserable, underdog, underprivileged, wretch. See RICH in Index.

unfortunateness *noun* See **misfortune.**

unfound *adjective* Not found : undetected, undiscovered, unexposed. See KNOWLEDGE in Index.

unfounded *adjective* See **baseless.**

unfoundedly *adverb* Without basis or foundation in fact : groundlessly, unwarrantedly. See REASON in Index.

unfrequented *adjective* See **lonely.**

unfriendly *adjective* See **hostile.**

unfruitful *adjective* See **barren.**

ungainly *adjective* See **awkward.**

ungovernable *adjective* See **unruly.**

ungovernableness *noun* See **unruliness.**

ungoverned *adjective* See **abandoned.**

ungraceful *adjective* See **awkward.**

ungracious *adjective* See **rude.**

ungraciousness *noun* See **unwelcome.**

ungrateful *adjective* See **thankless.**

unguarded *adjective* See **insecure.**

unhandy *adjective* See **awkward.**

unhappiness *noun* See **gloom.**

unhappy *adjective* See **depressed, unfortunate.**

unharmed *adjective* See **good, safe.**

unharmonious *adjective* See **inharmonious.**

unhealthy *adjective* See **corrupt, morbid, unwholesome.**

unheard-of *adjective* See **obscure.**

unheeding *adjective* See **mindless.**

unhesitating *adjective* See **implicit.**

unhinge *verb* See **derange.**

unhorse *verb* See **overthrow.**

unhospitable *adjective* See **forbidding.**

unhurried *adjective* See **deliberate.**

unhurt *adjective* See **good, safe.**

unification *noun* A bringing together into a whole : coalition, consolidation, union, unity. See PART in Index. — See also **combination.**

uniform *adjective* See **even[1], like[2].**

uniformity *noun* See **likeness.**

uniformness *noun* See **likeness.**

unify *verb* See **combine, harmonize.**

unimaginable *adjective* See **incredible.**

unimaginative *adjective* See **dull, sterile.**

unimpaired *adjective* See **good.**

unimpeded *adjective* See **clear.**

unimportance *noun* See **indifference.**

unimportant *adjective* See **little.**

unimpressionable *adjective* See **insensitive.**

uninformed *adjective* See **ignorant.**

uninhabited *adjective* See **unreserved.**

uninhibited *adjective* See **abandoned.**

uninitiate *noun* See **amateur.**

uninitiate *adjective* See **inexperienced.**

uninitiated *adjective* See **inexperienced.**

uninjured *adjective* See **good, safe.**

uninspired *adjective* See **dull, sterile.**

uninstructed *adjective* See **ignorant.**

unintelligent *adjective* See **mindless.**

unintelligible *adjective* See **incomprehensible.**

unintended *adjective* See **unintentional.**

unintentional *adjective* Not intended : inadvertent, undesigned, undevised, unintended, unmeant, unplanned, unwitting. See PLANNED in Index.

uninterest *noun* See **apathy.**

uninterested *adjective* See **apathetic, detached.**

uninteresting *adjective* See **boring.**

uninterrupted *adjective* See **continual.**

uninventive *adjective* See **sterile.**

uninvited *adjective* See **unwelcome.**

uninviting *adjective* See **forbidding.**

uninvolved *adjective* See **detached, neutral.**

union *noun* A group of people united in a relationship and having some interest, activity, or purpose in common : association, club, confederation, congress, federation, fellowship, fraternity, guild, league, order, organization, society, sorority. See GROUP in Index. — See also **alliance, combination, joint, unification, unity.**

unique *adjective* Without equal or rival : alone, incomparable, matchless, nonpareil, only, peerless, singular, unequaled, unexampled, unmatched, unparalleled, unrivaled. See SAME in Index. — See also **lone.**

uniqueness *noun* The quality or condition of being unique : oneness, singleness, singularity. See SAME in Index.

unit *noun* See **force.**

unite *verb* See **band[2], combine.**

unity *noun* **1.** The condition of being one : oneness, singleness, singularity. See PART in Index. **2.** An identity or coincidence of interests, purposes, or sympathies among the members of a group : oneness, solidarity, union. See AGREE in Index.

— See also **agreement, combination, unification.**

universal *adjective* **1.** So pervasive and all-inclusive as to exist in or affect the whole world : catholic, cosmic, cosmopolitan, ecumenical, global, pandemic, planetary, world-wide. See LIMITED, SPECIFIC in Index. **2.** Ever present in all places : omnipresent, ubiquitous. See LIMITED, SPECIFIC in Index. — See also **general.**

universal *noun* See **law.**

universalize *verb* To make universal : generalize. See SPECIFIC in Index.

universe *noun* The totality of all existing things : cosmos, creation, macrocosm, nature, world. See MATTER, PART in Index. — See also **mankind.**

unjust *adjective* See **unfair.**

unjustifiable *adjective* See **inexcusable.**

unjustness *noun* See **injustice.**

unkempt *adjective* See **messy.**

unknowing *adjective* See **ignorant.**

unknown *adjective* See **obscure.**

unlade *verb* See **unload.**

unlawful *adjective* Contrary to accepted, especially moral conventions : illicit. See RIGHT in Index. — See also **criminal, illegal, illegitimate.**

unlawfulness *noun* See **illegality.**

unlearned *adjective* See **ignorant, unscholarly.**

unlike *adjective* See **different.**

unlikely *adjective* See **doubtful.**

unlikeness *noun* See **difference.**

unlimited *adjective* See **endless, utter².**

unlimitedness *noun* See **infinity.**

unload *verb* To remove the cargo or load from : disburden, discharge, dump, unlade. See PUT IN in Index. — See also **sell off** at **sell.**

unloose *verb* See **undo.**

unloosen *verb* See **undo.**

unlovely *adjective* See **plain.**

unluckiness *noun* See **misfortune.**

unlucky *adjective* See **disappointing, fateful, unfortunate.**

unmanageability *noun* See **unruliness.**

unmanageable *adjective* See **awkward, unruly.**

unmanliness *noun* See **cowardice, effeminacy.**

unmanly *adjective* See **cowardly, effeminate.**

unmannered *adjective* See **genuine.**

unmannerly *adjective* See **rude.**

unmarked *adjective* See **clear.**

unmarred *adjective* See **good.**

unmarried *adjective* See **single.**

unmask *verb* See **reveal.**

unmatched *adjective* See **unique.**

unmeant *adjective* See **unintentional.**

unmentionable *adjective* See **unspeakable.**

unmerciful *adjective* See **merciless.**

unmindful *adjective* See **careless, mindless.**

unmistakable *adjective* See **sharp, unsubtle.**

unmitigated *adjective* See **utter².**

unmixed *adjective* See **pure, straight.**

unmovable *adjective* See **fixed.**

unmoved *adjective* See **cold, unsympathetic.**

unmoving *adjective* See **fixed, motionless.**

unmusical *adjective* See **inharmonious.**

unnamed *adjective* See **anonymous.**

unnatural *adjective* See **abnormal, eccentric, plastic, preternatural.**

unnaturalness *noun* See **abnormality.**

unnecessary *adjective* Not necessary : dispensable, inessential, needless, nonessential, uncalled-for, unessential, unneeded, unrequired. See NECESSARY in Index.

unneeded *adjective* See **unnecessary.**

unnegotiable *adjective* See **impracticable.**

unnerve *verb* See **enervate.**

unnoticeable *adjective* See **imperceptible, inconspicuous.**

unobjectionable *adjective* See **acceptable.**

unobservable *adjective* See **imperceptible.**

unobservant *adjective* See **mindless.**

unobstructed *adjective* See **clear.**

unobtrusive *adjective* See **inconspicuous, quiet.**

unoccupied *adjective* See **unreserved.**

unoffensive *adjective* See **harmless.**

unordinary *adjective* See **unusual.**

unoriginal *adjective* See **sterile.**

unostentatious *adjective* See **modest.**

unostentatiousness *noun* See **modesty.**

unpaid *adjective* Contributing one's time without pay : uncompensated, unrecompensed, unremunerated, unsalaried, voluntary. See PAY, WORK in Index. — See also **due.**

unpalatable *adjective* So unpleasant in flavor as to be inedible : distasteful, unappetizing, unsavory. See TASTE in Index. — See also **bitter.**

unparalleled *adjective* See **unique.**

unpardonable *adjective* See **inexcusable.**

unperceptive *adjective* See **blind.**

unperfected *adjective* See **rough.**

unpitying *adjective* See **unsympathetic.**

unplanned *adjective* See **random, unintentional.**

unpleasant *adjective* Not pleasant or agreeable : bad, disagreeable, displeasing, offensive, uncongenial, unsympathetic. *Informal:* icky. *Slang:* yucky. See GOOD, PAIN in Index.

unpolished *adjective* See **coarse, rough, rude, rustic.**

unpolitic *adjective* See **tactless.**

unpracticed *adjective* See **inexperienced, untried.**

unprecedented *adjective* See **new.**

unpredictable *adjective* See **capricious.**

unprejudiced *adjective* See **fair, neutral.**

unpremeditated *adjective* See **spontaneous.**

unpretentious *adjective* See **modest.**

unpretentiousness *noun* See **modesty.**

unprincipled *adjective* See **unscrupulous.**

unprocessed *adjective* See **crude.**

unproductive *adjective* See **barren.**

unprofessional *adjective* See **amateurish.**

unprofitable *adjective* See **futile.**

unprofitableness *noun* See **futility.**

unprogressive *adjective* Clinging to obsolete ideas : backward, conservative, reactionary. See POLITICS in Index.

unpropitious *adjective* See **bad.**

unprotected *adjective* See **helpless, insecure, open.**

unproved *adjective* See **untried.**

unqualified *adjective* See **inadequate, incompetent, unconditional, utter^2.**

unquestionable *adjective* See **authentic, certain, decided.**

unquestionably *adverb* See **yes.**

unquestioning *adjective* See **implicit**.

unquiet *adjective* See **restless**.

unravel *verb* See **resolve**.

unreachable *adjective* See **inaccessible**.

unreal *adjective* See **imaginary**.

unrealistic *adjective* See **idealistic**.

unrealizable *adjective* See **impossible**.

unreason *noun* The absence of reason : illogicality, illogicalness, irrationality, unreasonableness. See REASON in Index.

unreasonable *adjective* Not governed by or predicated on reason : illogical, irrational, unreasoned. *Idiom:* out of bounds. See REASON in Index. — See also **outrageous**.

unreasonableness *noun* See **unreason**.

unreasoned *adjective* See **unreasonable**.

unreceptiveness *noun* See **unwelcome**.

unrecompensed *adjective* See **unpaid**.

unreel *verb* See **play out** at **play**.

unrefined *adjective* See **coarse, crude**.

unrehearsed *adjective* See **extemporaneous**.

unrelenting *adjective* See **stubborn**.

unreliable *adjective* See **trick, undependable**.

unrelieved *adjective* See **utter²**.

unremarkable *adjective* See **ordinary**.

unremitting *adjective* See **continual**.

unremunerated *adjective* See **unpaid**.

unrepentant *adjective* See **remorseless**.

unrequired *adjective* See **unnecessary**.

unreserved *adjective* Not spoken for or occupied : free, open, uninhabited, unoccupied. See OWNED in Index. — See also **frank, implicit, outgoing, unconditional, utter²**.

unresolved *adjective* See **indefinite**.

unresponsive *adjective* See **apathetic, dull, frigid**.

unresponsiveness *noun* See **apathy**.

unrest *noun* A state of uneasiness and usually resentment brewing to an eventual explosion : ferment, Sturm und Drang, turmoil. See CALM, PEACE in Index. — See also **restlessness**.

unrestrained *adjective* See **abandoned, easygoing, loose**.

unrestraint *noun* See **abandon, ease**.

unrestricted *adjective* See **open**.

unrivaled or **unrivalled** *adjective* See **unique**.

unroll *verb* See **play out** at **play, spread**.

unromantic *adjective* See **realistic**.

unruffled *adjective* See **cool**.

unruliness *noun* The quality or condition of being unruly : disorderliness, fractiousness, indocility, intractability, intractableness, obstinacy, obstinateness, obstreperousness, recalcitrance, recalcitrancy, refractoriness, uncontrollability, uncontrollableness, ungovernableness, unmanageability, untowardness, wildness. See CONTROL, ORDER, PEACE, RESIST in Index.

unruly *adjective* Not submitting to discipline or control : disorderly, fractious, indocile, intractable, lawless, obstinate, obstreperous, recalcitrant, refractory, uncontrollable, undisciplined, ungovernable, unmanageable, untoward, wild. *Idiom:* out of line. See CONTROL, ORDER, PEACE, RESIST in Index.

unsafe *adjective* See **dangerous, insecure.**

unsaid *adjective* See **implicit, silent.**

unsalaried *adjective* See **unpaid.**

unsalutary *adjective* See **unwholesome.**

unsatisfactory *adjective* See **bad, unfavorable.**

unsavory *adjective* See **flat, unpalatable.**

unscathed *adjective* See **safe.**

unscholarly *adjective* Lacking the requisite scholarship or instruction : unlearned, unstudious. See KNOWLEDGE in Index.

unschooled *adjective* See **ignorant.**

unscrupulous *adjective* Lacking scruples or principles : conscienceless, ruthless, unconscionable, unethical, unprincipled. See HONEST in Index.

unseasonable *adjective* Not suitable for or characteristic of the season : untimely. See USUAL in Index.

unseasoned *adjective* See **inexperienced.**

unseeing *adjective* See **blind.**

unseemliness *noun* See **impropriety.**

unseemly *adjective* See **improper.**

unselfish *adjective* See **generous, selfless.**

unselfishness *noun* See **generosity.**

unserviceable *adjective* See **impracticable.**

unsettle *verb* See **agitate, disorder, upset.**

unsettled *adjective* See **anxious, changeable, due, indefinite, restless.**

unsettling *adjective* See **disturbing.**

unsex *verb* See **sterilize.**

unshakable *adjective* See **sound².**

unshaped *adjective* See **shapeless.**

unsightliness *noun* See **ugliness.**

unsightly *adjective* See **ugly.**

unsigned *adjective* See **anonymous.**

unskilled *adjective* See **amateurish, inefficient.**

unskillful *adjective* Clumsily lacking in the ability to do or perform : awkward, bumbling, clumsy, gauche, heavy-handed, inept, maladroit. See ABILITY in Index. — See also **amateurish, inefficient.**

unsleeping *adjective* See **wakeful.**

unsoiled *adjective* See **clean.**

unsophisticated *adjective* See **artless.**

unsought *adjective* See **unwelcome.**

unsound *adjective* See **erroneous, fallacious, infirm, insane, unwise.**

unsoundness *noun* See **infirmity.**

unsparing *adjective* See **generous.**

unsparingness *noun* See **generosity.**

unspeakable *adjective* **1.** That cannot be described : incommunicable, indefinable, indescribable, ineffable, inexpressible, undescribable, unutterable. *Idioms:* beyond description (or words), defying description. See WORDS in Index. **2.** That may not be spoken of or uttered : unmentionable. See DECENT, GOOD, WORDS in Index.

unspoken *adjective* See **implicit, silent.**

unstable *adjective* Not physically steady or firm : precarious, rickety, shaky, tottering, tottery, unsteady, wobbly. See FLEXIBLE in Index. — See also **capricious, changeable, insecure.**

unstableness *noun* The quality or condition of being physically unsteady : instability, precariousness, ricketiness, shakiness, unsteadiness, wobbliness. See FLEXIBLE in Index. — See also **instability.**

unstained *adjective* See **innocent.**

unsteadiness *noun* See **instability, unstableness.**

unsteady *adjective* See **capricious, changeable, insecure, uneven, unstable.**

unstinting *adjective* See **generous.**

unstirred *adjective* See **unsympathetic.**

unstudied *adjective* See **artless.**

unstudious *adjective* See **unscholarly.**

unsubstantial *adjective* See **immaterial, implausible, infirm, tenuous.**

unsubstantiality *noun* See **infirmity.**

unsubtle *adjective* Easily seen through due to a lack of subtlety : broad, clear, obvious, patent, plain, unmistakable. See CLEAR, SEE in Index.

unsuccess *noun* See **failure.**

unsuccessful *adjective* See **futile.**

unsuccessfulness *noun* See **failure.**

unsufferable *adjective* See **unbearable.**

unsuitability *noun* See **impropriety.**

unsuitable *adjective* See **improper, unfit.**

unsuitableness *noun* See **impropriety.**

unsuited *adjective* See **unfit.**

unsullied *adjective* See **clean, innocent.**

unsupportable *adjective* See **unbearable.**

unsure *adjective* See **ambiguous, doubtful, indefinite, insecure.**

unsureness *noun* See **instability.**

unsurpassable *adjective* See **ultimate.**

unsurpassed *adjective* See **best.**

unsusceptibility *noun* See **resistance.**

unsusceptible *adjective* See **insensitive, resistant.**

unswerving *adjective* See **concentrated.**

unsympathetic *adjective* Not sympathetic : uncaring, uncharitable, uncompassionate, unmoved, unpitying, unstirred, untouched. See FEELINGS in Index. — See also **unpleasant.**

unsystematic *adjective* See **disorderly.**

untactful *adjective* See **tactless.**

untainted *adjective* See **innocent.**

untamed *adjective* See **wild.**

untangle *verb* See **clear.**

untaught *adjective* See **ignorant.**

untested *adjective* See **untried.**

unthankful *adjective* See **thankless.**

unthanking *adjective* See **thankless.**

unthinkable *adjective* See **impossible, incredible.**

unthinking *adjective* See **careless, mindless, thoughtless.**

unthoughtful *adjective* See **thoughtless.**

unthoughtfulness *noun* See **thoughtlessness.**

unthrifty *adjective* See **improvident.**

untidiness *noun* See **disorderliness.**

untidy *adjective* See **careless, messy.**

untie *verb* See **undo.**

untighten *verb* See **ease.**

untimely *adjective* See **early, inconvenient, unseasonable.**

untiring *adjective* See **tireless.**

untouched *adjective* See **unsympathetic.**

untoward *adjective* See **improper, unfavorable, unfortunate, unruly.**

untowardness *noun* See **misfortune, unruliness.**

untried *adjective* Not tested or proved : undemonstrated, unpracticed, unproved, untested. See ABILITY, KNOWLEDGE in Index. — See also **inexperienced.**

untroubled *adjective* See **still.**

untroubledness *noun* See **stillness.**

untrue *adjective* See **erroneous, faithless, false.**

untrusting *adjective* See **distrustful**.

untrustworthy *adjective* See **undependable**.

untruth *noun* See **fallacy, lie²**.

untruthful *adjective* See **dishonest, false**.

untruthfulness *noun* See **mendacity**.

unusable *adjective* See **impracticable, useless**.

unused *adjective* See **idle**.

unusual *adjective* Not usual or ordinary : atypic, atypical, novel, unconventional, unordinary, unwonted. *Slang:* offbeat. See USUAL in Index. — See also **eccentric, infrequent, rare**.

unusually *adverb* In a manner or to a degree that is unusual : exceptionally, extraordinarily, remarkably, singularly, uncommonly. See USUAL in Index.

unutterable *adjective* See **unspeakable**.

unuttered *adjective* See **implicit, silent**.

unvarnished *adjective* See **bare**.

unvarying *adjective* See **even¹**.

unveil *verb* See **betray, reveal**.

unversed *adjective* See **inexperienced**.

unvoiced *adjective* See **silent**.

unwanted *adjective* See **objectionable, unwelcome**.

unwarranted *adjective* See **baseless**.

unwarrantedly *adverb* See **unfoundedly**.

unwashed *adjective* See **lowly**.

unwavering *adjective* See **firm¹**.

unwearied *adjective* See **tireless**.

unwed *adjective* See **single**.

unwelcome *adjective* Not welcome or wanted : undesirable, undesired, uninvited, unsought, unwanted, unwished-for. See LIKE in Index. — See also **objectionable**.

unwelcome *noun* Lack of cordiality and hospitableness : inhospitableness, inhospitality, ungraciousness, unreceptiveness, unwelcomeness. See LIKE in Index.

unwelcomeness *noun* See **unwelcome**.

unwell *adjective* See **sick**.

unwholesome *adjective* **1.** Not sustaining or promoting health : insalubrious, unhealthy, unsalutary. See HEALTH in Index. **2.** Morally detrimental : contaminative, corruptive, demoralizing, unhealthy. See RIGHT in Index. — See also **morbid, offensive**.

unwholesomeness *noun* See **impurity**.

unwieldy *adjective* See **awkward**.

unwilling *adjective* See **indisposed**.

unwillingness *noun* See **indisposition**.

unwind *verb* See **play out** at **play, rest¹**.

unwise *adjective* Not wise : ill-advised, ill-considered, impolitic, imprudent, indiscreet, injudicious, unsound. See WISE in Index.

unwished-for *adjective* See **unwelcome**.

unwitting *adjective* See **ignorant, unintentional**.

unwonted *adjective* See **unusual**.

unworkable *adjective* See **impossible, impracticable**.

unworkmanlike *adjective* See **inefficient**.

unworldly *adjective* See **artless, spiritual**.

unwritten *adjective* See **oral**.

unyielding *adjective* See **firm¹, rigid, severe, stubborn**.

up *adjective* See **elated**.

up *verb* See **raise**.

up-and-comer *noun* See **comer**.

up-and-coming *adjective* See **coming**.

upbeat *adjective* See **optimistic, positive.**

upbraid *verb* See **call down** at **call.**

upcoming *adjective* See **coming.**

update *verb* See **modernize.**

upgrade *verb* See **improve, promote.**

upgrade *noun* See **advancement, improvement.**

upheaval *noun* See **revolution.**

uphill *adjective* See **difficult.**

uphold *verb* See **elevate, support, sustain.**

upkeep *noun* See **living.**

uplift *verb* See **elate, elevate, exalt.**

uplift *noun* See **elation.**

upmost *adjective* See **top.**

upper *adjective* See **higher.**

upper class *noun* See **society.**

upper-class *adjective* See **noble.**

upper crust *noun* See **society.**

upper-crust *adjective* See **noble.**

upper hand *noun* See **advantage.**

uppermost *adjective* See **top.**

uppish *adjective* See **impudent, snobbish.**

uppishness *noun* See **impudence.**

uppity *adjective* See **impudent, snobbish.**

uppityness *noun* See **impudence.**

upraise *verb* See **elevate, erect.**

uprear *verb* See **elevate, erect.**

upright *adjective* See **erect, honest, vertical.**

uprightness *noun* See **good.**

uprise *verb* See **get up** at **get.**

uprising *noun* See **rebellion.**

uproar *noun* See **disturbance, noise, sensation, vociferation.**

uproot *verb* See **annihilate.**

upset *verb* To disturb the health or physiological functioning of : derange, disorder, turn, unsettle. See HEALTH in Index. — See also **agitate, disorder, disrupt, overturn.**

upset *noun* The act or an example of upsetting : disordering, disorgan-ization, disruption. See ORDER in Index. — See also **agitation.**

upset *adjective* See **upside-down.**

upsetting *adjective* See **disturbing.**

upshot *noun* See **effect.**

upside-down *adjective* Turned over completely : capsized, inverted, overturned, upset, upturned. See HORIZONTAL in Index. — See also **confused.**

upspring *verb* See **get up** at **get, stem.**

upstanding *adjective* See **erect, honest.**

upstandingness *noun* See **honesty.**

upsurge *verb* See **increase.**

upsurge *noun* See **increase.**

upswing *noun* See **increase.**

uptight *adjective* See **edgy.**

up to *adjective* See **equal.**

up-to-date *adjective* See **contemporary.**

up-to-the-minute *adjective* See **contemporary.**

upturn *noun* See **increase.**

upturned *adjective* See **upside-down.**

urban *adjective* See **city.**

urbane *adjective* See **cultured, suave.**

urbanity *noun* See **elegance.**

urbanize *verb* See **citify.**

urge *verb* To impel to action : exhort, press. See CAUSE, PUSH in Index. — See also **insist.**

urgent *adjective* See **burning, insistent.**

usable also **useable** *adjective* In a condition to be used : employable, serviceable, utilizable. See USED in Index. — See also **open.**

usage *noun* See **consumption, cus-tom, exercise.**

usance *noun* See **custom.**

use *verb* To put into action or use : actuate, apply, employ, exercise, exploit, implement, practice, utilize.

Idioms: avail oneself of, bring into play, bring to bear, make use of, put into practice, put to use. See USED in Index. — See also **abuse, operate.**

use up *verb* See **deplete, exhaust.**

use *noun* The quality of being suitable or adaptable to an end : account, advantage, avail, benefit, profit, usefulness, utility. See USED in Index. — See also **consumption, custom, duty, exercise.**

used *adjective* See **accustomed.**

useful *adjective* See **beneficial, convenient, practical.**

usefulness *noun* See **use.**

useless *adjective* Having no useful purpose : ineffectual, inutile, unusable, worthless. See USED in Index. — See also **futile, impracticable, ineffectual.**

uselessness *noun* See **futility, ineffectuality.**

user *noun* See **consumer.**

usher *verb* See **guide.**

usher in *verb* To make known the presence or arrival of : announce, herald, introduce, proclaim. See KNOWLEDGE, START in Index. — See also **introduce.**

usher *noun* See **guide.**

usual *noun* A regular or customary matter, condition, or course of events : commonplace, norm, ordinary, rule. See USUAL in Index.

usual *adjective* See **common, customary.**

usually *adverb* In an expected or customary manner; for the most part : commonly, consistently, customarily, frequently, generally, habitually, naturally, normally, often, regularly, routinely, typically. *Idioms:* as usual, per usual. See BIG, USUAL in Index.

usualness *noun* The quality or condition of being usual : customariness, habitualness, normalcy, nor-

mality, ordinariness, prevalence, regularity, routineness. See USUAL in Index.

usurp *verb* See **assume.**

usurpation *noun* The act of taking something for oneself : appropriation, arrogation, assumption, preemption, seizure. See GIVE in Index.

utensil *noun* See **tool.**

utilitarian *adjective* See **practical.**

utility *noun* See **use.**

utilizable *adjective* See **open, usable.**

utilization *noun* See **duty, exercise.**

utilize *verb* See **use.**

utmost *adjective* See **extreme, maximum, ultimate.**

utmost *noun* See **maximum.**

utopian *noun* See **dreamer.**

utopian *adjective* See **idealistic.**

utter[1] *verb* See **pronounce, say.**

utter[2] *adjective* Completely such, without qualification or exception : absolute, all-out, arrant, complete, consummate, crashing, damned, dead, downright, flat, out-and-out, outright, perfect, plain, pure, sheer[2], thorough, thoroughgoing, total, unbounded, unequivocal, unlimited, unmitigated, unqualified, unrelieved, unreserved. *Informal:* flat-out, positive. *Chiefly British:* blooming. See BIG, LIMITED in Index.

utterance *noun* See **expression, speech, voicing, word.**

uttered *adjective* See **vocal.**

utterly *adverb* See **completely.**

uttermost *adjective* See **extreme, maximum, ultimate.**

uttermost *noun* See **maximum.**

V

vacancy *noun* See **emptiness, nothingness.**

vacant *adjective* Lacking intelligent thought or content : blank, empty, empty-headed, inane, vacuous. See FULL in Index. — See also **empty, idle.**

vacate *verb* See **cancel, empty.**

vacation *noun* A regularly scheduled period spent away from work or duty, often in recreation : furlough, leave[2]. *Chiefly British:* holiday. See WORK in Index.

vacillant *adjective* See **hesitant.**

vacillate *verb* See **hesitate, sway, swing.**

vacillation *noun* See **hesitation.**

vacillatory *adjective* See **hesitant.**

vacuity *noun* See **emptiness, hole, nothingness.**

vacuous *adjective* See **empty, vacant.**

vacuousness *noun* See **emptiness.**

vacuum *noun* See **emptiness, nothingness.**

vagabond *adjective* See **nomadic.**

vagary *noun* See **fancy.**

vagrant *adjective* See **nomadic.**

vague *adjective* See **ambiguous, indefinite, unclear.**

vagueness *noun* The quality or state of being ambiguous : ambiguity, ambiguousness, cloudiness, equivocalness, indefiniteness, nebulousness, obscureness, obscurity, uncertainty, unclearness. See CLEAR in Index.

vain *adjective* Unduly preoccupied with one's own appearance : conceited, narcissistic. See SELF-LOVE in Index. — See also **egotistic, empty, futile.**

vainglorious *adjective* See **egotistic.**

vainglory *noun* See **egotism.**

vainness *noun* See **egotism, futility.**

valediction *noun* See **parting.**

valedictory *adjective* See **parting.**

valiance *noun* See **courage, heroism.**

valiancy *noun* See **courage, heroism.**

valiant *adjective* See **brave.**

valiantness *noun* See **courage.**

valid *adjective* See **authentic, sound[2].**

validate *verb* See **confirm, prove.**

validation *noun* See **confirmation.**

validity *noun* See **authenticity.**

valor *noun* See **courage, heroism.**

valorous *adjective* See **brave.**

valuable *adjective* Of great value : costly, inestimable, invaluable, precious, priceless, worthy. *Idioms:* beyond price, of great price. See VALUE in Index.

valuate *verb* See **estimate.**

valuation *noun* See **estimate, worth.**

value *noun* See **meaning, merit, worth.**

value *verb* See **admire, appreciate, estimate.**

valueless *adjective* See **worthless.**

vamoose *verb* See **run.**

vamp *noun* See **flirt, seductress.**

vampire *noun* See **fiend.**

vandalize *verb* See **trash.**

vanish *verb* See **disappear.**

vanished *adjective* No longer in use, force, or operation : dead, defunct, extinct, lost. See LIVE, NEW in Index.

vanishment *noun* See **disappearance.**

vanity *noun* See **egotism, futility.**

vanquish *verb* See **defeat, overwhelm.**

vanquishment *noun* See **defeat.**

vantage *noun* See **advantage, point of view.**

vapid *adjective* See **insipid.**

vapidity *noun* See **dullness, insipidity.**

vapidness *noun* See **dullness, insipidity.**

vaporize *verb* See **evaporate.**

vaporous *adjective* See **filmy.**

vapory *adjective* See **filmy.**

variable *adjective* See **capricious, changeable, uneven.**

variance *noun* See **conflict, variation.**

variant *noun* See **variation.**

variant *adjective* See **changeable, different.**

variation *noun* 1. The condition or fact of varying : difference, variance. See CHANGE, SAME in Index. 2. One that is slightly different from others of the same kind or designation : variant, variety, version. See SAME in Index. — See also **change.**

varicolored *adjective* See **multicolor.**

varied *adjective* See **various.**

variegate *verb* See **streak.**

variegated *adjective* See **multicolor, various.**

variegation *noun* See **variety.**

variety *noun* The quality of being made of many different elements, forms, kinds, or individuals : diverseness, diversification, diversity, heterogeneity, heterogeneousness, miscellaneousness, multifariousness, multiformity, multiplicity, variegation, variousness. *Biology:* polymorphism. See SAME in Index. — See also **assortment, kind², variation.**

various *adjective* Consisting of a number of different kinds : assorted, divers, diverse, diversified, heterogeneous, miscellaneous, mixed, motley, multifarious, multiform, sundry, varied, variegated. *Biology:* polymorphic, polymorphous. See SAME in Index. — See also

changeable, different, distinct, several, versatile.

variousness *noun* See **variety.**

varnish *verb* See **color.**

vary *verb* See **change, differ, go.**

vast *adjective* See **giant.**

vastness *noun* See **enormousness.**

vatic *adjective* See **prophetic.**

vatical *adjective* See **prophetic.**

vaticinal *adjective* See **prophetic.**

vaticinate *verb* See **prophesy.**

vaticination *noun* See **prophecy.**

vaticinator *noun* See **prophet.**

vault¹ *noun* See **grave¹.**

vault² *verb* See **jump.**

vault *noun* See **jump.**

vaunt *verb* See **boast.**

vaunt *noun* See **boast.**

vaunter *noun* See **braggart.**

vector *noun* See **heading.**

veer *verb* See **deviate, swerve, turn.**

vehemence *noun* See **intensity.**

vehemency *noun* See **intensity.**

vehement *adjective* See **intense.**

veil *noun* See **façade.**

veil *verb* See **cover, wrap.**

vein *noun* See **mood, streak, style.**

velocity *noun* See **speed.**

venal *adjective* See **corrupt, corruptible.**

vend *verb* See **peddle, sell.**

vender or **vendor** *noun* See **seller.**

veneer *noun* See **façade.**

veneer *verb* See **color.**

venerable *adjective* See **old.**

venerate *verb* See **adore.**

veneration *noun* See **adoration.**

venerational *adjective* See **reverent.**

vengeance *noun* See **retaliation.**

vengeful *adjective* See **vindictive.**

vengefulness *noun* See **vindictiveness.**

venial *adjective* See **pardonable.**

venom *noun* See **poison.**

venomous *adjective* See **malevolent, poisonous.**

venomousness *noun* See **malevolence.**

vent *verb* See **air, emit, say.**

vent *noun* See **hole.**

ventilate *verb* See **air.**

ventilation *noun* See **conference.**

venture *noun* See **adventure, project.**

venture *verb* See **gamble, hazard, presume, risk.**

venturer *noun* See **adventurer.**

venturesome *adjective* See **adventurous, dangerous.**

venturesomeness *noun* See **daring.**

venturous *adjective* See **adventurous, dangerous.**

venturousness *noun* See **daring.**

veracious *adjective* See **accurate, truthful.**

veraciousness *noun* See **veracity.**

veracity *noun* Correspondence with fact or truth : accuracy, correctness, exactitude, exactness, fidelity, truth, veraciousness, veridicality, verity. See TRUE in Index. —See also **truth.**

verbal *adjective* Relating to, consisting of, or having the nature of words : wordy. See WORDS in Index. —See also **literal, oral.**

verbalism *noun* See **wording.**

verbalization *noun* See **expression, speech.**

verbalize *verb* See **say, speak.**

verbatim *adjective* See **literal.**

verbiage *noun* See **wordiness.**

verbose *adjective* See **wordy.**

verboseness *noun* See **wordiness.**

verbosity *noun* See **wordiness.**

verboten *adjective* See **forbidden.**

verge *noun* A transitional interval beyond which some new action or different state of affairs is likely to begin or occur : borderline, brink, edge, point, threshold. See EDGE in Index. —See also **border.**

verge *verb* See **adjoin, border.**

verge on *verb* See **rival.**

veridical *adjective* See **accurate, truthful.**

veridicality *noun* See **veracity.**

verification *noun* See **confirmation.**

verify *verb* See **confirm, prove.**

verily *adverb* See **really.**

verisimilitude *noun* Appearance of truth or authenticity : believability, color, credibility, credibleness, creditability, creditableness, plausibility, plausibleness. See LIKELY in Index.

verity *noun* See **veracity.**

vernacular *noun* See **dialect, language.**

vernal *adjective* See **spring.**

versant *adjective* See **familiar.**

versatile *adjective* Having many aspects, uses, or abilities : all-around, all-round, many-sided, multifaceted, protean, various. See ABILITY, SAME in Index.

verse *noun* See **poem.**

versed *adjective* See **experienced, familiar.**

versicolor *adjective* See **multicolor.**

versicolored *adjective* See **multicolor.**

versifier *noun* See **poet.**

version *noun* See **paraphrase, story, variation.**

vertex *noun* See **height.**

vertical *adjective* At right angles to the horizon or to level ground : perpendicular, plumb, upright. See HORIZONTAL in Index.

vertiginous *adjective* See **dizzy, giddy.**

vertiginousness *noun* See **dizziness.**

vertigo *noun* See **dizziness.**

verve *noun* See **spirit, vigor.**

very *adverb* To a high degree : awfully, dreadfully, eminently, exceedingly, exceptionally, extra, extremely, greatly, highly, most, notably. *Informal:* awful. *Chiefly Regional:* mighty. See BIG in Index.

very *adjective* See **mere, precise, same.**

vesper *noun* See **evening.**

vestige *noun* See **trace.**

vestment *noun* See **habit.**

vet *noun* See **veteran.**

veteran *noun* One who has had long experience in a given activity or capacity : old hand. *Informal:* oldtimer, vet. See ABILITY, KNOWLEDGE in Index.

veteran *adjective* See **experienced.**

veto *verb* To prevent or forbid authoritatively : blackball, negative, turn down. *Slang:* nix. *Idiom:* turn thumbs down on. See ACCEPT in Index.

vex *verb* See **annoy.**

vexation *noun* See **annoyance.**

vexatious *adjective* Troubling the nerves or peace of mind, as by repeated vexations : annoying, bothersome, galling, irksome, irritating, nettlesome, plaguy, provoking, troublesome. See PAIN in Index.

viable *adjective* See **possible.**

vibrant *adjective* See **resonant, spirited.**

vibrate *verb* See **shake.**

vice *noun* See **corruption.**

vicinity *noun* See **environment, locality, neighborhood.**

vicious *adjective* See **cruel, evil, fierce, malevolent.**

viciousness *noun* See **malevolence.**

vicissitude *noun* See **difficulty.**

victim *noun* One that is made to suffer injury, loss, or death : casualty, prey. See HELP in Index. — See also **dupe, sacrifice.**

victimization *noun* See **cheat.**

victimize *verb* See **cheat, sacrifice.**

victimizer *noun* See **cheat.**

victor *noun* See **conqueror, winner.**

Victorian *adjective* See **genteel.**

Victorian *noun* See **prude.**

victorious *adjective* Relating to, having the nature of, or experiencing triumph : conquering, triumphal, triumphant, winning. See WIN in Index.

victory *noun* See **conquest.**

victual *noun* See **food.**

videlicet *adverb* See **namely.**

vie *verb* See **compete.**

view *noun* That which is or can be seen : lookout, outlook, panorama, perspective, prospect, scene, sight, vista. See SEE in Index. — See also **belief, examination, intention, look.**

view *verb* See **examine, look, regard.**

viewable *adjective* See **visible.**

viewer *noun* See **witness.**

viewpoint *noun* See **point of view.**

vigil *noun* See **lookout.**

vigilance *noun* See **alertness, lookout.**

vigilant *adjective* See **alert.**

vigor *noun* A quality of active mental and physical forcefulness : dash, punch, starch, verve, vigorousness, vim, vitality. *Informal:* snap. *Idiom:* vim and vigor. See ACTION, TIRED in Index. — See also **spirit.**

vigorous *adjective* Disposed to action : active, brisk, driving, dynamic, dynamical, energetic, enterprising, lively, peppy, sprightly, spry, zippy. *Informal:* snappy. See ACTION in Index. — See also **energetic, forceful, lusty.**

vigorously *adverb* See **hard.**

vigorousness *noun* See **vigor.**

vile *adjective* See **filthy, offensive, sordid.**

vilification *noun* See **libel.**

vilify *verb* See **libel.**

villain *noun* See **heavy.**

villainous *adjective* See **corrupt.**

villainousness *noun* See
corruption.

villainy *noun* See corruption.

villeinage also **villainage** *noun*
See slavery.

vim *noun* See spirit, vigor.

vincible *adjective* See vulnerable.

vinculum *noun* See bond.

vindicate *verb* See assert, avenge,
clear, defend, justify.

vindication *noun* See apology,
exculpation.

vindictive *adjective* Disposed to
seek revenge : revengeful, spiteful,
vengeful. See FORGIVENESS in
Index.

vindictiveness *noun* The quality
or condition of being vindictive :
revenge, spite, spitefulness, vengefulness. See FORGIVENESS in Index.

vintage *noun* Informal. A period of
origin : year. See TIME in Index.

vintage *adjective* Characterized
by enduring excellence, appeal, and
importance : classic, classical. See
GOOD in Index. — See also distinctive, old-fashioned.

violate *verb* 1. To spoil or mar the
sanctity of : defile, desecrate, pollute, profane. See CLEAN, RELIG-
ION, SACRED in Index. 2. To fail to
fulfill (a promise) or conform to (a
regulation) : breach, break, contravene, infringe, transgress. See DO in
Index. 3. To deprive of virginity :
defile, deflower. See SEX in Index.
— See also disobey, rape.

violation *noun* See breach,
sacrilege.

violence *noun* See force, intensity.

violent *adjective* See forcible,
intense, rough.

VIP *noun* See dignitary.

virago *noun* See scold.

virgin *noun* See innocent.

virgin *adjective* See chaste.

virginal *adjective* See chaste,
innocent.

virginity *noun* See chastity.

virile *adjective* See manly.

virtual *adjective* See implicit.

virtue *noun* A special feature or
quality that confers superiority :
beauty, distinction, excellence,
merit, perfection. See GOOD in
Index. — See also chastity, good,
merit.

virtuous *adjective* See chaste,
ethical.

virtuousness *noun* See chastity,
good.

virulence *noun* See resentment.

virulency *noun* See resentment.

virulent *adjective* Extremely
destructive or harmful : baneful,
deadly, malignant, noxious, pernicious, pestilent, pestilential. See
HELP in Index. — See also poisonous,
resentful.

virus *noun* See poison.

visage *noun* See expression, face.

vis-à-vis *noun* See counterpart.

visceral *adjective* See inner,
instinctive.

viscid *adjective* See viscous.

viscidity *noun* See viscosity.

viscose *adjective* See viscous.

viscosity *noun* The physical property of being viscous : glutinousness, viscidity. See SOLID in Index.

viscous *adjective* Having a heavy,
gluey quality : glutinous, mucilaginous, viscid, viscose. See SOLID in
Index.

visibility *noun* The quality, condition, or degree of being visible :
perceptibility, visuality, visualness.
See SEE in Index.

visible *adjective* Capable of being
seen : discernible, perceivable, perceptible, seeable, viewable, visual.
See SEE in Index. — See also
apparent.

vision noun **1.** The faculty of seeing : eye, eyesight, seeing, sight.
Archaic: light[1]. See SEE in Index.
2. Unusual or creative discernment
or perception : farsightedness, foresight, prescience. See FORESIGHT in
Index. — See also **dream, prophecy.**

vision verb See **imagine.**

visionary adjective Characterized
by foresight : farsighted, foresighted, prescient. See FORESIGHT
in Index. — See also **dreamy, idealistic, illusive, imaginary, prophetic.**

visionary noun See **dreamer.**

visit verb To go to or seek out the
company of in order to socialize :
call, come by, come over, drop by,
drop in, look in, look up, pop in, run
in, see, stop (by or in). *Idiom:* pay a
visit. See SEEK in Index. — See also
converse[1], inflict, stay[1].

visit noun An act or an instance of
going or coming to see another :
call, look-in, visitation. See SEEK in
Index. — See also **stay[1].**

visitant noun See **company, ghost.**

visitation noun See **trial, visit.**

visitor noun See **arrival, company.**

visor noun See **bill[2].**

vista noun See **view.**

visual adjective Serving, resulting
from, or relating to the sense of
sight : optic, optical. See SEE in
Index. — See also **visible.**

visuality noun See **visibility.**

visualize verb See **imagine.**

visualness noun See **visibility.**

vital adjective See **alive, deadly,
essential, lusty.**

vital force noun See **spirit.**

vitality noun See **spirit, vigor.**

vitalize verb See **energize, quicken.**

vitalizing adjective See **stimulating.**

vitiate verb See **abolish, corrupt,
injure.**

vitriolic adjective See **biting.**

vituperate verb See **revile.**

vituperation noun Harsh, often
insulting language : abuse, billingsgate, contumely, invective, obloquy,
railing, revilement, reviling, scurrility, scurrilousness. See PRAISE in
Index.

vituperative adjective See **abusive.**

vivacious adjective See **lively.**

vivaciousness noun See **spirit.**

vivacity noun See **spirit.**

vivid adjective See **colorful, graphic.**

vivify verb See **quicken.**

vivifying adjective See **stimulating.**

vixen noun See **scold.**

vocabulary noun **1.** An alphabetical list of words often defined or
translated : dictionary, glossary,
lexicon, wordbook. See WORDS in
Index. **2.** All the words of a language : lexicon, word-hoard. See
WORDS in Index. — See also
language.

vocal adjective **1.** Produced by the
voice : articulate, oral, sonant, spoken, uttered, voiced. See SOUNDS in
Index. **2.** Characterized by, containing, or functioning as a vowel or
vowels : vocalic, vowel. See
SOUNDS in Index. — See also
outspoken.

vocalic adjective See **vocal.**

vocalism noun See **voicing.**

vocalist noun A person who sings :
singer, songster, songstress, voice.
See PERFORMING ARTS in Index.

vocalization noun See **expression,
speech, voicing.**

vocalize verb See **pronounce, say,
sing, speak.**

vocation noun An inner urge to
pursue an activity or perform a service : calling, mission. See DESIRE
in Index. — See also **business.**

vociferate verb See **roar.**

vociferation noun Offensively loud
and insistent utterances, especially
of disapproval : clamor, hullabaloo,

outcry, rumpus, uproar. *Idiom:* hue
and cry. See LIKE, SOUNDS in Index.

vociferous *adjective* Offensively
loud and insistent : blatant, boisterous, clamorous, obstreperous,
strident. *Informal:* loudmouthed.
See SOUNDS in Index.

vogue *noun* See **fashion.**

voice *noun* The right or chance to
express an opinion or participate in a
decision : say, suffrage, vote.
Informal: say-so. See PARTICIPATE
in Index. — See also **expression,
vocalist.**

voice *verb* See **say.**

voiced *adjective* See **vocal.**

voiceless *adjective* See **dumb,
speechless.**

voicing *noun* The use of the speech
organs to produce sounds : articulation, enunciation, utterance, vocalism, vocalization. See SOUNDS,
WORDS in Index.

void *adjective* See **empty.**

void *noun* See **emptiness, gap,
hole, nothingness.**

void *verb* See **abolish, empty.**

voidance *noun* See **abolition.**

volatile *adjective* See **capricious.**

volatilize *verb* See **evaporate.**

volition *noun* See **will.**

volitional *adjective* See **voluntary.**

volley *noun* See **barrage.**

voluble *adjective* See **talkative.**

volume *noun* See **book, bulk,
publication.**

voluminous *adjective* See **full,
generous.**

voluntarily *adverb* Of one's own
free will : freely, spontaneously,
willfully, willingly. *Idioms:* of one's
own accord, on one's own volition.
See WILLING in Index.

voluntary *adjective* **1.** Done by
one's own choice : free, spontaneous, uncompelled, unforced, volitional, willful. See WILLING in

Index. **2.** Of or relating to free exercise of the will : volitional, willing.
See WILLING in Index. — See also
deliberate, unpaid.

voluntary *noun* See **volunteer.**

volunteer *noun* Someone who
offers his or her services freely :
voluntary. See WILLING, WORK in
Index.

volunteer *verb* See **offer.**

voluptuary *noun* See **sybarite.**

voluptuary *adjective* See
sybaritic.

voluptuous *adjective* See **sensual,
sensuous, sybaritic.**

voluptuousness *noun* See **sensuality, sensuousness.**

vomit *verb* To eject the contents of
the stomach through the mouth :
heave, throw up. *Slang:* puke. See
MOUTH in Index.

voodoo *verb* See **charm.**

voracious *adjective* Having an
insatiable appetite for an activity or
pursuit : avid, edacious, gluttonous, greedy, omnivorous, rapacious,
ravenous, unappeasable. See DESIRE
in Index. — See also **greedy,
ravenous.**

voracity *noun* The quality or condition of being voracious : avidity,
edacity, omnivorousness, rapaciousness, rapacity, ravenousness. See
DESIRE in Index.

votary *noun* See **devotee.**

vote *verb* See **elect.**

vote *noun* See **voice.**

voter *noun* See **elector.**

vouch *verb* See **certify.**

vouchsafe *verb* See **condescend,
grant.**

vow *noun* See **promise.**

vow *verb* See **pledge.**

vowel *adjective* See **vocal.**

voyage *noun* See **expedition.**

vulgar *adjective* See **coarse, lowly,
obscene.**

vulgarian *noun* See **boor**.

vulgarism *noun* See **corruption**.

vulgarity *noun* See **obscenity**.

vulgarness *noun* See **obscenity**.

vulnerability *noun* See **exposure**.

vulnerable *adjective* Open to attack and capture because of a lack of protection : assailable, attackable, pregnable, vincible. See STRONG in Index. — See also **liable**.

vulnerableness *noun* See **exposure**.

W

wacky also **whacky** *adjective* See **foolish, insane**.

wad *noun* See **fortune, heap, lump¹**.

wade *verb* See **plod**.

wade in or **into** *verb* See **attack, plunge**.

waffle *verb* See **equivocate**.

waffle *noun* See **equivocation**.

wag¹ *verb* To move to and fro vigorously and usually repeatedly : switch, waggle, wave. See REPETITION in Index.

wag² *noun* See **joker**.

wage *verb* To engage in (a war or campaign, for example) : carry on, carry out, conduct. See DO in Index.

wage *noun* Payment for work done : compensation, earnings, emolument, fee, hire, pay, remuneration, salary, stipend. See PAY in Index. — See also **due**.

wager *verb* See **bet, gamble**.

wager *noun* See **bet, gamble**.

waggish *adjective* See **playful**.

waggishness *noun* See **playfulness**.

waggle *verb* See **flap, wag¹, wiggle**.

wail *verb* See **bawl, cry, howl**.

wail *noun* See **howl**.

wailing *noun* See **cry**.

wait *verb* See **defer¹, expect, pause, remain**.

wait on or **upon** *verb* See **serve**.

wait *noun* An act or the time of waiting : waiting. See CONTINUE in Index.

waiting *noun* See **wait**.

waive *verb* See **abdicate, defer¹**.

waiver *noun* See **abdication, delay**.

wake¹ *verb* To cease sleeping : arouse, awake, awaken, rouse, stir¹, waken. See AWARENESS in Index.

wake *noun* A watch over the body of a dead person before burial : watch. See RITUAL in Index.

wake² *noun* See **train**.

wakeful *adjective* **1.** Not in a state of sleep : awake, unsleeping, wideawake. See AWARENESS in Index. **2.** Marked by an absence of sleep : sleepless, slumberless. See AWARENESS in Index. — See also **alert**.

wakefulness *noun* See **alertness**.

waken *verb* See **arouse, wake¹**.

wale *noun* See **welt**.

walk *noun* An act of walking, especially for pleasure : amble, meander (often used in plural), perambulation, promenade, ramble, saunter, stroll, wander. See MOVE in Index. — See also **constitutional**.

walk *verb* To go on foot : ambulate, foot, pace, step, tread. *Slang:* hoof. *Idiom:* foot it. See MOVE in Index.

walk out *verb* See **strike**.

walkaway *noun* See **breeze, runaway**.

walking stick *noun* See **stick**.

walkover *noun* See **breeze, runaway**.

wall *noun* A solid structure that encloses an area or separates one area from another : barrier, partition. See INCLUDE, THING in Index. — See also **bar**.

wall *verb* To separate with or as if with a wall : fence, partition. See INCLUDE in Index. — See also **bar, enclose.**

wallop *verb* See **hit, overwhelm.**

wallop *noun* *Informal.* The capacity to create a powerful effect : impact. *Informal:* punch. See AFFECT in Index. — See also **blow[2], kick, thrill.**

walloping *adjective* See **giant.**

wallow *verb* To move about in an indolent or clumsy manner : flounder, welter. See MOVE in Index. — See also **luxuriate.**

waltz *verb* See **breeze.**

wampum *noun* See **money.**

wan *adjective* See **haggard, pale.**

wan *verb* See **pale.**

wander *verb* See **digress, rove, stroll.**

wander *noun* See **walk.**

wandering *adjective* See **errant, erratic.**

wane *verb* See **fade, subside.**

wane *noun* The act or process of becoming less active or intense : abatement, ebb, letup, remission, slackening, subsidence. See INCREASE in Index.

wangle *verb* *Informal.* To make, achieve, or get through contrivance or guile : engineer, finesse, worm. *Informal:* finagle. See GET, MAKE in Index.

want *verb* See **choose, desire, lack.**

want *noun* See **absence, demand, poverty.**

wanting *adjective* See **absent, deficient, empty, insufficient.**

wanton *adjective* **1.** Marked by an absence of conventional restraint in sexual behavior; sexually unrestrained : easy, fast, libertine, light[2], loose, whorish. See SEX in Index. **2.** Not required, necessary, or warranted by the circumstances of

the case : gratuitous, supererogative, supererogatory, uncalled-for. See NECESSARY in Index. — See also **abandoned.**

wanton *noun* An immoral or licentious person : libertine, profligate, rake[1]. See SEX in Index. — See also **slut.**

wantonness *noun* See **abandon.**

war *noun* See **competition, conflict.**

war *verb* See **contend.**

war cry *noun* See **cry.**

ward *noun* See **defense, dependent, detention, guard.**

ward *verb* See **defend, prevent.**

ward off *verb* See **parry.**

warden *noun* See **jailer.**

warder *noun* See **jailer.**

ware *noun* See **good.**

warehouse *noun* See **depository.**

warfare *noun* See **competition, conflict.**

wariness *noun* See **alertness, caution.**

warlike *adjective* See **belligerent, military.**

warm *adjective* See **amiable, enthusiastic.**

warmed-over *adjective* See **trite.**

warmhearted *adjective* See **friendly.**

warmth *noun* See **amiability, heat.**

warn *verb* To notify (someone) of imminent danger or risk : admonish, alarm, alert, caution, forewarn. See WARN in Index.

warning *noun* Advice to beware, as of a person or thing : admonishment, admonition, caution, caveat, monition. See WARN in Index. — See also **alarm, example.**

warning *adjective* See **cautionary.**

warp *verb* See **bias, corrupt, distort.**

warp and woof *noun* See **texture.**

warrant *noun* See **basis, confirmation, guarantee, license, pawn[1], promise.**

warrant *verb* See **call for** at **call, confirm, guarantee.**

warranty *noun* See **guarantee.**

warrior *noun* See **fighter.**

wary *adjective* Trying attentively to avoid danger, risk, or error : careful, cautious, chary, circumspect, forehanded, gingerly, prudent. See CAREFUL in Index. — See also **alert.**

wash *verb* **1.** To make moist : bathe, dampen, moisten, wet. See DRY in Index. **2.** To flow against or along : bathe, lap, lave, lip. See DRY in Index. **3.** To move along with or be carried away by the action of water : drift, float. See MOVE in Index. **4.** To flow or move with a low slapping sound : bubble, burble, gurgle, lap, splash, swash. See MOVE, SOUNDS in Index. **5.** *Informal.* To prove valid under scrutiny : hold (up), prove out, stand up. *Idioms:* hold water, pass muster, ring true. See TRUE in Index.

wash up *verb* See **destroy.**

washed-up *adjective* See **through.**

washiness *noun* See **insipidity.**

washout *noun* See **failure.**

washy *adjective* See **dilute, insipid.**

waspish *adjective* See **ill-tempered.**

waste *verb* **1.** To use up foolishly or needlessly : consume, devour, dissipate, squander. See SAVE in Index. **2.** To spend (money) excessively and usually foolishly : consume, dissipate, fool away, fritter away, riot away, squander, throw away, trifle away. *Slang:* blow[1]. See SAVE in Index. — See also **consume, devastate, fade, idle, kill[1], lose, murder.**

waste *noun* See **barren, extravagance.**

wasted *adjective* Physically haggard : cadaverous, drawn, emaciated, gaunt, shrunken, skeletal.

Idiom: skin and bones. See BETTER, TIRED in Index.

wasteful *adjective* See **extravagant.**

wastefulness *noun* See **extravagance.**

wasteland *noun* See **barren.**

waster *noun* See **wastrel.**

wastrel *noun* **1.** A person who spends money or resources wastefully : prodigal, profligate, scattergood, spendthrift, waster. See SAVE in Index. **2.** A self-indulgent person who spends time avoiding work or other useful activity : bum[1], drone[1], fainéant, good-for-nothing, idler, layabout, loafer, ne'er-do-well, no-good, slugabed, sluggard. *Informal:* do-little, do-nothing, lazybones, slug[2]. *Slang:* slouch. See INDUSTRIOUS in Index.

watch *verb* To look at or on attentively or carefully : eye, observe, regard, scrutinize, survey. *Idioms:* have one's (or keep an) eye on, keep tabs on. See AWARENESS, SEE in Index. — See also **tend[2].**

watch out *verb* See **look out** at **look.**

watch over *verb* See **supervise.**

watch *noun* The act of observing, often for an extended time : observance, observation, scrutiny. See AWARENESS, SEE in Index. — See also **guard, lookout, turn, wake[1].**

watcher *noun* Someone who observes : beholder, bystander, looker-on, observer, onlooker, spectator. See AWARENESS, SEE in Index. — See also **tail.**

watchful *adjective* See **alert, careful.**

watchfulness *noun* See **alertness.**

water *verb* See **dilute, tear[2].**

watered-down *adjective* See **dilute.**

wateriness *noun* See **insipidity.**

waterish *adjective* See **dilute, insipid, pale.**

waterless *adjective* See **dry.**

waterloo *noun* See **fall.**

watershed *noun* See **basin.**

watery *adjective* See **dilute, insipid, pale.**

wave *verb* To have or cause to have a curved or sinuous form or surface : curl, curve, undulate. See STRAIGHT in Index. — See also **flap, flourish, wag**[1].

waver *verb* See **hesitate, sway, swing.**

wax *verb* See **become, increase.**

waxen *adjective* See **pale.**

way *noun* **1.** A course affording passage from one place to another : avenue, boulevard, drive, expressway, freeway, highway, path, road, roadway, route, street, superhighway, thoroughfare, thruway, turnpike. See MOVE, OPEN in Index. **2.** The approach used to do something : fashion, manner, method, mode, modus operandi, style, system, wise[2]. See MEANS in Index. — See also **behavior, custom, distance.**

waylay *verb* See **ambush.**

wayward *adjective* See **contrary.**

weak *adjective* See **dilute, faint, implausible, ineffectual, infirm, insecure.**

weaken *verb* To moderate or change a position or course of action as a result of pressure : ease off, relent, slacken, soften, yield. *Idiom:* give way (*or* ground). See STRONG in Index. — See also **dilute, enervate, fade.**

weakliness *noun* See **infirmity.**

weakling *noun* See **baby.**

weakly *adjective* See **infirm.**

weak-minded *adjective* See **backward, mindless.**

weakness *noun* An imperfection of character : failing, fault, foible, frailty, infirmity, shortcoming, weak point. See BETTER, HELP in Index. — See also **infirmity, taste.**

weak point *noun* See **weakness.**

weal[1] *noun* See **welfare.**

weal[2] *noun* See **welt.**

wealth *noun* See **heap, resource, riches.**

wealthy *adjective* See **rich.**

wear *verb* See **bite, fatigue.**

wear away *verb* See **bite.**

wear down *verb* See **fatigue.**

wear out *verb* See **exhaust, fatigue.**

wearied *adjective* See **exhausted.**

weariful *adjective* See **boring, exhausted.**

weariless *adjective* See **tireless.**

weariness *noun* See **dullness, exhaustion.**

wearing *adjective* See **tiring.**

wearisome *adjective* See **boring.**

weary *adjective* See **boring, exhausted, sick.**

weary *verb* See **bore, fatigue.**

wearying *adjective* See **tiring.**

weasel *noun* See **sneak.**

weasel *verb* See **equivocate.**

weasel word *noun* See **equivocation.**

weather *verb* See **survive.**

weave *verb* See **lurch, sway, wind**[2].

web *noun* **1.** An open fabric woven of strands that are interlaced and knotted at usually regular intervals : mesh, net[1], netting, network. See THING in Index. **2.** An interwoven or interrelated number of things : network, tissue. See GROUP in Index. — See also **tangle, texture.**

web *verb* See **catch.**

wed *verb* See **combine, marry.**

wedded *adjective* See **marital.**

wedding *noun* The act or ceremony by which two people become husband and wife : bridal, espousal, marriage, nuptial (often used in plural), spousal (often used in plural). See MARRIAGE in Index.

wedlock *noun* See **marriage.**

wee *adjective* See **tiny.**

weedy *adjective* See **thin.**

weeny *adjective* See **tiny.**

weep *verb* See **cry, drip, ooze.**

weeping *adjective* See **tearful.**

weeping *noun* See **cry.**

weepy *adjective* See **tearful.**

weigh *verb* See **count, ponder.**

weigh down *verb* See **depress.**

weigh on or **upon** *verb* See **haunt.**

weight *noun* The greatest part or portion : bulk, mass, preponderance, preponderancy. See BIG in Index. — See also **burden**[1], **heaviness, importance, influence, muscle.**

weight *verb* See **charge.**

weightiness *noun* See **gravity, heaviness, importance.**

weightless *adjective* See **light**[2].

weighty *adjective* See **burdensome, fat, grave**[2], **heavy, influential.**

weird *adjective* Of a mysteriously strange and usually frightening nature : eerie, uncanny, unearthly. *Informal:* spooky. See FEAR, USUAL in Index. — See also **eccentric, funny.**

weirdie also **weirdy** *noun* See **crackpot.**

weirdo *noun* See **crackpot.**

welcome *adjective* See **agreeable.**

welcome *noun* See **greeting.**

welcome *verb* See **accept, greet.**

welcoming *adjective* See **approachable.**

welfare *noun* A state of health, happiness, and prospering : prosperity, weal[1], well-being. See BETTER in Index. — See also **relief.**

welkin *noun* See **air.**

well[1] *noun* See **origin.**

well *verb* See **flow.**

well[2] *adverb* See **completely, considerably.**

well *adjective* See **advisable, healthy.**

well-being *noun* See **welfare.**

wellborn *adjective* See **noble.**

well-bred *adjective* See **courteous, cultured.**

well-developed *adjective* See **shapely.**

well-fixed *adjective* See **prosperous.**

well-founded *adjective* See **sane, sound**[2].

well-groomed *adjective* See **neat.**

well-grounded *adjective* See **sane, sound**[2].

well-heeled *adjective* See **prosperous.**

well-known *adjective* See **famous.**

well-liked *adjective* See **favorite.**

well-mannered *adjective* See **courteous.**

well-off *adjective* See **prosperous.**

well-timed *adjective* See **opportune.**

well-to-do *adjective* See **prosperous.**

well-worn *adjective* See **trite.**

welt *noun* A ridge or bump raised on the flesh, as by a lash or blow : wale, weal[2], wheal, whelk. See MARKS in Index. — See also **blow**[2].

welter *verb* See **wallow.**

wench *noun* See **slut.**

wend *verb* See **go.**

wet *adjective* Covered with or full of liquid : sodden, soggy, sopping, soppy. See DRY in Index.

wet *verb* To make thoroughly wet : douse, drench, saturate, soak, sodden, sop, souse. See DRY in Index. — See also **wash.**

wetland *noun* See **swamp.**

whack *verb* See **bang, hit, slap.**

whack *noun* See **blow**[2], **slap, try.**

wham *noun* See **blow²**, **slam**.

wham *verb* See **hit**.

whammy *noun* See **spell²**.

whatnot *noun* See **novelty**.

wheal *noun* See **welt**.

wheedle *verb* See **coax**.

wheel *noun* See **circle**, **revolution**.

wheel *verb* See **drive**, **swing**, **turn**.

whelk *noun* See **welt**.

whelm *verb* See **flood**.

wherefore *noun* See **cause**, **reason**.

wherewithal *noun* See **resource**.

whet *verb* See **sharpen**.

whiff *noun* See **shade**.

whiff *verb* See **smell**.

while *noun* See **bit¹**, **effort**.

while *verb* See **idle**.

whilom *adjective* See **late**.

whim *noun* See **fancy**.

whimper *verb* See **whine**.

whimsical *adjective* See **arbitrary**, **capricious**, **fanciful**.

whimsy also **whimsey** *noun* See **fancy**.

whine *verb* To cry with soft, intermittent, often plaintive sounds : pule, whimper. See SOUNDS in Index. — See also **complain**.

whiner *noun* See **grouch**.

whip *verb* See **beat**, **defeat**.

whipping *noun* See **beating**, **defeat**.

whipping boy *noun* See **scapegoat**.

whir *verb* See **hum**.

whir *noun* See **hum**.

whirl *verb* See **rush**, **spin**, **swirl**.

whirl *noun* See **drive**, **revolution**, **stir¹**, **try**.

whirlpool *noun* See **stir¹**.

whisk *verb* See **beat**, **rush**.

whisker *noun* See **shade**.

whisper *verb* See **confide**, **gossip**, **murmur**, **mutter**.

whisper *noun* See **murmur**, **shade**.

whisperer *noun* See **gossip**.

whispery *adjective* See **soft**.

whit *noun* See **bit¹**, **damn**.

white plague *noun* See **tuberculosis**.

whitewash *verb* See **color**, **extenuate**.

whiz also **whizz** *verb* See **hiss**, **hum**, **rush**.

whiz also **whizz** *noun* See **expert**, **hum**.

whole *adjective* Including every constituent or individual : all, complete, entire, gross, total. See PART in Index. — See also **complete**, **concentrated**, **good**, **healthy**, **round**.

whole *noun* An amount or quantity from which nothing is left out or held back : aggregate, all, entirety, everything, gross, sum, total, totality. *Informal:* work (used in plural). *Idioms:* everything but (or except) the kitchen sink, lock, stock, and barrel, the whole ball of wax (or kit and caboodle or megillah or nine yards or shebang). See PART in Index. — See also **system**.

wholehearted *adjective* See **implicit**.

wholeness *noun* See **completeness**, **health**, **soundness**.

wholesome *adjective* See **clean**, **healthful**, **healthy**.

wholly *adverb* See **completely**.

whoop *verb* See **roar**.

whoosh *verb* See **hiss**.

whop *noun* See **blow²**.

whop *verb* See **hit**.

whopper *noun* See **giant**, **lie²**.

whopping *adjective* See **giant**.

whore *noun* See **prostitute**, **slut**.

whorish *adjective* See **wanton**.

who's who or **Who's Who** *noun* See **society**.

why *noun* See **cause**, **intention**, **reason**.

wicked *adjective* See **evil**, **malevolent**, **troublesome**.

wickedness *noun* See **corruption**, **crime**, **evil**.

wide *adjective* See **broad, full.**

wide-awake *adjective* See **alert, wakeful.**

widen *verb* See **broaden, extend.**

wideness *noun* See **width.**

wide-ranging *adjective* See **general.**

wide-reaching *adjective* See **general.**

widespread *adjective* Spread out over a large area : far-flung. See WIDE in Index. — See also **common, general, prevailing.**

widget *noun* See **gadget.**

width *noun* The extent of something from side to side : breadth, broadness, wideness. See WIDE in Index.

wield *verb* See **exercise, handle.**

wiggle *verb* To move or proceed with short irregular motions up and down or from side to side : squiggle, squirm, waggle, worm, wriggle, writhe. See MOVE, REPETITION in Index.

wild *adjective* In a primitive state; not domesticated or cultivated; produced by nature : native, natural, rough, uncultivated, undomesticated, untamed. See WILD in Index. — See also **abandoned, frantic, rough, savage, uncivilized, unruly.**

wild *noun* An uninhabited region left in its natural state : bush, wilderness, wildness. See WILD in Index.

wilderness *noun* See **barren, wild.**

wildness *noun* See **abandon, unruliness, wild.**

wile *noun* See **trick.**

wile *verb* See **idle.**

wiliness *noun* See **art.**

will *noun* **1.** The mental faculty by which one deliberately chooses or decides : volition. See WILLING in Index. **2.** Unrestricted freedom to choose : discretion, pleasure. See FREE in Index. — See also **decision, liking.**

will *verb* See **choose, leave**[1].

willful also **wilfull** *adjective* See **deliberate, obstinate, voluntary.**

willfully also **wilfully** *adverb* See **voluntarily.**

willfulness also **wilfulness** *noun* See **obstinacy.**

willies *noun* See **jitter.**

willing *adjective* Disposed to accept or agree : acquiescent, agreeable, game, minded, ready. *Archaic:* fain. See WILLING in Index. — See also **voluntary.**

willingly *adverb* See **voluntarily, yes.**

will-o'-the-wisp *noun* See **illusion.**

willpower or **will power** *noun* See **decision.**

willy-nilly *adverb* See **helplessly.**

wilt *verb* To become limp, as from loss of freshness : droop, flag[2], sag. See BETTER in Index. — See also **slouch.**

wily *adjective* See **artful.**

win *verb* See **capture, earn, get.**

win over *verb* See **convince.**

win *noun* See **conquest.**

wince *verb* See **flinch.**

wince *noun* See **recoil.**

wind[1] *noun* A natural movement or current of air : air, blast, blow[1], breeze, gust, zephyr. *Archaic:* gale. See BREATH in Index.

wind *verb* See **air.**

wind[2] *verb* To move or proceed on a repeatedly curving course : coil, corkscrew, curl, entwine, meander, snake, spiral, twine, twist, weave, wreathe. See REPETITION, STRAIGHT in Index. — See also **insinuate.**

wind up *verb* See **close.**

windiness *noun* See **wordiness.**

winding *adjective* Repeatedly curving in alternate directions : anfractuous, flexuous, meandrous, serpentine, sinuous, snaky, tortuous. See REPETITION, STRAIGHT in Index.

windless *adjective* See **airless.**

window-dressing also **window dressing** *noun* See **façade.**

wind-up or **windup** *noun* See **end.**

windy *adjective* See **airy, inflated.**

wing *noun* See **branch, extension.**

wing *verb* See **fly, rush.**

wink *verb* See **blink, flash.**

wink at *verb* See **blink.**

wink *noun* See **blink, flash.**

winner *noun* One that wins a contest or competition : victor. See WIN in Index. — See also **conqueror.**

winning *adjective* See **attractive, victorious.**

winnow *verb* See **blow¹, sort.**

winsome *adjective* See **attractive.**

wintriness *noun* See **frigidness.**

wintry *adjective* See **frigid.**

wipe *verb* See **cancel.**

wipe out *verb* See **annihilate, eliminate, murder.**

wiped-out *adjective* See **drugged.**

wiretap *verb* See **tap².**

wisdom *noun* Deep, thorough, or mature understanding : insight, profundity, sagaciousness, sagacity, sageness, sapience. See WISE in Index. — See also **common sense, knowledge.**

wise¹ *adjective* Possessing or showing sound judgment and keen perception : knowing, sagacious, sage, sapient. See WISE in Index. — See also **aware, impudent, learned, sane, shrewd.**

wise² *noun* See **way.**

wiseacre *noun* See **smart aleck.**

wisecrack *noun* See **crack.**

wisecracker *noun* See **smart aleck.**

wise guy *noun* See **smart aleck.**

wisenheimer also **weisenheimer** *noun* See **smart aleck.**

wish *verb* See **choose, desire.**

wish *noun* See **desire.**

wishy-washiness *noun* See **insipidity.**

wishy-washy *adjective* See **insipid.**

wistful *adjective* See **depressed.**

wit *noun* See **discernment, humor, intelligence, joker, sanity.**

witch *noun* **1.** A woman who practices magic : enchantress, hag, lamia, sorceress. See SUPERNATURAL in Index. **2.** An ugly, frightening old woman : beldam, crone, hag. *Slang:* biddy. *Archaic:* trot. See BEAUTIFUL in Index. — See also **seductress.**

witch *verb* See **charm.**

witchcraft *noun* See **magic.**

witchery *noun* See **attraction, magic.**

witching *noun* See **magic.**

witching *adjective* See **magic, seductive.**

withdraw *verb* To pull back in : draw in, retract. See SHOW in Index. — See also **detach, go, remove, retract, retreat.**

withdrawal *noun* See **departure, retraction, retreat.**

withdrawn *adjective* See **cool.**

wither *verb* See **dry up** at **dry, languish, paralyze.**

withhold *verb* See **hold, refrain, refuse.**

with-it *adjective* See **fashionable.**

withstand *verb* See **endure, resist.**

witless *adjective* See **mindless.**

witling *noun* See **smart aleck.**

witness *noun* **1.** Someone who sees something occur : eyewitness, seer, viewer. See SEE in Index. **2.** One who testifies, especially in court : attestant, attester, testifier. *Law:* deponent. See LAW in Index. — See also **sign, testimony.**

witness *verb* See **certify, indicate, testify.**

witticism *noun* See **joke.**

wittiness noun See humor.

witting adjective See deliberate.

witty adjective See clever, humorous.

wizard noun See expert.

wizardly adjective See magic.

wizardry noun See magic.

wizen verb See dry up at dry.

wobble verb See hesitate, lurch, sway.

wobbliness noun See unstableness.

wobbly adjective See insecure, unstable.

woe noun See curse, distress, misery.

woebegone adjective See miserable, sorrowful.

woeful also **woful** adjective See miserable, sorrowful.

wolf noun See philanderer.

wolf verb See gulp.

wolfish adjective See fierce.

womanhood noun See femininity.

womanish adjective See effeminate, feminine.

womanishness noun See effeminacy.

womanize verb See philander.

womanizer noun See philanderer.

womankind noun See femininity.

womanliness noun See femininity.

womanly adjective See feminine.

womenfolk also **womenfolks** noun See femininity.

wonder noun The emotion aroused by something awe-inspiring or astounding : amaze, amazement, astonishment, awe, marvel, wonderment. *Archaic:* admiration, dread. See EXCITE, FEELINGS in Index.
— See also **doubt, marvel, miracle.**

wonder verb To have a feeling of great awe and rapt admiration : marvel. See EXCITE, FEELINGS in Index. — See also **doubt.**

wonderful adjective See fabulous, marvelous.

wonderment noun See marvel, wonder.

wondrous adjective See fabulous.

wont adjective See accustomed.

wont verb See accustom.

wont noun See custom.

wonted adjective See customary.

woo verb See court.

wooden adjective See dull, stiff.

wooer noun See beau.

woolgather verb See dream.

woolgathering adjective See dreamy.

woolly adjective See hairy.

wooziness noun See dizziness.

woozy adjective See dizzy.

word noun Something said : saying, statement, utterance. See WORDS in Index. — See also **argument, command, communication, gossip, news, promise, term.**

word verb See phrase.

wordage noun See wordiness, wording.

wordbook noun See vocabulary.

word-for-word adjective See literal.

word-hoard noun See vocabulary.

wordiness noun Words or the use of words in excess of those needed for clarity or precision : diffuseness, diffusion, long-windedness, pleonasm, prolixity, redundancy, verbiage, verboseness, verbosity, windiness, wordage. See EXCESS, STYLE, WORDS in Index.

wording noun Choice of words and the way in which they are used : diction, parlance, phrase, phraseology, phrasing, verbalism, wordage. See WORDS in Index.

wordless adjective See implicit, silent, speechless.

wordlessness noun See silence.

word of honor noun See promise.

word-of-mouth adjective See oral.

wordy *adjective* Using or containing an excessive number of words : diffuse, long-winded, periphrastic, pleonastic, prolix, redundant, verbose. See EXCESS, STYLE, WORDS in Index. — See also **verbal**.

work *noun* **1.** The technique, style, and quality of working : craftsmanship, workmanship. See WORK in Index. **2.** A building or complex in which an industry is located. Used in plural : factory, mill, plant. See MAKE, PLACE in Index. — See also **act, business, composition, labor, publication, whole**.

work *verb* **1.** To force to work : drive, task, tax. *Idiom:* crack the whip. See WORK in Index. **2.** To perform a function effectively : function, go, operate, run, take. See THRIVE in Index. **3.** To handle in a way so as to mix, form, and shape : knead, manipulate. See TOUCH in Index. **4.** To arrive at an answer to (a mathematical problem) : solve, work out. *Informal:* figure out. See REASON in Index. — See also **function, insinuate, labor, operate, succeed, till**.

work out *verb* See **arrange, design, exercise, succeed, work**.

work up *verb* See **provoke**.

workable *adjective* See **malleable, possible**.

workaday *adjective* See **everyday**.

workday *adjective* See **everyday**.

worked up *adjective* See **thrilled**.

worker *noun* See **employee, laborer**.

workhorse *noun* See **drudge**.

working *noun* See **behavior**.

working *adjective* See **active, employed**.

working girl *noun* See **laborer**.

workingman *noun* See **laborer**.

workingwoman *noun* See **laborer**.

workless *adjective* Out of work : jobless, unemployed. See WORK in Index.

workman *noun* See **laborer**.

workmanship *noun* See **work**.

workwoman *noun* See **laborer**.

world *noun* See **area, earth, environment, heap, mankind, universe**.

worldly *adjective* See **earthly, profane, sophisticated**.

worldly-wise *adjective* See **sophisticated**.

worldwide *adjective* See **universal**.

world without end *noun* See **endlessness**.

world without end *adjective* See **endless**.

worm *verb* See **crawl, insinuate, wangle, wiggle**.

worn *adjective* See **haggard**.

worn-down *adjective* See **exhausted**.

worn-out *adjective* See **exhausted, trite**.

worrisome *adjective* See **disturbing**.

worry *verb* To cause anxious uneasiness in : ail, cark, concern, distress, trouble. See CONCERN in Index. — See also **annoy, brood**.

worry *noun* See **anxiety, care**.

worrywart *noun* See **pessimist**.

worsen *verb* See **deteriorate**.

worship *verb* See **adore**.

worship *noun* See **adoration**.

worshipful *adjective* See **reverent**.

worst *verb* See **defeat**.

worth *noun* A measure of those qualities that determine merit, desirability, usefulness, or importance : account, valuation, value. See VALUE in Index. — See also **merit**.

worthiness *noun* See **qualification**.

worthless *adjective* Lacking all worth and value : drossy, good-for-nothing, inutile, no-good, valueless. *Informal:* no-account. *Slang:*

nothing. See VALUE in Index. — See also **useless.**

worthy *adjective* See **admirable, eligible, valuable.**

wound *noun* See **distress, trauma.**

wound *verb* See **distress, hurt, traumatize.**

wow *noun* See **hit.**

wrack¹ *noun* See **destruction.**

wrack² *noun* See **ruin.**

wrack *verb* See **destroy.**

wraith *noun* See **ghost.**

wrangle *verb* See **argue, brawl.**

wrangle *noun* See **argument.**

wrap *verb* **1.** To cover and tie (something), as with paper and string : do up, package. See PUT ON in Index. **2.** To surround and cover completely so as to obscure : cloak, clothe, enfold, enshroud, envelop, enwrap, infold, invest, shroud, veil. See SHOW in Index. **3.** To cover completely and closely, as with clothing or bandages : enfold, envelop, enwrap, infold, invest, roll, swaddle, swathe, wrap up. See PUT ON in Index. **4.** To put on warm clothes : bundle up, wrap up. See PUT ON in Index.

wrap up *verb* See **close, review, wrap.**

wrap *noun* A garment wrapped about a person : cloak, shawl, stole. See PUT ON in Index. — See also **wrapper.**

wrapper *noun* The material in which something is wrapped : wrap, wrapping (also used in plural). See PUT ON in Index.

wrapping *noun* See **wrapper.**

wrap-up *noun* See **end, summary.**

wrath *noun* See **fury.**

wrathful *adjective* See **furious.**

wrathfulness *noun* See **fury.**

wreak *verb* See **avenge, inflict.**

wreathe *verb* See **wind².**

wreck *verb* To damage, disable, or destroy (a seacraft) : shipwreck. See HELP in Index. — See also **destroy.**

wreck *noun* See **collapse, crash, destruction, ruin.**

wreckage *noun* See **breakage, destruction, ruin.**

wrecker *noun* See **ruin.**

wrench *verb* To alter the position of by a sharp, forcible twisting or turning movement : wrest, wring. See MOVE in Index. — See also **distort, extort, jerk, turn.**

wrench *noun* A tool with jaws for gripping and twisting : *Chiefly British:* spanner. See MACHINE in Index. — See also **jerk.**

wrest *verb* See **distort, extort, wrench.**

wrestle *verb* To contend with an opponent at close quarters, as by attempting to throw him or her : grapple, scuffle, tussle. *Idiom:* go to the mat with. See CONFLICT, TOUCH in Index. — See also **contend.**

wretch *noun* See **unfortunate.**

wretched *adjective* See **filthy, miserable.**

wretchedness *noun* See **distress, misery.**

wriggle *verb* See **wiggle.**

wring *verb* See **extort, wrench.**

wrinkle *verb* To make irregular folds in, especially by pressing or twisting : crease, crimp, crinkle, crumple, rimple, rumple. See SMOOTH in Index.

wrinkle *noun* *Informal.* A clever, unexpected new trick or method : gimmick, twist. *Informal:* kicker. *Slang:* angle², kick. See ABILITY, EXCITE, GOOD in Index. — See also **fold, line.**

write *verb* To form letters, characters, or words on a surface with an instrument : engross, indite, inscribe, scribe. See REMEMBER in Index. — See also **compose, publish.**

write down *verb* See **depreciate, list¹**.

write-down *noun* See **depreciation**.

writhe *verb* To twist and turn, as in pain, struggle, or embarrassment : agonize, squirm, toss, turn. See REPETITION in Index. — See also **wiggle**.

written *adjective* See **graphic**.

wrong *adjective* See **amiss, erroneous, evil, false, insane**.

wrong *adverb* Not in the right way or on the proper course : afield, amiss, astray, awry. See THRIVE in Index.

wrong *noun* See **crime, evil, injustice**.

wrong *verb* To do a wrong to; treat unjustly : aggrieve, oppress, outrage, persecute. See RIGHT in Index.

wrongdoing *noun* See **crime, misbehavior**.

wrongful *adjective* See **criminal, illegal**.

wry *adjective* See **cynical**.

XYZ

x *verb* See **cancel**.

yahoo *noun* See **boor**.

yak *noun* See **chatter**.

yak *verb* See **chatter**.

yank *verb* See **jerk**.

yank *noun* See **jerk**.

yap *verb* See **yelp**.

yap *noun* See **yelp**.

yard *noun* See **court**.

yardstick *noun* See **standard**.

yarn *noun* *Informal*. An entertaining and often oral account of a real or fictitious occurrence : anecdote, fable, story, tale. *Informal:* tall tale. See WORDS in Index.

yaw *verb* See **lurch, swerve**.

yawn *verb* **1.** To open the mouth wide with a deep inward breath, as when tired or bored : gape. See MOUTH in Index. **2.** To open wide : gap, gape. See WIDE in Index.

yawning *adjective* Open wide : abysmal, abyssal, cavernous, gaping. See WIDE in Index.

yawp also **yaup** *verb* See **roar, yelp**.

yawp also **yaup** *noun* See **yelp**.

yea *adverb* See **yes**.

yea *noun* See **yes**.

yeah *adverb* See **yes**.

year *noun* A period of time of approximately 12 months, especially that period during which the earth completes a single revolution around the sun : twelvemonth. See TIME in Index. — See also **age, vintage**.

yearn *verb* See **desire, feel**.

yearning *noun* See **desire**.

yeast *noun* See **catalyst, foam**.

yeast *verb* See **foam**.

yeasty *adjective* See **foamy**.

yell *verb* See **roar**.

yell *noun* See **shout**.

yellow *adjective* See **cowardly**.

yellow-bellied *adjective* See **cowardly**.

yellow-belly *noun* See **coward**.

yellowness *noun* See **cowardice**.

yellow streak *noun* See **cowardice**.

yelp *verb* To utter a shrill, short cry : squeal, yap, yawp, yip. See SOUNDS in Index.

yelp *noun* A shrill, short cry : squeal, yap, yawp, yip. See SOUNDS in Index.

yen *noun* See **desire**.

yenta *noun* See **gossip**.

yep *adverb* See **yes**.

yes *adverb* It is so; as you say or ask : absolutely, agreed, all right, assuredly, aye, gladly, indubitably, roger, undoubtedly, unquestionably,

willingly, yea. *Informal:* OK,
uh-huh, yeah, yep. *Slang:* right on.
See AFFIRM in Index.

yes *noun* An affirmative vote or
voter : aye, yea. See AFFIRM in
Index. — See also **acceptance.**

yes *verb* See **assent.**

yesterday *noun* See **past.**

yesteryear *noun* See **past.**

yet *adverb* See **additionally, earlier,
even**[1]**, still.**

yield *verb* See **abdicate, bear,
defer**[2]**, give in** at **give, relinquish,
return, succumb, weaken.**

yield *noun* The amount or quantity produced : output, production.
See BIG in Index. — See also **harvest.**

yielding *adjective* See **soft.**

yip *noun* See **yelp.**

yip *verb* See **yelp.**

yoke *noun* See **bond, couple,
slavery.**

yoke *verb* See **combine.**

yokel *noun* See **clodhopper.**

yore *noun* See **past.**

young *adjective* Being in an early
period of growth or development :
green, immature, infant, juvenile,
youthful. See YOUTH in Index.

young *noun* **1.** Young people collectively : youth. See YOUTH in
Index. **2.** The offspring, as of an animal or a bird, for example, that are
the result of one breeding season :
brood, litter. See KIN in Index.

youngster *noun* See **child.**

youth *noun* The time of life between
childhood and maturity : adolescence, greenness, juvenescence,
juvenility, puberty, salad days,
spring, youthfulness. See YOUTH in
Index. — See also **teenager, young.**

youthful *adjective* See **young.**

youthfulness *noun* See **youth.**

yowl *verb* See **bawl, cry, howl.**

yowl *noun* See **howl.**

yucky *adjective* See **unpleasant.**

yummy *adjective* See **delicious.**

zaftig or **zoftig** *adjective* See
plump[1]**.**

zaniness *noun* See **foolishness,
humor.**

zany *adjective* See **amusing, foolish.**

zany *noun* See **joker.**

zap *verb* See **kill**[1]**, murder.**

zeal *noun* See **enthusiasm.**

zealot *noun* See **devotee, enthusiast, extremist.**

zealous *adjective* See **enthusiastic.**

zealousness *noun* See **enthusiasm.**

zenith *noun* See **climax.**

zephyr *noun* See **breeze, wind**[1]**.**

zero *noun* See **nonentity, nothing.**

zero in *verb* See **aim.**

zero hour *noun* See **crisis.**

zest *noun* Spirited enjoyment :
gusto, relish. See PAIN in Index.
— See also **flavor.**

zesty *adjective* See **pungent.**

zigzag *verb* See **traverse.**

zilch *noun* See **nonentity, nothing.**

zillion *noun* See **heap.**

zip *noun* See **energy, spirit.**

zip *verb* See **breeze, rush.**

zippy *adjective* See **vigorous.**

zone *noun* See **area.**

zonked *adjective* See **drugged,
drunk.**

zoom *verb* See **rush.**

CATEGORY INDEX

ACCEPT *(cont.)*

reject
  refusal
  retraction
  snub
adjective
  impatient
  intolerant
  nice
verb
  banish
  blackball
  decline
  refuse
  repudiate
  retract
  snub
  veto

See also
  AFFIRM
  AGREE
  FORGIVENESS
  GIVE
  KEEP
  OFFER
  REQUEST
  RESIST

ACCOMPANIED

noun
  accompaniment (2)
  company
adjective
  accompanying
verb
  accompany
  bring
adverb
  together (2)

See also
  ABSENCE
  ASSEMBLE

ACTION
noun
  act

acting
activity
actor
behavior
bit[1]
business (2)
drive (2)
energy
feat
fuss
move
response
spirit
vigor
adjective
  active
  busy
  energetic
  lively
  rough
  spirited
  vigorous
verb
  act
  activate
  busy
  establish
  function
  fuss
  respond
  shoot
  tie up

inaction
noun
  abeyance
  inaction
  lethargy
adjective
  inactive
  languid
  latent
  lazy
  lethargic
verb
  cancel

See also
  ATTITUDE

AWARENESS
CONTINUE
DO
FEELINGS
MOVE
REPETITION
START
STRONG
THRIVE
TIME
TIRED
WORK

AFFECT
noun
  bias
  effect
  guidance
  heritage
  hold
  impact
  influence
  wallop
adjective
  influential
  insensitive
verb
  bias
  dispose
  nonplus
  overwhelm
  paralyze

ineffectiveness
noun
  ineffectuality
adjective
  ineffectual

See also
  ATTITUDE
  AWARENESS
  EXCITE
  FEELINGS
  MOVE
  PERSUASION
  SURPRISE
  USED

AFFIRM
noun
  acknowledgment
  argumentation
  assertion
  yes
adjective
  favorable
verb
  acknowledge (2)
  assert
  certify
adverb
  still
  yes

deny
noun
  denial
  no (2)
verb
  deny
  refute
adverb
  no

argue
verb
  argue

See also
  ACCEPT
  AGREE
  CERTAIN
  CONFLICT

AGREE
noun
  agreement (4)
  bargain
  complement
  compromise
  concession
  consistency
  engagement
  treaty
  unanimity
  unity
adjective
  accepted

agreeable
complementary
convenient
custom
unanimous
verb
  agree (2)
  arrange
  assent
  complement
  compromise
  contract
  fit¹ (2)
  flatter
  get along
  harmonize
  pledge (2)
  settle
  suit

disagree
noun
  gap
  impropriety
adjective
  discrepant
  improper
  incongruous
  inharmonious (2)
verb
  conflict
  differ
  haggle

See also
  ACCEPT
  AFFIRM
  ATTACK
  CONFLICT
  RIGHT
  SAME
  SUPPORT

ALLOW
noun
  license
  permission
adjective
  permissible

verb
  authorize
  conduct
  enable
  permit (3)

prevent
noun
  forbiddance
  prevention
adjective
  forbidden
  preventive (2)
verb
  forbid
  frustrate
  head off
  parry
  prevent

See also
  CRIMES
  LAW

APPROACH
noun
  advance
  approach
  bent
  charge
  comeback
  heading
  talent
adjective
  approachable
verb
  accost
  approach
  bear
  come
  go
  return
adverb
  back

retreat
noun
  bounce
  defection   *(cont.)*

APPROACH (cont.)

retreat
  defector
  departure
  deviation
  digression
  emigrant
  emigration
  émigré
  parting
  recoil
adjective
  digressive
  parting
verb
  bounce
  defect
  deviate
  digress
  double
  eject
  emigrate
  flinch
  go
  pass
  recede
  run

See also
  NEAR
  REACH
  TOUCH

ASK
noun
  appeal (2)
  appealer
  inquirer
  inquiry
  inquisitor
verb
  appeal
  ask (2)
  hint

answer
noun
  answer (2)

  retort
verb
  answer
  resolve

See also
  EXPLAIN
  INVESTIGATE
  REQUEST

ASSEMBLE
noun
  combination
  convention
  mixture
adjective
  combinational
verb
  attach
  beat
  combine
  mix

disassemble
noun
  analysis
  breach
  detachment
  division (2)
verb
  analyze
  cut
  detach (2)
  divide (2)
  separate
  take down
  tear¹

See also
  ACCOMPANIED
  CONNECT
  FREE
  GROUP
  INCREASE
  NEAR
  PART
  PUT ON

ATTACK
noun
  accusation

  accuser
  aggression
  aggressor
  ambush
  attack
  barrage
  beat
  beating
  belittlement
  belligerence
  blow²
  brawl
  defiance
  force
  indignity
  invasion
  libel
  retaliation
  sabotage
  siege
  slap
  thug
  tough
adjective
  abusive
  accusatorial
  aggressive
  belligerent (2)
  biting
  forcible
  libelous
  repressive
verb
  accuse
  afflict
  ambush
  attack
  barrage
  batter
  bawl out
  beat (2)
  belittle
  besiege (2)
  bite (2)
  blacken
  brawl
  call down

force
hit
implicate
insult
invade
lay for
libel
occupy
raid
retaliate
sabotage
seize
slap
slap around
thrash (2)

defend
noun
  apology
  cover
  defense
adjective
  tenable
verb
  assert
  defend

See also
  AGREE
  CONFLICT
  CRIMES
  HELP
  PAIN
  STRIKE
  WILLING

ATTITUDE

good attitude
noun
  amiability
  benevolence
  confidence
  consideration
  gallantry
  gravity
  modesty
  posture
  sentiment

temper
adjective
  affectionate
  aggressive
  airy
  amiable
  approachable
  benevolent
  broad
  companionable
  confident
  confidential
  friendly
  gallant
  gracious
  grave²
  humanitarian
  humble
  outgoing
  social

bad attitude
noun
  arrogance
  condescension
  cruelty
  cynic
  detachment
  impudence
  malevolence
  snob
adjective
  abrupt
  abusive
  accusatorial
  aggressive
  arrogant
  bleak
  boastful
  calculating
  cold (2)
  cold-blooded
  contrary
  cool
  cynical
  detached
  dry

ill-tempered
impatient
impudent
insensitive
malevolent
pedantic
resentful
snobbish
tepid
unctuous
verb
  condescend

neutral attitude
noun
  posture
  sentiment
  temper

See also
  ACTION
  AFFECT
  CONCERN
  FEELINGS
  HAPPY
  HELP
  HOT
  KIND
  LIKE
  LOVE
  PITY
  TIGHTEN
  TREAT WELL

AWARENESS
noun
  alertness
  guard
  lookout (2)
  revival
  sensation
  sensitiveness
  watch
  watcher
adjective
  active   *(cont.)*

AWARENESS (cont.)

alert
mindful
sensational
sensitive
wakeful (2)

verb

look out
revive
wake[1]
watch

unawareness

noun

blackout
daze
dizziness
nap
sleep
soporific
trance

adjective

absent-minded
absorbed
dead
dizzy
dull
giddy
sleeping
sleepy (2)
unconscious

verb

absorb
black out
daze
deaden
dull
inebriate
nap
retire
sleep
sleep in

See also

ABILITY
ACTION
AFFECT
CAREFUL

DRUGS
FEELINGS
KNOWLEDGE
REMEMBER
SEE
STRONG
TIRED

BE

noun

air
bearing
behavior
character
condition (2)
disposition
effect
environment
existence
heart
identity
presence
quality (2)
self
soul
streak
texture
thing
timber

adjective

actual
constitutional
effective
essential
implicit
innate

verb

act
amount
be
constitute
exist
lead
run

See also

FEELINGS

LIVE
REAL
SURFACE

BEAUTIFUL

noun

adornment
beauty
elegance
glitter (3)
harmony
proportion

adjective

beautiful
becoming
clean
clear
elegant
fresh
glorious
harmonious
shapely
sleek
symmetrical

verb

adorn
flatter
grace (2)
harmonize

ugly

noun

defect
deformity
mess
ugliness
witch

adjective

ghastly
plain
ugly

verb

deform

See also

BETTER
GOOD
PLAIN
RICH

BEINGS

noun
boy
germ
ghost
giant
human being
adjective
human

BELIEF

noun
confidence (2)
devotee
doctrine
myth (2)
theory (2)
adjective
confident
presumptive
reputed
supposed
verb
repute
speculate
suppose

unbelief
noun
disbelief
skeptic
adjective
incredible
incredulous
verb
disbelieve
adverb
skeptically

See also
LIKELY
OPINION
THOUGHTS

BETTER

noun
advance
best

bloom¹ (3)
improvement
progress
remedy
soundness
stability
trim
welfare
adjective
best (2)
better
choice
rare
ultimate
verb
bloom¹
fix up
perfect
touch up

worse
noun
decay
defect
deterioration
lapse
reverse
tatter
tatterdemalion
weakness
adjective
bad
defective
deficient
inferior
ruinous
shabby
tattered
wasted
verb
debase
decay
deteriorate
injure
relapse
wilt

See also
BEAUTIFUL

CHANGE
GOOD
HEALTH
HELP
IMPORTANT
INCREASE

BIG

noun
body
bulk
crowd (2)
deal
enormousness
flood
giant
heap (2)
intensity
size (2)
weight
adjective
alive
best
big (2)
bulky (2)
burning
double
extreme
generous
giant
grand
implicit
incalculable
intense
many
profuse
proportional
roomy
several
severe
sharp
sizable
staggering
steep¹
thick
thorough
towering   *(cont.)*

BIG *(cont.)*

ultimate
utter[2]
verb
double
pour
shower
surpass
teem
adverb
better
completely
considerably
even[1]
fairly
usually
very

small

noun
bit[1] (2)
damn
drop
flash
modesty
peanut
shade (2)
adjective
brief (2)
delicate
fine[1]
humble
imperceptible
insufficient
little (2)
meager
minimal
moderate
qualified
remote
tiny

amount

noun
degree (2)
distance (2)
extent
measurement

quantity
yield
verb
measure

See also
FAT
GET
IMPORTANT
INCREASE
LIMITED
LONG
NEAR
PART

BLOOD

noun
blood
adjective
bloody (2)
verb
bloody

See also
BODY

BODY

noun
body
brawn
constitution
head
heart
matter
nose
physicality
adjective
bodily
earthly
materialistic
physical (2)
sensational
sensory

spirit

noun
spirit
adjective
immaterial

inner
spiritual

See also
BLOOD
BREATH
MATTER

BREATH

noun
breath (2)
breeze
inspiration
pull
wind[1]
adjective
airy (2)
verb
air
blow[1]
breathe (3)
gasp
pant

breathlessness

adjective
airless (2)
verb
choke (2)

See also
BODY

CALM

noun
balance
calm
stillness
adjective
calm
cool
gentle
pastoral
still
verb
calm
pacify

agitation

noun
agitation (2)

agitator
disturbance
fuss
jitter
restlessness
state
stir[1]
throe
unrest
adjective
frantic
impatient
restless
rough
turbulent
verb
agitate (2)
boil
fuss (2)

See also
CONCERN
EASY
EXCITE
FEELINGS
HAPPY
ORDER
PAIN
PEACE
REPETITION
RESTRAINT
TIGHTEN

CARE FOR
noun
care
food
verb
bring up
dress
grow
nurse
serve
support
tend[2]

neglect
noun
neglect

verb
neglect

See also
CAREFUL
HELP

CAREFUL
noun
care
discernment
prudence
thoroughness
adjective
acute
attentive
careful (2)
close
critical
economical
shrewd
thorough
wary
verb
ease
edge
look out

careless
noun
abandon
extravagance
haste
negligence
temerity
adjective
airy
careless (2)
extravagant
improvident
light[2]
mindless
negligent
rash[1]
thoughtless

See also
AWARENESS
CARE FOR

KNOWLEDGE
PRECISE
THOUGHTS
WISE

CAUSE
noun
stimulus (2)
verb
exercise
get
provoke
urge

effect
noun
effect
verb
follow

See also
EXCITE
HELP
KIN
MAKE
START

CERTAIN
noun
certainty
decision
fate (2)
sureness
adjective
certain (2)
decided
definite
fated
sure (2)
verb
fate (2)
guarantee
adverb
absolutely

uncertain
noun
chance (2)
doubt *(cont.)*

CERTAIN *(cont.)*

uncertain
qualm
adjective
ambiguous (2)
debatable
doubtful
indefinite
verb
doubt
adverb
maybe
See also
AFFIRM
CHANGE
CLEAR
CONTINUE
FLEXIBLE
FORESIGHT
LUCK
MOVE
SAME
SURPRISE

CHANGE
noun
adaptation (2)
agitator
catalyst
change (3)
conversion
development
instability
reversal
revision
revolution
rotation
shakeup
transition
turn
variation
adjective
adaptable
capricious
changeable
insecure

mobile
verb
adapt
adjust
become
change (3)
convert
go
overturn
reverse
revise
revolutionize
rotate
shuffle
swerve
swing
turn

persist
noun
monotony
stability
adjective
ageless
consistent
firm[1]
irrevocable
verb
keep
stabilize
See also
BETTER
CERTAIN
CONTINUE
FLEXIBLE
MOVE
PUT IN
SAME

CHOICE
noun
appointee
appointment
choice (2)
elect
elector
adjective
optional

select
verb
appoint
choose
elect
See also
FREE
NECESSARY
WILLING

CLEAN
noun
innocent
purification (2)
purifier
purity
sterility
adjective
clean
innocent
neat
pure
purgative
sterile
straight
thoroughbred
verb
purify
refine
scrub
sterilize

dirty
noun
contaminant
contamination
corruption
dirtiness
filth
impurity
pit[1]
slime
adjective
corrupt
crude
dirty
filthy

impure (2)
muddy
slimy
sticky
verb
 adulterate
 blacken
 corrupt
 dirty
 muddy
 pollute
 stain
 taint
 violate

See also
 CRIMES
 MARKS

CLEAR
noun
 clarity
adjective
 clear (2)
 definite
 frank
 immediate
 sharp
 transparent
 unsubtle
verb
 clarify
 clear
adverb
 immediately

unclear
noun
 ambiguity
 equivocation
 gibberish (2)
 haze
 vagueness
adjective
 ambiguous (2)
 confused
 evasive
 filmy

turbid (2)
unclear
verb
 confuse
 equivocate
 obscure

See also
 CERTAIN
 LIGHT
 OPEN
 PUT ON
 SHOW

COLLECT
noun
 accumulation
 assembly
 assortment
 hoard
adjective
 concentrated
verb
 accumulate
 apply
 assemble (2)
 band²
 confer
 crowd
 gather
 glean
 hoard

distribute
noun
 allotment
 distribution (2)
verb
 allot
 appropriate
 assort
 distribute (2)
 lift
 scatter

See also
 EDGE
 GET
 GROUP
 ORDER

COLORS
noun
 color (2)
 complexion
 shade
 tint
adjective
 black
 blackish
 colorful
 dark
 fair (2)
 multicolor
 ruddy
verb
 color
 dip

colorless
adjective
 dull
 pale
verb
 pale

COMFORT
noun
 amenity
adjective
 livable

discomfort
noun
 inconvenience (2)
adjective
 bitter
 inconvenient
 uncomfortable
verb
 inconvenience

See also
 HELP

CONCERN
noun
 care
 concern   *(cont.)*

CONCERN (cont.)

consideration
eager beaver
enthusiasm (2)
enthusiast
extremist
morale
thing
adjective
concerned
eager
enthusiastic
extreme
verb
brood
care
eat up
worry

unconcern
noun
detachment
indifference
neglect
adjective
detached
perfunctory
verb
ignore
neglect

See also
ATTITUDE
CALM
FEELINGS
HAPPY
IMPORTANT
KIND
LOVE
TREAT WELL

CONFLICT
noun
argument
argumentativeness
collision
combat
competition (2)

competitor
conflict (2)
fight (2)
fighter
tilt
adjective
argumentative
competitive
verb
argue
collide
compete
contend
engage
wrestle

cooperation
noun
cooperation
adjective
cooperative
verb
cooperate

See also
AFFIRM
AGREE
ATTACK
HELP
RESIST

CONNECT
noun
alliance
ally
associate
attachment
basis
bond (2)
boy
boyfriend
company
contact
joint
junction
relation
sympathy
touch

adjective
allied
mutual
social
verb
ally
associate
bond
engage
reciprocate
relate
see

See also
ASSEMBLE
DEPENDENCE
GROUP
INCREASE
LOVE
NEAR
PUT ON
RELEVANT

CONTINUE
noun
continuation
endlessness
endurance
fidelity
immortality
insistence (2)
renewal
stability
thread
wait
adjective
bearable
chronic (2)
confirmed
continual
continuing
direct
endless
faithful
fast
hard
immortal

insistent
sound[2]
steady
stubborn
sure
tireless
verb
  bear up
  carry on
  continue
  endure (2)
  follow up
  harden
  immortalize
  insist (2)
  keep
  outlast
  remain
  renew

stop
noun
  abolition
  break
  end
  faithlessness
  gap
  grace
  reversal
  stop (2)
  suppression
  tie-up
adjective
  capricious
  faithless
  uneven
verb
  abandon
  abolish
  break
  break up
  cancel (2)
  dry up
  extinguish
  lapse
  lift
  pause

quit
retire
separate
stop (2)
strike
suppress
suspend
tie up

pause
noun
  break
  rest[1]
  truce
adjective
  intermittent
  temporary (2)
  transitory
verb
  blink
  break
  interrupt
  rest[1] (2)
adverb
  intermittently

See also
  ACTION
  CERTAIN
  CHANGE
  FLEXIBLE
  INCLUDE
  KEEP
  MOVE
  SAME
  START
  STRONG
  TIME
  USUAL

CONTROL
noun
  government
  grip
  monopoly
adjective
  governable
verb
  govern

handle
have
maneuver (2)
manipulate
operate
possess

uncontrol
noun
  unruliness
adjective
  naughty
  runaway
  unruly

See also
  DEPENDENCE
  OVER
  POLITICS

CONVEX
noun
  bill[2]
  bulge
  bump (2)
  nose
verb
  bulge
  poke

concave
noun
  cave
  depression
  hole
adjective
  hollow

See also
  GEOMETRY

CORRECT
noun
  accuracy
adjective
  accurate (2)
  corrective
verb
  correct   *(cont.)*

CORRECT *(cont.)*

incorrect
noun
blunder
botch
deviation
error
fallacy (2)
lapse
miscalculation
adjective
errant
erroneous
fallacious
verb
botch
confuse
deviate
err
miscalculate
misjudge

See also
HONEST
REAL
RIGHT
TRUE
USUAL

COUNT

noun
count
figure
score
total
verb
count
enumerate

See also
REASON

COURTESY

noun
amenity
bow[1]
ceremony

courtesy
gallantry
tact
adjective
ceremonious
correct
courteous
gallant
gracious

discourtesy

noun
impudence
thoughtlessness
adjective
coarse
impudent
rude
shameless
tactless
thoughtless

See also
GRATEFUL
INCLUDE
RESPECT
TREAT WELL

CRIMES

noun
accessory
annihilation
bribe
crime
criminal
illegality
larcenist
larceny
libel
plot
plunder
robbery
smuggler
thug
tough
trespass
adjective
corruptible

criminal
illegal
larcenous
libelous
verb
annihilate
break in
bribe
fix
implicate
kidnap
libel
plot
rob
sack[2]
smuggle
steal

See also
ALLOW
ATTACK
CLEAN
HELP
LAW
RIGHT
TREAT WELL

CULTURE

noun
culture (2)
mankind
adjective
artificial
cultural
cultured
earthly
manlike

nature

adjective
natural
uncivilized

See also
WILD

DECENT

adjective
clean

indecent
noun
  obscenity (2)
  swearword
adjective
  obscene
  racy
  unspeakable
verb
  swear

See also
  WORDS

DECIDE
noun
  crisis
  decision
  judge (2)
adjective
  decisive (2)
  definitive
  fateful
  set[1]
verb
  decide
  judge

hesitate
noun
  hesitation
adjective
  hesitant
verb
  hesitate
  swing

See also
  IMPORTANT

DEPENDENCE
noun
  parasite
adjective
  parasitic
verb
  freeload

independence
noun
  freedom

independence
adjective
  free
  independent (2)

See also
  CONNECT
  CONTROL

DESIRE
noun
  ambition
  appetite
  catch
  desire (2)
  envy
  greed
  sell
  toast
  vocation
  voracity
adjective
  ambitious
  desirable
  envious
  greedy (2)
  voracious
verb
  choose
  desire
  drink
  envy
  lust

See also
  LIKE
  SEX

DO
noun
  accomplishment
  act
  fulfillment
  function
  part
  performance
  practice
verb
  accomplish

act
commit
effect
fulfill
perform
practice
realize
satisfy
score
settle
wage

not do
noun
  failure
adjective
  insuperable
  invincible
verb
  defer[1]
  fail
  neglect
  violate

See also
  ACTION
  PARTICIPATE
  WORK

DRUGS
noun
  bender
  drug (2)
  drunkard
  drunkenness
  kick
adjective
  drugged
  drunk
verb
  befuddle
  drink
  drug

temperance
noun
  temperance

See also
  AWARENESS
  TRANSACTIONS

DRY
adjective
  absorbent
  dry (2)
  thirsty
verb
  dry
  dry up

wet
noun
  branch
  drink
  drool
  drop
  swamp
  sweat
  tear[2]
adjective
  damp
  sticky
  sweaty
  wet
verb
  drool
  pour
  steep[2]
  sweat
  tear[2]
  wash (2)
  wet

See also
  SOLID

EASY
noun
  breeze
  ease
  runaway
adjective
  easy
  light[2]
verb
  breeze
  ease (2)

hard

difficulty
predicament
problem
severity
trial
adjective
  awkward
  deep
  delicate
  difficult
  heavy
  severe
  thorny
  tight
  troublesome
adverb
  hard

See also
  CALM
  HEAVY
  PAIN
  PLAIN
  SIMPLE

EDGE
noun
  border (2)
  circumference
  end
  extreme
  extremist
  outline
  skirt
  verge
adjective
  extreme (2)
verb
  band[1]
  border

center
noun
  center (2)
  concentration
  moderation
  thick
adjective
  central

concentrated
inner (2)
middle
mild
moderate
verb
  concentrate

See also
  COLLECT

ENTER
noun
  admission
  arrival
  cut
  entrance[1]
  invasion
  pass
  plunge
  trespass
verb
  admit
  break in
  cut
  dig
  dip (2)
  enter
  insinuate
  intrude
  invade
  muscle
  penetrate
  plunge

exit
verb
  discharge

See also
  MOVE
  OPEN
  PARTICIPATE
  START
  WORK

EXCESS
noun
  excess (2)
  surplus
  wordiness
adjective
  excessive
  extravagant
  heavy
  profuse
  superfluous
  wordy
verb
  exceed
adverb
  unduly

insufficency
noun
  absence
  shortage
adjective
  absent
  deficient
  inadequate
  insufficient
  meager
  undermanned
verb
  fail

enough
noun
  enough
  satiation
adjective
  bare
  sufficient
verb
  satiate
  serve

See also
  FULL

EXCITE
noun
  absorption
  attention

  heat
  infatuation
  kick
  sensation
  thrill
  trick
  wonder
  wrinkle
adjective
  absorbed
  attentive
  dramatic
  fervid
  hot
  infatuated
  staggering
  stimulating
  thrilled
verb
  absorb
  arouse
  carry away
  climax
  engage
  fire
  grip
  interest
  provoke
  stagger
  startle
  tantalize
  wonder

bore
noun
  boredom
  dullness
  insipidity
  monotony
adjective
  boring
  dry
  dull
  insipid
  long[1]
  realistic
  trite

verb
  bore
interest
noun
  amusement (2)
adjective
  amusing
verb
  amuse

See also
  AFFECT
  CALM
  CAUSE
  FEAR
  FEELINGS
  HELP
  LIKE
  SURPRISE

EXPLAIN
noun
  account
  excuse
  explanation
adjective
  explainable
  explanatory
verb
  account for
  elaborate
  explain

baffle
adjective
  inexplicable
  mysterious

See also
  ASK
  KNOWLEDGE
  REGRET

EXPLOSION
noun
  blast
  eruption
  load
  outburst
verb
  break   *(cont.)*

EXPLOSION (cont.)
break out
burst
erupt
explode
fly

collapse
noun
breakdown
verb
cave in

See also
HELP

EXPRESS
noun
expression
face
frown
gesture
glare
smile
smirk
sneer
adjective
expressive
verb
blush
flourish
frown
gesture
glare
grimace
signal
smile
smirk
sneer

See also
SHOW

FAIR
noun
fairness
adjective
even[1]
fair
neutral
sportsmanlike
adverb
fair

unfair
noun
favor
adjective
favorable
unfair
verb
favor

See also
RIGHT

FAST
noun
haste
adjective
abrupt
brief
crash
fast
quick
adverb
fast
short

slow
noun
crawl
laggard
adjective
deliberate
gradual
slow
verb
crawl
delay

velocity
noun
speed
verb
speed

See also
TIME

FAT
noun
fat
adjective
fat
fatty
plump[1]
stocky

thin
adjective
gangling
thin
verb
reduce
thin

See also
BIG
THICK

FEAR
noun
caution
complex
coward
cowardice
dismay
fear
jitter
adjective
afraid
cowardly
crawly
fearful
horrible
weird
verb
crawl
dismay
fear
frighten

courage
noun
courage
hero
heroism
adjective
brave

See also
EXCITE
FEELINGS
SURPRISE

FEELINGS
noun
anger
annoyance (3)
anxiety
apathy
balance
emotion
enthusiasm
fury
gloom
glow
heart
heat
mood
morale
passion
resentment
sentimentality
temper (2)
theatrics
wonder
adjective
angry
anxious
apathetic
awkward
emotional (2)
fervid
furious
insensitive
moody
neutral
passionate
pitying
sentimental
spirited
testy
unsympathetic
verb
anger (2)
annoy (2)

complain
confuse
emotionalize
feel
greet
rave
sentimentalize
wonder

See also
ACTION
AFFECT
ATTITUDE
AWARENESS
BE
CALM
CONCERN
EXCITE
HAPPY
HOPE
KIND
PAIN
PITY
RELIGION
STRONG
SURPRISE
TIGHTEN
TIRED

FLEXIBLE
noun
flexibility
unstableness
adjective
flexible (2)
limp
malleable
unstable
rigid
adjective
inflexible
pedantic
rigid
stiff
verb
stiffen
See also
CERTAIN

CHANGE
CONTINUE
MOVE
RESIST
SAME
WILLING

FORESIGHT
noun
omen
precursor
prediction
prophecy
prophet
taste
threat
vision
adjective
predictive
prophetic
threatening
visionary
verb
adumbrate
foresee
predict
prophesy
threaten

See also
CERTAIN
PRECEDE
WARN

FORGIVENESS
noun
forgiveness
grace
adjective
justifiable
pardonable
verb
forgive

vindictiveness
noun
retaliation   *(cont.)*

FORGIVENESS *(cont.)*

vindictiveness
vindictiveness
adjective
inexcusable
vindictive
verb
avenge
retaliate

See also
ACCEPT
KIND
PITY

FORWARD
noun
advance
verb
advance

backward
noun
retreat
reversion
verb
back
recoil
retreat

See also
PRECEDE

FREE
noun
escape
freedom
liberty
will
adjective
clear
free
loose
verb
clear
discharge
emit
escape

excuse
free

unfree
noun
bond
detention
entanglement
jail
jailer
adjective
tight
verb
bar
catch
commit
constrain
enclose
enslave
hamper
hold
imprison
involve
jail
kidnap

See also
ASSEMBLE
CHOICE
OPEN
PARTICIPATE
RESTRAINT
TIGHTEN

FULL
noun
plug
satiation
adjective
full
heavy
verb
charge
crowd
fill (2)
flood (2)
heap
satiate

empty
noun
emptiness (3)
nothingness
adjective
empty (3)
lonely
vacant
verb
empty

capacity
verb
accommodate

See also
ABSENCE
EXCESS

GAMBLING
noun
bet
bettor
gamble
speculator
verb
bet
gamble (2)

See also
LUCK
TRANSACTIONS

GENDER
noun
effeminacy
femininity (2)
adjective
effeminate
feminine
manly

See also
SEX

GEOMETRY
noun
circle
revolution

adjective
oval
parallel
round
square

See also
CONVEX
HORIZONTAL
SHARP
SMOOTH
STRAIGHT

GET
noun
buy
catch
employment
gain
mercenary
recovery
adjective
available
profitable
verb
book
bring
buy
capture
catch
contract
develop
earn
employ
extort
find
get
hire
inherit
recover
run down
take
wangle

lose
noun
loss
adjective
lost

verb
drop
lose

See also
BIG
COLLECT
MONEY
PAY

GIVE
noun
administration
attribution
benevolence
conferment
courtesy
delivery
donation
donor
generosity
gift
grant
gratuity
adjective
benevolent
generous (3)
gifted
sacred
verb
administer
attribute
confer
contribute
devote
donate
entrust
fix
furnish
gift
give (3)
grant
hand down
impose
inflict
leave[1]
lend

pass
play out
sacrifice
satisfy
shower
submit
transfer
noun
adoption
consumer
consumption
dependent
deprivation
draft
greed
miser
pirate
plunder
robbery
seizure
usurpation
adjective
greedy
stingy
verb
adopt
assume
claim   •
deplete
deprive
dip
draft
drink
earn
hoard
pirate
resume
rob
sack[2]
seize
steal

reciprocity
verb
exchange

See also
ACCEPT
KEEP

GOOD

noun
amiability
chastity
delicacy
excellence
fire
marvel
masterpiece
merit
model
nonpareil
trick
virtue
wrinkle

adjective
acceptable
admirable
adorable
amiable
chaste
comfortable
convenient
decent
delicate
delicious
delightful
everyday
excellent
fabulous
good (2)
grand
ideal
marvelous
neat
ordinary
perfect
sound²
vintage

bad

noun
abnormality
boor
enormity
flagrancy
hole
infamy
joint
misbehavior
mischief (2)
prank¹
shame
smart aleck

adjective
abnormal
affected
airy
bad
corrupt
deplorable
filthy
flagrant
impure
insipid
morbid
naughty
ponderous
rude
shoddy
terrible
unfortunate
unpleasant
unspeakable

verb
misbehave

See also
BEAUTIFUL
BETTER
IMPORTANT
RIGHT
THRIVE

GRATEFUL

noun
appreciation
grace

adjective
grateful

ungrateful

adjective
thankless (2)

See also
COURTESY

GREETING

noun
greeting
regard

verb
accost
greet (2)

See also
MEET

GROUP

noun
alliance
blast
circle
citizen
class (2)
combine (2)
common
company (2)
conference
countryman
couple
crowd (3)
detachment
detail
family
force
gang
group
kind²
line
pair
party
trio
union
web

adjective
common
domestic
social
societal

verb
class
socialize

See also
ASSEMBLE

COLLECT
CONNECT
NEAR
ORDER

HANG
adjective
hanging
verb
hang (2)
slouch
trail
See also
POSTURE

HAPPEN
noun
circumstance
event
history (2)
plot
verb
chance
come (3)
occur
See also
SURPRISE

HAPPY
noun
delight
elation
exultation
fulfillment
happiness
heaven
adjective
cheerful
delightful
elated
exuberant
exultant
fulfilled
gay
glad (2)
light²

merry
verb
delight
elate
exult
light¹
rejoice

unhappy
noun
complaint
disappointment
distress
gloom
grief
grouch
misery
mutter
adjective
depressed
disappointing
disturbing
gloomy (2)
glum
lonely
miserable (2)
sad
sorrowful (2)
tearful
verb
complain
cry
depress
disappoint
distress
embitter
grieve
mutter
sulk

See also
ATTITUDE
CALM
CONCERN
FEELINGS
HOPE
LAUGHTER
LIKE
PAIN

HEALTH
noun
cure
health
recovery
treatment
adjective
curative
healthful
healthy
verb
cure
recover
treat

sickness
noun
black eye
disease
indisposition
seizure
sickness
tuberculosis
adjective
exhausted
sick
sickly (2)
tubercular
unwholesome
verb
collapse
languish
turn
upset

See also
BETTER
HELP
STRONG

HEAVY
noun
burden¹ (2)
gravity
heaviness
seriousness
task
adjective
burdensome *(cont.)*

HEAVY *(cont.)*

grave[2]
heavy (2)
serious

light
adjective
light[2]

See also
EASY
THICK
TIRED

HELP
noun
accessory
advantage (2)
assistant
capital
comfort
encouragement
favor
help
helper
interest
makeshift
panacea
patron
patronage
relief
renewal
rescue
resort
tonic
treatment
trump
adjective
auxiliary
beneficial
encouraging
obliging
positive
preservative
tonic
verb
adjust
advance

benefit
comfort
encourage (2)
energize
finance
fix
help
improve
oblige
patronize
profit
promote
refresh
renew
rescue (2)
restore
serve
sustain
treat

harm
noun
abuse
accident
annihilation
bar
black eye
breach
breakage
crash
curse
cut
defect
delay
destruction
disadvantage
disaster
distress
evil
harm
irritation
massacre
murder
murderer
poison
ruin
tear[1]

trauma
victim
weakness
adjective
cruel
destructive
fatal
grievous
harmful
helpless
murderous
poisonous
unfavorable
virulent
verb
abuse
afflict
annihilate (2)
batter
bend
blast
botch
break (3)
break up
bruise
chafe
consume
corrupt
crack
crash
cripple
crush (2)
cut
delay
destroy (2)
devastate
disable
discourage
eliminate
hamper
hang
hinder
hurt
injure
irritate
kill[1]
murder

overthrow
poison
shoot
slip
tamper
tear[1]
trample
trash
traumatize
wreck

harmless

adjective
harmless

See also
ATTACK
ATTITUDE
BETTER
CARE FOR
CAUSE
COMFORT
CONFLICT
CRIMES
EXCITE
EXPLOSION
HEALTH
HOPE
KIND
LIKE
LOVE
LUCK
MAKE
SUPPORT
TREAT WELL
USED
VALUE

HIGH

noun
air (2)
climax
elevation
height
hill
maximum
adjective
airy

climactic
elevated (2)
high (2)
higher
lofty
maximum
tall
top

low

noun
deep
low
adjective
low
verb
crouch

See also
OVER

HONEST

noun
honesty
adjective
accurate
artless
honest

dishonest

noun
act
affectation
art
cheat (2)
corruption
deceit
dishonesty
hypocrisy
hypocrite
indirection
insincerity
pretense (2)
trick
adjective
affected
artful
corrupt
dishonest

double
fallacious
hypocritical
insincere
plastic
shady
sly
unctuous
underhand
unscrupulous
verb
act
cheat
deceive
foist
pose
skin

See also
CORRECT
PERFORMING ARTS
PLAIN
RESPECT
RIGHT
TRUE

HOPE

noun
dream
dreamer
future
optimism
optimist
adjective
idealistic (2)
optimistic

despair

noun
despair
pessimist
adjective
despondent
gloomy
hopeless
verb
despair

See also
FEELINGS *(cont.)*

HOPE *(cont.)*

despair
  HAPPY
  HELP
  SURPRISE

HORIZONTAL
adjective
  flat
  transverse
verb
  lie[1]

vertical
adjective
  erect
  steep[1]
  vertical
verb
  erect

change of position
adjective
  upside-down
verb
  overturn
  right

See also
  GEOMETRY

HOT
noun
  burn
  fire
  heat (2)
adjective
  burning
  fervid
  hot (2)
  sticky
  tropical
verb
  burn (3)
  light[1]

cold
noun
  cold

frigidness
adjective
  bleak
  cold (3)
  cool
  frigid

lukewarm
adjective
  tepid

See also
  ATTITUDE
  KIND

IMPORTANT
noun
  dignitary
  eminence
  emphasis
  gravity
  importance
adjective
  big-league
  decisive
  essential
  grave[2]
  important
  influential
  pivotal
  primary
  ruling
verb
  count
  emphasize

unimportant
noun
  nonentity
  pettiness
  trivia
adjective
  petty

See also
  BEAUTIFUL
  BETTER
  BIG
  CONCERN

DECIDE
GOOD
KNOWLEDGE
OVER
STRONG

INCLUDE
noun
  integration
adjective
  built-in
verb
  build in
  contain (2)
  embody
  integrate (2)

exclude
noun
  aloneness
  detachment
  erasure
  individuality
  isolation
  seclusion
  segregation
  wall
adjective
  alone
  exclusive
  individual
  lone
  mere
  restricted
  sacred
  secluded
  select
  solitary
verb
  censor
  drop
  exclude
  isolate
  seclude
  sort
  wall
adverb
  alone

merely
separately
solely

See also
CONTINUE
COURTESY
KEEP
LIMITED
NEAR
TREAT WELL

INCREASE
noun
addition (2)
attachment
buildup
exaggeration
expansion
increase (2)
outbreak
adjective
accumulative
additional
auxiliary
coming
elevated
extensible
inflated
verb
add
amount
attach
deposit
double
elevate
exaggerate
explode
extend
gain
increase
intensify
lengthen
raise
restore (2)
return
rise

soar
adverb
additionally

decrease
noun
decrease
deduction
depreciation
fade-out
failure
fall
relief
wane
adjective
slow
verb
boil down
contract
cut back
decrease
deduct
deplete
depreciate
drain
exhaust
fade (3)
fade out
fall
go (2)
moderate
muffle
reduce
relieve
shade
shorten
slip
subside
thin

See also
ASSEMBLE
BETTER
BIG
CONNECT
LONG
PUT ON

INDUSTRIOUS
noun
diligence
efficiency
adjective
diligent
efficient

lazy
noun
laziness
wastrel
adjective
lazy
verb
idle (2)

See also
ABILITY
THRIVE

INGESTION
noun
bite
cook
delicacy
drop
feast
food (2)
harvest
serving
adjective
delicate
delicious
edible
greedy
hard
heavy
nutritious
nutritive
ravenous
raw
verb
bite
boil
consume
cook
eat   *(cont.)*

INGESTION (cont.)

gulp
live[1]
nourish
serve

See also
MOUTH
TASTE

INVESTIGATE
noun
analysis (2)
curiosity (2)
detective
examination (2)
exploration
feeler
inquirer
inquiry (2)
inquisitor
review
shakedown
snoop
spy
tail
test (3)
adjective
curious (2)
verb
analyze (2)
browse
examine
explore
feel out
interrogate
scour[1]
search
snoop
spy
tap[2]
test (3)

See also
ASK
KNOWLEDGE

KEEP
noun
conservation

conservative
depository
grave[1]
hold
treasury
adjective
conservative
sticky
verb
bank[2]
carry
conserve (2)
grasp
have
hold
maintain
restore (2)
return
save
stockpile
tie

release
noun
abandonment
abdication
dismissal
disposal
ejection
elimination (2)
adjective
abandoned
eliminative
verb
abandon
abdicate
discard
discharge
dismiss (3)
drop
eject
eliminate (2)
relinquish
retire
rid

See also
ACCEPT

CONTINUE
GIVE
INCLUDE
USUAL

KIN
noun
ancestor
ancestry
baby
child
derivative
descendant
family
father
genealogy
illegitimacy
kin
nobility
progeny
relative
shoot
young
adjective
ancestral
derivative
domestic
fatherly
illegitimate
related
verb
derive
descend
develop
father

See also
CAUSE
PRECEDE
START

KIND
noun
benevolence (2)
consideration
adjective
benevolent (2)

gentle
gracious
humanitarian

cruel
noun
cruelty
fiend
adjective
cruel
fiendish
fierce
merciless

See also
ATTITUDE
CONCERN
FEELINGS
FORGIVENESS
HELP
HOT
LIKE
LOVE
PITY
TREAT WELL

KNOWLEDGE
noun
ability
acknowledgment
acquaintance (2)
advertising
announcement (2)
awareness
celebrity
communication
education
eminence
fame
grasp
hint
information
informer
ken
knowledge
lore
news
notice

notoriety
presentation
promotion
recognition
table
tip³
veteran
adjective
artful
aware
contemporary
educated
eminent
familiar
famous
informed
learned
notorious
perceptible
practical
sophisticated
understandable
verb
acknowledge (2)
acquaint
advertise (2)
announce
break
come out (2)
communicate
feel
get around
inform (2)
know
notice
perceive
place
promote
recognize
register
usher in

ignorance
noun
ignorance (2)
innocent
nonsense

obscurity
adjective
anonymous
foolish
ignorant (3)
imperceptible
incomprehensible
mysterious
obscure
unfound
unscholarly
untried
verb
nonplus

See also
AWARENESS
CAREFUL
EXPLAIN
IMPORTANT
INVESTIGATE
SEE
SHOW
TEACH
THOUGHTS
UNDERSTAND
WISE
WORDS

LAUGHTER
noun
celebration
gaiety (2)
giggle
humor
joke
joker
laugh
ribbing
ridicule
sarcasm
satire
scream
sneer
takeoff
taunt
adjective
amusing   *(cont.)*

LAUGHTER (cont.)

clever
humorous
laughable
laughing
priceless
sarcastic

verb

break up
celebrate
chuckle
giggle
joke (2)
laugh
ridicule
sneer

See also
HAPPY
WORK

LAW

noun

accusation
accused
accuser
appeal
appealer
arrest
bond
bondsman
complainant
confirmation
court
exculpation
grant
guardian
holding
illegality
illegitimacy
informer
injustice (2)
judge
law (2)
lawsuit
lawyer
legality

libel
license
minor
minority
policeman
reversal
reward
ruling
sentence
sponsor
testimony
trial
witness

adjective

condemned
illegal
illegitimate
lawful
liable
libelous
litigable
minor

verb

accuse
arrest
clear
commit
condemn
confirm
hold
inform
inherit
judge
lapse
leave[1]
legalize
libel
lift
petition
police
present[2]
return
sign
sue
testify
transfer

See also
ALLOW
CRIMES
ORDER
POLITICS

LEFTOVER

noun

balance
deposit
destruction
end
ruin
trace

adjective

remaining

LIGHT

noun

beam
blink
fire
glare
glitter
gloss
illumination
light[1]

adjective

bright
brilliant
glossy

verb

beam
blink
flash
glare
gloss
glow
illuminate

darkness

noun

dark
night
shade

adjective

black

dark
dull
gloomy
nightly
shady (2)
verb
shade

See also
CLEAR
SEE

LIKE
noun
admirer
adoration (2)
attraction
bent
bias
delight
favorite
liking
lure (2)
public
taste
adjective
adorable
agreeable
attractive
biased
delightful
favorite
seductive
verb
admire
adore
attract
charm
delight
dispose
enjoy
like[1]
luxuriate
sweeten

dislike
noun
disapproval

disgust
dislike
drip
imposition
offense
prejudice
unwelcome
vociferation
adjective
bitter
crawly
damned
objectionable
offensive
unwelcome
verb
crawl
disapprove
disgust
dislike
offend

See also
ATTITUDE
DESIRE
EXCITE
HAPPY
HELP
KIND
LIKELY
LOVE
PAIN
PRAISE
VALUE

LIKELY
noun
chance
verisimilitude
adjective
inclined
liable
presumptive
probable
verb
tend[1]

unlikely
adjective
doubtful

implausible

See also
BELIEF
LIKE
OPINION
POSSIBLE
THOUGHTS
TRUE

LIMITED
noun
catch
environment
length
limit (2)
maximum
provision
restriction (2)
adjective
conditional
definite
local (2)
maximum
narrow
qualified
restricted (2)
verb
determine
limit

unlimited
noun
eternity
infinity
adjective
endless
eternal
implicit
indefinite
unconditional
universal (2)
utter[2]
adverb
absolutely
completely (2)

See also
BIG   *(cont.)*

LIMITED *(cont.)*

unlimited
INCLUDE
NECESSARY
RELEVANT
SPECIFIC

LIVE
noun
immortality
life
adjective
alive (2)
immortal
verb
quicken
revive
survive

die
noun
death
fatality (2)
fate
adjective
dead
deadly
ghastly
inanimate
vanished
verb
die
disappear
fate

See also
BE

LONG
noun
extension
adjective
long[1] (3)
verb
lengthen

short
verb
shorten

See also
BIG
INCREASE

LOVE
noun
admirer
adoration (2)
darling
devotee
friend
friendship
love (3)
reconciliation
sympathy
adjective
adorable
affectionate
darling
familiar
friendly
verb
adore (2)
reconcile

hatred
noun
enemy
enmity
estrangement
hate (2)
adjective
hateful
hostile
resentful
verb
estrange
hate

See also
ATTITUDE
CONCERN
CONNECT
HELP
KIND
LIKE
NEAR
SEX

SUPPORT
VALUE

LUCK
noun
luck
opportunity
adjective
favorable
happy
opportune

misfortune
noun
fate
jinx
misfortune
adjective
bad
fateful
unfortunate
verb
fate
jinx

chance
verb
toss

See also
CERTAIN
GAMBLING
HELP
SUPERNATURAL
SURPRISE
WARN

MACHINE
noun
behavior
device
furnishing
gadget
invention
stage
stick
tool
wrench

verb
  govern

See also
  MEANS

MAKE
noun
  builder (2)
  building
  composition
  invention (2)
  product
  work
verb
  build
  compose
  dig
  establish
  form
  invent
  make
  produce
  wangle

unmake
noun
  annihilation
verb
  annihilate (2)
  lift

See also
  CAUSE
  HELP

MARKS
noun
  character
  impression
  mark
  point
  prick
  score
  smear
  stain
  stigma
  ticket
  trace

  track
  trail
  welt
verb
  engrave (2)
  mark
  point
  speckle
  spot
  stain
  stigmatize
  streak
  ticket
  track

See also
  CLEAN
  STRIKE

MARRIAGE
noun
  engagement
  intended
  marriage
  spouse
  wedding
adjective
  eligible
  engaged
  marital
verb
  marry

unmarried
adjective
  single

See also
  SEX

MATTER
noun
  band¹
  beam
  body
  good
  material
  universe
adjective
  earthy

  physical

See also
  BODY
  SOLID
  THING

MEANING
noun
  idea
  import
  meaning
  moral
  subject
  thrust
adjective
  pithy
  pregnant
  thematic
verb
  imply
  mean¹

See also
  WORDS

MEANS
noun
  approach
  art
  go-between
  mean³
  outfit
  tactic
  ticket
  tool
  trick
  way
adjective
  artful
verb
  maneuver

See also
  ABILITY
  MACHINE

MEET
noun
  conferee   *(cont.)*

MEET (cont.)

conference
confrontation

verb

come across
confer
confront
cross
encounter
engage
meet[1]

See also
GREETING

MONEY

noun

bargain
bribe
buy
capital
collapse
combine
deposit
depreciation
failure
financier
fund
gain
living
money
peanut
speculator
take
tax
toll[1]

adjective

cheap
financial
free
independent
popular

verb

appropriate
bank[2]
bill[1]
bribe

buy
clean up
collapse
depreciate
earn
finance
return
ruin
secure

See also

GET
OWNED
PAY
RICH
SAVE
TRANSACTIONS
WORK

MOUTH

noun

bill[2]
drink
drool
mouth
swallow

verb

chew
drink
drool
swallow
vomit
yawn

See also

INGESTION

MOVE

noun

bounce (2)
constitutional
displacement
drive
driver
expedition
flow
jerk
jump (2)

motion
movement
removal
skip
smuggler
sneak
spate
spurt
stealth
throw
tourist
transportation
tread
tremor
trip
trot
walk
way

adjective

communicable
errant
migrant
migratory
mobile
nomadic
stealthy

verb

blunder
bounce (2)
communicate
cover
crawl
cross
disturb
drive (4)
edge
emit
flow (3)
fly (2)
glide
go
hike
jerk
journey
jump (2)
limp
lump[1]

lurch (2)
maneuver
migrate
mobilize
move (2)
ooze
overturn
plod
plunge
pour (2)
refer
remove
rove
run
rush
scramble
send
shed
shoot
shuffle
skip
slide (3)
slip
slither
slouch
smuggle (2)
sneak
spread (2)
spurt
stir[1] (2)
stride
stroll
strut
stumble
swing (2)
swirl
thrash
throw
toss
tramp
traverse (2)
trip
trot
turn (2)
walk
wallow
wash (2)

wiggle
wrench

halt
noun
  catch
adjective
  fixed
  motionless
verb
  catch
  fasten
  fix
  land (2)

See also
  ACTION
  AFFECT
  CERTAIN
  CHANGE
  CONTINUE
  ENTER
  FLEXIBLE
  PUSH
  PUT IN
  REPETITION
  SAME
  WORK

NATIVE
adjective
  constitutional
  domestic
  indigenous
  innate

foreign
noun
  foreigner
adjective
  foreign (2)

See also
  NEAR

NEAR
noun
  associate
  association

environment
locality
neighborhood
adjective
  adjoining
  close (2)
  coming
  confidential
  convenient
  immediate
  intimate[1]
  last[1]
  momentary
  tactical
  threatening
verb
  adjoin
  associate
  coincide
  snuggle
  threaten
adverb
  approximately
  close
  immediately
  late

far
noun
  detachment
  distance
adjective
  distant
  remote
adverb
  barely

distance
noun
  remove

See also
  APPROACH
  ASSEMBLE
  BIG
  CONNECT
  GROUP
  INCLUDE
  LOVE   *(cont.)*

NEAR *(cont.)*

distance
NATIVE
TOUCH

NECESSARY
noun
  condition
  demand
  need
adjective
  essential
verb
  demand
  must

unnecessary
adjective
  unnecessary
  wanton

See also
  CHOICE
  LIMITED
  OBLIGATION

NEW
noun
  contemporary
  novelty (2)
  renewal
adjective
  contemporary
  fresh
  modern
  new
verb
  modernize
  renew

old
noun
  obsoleteness
  obsoletism
  square
adjective
  high
  obsolete
  old (2)

old-fashioned
tacky²
vanished
verb
  obsolesce

See also
  TIME

OBLIGATION
noun
  debt
  duty
  fidelity
  guarantee
  promise
adjective
  obliged
  required
verb
  commit
  enforce
  guarantee
  impose
  pledge (2)
  require
  secure

See also
  NECESSARY
  RESIST

OFFER
noun
  offer
  offering
  proposal
verb
  go
  offer (2)
  propose

See also
  ACCEPT

OPEN
noun
  breach
  crack

gap
hole
prick
way
adjective
  clear
  open
  passable
verb
  air
  breach
  clear
  open

close
noun
  bar
  blind alley
adjective
  airless
verb
  close (2)
  close in
  hinder
  obstruct
  surround

See also
  CLEAR
  ENTER
  FREE
  PUT ON
  SHOW

OPINION
noun
  advice
  adviser
  belief (2)
  guess
  review
  thesis
adjective
  advisory
  arbitrary
verb
  advise
  believe (3)
  feel
  guess

review

See also
BELIEF
LIKELY
PERSPECTIVE
REASON
THOUGHTS

ORDER
noun
arrangement
balance
law
method
order
rule
series
adjective
methodical
neat
verb
arrange
balance (2)
belong
dress up
fold
line
methodize
set[1]
shuffle
thread
tidy (2)

disorder
noun
botch
disorder (2)
disorderliness
disturbance
heap
unruliness
upset
adjective
confused
disorderly
messy

shapeless
unruly
verb
confuse
disorder
disrupt
entangle
heap
sprawl
tousle

See also
CALM
COLLECT
GROUP
LAW
PEACE
PLANNED
SAME
SURFACE

OVER
noun
absolutism (2)
administration
advantage
authoritarian
authority (2)
boss (2)
bully
chief
command
demand
dictator
dominance
domination
employer
executive
muscle
nobility
society
superior
tyranny
adjective
absolute
administrative
authoritarian

authoritative
climactic
dictatorial
dominant
dominating
higher
highest
noble
principal
verb
administer (2)
bear
boss
command
conduct
control
demand
dictate
dominate (2)
enforce
govern
impose (2)
inflict
intimidate
seize
supervise
top
tyrannize

under
noun
base[1]
basis (2)
bearer
bottom (2)
burden[1] (3)
commonalty
employee
follower
pawn[2]
retinue
slavery
subordinate
sycophant
trash
adjective
bottom   *(cont.)*

OVER *(cont.)*

under
lowly
minor
servile
subordinate
verb
base[1]
bear
carry
charge
condescend (2)
fawn

See also
CONTROL
HIGH
IMPORTANT
POLITICS
PRECEDE

OWNED
noun
birthright (2)
claim
claimant
effect
holding
land
monopoly
owner
ownership
resource
riches
adjective
jealous
verb
carry
claim
command
enjoy

unowned
adjective
unreserved
verb
escape
lack

See also
PAY
TRANSACTIONS

PAIN
noun
annoyance (3)
embarrassment
offense
pain
thorn
throe
adjective
disturbing
offensive
painful
thorny
tormenting
unbearable
unpleasant
vexatious
verb
annoy (2)
embarrass
hurt
insult
offend
sting
torture

pleasure
noun
enjoyment
sensuousness
sybarite
zest
adjective
enjoyable
insinuating
sensuous
sybaritic
verb
please

See also
ATTACK
CALM
EASY

FEELINGS
HAPPY
LIKE

PART
noun
branch (4)
complement
cut
division (2)
element (3)
extension
figure
interest
lump[1]
quarter
section (2)
subsidiary
adjective
complementary
concentrated
double
partial
subordinate
verb
branch
complement
divide

whole
noun
completeness
complex
system
unification
unity
universe
whole
adjective
complete (3)
round
whole
verb
integrate
adverb
completely
through

See also
ASSEMBLE
BIG
START

PARTICIPATE
noun
entanglement
meddler
meddling
part
participant
participation
snoop
voice
adjective
contributive
meddling
social
verb
contribute
engage
experience
involve
join
meddle
participate
play along
snoop

abstain
verb
secede

See also
DO
ENTER
FREE

PAY
noun
deposit
payment
wage
adjective
even[1]
verb
compensate

pay
refund
reward
settle
treat

owe
noun
account
debt (2)
tax
toll[1]
adjective
due
unpaid

See also
GET
MONEY
OWNED
SAVE
TRANSACTIONS
WORK

PEACE
adjective
peaceable

conflict
noun
disorder
unrest
unruliness
adjective
disorderly
military (2)
unruly
verb
militarize

See also
CALM
ORDER

PERFORMING ARTS
noun
acting
actor
band[2]

booking
interpretation
lead
magic
mimic
player
scene
sketch
stage
vocalist
adjective
dramatic
verb
act
interpret
play (2)
stage

See also
HONEST
REAL

PERSPECTIVE
noun
phase
point of view
side
verb
regard

See also
OPINION

PERSUASION
noun
bribe
seducer
adjective
convincing
corruptible
seductive
verb
bribe
charm
coax
coerce
convince
persuade
seduce   *(cont.)*

PERSUASION *(cont.)*

dissuasion
verb
  dissuade

See also
  AFFECT
  SUGGEST

PITY
noun
  pity
adjective
  pitiful
  pitying
verb
  feel

See also
  ATTITUDE
  FEELINGS
  FORGIVENESS
  KIND

PLACE
noun
  air
  base[1]
  bearing
  court
  earth
  environment (2)
  expanse
  grave[1]
  haunt
  hide-out
  locality (2)
  place (3)
  point
  position (2)
  room
  scene
  side
  station
  stay[1]
  tenure
  work
adjective
  earthly

  heavenly
verb
  frequent
  inhabit
  keep
  lay[1]
  live[1]
  position
  set[1]
  station
  stay[1]

See also
  PUT IN
  TERRITORY

PLAIN
noun
  modesty
adjective
  bare
  conservative
  easygoing
  humble
  modest
  quiet
  rustic

fancy
noun
  bombast
  pretentiousness
  theatricalism
adjective
  affected
  arty
  elaborate
  exclusive
  fanciful
  formal
  genteel
  inflated
  ornate
  pompous
  showy
  sonorous
verb
  dress up

See also
  BEAUTIFUL
  HONEST
  PUT ON
  SELF-LOVE
  SIMPLE

PLANNED
noun
  arrangement
  design
  draft
  intention
  line
  plot
  program (2)
verb
  arrange
  design (2)
  draft
  have
  intend
  plot
  premeditate

unplanned
noun
  improvisation
adjective
  mindless
  random
  spontaneous
  unintentional
verb
  improvise

See also
  ORDER
  PREPARED
  PURPOSE
  SURPRISE

POLITICS
noun
  absolutism (2)
  agitator
  alarmist
  alliance

ally
citizen
crisis
elector
extremist
government (2)
liberal
mission
patronage
possession
reactionary
state
tax
ticket
treaty
tyranny
adjective
absolute
allied
extreme
governmental
inner
liberal
popular
reactionary
unprogressive
verb
ally
elect
establish
secede
socialize

See also
CONTROL
LAW
OVER

POSSIBLE
noun
possibility
potential
adjective
earthly
open
possible (2)
potential

impossible
adjective
impossible

See also
LIKELY

POSTURE
noun
position
posture
verb
balance
pose
posture
slouch
sprawl
squat
stoop
stride

See also
HANG

PRAISE
noun
acceptance
admirer
applause
boast
braggart
compliment
flattery
glory
praise
sycophant
testimonial
adjective
admirable
boastful
complimentary
verb
admire (2)
applaud
appreciate
approve
boast
compliment

flatter
honor
praise

blame
noun
accusation
accuser
blame
critic
rebuke
reflection
scapegoat
scold
smear
tirade
vituperation
adjective
accusatorial
blameworthy
critical
disparaging
verb
accuse
blame
call down
correct
deplore
nag
revile
slam

See also
LIKE
RELIGION
RESPECT
REWARD
SUPPORT
VALUE

PRECEDE
noun
ancestor (2)
ancestry
façade
face (2)
front
future   *(cont.)*

PRECEDE *(cont.)*
lead
leader
precedence
adjective
advance
advanced
ancestral
future
verb
face
lead
precede
adverb
earlier (3)

follow
noun
back
follower
order
tail
train
adjective
back
backward (2)
consecutive
following
last[1]
late
later
verb
defer[2]
dog
follow (3)
adverb
backward
late
later

See also
FORESIGHT
FORWARD
KIN
OVER
SEEK

PRECISE
noun
discrimination
adjective
discriminating
even[1]
fine[1]
precise
round
adverb
directly
even[1]

imprecise
noun
estimate
adjective
loose
verb
estimate

See also
CAREFUL
WISE

PREPARED
noun
preparation
adjective
ready
verb
gird
prepare
till

unprepared
noun
improvisation
adjective
extemporaneous
verb
improvise
adverb
unawares

See also
PLANNED

PROTECTION
noun
bill[2]

hole
home (2)
shelter
verb
harbor (2)
shade

exposure
noun
exposure
adjective
open
verb
expose

See also
SAFETY

PURPOSE
noun
intention
adjective
calculated
deliberate
firm[1]
verb
intend

purposelessness
adjective
aimless
erratic
mindless

See also
PLANNED
REASON
START
SURPRISE

PUSH
noun
pressure
push
verb
crowd
muscle
pressurize
push
urge

pull
noun
  jerk
  pull
verb
  jerk
  pull
See also
  MOVE
  PUT IN

PUT IN
verb
  establish
  introduce
  load
  ram

take out
verb
  pull
  unload

See also
  CHANGE
  MOVE
  PLACE
  PUSH

PUT ON
noun
  attire
  dress (3)
  habit
  wrap
  wrapper
verb
  clothe
  cover
  don
  dress
  dress up
  smear
  top
  wrap (3)

take off
noun
  nudity

  tatter
adjective
  bare
  nude
verb
  bare
  remove
  scrape
  scrub
  shed
  skin
  strip[1]

See also
  ASSEMBLE
  CLEAR
  CONNECT
  INCREASE
  OPEN
  PLAIN
  SHOW

REACH
verb
  extend
  fall
  reach (2)
  snap

unreachable
adjective
  inaccessible
  inconvenient

See also
  APPROACH

REAL
noun
  actuality
  circumstance
  existence
  fact
adjective
  accurate
  actual (2)
  factual
  real
  realistic (2)

adverb
  actually
  really

imaginary
noun
  character
  dream
  fiction
  hallucination
  illusion (2)
  imagination
  myth (2)
adjective
  artificial
  dreamy
  fallacious
  fictitious
  idealistic (2)
  illusive
  illusory
  imaginary
  mythical
  theoretical
verb
  dream
  sentimentalize

See also
  BE
  CORRECT
  PERFORMING ARTS
  TRUE

REASON
noun
  argument
  assumption
  calculation
  deduction
  logic
  reason
  sense
adjective
  logical (2)
  sane
  sound[2]
verb
  calculate   *(cont.)*

REASON *(cont.)*
derive
infer
resolve
work

unreason
noun
unreason
adjective
unreasonable
adverb
unfoundedly

See also
COUNT
OPINION
PURPOSE
SANE
START
THOUGHTS

REGRET
noun
apology
penitence
adjective
apologetic
remorseful
verb
regret

impenitence
adjective
remorseless

See also
EXPLAIN

RELEVANT
noun
business
· relevance
adjective
relevant
verb
apply
deal with

irrelevant
adjective
irrelevant

See also
CONNECT
LIMITED
SPECIFIC

RELIGION
noun
devotee
devotion
faith
grace
holiness
inspiration
missionary
myth
novice
offering
praise
prayer[1] (2)
preacher
purification
religion
sacrifice
separatist
adjective
condemned
divine[1] (2)
heavenly
holy (2)
impure
missionary
purgative
spiritual
verb
praise
pray
preach
purify
sacrifice
sanctify
violate

See also
FEELINGS

PRAISE
RESPECT
RITUAL
SACRED
SUPERNATURAL

REMEMBER
noun
celebration
list[1]
memorial
memory (2)
remembrance
toast
adjective
memorial
verb
celebrate
drink
immortalize
list[1]
memorialize
memorize
post[3]
recognize
remember (2)
schedule
time
write

forget
adjective
forgetful
verb
forget

See also
AWARENESS

REPETITION
noun
beat
circle
dancer
haunt
lapse
recurrence
repetition

reversion
revolution
rhythm
tremor (2)
adjective
recurrent
repetitive
rhythmical
tautological
tremulous
winding
verb
agitate
beat (4)
blink
bump
dance
flap (2)
flutter
haunt
recur
relapse
repeat (2)
return
shake (3)
spin (2)
sway
swing
swirl
toss
turn
wag¹
wiggle
wind²
writhe
adverb
anew

See also
ACTION
CALM
MOVE

REPRODUCTION
noun
pregnancy
reproduction

adjective
pregnant
reproductive (2)
verb
grow
reproduce

barrenness
noun
sterility
sterilization
verb
miscarry
sterilize

See also
RICH
SEX

REQUEST
noun
beggar
claim
dare
demand
supplicant
verb
address
beg
bill¹
call
claim
dare
demand
request

See also
ACCEPT
ASK

RESIST
noun
defiance
disobedience
obstinacy
opponent
rebel
rebellion
resistance (3)

stubbornness
unruliness
adjective
defiant
disobedient
firm¹
obstinate
rebellious
resistant (2)
stubborn
unruly
verb
defy
disobey
harden
rebel
resist
talk back

yield
noun
obedience (2)
surrender
adjective
deferential
obedient
passive
soft
verb
back down
defer²
give over
humor
succumb
surrender

See also
ACCEPT
CONFLICT
FLEXIBLE
OBLIGATION
RESPECT
WILLING

RESPECT
noun
distinction
eminence   *(cont.)*

RESPECT *(cont.)*

esteem
face
honor (2)
pride
trophy
adjective
admirable
eminent
holy
proud
reverent
verb
distinguish
pride

contempt
noun
condescension
crack
degradation
despisal
disgrace
disrespect
infamy
joke
mockery
ridicule
sarcasm
satire
sneer
stain
takeoff
taunt
adjective
biting
cynical
disdainful
disgraceful
disrespectful
sarcastic
shameless
verb
condescend
despise
disgrace
humble

ridicule
shame
sneer
stigmatize

standing
noun
reputation

See also
COURTESY
HONEST
PRAISE
RELIGION
RESIST
REWARD
RIGHT
RISE
SACRED
VALUE

RESTRAINT
noun
bit^2
chastity
modesty
reserve
shyness
temperance
adjective
chaste
conservative
modest
repressive
reserved
taciturn
temperate
verb
compose
refrain
repress
restrain

unrestraint
noun
abandon
bender
binge

blast
ease
liberty
license
room
adjective
abandoned
impure
outspoken
verb
revel

See also
CALM
FREE
TIGHTEN

REWARD
noun
decoration
reward (2)
verb
reward

punish
noun
beating
exile
fine^2
hell
punishment
sanction
adjective
damned
punishing
verb
beat
fine^2
punish
torture

deserve
noun
due

See also
PRAISE
RESPECT

RICH

noun
fertility
fortune
plenty
prosperity
riches

adjective
alive
big
fertile (2)
generous
luxurious
prosperous
rich

verb
bear (2)
bloom[1]
fertilize
teem

poor

noun
barren
beggary
depression
deprivation
hole
pauper
poverty
sterility
sterilization
tatterdemalion
trash
unfortunate

adjective
barren (2)
depressed
poor
sterile

verb
deplete
sterilize

See also
BEAUTIFUL
MONEY
REPRODUCTION

RIGHT

noun
decency
ethic (2)
good
innocent
justice

adjective
appropriate
ethical
exemplary
innocent (2)
just
justifiable

verb
call for
justify

wrong

noun
breach
crime (2)
evil
heavy
infamy
injustice (2)
outrage
pit[1]

adjective
evil
outrageous
shameless
sordid
unlawful
unwholesome

verb
fall
offend
shock[1]
wrong

See also
AGREE
CORRECT
CRIMES
FAIR
GOOD
HONEST

RESPECT
USUAL

RISE

noun
advancement
ascent (2)
exaltation
inclination
jump
lift
rise
takeoff

adjective
elevated
exalted
gradual

verb
ascend
elevate
erect
exalt
get up (2)
jump
lift
promote
rise (2)
take off

fall

noun
condescension
demotion
descent
drip
drop
fall (2)

adjective
descending

verb
condescend (2)
cut
demote
descend
drip
drop (3)
fall (2)
flop   *(cont.)*

RISE *(cont.)*

fall
lower[2]
seat
set[1]
settle
sink
traverse

See also
RESPECT

RITUAL
noun
ceremony
ritual
wake[1]
adjective
ritual

See also
RELIGION

SACRED
noun
adoration
sanctuary
adjective
sacred
verb
adore

profane
noun
sacrilege
swearword
adjective
impure
profane
sacrilegious
verb
swear
violate

See also
RELIGION
RESPECT

SAFETY
noun
cover

guard
refuge
safety
sanctity
adjective
safe (2)

danger
noun
adventure
adventurer
crisis
danger
daring
lure
pitfall
risk
threat
adjective
adventurous
critical
dangerous
helpless
insecure
verb
endanger
hazard
risk

See also
PROTECTION

SAME
noun
copy
counterpart
couple
double
echo (2)
echoism
equivalence
integration
likeness
mate
mimic
mimicry
mockery
model

parallel
peer[2]
precedent
sameness
takeoff
tie
adjective
echoic
equal (2)
even[1] (2)
imitative
like[2]
literal
same
symmetrical
twin
verb
copy
echo
equal
equalize
favor
follow (2)
identify
imitate
integrate
liken
rival
adverb
even[1]

different
noun
contrast
difference
distinction
inequality
uniqueness
variation (2)
variety
adjective
different
distinct
distinctive
uneven
unique
various
versatile

verb
  differ
  distinguish (2)

compare
adjective
  comparative
  typical
verb
  associate
  compare (2)

See also
  AGREE
  CERTAIN
  CHANGE
  CONTINUE
  FLEXIBLE
  MOVE
  ORDER
  SUBSTITUTE
  SUPPORT
  TRUE

SANE
noun
  sanity
adjective
  sane (2)

insane
noun
  insanity
adjective
  insane
verb
  derange

See also
  REASON
  USUAL
  WISE

SAVE
noun
  economy
adjective
  economical
verb
  economize

  save
  scrimp

waste
noun
  extravagance
  luxury
  wastrel
adjective
  extravagant
verb
  spend
  waste (2)

See also
  MONEY
  PAY
  TRANSACTIONS

SEA
noun
  sailor
adjective
  marine
  nautical

SEE
noun
  appearance
  eye
  gaze
  glance
  glare
  ken
  look
  notice
  squint
  view
  visibility
  vision
  watch
  watcher
  witness
adjective
  apparent
  graphic
  noticeable
  squinty

  unsubtle
  visible
  visual
verb
  appear
  catch
  discern
  foresee
  gaze
  glare (2)
  glimpse
  look
  notice
  see
  squint
  survey
  watch

not see
noun
  blindness
  blink
  fade-out
adjective
  blind (2)
  inconspicuous
verb
  blink (2)
  daze
  fade
  fade out

See also
  AWARENESS
  KNOWLEDGE
  LIGHT

SEEK
noun
  applicant
  application
  aspirant
  courtship
  drive
  insistence
  pursuit (2)
  target   *(cont.)*

SEEK *(cont.)*

visit
verb
  accost
  aim (2)
  apply
  aspire
  catch up
  court (2)
  grope
  hunt
  insist
  pursue
  seek
  target
  track
  visit

avoid
noun
  cut
  escape (2)
  fugitive
  recoil
adjective
  evasive
  fugitive
  stray
verb
  avoid
  cut
  evade
  flinch
  lose
  skirt

See also
  PRECEDE
  TRY

SELF
noun
  egoism
  egotist
  self
adjective
  corrupt
  egocentric
  egotistic

other
adjective
  selfless

See also
  SELF-LOVE

SELF-LOVE
noun
  egotism (2)
  egotist
  snob
adjective
  egotistic
  snobbish
  vain
verb
  strut

modesty
noun
  modesty
adjective
  humble

See also
  PLAIN
  SELF

SEX
asexual
noun
  chastity
  prude
adjective
  chaste
  frigid
  innocent

sexual
noun
  beau
  boyfriend
  courtship
  desire
  deviant
  flirt
  flirtation (2)
  gallant

heat
infatuation
lecher
love (2)
lover
philanderer
prostitute
seducer
seductress
sensuality
slut
wanton
adjective
  desirable
  erotic (2)
  flirtatious
  gay
  impure
  infatuated
  seductive
  sensual
  wanton
verb
  court
  flirt
  neck
  philander
  rape
  seduce
  take
  violate

See also
  DESIRE
  GENDER
  LOVE
  MARRIAGE
  REPRODUCTION

SHARP
noun
  edge (2)
  point
  prick
adjective
  acute
  pointed

sharp
thorny
verb
sharpen

dull
adjective
dull
verb
dull

See also
GEOMETRY

SHOW
noun
acknowledgment
display (2)
exhibition
expression
guide
hint
lead
nudity
precursor
reflection
representation
revelation
shade
sign (2)
adjective
designative
expressive
frank
nude
verb
adumbrate
air
bear
betray
come out
designate
develop
display
elaborate
evoke
express
guide

hint
indicate
instance
plot
prove
reflect
represent
reveal
scream
show (2)
strip¹
uncover

hide
noun
belittlement
burial
confidant
disappearance
disguise
façade
hide-out
mystery
secrecy
adjective
blind
confidential (2)
expressionless
implicit (2)
latent
secluded
secret
ulterior
verb
belittle
block
bury
censor (2)
confide
cover
disappear
disguise
extenuate
hide¹
hole up
lay for
obscure

soft-pedal
withdraw
wrap
adverb
secretly

See also
CLEAR
EXPRESS
KNOWLEDGE
OPEN
PUT ON
SURFACE
WORDS

SIMPLE
adjective
elementary
pastoral
verb
boil down

complex
noun
complexity
tangle
adjective
busy
complex (2)
verb
complicate

See also
EASY
PLAIN

SMELLS
good smells
noun
fragrance
adjective
fragrant
pungent
verb
scent
bad smells
adjective
moldy
smelly   *(cont.)*

SMELLS *(cont.)*

bad smells
verb
  smell

smell
noun
  smell (2)
  trail
verb
  smell

SMOOTH
adjective
  even[1]
  sleek
  slick
verb
  even[1]
  press

rough
noun
  fold
  irregularity
  line
adjective
  coarse (2)
  hairy
  irregular
  rough
verb
  fold
  wrinkle

See also
  GEOMETRY

SOLID
verb
  coagulate
  harden

liquid
noun
  foam
adjective
  foamy
verb
  evaporate

foam
melt
ooze

consistency
noun
  viscosity
adjective
  flat \
  thick
  viscous
verb
  thicken

See also
  DRY
  MATTER

SOUNDS

pleasant sounds
noun
  laugh
  melody
adjective
  harmonious
  laughing
  melodious (2)
  resonant
  soft
verb
  chuckle
  laugh
  listen
  ring[2]
  sing

unpleasant sounds
noun
  beat
  blast
  clash
  cry
  hiss
  howl
  hum
  mutter
  noise
  report

roar
scream
shout
snap
tread
vociferation
yelp
adjective
  harsh
  hoarse
  inharmonious
  loud
  vociferous
verb
  bang
  bawl
  blast
  clash
  crack
  crackle
  cry
  grind
  hiss
  howl
  hum
  mutter (2)
  rattle
  roar
  rumble
  scrape
  scream
  snap
  tramp
  whine
  yelp

neutral sounds or silence
noun
  beat
  drip
  echo
  echoism
  hearing (3)
  murmur
  silence
  sound[1]
  tap[1]

tone (2)
voicing
adjective
echoic
high
low
silent
taciturn
vocal (2)
verb
beat
echo
hear
muffle
murmur
silence
tap[1]
thud
wash

See also
WORDS

SPECIFIC
noun
name
adjective
detailed
graphic
mere
personal
private
special
specific
verb
call
enumerate
name (2)
stipulate
adverb
merely
namely

general
noun
public
adjective
general (3)

popular
prevailing
public
universal (2)
verb
socialize
universalize

See also
LIMITED
RELEVANT

START
noun
beginner
beginning
birth (2)
blame
cause (3)
center
dawn
foundation
germ
introduction
origin
original
originator
seed (3)
adjective
beginning
constitutional
dependent
early (2)
elementary
first
introductory
original
pilot
preliminary
primitive
rough
verb
begin
break out
broach
cause
come

consist
contribute
dawn
depend on
found
introduce (2)
light[1]
seed
start
stem
usher in

end
noun
arrival
cause
end
evening
fate
adjective
last[1] (3)
through (2)
verb
address
aim
arrive
arrive at
carry
close
fate
adverb
last[1]
through
ultimately

See also
ACTION
ATTACK
CAUSE
CONTINUE
ENTER
KIN
PART
PURPOSE
REASON
SURFACE
TIME
WORK

STRAIGHT

adjective
  accepted
  direct
adverb
  directly

bent

noun
  bend
  bias
  inclination
  irregularity
  loop
adjective
  bent
  bias
  biased
  crooked
  indirect
  irregular
  winding
verb
  bend (2)
  bias (2)
  incline
  lurch
  manipulate
  wave
  wind²

See also
  GEOMETRY

STRIKE

noun
  beat
  blow²
  shock¹
  slam
  slap
verb
  batter
  beat (2)
  glance
  hit
  parry
  slap

  slap around
  splash
  sprinkle
  thrash (2)

miss
adjective
  clear

See also
  ATTACK
  MARKS

STRONG

noun
  character
  decision
  force
  intensity
  muscle
  strength
adjective
  authoritative
  colorful
  deep
  emphatic (2)
  firm¹
  forceful
  hard
  heavy
  high
  influential
  intense
  lusty
  muscular
  powerful
  sound²
  straight
  strong (3)
verb
  confirm
  refresh
  toughen
adverb
  flatly
  hard (2)

weak
noun
  debilitation

  ineffectuality
  infirmity
  instability
adjective
  dilute
  faint
  fragile
  gentle
  ineffectual
  infirm
  insecure
  light²
  neutral
  pale
  tenuous
  trick
  vulnerable
verb
  dilute
  enervate
  fade
  weaken

See also
  ACTION
  AWARENESS
  CONTINUE
  FEELINGS
  HEALTH
  IMPORTANT
  TIRED

STYLE

good style
noun
  bearing
  class
  elegance
  fashion
  gravity
  poetry
  taste
adjective
  brief
  elegant
  elevated
  fashionable

pithy
smooth
suave
tasteful
tight

bad style

noun
bombast
corruption
theatricalism
theatrics
wordiness

adjective
dramatic
gaudy
tacky[2]
wordy

style

noun
style

adjective
sonorous

See also
WORDS

SUBSTITUTE

noun
acting
actor
change
compensation
copy
embodiment
example
flag[1]
makeshift
place
relief
representative
speaker
substitute
symbol

adjective
compensatory
symbolic
temporary

verb
act (2)
change (2)
compensate
embody
relieve
replace
represent (2)
substitute
supplant

See also
SAME

SUGGEST

noun
hint (2)
insinuation
suggestion

adjective
insinuating
suggestive

verb
hint
smack[2]

See also
PERSUASION

SUPERNATURAL

noun
charm
ghost
gibberish
magic
miracle
spell[2]
witch

adjective
magic
supernatural

See also
LUCK
RELIGION
WARN

SUPPORT

noun
endorsement

reference
sponsor
support

verb
back
confirm
defend
encourage
prove
support (2)

oppose

noun
objection
opponent
opposite
opposition

adjective
contrary
opposing
opposite

verb
contest
object
oppose
quibble

See also
AGREE
HELP
LOVE
PRAISE
SAME
TREAT WELL

SURFACE

noun
appearance
face (2)
form (2)
hide[2]
image
outline
shoal
skin (3)
terrain
trivia

adjective
apparent   *(cont.)*

SURFACE (cont.)
  frothy
  glib
  incidental
  shallow
  superficial
verb
  appear
  face
  form
adverb
  apparently

depth
noun
  depth
  essence
adjective
  deep (3)
  elemental
  essential
  radical
  underground
adverb
  essentially

See also
  BE
  ORDER
  SHOW
  START

SURPRISE
noun
  accident
  chance
adjective
  abrupt
  accidental
  amiss
  arbitrary (2)
  dramatic
  staggering
verb
  backfire
  stagger
  startle
  surprise
  take

expect
noun
  anticipation
  cliché
  expectation
adjective
  common
  due
  expectant
verb
  expect

See also
  AFFECT
  CERTAIN
  EXCITE
  FEAR
  FEELINGS
  HAPPEN
  HOPE
  LUCK
  PLANNED
  PURPOSE
  USUAL

TASTE
noun
  flavor (2)
  flavoring
adjective
  pungent
  sour
  sweet
verb
  flavor

bad taste
noun
  insipidity
adjective
  bad
  bitter
  flat (2)
  unpalatable

See also
  INGESTION

TEACH
noun
  education

  educator
  illumination
adjective
  didactic
  educable
  educational
  moral
  pedantic
verb
  educate
  illuminate
  impress
  indoctrinate (2)
  inform
  moralize
  socialize

learn
noun
  discovery
  student
adjective
  studious
verb
  discover
  learn
  study

See also
  KNOWLEDGE
  UNDERSTAND

TERRITORY
noun
  area (2)
  basin
  bay[1]
  beat
  border
  home
  lot
  neighborhood
  range
  reservation
  state
  territory
adjective
  territorial

See also
PLACE

THICK
noun
thickness
adjective
thick

thin
adjective
filmy

See also
FAT
HEAVY
WIDE

THING
noun
bouquet
matter
novelty
object
odds and ends
stick
thing
thread
wall
web

See also
MATTER

THOUGHTS
noun
advisement
depth
fancy
feeling
head
idea
imagination
inspiration
instinct
intelligence
psychology
survey
theory (2)

thinker
thought
adjective
instinctive
intellectual
mental
theoretical
thoughtful
verb
bear
brood
hear of
ignore
imagine
ponder
reconsider
review
speculate
think

See also
BELIEF
CAREFUL
KNOWLEDGE
LIKELY
OPINION
REASON
WISE

THRIVE
noun
efficiency
hit
prosperity
success
adjective
effective
efficient
flourishing
foolproof
good
prosperous
verb
clear
flourish (2)
prosper
succeed (2)

fail
noun
decay
failure (3)
fall
futility
adjective
amiss
bad
futile
impractical
verb
decay
fail (3)
malfunction
miscarry
adverb
wrong

exist
verb
manage
mess around
muddle
work

See also
ACTION
GOOD
INDUSTRIOUS
WIN

TIGHTEN
noun
constriction
adjective
edgy
taut
thick
tight (2)
verb
constrain
constrict
crowd (2)
squeeze (2)
tense
tie
tighten   *(cont.)*

TIGHTEN (cont.)

loosen

noun
ease
freedom

adjective
easygoing
full
loose
thin

verb
ease
thin
undo

See also
ATTITUDE
CALM
FEELINGS
FREE
RESTRAINT

TIME
noun
age (2)
contemporary (2)
delay (2)
flash
future
instant
lateness
life
morning
now
occasion
past
period (2)
siege
spring
summer
term
time (2)
turn
vintage
year
adjective
consecutive

contemporary
distant
early
following
future
inconvenient
instant
late
modern
past
posthumous
present[1]
punctual
simultaneous
spring
transitory
verb
delay
follow
go (2)
serve
spend
time (2)
adverb
directly
early
just
late (2)
now (3)
slow
together
ultimately
See also
ACTION
CONTINUE
FAST
NEW
START
YOUTH

TIRED
noun
exhaustion
adjective
exhausted
haggard

languid
restless
sick
tiring
wasted
verb
exhaust
fatigue
run down

fresh
noun
drive
vigor
adjective
tireless

See also
ACTION
AWARENESS
FEELINGS
HEAVY
STRONG

TOUCH
noun
brush[1]
brush[2]
contact
dig
embrace
kiss
tangibility
touch (4)
adjective
affecting
tactile
tangible
verb
affect[1]
brush[1]
caress
contact
dig
embrace
fiddle
grope
kiss

tamper
till
touch
work
wrestle

not touch

adjective
clear

See also
APPROACH
NEAR

TRANSACTIONS

noun
bargain
cost (3)
dealer
good
gratuity
pass
patron
patronage (2)
pawn[1]
pusher
seller
store
toll[1]

adjective
costly

verb
cost
hire
lease
pawn[1]
peddle
push
sell
sell off

See also
GAMBLING
MONEY
OWNED
PAY
SAVE
WORK

TREAT WELL

noun
consideration

adjective
attentive
favorite

verb
baby
favor

treat badly

noun
abuse

verb
abuse (2)
bait

treat

verb
deal with

See also
ATTITUDE
CONCERN
COURTESY
CRIMES
HELP
INCLUDE
KIND
SUPPORT

TRUE

noun
authenticity
certainty
confirmation
truth
veracity

adjective
accurate (2)
authentic
authoritative
believable
certain
genuine
true
truthful

verb
confirm

wash

adverb
actually
even[1]
really

false

noun
act
affectation
basis
counterfeit
fake
fallacy (2)
forger
liar
lie[2]
mendacity
pretense

adjective
affected
artificial
assumed
baseless
counterfeit
fallacious
false
fantastic
forced
perjurious

verb
act
assume
color
counterfeit
distort
equivocate
fake (2)
lie[2]
pretend

See also
CORRECT
HONEST
LIKELY
REAL
SAME
TRUST

TRUST
adjective
  dependable
  faithful
verb
  depend on
  entrust

distrust
noun
  betrayal
  betrayer
  defection
  distrust
  faithlessness
  treachery
  treason
adjective
  distrustful
  faithless
  treasonous
  undependable
verb
  betray
  defect
  distrust

See also
  TRUE

TRY
noun
  attempt
  drive
  try
adjective
  aggressive
verb
  attempt
  presume

See also
  SEEK

UNDERSTAND
noun
  sympathy
adjective
  understanding

verb
  interpret
  sympathize
  understand

misunderstand
noun
  misunderstanding
verb
  misunderstand

See also
  KNOWLEDGE
  TEACH

URBAN
noun
  city
adjective
  city
verb
  citify

rural
noun
  country
adjective
  country

USED
noun
  consumer
  consumption
  duty
  exercise
  use
adjective
  practical
  usable
verb
  handle
  resort
  take
  tie up
  use

unused
noun
  futility

obsoleteness
obsoletism
temperance
adjective
  futile
  idle
  impracticable
  obsolete
  useless
verb
  lose
  obsolesce

See also
  AFFECT
  HELP

USUAL
noun
  average
  convention
  custom
  decency
  fashion
  grind
  manner
  ritual
  routine
  standard
  usual
  usualness
adjective
  accepted
  accustomed (2)
  common
  conventional
  customary
  decent
  everyday
  fashionable
  ordinary
  orthodox
  strict
  trite
  typical
verb
  accustom

conventionalize
adverb
 usually

unusual
noun
 abnormality
 character
 deviant
 eccentricity
 freak
 impropriety (2)
adjective
 abnormal
 eccentric
 fantastic
 freakish
 funny
 improper (2)
 infrequent
 outrageous
 preternatural
 quaint
 rare
 steep¹
 unseasonable
 unusual
 weird
adverb
 infrequently
 unusually

See also
 CONTINUE
 CORRECT
 KEEP
 RIGHT
 SANE
 SURPRISE

VALUE
noun
 treasure
 worth
adjective
 admirable
 costly
 valuable

verb
 cherish

worthlessness
adjective
 cheap
 worthless
verb
 discredit

evaluation
noun
 class
 critic
 estimate
 merit
 quality
adjective
 critical
verb
 class
 estimate
 score

See also
 HELP
 LIKE
 LOVE
 PRAISE
 RESPECT

WARN
noun
 alarm
 alarmist
 example
 omen
 threat
 warning
adjective
 cautionary
 dark
 fateful
 forbidding
 malign
verb
 warn

invite
noun
 invitation

verb
 invite

See also
 FORESIGHT
 LUCK
 SUPERNATURAL

WIDE
noun
 width
adjective
 broad (3)
 widespread
 yawning
verb
 broaden
 spread
 yawn

narrow
noun
 constriction
adjective
 narrow
verb
 constrict

See also
 THICK

WILD
noun
 wild
adjective
 savage
 uncivilized
 wild

tame
adjective
 domestic
 gentle
verb
 domesticate
 gentle

See also
 CULTURE

WILLING

noun
volunteer
will

adjective
obliging
voluntary (2)
willing

adverb
voluntarily

unwilling

noun
imposition
indisposition

adjective
forced
indisposed

verb
impose (2)
inflict

adverb
helplessly

See also
ATTACK
CHOICE
FLEXIBLE
RESIST

WIN

noun
conqueror
conquest
defeat
favorite
runaway
suppression
trump
winner

adjective
invincible
victorious

verb
defeat
outwit
overwhelm
suppress
trump

lose

noun
degradation
surrender

verb
give in
humble
surrender

recovery

noun
comeback

verb
catch up

See also
THRIVE

WISE

noun
sage[1]
wisdom

adjective
advisable
advised
wise[1]

foolish

noun
crackpot
dupe

adjective
easy
unwise

See also
ABILITY
CAREFUL
KNOWLEDGE
PRECISE
SANE
THOUGHTS

WORDS

noun
application
argumentation
babble
bombast

book
call
chatter
command
comment
commentary (2)
communication
composition
conferee
conference (2)
confidant
conversation
conversationalist
coverage
crack
cry
curse
deliberation
dialect
discourse
draft
eloquence
entry
exclamation
expression (2)
feature
gibberish (2)
gossip (2)
head
history
impression
introduction
item
language (2)
letter
name
news
note
orator
oratory
paraphrase
pirate
plot
poem
poet
poetry
press

program
proverb
publication (2)
review
silence
speaker
speech (2)
stammer
story
summary
swearword
synopsis
talk
term
theme
thesis
vocabulary (2)
voicing
word
wordiness
wording
yarn

adjective

brief
conversational
descriptive
dumb
eloquent
glib
gossipy
graphic (2)
introductory
oral
oratorical
poetic
silent
sonorous
speechless
talkative
tautological
unspeakable (2)
verbal
wordy

verb

address (2)
air
announce

argue
babble
browse
call
chatter
command
comment
confer
confide
converse[1]
cover
curse
describe
discuss
draft
exclaim
gasp
ghost
gossip
introduce
name
paraphrase
phrase
pirate
present[2]
pronounce
publish (2)
rant
refer
review
say
signal
snap
speak
stammer
state
swear
talk back
telephone
translate

See also

DECENT
KNOWLEDGE
MEANING
SHOW
SOUNDS
STYLE

WORK

noun

drudge
effort
employee
employer
employment (2)
labor
laborer
mission
practice (2)
project
seriousness
task (2)
volunteer
work

adjective

employed
serious
unpaid
workless

verb

apply
attack
bone
employ
exercise
grind
labor
practice (2)
work

play

noun

blast
dance
party
play (2)
playfulness
plunge
prank[1]
toy
vacation

adjective

playful

verb

dance   *(cont.)*

WORK (cont.)

play
flirt
gambol
play

See also
ACTION
DO
ENTER
LAUGHTER
MONEY
MOVE
PAY
TRANSACTIONS

YOUTH
noun
baby (2)

child
minor
minority
squirt
teenager
young
youth
adjective
babyish
childish
minor
small
young

age
noun
age
senility

senior
adjective
senile
verb
age

maturity
noun
senior
adjective
aged
mature
senior
verb
mature

See also
TIME